MODELING FINANCIAL TIME SERIES WITH S-PLUS®

Springer
New York
Berlin
Heidelberg
Hong Kong
London
Milan
Paris
Tokyo

Eric Zivot   Jiahui Wang

MODELING FINANCIAL TIME SERIES WITH S-PLUS®

 Springer

Eric Zivot
Department of Economics
University of Washington
Seattle, WA 98195-3330
USA
ezivot@u.washington.edu

Jiahui Wang
Insightful Corporation
1700 Westlake Ave., N.
Seattle, WA 98109-9891
USA
jwang@insightful.com

Library of Congress Cataloging-in-Publication Data
Zivot, Eric.
    Modeling financial time series with S-Plus / Eric Zivot, Jiahui Wang.
       p.   cm.
    Includes bibliographical references and index.
    ISBN 0-387-95549-6 (pbk. : alk. paper)
    1. Finance—Mathematical models.   2. Time-series analysis.   3. Finance—Econometric
models.   4. S-Plus.   I. Wang, Jiahui.   II. Title.
HG106 .Z584   2003
332´.01´51955—dc21   2002026657

ISBN 0-387-95549-6   Printed on acid-free paper.

Printed in the United States of America.

9 8 7 6 5 4 3 2 1   SPIN 10887030

Typesetting: Pages created by authors using a Springer TEX macro package.

www.springer-ny.com

Springer-Verlag   New York Berlin Heidelberg
A member of BertelsmannSpringer Science+Business Media GmbH

Preface

What Is the Book and Why Was It Written?

This book is a guide to analyzing and modeling financial time series using
S-PLUS and S+FinMetrics. It is a unique blend of econometric theory, financial models, data analysis, and statistical programming. It serves as a
user's guide for Insightful's S+FinMetrics module of statistical functions
for financial time series analysis and financial econometrics as well as a general reference for models used in applied financial econometrics. The format
of the chapters in the book is to give a reasonably complete description of
a statistical model and how it works followed by illustrations of how to
analyze the model using S-PLUS and the functions in S+FinMetrics. In
this way, the book stands alone as an introduction to financial time series
analysis as well as a user's guide for S+FinMetrics. It also highlights the
general analysis of time series data using the new time series objects in
S-PLUS 6.

Intended Audience

This book is written for a wide audience of individuals who work, do research or study in the areas of empirical finance and financial econometrics.
The field of financial econometrics has exploded over the last decade, and
this book represents an integration of theory, methods and examples using the S-PLUS modeling language to facilitate the practice of financial
econometrics. This audience includes researchers and practitioners in the
finance industry, academic researchers in economics and finance, and ad-

vanced MBA and graduate students in economics and finance. Researchers and practitioners in the finance industry who already use S-PLUS and desire more functionality for analyzing and modeling financial data will find this text useful. It is also appropriate for financial analysts who may not be familiar with S-PLUS but who desire an integrated and open statistical modeling and programming environment for the analysis of financial data. This guide is useful for academic researchers interested in empirical finance and financial econometrics. Finally, this book may be used as a textbook or a textbook companion for advanced MBA and graduate level courses in empirical finance and financial econometrics.

Audience Background

It is assumed that the reader has a basic familiarity with S-PLUS at the level of Krause and Olson (2002) and a background in mathematical statistics at the level of Hogg and Craig (1994), is comfortable with linear algebra and linear regression, and has been exposed to basic time series concepts as presented in Harvey (1993) or Franses (1998). Most importantly, the book assumes that the reader is interested in modeling and analyzing financial time series.

Overview of the Book

The chapters in the book cover univariate and multivariate models for analyzing financial time series using S-PLUS and the functions in S+FinMetrics. Chapter one gives a general overview of the use of S-PLUS 6 and highlights certain aspects of the language for statistical modeling. Chapter two introduces the new time series objects in S-PLUS 6 and illustrates the specification, manipulation and visualization of these objects. Chapter three surveys time series concepts used throughout the book. Chapters four through eight cover a variety of topics in the modeling of univariate financial time series, including testing for unit roots, extreme value theory, time series regression models, GARCH models of volatility, and long memory models. Chapter nine introduces rolling analyses of time series models and covers related topics such as technical analysis of financial time series and moving average methods for high frequency data. Chapters ten through fifteen cover models for the analysis of multivariate financial time series. Topics include systems of regression equations, classical and Bayesian vector autoregressive models, cointegration, factor models, multivariate GARCH models, and state space models. Chapter 16 covers aspects of modeling time series arising from fixed income financial assets. Chapter 17, written by Victor Yohai and Jiahui Wang, describes robust REGARIMA models that allow for structural change.

What Is S+FinMetrics?

S+FinMetrics is an S-PLUS module for the econometric modeling and prediction of economic and financial time series. With some 600 functions, version 1.0 of S+FinMetrics offers the following functionality:

- Easy-to-use Trellis plots for multivariate time series

- Time series manipulations such as missing value interpolation, disaggregation, differences, distributed lags and polynomial distributed lags

- Rolling sample statistics such as variance, maximum, and minimum

- Moving average operators for both regularly spaced and irregularly spaced time series

- Common technical analysis measures and indicators

- Statistical tests for normality, autocorrelation, heteroskedasticity, multicollinearity, GARCH effects, and long memory

- Extreme value theory models based on generalized extreme value and generalized Pareto distributions as well as copulas

- Autoregressive distributed lag regression models

- White and Newey-West corrections for heteroskedasticity and serial correlation

- Robust estimation of REG-ARIMA models and robust detection of level shifts, trend breaks, and outliers

- Rolling and recursive regression

- Generic rolling models for back-testing

- Long memory fractional ARIMA and SEMIFAR models

- Univariate GARCH models including long memory FIGARCH and FIEGARCH models

- Multivariate GARCH models

- Linear and nonlinear systems of regression equations

- Classical and Bayesian vector autoregression models

- Tests for unit roots and cointegration

- Vector error correction models

- State space models and efficient estimation, prediction, smoothing, and simulation using the Kalman filter

- Statistical multifactor models for large data sets based on asymptotic principal components

- Term structure interpolation

S+FinMetrics incorporates functions from S+GARCH, the EVIS library of functions for modeling extreme values created by Alexander McNeil, the EVANESCE library of functions for modeling extreme values utilizing copulas created by Rene Carmona, and the *SsfPack* C library of state space modeling functions created by Siem Jan Koopman. S+GARCH was originally developed by Zhuanxin Ding, Hong-Ye Gao, Doug Martin, Jiahui Wang and Yihui Zhan. The S+FinMetrics function arima.rob was written by Ana Bianco, Marta Garcia Ben, Elena Martinez and Victor Yohai. The S+FinMetrics long memory modeling functions FAR, FARIMA, SEMIFAR and fgarch were developed by Jan Beran, Andrew Bruce, Don Percival, Alan Gibbs and Jiahui Wang and supported by NSF grant DMI-9801614 to Insightful Corporation (formerly MathSoft, Inc.). Hu McCulloch kindly provided the term structure data included with S+FinMetrics, and James MacKinnon provided data sets for the response surface critical values for the Dickey-Fuller and Phillips-Ouliaris distributions.

Contact Information and Website

The authors are responsible for all of the material in the book except the material on robust change detection, which was written by Victor Yohai. Eric Zivot is primarily responsible for chapters 2-6, 9-12 and 14-15 and Jiahui Wang is primarily responsible for chapters 1, 7-8, 13, and 16. The authors may be contacted by electronic mail at

    ezivot@u.washington.edu
    jwang@insightful.com

and welcome feedback and suggestions for improvements to the contents of the book. The website for the book is located on the Insightful Corporation website at

    http://www.insightful.com/support/finmetrics10

Acknowledgements

This book would not have been written without the support and encouragement from Insightful Corporation. The idea for the S+FinMetrics module was conceived by Douglas Martin and the authors. The development of S+FinMetrics was completed at Insightful by Jiahui Wang, Quan Wen and Hui Huang with help from many people. In particular, Jan Beran wrote many of the long memory functions while acting as a consultant to Insightful. Siem Jan Koopman helped to incorporate the *SsfPack* functions into S-PLUS and to write the chapter on state space models. Alexander McNeil and Rene Carmona graciously provided background material and S-PLUS examples for the material in the chapter on modeling extreme values. A number of people were helpful in proofreading the book and testing the software. Particular thanks go to Andrew Bruce, Chuck Curry, Zhuanxin Ding, Ruud Koning, Steve McKinney, David Weitzel, Quan Wen and Bingcheng Yan.

Typographical Conventions

This book obeys the following typographic conventions:

- The *italic* font is used for emphasis, and also for user-supplied variables within UNIX, DOS and S-PLUS commands.

- The typewriter font is used for S-PLUS functions, the output of S-PLUS functions and examples of S-PLUS sessions.

- S-PLUS objects of a specified class are expressed in typewriter font enclosed in quotations " ". For example, the S-PLUS timeSeries function creates objects of class "timeSeries".

Displayed S-PLUS commands are shown with the prompt character >. For example

```
> summary(ols.fit)
```

S-PLUS commands that require more than one line of input are displayed with the continuation prompt indicated by + or Continue string:. The S-PLUS output and plots in this book were generated from S+FinMetrics Version 1.0 and S-PLUS Version 6.0 release 2 for Windows. The S-PLUS output and "timeSeries" objects were generated with the options settings

```
> options(width=60)
> options(time.zone="GMT")
```

In some cases, parts of long output from S-PLUS functions is omitted and these lines are indicated by

```
...
```

Some of the output has been hand edited to avoid line overflow.

References

[1] FRANSES, P.H. (1998). *Time Series Models for Business and Economic Forecasting.* Cambridge University Press, Cambridge.

[2] HARVEY, A.C. (1993). *Time Series Models, Second Edition.* MIT Press, Cambridge.

[3] HOGG, R.V. AND A.T. CRAIG (1994). *Introduction to Mathematical Statistics, Fifth Edition.* Prentice Hall, New York.

[4] KRAUSE, A. AND M. OLSON (2002). *The Basics of S and S-PLUS, Third Edition.* Springer-Verlag, New York.

Contents

1
S and S-PLUS

1.1 Introduction

S-PLUS is a commercial software package developed by Insightful Corporation, based on the S language originally developed at Bell Laboratories (of AT&T and now Lucent Technologies) for statistical computation and visualization. Both S and S-PLUS have evolved through many versions. In 1999 John M. Chambers, the principal developer of S language, received the prestigious Software System Award from the Association for Computing Machinery (ACM), which has been awarded to UNIX, TEX, PostScript, TCP/IP and World Wide Web in the past.

The discussion of S language in this book is based on S-PLUS 6, which is supported on Microsoft Windows, Sun Solaris, and LINUX operating systems. In addition to *S-PLUS 6 Programmer's Guide*, there are many excellent books available introducing different aspects of S and S-PLUS (see Section 1.4 for a list of them), and refer to these books if you are not familiar with S or S-PLUS. This chapter has a rather limited goal: to introduce the object oriented approach of S language and summarize some modeling conventions that will be followed in this book. Section 1.2 introduces the concept of objects in S language, and Section 1.3 summarizes the usage of modeling functions in S-PLUS and S+FinMetrics. Finally, Section 1.4 points out some useful resources for learning and using S-PLUS.

1.2   S Objects

1.2.1   Assignment

As the S language evolved over time, different assignment operators have
been used, such as =, <-, <<-, and _ (underscore). This book will use the
assignment operator = whenever possible, because it is more intuitive and
requires only one key stroke. For example, in the command window of an
S-PLUS session, use the following command to assign the value of 3 to a
variable called a:

```
> a = 3
> a
[1] 3
```

When the name of the variable is typed at the command prompt, the value
of the variable is printed on screen with an index [1]. Since _ is reserved
as an assignment operator, it cannot be used in the names of any object.
Avoid the use of _ as an assignment operator, because the code may look
confusing to someone who is not familiar with S.

Although = has been chosen as the assignment operator whenever possible, only <- can be used as the assignment operator if the assignment is
inside a function call.[1] For example, suppose the user wants to assign the
value of 10 to the variable a, and use a to initialize a 5×5 matrix. If = is
used as the assignment operator, an error message appears:

```
> matrix(a = 10, 5, 5)
Problem in matrix: argument a= not matched: matrix(a = 10, 5, 5)
Use traceback() to see the call stack
```

But if the assignment operator <- is used, the desired behavior is achieved:

```
> matrix(a <- 10, 5, 5)
     [,1] [,2] [,3] [,4] [,5]
[1,]   10   10   10   10   10
[2,]   10   10   10   10   10
[3,]   10   10   10   10   10
[4,]   10   10   10   10   10
[5,]   10   10   10   10   10
> a
[1] 10
```

and 10 is successfully assigned as the value of a.

---

[1] The reason is that S-PLUS functions allow optional arguments with default values,
and = is used to set the default values in a function call.

1.2.2 Class

Since the S language is object oriented, everything in S-PLUS is an object with a *class*, and the class function can be used to find out the class of an object. For example:

```
> class(a)
[1] "integer"
```

thus the variable a has class "integer". Explicitly using the decimal point forces an integer number to be stored in double precision:

```
> b = 100000.
> class(b)
[1] "numeric"
```

A number with double precision in S-PLUS has class "numeric". In most situations S-PLUS is "smart" enough to perform computations in double precision if necessary. However, one has to be a little careful with integer arithmetic. For example, the following operation returns an NA:

```
> 100000 * 100000
[1] NA
```

because in this case, the multiplication is performed in integer mode, and the largest integer on a 32-bit machine is:

```
> 2^31 - 1
[1] 2147483647
```

which can be verified by querying the integer.max component of the machine constant object in S-PLUS:[2]

```
> .Machine$integer.max
[1] 2147483647
```

However, since the variable b created earlier is stored in double precision, the multiplication using b would return the desired result:

```
> b * b
[1] 1e+10
```

Together with "logical" and "character", "integer" and "numeric" objects are known as the *atomic* objects, upon which the user can build more complicated data structure, such as matrix, list, data frame, function, etc. For example, use the concatenation function c to combine the variables a and b into a vector, and use the matrix function to reshape it into a 2×1 matrix:

---

[2]See the on-line help file for .Machine for other components in the list.

```
> abMat = matrix(c(a,b), nrow=2)
> class(abMat)
[1] "matrix"
> abMat
       [,1]
[1,]  1e+01
[2,]  1e+05
```

As another example, although matrix is a built-in function in S-PLUS, it is just another object in S-PLUS:

```
> class(matrix)
[1] "function"
> matrix
function(data = NA, nrow = 1, ncol = 1, byrow = F, dimnames)
{
  if(missing(nrow))
    nrow <- ceiling(length(data)/ncol)
  else if(missing(ncol))
    ncol <- ceiling(length(data)/nrow)
  dim <- c(nrow, ncol)
  if(length(dim) != 2)
    stop("nrow and ncol should each be of length 1")
  value <- if(byrow) t(array(data, dim[2:1])) else
            array(data, dim)
  if(!missing(dimnames))
    value@.Dimnames <- dimnames
  value
}
```

The preceding output shows that matrix is just a "function" object. When the name of this object is typed, S-PLUS prints its function definition on the screen.

Most complicated S-PLUS objects are constructed as a list. For example, combine the variables a and b into a list as follows:

```
> abList = list(aComponent=a, bComponent=b)
> class(abList)
[1] "list"
> abList
$aComponent:
[1] 10

$bComponent:
[1] 1e+05
```

where the names aComponent and bComponent are given to a and b, respectively. Use the length function to find out the number of components in a list and the names function to extract the names of those components:

```
> length(abList)
[1] 2
> names(abList)
[1] "aComponent" "bComponent"
```

A particular component of a list can be extracted using the $ operator. For example:

```
> abList$aComponent
[1] 10
```

or the [[operator:

```
> abList[[2]]
[1] 1e+05
```

S-PLUS 6 is based on S language Version 4 (SV4). In SV4, a new class structure is introduced to build more complicated objects, as an alternative to using lists. One example is the "timeDate" objects in S-PLUS. For example, in the following example, use the timeDate function to parse a vector of character strings representing some dates:

```
> timeStamp = timeDate(c("1/1/2001", "1/2/2001", "1/3/2001"))
> timeStamp
[1] 01/01/2001 01/02/2001 01/03/2001
> class(timeStamp)
[1] "timeDate"
```

The names function cannot be used with these new class objects, which will be referred to as SV4 objects. Instead, use the slotNames function to extract the names of their components. For example:

```
> slotNames(timeStamp)
[1] ".Data"        ".Data.names"    ".Data.classes" "format"
[5] "time.zone"
```

A "timeDate" object has five slots. Instead of using the $ operator as for lists, use the @ operator to extract the component in a particular slot. For example:

```
> timeStamp@.Data
[[1]]:
[1] 14976 14977 14978

[[2]]:
[1] 0 0 0
```

The .Data slot of a "timeDate" object actually stores a list with two components.[3]

One difference between the list based objects and SV4 objects is that the list based objects are more flexible and thus prone to cause accidental programming errors if a programmer is not careful enough. In contrast, the SV4 objects are more stringently defined and can lead to robust software and computational efficiency. For example, the user can add or delete a component to a list at will:

```
> abList$anotherComponent = "a string component"
> abList
$aComponent:
[1] 10

$bComponent:
[1] 1e+05

$anotherComponent:
[1] "a string component"

> abList$aComponent = NULL
> abList
$bComponent:
[1] 1e+05

$anotherComponent:
[1] "a string component"
```

However, an SV4 object is strictly defined, and a component cannot be edited unless it is defined in its declaration:

```
> timeStamp@time.zone
[1] "GMT"
> timeStamp@time.zone = "Pacific"
> timeStamp@anotherSlot = "no way"
Problem in timeStamp@anotherSlot = "no way": Class "timeDate"
has no "anotherSlot" slot
Use traceback() to see the call stack
```

1.2.3 Method

Many S-PLUS functions are defined as *generic* in the sense that the user has the freedom of defining his or her own method for a particular class.

---

[3]The first component represents the Julian dates, and the second component represents the milliseconds elapsed since midnight of each day.

For example, the print and summary functions in S-PLUS are so generic that they work with any object and may generate different types of results depending on the class of the object.[4] For example:

```
> summary(abMat)
   Min. 1st Qu. Median   Mean 3rd Qu.    Max.
     10   25008  50005  50005   75002  100000
> summary(abList)
                  Length Class       Mode
      bComponent 1                   numeric
anotherComponent 1                   character
```

For a numeric matrix object, the summary method generates some sample statistics, while for a list object, the summary method summarizes the length and mode of each component.

In the above example, S-PLUS is "smart" enough to figure out the appropriate method to use for the generic summary function. If the name of the method function is known, the user can also call the method function directly. For example, if the user types matrix at the command prompt, S-PLUS will dispatch the print method for "function" objects because matrix is a "function" object. However, it can also call the function print.list on a "function" object to view the object using another format:

```
> print.list(matrix)
$data:
NA

$nrow:
[1] 1

$ncol:
[1] 1

$byrow:
F

$dimnames:

$"":
{
   if(missing(nrow))
```

---

[4] In fact, typing the name of an object at the command prompt, S-PLUS calls the print method of that object automatically. So any print methods rarely need to be called explicitly, except for Trellis graphics objects.

```
   nrow <- ceiling(length(data)/ncol)
 else if(missing(ncol))
   ncol <- ceiling(length(data)/nrow)
 dim <- c(nrow, ncol)
 if(length(dim) != 2)
   stop("nrow and ncol should each be of length 1")
 value <- if(byrow) t(array(data, dim[2:1])) else
         array(data, dim)
 if(!missing(dimnames))
   value@.Dimnames <- dimnames
 value
}
```

1.3   Modeling Functions in S+FinMetrics

In this book, many statistical and econometric examples are illustrated using modeling functions in S+FinMetrics. Some modeling functions in S+FinMetrics are named using upper case acronyms as they are known in the literature, because S is case sensitive and it distinguishes between upper case and lower case letters.

1.3.1   Formula Specification

For many modeling functions in S+FinMetrics, S formulas are used to specify the model to be estimated. Chambers and Hastie (1993) and *S-PLUS Guide to Statistics* provide detailed examples of how to specify models using formulas in S. This section points out some restrictions in formula specification so that the user can avoid some errors in using these functions. For illustrations, use the S-PLUS lm function as an example of modeling function.

If a formula is used to specify models in a modeling function, usually at least two arguments are supplied to the function: a formula object and a data object. The args function can always be used to find out the argument names of any function:

```
> args(lm)
function(formula, data, weights, subset, na.action, method =
        "qr", model = F, x = F, y = F, contrasts = NULL, ...)
NULL
```

The data object must be a "data.frame" object, or a "timeSeries" object with a "data.frame" in its data slot. First create a data frame using the S-PLUS data objects stack.x and stack.loss:

```
> stack.df = data.frame(Loss=stack.loss, stack.x)
```

```
> colIds(stack.df)
[1] "Loss"        "Air.Flow"    "Water.Temp" "Acid.Conc."
```

so the data frame `stack.df` has four columns with variable names as shown above.

To regress the variable `Loss` on `Air.Flow`, and `Water.Temp` using least squares, use the `lm` function as follows:

```
> test.mod = lm(Loss~Air.Flow + Water.Temp, data=stack.df)
> test.mod
Call:
lm(formula = Loss ~ Air.Flow + Water.Temp, data = stack.df)

Coefficients:
 (Intercept)   Air.Flow Water.Temp
   -50.35884 0.6711544    1.295351

Degrees of freedom: 21 total; 18 residual
Residual standard error: 3.238615
```

Notice that in the first `formula` object, `Loss` is on the left hand side of ~, so it represents the endogenous or response variable of the model; `Air.Flow` and `Water.Temp` are on the right hand side of ~, so they represent two independent or explanatory variables. An intercept or a constant term is also included automatically, as can be seen from the coefficient estimates in the output, which is generated by a call to the `print` method for "lm" objects:

```
> class(test.mod)
[1] "lm"
> oldClass(test.mod)
[1] "lm"
```

Note that since an "lm" object is a list based object, the user can also use the `oldClass` function to obtain its class. However, `oldClass` function does not work with SV4 objects. For example:

```
> oldClass(timeStamp)
NULL
```

The `data` argument can also be a "timeSeries" object with a data frame in its `data` slot. To illustrate this possibility, turn `stack.df` into a "timeSeries" object and call it `stack.ts`:

```
> stack.ts = timeSeries(stack.df)
> stack.ts
  Positions Loss Air.Flow Water.Temp Acid.Conc.
  01/01/1960 42   80       27         89
  01/02/1960 37   80       27         88
```

01/03/1960 37	75	25	90
01/04/1960 28	62	24	87
01/05/1960 18	62	22	87

...

Again, a linear model can be estimated using this data object just like in the previous example:

```
> test.mod = lm(Loss~Air.Flow + Water.Temp, data=stack.ts)
```

However, the **data** argument must have a data frame representation. The same function call will generate an error if the **data** argument is represented by a matrix:

```
> stack.mat = as.matrix(stack.df)
> lm(Loss~Air.Flow+Water.Temp, data=stack.mat)
Warning messages:
  Numerical expression has 84 elements: only the first used in:
  model.frame(formula, data, na.action, dots)
Problem: Invalid frame number, 42
Use traceback() to see the call stack
```

For most modeling functions such as lm, the **data** argument is actually an optional argument, which is not required. If the **data** argument is not supplied by the user, then the variables specified in the **formula** object must be on the search path. For example:

```
> lm(stack.loss~stack.x)
Call:
lm(formula = stack.loss ~ stack.x)

Coefficients:
 (Intercept) stack.xAir Flow stack.xWater Temp stack.xAcid Conc.
   -39.91967       0.7156402         1.295286         -0.1521225

Degrees of freedom: 21 total; 17 residual
Residual standard error: 3.243364
```

In addition, if the **data** argument is not supplied, the variables specified in the **formula** object must be either a vector or a matrix, and they cannot be a data frame nor a "timeSeries" object. For example:[5]

```
> stack.x.df = as.data.frame(stack.x)
> lm(stack.loss~stack.x.df)
Problem: Length of stack.x.df (variable 2) is 3 != length of
```

---

[5] In fact, many modeling functions in S+FinMetrics actually does allow a "timeSeries" object on the left hand side of the formula, but not the right hand side of the formula, if the **data** argument is not supplied. One example is the garch function.

```
others (21)
Use traceback() to see the call stack

> stack.loss.ts = timeSeries(stack.loss)
> lm(stack.loss.ts~stack.x)
Problem: Length of stack.loss.ts (variable 1) is 11 != length
of others (21)
Use traceback() to see the call stack
```

In S+FinMetrics, the formula is extended to support autoregressive specification, moving average specification, distributed lags and polynomial distributed lags for many modeling functions. These formulas will be illustrated in the appropriate chapters.

1.3.2 Method

In addition to print and summary functions, many other functions in S-PLUS are defined to be generic to work with modeling functions and objects, such as plot for diagnostic plots, coefficients or simply coef for extracting model coefficients, residuals for extracting model residuals, fitted.values or simply fitted for extracting model fitted values, predict for out of sample prediction, etc. For example, for the "lm" object test.mod, if the generic functions coef, predict or plot are applied, S-PLUS will figure out the appropriate method to use:

```
> coef(test.mod)
 (Intercept)  Air.Flow Water.Temp
   -50.35884 0.6711544   1.295351

> predict(test.mod, matrix(1, 5, 3))
[1] -48.39233 -48.39233 -48.39233 -48.39233 -48.39233

> plot(test.mod, ask=T)

Make a plot selection (or 0 to exit):

1: plot: All
2: plot: Residuals vs Fitted Values
3: plot: Sqrt of abs(Residuals) vs Fitted Values
4: plot: Response vs Fitted Values
5: plot: Normal QQplot of Residuals
6: plot: r-f spread plot
7: plot: Cook's Distances
Selection:
```

In addition to the above generic functions, S+FinMetrics defines three new generic functions for working with model objects: vcov for extracting the variance-covariance matrix of estimated parameters, simulate for generating simulations according to the estimated model, and cpredict for obtaining conditional forecasts of multivariate time series models.

1.4 S-PLUS Resources

1.4.1 Books

In addition to the S-PLUS manuals, there are a number of good books on using and programming in S and S-PLUS as well as data and statistical analysis using S-PLUS. The Insightful web page

http://www.insightful.com/support/splusbooks.asp

contains a listing of these books.

Using and Programming S-PLUS

Gentle introductions to S and S-PLUS are given in Spector (1994), Lam (2001) and Krause and Olson (2002). The details of version four of the S language are described in Chambers (1998), also known as the "green book". An indispensable guide to programming in the S language is Venables and Ripley (2000).

Data and Statistical Analysis in S-PLUS

S-PLUS provides extensive functionality for the statistical analysis of a wide variety of data, and many books have been written on the use of S-PLUS for particular applications. The following books describe statistical techniques that are useful for the analysis of financial data. Carmona (2001) and Chan (2002) describe the use of S-PLUS for the analysis of financial time series. An excellent guide to modern applied statistics using S-PLUS is Venables and Ripley (1999). Harrell (2001) gives a thorough treatment of regression models, including generalized linear models and survival model. Pinheiro and Bates (2000) detail the analysis of mixed effects (panel data) models. Therneau and Grambsch (2000) survey survival analysis models. Wilcox (1997), and Atkinson and Riani (2000) discuss robust statistical methods. Bruce and Gao (1996) describe wavelet analysis. Hastie, Tibshirani and Friedman (2001) cover aspects of statistical learning and data mining. Davison and Hinkley (1997) survey bootstrap methods, and Bowman and Azzalini (1997) disucss nonparametric and smoothing methods.

1.4.2   Internet

There is a wealth of information about S-PLUS available on the internet. The obvious place to start is the Insightful website at

http://www.insightful.com

S-News is an electronic mail discussion list for S and S-PLUS users. Information about S-News may be found at

http://www.biostat.wustl.edu/s-news/s-news-intro.html

StatLib is a repository for software and extensions for the S language, including many useful additions to S-PLUS. It can be found at

http://lib.stat.cmu.edu/S

Eric Zivot maintains a website containing links to websites for S-PLUS applications in econometrics and finance at

http://faculty.washington.edu/ezivot/splus.htm

1.5   References

[1] ATKINSON, A. AND M. RIANI (2000). *Robust Diagnostic Regression Analysis.* Springer-Verlag, New York.

[2] BOWMAN, A.W., AND A. AZZALINI (1997). *Applied Smoothing Techniques for Data Analysis:The Kernel Approach with S PLUS Illustrations.* Oxford University Press, Oxford.

[3] BRUCE, A. AND H.-Y. GAO (1996). *Applied Wavelet Analysis with S-PLUS.* Springer-Verlag, New York.

[4] CHAMBERS, J.M. (1998). *Programming with Data.* Springer-Verlag, New York.

[5] CHAMBERS, J. M., AND HASTIE, T. J. (1993). *Statistical Models in S.* Chapman & Hall.

[6] CARMONA, R. (2001). *Statistical Analysis of Financial Data, with an implementation in Splus.* Textbook under review.

[7] CHAN, N.H. (2002). *Time Series: Applications to Finance.* John Wiley & Sons, New York.

[8] DAVIDSON, A.C. AND D.V. HINKLEY (1997). *Bootstrap Methods and Their Application.* Cambridge University Press, Cambridge, UK.

[9] HARRELL, F.E. (2001). *Regression Modeling Strategies with Applications to Linear Models, Logistic Regression, and Survival Analysis.* Springer-Verlag, New York.

[10] HASTIE, T., R. TIBSHIRANI AND J. FRIEDMAN (2001). *The Elements of Statistical Learning: Data Mining, Inference and Prediction.* Springer-Verlag, New York.

[11] KRAUSE, A. AND M. OLSON (2002). *The Basics of S and S-PLUS, Third Edition.* Springer-Verlag, New York.

[12] LAM, L. (2001). *An Introduction to S-PLUS for Windows.* Candiensten, Amsterdam.

[13] PINHEIRO, J.C. AND D.M. BATES (2000). *Mixed-Effects Models in S and S-PLUS.* Springer-Verlag, New York.

[14] SPECTOR, P. (1994). *An Introduction to S and S-PLUS.* Duxbury Press, Belmont, CA.

[15] THERNEAU, T.M. AND P.M GRAMBSCH (2000). *Modeling Survival Data.* Springer-Verlag, New York.

[16] VENABLES, W.N. AND B.D. RIPLEY (1999). *Modern Applied Statistics with S-PLUS, Third Edition.* Springer-Verlag, New York.

[17] VENABLES, W.N. AND B.D. RIPLEY (1999). *S Programming.* Springer-Verlag, New York.

[18] WILCOX, P. (1997). *Introduction to Robust Estimation and Hypothesis Testing.* Academic Press, San Diego.

2
Time Series Specification, Manipulation, and Visualization in S-PLUS

2.1 Introduction

Time series data may be stored, manipulated and visualized in a variety of ways in S-PLUS[1]. This chapter discusses the basics of working with financial time series data in the form of S-PLUS "timeSeries" objects. It begins with a discussion of the specification of "timeSeries" and "timeDate" objects in S-PLUS and gives examples of how to specify common "timeDate" sequences for financial time series. Basic manipulations of financial time series are discussed and illustrated. These manipulations include aggregating and disaggregating time series, handling of missing values, creations of lags and differences and asset return calculations. The chapter ends with an overview of time series visualization tools and techniques, including the S-PLUS plotting functions for "timeSeries" as well as specialized plotting functions in S+FinMetrics.

2.2 The Specification of "timeSeries" Objects in S-PLUS

Financial time series data may be represented and analyzed in S-PLUS in a variety of ways. By far the most flexible way to analyze, manipulate

---

[1] Chapters 25-27 in the *S-PLUS Guide to Statistic (Vol. II)* discusses the analysis of time series in S-PLUS.

and visualize time series data is through the use of S-PLUS calendar-based "timeSeries" objects. A calendar-based "timeSeries" object, hereafter referred to as simply a "timeSeries" is an S version 4 (sv4) object that stores time and date information from a "timeDate" object in a positions slot and time series data from any rectangular data object (vector, matrix or data frame) in a data slot. Additionally, summary information about the time series may be stored in the title, documentation, units and attributes slots.

To illustrate a typical "timeSeries" object, consider the S+FinMetrics "timeSeries" object singleIndex.dat which contains monthly closing price data on Microsoft and the S&P 500 index over the period January 1990 through January 2001:

```
> class(singleIndex.dat)
[1] "timeSeries"

> slotNames(singleIndex.dat)
 [1] "data"              "positions"        "start.position"
 [4] "end.position"      "future.positions" "units"
 [7] "title"             "documentation"    "attributes"
[10] "fiscal.year.start" "type"

> singleIndex.dat@title
[1] "Monthly prices on Microsoft and S&P 500 Index"

> singleIndex.dat@documentation
[1] "Monthly closing prices over the period January 1900"
[2] "through January 2001 adjusted for dividends and stock"
[3] "splits.

> singleIndex.dat@units
[1] "Monthly price"

> singleIndex.dat[1:5,]
 Positions    MSFT   SP500
 Jan 1990   1.2847  329.08
 Feb 1990   1.3715  331.89
 Mar 1990   1.5382  339.94
 Apr 1990   1.6111  330.80
 May 1990   2.0278  361.23
```

The date information in the positions slot may be extracted directly or by using the positions extractor function:

```
> singleIndex.dat@positions[1:5]
[1] Jan 1990 Feb 1990 Mar 1990 Apr 1990 May 1990
```

```
> positions(singleIndex.dat)[1:5]
[1] Jan 1990 Feb 1990 Mar 1990 Apr 1990 May 1990
```

The generic start and end functions may be used to extract the start and end dates of a "timeSeries" object:

```
> start(singleIndex.dat)
[1] Jan 1990
> end(singleIndex.dat)
[1] Jan 2001
```

The date information in the positions slot is an object of class "timeDate"

```
> class(positions(singleIndex.dat))
[1] "timeDate"
```

Details on "timeDate" objects are given later on in this chapter.

The time series data in the data slot may be accessed directly or through the seriesData extractor function:

```
> singleIndex.dat@data[1:5,]
    MSFT   SP500
1 1.2847 329.08
2 1.3715 331.89
3 1.5382 339.94
4 1.6111 330.80
5 2.0278 361.23

> seriesData(singleIndex.dat)[1:5,]
    MSFT   SP500
1 1.2847 329.08
2 1.3715 331.89
3 1.5382 339.94
4 1.6111 330.80
5 2.0278 361.23
```

In general, the time series data in the data slot is a "rectangular" data object and is usually a data frame or a matrix. For example,

```
> class(seriesData(singleIndex.dat))
[1] "data.frame"
```

In fact, "timeSeries" objects themselves are "rectangular" data objects and so the functions numRows, numCols, colIds and rowIds may be used to extract useful information:

```
> is.rectangular(singleIndex.dat)
[1] T
> numRows(singleIndex.dat)
[1] 133
```

```
> numCols(singleIndex.dat)
[1] 2
> colIds(singleIndex.dat)
[1] "MSFT"  "SP500"
> rowIds(singleIndex.dat)[1:5]
[1] Jan 1990 Feb 1990 Mar 1990 Apr 1990 May 1990
```

2.2.1 Basic Manipulations

Basic manipulation of "timeSeries" objects may be done in the same
way as other S-PLUS objects. Mathematical operations may be applied to
"timeSeries" objects in the usual way and the result will be a "timeSeries"
object. Subscripting a "timeSeries" works in the same way as subscripting a data frame or matrix. For example, a "timeSeries" with the prices
on Microsoft may be extracted from singleIndex.dat using

```
> msft.p = singleIndex.dat[,"MSFT"]
> msft.p = singleIndex.dat[,1]
> msft.p@title = "Monthly closing price on Microsoft"
> msft.p@documentation =
+ c("Monthly closing price adjusted for stock",
+ "splits and dividends.")
> msft.p@units = "US dollar price"
> class(msft.p)
[1] "timeSeries"
```

Subsamples from a "timeSeries" may be extracted by creating an index of
logical values that are true for the times and dates of interest. For example,
consider creating a subsample from the "timeSeries" singleIndex.dat
over the period March 1992 through January 1993.

```
> smpl = (positions(singleIndex.dat) >= timeDate("3/1/1992") &
+ positions(singleIndex.dat) <= timeDate("1/31/1993"))
> singleIndex.dat[smpl,]
 Positions  MSFT SP500
 Mar 1992  4.938 403.7
 Apr 1992  4.594 414.9
 May 1992  5.042 415.4
 Jun 1992  4.375 408.1
 Jul 1992  4.547 424.2
 Aug 1992  4.656 414.0
 Sep 1992  5.031 417.8
 Oct 1992  5.547 418.7
 Nov 1992  5.820 431.4
 Dec 1992  5.336 435.7
 Jan 1993  5.406 438.8
```

Not all S-PLUS functions have methods to handle "timeSeries" objects. Some examples are the S-PLUS functions colMeans, colVars and colStdevs which compute the mean, variance and standard deviation value for each column of data:

```
> colMeans(singleIndex.dat)
[1] NA
```

For these functions, the extractor function seriesData should be used to extract the data slot of the "timeSeries" prior to applying the function:

```
> colMeans(seriesData(singleIndex.dat))
  MSFT SP500
 26.75 730.4
```

All of the S+FinMetrics modeling and support functions are designed to accept "timeSeries" objects in a uniform way.

2.2.2 S-PLUS "timeDate" Objects

Time and date information in S-PLUS may be stored in "timeDate" objects. The S-PLUS function timeDate is used to create "timeDate" objects. For example, to create a "timeDate" object for the date January 1, 2002 for the US Pacific time zone use

```
> td = timeDate("1/1/2002",in.format="%m/%d/%Y",
+ zone="Pacific")
```

The date information is specified in a character string and the optional arguments in.format and zone determine the input date format and the time zone, respectively. The input formats are single-element character vectors consisting of input fields which start with "%" and end with a letter. The default input date format may be viewed with

```
> options("time.in.format")
$time.in.format:
[1] "%m[/][.]%d[/][,]%y [%H[:%M[:%S[.%N]]][%p][[(]%3Z[)]]]"
```

and examples of common date formats can be found in the S-PLUS object format.timeDate

```
> names(format.timeDate)
 [1] "1/3/1998"
 [2] "3/1/1998"
...
[32] "03 Jan 1998 14:04:32 (PST)"
> format.timeDate[[1]]$input
[1] "%m/%d/%Y"
```

The result of timeDate is an object of class "timeDate"

```
> class(td)
[1] "timeDate"
> td
[1] 1/1/02 0:00:00 AM
> slotNames(td)
[1] ".Data"         ".Data.names"   ".Data.classes"
[4] "format"        "time.zone"
```

"timeDate" objects have a number of slots that are used to specify and control time and date information. Full details may be seen using

```
> ?class.timeDate
```

The .Data slot is a list with components giving the Julian date representation of the day and time within the day. The Julian day represents the number of days since January 1, 1960 and the Julian time within the day indicates the number of milliseconds since midnight Greenwich mean time (GMT)

```
> td@.Data
[[1]]:
[1] 15341

[[2]]:
[1] 28800000
```

Since the US Pacific Time Zone is 8 hours behind GMT, the number of milliseconds since Greenwich mean time is $8 * 60 * 60 * 1000 = 28,800,000$. The output display format of the date information is specified in the format slot

```
> ·td@format
[1] "%m/%d/%02y %H:%02M:%02S %p"
```

Like input formats, output formats are single-element character vectors consisting of output fields, which start with "%" and end with a letter, and other characters that are simply printed. The above format specifies printing the date as month/day/year and then hour:minute:second and AM or PM. The integers 02 before y, M and S fix the output width to 2 characters. All supported output fields are described in the help file for class.timeDate and a list of example output formats are given in the S-PLUS object format.timeDate. For example,

```
> names(format.timeDate)[18]
[1] "03 Jan 1998"
> format.timeDate[[18]]$output
[1] "%02d %b %Y"
```

Time Zone Issues

The time and date information stored in a "timeDate" object is aligned to the time zone specified in the time.zone slot

```
> td@time.zone
[1] "Pacific"
```

To modify the output format of a "timeDate" object to display time zone information simply add "%z"

```
> td@format = paste(td@format,"%z")
> td
[1] 1/1/02 0:00:00 AM Pacific
```

The object td is aligned to the US Pacific time zone. If the zone argument to timeDate is omitted when the "timeDate" object is created the default time zone in options('`time.zone")` is used[2]. For example,

```
> options("time.zone")
$time.zone:
[1] "Pacific"
> td2 = timeDate("Mar 02, 1963 08:00 PM",
+ in.format="%m %d, %Y %H:%M %p",
+ format="%b %02d, %Y %02I:%02M %p %z")
> td2
[1] Mar 02, 1963 08:00 PM Pacific
```

Note that the above example shows that the output format of the "timeDate" object can be specified when the object is created using the argument format.

All of the time zone specifications supported by S-PLUS are described in the help file for class.timeZone and these specifications are defined relative to times and dates given in GMT. The time zone specifications include daylight savings time in various areas around the world. To see how a time zone specification affects a timeDate object, consider what happens when the time zone for the object td is changed to US Eastern Time:

```
> td@time.zone = "Eastern"
> td
[1] 1/1/02 3:00:00 AM Eastern
> td@.Data
[[1]]:
```

---

[2]On Windows platforms, the time zone specification is obtained from the Windows regional settings. The examples in this section were created on a Windows computer in the U.S. Pacific time zone. Therefore, the default time zone taken from the Windows regional settings is "Pacific".

```
[1] 15341
```

```
[[2]]:
[1] 28800000
```

Since US Eastern Time is three hours ahead of US Pacific Time the displayed date is moved ahead three hours. That is, midnight US Pacific Time on January 1, 2002 is the same as 3 AM US Eastern Time on January 1, 2002. Notice that changing the time zone information does not alter the Julian date information in the .Data slot. To align the Julian date representation to reflect the number of milliseconds from GMT on US Eastern time the millisecond information in the second component of the .Data slot must be adjusted directly.

If a "timeDate" object is created in GMT then the S-PLUS function timeZoneConvert may be used to re-align the millisecond offset to a specified time zone. For example,

```
> tdGMT = timeDate("1/1/2002",zone="GMT",
+ format="%m/%d/%02y %H:%02M:%02S %p %z")
> tdGMT
[1] 1/1/02 0:00:00 AM GMT
> tdGMT@.Data
[[1]]:
[1] 15341

[[2]]:
[1] 0

> tdPST = timeZoneConvert(tdGMT,"PST")
> tdPST
[1] 1/1/02 0:00:00 AM PST
> tdPST@.Data
[[1]]:
[1] 15341

[[2]]:
[1] 28800000
```

Be aware that timeZoneConvert is not designed to convert the millisecond offsets from one arbitrary time zone other than GMT to another arbitrary time zone.

Mathematical Operations with "timeDate" Objects

Since "timeDate" objects have a Julian date representation, certain mathematical operations like addition and subtractions of numbers may be performed on them and the result will also be a "timeDate" object. For example,

```
> td1 = timeDate("1/1/2002",in.format="%m/%d/%Y",
+ zone="GMT",format="%m/%d/%04Y %H:%02M:%02S %p %z")
> td2 = timeDate("2/1/2002",in.format="%m/%d/%Y",
+ zone="GMT",format="%m/%d/%04Y %H:%02M:%02S %p %z")
> td1
[1] 1/1/2002 0:00:00 AM GMT
> td2
[1] 2/1/2002 0:00:00 AM GMT

> as.numeric(td1)
[1] 15341
> td1 + 1
[1] 1/2/2002 0:00:00 AM GMT
> td1 + 0.5
[1] 1/1/2002 12:00:00 PM GMT
> td1 - 1
[1] 12/31/2001 0:00:00 AM GMT
> 2*td1
[1] 30682
> td1+td2
[1] 2/2/2044 0:00:00 AM GMT
```

Adding two "timeDate" objects together creates another "timeDate" object with date given by the addition of the respective Julian dates. Subtraction of two "timeDate" objects, however, produces an sv4 object of class "timeSpan"

```
> td.diff = td2 - td1
> class(td.diff)
[1] "timeSpan"
> td.diff
[1] 31d 0h 0m 0s 0MS
> slotNames(td.diff)
[1] ".Data"         ".Data.names"    ".Data.classes"
[4] "format"
```

The "timeSpan" object td.diff gives the time difference between td1 and td2 - 31 days, 0 hours, 0 minutes, 0 seconds and 0 milliseconds. The Julian date information is kept in the .Data slot and the output format is in the format slot. Details about "timeSpan" objects is given in The *S-PLUS Guide to Statistics, Vol. II*, chapter 25.

2.2.3 Creating Common "timeDate" Sequences

Most historical financial time series are regularly spaced calendar-based time series; e.g. daily, monthly or annual time series. However, some financial time series are irregularly spaced. Two common examples of irregularly spaced financial time series are daily closing prices and intra-day transactions level data. There are a variety of time and date functions in S-PLUS that may be used to create regularly spaced and irregularly spaced "timeDate" sequences for essentially any kind of financial data. These functions are illustrated using the following examples[3].

Regularly and irregularly spaced sequences may be created using the S-PLUS functions timeCalendar, timeSeq and timeSequence. The function timeSeq is the most flexible. The following examples illustrate the use of these functions for creating common "timeDate" sequences.

Annual Sequences

Creating a "timeDate" sequence for an annual time series from 1900 to 1910 may be done in a variety of ways. Perhaps, the simplest way uses the S-PLUS timeCalendar function:

```
> td = timeCalendar(y=1900:1910,format="%Y")
> class(td)
[1] "timeDate"
> td
 [1] 1900 1901 1902 1903 1904 1905 1906 1907 1908 1909 1910
```

The timeCalendar function produces an object of class "timeDate". The argument format="%Y" specifies the output format of the "timeDate" object as a four digit year.

Since td contains a sequence of dates, the Julian date information for all of the dates is available in the .Data slot

```
> td@.Data
[[1]]:
 [1] -21914 -21549 -21184 -20819 -20454 -20088 -19723 -19358
 [9] -18993 -18627 -18262

[[2]]:
 [1] 0 0 0 0 0 0 0 0 0 0 0
```

An annual sequence from 1900 to 1910 may also be computed using the S-PLUS function timeSeq:

```
> timeSeq(from="1/1/1900", to="1/1/1910", by="years",
```

---

[3] To avoid problems with time zone specifications, all examples in this sections were created after setting the default time zone to GMT using options(time.zone="GMT").

```
+ format="%Y")
 [1] 1900 1901 1902 1903 1904 1905 1906 1907 1908 1909 1910
```

The argument by="years" specifies annual spacing between successive values in the sequence starting at 1/1/1900 and ending at 1/1/1910. The date formats for the starting and ending dates must conform to the default input format for "timeDate" objects (see options("time.in.format")).

Finally, an annual sequence from 1900 to 1910 may be created using the S-PLUS function timeSequence:

```
> tds = timeSequence("1/1/1900","1/1/1910",by="years",
+ format="%Y")
> class(tds)
[1] "timeSequence"
> tds
from:    1900
to:      1910
by:      +1yr
[1] 1900 1901 1902 ...   1910
```

timeSequence creates an object of class "timeSequence" which stores time and date information in a compact fashion. The "timeSequence" object may be converted to a "timeDate" object using the S-PLUS as function

```
> td = as(tds,"timeDate")
> td
 [1] 1900 1901 1902 1903 1904 1905 1906 1907 1908 1909 1910
```

Quarterly Sequences

A quarterly "timeDate" sequence from 1900:I through 1902:IV may be created using timeSeq with the by="quarters" option:

```
> timeSeq(from="1/1/1900", to="10/1/1902", by="quarters",
+ format="%Y:%Q")
 [1] 1900:I    1900:II   1900:III 1900:IV   1901:I    1901:II
 [7] 1901:III 1901:IV   1902:I    1902:II   1902:III 1902:IV
```

The output format character %Q displays the quarter information. Notice that the dates are specified as the first day of the quarter.

Monthly Sequences

Now consider creating a monthly "timeDate" sequence from January 1, 1900 through March 1, 1901. This may be done using timeCalendar

```
> timeCalendar(m=rep(1:12,length=15),y=rep(1900:1901,each=12,
+ length=15), format="%b %Y")
 [1] Jan 1900 Feb 1900 Mar 1900 Apr 1900 May 1900 Jun 1900
```

```
 [7] Jul 1900 Aug 1900 Sep 1900 Oct 1900 Nov 1900 Dec 1900
[13] Jan 1901 Feb 1901 Mar 1901
```

or timeSeq

```
> timeSeq(from="1/1/1900",to="3/1/1901",by="months",
+ format="%b %Y")
 [1] Jan 1900 Feb 1900 Mar 1900 Apr 1900 May 1900 Jun 1900
 [7] Jul 1900 Aug 1900 Sep 1900 Oct 1900 Nov 1900 Dec 1900
[13] Jan 1901 Feb 1901 Mar 1901
```

To create a monthly sequence of end of month values from December 31, 1899 through February 28, 1901, subtract 1 from the above calculation:

```
> timeSeq(from="1/1/1900",to="3/1/1901",by="months",
+ format="%b %Y") - 1
 [1] Dec 1899 Jan 1900 Feb 1900 Mar 1900 Apr 1900 May 1900
 [7] Jun 1900 Jul 1900 Aug 1900 Sep 1900 Oct 1900 Nov 1900
[13] Dec 1900 Jan 1901 Feb 1901
```

Weekly Sequences

Weekly sequences are best created using timeSeq with by="weeks". For example, a weekly sequence from Monday January 1, 1990 to Monday Feb 26, 1990 may be created using

```
> timeSeq(from="1/1/1990",to="3/1/1990",by="weeks",
+ format="%a %b %d, %Y")
[1] Mon Jan 1, 1990  Mon Jan 8, 1990  Mon Jan 15, 1990
[4] Mon Jan 22, 1990 Mon Jan 29, 1990 Mon Feb 5, 1990
[7] Mon Feb 12, 1990 Mon Feb 19, 1990 Mon Feb 26, 1990
```

To create a weekly sequence starting on a specific day, say Wednesday, make the starting date a Wednesday.

Daily Sequences

A regularly spaced daily sequence may be created using timeSeq with by = "days". For an irregularly spaced daily sequence of weekdays use timeSeq with by = "weekdays". For financial asset price data that trades on U.S. exchanges, the relevant "daily" sequence of dates is an irregularly spaced sequence based on business days. Business days are weekdays excluding certain holidays. For example, consider creating a daily "timeDate" sequence for the month of January, 2000 for a time series of asset prices that trade on the New York stock exchange (NYSE). The NYSE is not open on weekends and on certain holidays and these dates should be omitted from the "timeDate" sequence. The S-PLUS function holiday.NYSE returns the New York Stock Exchange holidays for a given year, 1885-present, according to the historical and current (as of 1998) schedule, not including special-event closure days or partial-day closures. The NYSE holidays for 2000 are

```
> holiday.NYSE(2000)
[1] 1/17/2000   2/21/2000   4/21/2000   5/29/2000   7/4/2000
[6] 9/4/2000    11/23/2000 12/25/2000
```

Martin Luther King day on Monday January 17th is the only weekday holiday. A "timeDate" sequence of business days excluding the holiday 1/17/2000 may be created using

```
> timeSeq(from="1/3/2000",to="1/31/2000",by="bizdays",
+ holidays=holiday.NYSE(2000),format="%a %b %d, %Y")
 [1] Mon Jan 3, 2000   Tue Jan 4, 2000   Wed Jan 5, 2000
 [4] Thu Jan 6, 2000   Fri Jan 7, 2000   Mon Jan 10, 2000
 [7] Tue Jan 11, 2000 Wed Jan 12, 2000 Thu Jan 13, 2000
[10] Fri Jan 14, 2000 Tue Jan 18, 2000 Wed Jan 19, 2000
[13] Thu Jan 20, 2000 Fri Jan 21, 2000 Mon Jan 24, 2000
[16] Tue Jan 25, 2000 Wed Jan 26, 2000 Thu Jan 27, 2000
[19] Fri Jan 28, 2000 Mon Jan 31, 2000
```

The argument holidays=holiday.NYSE(2000) in conjunction with by = "bizdays" instructs timeSeq to exclude the weekday dates associated with the NYSE holidays for 2000. Notice that the date Mon Jan 17, 2000 has been omitted from the sequence.

Intra-day Irregularly Spaced Sequences

Sequences of irregularly spaced intra-day dates may be created using the function timeCalendar. For example, consider creating a sequence of hourly observations only during the hypothetical trading hours from 9:00 AM to 3:00 PM from Monday January 3, 2000 through Tuesday January 4, 2000. Such a sequence may be created using timeCalendar as follows

```
> timeCalendar(h=rep(9:15,2),d=rep(3:4,each=7),
+ y=2000,format="%a %b %d, %Y %02I:%02M %p")
 [1] Mon Jan 3, 2000 09:00 AM Mon Jan 3, 2000 10:00 AM
 [3] Mon Jan 3, 2000 11:00 AM Mon Jan 3, 2000 12:00 PM
 [5] Mon Jan 3, 2000 01:00 PM Mon Jan 3, 2000 02:00 PM
 [7] Mon Jan 3, 2000 03:00 PM Tue Jan 4, 2000 09:00 AM
 [9] Tue Jan 4, 2000 10:00 AM Tue Jan 4, 2000 11:00 AM
[11] Tue Jan 4, 2000 12:00 PM Tue Jan 4, 2000 01:00 PM
[13] Tue Jan 4, 2000 02:00 PM Tue Jan 4, 2000 03:00 PM
```

In a similar fashion, a sequence of minute observations from 9:00 AM to 3:00 PM on Monday January 3, 2000 and Tuesday January 4, 2000 may be created using

```
> timeCalendar(min=rep(rep(0:59,6),2),
```

```
+ h=rep(9:14,each=60,length=360*2),
+ d=rep(3:4,each=360,length=360*2),
+ y=2000,format="%a %b %d, %Y %02I:%02M %p")
  [1] Mon Jan 3, 2000 09:00 AM Mon Jan 3, 2000 09:01 AM
  [3] Mon Jan 3, 2000 09:02 AM Mon Jan 3, 2000 09:03 AM
  ...
  [359] Mon Jan 3, 2000 02:58 PM Mon Jan 3, 2000 02:59 PM
  [361] Tue Jan 4, 2000 09:00 AM Tue Jan 4, 2000 09:01 AM
  ...
  [719] Tue Jan 4, 2000 02:58 PM Tue Jan 4, 2000 02:59 PM
```

2.2.4 Miscellaneous Time and Date Functions

In addition to the time and date functions discussed so far, S-PLUS has a number of miscellaneous time and date functions. In addition S+FinMetrics provides a few time and date functions. These are summarized in Table 2.1.

2.2.5 Creating "timeSeries" Objects

S-PLUS "timeSeries" objects are created with the timeSeries function. Typically a "timeSeries" is created from some existing data in a data frame or matrix and a "timeDate" object. For example,

```
> my.df = data.frame(x=abs(rnorm(10,mean=5)),
+ y=abs(rnorm(10,mean=10)))
> my.td = timeCalendar(y=1990:1999,format="%Y")
> my.ts = timeSeries(data=my.df,pos=my.td)
> my.ts
 Positions     x       y
 1990       4.250  11.087
 1991       5.290  11.590
 1992       5.594  11.848
 1993       5.138  10.426
 1994       5.205   9.678
 1995       4.804  11.120
 1996       5.726  11.616
 1997       6.124   9.781
 1998       3.981  10.725
 1999       6.006  10.341
```

Information about the "timeSeries" object may be added to the title, documentation and units slots:

```
> my.ts@title = "My timeSeries"
> my.ts@documentation = c("Simulated annual price data using ",
+ "the S-PLUS function rnorm")
```

S-PLUS function	Description
month.day.year	Converts calendar dates to Julian dates
julian	Converts Julian dates to calendar dates
quarters	Create an ordered factor corresponding to quarters
months	Create an ordered factor corresponding to months
days	Create an ordered factor corresponding to days
weekdays	Create an ordered factor corresponding to weekdays
years	Create an ordered factor corresponding to years
yeardays	Extract year day from date
hours	Extract hour from date
minutes	Extract minutes from date
seconds	Extract seconds from date
hms	Create data frame containing hours, minutes and seconds
mdy	Create data frame containing month, day and year
wdydy	Create data frame containing weekday, year day and year
leap.year	Determines if year number corresponds to a leap year
holidays	Generate a collection of holidays
holiday.fixed	Generate holidays that occur on fixed dates
holiday.weekday.number	Generate holidays that occur on weekdays
S+FinMetrics function	**Description**
days.count	Count number of days between two dates
is.weekday	Tests if date is a weekday
is.weekend	Tests if date is a weekend
is.bizday	Tests if date is a business day
imm.dates	Create International Monetary Market dates

TABLE 2.1. Miscellaneous time and date functions

```
> my.ts@units = c("US dollars","US dollars")
```

The title and units information is utilized in certain plot functions.

Creating "timeSeries" Objects from Time Series in Data Frames

Very often time series data that are in data frames have a date variable
with a formatted date string. The S-PLUS function timeDate has a variety of input formats that may be used to convert such date strings into
"timeDate" objects. For example, the S+FinMetrics data frame yhoo.df
contains daily high, low, open and close prices as well as volume information
for Yahoo stock for the month of February 2002

```
> yhoo.df[1:2,]
        Date  Open High   Low Close  Volume
1 1-Feb-02 17.26 17.3 16.35 16.68 6930100
2 4-Feb-02 16.55 16.6 15.60 15.75 8913700
```

The variable Date is a character vector containing the date strings. A
"timeDate" sequence created from the date strings in Date is

```
> td = timeDate(yhoo.df[,1],in.format="%d-%m-%y",
+ format="%a %b %d, %Y")
> td[1:2]
[1] Fri Feb 1, 2002 Mon Feb 4, 2002
```

A "timeSeries" object containing the data from yhoo.df is created using

```
> yhoo.ts = timeSeries(pos=td,data=yhoo.df[,-1])
> yhoo.ts[1:2,]
        Positions Open High   Low Close  Volume
 Fri Feb 1, 2002 17.26 17.3 16.35 16.68 6930100
 Mon Feb 4, 2002 16.55 16.6 15.60 15.75 8913700
```

High frequency data, however, is often recorded using nonstandard time
formats. For example, consider the transactions level data for the month of
December 1999 for 3M stock in the S+FinMetrics data frame highFreq3m.df

```
> highFreq3M.df[1:2,]
  trade.day trade.time trade.price
1         1      34412      94.688
2         1      34414      94.688
```

The variable trade.day contains the integer trading day of the month,
the variable trade.time contains the integer trade time recorded as the
number of seconds from midnight and the variable trade.price contains
the transaction price in dollars. A "timeDate" sequence may be easily
created from the trade day and trade time information as follows

```
> td = timeDate(julian=(highFreq3M.df$trade.day-1),
```

```
+ ms=highFreq3M.df$trade.time*1000,
+ in.origin=c(month=12,day=1,year=1999),zone="GMT")
> td[1:2]
[1] 12/1/99 9:33:32 AM 12/1/99 9:33:34 AM
```

The function timeDate can create a "timeDate" sequence using Julian date and millisecond information. The argument julian takes an integer vector containing the number of days since the date specified in the argument in.origin, and the argument ms takes an integer vector containing the number of milliseconds since midnight. In the above example, in.origin is specified as December 1, 1999 and the optional argument zone is used to set the time zone to GMT. A "timeSeries" object containing the high frequency data in highFreq3M.df is created using

```
> hf3M.ts = timeSeries(pos=td,data=highFreq3M.df)
```

2.2.6 Aggregating and Disaggregating Time Series

Often a regularly spaced financial time series of a given frequency may need to be aggregated to a coarser frequency or disaggregated to a finer frequency. In addition, aggregation and disaggregation may involve flow or stock variables. The S-PLUS functions aggregateSeries and align may be used for such purposes. To enhance and extend the disaggregation functionality in S-PLUS the S+FinMetrics function disaggregate is introduced.

Aggregating Time Series

Given a monthly "timeSeries" of end of month prices over a number of years, suppose one would like to create an annual time series consisting of the end of month December prices. Such a series may be easily constructed by subsetting using the S-PLUS function months:

```
> dec.vals = "Dec"==months(positions(singleIndex.dat))
> annual.p = singleIndex.dat[dec.vals,]
> annual.p
```

Positions	MSFT	SP500
Dec 1990	2.090	330.2
Dec 1991	4.635	417.1
Dec 1992	5.336	435.7
Dec 1993	5.039	466.4
Dec 1994	7.641	459.3
Dec 1995	10.969	615.9
Dec 1996	20.656	740.7
Dec 1997	32.313	970.4
Dec 1998	69.344	1229.2
Dec 1999	116.750	1469.3
Dec 2000	43.375	1320.3

Another way to create the above annual time series is to use the S-PLUS aggregateSeries function with a user-written function to pick off December values. One such function, based on the S-PLUS function hloc used to compute high, low, open and close values, is

```
pickClose = function(x)
{
# return closing values of a vector
     if(length(dim(x))) x = as.vector(as.matrix(x))
     len = length(x)
     if(!len)
          as(NA, class(x))
     else x[len]
}
```

The annual data is then constructed using aggregateSeries with optional arguments FUN=pickClose and by="years"

```
> annual.p = aggregateSeries(singleIndex.dat,
+ FUN=pickClose,by="years")
> positions(annual.p)@format = "%Y"
> annual.p
 Positions    MSFT   SP500
 1990         2.090  330.2
 1991         4.635  417.1
 1992         5.336  435.7
 1993         5.039  466.4
 1994         7.641  459.3
 1995        10.969  615.9
 1996        20.656  740.7
 1997        32.313  970.4
 1998        69.344 1229.2
 1999       116.750 1469.3
 2000        43.375 1320.3
 2001        61.063 1366.0
```

The function aggregateSeries passes to the function pickClose data from singleIndex.dat in blocks of year's length. The function pickClose simply picks off the last value for the year. Since singleIndex.dat only has data for January 2, 2001, the 2001 value for annual.p is this value.

The method described above may also be used to construct end-of-month closing price data from a "timeSeries" of daily closing price data. For example, the commands to create end of month closing prices from daily closing prices for Microsoft, taken from the S+FinMetrics "timeSeries" DowJones30, using aggregateSeries with FUN = pickClose and by = "months" are

```
> msft.daily.p = DowJones30[,"MSFT"]
> msft.daily.p@title = "Daily closing price on Microsoft"
> msft.daily.p@units = "Dollar price"
> msft.monthly.p = aggregateSeries(msft.daily.p,FUN=pickClose,
+ by="months",adj=0.99)
> msft.monthly.p[1:12]
  Positions  MSFT
  1/31/1991  2.726
  2/28/1991  2.882
  3/31/1991  2.948
  4/30/1991  2.750
  5/31/1991  3.049
  6/30/1991  2.838
  7/31/1991  3.063
  8/31/1991  3.552
  9/30/1991  3.708
 10/31/1991  3.912
 11/30/1991  4.052
 12/31/1991  4.635
```

The option `adj=0.99` adjusts the positions of the monthly data to the end of the month. Notice that the end of month dates are not necessarily the last trading days of the month.

The monthly closing price data may be extracted from the daily closing price data by clever use of subscripting[4]. One way to do this is

```
> end.month.idx =
+ which(diff(as.numeric(months(positions(msft.daily.p)))) != 0)
> msft.monthly.p = msft.daily.p[end.month.idx]
> msft.monthly.p[1:12]
  Positions  MSFT
  1/31/1991  2.726
  2/28/1991  2.882
  3/28/1991  2.948
  4/30/1991  2.750
  5/31/1991  3.049
  6/28/1991  2.838
  7/31/1991  3.063
  8/30/1991  3.552
  9/30/1991  3.708
 10/31/1991  3.912
 11/29/1991  4.052
 12/31/1991  4.635
```

---

[4]This method was suggested by Steve McKinney.

A common aggregation operation with financial price data is to construct
a *volume weighted average price* (vwap). This may be easily accomplished
with `aggregateSeries` and a user-specified function to compute the vwap.
For example, consider the daily open, high, low and close prices and volume
on Microsoft stock from October 2, 2000 through August 31, 2001 in the
S+FinMetrics "timeSeries" `msft.dat`.

```
> smpl = (positions(msft.dat) >= timeDate("10/1/2000") &
+ positions(msft.dat) <= timeDate("8/31/2001"))
> msft.dat[smpl,]
  Positions  Open   High   Low  Close     Volume
  10/2/2000 60.50  60.81 58.25 59.13   29281200
  ...
  8/31/2001 56.85  58.06 56.30 57.05   28950400
```

A function that can be used to aggregate open, high, low and close prices,
volume and compute the open and close vwap is

```
vol.wtd.avg.price = function(x) {
  VolumeSum = as.double(sum(x[, "Volume"]))
  nrowx = numRows(x)
  return(data.frame(Open = x[1, "Open"],
  High = max(x[, "High"]),
  Low = min(x[, "Low"]),
  Close = x[nrowx, "Close"],
  vwap.Open = sum(x[, "Open"] * x[, "Volume"])/VolumeSum,
  wap.Close = sum(x[, "Close"] * x[, "Volume"])/VolumeSum,
  Volume = VolumeSum))
}
```

Using `aggregateSeries` and the function `vol.wtd.avg.price` one can
compute the monthly open, high, low, close prices, volume, and open and
close vwap

```
> msft.vwap.dat = aggregateSeries(x = msft.dat[smpl,],
+ by = "months",FUN = vol.wtd.avg.price,
+ together = T)
> positions(msft.vwap.dat)@format="%b %Y"
> msft.vwap.dat[,-7]
  Positions  Open  High   Low Close vwap.Open vwap.Close
  Oct 2000  60.50 70.13 48.44 68.88 59.10        59.48
  Nov 2000  68.50 72.38 57.00 57.38 68.35        67.59
  ...
  Aug 2001  66.80 67.54 56.30 57.05 62.99        62.59
```

Disaggregating Time Series

Consider the problem of creating a daily "timeSeries" of inflation adjusted (real) prices on Microsoft stock over the period January 2, 1991 through January 2, 2001. To do this the daily nominal prices must be divided by a measure of the overall price level; e.g. the consumer price level (CPI). The daily nominal stock price data is in the "timeSeries" msft.daily.p created earlier and the CPI data is in the S+FinMetrics "timeSeries" CPI.dat. The CPI data, however, is only available monthly.

```
> start(CPI.dat)
[1] Jan 1913
> end(CPI.dat)
[1] Nov 2001
```

and represents the average overall price level during the month but is recorded at the end of the month. The CPI data from December 1990 through January 2001 is extracted using

```
> smpl = (positions(CPI.dat) >= timeDate("12/1/1990")
+ & positions(CPI.dat) <= timeDate("2/1/2001"))
> cpi = CPI.dat[smpl,]
> cpi[1:3]
 Positions    CPI
 Dec 1990   134.3
 Jan 1991   134.8
 Feb 1991   134.9
```

To compute real daily prices on Microsoft stock, the monthly CPI data in the "timeSeries" object cpi must be *disaggregated* to daily data. This disaggregation may be done in a number of ways. For example, the CPI for every day during the month of January, 1991 may be defined as the monthly CPI value for December, 1990 or the monthly CPI value for January, 1991. Alternatively, the daily values for January 1991 may be computed by linearly interpolating between the December, 1990 and January, 1991 values. The S-PLUS function align may be used to do each of these disaggregations.

The align function aligns a "timeSeries" object to a given set of positions and has options for the creation of values for positions in which the "timeSeries" does not have values. For example, the disaggregated CPI using the previous month's value for the current month's daily data is constructed using

```
> cpi.daily.before =
+ align(cpi,positions(msft.daily.p),how="before")
> cpi.daily.before[c(1:3,21:23)]
 Positions    CPI
  1/2/1991  134.3
```

```
   1/3/1991  134.3
   1/4/1991  134.3
  1/30/1991  134.3
  1/31/1991  134.8
   2/1/1991  134.8
```

The new positions to align the CPI values are the daily positions of the "timeSeries" msft.daily.p, and the argument how="before" specifies that the previous month's CPI data is to be used for the current month's daily CPI values. Similarly, the disaggregated CPI using the next month's value for the current month's daily data is constructed using

```
> cpi.daily.after =
+ align(cpi,positions(msft.daily.p),how="after")
> cpi.daily.after[c(1:3,21:23)]
 Positions    CPI
   1/2/1991 134.8
   1/3/1991 134.8
   1/4/1991 134.8
  1/30/1991 134.8
  1/31/1991 134.8
   2/1/1991 134.9
```

Finally, the disaggregated daily CPI using linear interpolation between the monthly values is constructed using

```
> cpi.daily.interp = align(cpi,positions(msft.daily.p),
+ how="interp")
> cpi.daily.interp[c(1:3,21:23)]
 Positions    CPI
   1/2/1991 134.3
   1/3/1991 134.3
   1/4/1991 134.4
  1/30/1991 134.8
  1/31/1991 134.8
   2/1/1991 134.8
```

The daily real prices on Microsoft stock using the interpolated daily CPI values are then

```
> msft.daily.rp = (msft.daily.p/cpi.daily.interp)*100
```

Disaggregating Time Series using the S+FinMetrics disaggregate Function

With economic and financial time series, it is sometimes necessary to distribute a flow variable or time average a stock variable that is observed at a low frequency to a higher frequency. For example, a variable of interest may only be observed on an annual basis and quarterly or monthly values are desired such that their sum is equal to the annual observation or their average is equal to the annual observation. The S+FinMetrics function disaggregate performs such disaggregations using two methods. The first method is based on cubic spline interpolation and is appropriate if the only information is on the series being disaggregated. The second method utilizes a generalized least squares (gls) fitting method due to Chow and Lin (1971) and is appropriate if information is available on one or more related series that are observed at the desired disaggregated frequency. The arguments expected by disaggregate are

```
> args(disaggregate)
function(data, k, method = "spline", how = "sum", x = NULL,
+ out.positions = NULL, ...)
```

where data is a vector, matrix or "timeSeries" of low frequency data, k is the number of disaggregtion periods, method determines the disaggregation method (spline or gls), how specifies if the disaggregated values sum to the aggregated values or are equal on average to the disaggregated values, x respresents any related observed data at the disaggregated frequency and out.positions represents a "timeDate" sequence for the resulting output.

To illustrate the use of disaggregate, consider the problem of disaggregating the annual dividend on the S&P 500 index to a monthly dividend. Since the annual dividend is a flow variable, the sum of the monthly dividends should equal the annual dividend. The annual S&P 500 dividend information over the period 1871 - 2000 is in the S+FinMetrics "timeSeries" shiller.annual. The disaggregated monthly dividend values such that their sum is equal to the annual values is created using

```
> monthly.dates = timeSeq(from="1/1/1871",to="12/31/2000",
+ by="months",format="%b %Y")
> div.monthly =
+ disaggregate(shiller.annual[,"dividend"],12,
+ out.positions=monthly.dates)
> div.monthly[1:12]
  Positions dividend
  Jan 1871  0.02999
  Feb 1871  0.01867
  Mar 1871  0.01916
  Apr 1871  0.01963
  May 1871  0.02009
  Jun 1871  0.02054
  Jul 1871  0.02097
  Aug 1871  0.02140
  Sep 1871  0.02181
  Oct 1871  0.02220
```

```
  Nov 1871   0.02259
  Dec 1871   0.02296
> sum(div.monthly[1:12])
[1] 0.26
> shiller.annual[1,"dividend"]
  Positions dividend
  1871        0.26
```

For the S&P 500 index, the index price is available in the S+FinMetrics monthly "timeSeries" shiller.dat. This information may be utilized in the disaggregation of the annual dividend using the gls method as follows

```
> smpl = positions(shiller.dat) <= timeDate("12/31/2000")
> price.monthly = as.matrix(seriesData(shiller.dat[smpl,"price"]))
> div2.monthly =
+ disaggregate(shiller.annual[,"dividend"], 12,
+ method="gls", x=price.monthly, out.positions=monthly.dates)
> div2.monthly[1:12]
  Positions dividend
  Jan 1871   0.006177
  Feb 1871   0.010632
  Mar 1871   0.014610
  Apr 1871   0.018104
  May 1871   0.021104
  Jun 1871   0,023569
  Jul 1871   0.025530
  Aug 1871   0.027043
  Sep 1871   0.028063
  Oct 1871   0.028508
  Nov 1871   0.028548
  Dec 1871   0.028111
> sum(div2.monthly[1:12])
[1] 0.26
> shiller.annual[1,"dividend"]
  Positions dividend
  1871        0.26
```

2.2.7 Merging Time Series

Often one would like to combine several "timeSeries" objects into a single "timeSeries" object. The S-PLUS functions c, concat and cbind do not operate on "timeSeries" objects. Instead, the S-PLUS function seriesMerge is used to combine or merge a collection of "timeSeries". To illustrate, consider creating a new "timeSeries" object consisting of the S+FinMetrics "timeSeries" CPI.dat and IP.dat containing monthly observations on the U.S. consumer price index and U.S. industrial production index, respectively:

```
> CPI.dat
  Positions      CPI
  Jan 1913      9.80
  Feb 1913      9.80
  ...
  Nov 2001    177.60
> IP.dat
  Positions       IP
  Jan 1919     7.628
  Feb 1919     7.291
  ...
  Nov 2001   137.139
```

Notice that the start date for CPI.dat is earlier than the start date for IP.dat, but the end dates are the same. A new "timeSeries" containing both CPI.dat and IP.dat with positions aligned to those for IP.dat using seriesMerge is

```
> IP.CPI.dat = seriesMerge(IP.dat,CPI.dat,
+ pos=positions(IP.dat))
> IP.CPI.dat[1:2,]
  Positions    IP  CPI
  Jan 1919  7.628 16.5
  Feb 1919  7.291 16.2
```

To create a "timeSeries" with positions given by the union of the positions for CPI.dat and IP.dat set pos="union" in the call to seriesMerge. Since IP.dat does not have observations for the dates January 1913 through December 1918, NA values for IP for these dates will be inserted in the new "timeSeries".

2.2.8 Dealing with Missing Values Using the S+FinMetrics Function interpNA

Occasionally, time series data contain missing or incorrect data values. One approach often used to fill-in missing values is interpolation[5]. The S-PLUS align function may be used for this purpose. The S+FinMetrics function interpNA performs similar missing value interpolation as align but is easier to use and is more flexible. The arguments expected by interpNA are

---

[5] More sophisticated imputation methods for dealing with missing values are available in the library S+MISSINGDATA which is included with S-PLUS.

```
> args(interpNA)
function(x, method = "spline")
```

where x is a rectangular object and method sets the interpolation method. Valid interpolation methods are "before", "after", "nearest", "linear" and (cubic) "spline". To illustrate the use of interpNA, note that the closing price for the Dow Jones Industrial Average in the S-PLUS "timeSeries" djia has a missing value on January 18, 1990:

```
> djia.close = djia[positions(djia) >= timeDate("1/1/1990"),
+ "close"]
> djia.close[10:12,]
  Positions  close
 01/17/1990 2659.1
 01/18/1990     NA
 01/19/1990 2677.9
```

To replace the missing value with an interpolated value based on a cubic spline use

```
> djia.close = interpNA(djia.close)
> djia.close[10:12,]
  Positions     1
 01/17/1990 2659.1
 01/18/1990 2678.7
 01/19/1990 2677.9
```

2.3   Time Series Manipulation in S-PLUS

There are several types of common manipulations and transformations that often need to be performed before a financial time series is to be analyzed. The most important transformations are the creation of lagged and differenced variables and the creation of returns from asset prices. The following sections describe how these operations may be performed in S-PLUS.

2.3.1   Creating Lags and Differences

Three common operations on time series data are the creation of lags, leads, and differences. The S-PLUS function shift may be used to create leads and lags, and the generic function diff may be used to create differences. However, these functions do not operate on "timeSeries" objects in the most convenient way. Consequently, the S+FinMetrics module contains the functions tslag and diff.timeSeries for creating lags/leads and differences.

Creating Lags and Leads Using the S+FinMetrics Function tslag

The S+FinMetrics function tslag creates a specified number of lag/leads of a rectangular data object. The arguments expected by tslag are

```
> args(tslag)
function(x, k = 1, trim = F)
```

where x is any rectangular object, k specifies the number of lags to be created (negative values create leads) and trim determines if NA values are to be trimmed from the result. For example, consider the "timeSeries" singleIndex.dat containing monthly prices on Microsoft and the S&P 500 index. The first five values are

```
> singleIndex.dat[1:5,]
 Positions   MSFT SP500
 Jan 1990  1.285 329.1
 Feb 1990  1.371 331.9
 Mar 1990  1.538 339.9
 Apr 1990  1.611 330.8
 May 1990  2.028 361.2
```

The "timeSeries" of lagged values using tslag are

```
> tslag(singleIndex.dat[1:5,])
 Positions MSFT.lag1 SP500.lag1
 Jan 1990        NA         NA
 Feb 1990     1.285      329.1
 Mar 1990     1.371      331.9
 Apr 1990     1.538      339.9
 May 1990     1.611      330.8
```

Notice that tslag creates a "timeSeries" containing the lagged prices on Microsoft and the S&P 500 index. The variable names are adjusted to indicate the type of lag created and since trim=F, NA values are inserted for the first observations. To create a "timeSeries" without NA values in the first position, use tslag with trim=T:

```
> tslag(singleIndex.dat[1:5,],trim=T)
 Positions MSFT.lag1 SP500.lag1
 Feb 1990     1.285      329.1
 Mar 1990     1.371      331.9
 Apr 1990     1.538      339.9
 May 1990     1.611      330.8
```

Leads are created by setting k equal to a negative number:

```
> tslag(singleIndex.dat[1:5,],k=-1)
 Positions MSFT.lead1 SP500.lead1
 Jan 1990    1.371       331.9
```

```
Feb 1990  1.538        339.9
Mar 1990  1.611        330.8
Apr 1990  2.028        361.2
May 1990    NA          NA
```

To create a "timeSeries" with multiple lagged values, simply specify the lags to create in the call to tslag. For example, specifying k=c(1,3) creates the first and third lag

```
> tslag(singleIndex.dat[1:5,],k=c(1,3))
 Positions MSFT.lag1 SP500.lag1 MSFT.lag3 SP500.lag3
 Jan 1990     NA        NA         NA        NA
 Feb 1990  1.285      329.1        NA        NA
 Mar 1990  1.371      331.9        NA        NA
 Apr 1990  1.538      339.9      1.285     329.1
 May 1990  1.611      330.8      1.371     331.9
```

Similarly, specifying k=-1:1 creates

```
> tslag(singleIndex.dat[1:5,],k=-1:1)
 Positions MSFT.lead1 SP500.lead1 MSFT.lag0 SP500.lag0
 Jan 1990  1.371      331.9       1.285     329.1
 Feb 1990  1.538      339.9       1.371     331.9
 Mar 1990  1.611      330.8       1.538     339.9
 Apr 1990  2.028      361.2       1.611     330.8
 May 1990    NA         NA        2.028     361.2
 MSFT.lag1 SP500.lag1
    NA         NA
 1.285      329.1
 1.371      331.9
 1.538      339.9
 1.611      330.8
```

Creating Differences Using the S+FinMetrics Function diff.timeSeries

The S+FinMetrics function diff.timeSeries is a method function for the generic S-PLUS function diff for objects of class "timeSeries" and creates a specified number of differences of a "timeSeries" object. The arguments expected by diff.timeSeries are

```
> args(diff.timeSeries)
function(x, lag = 1, differences = 1, trim = T, pad = NA)
```

where x represents a "timeSeries" object, lag specifies the number of lagged periods used in the difference, differences specifies the number of times to difference the series, trim determines if the resulting series is to have NA values removed and trimmed and pad specifies the value to be padded to the series in the positions where the differencing operation exceeds the start or the end positions. For example, consider again the "timeSeries" singleIndex.dat containing monthly prices on Microsoft and the S&P 500 index. Let P_t denote the price at time t. To create the first difference $\Delta P_t = P_t - P_{t-1}$ use diff with lag=1:

```
> diff(singleIndex.dat[1:5,],lag=1,trim=F)
 Positions    MSFT  SP500
 Jan 1990      NA     NA
 Feb 1990   0.0868   2.81
 Mar 1990   0.1667   8.05
 Apr 1990   0.0729  -9.14
 May 1990   0.4167  30.43
```

To create the difference $P_t - P_{t-2}$ and pad the result with zeros instead of NAs use diff with lag=2 and pad=0:

```
> diff(singleIndex.dat[1:5,],lag=2,trim=F,pad=0)
 Positions    MSFT  SP500
 Jan 1990   0.0000   0.00
 Feb 1990   0.0000   0.00
 Mar 1990   0.2535  10.86
 Apr 1990   0.2396  -1.09
 May 1990   0.4896  21.29
```

To create the 2nd difference $\Delta^2 P_t = \Delta(P_t - P_{t-1}) = P_t - 2P_{t-1} + P_{t-2}$ use diff with lag=1 and diff=2:

```
> diff(singleIndex.dat[1:5,],lag=1,diff=2,trim=F)
 Positions    MSFT   SP500
 Jan 1990      NA      NA
 Feb 1990      NA      NA
 Mar 1990   0.0799    5.24
 Apr 1990  -0.0938  -17.19
 May 1990   0.3438   39.57
```

Unlike tslag, diff.timeSeries does not rename the variables to indicate the differencing operation performed. Additionally, diff.timeSeries will not accept a vector of values for the arguments lag and differences.

2.3.2 Return Definitions

Simple Returns

Let P_t denote the price at time t of an asset that pays no dividends and let P_{t-1} denote the price at time $t-1$. Then the *simple net return* on an investment in the asset between times $t-1$ and t is defined as

$$R_t = \frac{P_t - P_{t-1}}{P_{t-1}} = \% \Delta P_t. \tag{2.1}$$

Writing $\frac{P_t - P_{t-1}}{P_{t-1}} = \frac{P_t}{P_{t-1}} - 1$, we can define the *simple gross return* as

$$1 + R_t = \frac{P_t}{P_{t-1}}. \tag{2.2}$$

Unless otherwise stated, references to returns mean net returns.

The simple two-period return on an investment in an asset between times $t-2$ and t is defined as

$$
\begin{aligned}
R_t(2) &= \frac{P_t - P_{t-2}}{P_{t-2}} = \frac{P_t}{P_{t-2}} - 1 \\
&= \frac{P_t}{P_{t-1}} \cdot \frac{P_{t-1}}{P_{t-2}} - 1 \\
&= (1 + R_t)(1 + R_{t-1}) - 1.
\end{aligned}
$$

Then the simple two-period gross return becomes

$$1 + R_t(2) = (1 + R_t)(1 + R_{t-1}) = 1 + R_{t-1} + R_t + R_{t-1}R_t,$$

which is a *geometric* (multiplicative) sum of the two simple one-period gross returns and not the simple sum of the one period returns. If, however, R_{t-1} and R_t are small then $R_{t-1}R_t \approx 0$ and $1 + R_t(2) \approx 1 + R_{t-1} + R_t$ so that $R_t(2) \approx R_{t-1} + R_t$.

In general, the k-period gross return is defined as the geometric average of k one period gross returns

$$
\begin{aligned}
1 + R_t(k) &= (1 + R_t)(1 + R_{t-1}) \cdots (1 + R_{t-k+1}) \tag{2.3} \\
&= \prod_{j=0}^{k-1}(1 + R_{t-j})
\end{aligned}
$$

and the k-period net return is

$$R_t(k) = \prod_{j=0}^{k-1}(1 + R_{t-j}) - 1. \tag{2.4}$$

Continuously Compounded Returns

Let R_t denote the simple one period return on an investment. The *continuously compounded one period return*, r_t, is defined as

$$r_t = \ln(1 + R_t) = \ln\left(\frac{P_t}{P_{t-1}}\right) \tag{2.5}$$

where $\ln(\cdot)$ is the natural log function. To see why r_t is called the continuously compounded return, take exponentials of both sides of (2.5) to give

$$e^{r_t} = 1 + R_t = \frac{P_t}{P_{t-1}}.$$

Rearranging gives

$$P_t = P_{t-1}e^{r_t},$$

so that r_t is the continuously compounded growth rate in prices between periods $t - 1$ and t. This is to be contrasted with R_t which is the simple growth rate in prices between periods $t-1$ and t without any compounding. Since $\ln\left(\frac{x}{y}\right) = \ln(x) - \ln(y)$ it follows that

$$
\begin{aligned}
r_t &= \ln\left(\frac{P_t}{P_{t-1}}\right) \\
&= \ln(P_t) - \ln(P_{t-1}) \\
&= p_t - p_{t-1}
\end{aligned}
$$

where $p_t = \ln(P_t)$. Hence, the continuously compounded one period return, r_t, can be computed simply by taking the first difference of the natural logarithms of prices between periods $t - 1$ and t.

Given a one period continuously compounded return r_t, it is straightforward to solve back for the corresponding simple net return R_t:

$$R_t = e^{r_t} - 1$$

Hence, nothing is lost by considering continuously compounded returns instead of simple returns.

The computation of multi-period continuously compounded returns is considerably easier than the computation of multi-period simple returns. To illustrate, consider the two period continuously compounded return defined as

$$r_t(2) = \ln(1 + R_t(2)) = \ln\left(\frac{P_t}{P_{t-2}}\right) = p_t - p_{t-2}.$$

Taking exponentials of both sides shows that

$$P_t = P_{t-2}e^{r_t(2)}$$

so that $r_t(2)$ is the continuously compounded growth rate of prices between periods $t - 2$ and t. Using $\frac{P_t}{P_{t-2}} = \frac{P_t}{P_{t-1}} \cdot \frac{P_{t-1}}{P_{t-2}}$ and the fact that $\ln(x \cdot y) = \ln(x) + \ln(y)$ it follows that

$$
\begin{aligned}
r_t(2) &= \ln\left(\frac{P_t}{P_{t-1}} \cdot \frac{P_{t-1}}{P_{t-2}}\right) \\
&= \ln\left(\frac{P_t}{P_{t-1}}\right) + \ln\left(\frac{P_{t-1}}{P_{t-2}}\right) \\
&= r_t + r_{t-1}.
\end{aligned}
$$

Hence the continuously compounded two period return is just the sum of the two continuously compounded one period returns.

The continuously compounded k-period return is defined as

$$r_t(k) = \ln(1 + R_t(k)) = \ln\left(\frac{P_t}{P_{t-k}}\right) = p_t - p_{t-k}. \qquad (2.6)$$

Using similar manipulations to the ones used for the continuously compounded two period return the continuously compounded k-period return may be expressed as the sum of k continuously compounded one period returns:

$$r_t(k) = \sum_{j=0}^{k-1} r_{t-j}. \qquad (2.7)$$

The additivitity of continuously compounded returns to form multiperiod returns is an important property for statistical modeling purposes.

2.3.3 Computing Asset Returns Using the S+FinMetrics Function getReturns

Given a data set with asset prices the S+FinMetrics function getReturns may be used to compute discrete and continuously compounded returns. The arguments to getReturns are

```
> args(getReturns)
function(x, type = "continuous", percentage = F, trim = T)
```

where x is any rectangular data object and type specifies the type of returns to compute (discrete or continuously compounded). To illustrate, the S+FinMetrics "timeSeries" singleIndex.dat contains monthly closing prices on Microsoft stock and the S&P 500 index, adjusted for stock splits and dividends, over the period January 1990 through January 2001.

```
> colIds(singleIndex.dat)
[1] "MSFT"  "SP500"
> singleIndex.dat[1:3,]
 Positions   MSFT  SP500
 Jan 1990  1.2847 329.08
 Feb 1990  1.3715 331.89
 Mar 1990  1.5382 339.94
```

A "timeSeries" of simple one-period discrete returns expressed as percentages is computed as

```
> ret.d = getReturns(singleIndex.dat,type="discrete",
+ percentage=T)
> ret.d[1:3,]
 Positions   MSFT    SP500
 Feb 1990   6.756   0.8539
 Mar 1990  12.155   2.4255
```

```
Apr 1990    4.739 -2.6887
```

By default the first observation in the "timeSeries" is trimmed. To retain the first (NA) observation use the optional argument trim=F

```
> ret.d = getReturns(singleIndex.dat,type="discrete",trim=F)
> ret.d[1:3,]
Positions     MSFT       SP500
Jan 1990        NA          NA
Feb 1990  0.067564  0.008539
Mar 1990  0.121546  0.024255
```

Continuously compounded returns are created by specifying the optional argument type="continuous"

```
> ret.cc = getReturns(singleIndex.dat,type="continuous")
> ret.cc[1:3,]
Positions     MSFT        SP500
Feb 1990  0.065380   0.0085027
Mar 1990  0.114708   0.0239655
Apr 1990  0.046304  -0.0272552
```

Multiperiod returns may be computed from a "timeSeries" of one period returns using the S-PLUS function aggregateSeries. Multipcriod returns may be either overlapping or non-overlapping. For example, consider computing a monthly "timeSeries" of overlapping annual continuously compounded returns from the monthly continuously compounded returns in the "timeSeries" ret.cc using aggregateSeries:

```
> ret12.cc = aggregateSeries(ret.cc,moving=12,FUN=sum)
> ret12.cc[1:3,]
Positions    MSFT     SP500
Feb 1990  0.75220  0.044137
Mar 1990  0.74254  0.100749
Apr 1990  0.65043  0.098743
> colSums(seriesData(ret.cc[1:12,]))
   MSFT      SP500
0.7522   0.044137
```

The argument moving=12 and FUN=sum tells aggregateSeries to compute a moving sum of twelve returns. Hence, the annual return reported for Feb 1990 is the sum of the twelve monthly returns from February 1990 through January 1991. Non-overlapping annual returns are computed from the monthly returns using aggregateSeries with the option by="years"

```
> ret12.cc = aggregateSeries(ret.cc,by="years",FUN=sum)
> ret12.cc[1:3,]
Positions    MSFT      SP500
Jan 1990  0.48678  0.0034582
```

```
 Jan 1991  0.79641 0.2335429
 Jan 1992  0.14074 0.0436749
> colSums(seriesData(ret.cc[1:11,]))
    MSFT      SP500
 0.48678 0.0034582
```

The "timeSeries" ret12.cc is now an annual series of non-overlapping
annual returns. Notice that the annual return for January 1990 is computed
using only the eleven returns from February 1990 through December 1990.

Multiperiod discrete returns (2.4) may be computed using the function
aggregateSeries with FUN=prod. For example, a monthly "timeSeries"
of overlapping annual discrete returns is computed as

```
> ret12.d = aggregateSeries((1+ret.d),moving=12,FUN=prod)-1
> ret12.d[1:3,]
 Positions    MSFT     SP500
 Feb 1990  1.12166 0.045126
 Mar 1990  1.10128 0.105999
 Apr 1990  0.91646 0.103783
> prod(seriesData(1+ret.d[1:12,1]))-1
[1] 1.1217
```

Notice that 1 is added to the return data and 1 is subtracted from the result
in order to compute (2.4) properly. Non-overlapping multiperiod discrete
returns may be computed using

```
> ret12.d = aggregateSeries((1+ret.d),by="years",FUN=prod)-1
> ret12.d[1:3,]
 Positions  MSFT    SP500
 Jan 1990     NA       NA
 Jan 1991  1.2176 0.26307
 Jan 1992  0.1511 0.04464
```

2.4   Visualizing Time Series in S-PLUS

Time series data in "timeSeries" objects may be visualized by using the
S-PLUS generic plot function, the S-PLUS trellisPlot function, or by
using the S+FinMetrics plotting functions based on Trellis graphics.

2.4.1   Plotting "timeSeries" Using the S-PLUS Generic plot Function

The S-PLUS generic plot function has a method function, plot.timeSeries,
for plotting "timeSeries" objects. To illustrate, consider the monthly closing prices of Microsoft stock over the period January 1990 to January 2001
in the "timeSeries" object msft.p created earlier:

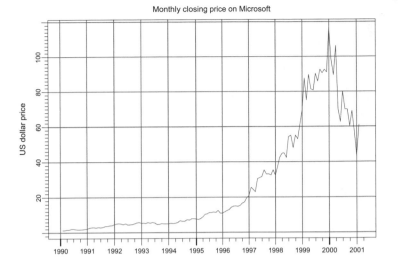

FIGURE 2.1. Monthly closing prices on Microsoft stock created using plot.timeSeries.

```
> msft.p@title
[1] "Monthly closing price on Microsoft"
> msft.p@units
[1] "US dollar price"
```

Figure 2.1 shows the output produced by the generic **plot** function

```
> plot(msft.p)
```

Notice how the information in the **title** and **units** slots is utilized in the plot. To eliminate the horizontal and vertical grid lines specify **reference.grid=F** in the call to **plot**. To show the price data on a logarithmic scale specify **log.axes="y"** in the call to **plot**.

Multiple series (on the same scale) may also be plotted together on the same plot using **plot**[6]. For example, the prices for Microsoft and the S&P 500 index in the "**timeSeries**" **singleIndex.dat** may be plotted together using

```
> plot(singleIndex.dat,plot.args=list(lty=c(1,3)))
> legend(0.1,1400,legend=colIds(singleIndex.dat),lty=c(1,3))
```

---

[6] To create a scatterplot of two "timeSeries" use the extractor function **seriesData** possibly in conjunction with the coersion function **as.matrix** on the "timeSeries" objects in the call to **plot**. Alternatively, the S+FinMetrics function **rvfPlot** may be used.

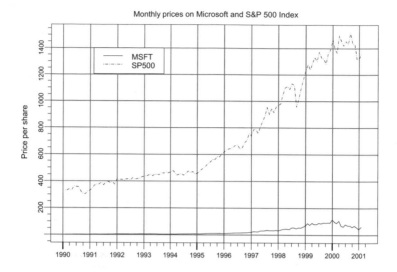

FIGURE 2.2. Monthly closing prices on Microsoft and the S&P 500 index created using plot.timeSeries.

The plot is illustrated in Figure 2.2. Notice how the line types are specified as a list argument to the optional argument plot.args. In the placement of the legend, the x-axis units are treated as values in the unit interval.

Multipanel plots may be created by specifying the plot layout using the S-PLUS function par. Figure 2.3 shows a two panel plot of the price data in singleIndex.dat produced using

```
> par(mfrow=c(2,1))
> plot(singleIndex.dat[,"MSFT"],
+ main="Monthly price on Microsoft")
> plot(singleIndex.dat[,"SP500"],
+ main="Monthly price on S&P 500 index")
```

Two specialized plot types for financial data can be made with the function plot.timeSeries. The first is a high/low/open/close (hloc) plot and the second is a stackbar plot. These plots are made by setting plot.type = "hloc" or plot.type = "stackbar" in the call to plot.timeSeries. For a hloc plot, the "timeSeries" to be plotted must have hloc information or such information must be created using aggregateSeries with the S-PLUS function hloc. Stackbar plots are generally used for plotting asset volume information. To illustrate these plot types, consider the monthly data from the Dow Jones Industrial Averages in the S-PLUS "timeSeries" djia:

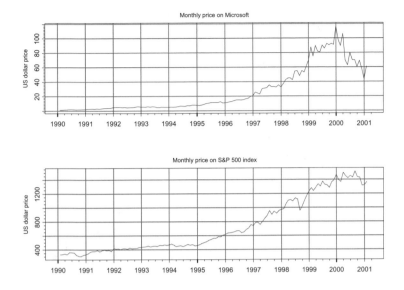

FIGURE 2.3. Two panel plot created using `par(mfrow=c(2,1))` in conjunction with `plot.timeSeries`.

```
> colIds(djia)
[1] "open"    "high"    "low"     "close"   "volume"
```

Figure 2.4 gives a multipanel plot showing high, low, open, close and volume information created by

```
> smpl = (positions(djia) >= timeDate("9/1/1987") &
+ positions(djia) <= timeDate("11/30/1987"))
> par(mfrow=c(2,1))
> plot(djia[smpl,1:4],plot.type="hloc")
> plot(djia[smpl,5],plot.type="stackbar")
```

Lines may be added to an existing time series plot using the S-PLUS function `lines.render` and stackbar information may be added using the S-PLUS function `stackbar.render`. See chapter 26 in the *S-PLUS Guide to Statistics Vol. II* for details on using these functions.

2.4.2 Plotting "timeSeries" Using the S+FinMetrics Trellis Plotting Functions

S+FinMetrics provides several specialized Trellis-based plotting functions for "timeSeries" objects. These functions extend the S-PLUS function `TrellisPlot.timeSeries` and are summarized in Table 2.2.

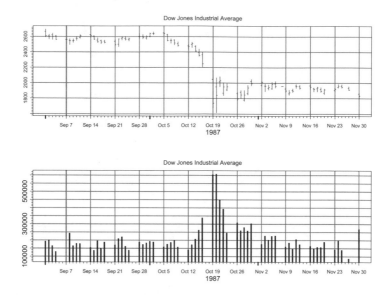

FIGURE 2.4. Monthly high, low, open, close and volume information for the Dow Jones Industrial Average using `plot.timeSeries` with `type="hloc"` and `type="stackbar"`.

Function	Description
seriesPlot	Trellis time series plot
histPlot	Trellis histogram plot
qqPlot	Trellis qq-plot for various distributions

TABLE 2.2. S+FinMetrics Trellis plotting functions

All of the functions in the table can create multi-panel plots with text labels in the panel strips. For the following examples, monthly return data on six stocks from the S+FinMetrics "timeSeries" DowJones30 will be used. This data is created using

```
> DJ.ret = getReturns(DowJones30[,1:6], percentage=T)
> colIds(DJ.ret)
[1] "AA"  "AXP" "T"   "BA"  "CAT" "C"
```

The function seriesPlot may be used to create single panel or multipanel time plots. To create the multi-panel time plot of the six Dow Jones 30 assets shown in Figure 2.5 use

```
> seriesPlot(DJ.ret,one.plot=F,strip.text=colIds(DJ.ret),
+ main="Monthly returns on six Dow Jones 30 stocks")
```

Monthly returns on six Dow Jones 30 stocks

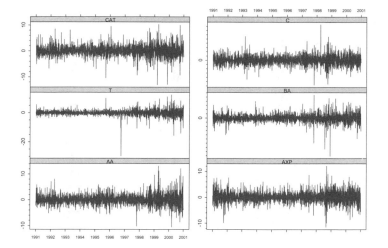

FIGURE 2.5. Multi-panel time plot created using the S+FinMetrics function seriesPlot.

Notice that each time plot has a different scale.

The function histPlot may be used to create either a single panel histogram of one data series or a multi-panel plot of histograms for multiple series. The multi-panel plot in Figure 2.6 is created using

```
> histPlot(DJ.ret,strip.text=colIds(DJ.ret),
+ main="Histograms of returns on six Dow Jones 30 stocks")
```

Notice that each histogram uses the same bins.

Single panel or multi-panel Trellis-based qq-plots using Gaussian, Student-t, and double exponential distributions may be created using the function qqPlot. To illustrate, consider computing qq-plots for the six Dow Jones 30 assets using six Student-t reference distributions with degrees of freedom equal to 5, 6, 7, 8, 9 and 10. These qq-plots, shown in Figure 2.7, are created using

```
> s.text = paste(colIds(DJ.ret),5:10,sep=" ","df")
> qqPlot(DJ.ret,strip.text=s.text,
+ distribution="t",dof=c(5,6,7,8,9,10), id.n=FALSE,
+ main="Student-t QQ-plots for returns on six Dow Jones 30 stocks")
```

Notice how the degress of freedom for each Student-t distribution along with the asset name is indicated in the strip text. The optional argument id.n=FALSE suppresses the identification of outliers on the qq-plots.

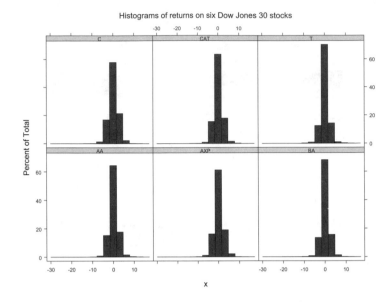

FIGURE 2.6. Multi-panel histogram plot created using the S+FinMetrics function histPlot.

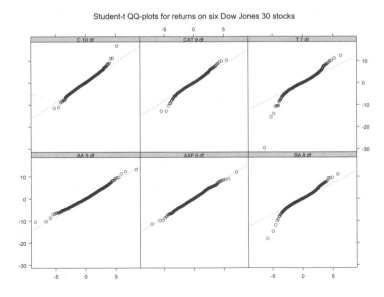

FIGURE 2.7. Multi-panel qq-plots created using the S+FinMetrics function qqPlot.

2.5   References

[1] Chow, G., and Lin, A. (1971). "Best Linear Unbiased Interpolation, Distribution, and Extrapolation of Time Series by Related Series", *Review of Economics & Statistics*, 53, 372-375.

3
Time Series Concepts

3.1 Introduction

This chapter provides background material on time series concepts that are used throughout the book. These concepts are presented in an informal way, and extensive examples using S-PLUS are used to build intuition. Section 3.2 discusses time series concepts for stationary and ergodic univariate time series. Topics include testing for white noise, linear and autoregressive moving average (ARMA) process, estimation and forecasting from ARMA models, and long-run variance estimation. Section 3.3 introduces univariate nonstationary time series and defines the important concepts of $I(0)$ and $I(1)$ time series. Section 3.4 explains univariate long memory time series. Section 3.5 covers concepts for stationary and ergodic multivariate time series, introduces the class of vector autoregression models, and discusses long-run variance estimation.

Rigorous treatments of the time series concepts presented in this chapter can be found in Fuller (1996) and Hamilton (1994). Applications of these concepts to financial time series are provided by Campbell, Lo and MacKinlay (1997), Mills (1999), Gourieroux and Jasiak (2001), Tsay (2001), Alexander (2001) and Chan (2002).

3.2 Univariate Time Series

3.2.1 Stationary and Ergodic Time Series

Let $\{y_t\} = \{\ldots y_{t-1}, y_t, y_{t+1}, \ldots\}$ denote a sequence of random variables indexed by some time subscript t. Call such a sequence of random variables a *time series*.

The time series $\{y_t\}$ is *covariance stationary* if

$$
\begin{aligned}
E[y_t] &= \mu \text{ for all } t \\
cov(y_t, y_{t-j}) &= E[(y_t - \mu)(y_{t-j} - \mu)] = \gamma_j \text{ for all } t \text{ and any } j
\end{aligned}
$$

For brevity, call a covariance stationary time series simply a *stationary* time series. Stationary time series have time invariant first and second moments. The parameter γ_j is called the jth order or lag j *autocovariance* of $\{y_t\}$ and a plot of γ_j against j is called the *autocovariance function*. The *autocorrelations* of $\{y_t\}$ are defined by

$$
\rho_j = \frac{cov(y_t, y_{t-j})}{\sqrt{var(y_t)var(y_{t-j})}} = \frac{\gamma_j}{\gamma_0}
$$

and a plot of ρ_j against j is called the *autocorrelation function* (ACF). Intuitively, a stationary time series is defined by its mean, variance and ACF. A useful result is that any function of a stationary time series is also a stationary time series. So if $\{y_t\}$ is stationary then $\{z_t\} = \{g(y_t)\}$ is stationary for any function $g(\cdot)$.

The lag j *sample autocovariance* and lag j *sample autocorrelation* are defined as

$$
\hat{\gamma}_j = \frac{1}{T} \sum_{t=j+1}^{T} (y_t - \bar{y})(y_{t-j} - \bar{y}) \tag{3.1}
$$

$$
\hat{\rho}_j = \frac{\hat{\gamma}_j}{\hat{\gamma}_0} \tag{3.2}
$$

where $\bar{y} = \frac{1}{T} \sum_{t=1}^{T} y_t$ is the sample mean. The sample ACF (SACF) is a plot of $\hat{\rho}_j$ against j.

A stationary time series $\{y_t\}$ is *ergodic* if sample moments converge in probability to population moments; i.e. if $\bar{y} \xrightarrow{p} \mu, \hat{\gamma}_j \xrightarrow{p} \gamma_j$ and $\hat{\rho}_j \xrightarrow{p} \rho_j$.

Example 1 *Gaussian white noise (GWN) processes*

Perhaps the most simple stationary time series is the *independent Gaussian white noise* process $y_t \sim iid\ N(0, \sigma^2) \equiv GWN(0, \sigma^2)$. This process has $\mu = \gamma_j = \rho_j = 0$ $(j \neq 0)$. To simulate a $GWN(0, 1)$ process in S-PLUS use the `rnorm` function:

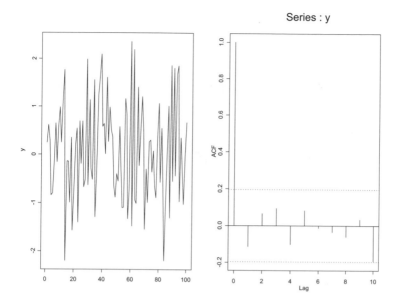

FIGURE 3.1. Simulated Gaussian white noise process and SACF.

```
> set.seed(101)
> y = rnorm(100,sd=1)
```

To compute the sample moments $\bar{y}$, $\hat{\gamma}_j$, $\hat{\rho}_j$ ($j = 1, \ldots, 10$) and plot the data and SACF use

```
> y.bar = mean(y)
> g.hat = acf(y,lag.max=10,type="covariance",plot=F)
> r.hat = acf(y,lag.max=10,type="correlation",plot=F)
> par(mfrow=c(1,2))
> tsplot(y,ylab="y")
> acf.plot(r.hat)
```

By default, as shown in Figure 3.1, the SACF is shown with 95% confidence limits about zero. These limits are based on the result (c.f. Fuller (1996) pg. 336) that if $\{y_t\} \sim iid\ (0, \sigma^2)$ then

$$\hat{\rho}_j \overset{A}{\sim} N\left(0, \frac{1}{T}\right),\ j > 0.$$

The notation $\hat{\rho}_j \overset{A}{\sim} N\left(0, \frac{1}{T}\right)$ means that the distribution of $\hat{\rho}_j$ is approximated by normal distribution with mean 0 and variance $\frac{1}{T}$ and is based on the central limit theorem result $\sqrt{T}\hat{\rho}_j \overset{d}{\to} N(0, 1)$. The 95% limits about zero are then $\pm\frac{1.96}{\sqrt{T}}$.

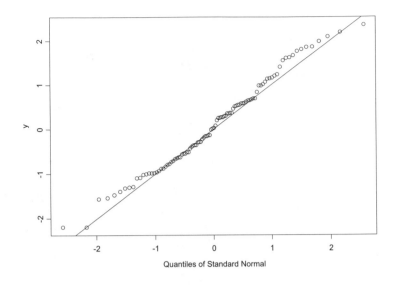

FIGURE 3.2. Normal qq-plot for simulated GWN.

Two slightly more general processes are the independent *white noise* (IWN) process, $y_t \sim IWN(0, \sigma^2)$, and the *white noise* (WN) process, $y_t \sim WN(0, \sigma^2)$. Both processes have mean zero and variance σ^2, but the IWN process has independent increments, whereas the WN process has uncorrelated increments.

Testing for Normality

In the previous example, $y_t \sim GWN(0, 1)$. There are several statistical methods that can be used to see if an *iid* process y_t is Gaussian. The most common is the normal quantile-quantile plot or *qq-plot*, a scatterplot of the standardized empirical quantiles of y_t against the quantiles of a standard normal random variable. If y_t is normally distributed, then the quantiles will lie on a 45 degree line. A normal qq-plot with 45 degree line for y_t may be computed using the S-PLUS functions qqnorm and qqline

```
> qqnorm(y)
> qqline(y)
```

Figure 3.2 shows the qq-plot for the simulated GWN data of the previous example. The quantiles lie roughly on a straight line. The S+FinMetrics function qqPlot may be used to create a Trellis graphics qq-plot.

The qq-plot is an informal graphical diagnostic. Two popular formal statistical tests for normality are the *Shapiro-Wilks* test and the *Jarque-*

Bera test. The Shapiro-Wilk's test is a well-known goodness of fit test for the normal distribution. It is attractive because it has a simple, graphical interpretation: one can think of it as an approximate measure of the correlation in a normal quantile-quantile plot of the data. The Jarque-Bera test is based on the result that a normally distributed random variable has skewness equal to zero and kurtosis equal to three. The Jarque-Bera test statistic is

$$JB = \frac{T}{6} \left(\widehat{skew}^2 + \frac{(\widehat{kurt} - 3)^2}{4} \right) \tag{3.3}$$

where $\widehat{skew}$ denotes the sample skewness and $\widehat{kurt}$ denotes the sample kurtosis. Under the null hypothesis that the data is normally distributed

$$JB \overset{A}{\sim} \chi^2(2).$$

Example 2 *Testing for normality using the S+FinMetrics function* normalTest

The Shapiro-Wilks and Jarque-Bera statistics may be computed using the S+FinMetrics function normalTest. For the simulated GWN data of the previous example, these statistics are

```
> normalTest(y, method="sw")
Test for Normality: Shapiro-Wilks

Null Hypothesis: data is normally distributed

Test Statistics:

Test Stat 0.9703
  p.value 0.1449

Dist. under Null: normal
   Total Observ.: 100

> normalTest(y, method="jb")

Test for Normality: Jarque-Bera

Null Hypothesis: data is normally distributed

Test Statistics:

Test Stat 1.8763
  p.value 0.3914
```

```
Dist. under Null: chi-square with 2 degrees of freedom
    Total Observ.: 100
```

The null of normality is not rejected using either test.

Testing for White Noise

Consider testing the null hypothesis

$$H_0 : y_t \sim WN(0, \sigma^2)$$

against the alternative that y_t is not white noise. Under the null, all of the autocorrelations ρ_j for $j > 0$ are zero. To test this null, Box and Pierce (1970) suggested the *Q-statistic*

$$Q(k) = T \sum_{j=1}^{k} \hat{\rho}_j^2 \tag{3.4}$$

where $\hat{\rho}_j$ is given by (3.2). Under the null, $Q(k)$ is asymptotically distributed $\chi^2(k)$. In a finite sample, the Q-statistic (3.4) may not be well approximated by the $\chi^2(k)$. Ljung and Box (1978) suggested the *modified Q-statistic*

$$MQ(k) = T(T+2) \sum_{j=1}^{k} \frac{\hat{\rho}_j^2}{T-k} \tag{3.5}$$

which is better approximated by the $\chi^2(k)$ in finite samples.

Example 3 *Daily returns on Microsoft*

Consider the time series behavior of daily continuously compounded returns on Microsoft for 2000. The following S-PLUS commands create the data and produce some diagnostic plots:

```
> r.msft = getReturns(DowJones30[,"MSFT"],type="continuous")
> r.msft@title = "Daily returns on Microsoft"
> sample.2000 = (positions(r.msft) > timeDate("12/31/1999")
+ & positions(r.msft) < timeDate("1/1/2001"))
> par(mfrow=c(2,2))
> plot(r.msft[sample.2000],ylab="r.msft")
> r.acf = acf(r.msft[sample.2000])
> hist(seriesData(r.msft))
> qqnorm(seriesData(r.msft))
```

The daily returns on Microsoft resemble a white noise process. The qq-plot, however, suggests that the tails of the return distribution are fatter than the normal distribution. Notice that since the hist and qqnorm functions do not have methods for "timeSeries" objects the extractor function seriesData is required to extract the data frame from the data slot of r.msft.

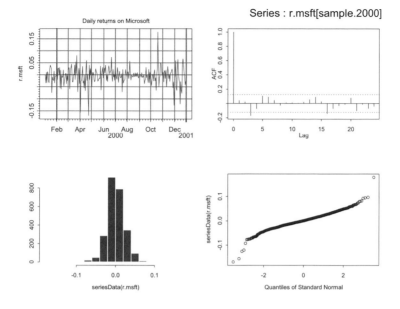

FIGURE 3.3. Daily returns on Microsoft with diagnostic plots.

The S+FinMetrics functions histPlot and qqPlot will produce a histogram and qq-plot for a "timeSeries" object using Trellis graphics. For example,

```
> histPlot(r.msft,strip.text="MSFT monthly return")
> qqPlot(r.msft,strip.text="MSFT monthly return")
```

However, Trellis plots cannot be displayed in a multipanel plot created using par.

The S+FinMetrics function autocorTest may be used to compute the Q-statistic and modified Q-statistic to test the null that the returns on Microsoft follow a white noise process:

```
> autocorTest(r.msft, lag.n=10, method="lb")

Test for Autocorrelation: Ljung-Box
Null Hypothesis: no autocorrelation

Test Statistics:

Test Stat 11.7746
  p.value   0.3004

Dist. under Null: chi-square with 10 degrees of freedom
```

`Total Observ.: 2527`

The argument `lag.n=10` specifies that $k = 10$ autocorrelations are used in computing the statistic, and `method="lb"` specifies that the modified Box-Pierce statistic (3.5) be computed. To compute the simple Box-Pierce statistic, specify `method="bp"`. The results indicate that the white noise null cannot be rejected.

3.2.2 Linear Processes and ARMA Models

Wold's decomposition theorem (c.f. Fuller (1996) pg. 96) states that any covariance stationary time series $\{y_t\}$ has a *linear process* or infinite order moving average representation of the form

$$y_t = \mu + \sum_{k=0}^{\infty} \psi_k \varepsilon_{t-k} \tag{3.6}$$

$$\psi_0 = 1, \ \sum_{k=0}^{\infty} \psi_k^2 < \infty$$

$$\varepsilon_t \sim WN(0, \sigma^2)$$

In the Wold form, it can be shown that

$$E[y_t] = \mu$$

$$\gamma_0 = var(y_t) = \sigma^2 \sum_{k=0}^{\infty} \psi_k^2$$

$$\gamma_j = cov(y_t, y_{t-j}) = \sigma^2 \sum_{k=0}^{\infty} \psi_k \psi_{k+j}$$

$$\rho_j = \frac{\sum_{k=0}^{\infty} \psi_k \psi_{k+j}}{\sum_{k=0}^{\infty} \psi_k^2}$$

Hence, the pattern of autocorrelations in any stationary and ergodic time series $\{y_t\}$ is determined by the moving average weights $\{\psi_j\}$ in its Wold representation. To ensure convergence of the linear process representation to a stationary and ergodic process with nice properties, it is necessary to further restrict the behavior of the moving average weights $\{\psi_j\}$. A standard assumption used in the econometrics literature (c.f. Hamilton (1994) pg. 504) is *1-summability*

$$\sum_{j=0}^{\infty} j|\psi_j| = 1 + 2|\psi_2| + 3|\psi_3| + \cdots < \infty.$$

The moving average weights in the Wold form are also called *impulse responses* since

$$\frac{\partial y_{t+s}}{\partial \varepsilon_t} = \psi_s, s = 1, 2, \ldots$$

For a stationary and ergodic time series $\lim_{s \to \infty} \psi_s = 0$ and the *long-run cumulative impulse response* $\sum_{s=0}^{\infty} \psi_s < \infty$. A plot of ψ_s against s is called the *impulse response function* (IRF).

The general Wold form of a stationary and ergodic time series is handy for theoretical analysis but is not practically useful for estimation purposes. A very rich and practically useful class of stationary and ergodic processes is the *autoregressive-moving average* (ARMA) class of models made popular by Box and Jenkins (1976). ARMA(p, q) models take the form of a *pth* order stochastic difference equation

$$
\begin{aligned}
y_t - \mu &= \phi_1(y_{t-1} - \mu) + \cdots + \phi_p(y_{t-p} - \mu) \quad (3.7) \\
&\quad + \varepsilon_t + \theta_1 \varepsilon_{t-1} + \cdots + \theta_q \varepsilon_{t-q} \\
\varepsilon_t &\sim WN(0, \sigma^2)
\end{aligned}
$$

ARMA(p, q) models may be thought of as parsimonious approximations to the general Wold form of a stationary and ergodic time series. More information on the properties of ARMA(p, q) process and the procedures for estimating and forecasting these processes using S-PLUS are in the *S-PLUS Guide to Statistics Vol. II*, chapter 27, Venables and Ripley (1999) chapter 13, and Meeker (2001)[1].

Lag Operator Notation

The presentation of time series models is simplified using *lag operator* notation. The lag operator L is defined such that for any time series $\{y_t\}$, $Ly_t = y_{t-1}$. The lag operator has the following properties: $L^2 y_t = L \cdot L y_t = y_{t-2}$, $L^0 = 1$ and $L^{-1} y_t = y_{t+1}$. The operator $\Delta = 1 - L$ creates the first difference of a time series: $\Delta y_t = (1 - L)y_t = y_t - y_{t-1}$. The ARMA$(p, q)$ model (3.7) may be compactly expressed using lag polynomials. Define $\phi(L) = 1 - \phi_1 L - \cdots - \phi_p L^p$ and $\theta(L) = 1 + \theta_1 L + \cdots + \theta_q L^q$. Then (3.7) may be expressed as

$$
\phi(L)(y_t - \mu) = \theta(L)\varepsilon_t
$$

Similarly, the Wold representation in lag operator notation is

$$
\begin{aligned}
y_t &= \mu + \psi(L)\varepsilon_t \\
\psi(L) &= \sum_{k=0}^{\infty} \psi_k L^k, \ \psi_0 = 1
\end{aligned}
$$

and the long-run cumulative impulse response is $\psi(1)$ (i.e. evaluate $\psi(L)$ at $L = 1$). With ARMA(p, q) models the Wold polynomial $\psi(L)$ is approx-

---

[1]William Meeker also has a library of time series functions for the analysis of ARMA models available for download at
http://www.public.iastate.edu/~stat451/splusts/splusts.html.

imated by the ratio of the AR and MA polynomials

$$\psi(L) = \frac{\theta(L)}{\phi(L)}$$

3.2.3 Autoregressive Models

AR(1) Model

A commonly used stationary and ergodic time series in financial modeling is the AR(1) process

$$y_t - \mu = \phi(y_{t-1} - \mu) + \varepsilon_t, \ t = 1, \ldots, T$$

where $\varepsilon_t \sim WN(0, \sigma^2)$ and $|\phi| < 1$. The above representation is called the *mean-adjusted form*. The *characteristic equation* for the AR(1) is

$$\phi(z) = 1 - \phi z = 0 \tag{3.8}$$

so that the root is $z = \frac{1}{\phi}$. Stationarity is satisfied provided the absolute value of the root of the characteristic equation (3.8) is greater than one: $|\frac{1}{\phi}| > 1$ or $|\phi| < 1$. In this case, it is easy to show that $E[y_t] = \mu$, $\gamma_0 = \frac{\sigma^2}{1-\phi^2}$, $\psi_j = \rho_j = \phi^j$ and the Wold representation is

$$y_t = \mu + \sum_{j=0}^{\infty} \rho^j \varepsilon_{t-j}.$$

Notice that for the AR(1) the ACF and IRF are identical. This is not true in general. The long-run cumulative impulse response is $\psi(1) = \frac{1}{1-\phi}$.

The AR(1) model may be re-written in *components form* as

$$
\begin{aligned}
y_t &= \mu + u_t \\
u_t &= \phi u_{t-1} + \varepsilon_t
\end{aligned}
$$

or in *autoregression form* as

$$
\begin{aligned}
y_t &= c + \phi y_{t-1} + \varepsilon_t \\
c &= \mu(1 - \phi)
\end{aligned}
$$

An AR(1) with $\mu = 1$, $\phi = 0.75$, $\sigma^2 = 1$ and $T = 100$ is easily simulated in S-PLUS using the components form:

```
> set.seed(101)
> e = rnorm(100,sd=1)
> e.start = rnorm(25,sd=1)
> y.ar1 = 1 + arima.sim(model=list(ar=0.75), n=100,
```

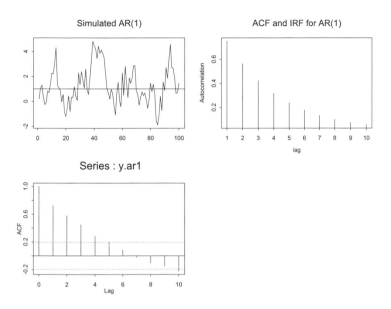

FIGURE 3.4. Simulated AR(1), ACF, IRF and SACF.

```
+ innov=e, start.innov=e.start)
> mean(y.ar1)
[1] 1.271
> var(y.ar1)
[1] 2.201
```

The ACF and IRF may be computed as

```
> gamma.j = rep(0.75,10)^seq(10)
```

The simulated data, ACF and SACF are illustrated in Figure 3.4 using

```
> par(mfrow=c(2,2))
> tsplot(y.ar1,main="Simulated AR(1)")
> abline(h=1)
> tsplot(gamma.j, type="h", main="ACF and IRF for AR(1)",
+ ylab="Autocorrelation", xlab="lag")
> tmp = acf(y.ar1, lag.max=10)
```

Notice that $\{y_t\}$ exhibits *mean-reverting* behavior. That is, $\{y_t\}$ fluctuates about the mean value $\mu = 1$. The ACF and IRF decay at a geometric rate. The decay rate of the IRF is sometimes reported as a *half-life* – the lag j^{half} at which the IRF reaches $\frac{1}{2}$. For the AR(1) with positive ϕ, it can be shown that $j^{half} = \ln(0.5)/\ln(\phi)$. For $\phi = 0.75$, the half-life is

```
> log(0.5)/log(0.75)
```

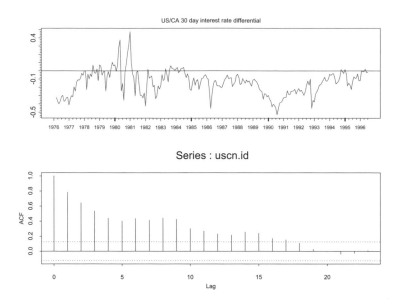

FIGURE 3.5. US/CA 30 day interest rate differential and SACF.

[1] 2.409

Many economic and financial time series are well characterized by an AR(1) process. Leading examples in finance are valuation ratios (dividend-price ratio, price-earning ratio etc), real exchange rates, interest rates, and interest rate differentials (spreads). To illustrate, consider the 30-day US/CA interest rate differential[2] constructed from the S+FinMetrics "timeSeries" object lexrates.dat:

```
> uscn.id = 100*(lexrates.dat[,"USCNF"]-
+ lexrates.dat[,"USCNS"])
> colIds(uscn.id) = "USCNID"
> uscn.id@title = "US/CA 30 day interest rate differential"
> par(mfrow=c(2,1))
> plot(uscn.id,reference.grid=F)
> abline(h=0)
> tmp = acf(uscn.id)
```

The interest rate differential is clearly persistent: autocorrelations are significant at the 5% level up to 15 months.

---

[2] By covered interest rate parity, the nominal interest rate differential between risk free bonds from two countries is equal to the difference between the nominal forward and spot exchange rates.

AR(p) Models

The AR(p) model in mean-adjusted form is

$$y_t - \mu = \phi_1(y_{t-1} - \mu) + \cdots + \phi_p(y_{t-p} - \mu) + \varepsilon_t$$

or, in lag operator notation,

$$\phi(L)(y_t - \mu) = \varepsilon_t$$

where $\phi(L) = 1 - \phi_1 L - \cdots - \phi_p L^p$. The autoregressive form is

$$\phi(L)y_t = c + \varepsilon_t.$$

It can be shown that the AR(p) is stationary and ergodic provided the roots of the *characteristic equation*

$$\phi(z) = 1 - \phi_1 z - \phi_2 z^2 - \cdots - \phi_p z^p = 0 \qquad (3.9)$$

lie outside the complex unit circle (have modulus greater than one). A necessary condition for stationarity that is useful in practice is that $|\phi_1 + \cdots + \phi_p| < 1$. If (3.9) has complex roots then y_t will exhibit sinusoidal behavior. In the stationary AR(p), the constant in the autoregressive form is equal to $\mu(1 - \phi_1 - \cdots - \phi_p)$.

The moments of the AR(p) process satisfy the *Yule-Walker equations*

$$
\begin{aligned}
\gamma_0 &= \phi_1\gamma_1 + \phi_2\gamma_2 + \cdots + \phi_p\gamma_p + \sigma^2 \qquad (3.10)\\
\gamma_j &= \phi_1\gamma_{j-1} + \phi_2\gamma_{j-2} + \cdots + \phi_p\gamma_{j-p}
\end{aligned}
$$

A simple recursive algorithm for finding the Wold representation is based on matching coefficients in $\phi(L)$ and $\psi(L)$ such that $\phi(L)\psi(L) = 1$. For example, in the AR(2) model

$$(1 - \phi_1 L - \phi_2 L^2)(1 + \psi_1 L + \psi_2 L^2 + \cdots) = 1$$

implies

$$
\begin{aligned}
\psi_1 &= 1\\
\psi_2 &= \phi_1\psi_1 + \phi_2\\
\psi_3 &= \phi_1\psi_2 + \phi_2\psi_1\\
&\vdots\\
\psi_j &= \phi_1\psi_{j-1} + \phi_2\psi_{j-2}
\end{aligned}
$$

Partial Autocorrelation Function

The *partial autocorrelation function* (PACF) is a useful tool to help identify AR(p) models. The PACF is based on estimating the sequence of AR

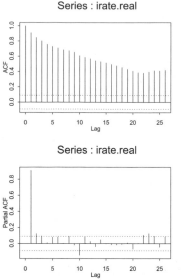

FIGURE 3.6. Monthly U.S. real interest rate, SACF and SPACF.

models

$$z_t = \phi_{11}z_{t-1} + \varepsilon_{1t}$$
$$z_t = \phi_{21}z_{t-1} + \phi_{22}z_{t-2} + \varepsilon_{2t}$$
$$\vdots$$
$$z_t = \phi_{p1}z_{t-1} + \phi_{p2}z_{t-2} + \cdots + \phi_{pp}z_{t-p} + \varepsilon_{pt}$$

where $z_t = y_t - \mu$ is the demeaned data. The coefficients ϕ_{jj} for $j = 1, \ldots, p$ (i.e., the last coefficients in each $AR(p)$ model) are called the partial autocorrelation coefficients. In an $AR(1)$ model the first partial autocorrelation coefficient ϕ_{11} is non-zero, and the remaining partial autocorrelation coefficients ϕ_{jj} for $j > 1$ are equal to zero. Similarly, in an $AR(2)$, the first and second partial autocorrelation coefficients ϕ_{11} and ϕ_{22} are non-zero and the rest are zero for $j > 2$. For an $AR(p)$ all of the first p partial autocorrelation coefficients are non-zero, and the rest are zero for $j > p$. The sample partial autocorrelation coefficients up to lag p are essentially obtained by estimating the above sequence of p AR models by least squares and retaining the estimated coefficients $\hat{\phi}_{jj}$.

Example 4 *Monthly real interest rates*

The "timeSeries" object varex.ts in the S+FinMetrics module contains monthly data on real stock returns, real interest rates, inflation and real output growth.

```
> colIds(varex.ts)
[1] "MARKET.REAL" "RF.REAL"      "INF"          "IPG"
```

Figure 3.6 shows the real interest rate, RF.REAL, over the period January 1961 through December 2000 produced with the S-PLUS commands

```
> smpl = (positions(varex.ts) > timeDate("12/31/1960"))
> irate.real = varex.ts[smpl,"RF.REAL"]
> par(mfrow=c(2,2))
> acf.plot(acf(irate.real, plot=F))
> plot(irate.real, main="Monthly Real Interest Rate")
> tmp = acf(irate.real, type="partial")
```

The SACF and SPACF indicate that the real interest rate might be modeled as an AR(2) or AR(3) process.

3.2.4 Moving Average Models

MA(1) Model

The MA(1) model has the form

$$y_t = \mu + \varepsilon_t + \theta\varepsilon_{t-1}, \ \varepsilon_t \sim WN(0,\sigma^2)$$

For any finite θ the MA(1) is stationary and ergodic. The moments are $E[y_t] = \mu$, $\gamma_0 = \sigma^2(1+\theta^2)$, $\gamma_1 = \sigma^2\theta$, $\gamma_j = 0$ for $j > 1$ and $\rho_1 = \theta/(1+\theta^2)$. Hence, the ACF of an MA(1) process cuts off at lag one, and the maximum value of this correlation is ± 0.5.

There is an identification problem with the MA(1) model since $\theta = 1/\theta$ produce the same value of ρ_1. The MA(1) is called *invertible* if $|\theta| < 1$ and is called *non-invertible* if $|\theta| \geq 1$. In the invertible MA(1), the error term ε_t has an infinite order AR representation of the form

$$\varepsilon_t = \sum_{j=0}^{\infty} \theta^{*j}(y_{t-j} - \mu)$$

where $\theta^* = -\theta$ so that ε_t may be thought of as a prediction error based on past values of y_t. A consequence of the above result is that the PACF for an invertible MA(1) process decays towards zero at an exponential rate.

Example 5 *Signal plus noise model*

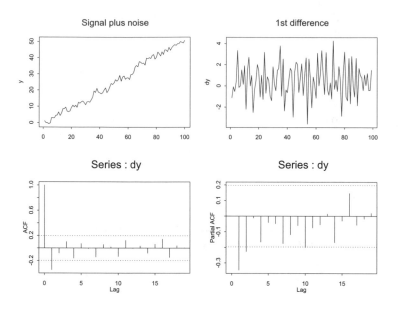

FIGURE 3.7. Simulated data, SACF and SPACF from signal plus noise model.

MA(1) models often arise through data transformations like aggregation and differencing[3]. For example, consider the signal plus noise model

$$y_t = z_t + \varepsilon_t, \ \varepsilon_t \sim WN(0, \sigma_\varepsilon^2)$$
$$z_t = z_{t-1} + \eta_t, \ \eta_t \sim WN(0, \sigma_\eta^2)$$

where ε_t and η_t are independent. For example, z_t could represent the fundamental value of an asset price and ε_t could represent an *iid* deviation about the fundamental price. A stationary representation requires differencing y_t:

$$\Delta y_t = \eta_t + \varepsilon_t - \varepsilon_{t-1}$$

It can be shown, e.g. Harvey (1993), that Δy_t is an MA(1) process with $\theta = \frac{-(q+2)+\sqrt{q^2+4q}}{2}$ where $q = \frac{\sigma_\varepsilon^2}{\sigma_\eta^2}$ is the signal-to-noise ratio and $\rho_1 = \frac{-1}{q+2} < 0$.

Simulated data with $\sigma_\varepsilon^2 = 1$ and $\sigma_\eta^2 = (0.5)^2$ created with the S-PLUS commands

```
> set.seed(112)
> eps = rnorm(100,1)
> eta = rnorm(100,0.5)
```

----

[3] MA(1) type models for asset returns often occur as the result of no-trading effects or bid-ask bounce effects. See Campbell, Lo and MacKinlay (1997) chapter 3 for details.

```
> z = cumsum(eta)
> y = z + eps
> dy = diff(y)
> par(mfrow=c(2,2))
> tsplot(y, main="Signal plus noise",ylab="y")
> tsplot(dy, main="1st difference",ylab="dy")
> tmp = acf(dy)
> tmp = acf(dy,type="partial")
```

are illustrated in Figure 3.7. The signal-to-noise ratio $q = 1.4142$ implies a
first lag autocorrelation of $\rho_1 = -0.293$. This negative correlation is clearly
reflected in the SACF.

MA(q) Model

The MA(q) model has the form

$$y_t = \mu + \varepsilon_t + \theta_1\varepsilon_{t-1} + \cdots + \theta_q\varepsilon_{t-q}, \text{ where } \varepsilon_t \sim WN(0, \sigma^2)$$

The MA(q) model is stationary and ergodic provided $\theta_1, \ldots, \theta_q$ are finite.
It is *invertible* if all of the roots of the MA characteristic polynomial

$$\theta(z) = 1 + \theta_1 z + \cdots \theta_q z^q = 0 \tag{3.11}$$

lie outside the complex unit circle. The moments of the MA(q) are

$$
\begin{aligned}
E[y_t] &= \mu \\
\gamma_0 &= \sigma^2(1 + \theta_1^2 + \cdots + \theta_q^2) \\
\gamma_j &= \begin{cases} (\theta_j + \theta_{j+1}\theta_1 + \theta_{j+2}\theta_2 + \cdots + \theta_q\theta_{q-j})\sigma^2 \text{ for } j = 1, 2, \ldots, q \\ 0 \text{ for } j > q \end{cases}
\end{aligned}
$$

Hence, the ACF of an MA(q) is non-zero up to lag q and is zero afterwards.
As with the MA(1), the PACF for an invertible MA(q) will show exponential decay and possibly pseudo cyclical behavior if the roots of (3.11) are
complex.

Example 6 *Overlapping returns and MA(q) models*

MA(q) models often arise in finance through data aggregation transformations. For example, let $R_t = \ln(P_t/P_{t-1})$ denote the monthly continuously compounded return on an asset with price P_t. Define the an-
nual return at time t using monthly returns as $R_t(12) = \ln(P_t/P_{t-12}) = \sum_{j=0}^{11} R_{t-j}$. Suppose $R_t \sim WN(\mu, \sigma^2)$ and consider a sample of monthly
returns of size T, $\{R_1, R_2, \ldots, R_T\}$. A sample of annual returns may be cre-
ated using *overlapping* or *non-overlapping* returns. Let $\{R_{12}(12), R_{13}(12),$
$\ldots, R_T(12)\}$ denote a sample of $T^* = T - 11$ monthly overlapping annual
returns and $\{R_{12}(12), R_{24}(12), \ldots, R_T(12)\}$ denote a sample of $T/12$ non-
overlapping annual returns. Researchers often use overlapping returns in

analysis due to the apparent larger sample size. One must be careful using overlapping returns because the monthly annual return sequence $\{R_t(12)\}$ is not a white noise process even if the monthly return sequence $\{R_t\}$ is. To see this, straightforward calculations give

$$
\begin{aligned}
E[R_t(12)] &= 12\mu \\
\gamma_0 &= var(R_t(12)) = 12\sigma^2 \\
\gamma_j &= cov(R_t(12), R_{t-j}(12)) = (12 - j)\sigma^2 \text{ for } j < 12 \\
\gamma_j &= 0 \text{ for } j \geq 12
\end{aligned}
$$

Since $\gamma_j = 0$ for $j \geq 12$ notice that $\{R_t(12)\}$ behaves like an MA(11) process

$$
\begin{aligned}
R_t(12) &= 12\mu + \varepsilon_t + \theta_1\varepsilon_{t-1} + \cdots + \theta_{11}\varepsilon_{t-11} \\
\varepsilon_t &\sim WN(0, \sigma^2)
\end{aligned}
$$

To illustrate, consider creating annual overlapping continuously compounded returns on the S&P 500 index over the period February 1990 through January 2001. The S+FinMetrics "timeSeries" singleIndex.dat contains the S&P 500 price data and the continuously compounded monthly returns are computed using the S+FinMetrics function getReturns

```
> sp500.mret = getReturns(singleIndex.dat[,"SP500"],
+ type="continuous")
> sp500.mret@title = "Monthly returns on S&P 500 Index"
```

The monthly overlapping annual returns are easily computed using the S-PLUS function aggregateSeries

```
> sp500.aret = aggregateSeries(sp500.mret,moving=12,FUN=sum)
> sp500.aret@title = "Monthly Annual returns on S&P 500 Index"
```

The optional argument moving=12 specifies that the sum function is to be applied to moving blocks of size 12. The data together with the SACF and PACF of the monthly annual returns are displayed in Figure 3.8.

The SACF has non-zero values up to lag 11. Interestingly, the SPACF is very small at all lags except the first.

3.2.5 ARMA(p,q) Models

The general ARMA(p, q) model in mean-adjusted form is given by (3.7). The regression formulation is

$$
y_t = c + \phi_1 y_{t-1} + \cdots + \phi_p y_{t-p} + \varepsilon_t + \theta\varepsilon_{t-1} + \cdots + \theta\varepsilon_{t-q} \tag{3.12}
$$

It is stationary and ergodic if the roots of the characteristic equation $\phi(z) = 0$ lie outside the complex unit circle, and it is invertible if the roots of the

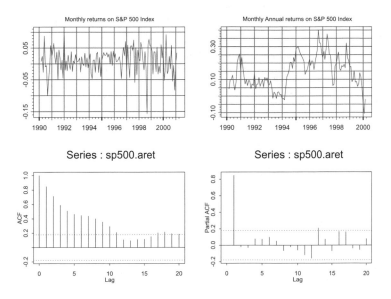

FIGURE 3.8. Monthly non-overlapping and overlapping annual returns on the S&P 500 index.

MA characteristic polynomial $\theta(z) = 0$ lie outside the unit circle. It is assumed that the polynomials $\phi(z) = 0$ and $\theta(z) = 0$ do not have canceling or common factors. A stationary and ergodic ARMA(p, q) process has a mean equal to

$$\mu = \frac{c}{1 - \phi_1 - \cdots - \phi_p} \tag{3.13}$$

and its autocovariances, autocorrelations and impulse response weights satisfy the recursive relationships

$$\begin{aligned}
\gamma_j &= \phi_1 \gamma_{j-1} + \phi_2 \gamma_{j-2} + \cdots + \phi_p \gamma_{j-p} \\
\rho_j &= \phi_1 \rho_{j-1} + \phi_2 \rho_{j-2} + \cdots + \phi_p \rho_{j-p} \\
\psi_j &= \phi_1 \psi_{j-1} + \phi_2 \psi_{j-2} + \cdots + \phi_p \psi_{j-p}
\end{aligned}$$

The general form of the ACF for an ARMA(p, q) process is complicated. See Hamilton (1994) chapter five for details. In general, for an ARMA(p, q) process, the ACF behaves like the ACF for an AR(p) process for $p > q$, and the PACF behaves like the PACF for an MA(q) process for $q > p$. Hence, both the ACF and PACF eventually show exponential decay.

ARMA(p, q) models often arise from certain aggregation transformations of simple time series models. An important result due to Granger and Morris (1976) is that if y_{1t} is an ARMA(p_1, q_1) process and y_{2t} is an ARMA(p_2, q_2) process, which may be contemporaneously correlated with y_{1t}, then $y_{1t} + y_{2t}$ is an ARMA(p, q) process with $p = p_1 + p_2$ and $q = \max(p_1 + q_2, q_1 + p_2)$. For example, if y_{1t} is an AR(1) process and y_2 is a AR(1) process, then $y_1 + y_2$ is an ARMA(2,1) process.

High order ARMA(p, q) processes are difficult to identify and estimate in practice and are rarely used in the analysis of financial data. Low order ARMA(p, q) models with p and q less than three are generally sufficient for the analysis of financial data.

ARIMA(p, d, q) Models

The specification of the ARMA(p, q) model (3.7) assumes that y_t is stationary and ergodic. If y_t is a trending variable like an asset price or a macroeconomic aggregate like real GDP, then y_t must be transformed to stationary form by eliminating the trend. Box and Jenkins (1976) advocate removal of trends by differencing. Let $\Delta = 1 - L$ denote the *difference operator*. If there is a linear trend in y_t then the first difference $\Delta y_t = y_t - y_{t-1}$ will not have a trend. If there is a quadratic trend in y_t, then Δy_t will contain a linear trend but the second difference $\Delta^2 y_t = (1 - 2L + L^2)y_t = y_t - 2y_{t-1} + y_{t-2}$ will not have a trend. The class of ARMA(p, q) models where the trends have been transformed by differencing d times is denoted ARIMA(p, d, q)[4].

3.2.6   Estimation of ARMA Models and Forecasting

ARMA(p, q) models are generally estimated using the technique of maximum likelihood, which is usually accomplished by putting the ARMA(p, q) in state-space form from which the prediction error decomposition of the log-likelihood function may be constructed. Details of this process are given in Harvey (1993). An often ignored aspect of the maximum likelihood estimation of ARMA(p, q) models is the treatment of initial values. These initial values are the first p values of y_t and q values of ε_t in (3.7). The *exact likelihood* utilizes the stationary distribution of the initial values in the construction of the likelihood. The *conditional likelihood* treats the p initial values of y_t as fixed and often sets the q initial values of ε_t to zero. The exact maximum likelihood estimates (MLEs) maximize the exact log-likelihood, and the conditional MLEs maximize the conditional log-likelihood. The exact and conditional MLEs are asymptotically equivalent but can differ substantially in small samples, especially for models that are close to being nonstationary or noninvertible.[5]

---

[4] More general ARIMA(p, d, q) models allowing for seasonality are discussed in chapter 27 of the *S-PLUS Guide to Statistics, Vol. II*.

[5] As pointed out by Venables and Ripley (1999) page 415, the maximum likelihood estimates computed using the S-PLUS function `arima.mle` are conditional MLEs. Exact MLEs may be easily computed using the S+FinMetrics state space modeling functions.

For pure AR models, the conditional MLEs are equivalent to the least squares estimates from the model

$$y_t = c + \phi_1 y_{t-1} + \cdots + \phi_p y_{t-p} + \varepsilon_t \qquad (3.14)$$

Notice, however, that c in (3.14) is not an estimate of $E[y_t] = \mu$. The least squares estimate of μ is given by plugging in the least squares estimates of $c, \phi_1, \ldots, \phi_p$ into (3.13).

Model Selection Criteria

Before an ARMA(p, q) may be estimated for a time series y_t, the AR and MA orders p and q must be determined by visually inspecting the SACF and SPACF for y_t. Alternatively, statistical *model selection criteria* may be used. The idea is to fit all ARMA(p, q) models with orders $p \le p_{max}$ and $q \le q_{max}$ and choose the values of p and q which minimizes some model selection criteria. Model selection criteria for ARMA(p, q) models have the form

$$MSC(p, q) = \ln(\tilde{\sigma}^2(p, q)) + c_T \cdot \varphi(p, q)$$

where $\tilde{\sigma}^2(p, q)$ is the MLE of $var(\varepsilon_t) = \sigma^2$ *without a degrees of freedom correction* from the ARMA(p, q) model, c_T is a sequence indexed by the sample size T, and $\varphi(p, q)$ is a penalty function which penalizes large ARMA(p, q) models. The two most common information criteria are the Akaike (AIC) and Schwarz-Bayesian (BIC):

$$
\begin{aligned}
AIC(p, q) &= \ln(\tilde{\sigma}^2(p, q)) + \frac{2}{T}(p + q) \\
BIC(p, q) &= \ln(\tilde{\sigma}^2(p, q)) + \frac{\ln T}{T}(p + q)
\end{aligned}
$$

The AIC criterion asymptotically overestimates the order with positive probability, whereas the BIC estimate the order consistently under fairly general conditions if the true orders p and q are less than or equal to p_{max} and q_{max}. However, in finite samples the BIC generally shares no particular advantage over the AIC.

Forecasting Algorithm

Forecasts from an ARIMA(p, d, q) model are straightforward. The model is put in state space form, and optimal h-step ahead forecasts along with forecast standard errors (not adjusted for parameter uncertainty) are produced using the Kalman filter algorithm. Details of the method are given in Harvey (1993).

Estimation and Forecasting ARIMA(p, d, q) Models Using the S-PLUS Function `arima.mle`

Conditional MLEs may be computed using the S-PLUS function `arima.mle`. The form of the ARIMA(p, d, q) assumed by `arima.mle` is

$$
\begin{aligned}
y_t &= \phi_1 y_{t-1} + \cdots + \phi_p y_{t-p} \\
&\quad + \varepsilon_t - \theta_1 \varepsilon_{t-1} - \cdots - \theta_q \varepsilon_{t-q} \\
&\quad + \beta' \mathbf{x}_t
\end{aligned}
$$

where $\mathbf{x}_t$ represents additional explanatory variables. It is assumed that y_t has been differenced d times to remove any trends and that the unconditional mean μ has been subtracted out so that y_t is demeaned. Notice that `arima.mle` assumes that the signs on the MA coefficients θ_j are the opposite to those in (3.7).

The arguments expected by `arima.mle` are

```
> args(arima.mle)
function(x, model = NULL, n.cond = 0, xreg = NULL, ...)
```

where x is a univariate "timeSeries" or vector, model is a list object describing the specification of the ARMA model, n.cond sets the number of initial observations on which to condition in the formation of the log-likelihood, and xreg is a "timeSeries", vector or matrix of additional explanatory variables. By default, `arima.mle` assumes that the ARIMA(p, d, q) model is stationary and in mean-adjusted form with an estimate of μ subtracted from the observed data y_t. To estimate the regression form (3.12) of the ARIMA(p, q) model, simply set xreg=1. ARIMA(p, d, q) models are specified using list variables the form

```
> mod.list = list(order=c(1,0,1))
> mod.list = list(order=c(1,0,1),ar=0.75,ma=0)
> mod.list = list(ar=c(0.75,-0.25),ma=c(0,0))
```

The first list simply specifies an ARMA(1,0,1)/ARMA(1,1) model. The second list specifies an ARMA(1,0,1) as well as starting values for the AR and MA parameters ϕ and θ. The third list implicitly determines an ARMA(2,2) model by giving the starting values for the AR and MA parameters. The function `arima.mle` produces an object of class "arima" for which there are `print` and `plot` methods. Diagnostics from the fit can be created with the S-PLUS function `arima.diag`, and forecasts may be produced using `arima.forecast`.

Example 7 *Estimation of ARMA model for US/CA interest rate differential*

Consider estimating an ARMA(p, q) for the monthly US/CA interest rate differential data in the "timeSeries" `uscn.id` used in a previous example. To estimate an ARMA(1,1) model for the demeaned interest rate differential with starting values $\phi = 0.75$ and $\theta = 0$ use

```
> uscn.id.dm = uscn.id - mean(uscn.id)
> arma11.mod = list(ar=0.75,ma=0)
> arma11.fit = arima.mle(uscn.id.dm,model=arma11.mod)
> class(arma11.fit)
[1] "arima"
```

The components of arma11.fit are

```
> names(arma11.fit)
 [1] "model"      "var.coef"  "method"     "series"
 [5] "aic"        "loglik"    "sigma2"     "n.used"
 [9] "n.cond"     "converged" "conv.type" "call"
```

To see the basic fit simply type

```
> arma11.fit
Call: arima.mle(x = uscn.id.dm, model = arma11.mod)
Method:  Maximum Likelihood
Model :  1 0 1

Coefficients:
      AR :  0.82913
      MA :  0.11008


Variance-Covariance Matrix:
          ar(1)      ma(1)
ar(1) 0.002046 0.002224
ma(1) 0.002224 0.006467


Optimizer has  converged
Convergence Type: relative function convergence
AIC: -476.25563
```

The conditional MLEs are $\hat{\phi}_{cmle} = 0.829$ and $\hat{\theta}_{cmle} = -0.110$. Standard errors for these parameters are given by the square roots of the diagonal elements of variance-covariance matrix

```
> std.errs = sqrt(diag(arma11.fit$var.coef))
> names(std.errs) = colIds(arma11.fit$var.coef)
> std.errs
   ar(1)    ma(1)
 0.04523 0.08041
```

It appears that the $\hat{\theta}_{cmle}$ is not statistically different from zero.

To estimate the ARMA(1,1) for the interest rate differential data in regression form (3.12) with an intercept use

```
> arma11.fit2 = arima.mle(uscn.id,model=arma11.mod,xreg=1)
> arma11.fit2
Call: arima.mle(x = uscn.id, model = arma11.mod, xreg = 1)
Method:  Maximum Likelihood
Model :  1 0 1

Coefficients:
     AR : 0.82934
     MA : 0.11065

Variance-Covariance Matrix:
         ar(1)    ma(1)
ar(1) 0.002043 0.002222
ma(1) 0.002222 0.006465
Coeffficients for regressor(s): intercept
[1] -0.1347

Optimizer has   converged
Convergence Type: relative function convergence
AIC: -474.30852
```

The conditional MLEs for ϕ and θ are essentially the same as before, and the MLE for c is $\hat{c}_{cmle} = -0.1347$. Notice that the reported variance-covariance matrix only gives values for the estimated ARMA coefficients $\hat{\phi}_{cmle}$ and $\hat{\theta}_{cmle}$.

Graphical diagnostics of the fit produced using the plot method

```
> plot(arma11.fit)
```

are illustrated in Figure 3.9. There appears to be some high order serial correlation in the errors as well as heteroskedasticity.

The h-step ahead forecasts of future values may be produced with the S-PLUS function arima.forecast. For example, to produce monthly forecasts for the demeaned interest rate differential from July 1996 through June 1997 use

```
> fcst.dates = timeSeq("7/1/1996", "6/1/1997",
+ by="months", format="%b %Y")
> uscn.id.dm.fcst = arima.forecast(uscn.id.dm, n=12,
+ model=arma11.fit$model, future.positions=fcst.dates)
> names(uscn.id.dm.fcst)
[1] "mean"    "std.err"
```

The object uscn.id.dm.fcst is a list whose first component is a "timeSeries" containing the h-step forecasts, and the second component is a "timeSeries" containing the forecast standard errors:

```
> uscn.id.dm.fcst[[1]]
```

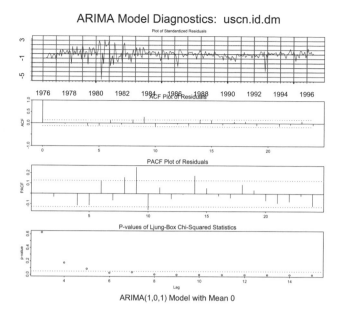

FIGURE 3.9. Residual diagnostics from ARMA(1,1) fit to US/CA interest rate differentials.

Positions	1
Jul 1996	0.09973
Aug 1996	0.08269
Sep 1996	0.06856
Oct 1996	0.05684
Nov 1996	0.04713
Dec 1996	0.03908
Jan 1997	0.03240
Feb 1997	0.02686
Mar 1997	0.02227
Apr 1997	0.01847
May 1997	0.01531
Jun 1997	0.01270

The data, forecasts and 95% forecast confidence intervals shown in Figure 3.10 are produced by

```
> smpl = positions(uscn.id.dm) >= timeDate("6/1/1995")
> plot(uscn.id.dm[smpl,],uscn.id.dm.fcst$mean,
+ uscn.id.dm.fcst$mean+2*uscn.id.dm.fcst$std.err,
+ uscn.id.dm.fcst$mean-2*uscn.id.dm.fcst$std.err,
+ plot.args=list(lty=c(1,4,3,3)))
```

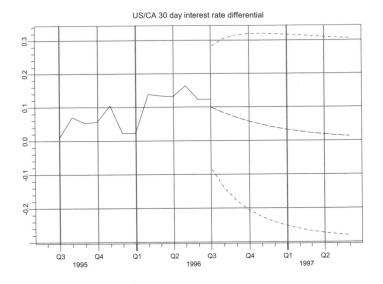

FIGURE 3.10. Forecasts for 12 months for the series uscn.id.dm.

Estimating AR(p) by Least Squares Using the S+FinMetrics Function
OLS

As previously mentioned, the conditional MLEs for an AR(p) model may
be computed using least squares. The S+FinMetrics function OLS, which
extends the S-PLUS function lm to handle general time series regression,
may be used to estimate an AR(p) in a particularly convenient way. The
general use of OLS is discussed in Chapter 6, and its use for estimating an
AR(p) is only mentioned here. For example, to estimate an AR(2) model
for the US/CA interest rate differential use

```
> ar2.fit = OLS(USCNID~ar(2), data=uscn.id)
> ar2.fit

Call:
OLS(formula = USCNID ~ar(2), data = uscn.id)

Coefficients:
 (Intercept)    lag1     lag2
 -0.0265      0.7259   0.0758

Degrees of freedom: 243 total; 240 residual
Time period: from Apr 1976 to Jun 1996
Residual standard error: 0.09105
```

The least squares estimates of the AR coefficients are $\hat{\phi}_1 = 0.7259$ and $\hat{\phi}_2 = 0.0758$. Since $\hat{\phi}_1 + \hat{\phi}_2 < 1$ the estimated AR(2) model is stationary. To be sure, the roots of $\phi(z) = 1 - \hat{\phi}_1 z - \hat{\phi}_2 z^2 = 0$ are

```
> abs(polyroot(c(1,-ar2.fit$coef[2:3])))
[1]  1.222 10.798
```

are outside the complex unit circle.

3.2.7 Martingales and Martingale Difference Sequences

Let $\{y_t\}$ denote a sequence of random variables and let $I_t = \{y_t, y_{t-1}, \ldots\}$ denote a set of conditioning information or *information set* based on the past history of y_t. The sequence $\{y_t, I_t\}$ is called a *martingale* if

- $I_{t-1} \subset I_t$ (I_t is a filtration)

- $E[|y_t|] < \infty$

- $E[y_t | I_{t-1}] = y_{t-1}$ (martingale property)

The most common example of a martingale is the random walk model

$$y_t = y_{t-1} + \varepsilon_t, \ \varepsilon_t \sim WN(0, \sigma^2)$$

where y_0 is a fixed initial value. Letting $I_t = \{y_t, \ldots, y_0\}$ implies $E[y_t | I_{t-1}] = y_{t-1}$ since $E[\varepsilon_t | I_{t-1}] = 0$.

Let $\{\varepsilon_t\}$ be a sequence of random variables with an associated information set I_t. The sequence $\{\varepsilon_t, I_t\}$ is called a *martingale difference sequence* (MDS) if

- $I_{t-1} \subset I_t$

- $E[\varepsilon_t | I_{t-1}] = 0$ (MDS property)

If $\{y_t, I_t\}$ is a martingale, a MDS $\{\varepsilon_t, I_t\}$ may be constructed by defining

$$\varepsilon_t = y_t - E[y_t | I_{t-1}]$$

By construction, a MDS is an uncorrelated process. This follows from the *law of iterated expectations*. To see this, for any $k > 0$

$$
\begin{aligned}
E[\varepsilon_t \varepsilon_{t-k}] &= E[E[\varepsilon_t \varepsilon_{t-k} | I_{t-1}]] \\
&= E[\varepsilon_{t-k} E[\varepsilon_t | I_{t-1}]] \\
&= 0
\end{aligned}
$$

In fact, if z_n is any function of the past history of ε_t so that $z_n \in I_{t-1}$ then

$$E[\varepsilon_t z_n] = 0$$

Although a MDS is an uncorrelated process, it does not have to be an independent process. That is, there can be dependencies in the higher order moments of ε_t. The *autoregressive conditional heteroskedasticity* (ARCH) process in the following example is a leading example in finance.

MDSs are particularly nice to work with because there are many useful convergence results (laws of large numbers, central limit theorems etc.). White (1984), Hamilton (1994) and Hayashi (2000) describe the most useful of these results for the analysis of financial time series.

Example 8 *ARCH process*

A well known stylized fact about high frequency financial asset returns is that volatility appears to be autocorrelated. A simple model to capture such volatility autocorrelation is the ARCH process due to Engle (1982). To illustrate, let r_t denote the daily return on an asset and assume that $E[r_t] = 0$. An ARCH(1) model for r_t is

$$
\begin{align}
r_t &= \sigma_t z_t \tag{3.15} \\
z_t &\sim \; iid \; N(0,1) \\
\sigma_t^2 &= \omega + \alpha r_{t-1}^2 \tag{3.16}
\end{align}
$$

where $\omega > 0$ and $0 < \alpha < 1$. Let $I_t = \{r_t, \ldots\}$. The S+FinMetrics function simulate.garch may be used to generate simulations from above ARCH(1) model. For example, to simulate 250 observations on r_t with $\omega = 0.1$ and $\alpha = 0.8$ use

```
> rt = simulate.garch(model=list(a.value=0.1, arch=0.8),
+        n=250, rseed=196)
> class(rt)
[1] "structure"
> names(rt)
[1] "et"        "sigma.t"
```

Notice that the function simulate.garch produces simulated values of both r_t and σ_t. These values are shown in Figure 3.11.

To see that $\{r_t, I_t\}$ is a MDS, note that

$$
\begin{align}
E[r_t | I_{t-1}] &= E[z_t \sigma_t | I_{t-1}] \\
&= \sigma_t E[z_t | I_{t-1}] \\
&= 0
\end{align}
$$

Since r_t is a MDS, it is an uncorrelated process. Provided $|\alpha| < 1$, r_t is a mean zero covariance stationary process. The unconditional variance of r_t is given by

$$
\begin{align}
var(r_t) &= E[r_t^2] = E[E[z_t^2 \sigma_t^2 | I_{t-1}]] \\
&= E[\sigma_t^2 E[z_t^2 | I_{t-1}] = E[\sigma_t^2]
\end{align}
$$

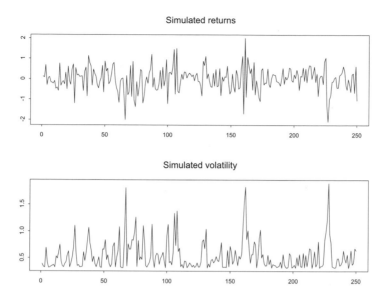

FIGURE 3.11. Simulated values from ARCH(1) process with $\omega = 1$ and $\alpha = 0.8$.

since $E[z_t^2|I_{t-1}] = 1$. Utilizing (3.16) and the stationarity of r_t, $E[\sigma_t^2]$ may be expressed as

$$E[\sigma_t^2] = \frac{\omega}{1 - \alpha}$$

Furthermore, by adding ε_t^2 to both sides of (3.16) and rearranging it follows that r_t^2 has an AR(1) representation of the form

$$\varepsilon_t^2 = \omega + \alpha\varepsilon_{t-1}^2 + v_t$$

where $v_t - \varepsilon_t^2 - \sigma_t^2$ is a MDS.

3.2.8 Long-run Variance

Let y_t be a stationary and ergodic time series. Anderson's central limit theorem for stationary and ergodic processes (c.f. Hamilton (1994) pg. 195) states

$$\sqrt{T}(\bar{y} - \mu) \xrightarrow{d} N(0, \sum_{j=-\infty}^{\infty} \gamma_j)$$

or

$$\bar{y} \stackrel{A}{\sim} N\left(\mu, \frac{1}{T}\sum_{j=-\infty}^{\infty} \gamma_j\right)$$

The sample size, T, times the *asymptotic variance* of the sample mean is often called the *long-run variance* of y_t[6] :

$$lrv(y_t) = T \cdot avar(\bar{y}) = \sum_{j=-\infty}^{\infty} \gamma_j.$$

Since $\gamma_{-j} = \gamma_j$, $lrv(y_t)$ may be alternatively expressed as

$$lrv(y_t) = \gamma_0 + 2\sum_{j=1}^{\infty} \gamma_j.$$

Using the long-run variance, an asymptotic 95% confidence interval for μ takes the form

$$\bar{y} \pm 1.96 \cdot \sqrt{T^{-1}\widehat{lrv}(y_t)}$$

where $\widehat{lrv}(y_t)$ is a consistent estimate of $lrv(y_t)$.

Estimating the Long-Run Variance

If y_t is a linear process, it may be shown that

$$\sum_{j=-\infty}^{\infty} \gamma_j = \sigma^2 \left(\sum_{j=0}^{\infty} \psi_j\right)^2 = \sigma^2 \psi(1)^2$$

and so

$$lrv(y_t) = \sigma^2 \psi(1)^2 \tag{3.17}$$

Further, if $y_t \sim \text{ARMA}(p,q)$ then

$$\psi(1) = \frac{1 + \theta_1 + \cdots + \theta_q}{1 - \phi_1 - \cdots - \phi_p} = \frac{\theta(1)}{\phi(1)}$$

so that

$$lrv(y_t) = \frac{\sigma^2 \theta(1)^2}{\phi(1)^2}. \tag{3.18}$$

A consistent estimate of $lrv(y_t)$ may then be computed by estimating the parameters of the appropriate ARMA(p,q) model and substituting these estimates into (3.18). Alternatively, the ARMA(p,q) process may be approximated by a high order AR(p^*) process

$$y_t = c + \phi_1 y_{t-1} + \cdots + \phi_{p^*} y_{t-p^*} + \varepsilon_t$$

---

[6] Using spectral methods, $lrv(\bar{y})$ has the alternative representation

$$lrv(\bar{y}) = \frac{1}{T} 2\pi f(0)$$

where $f(0)$ denotes the spectral density of y_t evaluated at frequency 0.

where the lag length p^* is chosen such that ε_t is uncorrelated. This gives rise to the *autoregressive long-run variance* estimate

$$lrv_{AR}(y_t) = \frac{\sigma^2}{\phi^*(1)^2}. \tag{3.19}$$

A consistent estimate of $lrv(y_t)$ may also be computed using some non-parametric methods. An estimator made popular by Newey and West (1987) is the weighted autocovariance estimator

$$\widehat{lrv}_{NW}(y_t) = \hat{\gamma}_0 + 2 \sum_{j=1}^{M_T} w_{j,T} \cdot \hat{\gamma}_j \tag{3.20}$$

where $w_{j,T}$ are weights which sum to unity and M_T is a truncation lag parameter that satisfies $M_T = O(T^{1/3})$. For MA(q) processes, $\gamma_j = 0$ for $j > q$ and Newey and West suggest using the *rectangular* weights $w_{j,T} = 1$ for $j \le M_T = q$; 0 otherwise. For general linear processes, Newey and West suggest using the *Bartlett* weights $w_{j,T} = 1 - \frac{j}{M_T+1}$ with M_T equal to the integer part of $4(T/100)^{2/9}$.

Example 9 *Long-run variance of AR(1)*

Let y_t be an AR(1) process created using

```
> set.seed(101)
> e = rnorm(100,sd=1)
> y.ar1 = 1 + arima.sim(model=list(ar=0.75),innov=e)
```

Here $\psi(1) = \frac{1}{\phi(1)} = \frac{1}{1-\phi}$ and

$$lrv(y_t) = \frac{\sigma^2}{(1-\phi)^2}.$$

For $\phi = 0.75$, $\sigma^2 = 1$, $lrv(y_t) = 16$ implies for $T = 100$ an asymptotic standard error for $\bar{y}$ equal to $SE(\bar{y}) = 0.40$. If $y_t \sim WN(0,1)$, then the asymptotic standard error for $\bar{y}$ is $SE(\bar{y}) - 0.10$.

$lrv_{AR}(y_t)$ may be easily computed in S-PLUS using OLS to estimate the AR(1) parameters:

```
> ar1.fit = OLS(y.ar1~ar(1))
> rho.hat = coef(ar1.fit)[2]
> sig2.hat = sum(residuals(ar1.fit)^2)/ar1.fit$df.resid
> lrv.ar1 = sig2.hat/(1-rho.hat)^2
> as.numeric(lrv.ar1)
[1] 13.75
```

Here $lrv_{AR}(y_t) = 13.75$, and an estimate for $SE(\bar{y})$ is $\widehat{SE}_{AR}(\bar{y}) = 0.371$.

The S+FinMetrics function `asymp.var` may be used to compute the nonparameteric Newey-West estimate $lrv_{NW}(y_t)$. The arguments expected by `asymp.var` are

```
> args(asymp.var)
function(x, bandwidth, window = "bartlett", na.rm = F)
```

where x is a "timeSeries", bandwidth sets the truncation lag M_T in (3.20) and window specifies the weight function. Newey and West suggest setting the bandwidth using the sample size dependent rule

$$M_T = 4(T/100)^{2/9}$$

which is equal to 4 in the present case. The Newey-West long-run variance estimate is then

```
> lrv.nw = asymp.var(y.ar1, bandwidth=4)
> lrv.nw
[1] 7.238
```

and the Newey-West estimate of $SE(\bar{y})$ is $\widehat{SE}_{NW}(\bar{y}) = 0.269$.

3.3 Univariate Nonstationary Time Series

A univariate time series process $\{y_t\}$ is called *nonstationary* if it is not stationary. Since a stationary process has time invariant moments, a nonstationary process must have some time dependent moments. The most common forms of nonstationarity are caused by time dependence in the mean and variance.

Trend Stationary Process

$\{y_t\}$ is a *trend stationary* process if it has the form

$$y_t = TD_t + x_t$$

where TD_t are deterministic trend terms (constant, trend, seasonal dummies etc) that depend on t and $\{x_t\}$ is stationary. The series y_t is nonstationary because $E[TD_t] = TD_t$ which depends on t. Since x_t is stationary, y_t never deviates too far away from the deterministic trend TD_t. Hence, y_t exhibits *trend reversion*. If TD_t were known, y_t may be transformed to a stationary process by subtracting off the deterministic trend terms:

$$x_t = y_t - TD_t$$

Example 10 *Trend stationary AR(1)*

A trend stationary AR(1) process with $TD_t = \mu + \delta t$ may be expressed in three equivalent ways

$$
\begin{aligned}
y_t &= \mu + \delta t + u_t, u_t = \phi u_{t-1} + \varepsilon_t \\
y_t - \mu - \delta t &= \phi(y_{t-1} - \mu - \delta(t-1)) + \varepsilon_t \\
y_t &= c + \beta t + \phi y_{t-1} + \varepsilon_t
\end{aligned}
$$

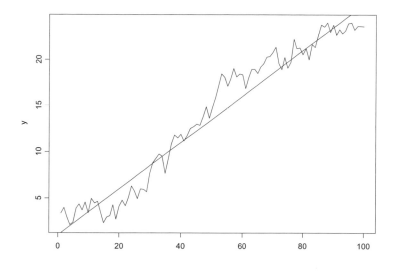

FIGURE 3.12. Simulated trend stationary process.

where $|\phi| < 1$, $c = \mu(1 - \phi) + \delta$, $\beta = \delta(1 - \phi)t$ and $\varepsilon_t \sim WN(0, \sigma^2)$. Figure 3.12 shows $T = 100$ observations from a trend stationary AR(1) with $\mu = 1$, $\delta = 0.25$, $\phi = 0.75$ and $\sigma^2 = 1$ created with the S-PLUS commands

```
> set.seed(101)
> y.tsar1 = 1 + 0.25*seq(100) +
+ arima.sim(model=list(ar=0.75),n=100)
> tsplot(y.tsar1,ylab="y")
> abline(a=1,b=0.25)
```

The simulated data show clear trend reversion.

Integrated Processes

$\{y_t\}$ is an *integrated process* of order 1, denoted $y_t \sim I(1)$, if it has the form

$$y_t = y_{t-1} + u_t \tag{3.21}$$

where u_t is a stationary time series. Clearly, the first difference of y_t is stationary

$$\Delta y_t = u_t$$

Because of the above property, $I(1)$ processes are sometimes called *difference stationary* processes. Starting at y_0, by recursive substitution y_t has the representation of an *integrated sum* of stationary innovations

$$y_t = y_0 + \sum_{j=1}^{t} u_j. \tag{3.22}$$

The integrated sum $\sum_{j=1}^{t} u_j$ is called a *stochastic trend* and is denoted TS_t. Notice that

$$TS_t = TS_{t-1} + u_t$$

where $TS_0 = 0$. In contrast to a deterministic trend, changes in a stochastic trend are not perfectly predictable.

Since the stationary process u_t does not need to be differenced, it is called an integrated process of order zero and is denoted $u_t \sim I(0)$. Recall, from the Wold representation (3.6) a stationary process has an infinite order moving average representation where the moving average weights decline to zero at a geometric rate. From (3.22) it is seen that an $I(1)$ process has an infinite order moving average representation where all of the weights on the innovations are equal to 1.

If $u_t \sim IWN(0, \sigma^2)$ in (3.21) then y_t is called a *random walk*. In general, an $I(1)$ process can have serially correlated and heteroskedastic innovations u_t. If y_t is a random walk and assuming y_0 is fixed then it can be shown that

$$\begin{aligned} \gamma_0 &= \sigma^2 t \\ \gamma_j &= (t-j)\sigma^2 \\ \rho_j &= \sqrt{\frac{t-j}{t}} \end{aligned}$$

which clearly shows that y_t is nonstationary. Also, if t is large relative to j then $\rho_j \approx 1$. Hence, for an $I(1)$ process, the ACF does not decay at a geometric rate but at a linear rate as j increases.

An $I(1)$ process with drift has the form

$$y_t = \mu + y_{t-1} + u_t, \text{ where } u_t \sim I(0)$$

Starting at $t = 0$ an $I(1)$ process with drift μ may be expressed as

$$\begin{aligned} y_t &= y_0 + \mu t + \sum_{j=1}^{t} u_t \\ &= TD_t + TS_t \end{aligned}$$

so that it may be thought of as being composed of a deterministic linear trend $TD_t = y_0 + \mu t$ as well as a stochastic trend $TS_t = \sum_{j=1}^{t} u_j$.

An $I(d)$ process $\{y_t\}$ is one in which $\Delta^d y_t \sim I(0)$. In finance and economics data series are rarely modeled as $I(d)$ process with $d > 2$. Just as an $I(1)$ process with drift contains a linear deterministic trend, an $I(2)$ process with drift will contain a quadratic trend.

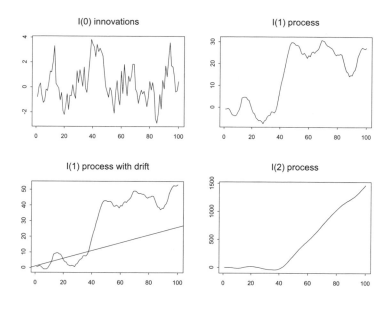

FIGURE 3.13. Simulated $I(d)$ processes for $d = 0$, 1 and 2.

Example 11 *Simulated I(1) processes*

Consider the simulation of $T = 100$ observations from various $I(1)$ processes where the innovations u_t follow an AR(1) process $u_t = 0.75u_{t-1} + \varepsilon_t$ with $\varepsilon_t \sim GWN(0,1)$.

```
> set.seed(101)
> u.ar1 = arima.sim(model=list(ar=0.75), n=100)
> y1 = cumsum(u.ar1)
> y1.d = 1 + 0.25*seq(100)+ y1
> y2 = rep(0,100)
> for (i in 3:100) {
+    y2[i] = 2*y2[i-1] - y2[i-2] + u.ar1[i]
+ }
```

The simulated data are illustrated in Figure 3.13 .

Example 12 *Financial time series*

Many financial time series are well characterized by $I(1)$ processes. The leading example of an $I(1)$ process with drift is the logarithm of an asset price. Common examples of $I(1)$ processes without drifts are the logarithms of exchange rates, nominal interest rates, and inflation rates. Notice that if inflation is constructed as the the difference in the logarithm of a price index and is an $I(1)$ process, then the logarithm of the price index is an

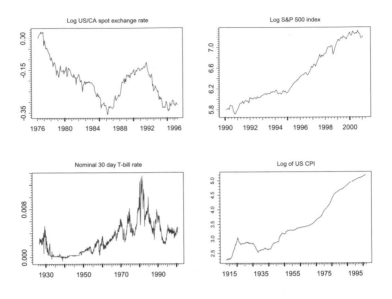

FIGURE 3.14. Monthly financial time series.

$I(2)$ process. Examples of these data are illustrated in Figure 3.14. The exchange rate is the monthly log of the US/CA spot exchange rate taken from the S+FinMetrics "timeSeries" lexrates.dat, the asset price of the monthly S&P 500 index taken from the S+FinMetrics "timeSeries" object singleIndex.dat, the nominal interest rate is the 30 day T-bill rate taken from the S+FinMetrics "timeSeries" object rf.30day, and the monthly consumer price index is taken from the S+FinMetrics "timeSeries" object CPI.dat.

3.4 Long Memory Time Series

If a time series y_t is $I(0)$ then its ACF declines at a geometric rate. As a result, $I(0)$ process have *short memory* since observations far apart in time are essentially independent. Conversely, if y_t is $I(1)$ then its ACF declines at a linear rate and observations far apart in time are not independent. In between $I(0)$ and $I(1)$ processes are so-called *fractionally integrated* $I(d)$ process where $0 < d < 1$. The ACF for a fractionally integrated processes declines at a polynomial (hyperbolic) rate, which implies that observations far apart in time may exhibit weak but non-zero correlation. This weak correlation between observations far apart is often referred to as *long memory*.

A fractionally integrated white noise process y_t has the form

$$(1 - L)^d y_t = \varepsilon_t, \ \varepsilon_t \sim WN(0, \sigma^2) \tag{3.23}$$

where $(1 - L)^d$ has the binomial series expansion representation (valid for any $d > -1$)

$$
\begin{aligned}
(1 - L)^d &= \sum_{k=0}^{\infty} \binom{d}{k} (-L)^k \\
&= 1 - dL + \frac{d(d-1)}{2!} L^2 - \frac{d(d-1)(d-2)}{3!} L^3 + \cdots
\end{aligned}
$$

If $d = 1$ then y_t is a random walk and if $d = 0$ then y_t is white noise. For $0 < d < 1$ it can be shown that

$$\rho_k \propto k^{2d-1}$$

as $k \to \infty$ so that the ACF for y_t declines hyperbolically to zero at a speed that depends on d. Further, it can be shown y_t is stationary and ergodic for $0 < d < 0.5$ and that the variance of y_t is infinite for $0.5 \leq d < 1$.

Example 13 *Simulated fractional white noise*

The S+FinMetrics function `simulate.FARIMA` may be used to generate simulated values from a fractional white noise process. To simulate 500 observations from (3.23) with $d = 0.3$ and $\sigma^2 = 1$ use

```
> set.seed(394)
> y.fwn = simulate.FARIMA(list(d=0.3), 500)
```

Figure 3.15 shows the simulated data along with the sample ACF created using

```
> par(mfrow=c(2,1))
> tsplot(y.fwn)
> tmp = acf(y.fwn,lag.max=50)
```

Notice how the sample ACF slowly decays to zero.

A fractionally integrated process with stationary and ergodic ARMA(p, q) errors

$$(1 - L)^d y_t = u_t, \ u_t \sim ARMA(p, q)$$

is called an *autoregressive fractionally integrated moving average* (ARFIMA) process. The modeling of long memory process is described in detail in Chapter 8.

Example 14 *Long memory in financial time series*

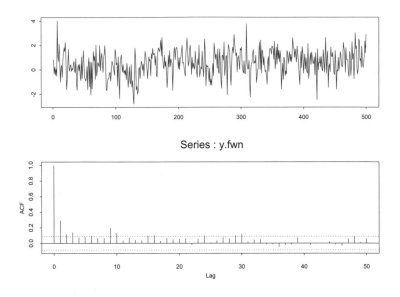

Series : y.fwn

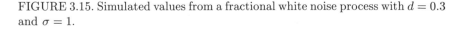

FIGURE 3.15. Simulated values from a fractional white noise process with $d = 0.3$ and $\sigma = 1$.

Long memory behavior has been observed in certain types of financial time series. Ding, Granger and Engle (1993) find evidence of long memory in the absolute value of daily stock returns. Baillie and Bollerslev (1994) find evidence for long memory in the monthly interest rate differentials between short term U.S. government bonds and short term foreign government bonds. To illustrate, consider the absolute values of the daily returns on Microsoft over the 10 year period 1/2/1991 - 1/2/2001 taken from the S+FinMetrics "timeSeries" DowJones30

```
> msft.aret = abs(getReturns(DowJones30[,"MSFT"]))
```

Consider also the monthly US/CA 30-day interest rate differential over the period February 1976 through June 1996 in the "timeSeries" uscn.id constructed earlier and taken from the S+FinMetrics "timeSeries" object lexrates.dat. Figure 3.16 shows the SACFs these series create by

```
> par(mfrow=c(2,1))
> tmp = acf(msft.aret, lag.max=100)
> tmp = acf(uscn.id, lag.max=50)
```

For the absolute return series, notice the large number of small but apparently significant autocorrelations at very long lags. This is indicative of long memory. For the interest rate differential series, the ACF appears to decay fairly quickly, so the evidence for long memory is not as strong.

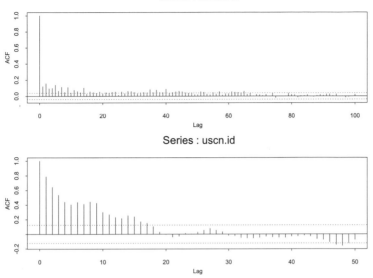

FIGURE 3.16. SACFs for the absolute value of daily returns on Microsoft and the monthly 30-day interest rate differential between U.S. bonds and Canadian bonds.

3.5 Multivariate Time Series

Consider n time series variables $\{y_{1t}\}, \ldots, \{y_{nt}\}$. A *multivariate time series* is the $(n \times 1)$ vector time series $\{\mathbf{Y}_t\}$ where the ith row of $\{\mathbf{Y}_t\}$ is $\{y_{it}\}$. That is, for any time t, $\mathbf{Y}_t = (y_{1t}, \ldots, y_{nt})'$. Multivariate time series analysis is used when one wants to model and explain the interactions and co-movements among a group of time series variables. In finance, multivariate time series analysis is used to model systems of asset returns, asset prices and exchange rates, the term structure of interest rates, asset returns/prices, and economic variables etc. Many of the time series concepts described previously for univariate time series carry over to multivariate time series in a natural way. Additionally, there are some important time series concepts that are particular to multivariate time series. The following sections give the details of these extensions and provide examples using S-PLUS and S+FinMetrics.

3.5.1 Stationary and Ergodic Multivariate Time Series

A multivariate time series $\mathbf{Y}_t$ is covariance stationary and ergodic if all of its component time series are stationary and ergodic. The mean of $\mathbf{Y}_t$ is defined as the $(n \times 1)$ vector

$$E[\mathbf{Y}_t] = \boldsymbol{\mu} = (\mu_1, \ldots, \mu_n)'$$

where $\mu_i = E[y_{it}]$ for $i = 1, \ldots, n$. The variance/covariance matrix of $\mathbf{Y}_t$ is the $(n \times n)$ matrix

$$
\begin{aligned}
var(\mathbf{Y}_t) \quad &= \quad \Gamma_0 = E[(\mathbf{Y}_t - \boldsymbol{\mu})(\mathbf{Y}_t - \boldsymbol{\mu})'] \\
&= \begin{pmatrix}
var(y_{1t}) & cov(y_{1t}, y_{2t}) & \cdots & cov(y_{1t}, y_{nt}) \\
cov(y_{2t}, y_{1t}) & var(y_{2t}) & \cdots & cov(y_{2t}, y_{nt}) \\
\vdots & \vdots & \ddots & \vdots \\
cov(y_{nt}, y_{1t}) & cov(y_{nt}, y_{2t}) & \cdots & var(y_{nt})
\end{pmatrix}
\end{aligned}
$$

The matrix Γ_0 has elements $\gamma_{ij}^0 = cov(y_{it}, y_{jt})$. The correlation matrix of Y_t is the $(n \times n)$ matrix

$$corr(\mathbf{Y}_t) = \mathbf{R}_0 = \mathbf{D}^{-1}\Gamma_0\mathbf{D}^{-1}$$

where $\mathbf{D}$ is an $(n \times n)$ diagonal matrix with j^{th} diagonal element $(\gamma_{jj}^0)^{1/2} = SD(y_{jt})$. The parameters μ, Γ_0 and $\mathbf{R}_0$ are estimated from data $(\mathbf{Y}_1, \ldots, \mathbf{Y}_T)$ using the sample moments

$$
\bar{\mathbf{Y}} \quad = \quad \frac{1}{T}\sum_{t=1}^{T}\mathbf{Y}_t
$$

$$
\hat{\Gamma}_0 \quad = \quad \frac{1}{T}\sum_{t=1}^{T}(\mathbf{Y}_t - \bar{\mathbf{Y}})(\mathbf{Y}_t - \bar{\mathbf{Y}})'
$$

$$
\hat{\mathbf{R}}_0 \quad = \quad \hat{\mathbf{D}}^{-1}\hat{\Gamma}_0\hat{\mathbf{D}}^{-1}
$$

where $\mathbf{D}$ is the $(n \times n)$ diagonal matrix with the sample standard deviations of y_{jt} along the diagonal. In order for the sample variance matrix $\hat{\Gamma}_0$ and correlation matrix $\hat{\mathbf{R}}_0$ to be positive definite, the sample size T must be greater than the number of component time series n.

Example 15 *System of asset returns*

The S+FinMetrics "timeSeries" object DowJones30 contains daily closing prices on the 30 assets in the Dow Jones index. An example of a stationary and ergodic multivariate time series is the continuously compounded returns on the first four assets in this index:

```
> Y = getReturns(DowJones30[,1:4],type="continuous")
> colIds(Y)
[1] "AA"  "AXP" "T"   "BA"
```

The S-PLUS function colMeans may be used to efficiently compute the mean vector of $\mathbf{Y}$

```
> colMeans(seriesData(Y))
      AA        AXP            T           BA
0.0006661  0.0009478  -0.00002873  0.0004108
```

The function `colMeans` does not have a method for "`timeSeries`" objects so the extractor function `seriesData` is used to extract the data slot of the variable Y. The S-PLUS functions `var` and `cor`, which do have methods for "`timeSeries`" objects, may be used to compute $\hat{\Gamma}_0$ and $\hat{R}_0$

```
> var(Y)
            AA         AXP           T          BA
AA  0.00041096  0.00009260  0.00005040  0.00007301
AXP 0.00009260  0.00044336  0.00008947  0.00009546
 T  0.00005040  0.00008947  0.00040441  0.00004548
BA  0.00007301  0.00009546  0.00004548  0.00036829
> cor(Y)
        AA     AXP       T      BA
AA  1.0000  0.2169  0.1236  0.1877
AXP 0.2169  1.0000  0.2113  0.2362
 T  0.1236  0.2113  1.0000  0.1179
BA  0.1877  0.2362  0.1179  1.0000
```

If only the variances or standard deviations of $\mathbf{Y}_t$ are needed the S-PLUS functions `colVars` and `colStdevs` may be used

```
> colVars(seriesData(Y))
      AA        AXP          T          BA
0.000411  0.0004434  0.0004044  0.0003683
> colStdevs(seriesData(Y))
      AA        AXP         T         BA
0.020272  0.021056  0.02011  0.019191
```

Cross Covariance and Correlation Matrices

For a univariate time series y_t the autocovariances γ_k and autocorrelations ρ_k summarize the linear time dependence in the data. With a multivariate time series $\mathbf{Y}_t$ each component has autocovariances and autocorrelations but there are also cross lead-lag covariances and correlations between all possible pairs of components. The autocovariances and autocorrelations of y_{jt} for $j = 1, \ldots, n$ are defined as

$$\gamma_{jj}^k = cov(y_{jt}, y_{jt-k}),$$

$$\rho_{jj}^k = corr(y_{jt}, y_{jt-k}) = \frac{\gamma_{jj}^k}{\gamma_{jj}^0}$$

and these are symmetric in k: $\gamma_{jj}^k = \gamma_{jj}^{-k}$, $\rho_{jj}^k = \rho_{jj}^{-k}$. The *cross lag covariances* and *cross lag correlations* between y_{it} and y_{jt} are defined as

$$\gamma_{ij}^k = cov(y_{it}, y_{jt-k}),$$

$$\rho_{ij}^k = corr(y_{jt}, y_{jt-k}) = \frac{\gamma_{ij}^k}{\sqrt{\gamma_{ii}^0 \gamma_{jj}^0}}$$

and they are not necessarily symmetric in k. In general,

$$\gamma_{ij}^k = cov(y_{it}, y_{jt-k}) \neq cov(y_{it}, y_{jt+k}) = cov(y_{jt}, y_{it-k}) = \gamma_{ij}^{-k}$$

If $\gamma_{ij}^k \neq 0$ for some $k > 0$ then y_{jt} is said to *lead* y_{it}. Similarly, if $\gamma_{ij}^{-k} \neq 0$ for some $k > 0$ then y_{it} is said to *lead* y_{jt}. It is possible that y_{it} leads y_{jt} and vice-versa. In this case, there is said to be *feedback* between the two series.

All of the lag k cross covariances and correlations are summarized in the $(n \times n)$ lag k cross covariance and lag k cross correlation matrices

$$\boldsymbol{\Gamma}_k = E[(\mathbf{Y}_t - \boldsymbol{\mu})(\mathbf{Y}_{t-k} - \boldsymbol{\mu})']$$

$$= \begin{pmatrix} cov(y_{1t}, y_{1t-k}) & cov(y_{1t}, y_{2t-k}) & \cdots & cov(y_{1t}, y_{nt-k}) \\ cov(y_{2t}, y_{1t-k}) & cov(y_{2t}, y_{2t-k}) & \cdots & cov(y_{2t}, y_{nt-k}) \\ \vdots & \vdots & \ddots & \vdots \\ cov(y_{nt}, y_{1t-k}) & cov(y_{nt}, y_{2t-k}) & \cdots & cov(y_{nt}, y_{nt-k}) \end{pmatrix}$$

$$\mathbf{R}_k = \mathbf{D}^{-1}\boldsymbol{\Gamma}_k\mathbf{D}^{-1}$$

The matrices $\boldsymbol{\Gamma}_k$ and $\mathbf{R}_k$ are not symmetric in k but it is easy to show that $\boldsymbol{\Gamma}_{-k} = \boldsymbol{\Gamma}_k'$ and $\mathbf{R}_{-k} = \mathbf{R}_k'$. The matrices $\boldsymbol{\Gamma}_k$ and $\mathbf{R}_k$ are estimated from data $(\mathbf{Y}_1, \ldots, \mathbf{Y}_T)$ using

$$\hat{\boldsymbol{\Gamma}}_k = \frac{1}{T} \sum_{t=k+1}^{T} (\mathbf{Y}_t - \bar{\mathbf{Y}})(\mathbf{Y}_{t-k} - \bar{\mathbf{Y}})'$$

$$\hat{\mathbf{R}}_k = \hat{\mathbf{D}}^{-1}\hat{\boldsymbol{\Gamma}}_k\hat{\mathbf{D}}^{-1}$$

Example 16 *Lead-lag covariances and correlations among asset returns*

Consider computing the cross lag covariances and correlations for $k = 0, \ldots, 5$ between the first two Dow Jones 30 asset returns in the "timeSeries" Y. These covariances and correlations may be computed using the S-PLUS function acf

```
> Ghat = acf(Y[,1:2],lag.max=5,type="covariance",plot=F)
> Rhat = acf(Y[,1:2],lag.max=5,plot=F)
```

Ghat and Rhat are objects of class "acf" for which there is only a print method. For example, the estimated cross lag autocorrelations are

```
> Rhat
Call: acf(x = Y[, 1:2], lag.max = 5, plot = F)

Autocorrelation matrix:
  lag   AA.AA   AA.AXP AXP.AXP
1   0  1.0000  0.2169  1.0000
2   1  0.0182  0.0604 -0.0101
3   2 -0.0556 -0.0080 -0.0710
4   3  0.0145 -0.0203 -0.0152
5   4 -0.0639  0.0090 -0.0235
6   5  0.0142 -0.0056 -0.0169


  lag  AXP.AA
1   0  0.2169
2  -1 -0.0015
3  -2 -0.0187
4  -3 -0.0087
5  -4 -0.0233
6  -5  0.0003
```

The function `acf.plot` may be used to plot the cross lag covariances and correlations produced by `acf`.

```
> acf.plot(Rhat)
```

Figure 3.17 shows these cross lag correlations. The matrices $\hat{\boldsymbol{\Gamma}}_k$ and $\hat{\mathbf{R}}_k$ may be extracted from `acf` component of `Ghat` and `Rhat`, respectively. For example,

```
> Ghat$acf[1,,]
            [,1]        [,2]
[1,] 0.00041079 0.00009256
[2,] 0.00009256 0.00044318
> Rhat$acf[1,,]
        [,1]   [,2]
[1,] 1.0000 0.2169
[2,] 0.2169 1.0000
> Ghat$acf[2,,]
            [,1]        [,2]
[1,]   7.488e-006   2.578e-005
[2,]  -6.537e-007  -4.486e-006
> Rhat$acf[2,,]
          [,1]      [,2]
[1,]   0.018229  0.06043
[2,]  -0.001532 -0.01012
```

extracts $\hat{\boldsymbol{\Gamma}}_1$, $\hat{\mathbf{R}}_1$, $\hat{\boldsymbol{\Gamma}}_2$ and $\hat{\mathbf{R}}_2$.

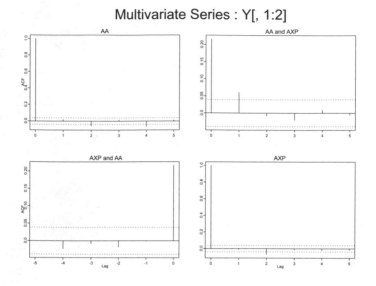

FIGURE 3.17. Cross lag correlations between the first four Dow Jones 30 asset returns.

3.5.2 Multivariate Wold Representation

Any $(n \times 1)$ covariance stationary multivariate time series $\mathbf{Y}_t$ has a Wold or linear process representation of the form

$$
\begin{aligned}
\mathbf{Y}_t &= \boldsymbol{\mu} + \boldsymbol{\varepsilon}_t + \boldsymbol{\Psi}_1\boldsymbol{\varepsilon}_{t-1} + \boldsymbol{\Psi}_2\boldsymbol{\varepsilon}_{t-2} + \cdots \qquad (3.24) \\
&= \boldsymbol{\mu} + \sum_{k=0}^{\infty} \boldsymbol{\Psi}_k\boldsymbol{\varepsilon}_{t-k}
\end{aligned}
$$

where $\boldsymbol{\Psi}_0 = \mathbf{I}_n$ and $\boldsymbol{\varepsilon}_t$ is a multivariate white noise process with mean zero and variance matrix $E[\boldsymbol{\varepsilon}_t\boldsymbol{\varepsilon}_t'] = \boldsymbol{\Sigma}$. In (3.24), $\boldsymbol{\Psi}_k$ is an $(n \times n)$ matrix with (i, j)th element ψ_{ij}^k. In lag operator notation, the Wold form is

$$
\begin{aligned}
Y_t &= \boldsymbol{\mu} + \boldsymbol{\Psi}(L)\varepsilon_t \\
\boldsymbol{\Psi}(L) &= \sum_{k=0}^{\infty} \boldsymbol{\Psi}_k L^k
\end{aligned}
$$

The moments of $\mathbf{Y}_t$ are given by

$$
\begin{aligned}
E[Y_t] &= \mu \\
var(Y_t) &= \sum_{k=0}^{\infty} \boldsymbol{\Psi}_k \boldsymbol{\Sigma} \boldsymbol{\Psi}_k'
\end{aligned}
$$

VAR Models

The most popular multivariate time series model is the *vector autoregressive*
(VAR) model. The VAR model is a multivariate extension of the univariate
autoregressive model. For example, a bivariate VAR(1) model has the form

$$
\begin{pmatrix} y_{1t} \\ y_{2t} \end{pmatrix} = \begin{pmatrix} c_1 \\ c_2 \end{pmatrix} + \begin{pmatrix} \pi_{11}^1 & \pi_{12}^1 \\ \pi_{21}^1 & \pi_{22}^1 \end{pmatrix} \begin{pmatrix} y_{1t-1} \\ y_{2t-1} \end{pmatrix} + \begin{pmatrix} \varepsilon_{1t} \\ \varepsilon_{2t} \end{pmatrix}
$$

or

$$
\begin{aligned}
y_{1t} &= c_1 + \pi_{11}^1 y_{1t-1} + \pi_{12}^1 y_{2t-1} + \varepsilon_{1t} \\
y_{2t} &= c_2 + \pi_{21}^1 y_{1t-1} + \pi_{22}^1 y_{2t-1} + \varepsilon_{2t}
\end{aligned}
$$

where

$$
\begin{pmatrix} \varepsilon_{1t} \\ \varepsilon_{2t} \end{pmatrix} \sim iid \left(\begin{pmatrix} 0 \\ 0 \end{pmatrix}, \begin{pmatrix} \sigma_{11} & \sigma_{12} \\ \sigma_{12} & \sigma_{22} \end{pmatrix} \right)
$$

In the equations for y_1 and y_2, the lagged values of both y_1 and y_2 are
present.

The general VAR(p) model for $\mathbf{Y}_t = (y_{1t}, y_{2t}, \ldots, y_{nt})'$ has the form

$$
\mathbf{Y}_t = \mathbf{c} + \mathbf{\Pi}_1 \mathbf{Y}_{t-1} + \mathbf{\Pi}_2 \mathbf{Y}_{t-2} + \cdots + \mathbf{\Pi}_p \mathbf{Y}_{t-p} + \boldsymbol{\varepsilon}_t, \; t = 1, \ldots, T \quad (3.25)
$$

where $\mathbf{\Pi}_i$ are $(n \times n)$ coefficient matrices and $\boldsymbol{\varepsilon}_t$ is an $(n \times 1)$ unobservable
zero mean white noise vector process with covariance matrix $\mathbf{\Sigma}$. VAR mod-
els are capable of capturing much of the complicated dynamics observed
in stationary multivariate time series. Details about estimation, inference,
and forecasting with VAR models are given in chapter eleven.

3.5.3 Long Run Variance

Let $\mathbf{Y}_t$ be an $(n \times 1)$ stationary and ergodic multivariate time series with
$E[\mathbf{Y}_t] = \boldsymbol{\mu}$. Anderson's central limit theorem for stationary and ergodic
process states

$$
\sqrt{T}(\bar{\mathbf{Y}} - \boldsymbol{\mu}) \xrightarrow{d} N \left(\mathbf{0}, \sum_{j=-\infty}^{\infty} \mathbf{\Gamma}_j \right)
$$

or

$$
\bar{\mathbf{Y}} \overset{A}{\sim} N \left(\boldsymbol{\mu}, \frac{1}{T} \sum_{j=-\infty}^{\infty} \mathbf{\Gamma}_j \right)
$$

Hence, the *long-run variance* of $\mathbf{Y}_t$ is T times the asymptotic variance of
$\bar{\mathbf{Y}}$:

$$
lrv(\mathbf{Y}_t) = T \cdot avar(\bar{\mathbf{Y}}) = \sum_{j=-\infty}^{\infty} \mathbf{\Gamma}_j
$$

Since $\boldsymbol{\Gamma}_{-j} = \boldsymbol{\Gamma}'_j$, $lrv(\mathbf{Y}_t)$ may be alternatively expressed as

$$lrv(\mathbf{Y}_t) = \boldsymbol{\Gamma}_0 + \sum_{j=1}^{\infty} (\boldsymbol{\Gamma}_j + \boldsymbol{\Gamma}'_j)$$

Using the Wold representation of $\mathbf{Y}_t$ it can be shown that

$$lrv(\mathbf{Y}_t) = \boldsymbol{\Psi}(1)\boldsymbol{\Sigma}\boldsymbol{\Psi}(1)'$$

where $\boldsymbol{\Psi}(1) = \sum_{k=0}^{\infty} \boldsymbol{\Psi}_k$.

VAR Estimate of the Long-Run Variance

The Wold representation (3.24) may be approximated by high order VAR(p^*) model

$$\mathbf{Y}_t = \mathbf{c} + \boldsymbol{\Phi}_1 \mathbf{Y}_{t-1} + \cdots + \boldsymbol{\Phi}_{p^*} \mathbf{Y}_{t-p^*} + \boldsymbol{\varepsilon}_t$$

where the lag length p^* is chosen such $p^* = O(T^{1/3})$. This gives rise to the *autoregressive long-run variance matrix* estimate

$$\widehat{lrv}_{AR}(\mathbf{Y}_t) = \hat{\boldsymbol{\Psi}}(1)\hat{\boldsymbol{\Sigma}}\hat{\boldsymbol{\Psi}}(1)' \tag{3.26}$$

$$\hat{\boldsymbol{\Psi}}(1) = (\mathbf{I}_n - \hat{\boldsymbol{\Phi}}_1 - \cdots - \hat{\boldsymbol{\Phi}}_p)^{-1} \tag{3.27}$$

$$\hat{\boldsymbol{\Sigma}} = \frac{1}{T} \sum_{t=1}^{T} \hat{\boldsymbol{\varepsilon}}_t \hat{\boldsymbol{\varepsilon}}'_t \tag{3.28}$$

where $\hat{\boldsymbol{\Phi}}_k$ ($k = 1, \ldots, p^*$) are estimates of the VAR parameter matrices.

Non-parametric Estimate of the Long-Run Variance

A consistent estimate of $lrv(\mathbf{Y}_t)$ may be computed using non-parametric methods. A popular estimator is the Newey-West weighted autocovariance estimator

$$\widehat{lrv}_{NW}(\mathbf{Y}_t) = \hat{\boldsymbol{\Gamma}}_0 + \sum_{j=1}^{M_T} w_{j,T} \cdot \left(\hat{\boldsymbol{\Gamma}}_j + \hat{\boldsymbol{\Gamma}}'_j \right) \tag{3.29}$$

where $w_{j,T}$ are weights which sum to unity and M_T is a truncation lag parameter that satisfies $M_T = O(T^{1/3})$.

Example 17 *Newey-West estimate of long-run variance matrix for stock returns*

The S+FinMetrics function `asymp.var` may be used to compute the Newey-West long-run variance estimate (3.29) for a multivariate time series. The long-run variance matrix for the first four Dow Jones assets in the "`timeSeries`" Y is

```
> M.T = floor(4*(nrow(Y)/100)^(2/9))
> lrv.nw = asymp.var(Y,bandwidth=M.T)
> lrv.nw
            AA         AXP         T          BA
 AA 0.00037313 0.00008526 3.754e-005 6.685e-005
AXP 0.00008526 0.00034957 7.937e-005 1.051e-004
  T 0.00003754 0.00007937 3.707e-004 7.415e-006
 BA 0.00006685 0.00010506 7.415e-006 3.087e-004
```

3.6   References

[1] ALEXANDER, C. (2001). *Market Models. A Guide to Financial Data Analysis.* John Wiley & Sons, Chichester, UK.

[2] BAILLE, R.T. AND T. BOLLERSLEV (1994). "The Long Memory of the Forward Premium," *Journal of International Money and Finance,* 13, 555-571.

[3] BOX, G.E.P. AND G.M. JENKINS (1976). *Time Series Analysis, Forecasting and Control. Revised Edition.* Holden Day, San Francisco.

[4] CAMPBELL, J.Y., A.W. LO, A.C. MACKINLAY (1997). *The Econometrics of Financial Markets.* Princeton University Press, New Jersey.

[5] BOX, G.E.P., AND D.A. PIERCE (1970). "Distribution of Residual Autocorrelations in Autoregressive-integrated Moving Average Time Series Models," *Journal of the American Statistical Association,* 65, 1509-1526.

[6] CHAN, N.H. (2002). *Time Series: Applicatios to Finance.* John Wiley & Sons, New York.

[7] DING, Z., C.W.J. GRANGER AND R.F. ENGLE (1993). "A Long Memory Property of Stock Returns and a New Model," *Journal of Empirical Finance,* 1, 83-106.

[8] ENGLE, R.F. (1982). "Autoregressive Conditional Heteroskedasticity with Estimates of the Variance of United Kingdom Inflations," *Econometrica,* 50, 987-1097.

[9] FULLER, W.A. (1996). *Introduction to Statistical Time Series, Second Edition.* John Wiley & Sons, New York.

[10] GOURIEROUX, C AND J. JASIAK (2001). *Financial Econometrics.* Princeton University Press, New Jersey.

[11] GRANGER, C.W.J. AND M.J. MORRIS (1976). "Time Series Modeling and Interpretation," *Journal of the Royal Statistical Society*, Series A, 139, 246-257.

[12] HAMILTON, J.D. (1994). *Time Series Analysis*. Princeton University Press, New Jersey.

[13] HARVEY, A.C. (1993). *Time Series Models, Second Edition*. MIT Press, Massachusetts.

[14] HAYASHI, F. (2000). *Econometrics*. Princeton University Press, New Jersey.

[15] LJUNG, T. AND G.E.P. BOX (1979). "The Likelihood Function for a Stationary Autoregressive Moving Average Process," *Biometrika*, 66, 265-270.

[16] MILLS, T.C. (1999). *The Econometric Modeling of Financial Time Series, Second Edition*. Cambridge University Press, Cambridge, UK.

[17] NEWEY, W.K. AND K.D. WEST (1987). "A Simple Positive Semidefinite Heteroskedasticity and Autocorrelation Consistent Covariance Matrix," *Econometrica*, 55, 703-708.

[18] TSAY, R.S. (2001). *Analysis of Financial Time Series*, John Wiley & Sons, New York.

[19] VENABLES, W.N. AND B.D. RIPLEY (1999). *Modern Applied Statistics with S-PLUS*, Third Edition. Springer-Verlag, New York.

[20] WHITE, H. (1984). *Asymptotic Theory for Econometrians*. Academic Press, San Diego.

4
Unit Root Tests

4.1 Introduction

Many economic and financial time series exhibit trending behavior or non-stationarity in the mean. Leading examples are asset prices, exchange rates and the levels of macroeconomic aggregates like real GDP. An important econometric task is determining the most appropriate form of the trend in the data. For example, in ARMA modeling the data must be transformed to stationary form prior to analysis. If the data are trending, then some form of trend removal is required.

Two common trend removal or de-trending procedures are first differencing and time-trend regression. First differencing is appropriate for $I(1)$ time series and time-trend regression is appropriate for trend stationary $I(0)$ time series. Unit root tests can be used to determine if trending data should be first differenced or regressed on deterministic functions of time to render the data stationary. Moreover, economic and finance theory often suggests the existence of long-run equilibrium relationships among nonstationary time series variables. If these variables are $I(1)$, then cointegration techniques can be used to model these long-run relations. Hence, pre-testing for unit roots is often a first step in the cointegration modeling discussed in Chapter 12. Finally, a common trading strategy in finance involves exploiting mean-reverting behavior among the prices of pairs of assets. Unit root tests can be used to determine which pairs of assets appear to exhibit mean-reverting behavior.

This chapter is organized as follows. Section 4.2 reviews $I(1)$ and trend stationary $I(0)$ time series and motivates the unit root and stationary tests described in the chapter. Section 4.3 describes the class of autoregressive unit root tests made popular by David Dickey, Wayne Fuller, Pierre Perron and Peter Phillips. Section 4.4 describes the stationarity tests of Kwiatkowski, Phillips, Schmidt and Shinn (1992).

In this chapter, the technical details of unit root and stationarity tests are kept to a minimum. Excellent technical treatments of nonstationary time series may be found in Hamilton (1994), Hatanaka (1995), Fuller (1996) and the many papers by Peter Phillips. Useful surveys on issues associated with unit root testing are given in Stock (1994), Maddala and Kim (1998) and Phillips and Xiao (1998).

4.2   Testing for Nonstationarity and Stationarity

To understand the econometric issues associated with unit root and stationarity tests, consider the stylized trend-cycle decomposition of a time series y_t:

$$
\begin{aligned}
y_t &= TD_t + z_t \\
TD_t &= \kappa + \delta t \\
z_t &= \phi z_{t-1} + \varepsilon_t, \ \varepsilon_t \sim WN(0, \sigma^2)
\end{aligned}
$$

where TD_t is a deterministic linear trend and z_t is an AR(1) process. If $|\phi| < 1$ then y_t is $I(0)$ about the deterministic trend TD_t. If $\phi = 1$, then $z_t = z_{t-1} + \varepsilon_t = z_0 + \sum_{j=1}^{t} \varepsilon_j$, a stochastic trend and y_t is $I(1)$ with drift. Simulated $I(1)$ and $I(0)$ data with $\kappa = 5$ and $\delta = 0.1$ are illustrated in Figure 4.1. The $I(0)$ data with trend follows the trend $TD_t = 5 + 0.1t$ very closely and exhibits trend reversion. In contrast, the $I(1)$ data follows an upward drift but does not necessarily revert to TD_t.

Autoregressive *unit root tests* are based on testing the null hypothesis that $\phi = 1$ (difference stationary) against the alternative hypothesis that $\phi < 1$ (trend stationary). They are called unit root tests because under the null hypothesis the autoregressive polynomial of z_t, $\phi(z) = (1 - \phi z) = 0$, has a root equal to unity.

Stationarity tests take the null hypothesis that y_t is trend stationary. If y_t is then first differenced it becomes

$$
\begin{aligned}
\Delta y_t &= \delta + \Delta z_t \\
\Delta z_t &= \phi \Delta z_{t-1} + \varepsilon_t - \varepsilon_{t-1}
\end{aligned}
$$

Notice that first differencing y_t, when it is trend stationary, produces a unit moving average root in the ARMA representation of Δz_t. That is, the

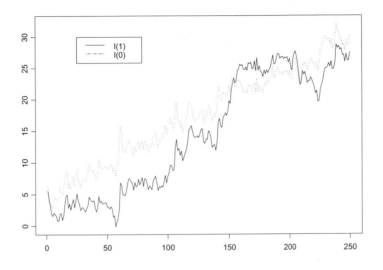

FIGURE 4.1. Simulated trend stationary ($I(0)$) and difference stationary ($I(1)$) processes.

ARMA representation for Δz_t is the non-invertible ARMA(1,1) model

$$\Delta z_t = \phi \Delta z_{t-1} + \varepsilon_t + \theta \varepsilon_{t-1}$$

with $\theta = -1$. This result is known as *overdifferencing*. Formally, stationarity tests are based on testing for a unit moving average root in Δz_t.

Unit root and stationarity test statistics have nonstandard and nonnormal asymptotic distributions under their respective null hypotheses. To complicate matters further, the limiting distributions of the test statistics are affected by the inclusion of deterministic terms in the test regressions. These distributions are functions of standard Brownian motion (Wiener process), and critical values must be tabulated by simulation techniques. MacKinnon (1996) provides response surface algorithms for determining these critical values, and various S+FinMetrics functions use these algorithms for computing critical values and p-values.

4.3 Autoregressive Unit Root Tests

To illustrate the important statistical issues associated with autoregressive unit root tests, consider the simple AR(1) model

$$y_t = \phi y_{t-1} + \varepsilon_t, \text{ where } \varepsilon_t \sim WN(0, \sigma^2)$$

The hypotheses of interest are

$$H_0 \quad : \quad \phi = 1 \text{ (unit root in } \phi(z) = 0) \Rightarrow y_t \sim I(1)$$
$$H_1 \quad : \quad |\phi| < 1 \Rightarrow y_t \sim I(0)$$

The test statistic is

$$t_{\phi=1} = \frac{\hat{\phi} - 1}{SE(\hat{\phi})}$$

where $\hat{\phi}$ is the least squares estimate and $SE(\hat{\phi})$ is the usual standard error estimate[1]. The test is a one-sided left tail test. If $\{y_t\}$ is stationary (i.e., $|\phi| < 1$) then it can be shown (c.f. Hamilton (1994) pg. 216)

$$\sqrt{T}(\hat{\phi} - \phi) \xrightarrow{d} N(0, (1 - \phi^2))$$

or

$$\hat{\phi} \overset{A}{\sim} N\left(\phi, \frac{1}{T}(1 - \phi^2)\right)$$

and it follows that $t_{\phi=1} \overset{A}{\sim} N(0,1)$. However, under the null hypothesis of nonstationarity the above result gives

$$\hat{\phi} \overset{A}{\sim} N(1, 0)$$

which clearly does not make any sense. The problem is that under the unit root null, $\{y_t\}$ is not stationary and ergodic, and the usual sample moments do not converge to fixed constants. Instead, Phillips (1987) showed that the sample moments of $\{y_t\}$ converge to random functions of Brownian motion[2]:

$$T^{-3/2} \sum_{t=1}^{T} y_{t-1} \xrightarrow{d} \sigma \int_0^1 W(r)dr$$

$$T^{-2} \sum_{t=1}^{T} y_{t-1}^2 \xrightarrow{d} \sigma^2 \int_0^1 W(r)^2 dr$$

$$T^{-1} \sum_{t=1}^{T} y_{t-1}\varepsilon_t \xrightarrow{d} \sigma^2 \int_0^1 W(r)dW(r)$$

---

[1] The AR(1) model may be re-written as $\Delta y_t = \pi y_{t-1} + u_t$ where $\pi = \phi - 1$. Testing $\phi = 1$ is then equivalent to testing $\pi = 0$. Unit root tests are often computed using this alternative regression and the S+FinMetrics function unitroot follows this convention.

[2] A Wiener process $W(\cdot)$ is a continuous-time stochastic process, associating each date $r \in [0,1]$ a scalar random variable $W(r)$ that satisfies: (1) $W(0) = 0$; (2) for any dates $0 \le t_1 \le \cdots \le t_k \le 1$ the changes $W(t_2) - W(t_1), W(t_3) - W(t_2), \ldots, W(t_k) - W(t_{k-1})$ are independent normal with $W(s) - W(t) \sim N(0, (s - t))$; (3) $W(s)$ is continuous in s.

where $W(r)$ denotes a standard Brownian motion (Wiener process) defined on the unit interval. Using the above results Phillips showed that under the unit root null $H_0 : \phi = 1$

$$T(\hat{\phi} - 1) \xrightarrow{d} \frac{\int_0^1 W(r)dW(r)}{\int_0^1 W(r)^2 dr} \tag{4.1}$$

$$t_{\phi=1} \xrightarrow{d} \frac{\int_0^1 W(r)dW(r)}{\left(\int_0^1 W(r)^2 dr\right)^{1/2}} \tag{4.2}$$

The above yield some surprising results:

- $\hat{\phi}$ is *super-consistent*; that is, $\hat{\phi} \xrightarrow{p} \phi$ at rate T instead of the usual rate $T^{1/2}$.

- $\hat{\phi}$ is not asymptotically normally distributed and $t_{\phi=1}$ is not asymptotically standard normal.

- The limiting distribution of $t_{\phi=1}$ is called the Dickey-Fuller (DF) distribution and does not have a closed form representation. Consequently, quantiles of the distribution must be computed by numerical approximation or by simulation[3].

- Since the *normalized bias* $T(\hat{\phi} - 1)$ has a well defined limiting distribution that does not depend on nuisance parameters it can also be used as a test statistic for the null hypothesis $H_0 : \phi = 1$.

4.3.1 Simulating the DF and Normalized Bias Distributions

As mentioned above, the DF and normalized bias distributions must be obtained by simulation methods. To illustrate, the following S-PLUS function wiener produces one random draw from the functions of Brownian motion that appear in the limiting distributions of $t_{\phi=1}$ and $T(\hat{\phi} - 1)$:

```
wiener = function(nobs) {
    e = rnorm(nobs)
    y = cumsum(e)
    ym1 = y[1:(nobs-1)]
    intW2 = nobs^(-2) * sum(ym1^2)
    intWdW = nobs^(-1) * sum(ym1*e[2:nobs])
    ans = list(intW2=intW2,
               intWdW=intWdW)
```

---

[3]Dickey and Fuller (1979) first considered the unit root tests and derived the asymptotic distribution of $t_{\phi=1}$. However, their representation did not utilize functions of Wiener processes.

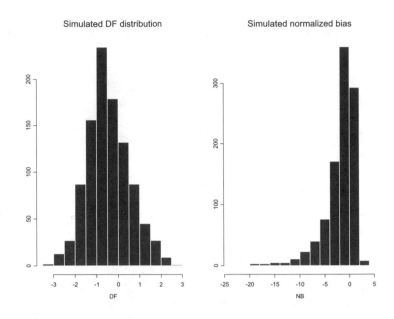

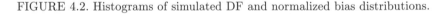

FIGURE 4.2. Histograms of simulated DF and normalized bias distributions.

```
    ans
}
```

A simple loop then produces the simulated distributions:

```
> nobs = 1000
> nsim = 1000
> NB = rep(0,nsim)
> DF = rep(0,nsim)
> for (i in 1:nsim) {
+     BN.moments = wiener(nobs)
+     NB[i] = BN.moments$intWdW/BN.moments$intW2
+     DF[i] = BN.moments$intWdW/sqrt(BN.moments$intW2)
}
```

Figure 4.2 shows the histograms and density estimates of the simulated distributions. The DF density is slightly left-skewed relative to the standard normal, and the normalized bias density is highly left skewed and non-normal. Since the alternative is one-sided, the test statistics reject if they are sufficiently negative. For the DF and normalized bias densities the empirical 1%, 5% and 10% quantiles are

```
> quantile(DF,probs=c(0.01,0.05,0.1))
    1%     5%    10%
 -2.451 -1.992 -1.603
```

```
> quantile(NB,probs=c(0.01,0.05,0.1))
    1%    5%    10%
 -11.94 -8.56 -5.641
```

For comparison purposes, note that the 5% quantile from the standard normal distribution is -1.645.

The simulation of critical values and p-values from (4.1) and (4.2) is straightforward but time consuming. The `punitroot` and `qunitroot` functions in S+FinMetrics produce p-values and quantiles of the DF and normalized bias distributions based on MacKinnon's (1996) response surface methodology. The advantage of the response surface methodology is that accurate p-values and quantiles appropriate for a given sample size can be produced. For example, the 1%, 5% and 10% quantiles for (4.2) and (4.1) based on a sample size of 100 are

```
> qunitroot(c(0.01,0.05,0.10), trend="nc", statistic="t",
+ n.sample=100)
[1] -2.588 -1.944 -1.615
> qunitroot(c(0.01,0.05,0.10), trend="nc", statistic="n",
+ n.sample=100)
[1] -13.086  -7.787  -5.565
```

The argument `trend="nc"` specifies that no constant is included in the test regression. Other valid options are `trend="c"` for constant only and `trend="ct"` for constant and trend. These trend cases are explained below. To specify the normalized bias distribution, set `statistic="n"`. For asymptotic quantiles set `n.sample=0`.

Similarly, the p-value of -1.645 based on the DF distribution for a sample size of 100 is computed as

```
> punitroot(-1.645, trend="nc", statistic="t")
[1] 0.0945
```

4.3.2 Trend Cases

When testing for unit roots, it is crucial to specify the null and alternative hypotheses appropriately to characterize the trend properties of the data at hand. For example, if the observed data does not exhibit an increasing or decreasing trend, then the appropriate null and alternative hypotheses should reflect this. The trend properties of the data *under the alternative hypothesis* will determine the form of the test regression used. Furthermore, the type of deterministic terms in the test regression will influence the asymptotic distributions of the unit root test statistics. The two most common trend cases are summarized below and illustrated in Figure 4.3.

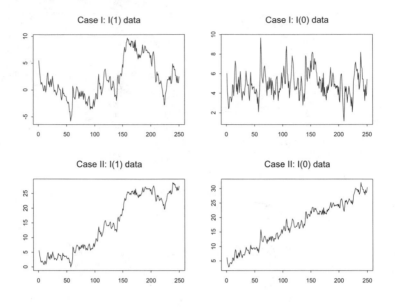

FIGURE 4.3. Simulated $I(1)$ and $I(0)$ data under trend cases I and II.

Case I: Constant Only

The test regression is

$$y_t = c + \phi y_{t-1} + \varepsilon_t$$

and includes a constant to capture the nonzero mean under the alternative. The hypotheses to be tested are

$$H_0 \quad : \quad \phi = 1 \;\Rightarrow\; y_t \sim I(1) \text{ without drift}$$
$$H_1 \quad : \quad |\phi| < 1 \Rightarrow y_t \sim I(0) \text{ with nonzero mean}$$

This formulation is appropriate for non-trending financial series like interest rates, exchange rates, and spreads. The test statistics $t_{\phi=1}$ and $T(\hat{\phi} - 1)$ are computed from the above regression. Under $H_0 : \phi = 1$ the asymptotic distributions of these test statistics are different from (4.2) and (4.1) and are influenced by the presence but not the coefficient value of the constant in the test regression. Quantiles and p-values for these distributions can be computed using the S+FinMetrics functions punitroot and qunitroot with the trend="c" option:

```
> qunitroot(c(0.01,0.05,0.10), trend="c", statistic="t",
+ n.sample=100)
[1] -3.497 -2.891 -2.582
> qunitroot(c(0.01,0.05,0.10), trend="c", statistic="n",
+ n.sample=100)
```

```
[1] -19.49 -13.53 -10.88
> punitroot(-1.645, trend="c", statistic="t", n.sample=100)
[1] 0.456
> punitroot(-1.645, trend="c", statistic="n", n.sample=100)
[1] 0.8172
```

For a sample size of 100, the 5% left tail critical values for $t_{\phi=1}$ and $T(\hat{\phi}-1)$ are -2.891 and -13.53, respectively, and are quite a bit smaller than the 5% critical values computed when `trend="nc"`. Hence, inclusion of a constant pushes the distributions of $t_{\phi=1}$ and $T(\hat{\phi}-1)$ to the left.

Case II: Constant and Time Trend

The test regression is

$$y_t = c + \delta t + \phi y_{t-1} + \varepsilon_t$$

and includes a constant and deterministic time trend to capture the deterministic trend under the alternative. The hypotheses to be tested are

$$H_0 \quad : \quad \phi = 1 \Rightarrow y_t \sim I(1) \text{ with drift}$$
$$H_1 \quad : \quad |\phi| < 1 \Rightarrow y_t \sim I(0) \text{ with deterministic time trend}$$

This formulation is appropriate for trending time series like asset prices or the levels of macroeconomic aggregates like real GDP. The test statistics $t_{\phi=1}$ and $T(\hat{\phi}-1)$ are computed from the above regression. Under H_0 : $\phi = 1$ the asymptotic distributions of these test statistics are different from (4.2) and (4.1) and are influenced by the presence but not the coefficient values of the constant and time trend in the test regression. Quantiles and p-values for these distributions can be computed using the S+FinMetrics functions `punitroot` and `qunitroot` with the `trend="ct"` option:

```
> qunitroot(c(0.01,0.05,0.10), trend="ct", statistic="t",
+ n.sample=100)
[1] -4.052 -3.455 -3.153
> qunitroot(c(0.01,0.05,0.10), trend="ct", statistic="n",
+ n.sample=100)
[1] -27.17 -20.47 -17.35
> punitroot(-1.645, trend="ct", statistic="t", n.sample=100)
[1] 0.7679
> punitroot(-1.645, trend="ct", statistic="n", n.sample=100)
[1] 0.9769
```

Notice that the inclusion of a constant and trend in the test regression further shifts the distributions of $t_{\phi=1}$ and $T(\hat{\phi}-1)$ to the left. For a sample size of 100, the 5% left tail critical values for $t_{\phi=1}$ and $T(\hat{\phi}-1)$ are now -3.455 and -20.471.

4.3.3 Dickey-Fuller Unit Root Tests

The unit root tests described above are valid if the time series y_t is well characterized by an AR(1) with white noise errors. Many financial time series, however, have a more complicated dynamic structure than is captured by a simple AR(1) model. Said and Dickey (1984) augment the basic autoregressive unit root test to accommodate general ARMA(p, q) models with unknown orders and their test is referred to as the *augmented Dickey-Fuller* (ADF) test. The ADF test tests the null hypothesis that a time series y_t is $I(1)$ against the alternative that it is $I(0)$, assuming that the dynamics in the data have an ARMA structure. The ADF test is based on estimating the test regression

$$y_t = \boldsymbol{\beta}'\mathbf{D}_t + \phi y_{t-1} + \sum_{j=1}^{p} \psi_j \Delta y_{t-j} + \varepsilon_t \qquad (4.3)$$

where $\mathbf{D}_t$ is a vector of deterministic terms (constant, trend etc.). The p lagged difference terms, Δy_{t-j}, are used to approximate the ARMA structure of the errors, and the value of p is set so that the error ε_t is serially uncorrelated. The error term is also assumed to be homoskedastic. The specification of the deterministic terms depends on the assumed behavior of y_t under the alternative hypothesis of trend stationarity as described in the previous section. Under the null hypothesis, y_t is $I(1)$ which implies that $\phi = 1$. The ADF t-statistic and normalized bias statistic are based on the least squares estimates of (4.3) and are given by

$$ADF_t = t_{\phi=1} = \frac{\hat{\phi} - 1}{SE(\phi)}$$

$$ADF_n = \frac{T(\hat{\phi} - 1)}{1 - \hat{\psi}_1 - \cdots - \hat{\psi}_p}$$

An alternative formulation of the ADF test regression is

$$\Delta y_t = \boldsymbol{\beta}'\mathbf{D}_t + \pi y_{t-1} + \sum_{j=1}^{p} \psi_j \Delta y_{t-j} + \varepsilon_t \qquad (4.4)$$

where $\pi = \phi - 1$. Under the null hypothesis, Δy_t is $I(0)$ which implies that $\pi = 0$. The ADF t-statistic is then the usual t-statistic for testing $\pi = 0$ and the ADF normalized bias statistic is $T\hat{\pi}/(1 - \hat{\psi}_1 - \cdots - \hat{\psi}_p)$. The test regression (4.4) is often used in practice because the ADF t-statistic is the usual t-statistic reported for testing the significance of the coefficient y_{t-1}. The S+FinMetrics function unitroot follows this convention.

Choosing the Lag Length for the ADF Test

An important practical issue for the implementation of the ADF test is the specification of the lag length p. If p is too small then the remaining serial

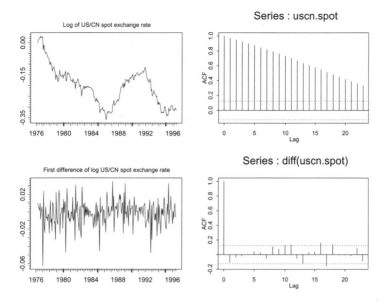

FIGURE 4.4. US/CN spot rate, first difference and SACF.

correlation in the errors will bias the test. If p is too large then the power of the test will suffer. Ng and Perron (1995) suggest the following data dependent lag length selection procedure that results in stable size of the test and minimal power loss. First, set an upper bound p_{max} for p. Next, estimate the ADF test regression with $p = p_{max}$. If the absolute value of the t-statistic for testing the significance of the last lagged difference is greater than 1.6 then set $p = p_{max}$ and perform the unit root test. Otherwise, reduce the lag length by one and repeat the process.

A useful rule of thumb for determining p_{max}, suggested by Schwert (1989), is

$$p_{max} = \left[12 \cdot \left(\frac{T}{100} \right)^{1/4} \right] \tag{4.5}$$

where $[x]$ denotes the integer part of x. This choice allows p_{max} to grow with the sample so that the ADF test regressions (4.3) and (4.4) are valid if the errors follow an ARMA process with unknown order.

Example 18 *Testing for a unit root in exchange rate data using ADF tests*

To illustrate the ADF test procedure, consider testing for a unit root in the logarithm of the US/CA monthly spot exchange rate, denoted s_t, over the 30 year period 1976 - 1996. Figure 4.4 shows $s_t, \Delta s_t$ as well as the sample autocorrelations for these series. The data and plots are created with the S-PLUS commands

```
> uscn.spot = lexrates.dat[,"USCNS"]
> uscn.spot@title = "Log US/CN spot exchange rate"
> par(mfrow=c(2,2))
> plot.timeSeries(uscn.spot, reference.grid=F,
+ main="Log of US/CN spot exchange rate")
> xx = acf(uscn.spot)
> plot.timeSeries(diff(uscn.spot), reference.grid=F,
+ main="First difference of log US/CN spot exchange rate")
> xx = acf(diff(uscn.spot))
```

Clearly, s_t exhibits random walk like behavior with no apparent positive or negative drift. However, Δs_t behaves very much like a white noise process. The appropriate trend specification is to include a constant in the test regression. Regarding the maximum lag length for the Ng-Perron procedure, given the lack of serial correlation in Δs_t a conservative choice is $p_{max} = 6$. The ADF t-statistic computed from the test regression with a constant and $p = 6$ lags can be computed using the S+FinMetrics function unitroot as follows

```
> adft.out = unitroot(uscn.spot, trend="c", statistic="t",
+ method="adf", lags=6)
> class(adft.out)
[1] "unitroot"
```

The output of unitroot is an object of class "unitroot" for which there are print and summary methods. Typing the name of the object invokes the print method and displays the basic test result

```
> adft.out
Test for Unit Root: Augmented DF Test

Null Hypothesis: there is a unit root
   Type of Test: t-test
 Test Statistic: -2.6
        P-value: 0.09427

Coefficients:
    lag1    lag2    lag3    lag4    lag5    lag6 constant
 -0.0280 -0.1188 -0.0584 -0.0327 -0.0019  0.0430 -0.0075

Degrees of freedom: 239 total; 232 residual
Time period: from Aug 1976 to Jun 1996
Residual standard error: 0.01386
```

With $p = 6$ the ADF t-statistic is -2.6 and has a p-value (computed using punitroot) of 0.094. Hence we do not reject the unit root null at the 9.4% level. The small p-value here may be due to the inclusion of superfluous lags.

To see the significance of the lags in the test regression, use the summary method

```
> summary(adft.out)
Test for Unit Root: Augmented DF Test

Null Hypothesis: there is a unit root
   Type of Test: t test
 Test Statistic: -2.6
        P-value: 0.09427

Coefficients:
            Value Std. Error t value Pr(>|t|)
    lag1 -0.0280  0.0108     -2.6004  0.0099
    lag2 -0.1188  0.0646     -1.8407  0.0669
    lag3 -0.0584  0.0650     -0.8983  0.3700
    lag4 -0.0327  0.0651     -0.5018  0.6163
    lag5 -0.0019  0.0651     -0.0293  0.9766
    lag6  0.0430  0.0645      0.6662  0.5060
constant -0.0075  0.0024     -3.0982  0.0022

Regression Diagnostics:

        R-Squared 0.0462
Adjusted R-Squared 0.0215
Durbin-Watson Stat 2.0033

Residual standard error: 0.01386 on 235 degrees of freedom
F-statistic: 1.874 on 6 and 232 degrees of freedom, the
p-value is 0.08619
Time period: from Aug 1976 to Jun 1996
```

The results indicate that too many lags have been included in the test regression. Following the Ng-Perron backward selection procedure $p = 2$ lags are selected. The results are

```
> adft.out = unitroot(uscn.spot, trend="c", lags=2)
> summary(adft.out)
Test for Unit Root: Augmented DF Test

Null Hypothesis: there is a unit root
   Type of Test: t test
 Test Statistic: -2.115
        P-value: 0.2392

Coefficients:
```

```
          Value  Std. Error  t value  Pr(>|t|)
    lag1 -0.0214  0.0101      -2.1146  0.0355
    lag2 -0.1047  0.0635      -1.6476  0.1007
constant -0.0058  0.0022      -2.6001  0.0099
```

Regression Diagnostics:

```
          R-Squared 0.0299
Adjusted R-Squared 0.0218
Durbin-Watson Stat 2.0145
```

Residual standard error: 0.01378 on 239 degrees of freedom
F-statistic: 3.694 on 2 and 240 degrees of freedom, the
p-value is 0.02629
Time period: from Apr 1976 to Jun 1996

With 2 lags the ADF t-statistic is -2.115, the p-value 0.239 and we have greater evidence for a unit root in s_t. A similar result is found with the ADF normalized bias statistic

```
> adfn.out = unitroot(uscn.spot, trend="c", lags=2,
+ statistic="n")
> adfn.out
Test for Unit Root: Augmented DF Test

Null Hypothesis: there is a unit root
   Type of Test: normalized test
 Test Statistic: -5.193
        P-value: 0.4129

Coefficients:
    lag1    lag2 constant
 -0.0214 -0.1047 -0.0058

Degrees of freedom: 243 total; 240 residual
Time period: from Apr 1976 to Jun 1996
Residual standard error: 0.01378
```

Example 19 *Testing for a unit root in log stock prices*

The log levels of asset prices are usually treated as $I(1)$ with drift. Indeed, the random walk model of stock prices is a special case of an $I(1)$ process. Consider testing for a unit root in the log of the monthly S&P 500 index, p_t, over the period January 1990 through January 2001. The data is taken from the S+FinMetrics "timeSeries" singleIndex.dat. The data and various plots are created with the S-PLUS commands

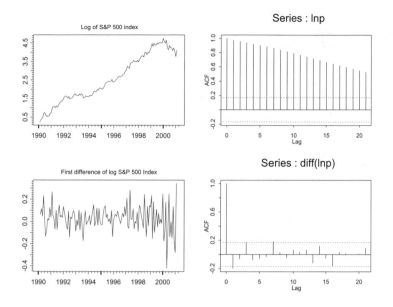

FIGURE 4.5. Log prices on the S&P 500 index, first difference and SACF.

```
> lnp = log(singleIndex.dat[,1])
> lnp@title = "Log of S&P 500 Index"
> par(mfrow=c(2,2))
> plot.timeSeries(lnp, reference.grid=F,
+ main="Log of S&P 500 index")
> acf.plot(acf(lnp,plot=F))
> plot.timeSeries(diff(lnp), reference.grid=F,
+ main="First difference of log S&P 500 Index")
> acf.plot(acf(diff(lnp),plot=F))
```

and are illustrated in Figure 4.5. Clearly, the p_t is nonstationary due to the positive trend. Also, there appears to be some negative autocorrelation at lag one in Δp_t. The null hypothesis to be tested is that p_t is $I(1)$ with drift, and the alternative is that the p_t is $I(0)$ about a deterministic time trend. The ADF t-statistic to test these hypotheses is computed with a constant and time trend in the test regression and four lags of Δp_t (selecting using the Ng-Perron backward selection method)

```
> adft.out = unitroot(lnp, trend="ct", lags=4)
> summary(adft.out)

Test for Unit Root: Augmented DF Test

Null Hypothesis: there is a unit root
```

```
      Type of Test: t test
   Test Statistic: -1.315
          P-value: 0.8798
```

```
Coefficients:
              Value Std. Error t value Pr(>|t|)
     lag1 -0.0540   0.0410    -1.3150  0.1910
     lag2 -0.1869   0.0978    -1.9111  0.0583
     lag3 -0.0460   0.0995    -0.4627  0.6444
     lag4  0.1939   0.0971     1.9964  0.0481
 constant  0.1678   0.1040     1.6128  0.1094
     time  0.0015   0.0014     1.0743  0.2848
```

```
Regression Diagnostics:

          R-Squared 0.1016
 Adjusted R-Squared 0.0651
 Durbin-Watson Stat 1.9544
```

```
Residual standard error: 0.1087 on 125 degrees of freedom
F-statistic: 2.783 on 5 and 123 degrees of freedom, the
p-value is 0.0204
Time period: from May 1990 to Jan 2001
```

$ADF_t = -1.315$ and has a p-value of 0.8798, so one clearly does not reject the null that p_t is $I(1)$ with drift.

4.3.4   Phillips-Perron Unit Root Tests

Phillips and Perron (1988) developed a number of unit root tests that have become popular in the analysis of financial time series. The Phillips-Perron (PP) unit root tests differ from the ADF tests mainly in how they deal with serial correlation and heteroskedasticity in the errors. In particular, where the ADF tests use a parametric autoregression to approximate the ARMA structure of the errors in the test regression, the PP tests ignore any serial correlation in the test regression. The test regression for the PP tests is

$$\Delta y_t = \beta' \mathbf{D}_t + \pi y_{t-1} + u_t$$

where u_t is $I(0)$ and may be heteroskedastic. The PP tests correct for any serial correlation and heteroskedasticity in the errors u_t of the test regression by directly modifying the test statistics $t_{\pi=0}$ and $T\hat{\pi}$. These modified statistics, denoted Z_t and Z_π, are given by

$$Z_t = \left(\frac{\hat{\sigma}^2}{\hat{\lambda}^2}\right)^{1/2} \cdot t_{\pi=0} - \frac{1}{2}\left(\frac{\hat{\lambda}^2 - \hat{\sigma}^2}{\hat{\lambda}^2}\right) \cdot \left(\frac{T \cdot SE(\hat{\pi})}{\hat{\sigma}^2}\right)$$

$$Z_\pi = T\hat{\pi} - \frac{1}{2}\frac{T^2 \cdot SE(\hat{\pi})}{\hat{\sigma}^2}(\hat{\lambda}^2 - \hat{\sigma}^2)$$

The terms $\hat{\sigma}^2$ and $\hat{\lambda}^2$ are consistent estimates of the variance parameters

$$\sigma^2 = \lim_{T\to\infty} T^{-1}\sum_{t=1}^{T} E[u_t^2]$$

$$\lambda^2 = \lim_{T\to\infty} \sum_{t=1}^{T} E\left[T^{-1}S_T^2\right]$$

where $S_T = \sum_{t=1}^{T} u_t$. The sample variance of the least squares residual $\hat{u}_t$ is a consistent estimate of σ^2, and the Newey-West long-run variance estimate of u_t using $\hat{u}_t$ is a consistent estimate of λ^2.

Under the null hypothesis that $\pi = 0$, the PP Z_t and Z_π statistics have the same asymptotic distributions as the ADF t-statistic and normalized bias statistics. One advantage of the PP tests over the ADF tests is that the PP tests are robust to general forms of heteroskedasticity in the error term u_t. Another advantage is that the user does not have to specify a lag length for the test regression.

Example 20 *Testing for a unit root in exchange rates using the PP tests*

Recall the arguments for the S+FinMetrics unitroot function are

```
> args(unitroot)
function(x, trend = "c", method = "adf",
statistic = "t",lags = 1, bandwidth = NULL,
window = "bartlett", asymptotic = F, na.rm = F)
```

The PP statistics may be computed by specifying the optional argument method="pp". When method="pp" is chosen, the argument window specifies the weight function and the argument bandwidth determines the lag truncation parameter used in computing the long-run variance parameter λ^2. The default bandwidth is the integer part of $(4 \cdot (T/100))^{2/9}$ where T is the sample size.

Now, consider testing for a unit root in the log of the US/CN spot exchange rate using the PP Z_t and Z_π statistics:

```
> unitroot(uscn.spot, trend="c", method="pp")
Test for Unit Root: Phillips-Perron Test
```

```
Null Hypothesis: there is a unit root
   Type of Test: t-test
 Test Statistic: -1.97
        P-value: 0.2999

Coefficients:
    lag1 constant
 -0.0202 -0.0054

Degrees of freedom: 244 total; 242 residual
Time period: from Mar 1976 to Jun 1996
Residual standard error: 0.01383

> unitroot(uscn.spot, trend="c", method="pp", statistic="n")
Test for Unit Root: Phillips-Perron Test

Null Hypothesis: there is a unit root
   Type of Test: normalized test
 Test Statistic: -4.245
        P-value: 0.5087

Coefficients:
    lag1 constant
 -0.0202 -0.0054

Degrees of freedom: 244 total; 242 residual
Time period: from Mar 1976 to Jun 1996 .
Residual standard error: 0.01383
```

As with the ADF tests, the PP tests do not reject the null that the log of the US/CN spot rate is $I(1)$ at any reasonable significance level.

4.3.5 Some Problems with Unit Root Tests

The ADF and PP tests are asymptotically equivalent but may differ substantially in finite samples due to the different ways in which they correct for serial correlation in the test regression. In particular, Schwert (1989) finds that if Δy_t has an ARMA representation with a large and negative MA component, then the ADF and PP tests are severely size distorted (reject $I(1)$ null much too often when it is true) and that the PP tests are more size distorted than the ADF tests. Recently, Perron and Ng (1996) have suggested useful modifications to the PP tests to mitigate this size distortion.

In general, the ADF and PP tests have very low power against $I(0)$ alternatives that are close to being $I(1)$. That is, unit root tests cannot distinguish highly persistent stationary processes from nonstationary processes very well. Also, the power of unit root tests diminish as deterministic terms are added to the test regressions. That is, tests that include a constant and trend in the test regression have less power than tests that only include a constant in the test regression. For maximum power against very persistent alternatives the recent tests proposed by Elliot, Rothenberg and Stock (1996) should be used.

4.4   Stationarity Tests

The ADF and PP unit root tests are for the null hypothesis that a time series y_t is $I(1)$. Stationarity tests, on the other hand, are for the null that y_t is $I(0)$. The most commonly used stationarity test, the KPSS test, is due to Kwiatkowski, Phillips, Schmidt and Shin (1992). They derive their test by starting with the model

$$
\begin{aligned}
y_t &= \beta' \mathbf{D}_t + \mu_t + u_t \\
\mu_t &= \mu_{t-1} + \varepsilon_t, \ \varepsilon_t \sim WN(0, \sigma_\varepsilon^2)
\end{aligned}
\tag{4.6}
$$

where $\mathbf{D}_t$ contains deterministic components (constant or constant plus time trend), u_t is $I(0)$ and may be heteroskedastic. Notice that μ_t is a pure random walk with innovation variance σ_ε^2. The null hypothesis that y_t is $I(0)$ is formulated as $H_0 : \sigma_\varepsilon^2 = 0$, which implies that μ_t is a constant. Although not directly apparent, this null hypothesis also implies a unit moving average root in the ARMA representation of Δy_t. The KPSS test statistic is the Lagrange multiplier (LM) or score statistic for testing $\sigma_\varepsilon^2 = 0$ against the alternative that $\sigma_\varepsilon^2 > 0$ and is given by

$$
KPSS = \left(T^{-2} \sum_{t=1}^{T} \hat{S}_t^2 \right) / \hat{\lambda}^2
\tag{4.7}
$$

where $\hat{S}_t = \sum_{j=1}^{t} \hat{u}_j$, $\hat{u}_t$ is the residual of a regression of y_t on $\mathbf{D}_t$ and $\hat{\lambda}^2$ is a consistent estimate of the long-run variance of u_t using $\hat{u}_t$. Under the null that y_t is $I(0)$, Kwiatkowski, Phillips, Schmidt and Shin show that KPSS converges to a function of standard Brownian motion that depends on the form of the deterministic terms $\mathbf{D}_t$ but not their coefficient values β. In particular, if $\mathbf{D}_t = 1$ then

$$
KPSS \rightarrow \int_0^1 V_1(r) dr
\tag{4.8}
$$

where $V_1(r) = W(r) - rW(1)$ and $W(r)$ is a standard Brownian motion for $r \in [0, 1]$. If $\mathbf{D}_t = (1, t)'$ then

$$
KPSS \rightarrow \int_0^1 V_2(r) dr
\tag{4.9}
$$

	Right tail quantiles				
Distribution	0.90	0.925	0.950	0.975	0.99
$\int_0^1 V_1(r)dr$	0.349	0.396	0.446	0.592	0.762
$\int_0^1 V_2(r)dr$	0.120	0.133	0.149	0.184	0.229

TABLE 4.1. Quantiles of the distribution of the KPSS statistic

where $V_2(r) = W(r) + r(2 - 3r)W(1) + 6r(r^2 - 1) \int_0^1 W(s)ds$. Critical values from the asymptotic distributions (4.8) and (4.9) must be obtained by simulation methods, and these are summarized in Table 4.1.

The stationary test is a one-sided right-tailed test so that one rejects the null of stationarity at the $100 \cdot \alpha\%$ level if the KPSS test statistic (4.7) is greater than the $100 \cdot (1 - \alpha)\%$ quantile from the appropriate asymptotic distribution (4.8) or (4.9).

4.4.1 Simulating the KPSS Distributions

The distributions in (4.8) and (4.9) may be simulated using methods similar to those used to simulate the DF distribution. The following S-PLUS code is used to create the quantiles in Table 4.1:

```
wiener2 = function(nobs) {
    e = rnorm(nobs)
# create detrended errors
    e1 = e - mean(e)
    e2 = residuals(OLS(e~seq(1,nobs)))
# compute simulated Brownian Bridges
    y1 = cumsum(e1)
    y2 = cumsum(e2)
    intW2.1 = nobs^(-2) * sum(y1^2)
    intW2.2 = nobs^(-2) * sum(y2^2)
    ans = list(intW2.1=intW2.1,
               intW2.2=intW2.2)
    ans
}
#
# simulate KPSS distributions
#
> nobs = 1000
> nsim = 10000
> KPSS1 = rep(0,nsim)
> KPSS2 = rep(0,nsim)
> for (i in 1:nsim) {
    BN.moments = wiener2(nobs)
    KPSS1[i] = BN.moments$intW2.1
```

```
    KPSS2[i] = BN.moments$intW2.2
}
#
# compute quantiles of distribution
#
> quantile(KPSS1, probs=c(0.90,0.925,0.95,0.975,0.99))
    90.0%   92.5%   95.0%   97.5%   99.0%
 0.34914 0.39634 0.46643 0.59155 0.76174
> quantile(KPSS2, probs=c(0.90,0.925,0.95,0.975,0.99))
    90.0%   92.5%   95.0%  97.5%   99.0%
 0.12003 0.1325 0.14907 0.1841 0.22923
```

Currently, only asymptotic critical values are available for the KPSS test.

4.4.2 Testing for Stationarity Using the *S+FinMetrics* Function *stationaryTest*

The S+FinMetrics function stationaryTest may be used to test the null hypothesis that a time series y_t is $I(0)$ based on the KPSS statistic (4.7). The function stationaryTest has arguments

```
> args(stationaryTest)
function(x, trend = "c", bandwidth = NULL, na.rm = F)
```

where x represents a univariate vector or "timeSeries". The argument trend specifies the deterministic trend component in (4.6) and valid choices are "c" for a constant and "ct" for a constant and time trend. The argument bandwidth determines the lag truncation parameter used in computing the long-run variance parameter λ^2. The default bandwidth is the integer part of $(4 \cdot (T/100))^{2/9}$ where T is the sample size. The output of stationaryTest is an object of class "stationaryTest" for which there is only a print method. The use of stationaryTest is illustrated with the following example.

Example 21 *Testing for stationarity in exchange rates*

Consider the US/CN spot exchange data used in the previous examples. To test the null that s_t is $I(0)$, the KPSS statistic is computed using a constant in (4.6):

```
> kpss.out = stationaryTest(uscn.spot, trend="c")
> class(kpss.out)
[1] "stationaryTest"
> kpss.out
```

```
Test for Stationarity: KPSS Test
```

Null Hypothesis: stationary around a constant

Test Statistics:
    USCNS
 1.6411**

 * : significant at 5% level
** : significant at 1% level

 Total Observ.: 245
    Bandwidth : 5

The KPSS statistic is 1.641 and is greater than the 99% quantile, 0.762, from Table.4.1. Therefore, the null that s_t is $I(0)$ is rejected at the 1% level.

4.5   References

[1] DICKEY, D. AND W. FULLER (1979). "Distribution of the Estimators for Autoregressive Time Series with a Unit Root," *Journal of the American Statistical Association,* 74, 427-431.

[2] DICKEY, D. AND W. FULLER (1981). "Likelihood Ratio Statistics for Autoregressive Time Series with a Unit Root," *Econometrica,* 49, 1057-1072.

[3] ELLIOT, G., T.J. ROTHENBERG, AND J.H. STOCK (1996). "Efficient Tests for an Autoregressive Unit Root," *Econometrica,* 64, 813-836.

[4] FULLER, W. (1996). *Introduction to Statistical Time Series, Second Edition.* John Wiley, New York.

[5] HAMILTON, J. (1994). *Time Series Analysis.* Princeton University Press, New Jersey.

[6] HATANAKA, T. (1995). *Time-Series-Based Econometrics: Unit Roots and Co-Integration.* Oxford University Press, Oxford.

[7] KWIATKOWSKI, D., P.C.B. PHILLIPS, P. SCHMIDT AND Y. SHIN (1992). "Testing the Null Hypothesis of Stationarity Against the Alternative of a Unit Root," *Journal of Econometrics,* 54, 159-178.

[8] MACKINNON, J. (1996). "Numerical Distribution Functions for Unit Root and Cointegration Tests," *Journal of Applied Econometrics,* 11, 601-618.

[9] MADDALA, G.S. AND I.-M. KIM (1998). *Unit Roots, Cointegration and Structural Change.* Oxford University Press, Oxford.

[10] NG, S., AND P. PERRON (1995). "Unit Root Tests in ARMA Models with Data-Dependent Methods for the Selection of the Truncation Lag," *Journal of the American Statistical Association,* 90, 268-281.

[11] PERRON, P. AND S. NG. (1996). "Useful Modifications to Some Unit Root Tests with Dependent Errors and their Local Asymptotic Properties," *Review of Economic Studies,* 63, 435-463.

[12] PHILLIPS, P.C.B. (1987). "Time Series Regression with a Unit Root," *Econometrica,* 55, 227-301.

[13] PHILLIPS, P.C.B. AND P. PERRON (1988). "Testing for Unit Roots in Time Series Regression," *Biometrika,* 75, 335-346.

[14] PHILLIPS, P.C.B. AND Z. XIAO (1998). "A Primer on Unit Root Testing," *Journal of Economic Surveys,* 12, 423-470.

[15] SCHWERT, W. (1989). "Test for Unit Roots: A Monte Carlo Investigation," *Journal of Business and Economic Statistics,* 7, 147-159.

[16] SAID, S.E. AND D. DICKEY (1984). "Testing for Unit Roots in Autoregressive Moving-Average Models with Unknown Order," *Biometrika,* 71, 599-607.

[17] STOCK, J.H. (1994). "Units Roots, Structural Breaks and Trends," in R.F. Engle and D.L. McFadden (eds.), *Handbook of Econometrics, Volume IV.* North Holland, New York.

5
Modeling Extreme Values

5.1 Introduction

One of the goals of financial risk management is the accurate calculation of the magnitudes and probabilities of large potential losses due to extreme events such as stock market crashes, currency crises, trading scandals, or large bond defaults. In statistical terms, these magnitudes and probabilities are *high quantiles* and *tail probabilities* of the probability distribution of losses. The importance of risk management in finance cannot be overstated. The catastrophes of October 17, 1987, Long-Term Capital Management, Barings PLC, Metallgesellschaft, Orange County and Daiwa clearly illustrate the losses that can occur as the result of extreme market movements[1]. The objective of extreme value analysis in finance is to quantify the probabilistic behavior of unusually large losses and to develop tools for managing extreme risks.

Traditional parametric and nonparametric methods for estimating distributions and densities work well in areas of the empirical distribution where there are many observations, but they often give very poor fits to the extreme tails of the distribution. This result is particularly troubling because the management of extreme risk often requires estimating quantiles and tail probabilities beyond those observed in the data. The methods of extreme value theory focus on modeling the tail behavior of a loss distribution using only extreme values rather than all of the data.

---

[1] See Jorian (2001) for a detailed description of these financial disasters.

This chapter is organized as follows. Section 5.2 covers the modeling of block maximum and minimum values using the generalized extreme value (GEV) distribution. The maximum likelihood estimator for the parameters of the GEV distribution is derived and analyzed, and graphical diagnostics for evaluating the fit are discussed. The use of the GEV distribution is illustrated with examples from finance, and the concept of return level is introduced. Section 5.3 discusses the modeling of extremes over high thresholds or "peaks over thresholds". This technique is well suited for the estimation of common risk measures like value-at-risk and expected shortfall. Parametric models utilizing the generalized Pareto distribution as well as non-parametric models are presented.

Two excellent textbooks on extreme value theory are Embrechts, Klüppelberg and Mikosch (1997) and Coles (2001). Both books provide many examples utilizing S-PLUS. Less rigorous treatments of extreme value theory with many examples in finance are given in Alexander (2001), Jorian (2001) and Tsay (2001). Useful surveys of extreme value theory applied to finance and risk management are given in Diebold, Schuermann and Stroughair (1997), Danielsson and de Vries (2001), McNeil (1998) and Longin (2000).

The S+FinMetrics functions for modeling extreme values described in this chapter are based on the functions in the *EVIS* (Extreme Values In S-PLUS) library written by Alexander McNeil at ETH Zurich. S+FinMetrics also contains functions for modeling multivariate extremes based on the functions in the *EVANESCE* library written by Rene Carmona. These functions are described in Carmona (2001) and Carmona and Morrison (2001).

5.2   Modeling Maxima and Worst Cases

To motivate the importance of the statistical modeling of extreme losses in finance, consider the following example taken from McNeil (1998). Figure 5.1 shows the daily closing prices and percentage changes in the S&P 500 index over the period January 5, 1960 through October 16, 1987 taken from the S+FinMetrics "timeSeries" object sp.raw

```
> spto87 = getReturns(sp.raw, type="discrete", percentage=T)
> par(mfrow=c(2,1))
> plot(sp.raw, main="Daily Closing Prices")
> plot(spto87, main="Daily Percentage Returns")
```

Before the October crash, the stock market was unusually volatile with several large price drops in the index resulting in large negative returns. Of interest is the characterization of the worst case scenario for a future fall in S&P 500 index utilizing the historical data prior to the crash given in Figure 5.1. To do this, the following two questions will be addressed:

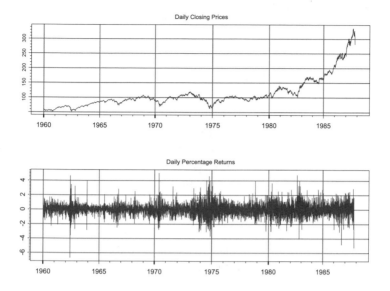

FIGURE 5.1. Daily closing prices and percentage returns on the S&P 500 Index from January, 1960 through October 16, 1987.

- What is the probability that next year's annual maximum negative return exceeds all previous negative returns? In other words, what is the probability that next year's maximum negative return is a new *record*?

- What is the 40-year *return level* of the negative returns? That is, what is the negative return which, on average, should only be exceeded in one year every forty years?

To answer these questions, the distribution of extreme negative returns on S&P 500 index is required. The distribution theory required to analyze maximum values is briefly discussed in the next section.

5.2.1   The Fisher-Tippet Theorem and the Generalized Extreme Value Distribution

Let $X_1, X_2, \ldots$ be *iid* random variables representing risks or losses with an unknown cumulative distribution function (CDF) $F(x) = \Pr\{X_i \leq x\}$. Examples of the random risks X_i are losses or negative returns on a financial asset or portfolio, operational losses, catastrophic insurance claims, and credit losses. Throughout this chapter, a loss is treated as a positive number and *extreme* events occur when losses take values in the right *tail* of the loss distribution F. Define $M_n = \max(X_1, \ldots, X_n)$ as the worst-case loss in a sample of n losses. An important part of *extreme value theory* focuses on the distribution of M_n. From the *iid* assumption, the CDF of M_n is

$$\Pr\{M_n \leq x\} = \Pr\{X_1 \leq x, \ldots, X_n \leq x\} = \prod_{i=1}^{n} F(x) = F^n(x)$$

Since F^n is assumed to be unknown and the empirical distribution function is often a very poor estimator of $F^n(x)$, an asymptotic approximation to F^n based on the *Fisher-Tippet Theorem* (Fisher and Tippett, 1928) is used to make inferences on M_n. Furthermore, since $F^n(x) \to 0$ or 1 as $n \to \infty$ and x is fixed, the asymptotic approximation is based on the standardized maximum value

$$Z_n = \frac{M_n - \mu_n}{\sigma_n} \tag{5.1}$$

where $\sigma_n > 0$ and μ_n are sequences of real numbers such that σ_n is interpreted as a scale measure and μ_n is interpreted as a location measure. The Fisher-Tippet Theorem states that if the standardized maximum (5.1) converges to some non-degenerate distribution function, it must be a *generalized extreme value* (GEV) distribution of the form

$$H_\xi(z) = \begin{cases} \exp\left\{-(1+\xi z)^{-1/\xi}\right\} & \xi \neq 0, \ 1 + \xi z > 0 \\ \exp\left\{-\exp(-z)\right\} & \xi = 0, \ -\infty \leq z \leq \infty \end{cases} \tag{5.2}$$

If (5.1) converges to (5.2), then the CDF F of the underlying data is in the *domain of attraction* of H_ξ. The Fisher-Tippet Theorem is the analog of the *Central Limit Theorem* for extreme values. Whereas the Central Limit Theorem applies to normalized sums of random variables, the Fisher-Tippet Theorem applies to standardized maxima of random variables. The parameter ξ is a *shape* parameter and determines the tail behavior of H_ξ. The parameter $\alpha = 1/\xi$ is called the *tail index* if $\xi > 0$.

The tail behavior of the distribution F of the underlying data determines the shape parameter ξ of the GEV distribution (5.2). If the tail of F declines exponentially, then H_ξ is of the *Gumbel* type and $\xi = 0$. Distributions in the domain of attraction of the Gumbel type are *thin tailed* distributions such as the normal, log-normal, exponential, and gamma. For these distributions, all moments usually exist. If the tail of F declines by a power function, i.e.

$$1 - F(x) = x^{-1/\xi} L(x)$$

for some slowly varying function $L(x)$, then H_ξ is of the *Fréchet* type and $\xi > 0$[2]. Distributions in the domain of attraction of the Fréchet type include *fat tailed* distributions like the Pareto, Cauchy, Student-t, alpha-stable with

---

[2] A function L on $(0, \infty)$ is slowly varying if $\lim_{x \to \infty} L(tx)/L(x) = 1$ for $t > 0$.

characteristic exponent in $(0, 2)$, as well as various mixture models. Not all moments are finite for these distributions. In fact, it can be shown that $E[X^k] = \infty$ for $k \geq \alpha = 1/\xi$. Last, if the tail of F is finite then H_ξ is of the *Weibull* type and $\xi < 0$. Distributions in the domain of attraction of the Weibull type include distributions with bounded support such as the uniform and beta distributions. All moments exist for these distributions.

The Fisher-Tippet Theorem applies to *iid* observations. However, the GEV distribution (5.2) may be shown (e.g. Embrechts et. al. (1997)) to be the correct limiting distribution for maxima computed from stationary time series including stationary GARCH-type processes.

The GEV distribution (5.2) characterizes the limiting distribution of the standardized maximum (5.1). It turns out that the GEV distribution (5.2) is invariant to location and scale transformations such that for location and scale parameters μ and $\sigma > 0$

$$H_\xi(z) = H_\xi\left(\frac{x - \mu}{\sigma}\right) = H_{\xi,\mu,\sigma}(x) \tag{5.3}$$

The Fisher-Tippet Theorem may then be interpreted as follows. For large enough n

$$\Pr\left\{Z_n < z\right\} = \Pr\left\{\frac{M_n - \mu_n}{\sigma_n} < z\right\} \approx H_\xi(z)$$

Letting $x = \sigma_n z + \mu_n$ then

$$\Pr\{M_n < x\} \approx H_{\xi,\mu,\sigma}\left(\frac{x - \mu_n}{\sigma_n}\right) = H_{\xi,\mu_n,\sigma_n}(x) \tag{5.4}$$

The result (5.4) is used in practice to make inferences about the maximum loss M_n.

Example 22 *Plots of GEV distributions*

The S+FinMetrics/EVIS functions pgev, qgev, dgev and rgev compute cumulative probability, quantiles, density, and random generation, respectively, from the GEV distribution (5.3) for $\xi \neq 0$ and general values for x, μ and σ. For example, the S-PLUS code to compute and plot the GEV CDF H_ξ and the pdf h_ξ for a Fréchet ($\xi = 0.5$), Weibull ($\xi = -0.5$) and Gumbell ($\xi = 0$) is

```
> z.vals = seq(-5, 5, length=200)
> cdf.f = ifelse((z.vals > -2), pgev(z.vals,xi=0.5), 0)
> cdf.w = ifelse((z.vals < 2), pgev(z.vals,xi=-0.5), 1)
> cdf.g = exp(-exp(-z.vals))
> plot(z.vals, cdf.w, type="l", xlab="z", ylab="H(z)")
> lines(z.vals, cdf.f, type="l", lty=2)
> lines(z.vals, cdf.g, type="l", lty=3)
> legend(-5, 1, legend=c("Weibull H(-0.5,0,1)",
```

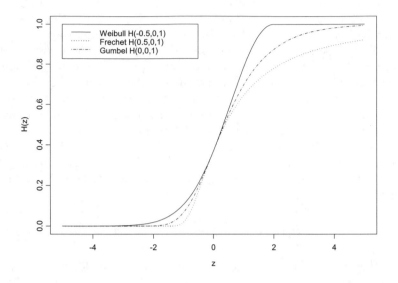

FIGURE 5.2. Generalized extreme value CDFs H_ξ for Fréchet ($\xi = -0.5$), Weibull ($\xi = 0.5$) and Gumbell ($\xi = 0$).

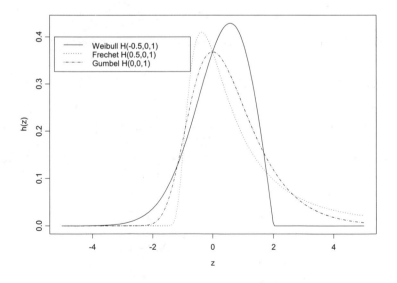

FIGURE 5.3. Generalized extreme value pdfs h_ξ for Fréchet ($\xi = -0.5$), Weibull ($\xi = 0.5$) and Gumbell ($\xi = 0$).

```
+ "Frechet H(0.5,0,1)","Gumbel H(0,0,1)"), lty=1:3)
> # pdfs
> pdf.f = ifelse((z.vals > -2), dgev(z.vals,xi=0.5), 0)
> pdf.w = ifelse((z.vals < 2), dgev(z.vals,xi=-0.5), 0)
> pdf.g = exp(-exp(-z.vals))*exp(-z.vals)
> plot(z.vals, pdf.w, type="l", xlab="z", ylab="h(z)")
> lines(z.vals, pdf.f, type="l", lty=2)
> lines(z.vals, pdf.g, type="l", lty=3)
> legend(-5.25, 0.4, legend=c("Weibull H(-0.5,0,1)",
+ "Frechet H(0.5,0,1)","Gumbel H(0,0,1)"), lty=1:3)
```

The CDF and pdf values are illustrated in Figures 5.2 and 5.3. Notice that the Fréchet is only defined for $z > -2$, and that the Weibull is only defined for $z < 2$.

5.2.2 Estimation of the GEV Distribution

The GEV distribution (5.4) depends on three parameters: the shape parameter ξ and the standardizing constants σ_n and μ_n. These parameters may be estimated using parametric maximum likelihood estimation (MLE). The S+FinMetrics/EVIS functions gev and gumbel fit the GEV distribution (5.2) by MLE to block maxima data. The calculation of the parametric MLE is briefly described below and illustrated with examples.

Parametric Maximum Likelihood Estimator

Let $X_1, \ldots, X_T$ be identically distributed losses from a sample of size T with unknown CDF F and let M_T denote the sample maximum. For inference on M_T using (5.4) the parameters ξ, σ_T and μ_T must be estimated. Since there is only one value of M_T for the entire sample, it is not possible to form a likelihood function for ξ, σ_T and μ_T. However, if interest is on the maximum of X over a large finite subsample or block of size $n < T$, M_n, then a sub-sampling method may be used to form the likelihood function for the parameters ξ, σ_n and μ_n of the GEV distribution for M_n. To do this, the sample is divided into m non-overlapping blocks of essentially equal size $n = T/m$

$$[X_1, \ldots, X_n | X_{n+1}, \ldots, X_{2n} | \ldots | X_{(m-1)n+1}, \ldots, X_{mn}]$$

and $M_n^{(j)}$ is defined as the maximum value of X_i in block $j = 1, \ldots, m$. The likelihood function for the parameters ξ, σ_n and μ_n of the GEV distribution (5.4) is then constructed from the sample of block maxima $\{M_n^{(1)}, \ldots, M_n^{(m)}\}$. It is assumed that the block size n is sufficiently large so that the Fisher-Tippet Theorem holds.

The log likelihood function assuming *iid* observations from a GEV distribution with $\xi \neq 0$ is

$$l(\mu, \sigma, \xi) = -m \ln(\sigma) - (1 + 1/\xi) \sum_{i=1}^{m} \ln \left[1 + \xi \left(\frac{M_n^{(i)} - \mu}{\sigma}\right)\right]$$

$$- \sum_{i=1}^{m} \left[1 + \xi \left(\frac{M_n^{(i)} - \mu}{\sigma}\right)\right]^{-1/\xi}$$

such that

$$1 + \xi \left(\frac{M_n^{(i)} - \mu}{\sigma}\right) > 0$$

The log-likelihood for the case $\xi = 0$ (Gumbel family) is

$$l(\mu, \sigma) = -m \ln(\sigma) - \sum_{i=1}^{m} \left(\frac{M_n^{(i)} - \mu}{\sigma}\right)$$

$$- \sum_{i=1}^{m} \exp \left[-\left(\frac{M_n^{(i)} - \mu}{\sigma}\right)\right]$$

Details of the maximum likelihood estimation are discussed in Embrechts et. al. (1997) and Coles (2001). For $\xi > -0.5$ the MLEs for μ, σ and ξ are consistent and asymptotically normally distributed with asymptotic variance given by the inverse of the observed information matrix. The finite sample properties of the MLE will depend on the number of blocks m and the block size n, see McNeil (1998) for an illustration. There is a trade-off between bias and variance. The bias of the MLE is reduced by increasing the block size n, and the variance of the MLE is reduced by increasing the number of blocks m.

Example 23 *MLE of GEV CDF for block maxima from daily S&P 500 returns*

Consider determining the appropriate GEV distribution for the daily negative returns on S&P 500 index discussed at the beginning of this section. A normal qq-plot of the returns computed using

```
> qqPlot(spto87,strip.text="Daily returns on S&P 500",
+ xlab="Quantiles of standard normal",
+ ylab="Quantiles of S&P 500")
```

is shown in Figure 5.4. The returns clearly have fatter tails than the normal distribution which suggests the Fréchet family of GEV distributions with $\xi > 0$ for the block maximum of negative returns.

Before the GEV distribution is fit by MLE, consider first some exploratory data analysis on the annual block maxima of daily negative

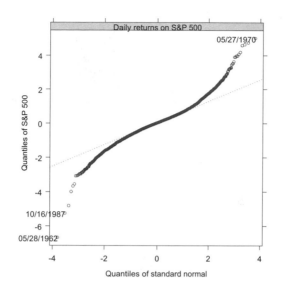

FIGURE 5.4. Normal qq-plot for the daily percentage returns on the S&P 500 index over the period January 5, 1960 through October 16, 1987.

returns. The block maxima may be easily computed using the function aggregateSeries:

```
> annualMax.sp500 = aggregateSeries(-spto87, by="years",
+ FUN=max)
```

Figure 5.5 created using

```
> Xn = sort(seriesData(annualMax.sp500))
> par(mfrow=c(2,2))
> plot(annualMax.sp500)
> hist(seriesData(annualMax.sp500),xlab="Annual maximum")
> plot(Xn,-log(-log(ppoints(Xn))),xlab="Annual maximum")
> tmp = records(-spto87)
```

gives several graphical summaries of the annual block maxima. The largest daily negative return in an annual block is 6.68% occurring in 1962. The histogram resembles a Fréchet density (see example above). The qq-plot uses the Gumbel, H_0, as the reference distribution. For this distribution, the quantiles satisfy $H_0^{-1}(p) = -\ln(-\ln(p))$. The downward curve in the plot indicates a GEV distribution with $\xi > 0$. The plot of record development is created with the S+FinMetrics/EVIS function records and illustrates the developments of records (new maxima) for the daily negative returns along with the expected number of records for *iid* data, see Embrechts et.

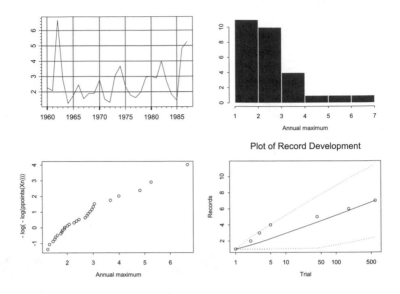

FIGURE 5.5. Annual block maxima, histogram, Gumbel qq-plot and records summary for the daily returns on the S&P 500.

al. (1997) section 6.2.5. Apart from the somewhat large number of records early on, the number of records appears consistent with *iid* behavior.

The MLEs for the parameters of the GEV distribution with $\xi \neq 0$ using block maxima may be computed using the S+FinMetrics/EVIS function gev. For example, to compute the MLEs using annual blocks from the daily (negative) returns on S&P 500 index use

```
> gev.fit.year = gev(-spto87, block="year")
> class(gev.fit.year)
[1] "gev"
```

The argument block determines the blocking method for the supplied data. An integer value for block gives the number of observations in each block. If the data supplied are a "timeSeries" then the value of block can be also be the character strings "year", "semester", "quarter" or "month". If no value for block is given then the data are interpreted as block maxima.

The function gev returns an sv3 object of class "gev" for which there is only a plot method. The components of gev.fit.year are

```
> names(gev.fit.year)
 [1] "n.all"      "n"          "call"       "block"
 [5] "data"       "par.ests"   "par.ses"    "varcov"
 [9] "converged"  "nllh.final"
```

and a description of these components is given in the online help for
gev.object. The component n gives the number of blocks m:

```
> gev.fit.year$n
[1] 28
```

The block maxima $M_n^{(i)}$ $(i = 1, \ldots, m)$ are in the data component. Since
the data supplied to gev are in a "timeSeries", the block maxima in
gev.fit.year$data are also a "timeSeries". The MLEs and asymptotic
standard errors for the parameters μ, σ and ξ are in the components
par.ests and par.ses:

```
> gev.fit.year$par.ests
     xi  sigma     mu
 0.3344 0.6716 1.975
> gev.fit.year$par.ses
     xi  sigma     mu
 0.2081 0.1308 0.1513
```

The MLE for ξ is 0.334 with asymptotic standard $\widehat{SE}(\hat{\xi}) = 0.208$. An
asymptotic 95% confidence interval for ξ is $[-0.081, 0.751]$ and indicates
considerably uncertainty about the value of ξ.

The fit to the GEV distribution may be evaluated graphically using the
plot method:

```
> plot(gev.fit.year)

Make a plot selection (or 0 to exit):
1: plot: Scatterplot of Residuals
2: plot: QQplot of Residuals
Selection:
```

Plot options 1 and 2 are illustrated in Figure 5.6. The plots show aspects
of the *crude* residuals

$$W_i = \left(1 + \hat{\xi} \frac{M_n^{(i)} - \hat{\mu}}{\hat{\sigma}}\right)^{-1/\xi}$$

which should be *iid* unit exponentially distributed random variables if the
fitted model is correct. The scatterplot of the residuals, with a lowest estimate of trend, does not reveal any significant unmodeled trend in the data.
The qq-plot, using the exponential distribution as the reference distribution, is linear and appears to validate the GEV distribution.

Using the MLEs of the GEV distribution fit to the annual block maxima
of the (negative) daily returns on S&P 500 index, the question

- What is the probability that next year's annual maximum negative
  return exceeds all previous negative returns?

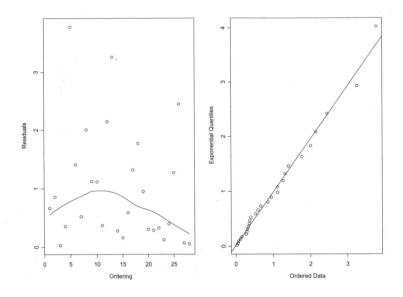

FIGURE 5.6. Residual plots from GEV distribution fit to annual block maxima of daily negative return on the S&P 500 index.

may be answered using (5.4). Since the largest block maxima is 6.68%, this probability is estimated using

$$\Pr\left(M_{260}^{(29)} > \max\left(M_{260}^{(1)}, \ldots, M_{260}^{(28)}\right)\right) = 1 - H_{\hat{\xi}, \hat{\mu}, \hat{\sigma}} \ (6.68)$$

Using the S+FinMetrics/EVIS function pgev, the result is

```
> 1- pgev(max(gev.fit.year$data),
+ xi=gev.fit.year$par.ests["xi"],
+ mu=gev.fit.year$par.ests["mu"],
+ sigma=gev.fit.year$par.ests["sigma"])
 0.02677
```

That is, there is a 2.7% chance that a new record maximum daily negative return will be established during the next year.

The above analysis is based on annual block maxima. The GEV distribution fit to quarterly block maxima is obtained using

```
> gev.fit.quarter= gev(-spto87,block="quarter")
> gev.fit.quarter$n
[1] 112
> gev.fit.quarter$par.ests
    xi  sigma    mu
 0.191 0.5021 1.401
```

```
> gev.fit.quarter$par.ses
      xi    sigma        mu
 0.06954  0.0416  0.05296
```

The MLEs for ξ, μ and σ using quarterly blocks are slightly smaller than the MLEs using annual blocks. Notice, however, that the estimated asymptotic standard errors are much smaller using quarterly block. In particular, an asymptotic 95% confidence interval for ξ is $[0.052, 0.330]$ and contains only positive values for ξ indicating a fat-tailed distribution. An estimate of the probability that next quarter's maximum exceeds all previous maxima is

```
> 1- pgev(max(gev.fit.quarter$data),
+ xi=gev.fit.quarter$par.ests["xi"],
+ mu=gev.fit.quarter$par.ests["mu"],
+ sigma=gev.fit.quarter$par.ests["sigma"])
 0.003138
```

As expected, this probability is smaller than the corresponding probability computed for annual maxima.

5.2.3 Return Level

For $\alpha \in (0,1)$ the $100 \cdot \alpha\%$ quantile of a continuous distribution with distribution function F is the value q_α such that

$$q_\alpha = F^{-1}(\alpha).$$

A useful risk measure for block maxima that is related to a high quantile is the so-called *return level*. The k n-block return level, $R_{n,k}$, is defined to be that level which is exceeded in one out of every k blocks of size n. That is, $R_{n,k}$ is the loss value such that

$$\Pr\{M_n > R_{n,k}\} = 1/k \tag{5.5}$$

The n-block in which the return level is exceeded is called a *stress period*. If the distribution of the maxima M_n in blocks of length n is characterized by (5.4) then $R_{n,k}$ is simply the $1 - 1/k$ quantile of this distribution:

$$R_{n,k} \approx H_{\xi,\mu,\sigma}^{-1}(1 - 1/k) = \mu - \frac{\sigma}{\xi}\left(1 - (-\log(1 - 1/k))^{-\xi}\right) \tag{5.6}$$

By the invariance property of maximum likelihood estimation, given the MLEs for the parameters ξ, μ and σ, the MLE for $R_{n,k}$ is

$$\hat{R}_{n,k} = \hat{\mu} - \frac{\hat{\sigma}}{\hat{\xi}}\left(1 - (-\log(1 - 1/k))^{-\hat{\xi}}\right)$$

An asymptotically valid confidence interval for $R_{n,k}$ may be computed using the *delta method* (see Greene (2000) page 118) or from the concentrated/profile log-likelihood function. Given that (5.6) is a highly nonlinear function of σ, μ and ξ, the delta method is not recommended. Details of constructing a confidence interval for $R_{n,k}$ based on the profile log-likelihood are given in chapter three of Coles (2001) and the appendix of McNeil (1998).

The return level probability in (5.5) is based on the GEV distribution $H_{\xi,\mu,\sigma}$ of the maxima M_n. For *iid* losses X with CDF F, $H_{\xi,\mu,\sigma} \approx F^n$ so that

$$F(R_{n,k}) = \Pr\{X \leq R_{n,k}\} \approx (1 - 1/k)^{1/n} \tag{5.7}$$

Hence, for *iid* losses the return level $R_{n,k}$ is approximately the $(1 - 1/k)^{1/n}$ quantile of the loss distribution F.

Example 24 *Return levels for S&P 500 negative returns*

Given the MLEs for the GEV distribution fit to the annual block maxima of the (negative) daily returns on S&P 500 index, the question

- What is the 40-year *return level* of the index returns?

may be answered using (5.6). The S+FinMetrics/EVIS function rlevel.gev computes (5.6) as well as an asymptotic 95% confidence interval based on the profile likelihood using the information from a "gev" object. To compute the 40 year return level for the S&P 500 returns from the "gev" object gev.fit.year and to create a plot of the 95% confidence interval use

```
> rlevel.gev(gev.fit.year, k.blocks=40, type="profile")
> class(rlevel.year.40)
[1] "list"
> names(rlevel.year.40)
[1] "Range"  "rlevel"
> rlevel.year.40$rlevel
[1] 6.833
```

When type="profile", the function rlevel.gev returns a list object, containing the return level and range information used in the construction of the profile log-likelihood confidence interval, and produces a plot of the profile log-likelihood confidence interval for the return level. The estimate of the 40 year return level is 6.83%. Assuming *iid* returns and using (5.7), the estimated return level of 6.83% is approximately the 99.99% quantile of the daily return distribution. An asymptotic 95% confidence interval for the true return level is illustrated in Figure 5.7. Notice the asymmetric shape of the asymptotic confidence interval. Although the point estimate of the return level is 6.83%, the upper endpoint of the 95% confidence interval is about 21%. This number may seem large; however, on Monday October 19th 1987 S&P 500 index closed down 20.4%.

By default, the function rlevel.gev produces a plot of the asymptotic 95% confidence level. Alternatively, if rlevel.gev is called with the optional argument type="RetLevel":

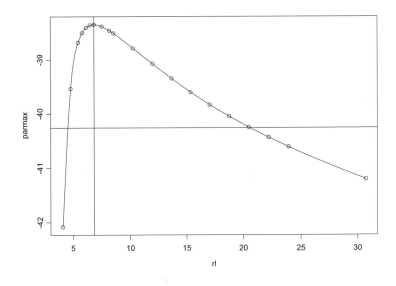

FIGURE 5.7. Asymptotic 95% confidence interval for the 40 year return level based on the profile log-likelihood function.

```
> rlevel.year.40 = rlevel.gev(gev.fit.year, k.blocks=40,
+ type="RetLevel")
> names(rlevel.year.40)
[1] "LowerCB" "rlevel"  "UpperCB"
> rlevel.year.40
$LowerCB:
[1] 4.646

$rlevel:
[1] 6.833

$UpperCB:
[1] 20.5
```

A plot of the estimated return level along with the block maxima, as shown in Figure 5.8, is created, and the components of the returned list are the estimated return level along with the end points of the 95% confidence interval.

The 40 year return level may also be estimated from the GEV distribution fit to quarterly maxima. Since 40 years is 160 quarters, the 40 year return level computed from the "gev" object gev.fit.quarter is

```
> rlevel.160.q = rlevel.gev(gev.fit.quarter, k.blocks=160,
```

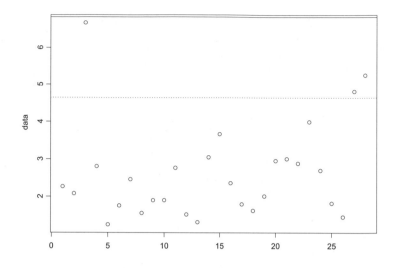

FIGURE 5.8. Estimated 40-year return level with 95% confidence band for the S&P 500 daily negative returns.

```
+ type="RetLevel")
> rlevel.160.q
$LowerCB:
[1]  4.433

$rlevel:
[1]  5.699

$UpperCB:
[1]  8.549
```

Here, the estimated return level and asymptotic 95% confidence interval are smaller than the corresponding quantities estimated from annual data.

5.3   Modeling Extremes Over High Thresholds

Modeling only block maxima data is inefficient if other data on extreme values are available. A more efficient alternative approach that utilizes more data is to model the behavior of extreme values above some high threshold. This method is often called *peaks over thresholds* (POT). Another advantage of the POT approach is that common risk measures like *Value-at-Risk* (VaR) and *expected shortfall* (ES) may easily be computed[3].

To illustrate the concepts of VaR and ES, review the daily S&P 500 returns analyzed in the previous section. Suppose the S&P 500 is the only asset in a large portfolio for an investor and that the random variable X with CDF F represents the daily loss on the portfolio. The daily VaR on the portfolio is simply a high quantile of the distribution F of daily losses. For example, the daily 1% VaR on the portfolio is the 99% quantile of X

$$VaR_{.99} = F^{-1}(0.99).$$

That is, with 1% probability the loss in portfolio value over a day will exceed $VaR_{.99}$. Often the high quantile $VaR_{.99}$ is computed assuming $X \sim N(\mu, \sigma^2)$. In this case, the calculation of $VaR_{.99}$ reduces to the simple formula

$$VaR_{.99} = \mu + \sigma \cdot q_{.99} \qquad (5.8)$$

where $q_{.99}$ is the 99% quantile of the standard normal distribution. The distribution of daily portfolio losses, however, generally has fatter tails than the normal distribution so that (5.8) may severely under-estimate $VaR_{.99}$. Estimates of VaR based on the POT methodology are much more reliable.

The ES on the portfolio is the average loss given that VaR has been exceeded. For example, the 1% ES is the conditional mean of X given that $X > VAR_{.99}$

$$ES_{.99} = E[X|X > VaR_{.99}]$$

If $X \sim N(\mu, \sigma^2)$ then $ES_{.99}$ may be computed as the mean of a truncated normal random variable:

$$ES_{.99} = \mu + \sigma \cdot \frac{\phi(z)}{1 - \Phi(z)} \qquad (5.9)$$

where $z = (VaR_{.99} - \mu)/\sigma$, $\phi(z)$ is the standard normal density function and $\Phi(z)$ is the standard normal CDF. Again, if the distribution of losses has fatter tails than the normal, then (5.9) will underestimate $ES_{.99}$. The POT methodology estimates the distribution of losses over a threshold and produces an estimate of ES as a by-product of the estimation.

For another example, consider the "timeSeries" danish representing Danish fire loss data in S+FinMetrics, which is analyzed in McNeil (1999). The data in danish consist of 2167 daily insurance claims for losses exceeding one million Danish Krone from January 3, 1980 through December 31, 1990. The reported loss is an inflation adjusted total loss for the event concerned and includes damages to buildings, damage to contents of buildings as well as loss of profits. Figure 5.9 created using

---

[3]Notice that VaR and ES are based on the distribution of the losses and not on the distribution of the maximum losses. The analysis of block maxima based on the GEV distribution allowed inferences to be made only on the maxima of returns. The POT analysis will allow inferences to be made directly on the distribution of losses.

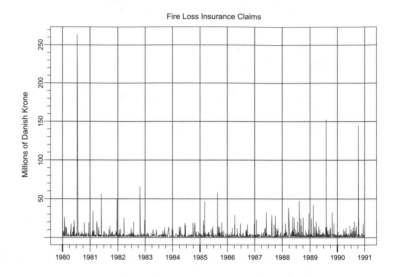

FIGURE 5.9. Large fire loss insurance claims.

```
> plot(danish, ain="Fire Loss Insurance Claims",
+ ylab="Millions of Danish Krone")
```

shows the data and reveals several extreme losses. For risk management purposes, insurance companies may be interested in the frequency of occurrence of large claims above some high threshold as well as the average value of the claims that exceed the high threshold. Additionally, they may be interested in daily VaR and ES. The statistical models for extreme values above a high threshold may be used to address these issues.

5.3.1   The Limiting Distribution of Extremes Over High Thresholds and the Generalized Pareto Distribution

As with the analysis of block maxima, let $X_1, X_2, \ldots$ be a sequence of *iid* random variables representing risks or losses with an unknown CDF F and let $M_n = \max\{X_1, \ldots, X_n\}$. A natural measure of extreme events are values of the X_i that exceed a high threshold u. Define the *excess distribution* above the threshold u as the conditional probability:

$$F_u(y) = \Pr\{X - u \le y | X > u\} = \frac{F(y+u) - F(u)}{1 - F(u)}, \ y > 0 \qquad (5.10)$$

For the class of distributions F such that the CDF of the standardized value of M_n converges to a GEV distribution (5.2), it can be shown (c.f.

Embrechts et. al. (1997)) that for large enough u there exists a positive function $\beta(u)$ such that the excess distribution (5.10) is well approximated by the *generalized Pareto distribution* (GPD)

$$G_{\xi,\beta(u)}(y) = \begin{cases} 1 - (1 + \xi y/\beta(u)) & \text{for } \xi \neq 0 \\ 1 - \exp(-y/\beta(u)) & \text{for } \xi = 0 \end{cases} , \quad \beta(u) > 0 \qquad (5.11)$$

defined for $y \geq 0$ when $\xi \geq 0$ and $0 \leq y \leq -\beta(u)/\xi$ when $\xi < 0$.

Remarks:

- Operationally, for a sufficiently high threshold u, $F_u(y) \approx G_{\xi,\beta(u)}(y)$ for a wide class of loss distributions F. To implement this result, the threshold value u must be specified and estimates of the unknown parameters ξ and $\beta(u)$ must be obtained.

- There is a close connection between the limiting GEV distribution for block maxima and the limiting GPD for threshold excesses. For a given value of u, the parameters ξ, μ and σ of the GEV distribution determine the parameters ξ and $\beta(u)$. In particular, the shape parameter ξ of the GEV distribution is the same shape parameter ξ in the GPD and is independent of the threshold value u. Consequently, if $\xi < 0$ then F is in the Weibull family and $G_{\xi,\beta(u)}$ is a *Pareto type II* distribution; if $\xi = 0$ then F is in the Gumbel family and $G_{\xi,\beta(u)}$ is an *exponential* distribution; and if $\xi > 0$ then F is in the Fréchet family and $G_{\xi,\beta(u)}$ is a *Pareto* distribution.

- For $\xi > 0$, the most relevant case for risk management purposes, it can be shown that $E[X^k] = \infty$ for $k \geq \alpha = 1/\xi$. For example, if $\xi = 0.5$ then $E[X^2] = \infty$ and the distribution of losses, X, does not have finite variance. If $\xi = 1$ then $E[X] = \infty$.

- Consider a limiting GPD with shape parameter ξ and scale parameter $\beta(u_0)$ for an excess distribution F_{u_0} with threshold u_0. For an arbitrary threshold $u > u_0$, the excess distribution F_u has a limiting GPD distribution with shape parameter ξ and scale parameter $\beta(u) = \beta(u_0) + \xi(u - u_0)$. Alternatively, for any $y > 0$ the excess distribution F_{u_0+y} has a limiting GPD distribution with shape parameter ξ and scale parameter $\beta(u_0) + \xi y$.

Example 25 *Plots of GPDs*

The S+FinMetrics/EVIS functions pgpd, qgpd, dgpd and rgpd compute cumulative probability, quantiles, density and random number generation, respectively, from the GPD (5.11) for $\xi \neq 0$ and general values for $\beta(u)$. For example, the S-PLUS code to compute and plot the CDFs and pdfs with $\beta(u) = 1$ for a Pareto ($\xi = -0.5$), exponential ($\xi = 0$) and Pareto type II ($\xi = -0.5$) is

```
> par(mfrow=c(1,2))
> y.vals = seq(0,8,length=200)
> cdf.p = pgpd(y.vals, xi=0.5)
> cdf.p2 = ifelse((y.vals < 2), pgpd(y.vals,xi=-0.5), 1)
> cdf.e = 1-exp(-z.vals)
> plot(y.vals, cdf.p, type="l", xlab="y", ylab="G(y)",
+ ylim=c(0,1))
> lines(y.vals, cdf.e, type="l", lty=2)
> lines(y.vals, cdf.p2, type="l", lty=3)
> legend(1,0.2,legend=c("Pareto G(0.5,1)","Exponential G(0,1)",
+ "Pareto II G(0.5,1)"),lty=1:3)
> # PDFs
> pdf.p = dgpd(y.vals, xi=0.5)
> pdf.p2 = ifelse((y.vals < 2), dgpd(y.vals,xi=-0.5), 0)
> pdf.e = exp(-y.vals)
> plot(y.vals, pdf.p, type="l", xlab="y", ylab="g(y)",
+ ylim=c(0,1))
> lines(y.vals, pdf.e, type="l", lty=2)
> lines(y.vals, pdf.p2, type="l", lty=3)
> legend(2,1,legend=c("Pareto g(0.5,1)","Exponential g(0,1)",
+ "Pareto II g(-0.5,1)"),lty=1:3)
```

The CDFs and pdfs are illustrated in Figure 5.10. Notice that the Pareto type II is only defined for $y < 2$.

Example 26 *qq-plots to determine tail behavior*

A simple graphical technique infers the tail behavior of observed losses is to create a qq-plot using the exponential distribution as a reference distribution. If the excesses over thresholds are from a thin-tailed distribution, then the GPD is exponential with $\xi = 0$ and the qq-plot should be linear. Departures from linearity in the qq-plot then indicate either fat-tailed behavior ($\xi > 0$) or bounded tails ($\xi < 0$). The S+FinMetrics/EVIS function qplot may be used to create a qq-plot using a GPD as a reference distribution. For example, to create qq-plots with the exponential distribution as the reference distribution for the S&P 500 negative returns over the threshold $u = 1$ and the Danish fire loss data over the threshold $u = 10$ use

```
> par(mfrow=c(1,2))
> qplot(-spto87, threshold=1, main="S&P 500 negative returns")
> qplot(danish, threshold=10, main="Danish fire losses")
```

Figure 5.11 shows these qq-plots. There is a slight departure from linearity for the negative S&P 500 returns and a rather large departure from linearity for the Danish fire losses.

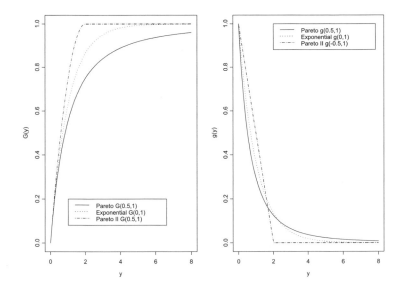

FIGURE 5.10. Generalized Pareto CDFs, $G_{\xi,1}$, and pdfs, $g_{\xi,1}$, for Pareto ($\xi = 0.5$), exponential ($\xi = 0$) and Pareto type II ($\xi = -0.5$).

Mean Excess Function

Suppose the threshold excess $X - u_0$ follows a GPD with parameters $\xi < 1$ and $\beta(u_0)$. Then the *mean excess* over the threshold u_0 is

$$E[X - u_0 | X > u_0] = \frac{\beta(u_0)}{1 - \xi}. \tag{5.12}$$

For any $u > u_0$, define the *mean excess function* $e(u)$ as

$$e(u) = E[X - u | X > u] = \frac{\beta(u_0) + \xi(u - u_0)}{1 - \xi}. \tag{5.13}$$

Alternatively, for any $y > 0$

$$e(u_0 + y) = E[X - (u_0 + y) | X > u_0 + y] = \frac{\beta(u_0) + \xi y}{1 - \xi}. \tag{5.14}$$

Notice that for a given value of ξ, the mean excess function is a linear function of $y = u - u_0$. This result motivates a simple graphical way to infer the appropriate threshold value u_0 for the GPD. Define the *empirical mean excess function*

$$e_n(u) = \frac{1}{n_u} \sum_{i=1}^{n_u} (x_{(i)} - u) \tag{5.15}$$

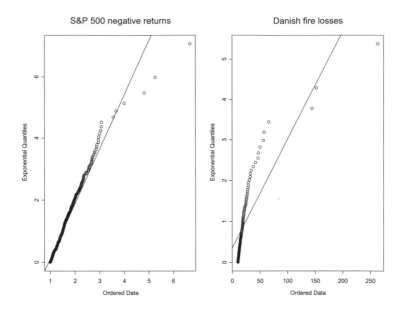

FIGURE 5.11. QQ-plots with exponential reference distribution for the S&P 500 negative returns over the threshold $u = 1$ and the Danish fire losses over the threshold $u = 10$.

where $x_{(i)}$ $(i = 1, \ldots, n_u)$ are the values of x_i such that $x_i > u$. The *mean excess plot* is a plot of $e_n(u)$ against u and should be linear in u for $u > u_0$.

Example 27 *Mean excess plots for S&P 500 and fire loss data*

The **S+FinMetrics/EVIS** function `meplot` computes the empirical mean excess function (5.15) and creates the mean excess plot. The mean excess functions and mean excess plots for the S&P 500 negative returns and the Danish fire losses are computed using

```
> me.sp500 = meplot(-spto87)
> me.dainsh = meplot(danish)
> class(me.sp500)
[1] "data.frame"
> colIds(me.sp500)
[1] "threshold" "me"
```

The function `meplot` returns a data frame containing the thresholds u and the mean excesses $e_n(u)$ and produces a mean excess plot. The mean excess plots for the S&P 500 and Danish data are illustrated in Figures 5.12 and 5.13. The mean excess plot for the S&P 500 negative returns is linear in u for $u < -1$ and for $u > 1$. The plot for the fire loss data appears to be linear for almost all values of u.

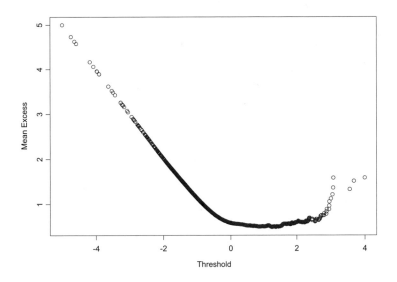

FIGURE 5.12. Mean excess plot for the S&P 500 negative returns.

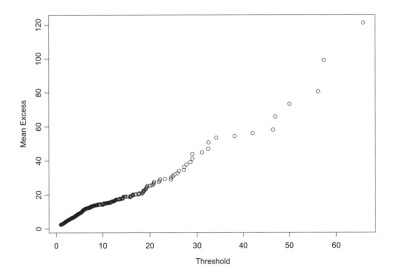

FIGURE 5.13. Mean excess plot for the Danish fire loss data.

5.3.2 Estimating the GPD by Maximum Likelihood

Let $x_1, \ldots, x_n$ be *iid* sample of losses with unknown CDF F. For a given high threshold u, extreme values are those x_i values for which $x_i - u > 0$. Denote these values $x_{(1)}, \ldots, x_{(k)}$ and define the threshold excesses as $y_i = x_{(i)} - u$ for $i = 1, \ldots, k$. The results of the previous section imply that if u is large enough then $\{y_1, \ldots, y_k\}$ may be thought of as a random sample from a GPD with unknown parameters ξ and $\beta(u)$. For $\xi \neq 0$, the log-likelihood function based on (5.11) is

$$l(\xi, \beta(u)) = -k \ln(\beta(u)) - (1 + 1/\xi) \sum_{i=1}^{k} \ln(1 + \xi y_i / \beta(u))$$

provided $y_i \geq 0$ when $\xi > 0$ and $0 \leq y_i \leq -\beta(u)/\xi$ when $\xi < 0$. For $\xi = 0$ the log-likelihood function is

$$l(\beta(u)) = -k \ln(\beta(u)) - \beta(u)^{-1} \sum_{i=1}^{k} y_i.$$

5.3.3 Estimating the Tails of the Loss Distribution

For a sufficiently high threshold u, $F_u(y) \approx G_{\xi, \beta(u)}(y)$. Using this result in (5.10) and setting $x = u + y$, an approximation to the tails of the loss distribution $F(x)$ for $x > u$ is given by

$$F(x) = (1 - F(u))G_{\xi, \beta(u)}(y) + F(u) \tag{5.16}$$

The CDF value $F(u)$ may be estimated non-parametrically using the empirical CDF

$$\hat{F}(u) = \frac{(n - k)}{n} \tag{5.17}$$

where k denotes the number of exceedences over the threshold u. Combining the parametric representation (5.11) with the non-parametric estimate (5.17) gives the resulting estimate of (5.16)

$$\hat{F}(x) = 1 - \frac{k}{n} \left(1 + \hat{\xi} \cdot \frac{x - u}{\hat{\beta}(u)} \right) \tag{5.18}$$

where $\hat{\xi}$ and $\hat{\beta}(u)$ denote the MLEs of ξ and $\beta(u)$, respectively.

Example 28 *Estimating the GPD for the S&P 500 negative returns*

Maximum likelihood estimation of the parameters ξ and $\beta(u)$ of the GPD (5.11) may be computed using the S+FinMetrics/EVIS function gpd. In order to compute the MLE, a threshold value u must be specified. The threshold should be large enough so that the GPD approximation is valid but low enough so that a sufficient number of observations k are available for a precise fit.

To illustrate, consider fitting GPD to the negative returns on the S&P 500 index. The S+FinMetrics/EVIS function gpd may be used to compute the MLEs for the GPD (5.11) for a given threshold u. The mean excess plot for the S&P 500 returns in Figure 5.12 suggests a value of $u = 1$ may be appropriate for the GPD approximation to be valid. The MLE using $u = 1$ is computed using

```
> gpd.sp500.1 = gpd(-spto87, threshold=1)
> class(gpd.sp500.1)
[1] "gpd"
```

The function gpd returns an object of class "gpd" for which there is only a plot method. The components of a "gpd" object are

```
> names(gpd.sp500.1)
 [1] "n"                    "data"
 [3] "upper.exceed"         "lower.exceed"
 [5] "upper.thresh"         "lower.thresh"
 [7] "p.less.upper.thresh"  "p.larger.lower.thresh"
 [9] "n.upper.exceed"       "n.lower.exceed"
[11] "upper.method"         "lower.method"
[13] "upper.par.ests"       "lower.par.ests"
[15] "upper.par.ses"        "lower.par.ses"
[17] "upper.varcov"         "lower.varcov"
[19] "upper.info"           "lower.info"
[21] "upper.converged"      "lower.converged"
[23] "upper.nllh.final"     "lower.nllh.final"
```

and a description of these components is given in the online help for gpd.object. The threshold information is

```
> gpd.sp500.1$upper.thresh
[1] 1
> gpd.sp500.1$n.upper.exceed
[1] 595
> gpd.sp500.1$p.less.upper.thresh
[1] 0.9148
```

The MLEs for ξ and $\beta(1)$ and asymptotic standard errors are

```
> gpd.sp500.1$upper.par.ests
     xi    beta
 0.06767 0.4681
> gpd.sp500.1$upper.par.ses
     xi     beta
```

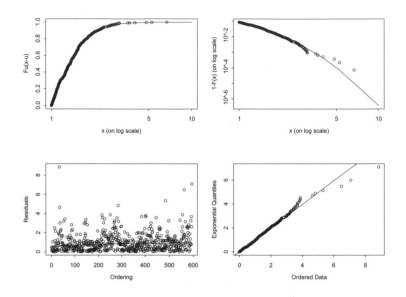

FIGURE 5.14. Diagnostic plots for GPD fit to daily negative returns on S&P 500 index.

```
0.03973 0.02669
```

Notice that $\hat{\xi} = 0.068$ is fairly close to zero and indicates that the return distribution is not so heavy-tailed. Also, the GPD estimate of ξ is quite a bit smaller than the GEV estimate $\hat{\xi} = 0.334$ based on annual data, but it is very close to the GEV estimate $\hat{\xi} = 0.069$ based on quarterly data.

Diagnostic plots of the GDP fit are created using the `plot` method

```
> plot(gpd.sp500.1)

Make a plot selection (or 0 to exit):
1: plot: Excess Distribution
2: plot: Tail of Underlying Distribution
3: plot: Scatterplot of Residuals
4: plot: QQplot of Residuals
Selection:
```

The four plot options are depicted in Figure 5.14. The first plot option shows the GPD estimate of the excess distribution, and the second plot option shows the tail estimate (5.18). The GPD appears to fit the distribution of threshold excesses fairly well. Note, the S+FinMetrics/EVIS function `tailplot` may be used to compute plot option 2 directly.

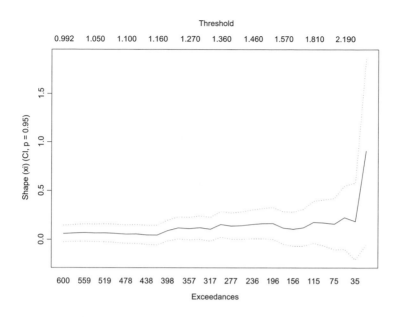

FIGURE 5.15. Estimates of shape parameter ξ for S&P 500 negative returns as a function of the threshold value u.

The S+FinMetrics/EVIS function shape can be used to create a plot showing how the MLE of the shape parameter ξ varies with the selected threshold u:

```
> shape(-spto87, end=600)
```

The optional argument end=600 specifies the maximum number of threshold exceedences to consider. The resulting plot is shown in Figure 5.15. The estimates of ξ are fairly stable and close to zero for thresholds values less than 2.

Example 29 *Estimating the GPD for the Danish fire loss data*

The mean excess plot in Figure 5.13 suggests a threshold value of $u = 10$. The MLEs of the GPD parameters for the Danish fire loss data using a high threshold of 10 million Krone are computed using

```
> gpd.fit.10 = gpd(danish, threshold=10)
> gpd.danish.10 = gpd(danish, threshold=10)
> gpd.danish.10$n.upper.exceed
[1] 109
> gpd.danish.10$p.less.upper.thresh
[1] 0.9497
> gpd.danish.10$upper.par.ests
```

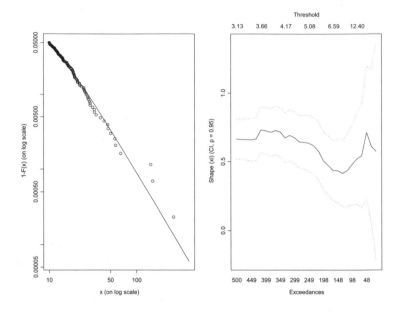

FIGURE 5.16. Diagnostic plots from GPD fit to Danish fire loss data.

```
    xi   beta
 0.497 6.975
> gpd.danish.10$upper.par.ses
     xi   beta
 0.1363 1.113
```

The estimate of ξ shows heavy tails and suggests that the variance may not be finite. The diagnostic plots in Figure 5.16, created using

```
> par(mfrow=c(1,2))
> tailplot(gpd.danish.10)
> shape(danish)
```

show that the GPD fits the data well and that the estimates of ξ are fairly stable for a wide range of threshold values.

5.3.4   Risk Measures

As mentioned in the introduction to this section, two common risk measures are *Value-at-Risk* (VaR) and *expected shortfall* (ES). VaR is a high quantile of the loss distribution. That is, for $0.95 \leq q < 1$, say, VaR_q is the qth quantile of the distribution F

$$VaR_q = F^{-1}(q) \tag{5.19}$$

where F^{-1} is the inverse of F. For a given probability $q > F(u)$, an estimate
of (5.19) based on inverting the tail estimation formula (5.18) is

$$\widehat{VaR}_q = u + \frac{\hat{\beta}(u)}{\hat{\xi}} \left(\left(\frac{n}{k}(1-q) \right)^{-\hat{\xi}} - 1 \right) \tag{5.20}$$

Expected shortfall is the expected loss size, given that VaR_q is exceeded

$$ES_q = E[X|X > VaR_q] \tag{5.21}$$

The measure ES_q is related to VaR_q via

$$ES_q = VaR_q + E[X - VaR_q|X > VaR_q]. \tag{5.22}$$

where the second term in (5.22) is simply the mean of the excess distribution
$F_{VaR_q}(y)$ over the threshold VaR_q. By the translation property of the GPD
distribution, the GPD approximation to $F_{VaR_q}(y)$ has shape parameter ξ
and scale parameter $\beta(u) + \xi(VaR_q - u)$. Consequently, using (5.13)

$$E[X - VaR_q|X > VaR_q] = \frac{\beta(u) + \xi(VaR_q - u)}{1 - \xi} \tag{5.23}$$

provided $\xi < 1$. Combining (5.23) with (5.20) and substituting into (5.22)
gives the GPD approximation to ES_q

$$\widehat{ES}_q = \frac{\widehat{VaR}_q}{1 - \hat{\xi}} + \frac{\hat{\beta}(u) - \hat{\xi}u}{1 - \hat{\xi}}. \tag{5.24}$$

Example 30 *Computing VaR and ES for negative S&P 500 returns*

The S+FinMetrics/EVIS function `riskmeasures` computes estimates of
VaR_q and ES_q based on the GPD approximations (5.20) and (5.24), respectively, using the information from a "gpd" object. For example, the
VaR_q and ES_q estimates for the negative S&P 500 negative returns for
$q = 0.95, 0.99$ are computed using

```
> riskmeasures(gpd.sp500.1, c(0.95,0.99))
        p quantile  sfall
[1,] 0.95   1.2539 1.7744
[2,] 0.99   2.0790 2.6594
```

That is, with 5% probability the daily return could be as low as -1.254%
and, given that the return is less than 1.254%, the average return value is
-1.774%. Similarly, with 1% probability the daily return could be as low
as -2.079% with an average return of -2.659% given that the return is
less than -2.079%.

It is instructive to compare these results to those based on the assumption of normally distributed returns. Using the formulas (5.8) and (5.9),
estimates of VaR_q and ES_q for $q = 0.95, 0.99$ are computed using

```
> sp500.mu = mean(-spto87)
> sp500.sd = sqrt(var(-spto87))
> var.95 = sp500.mu + sp500.sd*qnorm(0.95)
> var.99 = sp500.mu + sp500.sd*qnorm(0.99)
> var.95
[1] 1.299
> var.99
[1] 1.848

> z95 = (var.95 - sp500.mu)/sp500.sd
> z99 = (var.99 - sp500.mu)/sp500.sd
> es.95 = sp500.mu + sp500.sd*dnorm(z95)/(1-pnorm(z95))
> es.99 = sp500.mu + sp500.sd*dnorm(z99)/(1-pnorm(z99))
> es.95
[1] 1.636
> es.99
[1] 2.121
```

The estimates of VaR_q and ES_q based on the normal distribution are fairly close to the estimates based on the GPD. This result is to be expected since $\hat{\xi} = 0.068$ is close zero.

Example 31 *Computing VaR and ES for Danish fire loss data*

The VaR_q and ES_q estimates for the Danish fire loss data for $q = 0.95, 0.99$ are

```
> riskmeasures(gpd.danish.10, c(0.95,0.99))
         p quantile sfall
[1,] 0.95   10.042 23.95
[2,] 0.99   27.290 58.24
```

The estimates of VaR_q and ES_q based on the normal distribution are

```
> danish.mu = mean(danish)
> danish.sd = sqrt(var(danish))
> var.95 = danish.mu + danish.sd*qnorm(0.95)
> var.99 = danish.mu + danish.sd*qnorm(0.99)
> var.95
[1] 17.38
> var.99
[1] 23.18

> z95 = (var.95 - danish.mu)/danish.sd
> z99 = (var.99 - danish.mu)/danish.sd
> es.95 = danish.mu + danish.sd*dnorm(z95)/(1-pnorm(z95))
> es.99 = danish.mu + danish.sd*dnorm(z99)/(1-pnorm(z99))
> es.95
```

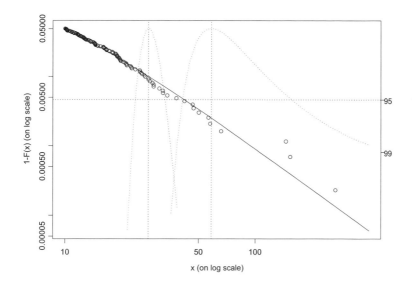

FIGURE 5.17. Asymptotic confidence intervals for $VaR_{.99}$ and $ES_{.99}$ based on the GPD fit to the Danish fire loss data.

```
[1] 20.93
> es.99
[1] 26.06
```

In this case, because $\hat{\xi} = 0.497$, the estimates based on the GPD and normal distribution differ considerably.

Estimates and asymptotically valid confidence intervals for VaR_q and ES_q may be computed using the S+FinMetrics/EVIS function gpd.q and gpd.sfall, respectively. Wald-type confidence intervals based on the delta method or likelihood ratio-type confidence intervals based on the profile log-likelihood function may be computed, and these confidence intervals may be visualized on a plot with the tail estimate (5.18). First create plot of the excess distribution using the S+FinMetrics/EVIS function tailplot

```
> tailplot(gpd.danish.10)
```

After the plot has been created, the asymptotic confidence intervals for VaR_q and ES_q may be added using

```
> gpd.q(0.99,plot=T)
> gpd.sfall(0.99,plot=T)
```

The combined plots are illustrated in Figure 5.17. Notice, in particular, the wide asymmetric confidence interval for $ES_{.99}$. This result is due to the

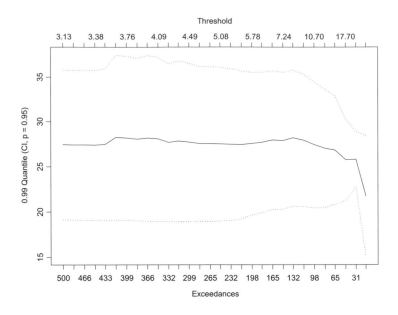

FIGURE 5.18. $VaR_{.99}$ estimates as a function of u for the Danish fire loss data.

uncertainty created by only a few observations in the extreme tails of the distribution.

The sensitivity of the VaR_q estimates to changes in the threshold u may be investigated using the S+FinMetrics/EVIS function quant. For example, to see how the $VaR_{.99}$ estimates vary with u use

```
> quant(danish, p=0.99)
```

which produces the graph in Figure 5.18. The $VaR_{.99}$ estimates are stable for $u < 20$.

5.4 Hill's Non-parametric Estimator of Tail Index

The shape parameter ξ, or equivalently, the tail index $a = 1/\xi$, of the GEV and GPD distributions (5.2) and (5.11) may be estimated non-parametrically in a number of ways. A popular method due to Hill (1975) applies to the case where $\xi > 0$ ($\alpha > 0$) so that the data is generated by some fat-tailed distribution in the domain of attraction of a Fréchet type GEV. To describe the Hill estimator, consider a sample of losses $X_1, \ldots, X_T$ and define the order statistics as

$$X_{(1)} \geq X_{(2)} \geq \cdots \geq X_{(T)}$$

For a positive integer k, the *Hill estimator* of ξ is defined as

$$\hat{\xi}^{Hill}(k) = \frac{1}{k} \sum_{j=1}^{k} \left(\log X_{(j)} - \log X_{(k)} \right) \tag{5.25}$$

and the Hill estimator of α is

$$\hat{\alpha}^{Hill}(k) = 1/\hat{\xi}^{Hill}(k) \tag{5.26}$$

The Hill estimators of ξ and α depend on the integer k. Notice that k in (5.26) plays the same role as k in (5.17) for the analysis of the GPD. It can be shown that if F is in the domain of attraction of a GEV distribution, then $\hat{\xi}^{Hill}(k)$ converges in probability to ξ as $k \to \infty$ and $\frac{k}{n} \to 0$, and that $\hat{\xi}^{Hill}(k)$ is asymptotically normally distributed with asymptotic variance

$$avar(\hat{\xi}^{Hill}(k)) = \frac{\xi^2}{k}$$

By the delta method, $\hat{\alpha}^{Hill}(k)$ is asymptotically normally distributed with asymptotic variance

$$avar(\hat{\alpha}^{Hill}(k)) = \frac{\alpha^2}{k}$$

In practice, the Hill estimators $\hat{\xi}^{Hill}(k)$ or $\hat{\alpha}^{Hill}(k)$ are often plotted against k to find the value of k such that the estimator appears stable.

5.4.1 Hill Tail and Quantile Estimation

Suppose that the loss distribution F is such that $1 - F(x) = x^{-\alpha} L(x)$ with $\alpha = 1/\xi > 0$, where $L(x)$ is a slowly varying function. Let $x > X_{(k+1)}$ where $X_{(k+1)}$ is a high order statistic. Then the Hill estimator of $F(x)$ is given by

$$\hat{F}^{Hill}(x) = 1 - \frac{k}{n} \left(\frac{x}{X_{(k+1)}} \right)^{-\hat{\alpha}^{Hill}(k)} , \quad x > X_{(k+1)} \tag{5.27}$$

Inverting the Hill tail estimator (5.27) gives the Hill quantile estimator

$$\hat{x}_{q,k}^{Hill} = X_{(k+1)} - X_{(k+1)} \left(\left(\frac{n}{k}(1-q) \right)^{-\hat{\xi}^{Hill}(k)} - 1 \right) \tag{5.28}$$

where $q > 1 - k/n$. The Hill quantile estimator (5.28) is very similar to the MLE GPD quantile estimator (5.20) with $u = X_{(k+1)}$.

Example 32 *Nonparametric estimation of ξ for Danish fire loss data*

The Hill estimates of α, ξ and the quantile $x_{q,k}$ may be computed and plotted using the S+FinMetrics/EVIS function hill. The arguments expected by hill are

```
> args(hill)
function(data, option = "alpha", start = 15, end = NA,
p = NA, ci = 0.95, plot = T, reverse = F,
auto.scale = T, labels = T, ...)
```

where data is a univariate numeric vector or "timeSeries", option determines if α ("alpha"), ξ ("xi") or $x_{q,k}$ ("quantile") is to be computed, start and end specify the starting and ending number of order statistics to use in computing the estimates, p specifies the probability required when option="quantile", ci determines the probability for asymptotic confidence bands, and plot determines if a plot is to be created. To illustrate the use of hill, consider the computation of (5.25) for the Danish fire loss data using all of the order statistics less than $X_{(15)}$

```
> hill.danish = hill(danish, option="xi")
> class(hill.danish)
[1] "data.frame"
> names(hill.danish)
[1] "xi"         "orderStat" "threshold"
```

The function hill returns a data frame with components xi containing the estimates of ξ, orderStat containing the order statistic labels k, and threshold containing the order statistic or threshold values $X_{(k)}$. Since the default option plot=T is used, hill also produces the plot shown in Figure 5.19. For $k > 120$ ($X_{(k)} < 9$), $\hat{\xi}^{Hill}(k)$ is fairly stable around 0.7. The GPD estimate of ξ with threshold $u = 10$ is 0.497. The Hill estimates for threshold values near 10 are

```
> idx = (hill.danish$threshold >= 9.8 &
+ hill.danish$threshold <= 10.2)
> hill.danish[idx,]
          xi orderStat threshold
2059 0.6183       109     9.883
2060 0.6180       108    10.011
2061 0.6173       107    10.072
2062 0.6191       106    10.137
2063 0.6243       105    10.178
2064 0.6285       104    10.185
```

The 99% quantile estimates (5.28) for $15 \leq k \leq 500$ are computed using

```
> hill.danish.q = hill(danish, option="quantile", p=0.99,
+ end=500)
```

and are illustrated in Figure 5.20. For threshold values around 10, the Hill

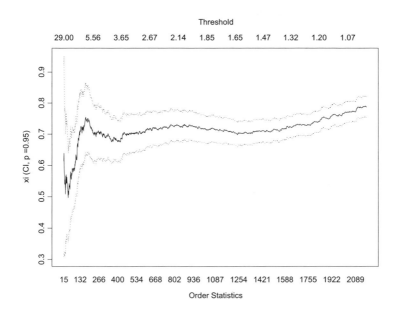

FIGURE 5.19. Hill estimates of ξ for the Danish fire loss data.

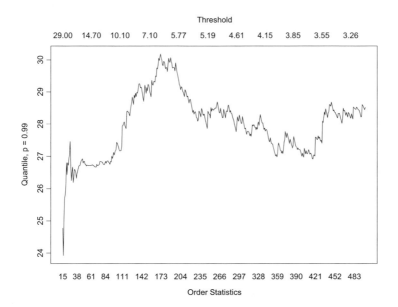

FIGURE 5.20. Hill estimates of 1% quantile of Danish fire loss data.

estimates of the 99% quantile are similar to the MLE GPD estimates shown in Figure 5.18.

5.5 References

[1] ALEXANDER, C. (2001). *Market Models: A Guide to Financial Data Analysis*, John Wiley and Sons.

[2] CARMONA, R. (2001). *Statistical Analysis of Financial Data, with an implementation in Splus.* Textbook under review.

[3] CARMONA, R. AND J. MORRISSON (2001). "Heavy Tails and Copulas with Evanesce," ORFE Tech. Report, Princeton University.

[4] COLES, S (2001). *An Introduction to Statistical Modeling of Extreme Values.* Springer-Verlag, London.

[5] DANIELSSON, J. AND C.G. DE VRIES (1997). "Tail Index and Quantile Estimation with Very High Frequency Data," *Journal of Empirical Finance*, 4, 241-257.

[6] DIEBOLD, F.X., T. SCHUERMANN, AND J.D. STROUGHAIR (1997), "Pitfalls and Opportunities in the Use of Extreme Value Theory in Risk Management," *Advances in Computational Management Science* 2, 3-12.

[7] EMBRECHTS, P. C. KLOPPELBERG, AND T. MIKOSCH (1997). *Modelling Extremal Events.* Springer-Verlag, Berlin.

[8] FISHER, R. AND L. TIPPETT (1928). "Limiting Forms of the Frequency Distribution of the Largest or Smallest Member of a Sample," *Proceedings of the Cambridge Philosophical Society* 24, 180-190.

[9] GREENE, W. (2000). *Econometric Analysis, Fourth Edition.* Prentice Hall, Upper Saddle River.

[10] HILL, B.M. (1975). "A Simple General Approach to Inference about the Tail of a Distribution," *The Annals of Statistics*, 3, 1163-1174.

[11] JORIAN, P. (2001). *Value at Risk, Second Edition.* McGraw-Hill, New York.

[12] LONGIN, F.M. (2000). "From Value-at-Risk to Stress Testing: The Extreme Value Approach," *Journal of Banking an Finance* 24, 1097-1130.

[13] MCNEIL, A.J. (1998). "On Extremes and Crashes," *RISK*, January, page 99.

[14] MCNEIL, A.J. (1998). "Calculating Quantile Risk Measures for Financial Returns using Extreme Value Theory," unpublished manuscript, Department Mathematik, ETH Zentrum.

[15] MCNEIL, A.J. (1999). "Extreme Value Theory for Risk Managers," in *Internal Modelling and CAD II,* published by RISK Books, 93-113.

[16] MCNEIL, A.J. AND R. FREY (2000). "Estimation of Tail-Related Risk Measures for Heteroskedastic Financial Time Series: An Extreme Value Approach," *Journal of Empirical Finance* 7, 271-300.

[17] MCNEIL A.J. AND T. SALADIN (2000). "Developing Scenarios for Future Extreme Losses Using the POT Method," in *Extremes and Integrated Risk Management* , edited by Embrechts PME, published by RISK books, London.

[18] TSAY, R.S. (2001). *Analysis of Financial Time Series,* John Wiley & Sons, New York.

6
Time Series Regression Modeling

6.1 Introduction

Time series regression techniques are widely used in the analysis of financial data and for estimating and testing models for asset prices and returns like the capital asset pricing model and the arbitrage pricing model. They are used to uncover and exploit predictive relationships between financial variables. For example, the predictability of asset returns using valuation ratios like dividend/price, earnings/price and book/market is usually established using time series regression techniques, and the resulting regression models are used to forecast future returns. Time series regression techniques are also used for testing the informational efficiency of financial markets. Market efficiency often implies that certain financial variables should not be predictable based on observable information, and time series regression techniques may be used to verify efficiency implications.

Regression modeling with financial time series requires some care because the time series properties of the data can influence the properties of standard regression estimates and inference methods. In general, standard regression techniques are appropriate for the analysis of $I(0)$/stationary data. For example, asset returns are often treated as stationary and ergodic, and standard regression techniques are then used to estimate models involving asset returns. For nonstationary trending data like asset prices, however, standard regression techniques may or may not be appropriate depending on the nature of the trend. This chapter discusses regression modeling techniques appropriate for $I(0)$/stationary and introduces and illustrates the use of various S+FinMetrics functions designed for time series regression analysis.

The rest of the chapter is organized as follows: Section 6.2 gives an overview of the linear time series regression model and covers estimation, goodness of fit, inference and residual diagnostics. Section 6.3 introduces the S+FinMetrics function OLS that extends the S-PLUS linear model function lm to handle general time series regression and illustrates the use of OLS through examples. Section 6.4 reviews dynamic regression models involving distributed lags of the dependent and explanatory variables and gives examples of how OLS may be used analyze these models. Section 6.5 discusses heteroskedasticity and autocorrelation consistent coefficient covariance matrices and their use in constructing robust standard errors for estimated regression coefficients. Section 6.6 ends the chapter with a discussion of recursive regression techniques for assessing the parameter stability of time series regression models.

In this chapter, the technical details of time series regression are kept to a minimum. Excellent treatments of time series regression models from an econometric perspective are given in Hamilton (1994) and Hayashi (2000). Many applications of time series regression to financial data can be found in Mills (1999).

6.2   Time Series Regression Model

Consider the *linear time series regression model*

$$y_t = \beta_0 + \beta_1 x_{1t} + \cdots + \beta_k x_{kt} + \varepsilon_t = \mathbf{x}_t'\boldsymbol{\beta} + \varepsilon_t, \ t = 1, \ldots, T \qquad (6.1)$$

where $\mathbf{x}_t = (1, x_{1t}, \ldots, x_{kt})'$ is a $(k+1) \times 1$ vector of explanatory variables, $\boldsymbol{\beta} = (\beta_0, \beta_1, \ldots, \beta_k)'$ is a $(k+1) \times 1$ vector of coefficients, and ε_t is a random error term. In matrix form the model is expressed as

$$\mathbf{y} = \mathbf{X}\boldsymbol{\beta} + \boldsymbol{\varepsilon} \qquad (6.2)$$

where $\mathbf{y}$ and $\boldsymbol{\varepsilon}$ are $(T \times 1)$ vectors and $\mathbf{X}$ is a $(T \times (k+1))$ matrix.

The standard assumptions of the time series regression model are (e.g. Hayashi (2000), chapters 1 and 2):

- the linear model (6.1) is correctly specified.

- $\{y_t, \mathbf{x}_t\}$ is jointly stationary and ergodic.

- the regressors $\mathbf{x}_t$ are *predetermined*: $E[x_{is}\varepsilon_t] = 0$ for all $s \leq t$ and $i = 1, \ldots, k$.

- $E[\mathbf{x}_t\mathbf{x}_t'] = \boldsymbol{\Sigma}_{XX}$ is of full rank $k + 1$.

- $\{\mathbf{x}_t \varepsilon_t\}$ is an uncorrelated process with finite $(k+1) \times (k+1)$ covariance matrix $E[\varepsilon_t^2 \mathbf{x}_t \mathbf{x}_t'] = \mathbf{S} = \sigma^2 \boldsymbol{\Sigma}_{XX}$.

The second assumption rules out trending regressors, the third rules out endogenous regressors but allows lagged dependent variables, the fourth avoids redundant regressors or exact multicolinearity, and the fifth implies that the error term is a serially uncorrelated process with constant unconditional variance σ^2. In the time series regression model, the regressors $\mathbf{x}_t$ are random and the error term ε_t is not assumed to be normally distributed.

6.2.1 Least Squares Estimation

Ordinary least squares (OLS) estimation is based on minimizing the sum of squared residuals

$$SSR(\boldsymbol{\beta}) = \sum_{t=1}^{T} (y_t - \mathbf{x}_t' \boldsymbol{\beta})^2 = \sum_{t=1}^{T} \varepsilon_t^2$$

and produces the fitted model

$$y_t = \mathbf{x}_t' \hat{\boldsymbol{\beta}} + \hat{\varepsilon}_t, \ t = 1, \ldots, T$$

where $\hat{\boldsymbol{\beta}} = (\mathbf{X}'\mathbf{X})^{-1}\mathbf{X}'\mathbf{y}$ and $\hat{\varepsilon}_t = y_t - \hat{y}_t = y_t - \mathbf{x}_t'\hat{\boldsymbol{\beta}}$. The error variance is estimated as $\hat{\sigma}^2 = \hat{\varepsilon}'\hat{\varepsilon}/(T - k - 1)$.

Under the assumptions described above, the OLS estimates $\hat{\boldsymbol{\beta}}$ are consistent and asymptotically normally distributed. A consistent estimate of the asymptotic variance of $\hat{\boldsymbol{\beta}}$, $avar(\hat{\boldsymbol{\beta}})$, is given by[1]

$$\widehat{avar}(\hat{\boldsymbol{\beta}}) = \hat{\sigma}^2 (\mathbf{X}'\mathbf{X})^{-1} \tag{6.3}$$

Estimated standard errors for $\hat{\beta}_i$ $(i = 0, ..., k)$, denoted $\widehat{SE}(\hat{\beta}_i)$, are given by the square root of the diagonal elements of (6.3).

6.2.2 Goodness of Fit

Goodness of fit is summarized by the R^2 of the regression

$$R^2 = 1 - \frac{\hat{\varepsilon}'\hat{\varepsilon}}{(\mathbf{y} - \bar{y}\mathbf{1})'(\mathbf{y} - \bar{y}\mathbf{1})}$$

---

[1] The following convention is used throughout this book. A consistent and asymptotically normal estimator $\hat{\boldsymbol{\beta}}$ satisfies $\sqrt{T}(\hat{\boldsymbol{\beta}} - \boldsymbol{\beta}) \overset{d}{\to} N(0, \mathbf{V})$ where $\overset{d}{\to}$ denotes convergence in distribution. Call $\mathbf{V}$ the asymptotic variance of $\sqrt{T}(\hat{\boldsymbol{\beta}} - \boldsymbol{\beta})$ and $T^{-1}\mathbf{V}$ the asymptotic variance of $\hat{\boldsymbol{\beta}}$. Use the notation $\hat{\boldsymbol{\beta}} \overset{A}{\sim} N(\boldsymbol{\beta}, T^{-1}\mathbf{V})$ to denote the asymptotic approximating distribution of $\hat{\boldsymbol{\beta}}$ and $\widehat{avar}(\hat{\boldsymbol{\beta}})$ to denote the asymptotic variance $T^{-1}\mathbf{V}$.

where $\bar{y}$ is the sample mean of y_t and $\mathbf{1}$ is a $(T \times 1)$ vector of 1's. R^2 measures the percentage of the variability of y_t that is explained by the regressors, $\mathbf{x}_t$. The usual R^2 has the undesirable feature of never decreasing as more variables are added to the regression, even if the extra variables are irrelevant. To remedy this, the R^2 statistic may be adjusted for degrees of freedom giving

$$R_a^2 = 1 - \frac{\hat{\varepsilon}'\hat{\varepsilon}/(T-k)}{(\mathbf{y} - \bar{y}\mathbf{1})'(\mathbf{y} - \bar{y}\mathbf{1})/(T-1)} = \frac{\hat{\sigma}^2}{\widehat{var}(y_t)}$$

The *adjusted* R^2, R_a^2, may decrease with the addition of variables with low explanatory power. If fact, it can be shown, e.g. Greene (2000) pg. 240, that R_a^2 will fall (rise) when a variable is deleted from the regression if the absolute value of the t-statistic associated with this variable is greater (less) than 1.

6.2.3 Hypothesis Testing

The simple null hypothesis

$$H_0 : \beta_i = \beta_i^0$$

is tested using the *t-ratio*

$$t = \frac{\hat{\beta}_i - \beta_i^0}{\widehat{SE}(\hat{\beta}_i)} \tag{6.4}$$

which is asymptotically distributed $N(0,1)$ under the null. With the additional assumption of *iid* Gaussian errors and regressors independent of the errors for all t, $\hat{\boldsymbol{\beta}}$ is normally distributed in finite samples and the t-ratio is distributed Student-t with $T - k - 1$ degrees of freedom.

Linear hypotheses of the form

$$H_0 : \mathbf{R}\boldsymbol{\beta} = \mathbf{r} \tag{6.5}$$

where $\mathbf{R}$ is a fixed $q \times (k+1)$ matrix of rank q and $\mathbf{r}$ is a fixed $q \times 1$ vector are tested using the *Wald statistic*

$$Wald = (\mathbf{R}\hat{\boldsymbol{\beta}} - \mathbf{r})' \left[\mathbf{R}\widehat{avar}(\hat{\boldsymbol{\beta}})\mathbf{R}' \right]^{-1} (\mathbf{R}\hat{\boldsymbol{\beta}} - \mathbf{r}) \tag{6.6}$$

Under the null, the Wald statistic is asymptotically distributed $\chi^2(q)$. Under the additional assumption of *iid* Gaussian errors and regressors independent of the errors for all t, $Wald/q$ is distributed $F(q, T - k - 1)$ in finite samples.

The statistical significance of all of the regressors excluding the constant is captured by the F-statistic

$$F = \frac{R^2/k}{(1 - R^2)/(T-k-1)}$$

which is distributed $F(k, T - k - 1)$ under the null hypothesis that all slope coefficients are zero and the errors are *iid* Gaussian.

6.2.4   Residual Diagnostics

In the time series regression models, several residual diagnostic statistics are usually reported along with the regression results. These diagnostics are used to evaluate the validity of some of the underlying assumptions of the model and to serve as warning flags for possible misspecification. The most common diagnostic statistics are based on tests for normality and serial correlation in the residuals of (6.1).

The most common diagnostic for serial correlation based on the estimated residuals $\hat{\varepsilon}_t$ is the *Durbin-Watson statistic*

$$DW = \frac{\sum_{t=2}^{T}(\hat{\varepsilon}_t - \hat{\varepsilon}_{t-1})^2}{\sum_{t=1}^{T}\hat{\varepsilon}_t^2}.$$

It is easy to show that $DW \approx 2(1 - \hat{\rho})$, where $\hat{\rho}$ is the estimated correlation between and $\hat{\varepsilon}_t$ and $\hat{\varepsilon}_{t-1}$. Hence, values of DW range between 0 and 4. Values of DW around 2 indicate no serial correlation in the errors, values less than 2 suggest positive serial correlation, and values greater than 2 suggest negative serial correlation[2]. Another common diagnostic for serial correlation is the Ljung-Box modified Q statistic discussed in Chapter 3.

Although error terms in the time series regression model are not assumed to be normally distributed, severe departures from normality may cast doubt on the validity of the asymptotic approximations utilized for statistical inference especially if the sample size is small. Therefore, another diagnostic statistic commonly reported is the Jarque-Bera test for normality discussed in Chapter 3.

6.3   Time Series Regression Using the S+FinMetrics Function OLS

Ordinary least squares estimation of the time series regression model (6.1) in S-PLUS is carried out with the S+FinMetrics function OLS. OLS extends the S-PLUS linear model function lm to handle time series regression in a

---

[2] The DW statistic is an optimal test only for the special case that ε_t in (1) follows an AR(1) process and that the regressors $\mathbf{x}_t$ are fixed. Critical values for the bounding distribution of DW in this special case are provided in most econometrics textbooks. However, in practice there is often little reason to believe that ε_t follows an AR(1) process and the regressors are rarely fixed and so the DW critical values are of little practical use.

more natural way. The arguments expected by OLS are similar to those for lm:

```
> args(OLS)
function(formula, data, weights, subset, na.rm = F, method
= "qr", contrasts = NULL, start = NULL, end = NULL,...)
```

The main arguments are formula, which is an S-PLUS formula with the response variable(s) on the left hand side of the ~ character and the response variables separated by + on the right hand side[3], and data, which is "timeSeries" or data frame in which to interpret the variables named in the formula and subset arguments. The other arguments will be explained and their use will be illustrated in the examples to follow.

OLS produces an object of class "OLS" for which there are print, summary, plot and predict methods as well as extractor functions coefficients (coef), residuals (resid), fitted.values (fitted), vcov and IC. The extractor functions coef, resid and fitted are common to many S-PLUS model objects. Note that if "timeSeries" objects are used in the regression then the extracted residuals and fitted values are also "timeSeries" objects. The extractor functions vcov, which extracts $\widehat{avar}(\hat{\beta})$, and IC, which extracts information criteria, are specific to S+FinMetrics model objects and work similarly to the extractor functions vcov and AIC from the MASS library.

There are several important differences between lm and OLS. First, the argument formula is modified to accept lagged values of the dependent variable through the use of AR terms and lagged values of regressors through the use of the S+FinMetrics functions tslag and pdl. Second, subset regression for "timeSeries" data is simplified through the use of the start and end options. Third, summary output includes time series diagnostic measures and standard econometric residual diagnostic tests may be computed from OLS objects. Fourth, heteroskedasticity consistent as well as heteroskedasticity and autocorrelation consistent coefficient covariance matrices may be computed from OLS objects.

The use of OLS for time series regression with financial data is illustrated with the following examples

Example 33 *Estimating and testing the capital asset pricing model*

The famous *Capital Asset Pricing Model* (CAPM) due to Sharpe, Litner and Mosen is usually estimated using the *excess return single index model*

$$R_{it} - r_{ft} = \alpha_i + \beta_i(R_{Mt} - r_{ft}) + \varepsilon_{it}, \ i = 1,\dots,N; t = 1,\dots,T \quad (6.7)$$

where R_{it} is the return on asset i $(i = 1,\dots,N)$ between time periods $t - 1$ and t, R_{Mt} is the return on a *market index* portfolio between time

---

[3]See Chapter 1 for details on specifying formulas in S-PLUS.

periods $t-1$ and t, r_{ft} denotes the rate of return between times $t-1$ and t on a risk-free asset, and ε_{it} is a normally distributed random error such that $\varepsilon_{it} \sim GWN(0, \sigma_i^2)$. The market index portfolio is usually some well diversified portfolio like the S&P 500 index, the Wilshire 5000 index or the CRSP[4] equally or value weighted index. In practice, r_{ft} is taken as the T-bill rate to match the investment horizon associated with R_{it}. The CAPM is an equilibrium model for asset returns and, if R_{Mt} is the value-weighted portfolio of all publicly traded assets, it imposes the relationship

$$E[R_{it}] - r_{ft} = \beta_i(E[R_{Mt}] - r_{ft}).$$

In other words, the above states that the *risk premium* on asset i is equal to its beta, β_i, times the risk premium on the market portfolio. Hence, β_i is the appropriate risk measure for asset i. In the excess returns single index model, the CAPM imposes the testable restriction that $\alpha_i = 0$ for all assets.

The intuition behind the CAPM is as follows. The market index R_{Mt} captures "macro" or market-wide systematic risk factors that affect all returns in one way or another. This type of risk, also called *covariance risk, systematic risk* and *market risk*, cannot be eliminated in a well diversified portfolio. The beta of an asset captures the magnitude of this nondiversifiable risk. The random error term ε_{it} represents random "news" that arrives between time $t-1$ and t that captures "micro" or firm-specific risk factors that affect an individual asset's return that are not related to macro events. For example, ε_{it} may capture the news effects of new product discoveries or the death of a CEO. This type of risk is often called *firm specific risk, idiosyncratic risk, residual risk* or *non-market risk*. This type of risk can be eliminated in a well diversified portfolio. The CAPM says that in market equilibrium the risk premium on any asset is directly related to the magnitude of its nondiversifiable risk (beta). Diversifiable risk is not priced; i.e., diversifiable risk does not command a risk premium because it can be eliminated by holding a well diversified portfolio.

In the CAPM, the independence between R_{Mt} and ε_{it} allows the unconditional variability of an asset's return R_{it} to be decomposed into the variability due to the market index, $\beta_i^2 \sigma_M^2$, plus the variability of the firm specific component, σ_i^2. The proportion of the variance R_{it} explained by the variability in the market index is the usual regression R^2 statistic. Accordingly, $1 - R^2$ is then the proportion of the variability of R_{it} that is due to firm specific factors. One can think of R^2 as measuring the proportion of risk in asset i that cannot be diversified away when forming a portfolio and $1 - R^2$ as the proportion of risk that can be diversified away.

---

[4]CRSP refers to the Center for Research in Security Prices at the University of Chicago.

Estimating the CAPM Using the S+FinMetrics Function OLS

Consider the estimation of the CAPM regression (6.7) for Microsoft using monthly data over the ten year period January 1990 through January 2000. The S&P 500 index is used for the market proxy, and the 30 day T-bill rate is used for the risk-free rate. The S+FinMetrics "timeSeries" singleIndex.dat contains the monthly price data for Microsoft, and the S&P 500 index and the "timeSeries" rf.30day contains the monthly 30 day T-bill rate. The excess return data are created using

```
> colIds(singleIndex.dat)
[1] "MSFT"  "SP500"
> colIds(rf.30day)
[1] "RF"
> ret.ts = getReturns(singleIndex.dat, type="continuous")
> excessRet.ts = seriesMerge(ret.ts,log(1+rf.30day))
> excessRet.ts[,"MSFT"] = excessRet.ts[,"MSFT"] -
+ excessRet.ts[,"RF"]
> excessRet.ts[,"SP500"] = excessRet.ts[,"SP500"] -
+ excessRet.ts[,"RF"]
> excessRet.ts = excessRet.ts[,1:2]
```

Time plots and a scatterplot of the excess returns created by

```
> par(mfrow=c(2,1))
> plot(excessRet.ts, plot.args=list(lty=c(1,3)),
+ main="Monthly excess returns on Microsoft and S&P 500 Index")
> legend(0, -0.2, legend=c("MSFT","S&P 500"), lty=c(1,3))
> plot(seriesData(excessRet.ts[,"SP500"]),
+ seriesData(excessRet.ts[,"MSFT"]),
+ main="Scatterplot of Returns",
+ xlab="SP500", ylab="MSFT")
```

are given in Figure 6.1. The returns on Microsoft and the S&P 500 index appear stationary and ergodic and tend to move in the same direction over time with the returns on Microsoft being more volatile than the returns on the S & P 500 index. The estimate of the CAPM regression for Microsoft using OLS is:

```
> ols.fit = OLS(MSFT~SP500, data=excessRet.ts)
> class(ols.fit)
[1] "OLS"
```

OLS produces an object of class "OLS" with the following components

```
> names(ols.fit)
 [1] "R"          "coef"      "df.resid"   "fitted"
 [5] "residuals"  "assign"    "contrasts"  "ar.order"
 [9] "terms"      "call"
```

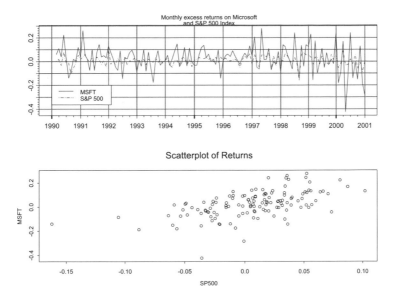

FIGURE 6.1. Monthly excess returns on Microsoft and the S&P 500 index.

The results of the OLS fit are displayed using the generic print and summary methods. The print method produces minimal output:

```
> ols.fit
Call:
OLS(formula = MSFT ~SP500, data = excessRet.ts)

Coefficients:
 (Intercept)  SP500
  0.0128      1.5259

Degrees of freedom: 131 total; 129 residual
Time period: from Feb 1990 to Dec 2000
Residual standard error: 0.09027
```

Notice that since the object specified in data is a "timeSeries", the start and end dates of the estimation sample are printed. The summary method produces the standard econometric output:

```
> summary(ols.fit)
Call:
OLS(formula = MSFT ~SP500, data = excessRet.ts)

Residuals:
```

```
     Min      1Q  Median      3Q     Max
 -0.3835 -0.0566  0.0023  0.0604  0.1991
```

Coefficients:
```
              Value Std. Error t value Pr(>|t|)
(Intercept) 0.0128 0.0080       1.6025   0.1115
      SP500 1.5259 0.1998       7.6354   0.0000
```

Regression Diagnostics:

```
          R-Squared 0.3113
 Adjusted R-Squared 0.3059
 Durbin-Watson Stat 2.1171
```

Residual Diagnostics:
```
                  Stat P-Value
 Jarque-Bera 41.6842  0.0000
   Ljung-Box 11.9213  0.9417
```

Residual standard error: 0.09027 on 129 degrees of freedom
Time period: from Feb 1990 to Dec 2000
F-statistic: 58.3 on 1 and 129 degrees of freedom, the
p-value is 4.433e-012

The estimated value for β for Microsoft is 1.526 with an estimated standard error $\widehat{SE}(\hat{\beta}) = 0.200$. An approximate 95% confidence interval for β is $\hat{\beta} \pm 2 \cdot \widehat{SE}(\hat{\beta}) = [1.126, 1.926]$, and so Microsoft is judged to be riskier than the S&P 500 index. The estimated value of α is 0.013 with an estimated standard error of $\widehat{SE}(\hat{\alpha}) = 0.008$. An approximate 95% confidence interval for α is $\hat{\alpha} \pm 2 \cdot \widehat{SE}(\hat{\alpha}) = [-0.003, 0.029]$. Since $\alpha = 0$ is in the confidence interval the CAPM restriction hold for Microsoft. The percentage of nondiversifiable (market specific) risk is $R^2 = 0.31$ and the percentage of diversifiable (firm specific) risk is $1 - R^2 = 0.69$. The estimated magnitude of diversifiable risk is $\hat{\sigma} = 0.090$ or 9% per month. Notice that the Jarque-Bera statistic indicates that the residuals from the CAPM regression are not normally distributed. The DW and Ljung-Box statistics, however, indicate that the residuals are serially uncorrelated (at least at the first lag).

The extractor functions for an "OLS" object are used to extract the vectors of estimated coefficients $\hat{\beta}$, fitted values $\hat{y}$, residuals $\hat{\varepsilon}$ and asymptotic variance matrix $\widehat{avar}(\hat{\beta})$:

```
> coef(ols.fit)
 (Intercept) SP500
     0.01281 1.526
```

```
> fitted(ols.fit)[1:3]
 Positions        1
 Feb 1990    0.01711
 Mar 1990    0.03965
 Apr 1990   -0.03927

> resid(ols.fit)[1:3]
 Positions        1
 Feb 1990   0.04258
 Mar 1990   0.06868
 Apr 1990   0.07870

> vcov(ols.fit)
             (Intercept)        SP500
(Intercept)   0.00006393 -0.0002618
      SP500 -0.00026181  0.0399383
```

Notice that to use the extractor functions residuals and fitted.values one only has to type resid and fitted. Since the data used for estimation is a "timeSeries" object, the extracted residuals and fitted values are also "timeSeries" objects.

To illustrate the use of the extractor functions, the t-statistics for testing the null hypothesis that the intercept is zero and the slope is unity are

```
> (coef(ols.fit)-c(0,1))/sqrt(diag(vcov(ols.fit)))
 (Intercept) SP500
       1.603 2.631
```

and summary statistics for the residuals using the S+FinMetrics function summaryStats are

```
> summaryStats(residuals(ols.fit))

Sample Quantiles:
     min         1Q    median       3Q      max
 -0.3835 -0.05661 0.002342 0.06037 0.1991

Sample Moments:
        mean       std skewness kurtosis
 -7.204e-018 0.08993  -0.7712    5.293

Number of Observations:   131
```

Testing Linear Restrictions

The CAPM regression (6.7) in matrix form is (6.2) with $\mathbf{x}_t = (1, R_{Mt} - r_{ft})'$ and $\boldsymbol{\beta} = (\alpha, \beta)'$. Consider testing the joint null hypothesis $H_0 : \alpha = 0$ and

$\beta = 1$. This hypothesis imposes two linear restrictions on the parameter vector $\boldsymbol{\beta} = (\alpha, \beta)'$ that may be written in the form (6.5) with

$$\mathbf{R} = \begin{pmatrix} 1 & 0 \\ 0 & 1 \end{pmatrix}, \ \mathbf{r} = \begin{pmatrix} 0 \\ 1 \end{pmatrix}$$

The Wald statistic (6.6) may be computed directly as

```
> Rmat = diag(2)
> rvec = c(0,1)
> bhat = coef(ols.fit)
> avarRbhat = Rmat%*%vcov(ols.fit)%*%t(Rmat)
> wald.stat =
+ t(Rmat%*%bhat-rvec)%*%solve(avarRbhat)%*%(Rmat%*%bhat-rvec)
> as.numeric(wald.stat)
[1] 11.17
> p.value = 1 - pchisq(wald.stat,2)
> p.value
[1] 0.003745
```

The small p-value suggests that null $H_0 : \alpha = 0$ and $\beta = 1$ should be rejected at any reasonable significance level. The F-statistic version of the Wald statistic based on normal errors is

```
> F.stat = wald.stat/2
> p.value = 1 - pf(F.stat,2,ols.fit$df.resid)
> p.value
[1] 0.004708
```

and also suggests rejection of the null hypothesis.

The F-statistic version of the Wald statistic for general linear restrictions of the form (6.5) may be conveniently computed using the S+FinMetrics function waldTest. For example,

```
> waldTest(ols.fit,Intercept==0,SP500==1)

Wald Test of Coefficients:

 Null Hypothesis: constraints are true
  Test Statistic: 5.587
Dist. under Null: F with ( 2 , 129 ) degrees of freedom
          P-value: 0.004708
```

produces the F-statistic version of the Wald test for the null hypothesis $H_0 : \alpha = 0$ and $\beta = 1$. Notice how the restrictions under the null being tested are reflected in the call to waldTest. More complicated linear restrictions like $H_0 : \alpha + 2\beta = 2$ are also easily handled

```
> waldTest(ols.fit,Intercept-2*SP500==2)
```

```
Wald Test of Coefficients:

 Null Hypothesis: constraints are true
  Test Statistic: 157.8
Dist. under Null: F with ( 1 , 129 ) degrees of freedom
          P-value: 0
```

Likelihood ratio (LR) statistics for testing linear hypotheses may also be computed with relative ease since the OLS estimates are the maximum likelihood estimates assuming the errors have a normal distribution. The log-likelihood value of the OLS fit assuming normal errors may be extracted using the S+FinMetrics function IC. For example, the log-likelihood for the unrestricted CAPM fit is

```
> IC(ols.fit, "loglike")
[1] 130.2
```

Consider testing the CAPM restriction $H_0 : \alpha = 0$ using a LR statistic. The restricted OLS fit, imposing $\alpha = 0$, is computed using

```
> ols.fit2 = OLS(MSFT~SP500-1,data=excessRet.ts)
```

The LR statistic is then computed as

```
> LR = -2*(IC(ols.fit2,"loglike")-IC(ols.fit,"loglike"))
> LR
[1] 2.571
> 1 - pchisq(LR,1)
[1] 0.1089
```

Given the p-value of 0.109, the CAPM restriction is not rejected at the 10% significance level.

Graphical Diagnostics

Graphical summaries of the OLS fit are produced with the generic plot function. By default, plot produces a menu of plot choices:

```
> plot(ols.fit)
Make a plot selection (or 0 to exit):

1: plot: all
2: plot: response vs fitted values
3: plot: response and fitted values
4: plot: normal QQ-plot of residuals
5: plot: residuals
6: plot: standardized residuals
7: plot: residual histogram
8: plot: residual ACF
```

Plot Function	Description
xygPlot	Trellis xyplot with grid and strip.text options
rvfPplot	Trellis response vs. fitted plot with grid and strip.text options
rafPlot	Trellis plot of response and fitted values
histPlot	Trellis density estimate with strip.text options
qqPlot	Trellis QQ-plot with grid and strip.text options
residPlot	Trellis plot of residuals
acfPlot	Trellis ACF plot

TABLE 6.1. S+FinMetrics utility Trellis plotting functions

```
9: plot: residual PACF
10: plot: residual^2 ACF
11: plot: residual^2 PACF
Selection:
```

The plot choices are different from those available for "lm" objects and focus on time series diagnostics. All plots are generated using Trellis graphics[5]. Table 6.1 summarizes the utility plot functions used to create the various OLS plots. See the help files for more information about the plot functions. Figures 6.2 and 6.3 illustrate plot choices 3 (response and fitted) and 8 (residual ACF). From the response and fitted plot, it is clear that the return on the S&P 500 index is a weak predictor of return on Microsoft. The residual ACF plot indicates that the residuals do not appear to be autocorrelated, which supports the results from the residual diagnostics reported using summary.

Individual plots can be created directly, bypassing the plot menu, using the which.plot option of plot.OLS. For example, the following command creates a normal qq-plot of the residuals:

```
> plot(ols.fit,which.plot=3)
```

Notice that number used for the qq-plot specified by which.plot is one less than the value specified in the menu. The qq-plot may also be created by calling the Trellis utility plot function qqPlot directly:

```
> qqPlot(resid(ols.fit), strip.text="ols.fit",
+ xlab="Quantile of Standard Normal",
+ ylab="Residuals",main="Normal QQ Plot")
```

Residual Diagnostics

The residual diagnostics reported by summary may be computed directly from an "OLS" object. The normalTest and autocorTest functions in

---

[5] Unfortunately, the Trellis plots cannot be easily combined into multipanel plots.

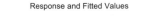

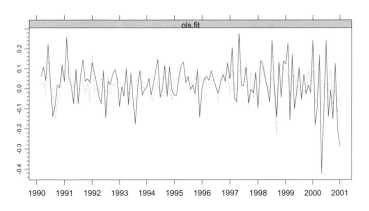

FIGURE 6.2. Response and fitted values from the OLS fit to the CAPM regression for Microsoft.

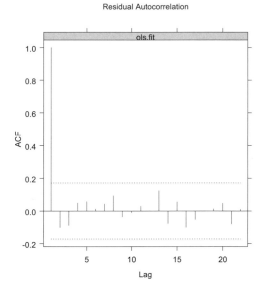

FIGURE 6.3. Residual ACF plot from the OLS fit to the CAPM regression for Microsoft.

S+FinMetrics may be used to compute test statistics for normality and autocorrelation from the residuals of an OLS fit. For example, to compute the Jarque-Bera normality test and the Ljung-Box test from the residuals of the CAPM regression use

```
> normalTest(ols.fit,method="jb")
```

Test for Normality: Jarque-Bera

Null Hypothesis: data is normally distributed

Test Statistics:

Test Stat 41.68
  p.value   0.00

Dist. under Null: chi-square with 2 degrees of freedom
    Total Observ.: 131

```
> autocorTest(ols.fit,method="lb")
```

Test for Autocorrelation: Ljung-Box

Null Hypothesis: no autocorrelation

Test Statistics:

Test Stat 11.9213
  p.value   0.9417

Dist. under Null: chi-square with 21 degrees of freedom
    Total Observ.: 131

Subset Regression

The estimated β for Microsoft uses all of the data over the 11 year period from January 1990 to December 2000. It is generally thought that β does not stay constant over such a long time period. To estimate β using only the most recent five years of data the start option of OLS may be utilized

```
> OLS(MSFT~SP500, data=excessRet.ts,
+ start="Jan 1996", in.format="%m %Y")

Call:
OLS(formula = MSFT ~SP500, data = excessRet.ts, start =
"Jan 1996", in.format = "%m %Y")
```

```
Coefficients:
 (Intercept)   SP500
   0.0035     1.7828
```

```
Degrees of freedom: 60 total; 58 residual
Time period: from Jan 1996 to Dec 2000
Residual standard error: 0.1053
```

Notice that date string passed to **start** uses the same display format as the "timeDate" objects in the **positions** slot of **excessRet.ts**, and that this format is specified directly using **in.format="%m %Y"**. Estimation over general sub-periods follows by specifying both the start date and the end date of the sub-period in the call to **OLS**.

Regression estimates may be computed over general subsets by using the optional argument **subset** to specify which observations should be used in the fit. Subsets can be specified using a logical vector (which is replicated to have length equal to the number of observations), a numeric vector indicating the observation numbers to be included, or a character vector of the observation names that should be included. For example, to estimate the CAPM only for the observations for which the excess return on the S&P 500 is positive, use

```
> OLS(MSFT~SP500, data=excessRet.ts, subset=(SP500>=0))
```

```
Call:
OLS(formula = MSFT ~SP500, data = excessRet.ts, subset = (
SP500 >= 0))
```

```
Coefficients:
 (Intercept)   SP500
   0.0231     1.3685
```

```
Degrees of freedom: 80 total; 78 residual
Residual standard error: 0.08341
```

Regression with Dummy Variables

In the analysis of asset returns, it is often noticed that excess returns are higher in January than in any other month. To investigate this claim, a dummy variable is created which equals 1 if the month is January and 0 otherwise:

```
> is.Jan = (months(positions(excessRet.ts))=="Jan")
> Jan.dum = timeSeries(pos=positions(excessRet.ts),
+ data=as.integer(is.Jan))
```

Next, the January dummy variable is added to the time series of excess returns:

```
> newdat.ts = seriesMerge(excessRet.ts,Jan.dum)
> colIds(newdat.ts)[3] = "Jan.dum"
```

The CAPM regression allowing for a different intercept in January is

```
> summary(OLS(MSFT~SP500+Jan.dum, data=newdat.ts))
```

```
Call:
OLS(formula = MSFT ~SP500 + Jan.dum, data = newdat.ts)

Residuals:
    Min    1Q Median     3Q    Max
 -0.3804 -0.0532 0.0065 0.0604 0.2032

Coefficients:
             Value Std. Error t value Pr(>|t|)
(Intercept) 0.0090 0.0082      1.0953  0.2755
      SP500 1.5085 0.1986      7.5972  0.0000
    Jan.dum 0.0513 0.0295      1.7371  0.0848

Regression Diagnostics:

        R-Squared 0.3271
Adjusted R-Squared 0.3166
Durbin-Watson Stat 2.0814

Residual Diagnostics:
               Stat P-Value
Jarque-Bera 43.4357  0.0000
  Ljung-Box 12.1376  0.9358

Residual standard error: 0.08958 on 128 degrees of freedom
Time period: from Feb 1990 to Dec 2000
F-statistic: 31.11 on 2 and 128 degrees of freedom, the
p-value is 9.725e-012
```

The coefficient on the January dummy is positive and significant at the 9% level indicating that excess returns are slightly higher in January than in other months. To allow for a different intercept and slope in the regression, use

```
> summary(OLS(MSFT~SP500*Jan.dum, data=newdat.ts))
```

```
Call:
```

```
OLS(formula = MSFT ~SP500 * Jan.dum, data = tmp1.ts)
```

Residuals:
```
     Min      1Q   Median      3Q      Max
 -0.3836 -0.0513   0.0047  0.0586   0.2043
```

Coefficients:
```
                Value Std. Error t value Pr(>|t|)
  (Intercept) 0.0095 0.0082       1.1607  0.2479
        SP500 1.4307 0.2017       7.0917  0.0000
      Jan.dum 0.0297 0.0317       0.9361  0.3510
SP500:Jan.dum 1.6424 0.9275       1.7707  0.0790
```

Regression Diagnostics:

```
         R-Squared 0.3433
Adjusted R-Squared 0.3278
Durbin-Watson Stat 2.0722
```

Residual Diagnostics:
```
                Stat P-Value
Jarque-Bera 51.4890  0.0000
  Ljung-Box 12.7332  0.9177
```

Residual standard error: 0.08884 on 127 degrees of freedom
Time period: from Feb 1990 to Dec 2000
F-statistic: 22.13 on 3 and 127 degrees of freedom, the
p-value is 1.355e-011

Notice that the formula uses the short-hand notation A*B = A+B+A:B. Interestingly, when both the slope and intercept are allowed to be different in January only the slope is significantly higher.

Predictions

Predictions or forecasts from an OLS fit may be computed using the generic predict function. For example, consider computing forecasts of the excess return on Microsoft conditional on specified values for the S&P 500 excess return based on the CAPM fit. The excess returns on the S&P 500 for the conditioinal forecasts are

```
> sp500.new = data.frame(c(-0.2,0,2))
> colIds(sp500.new) = "SP500"
```

These new data values must be in a data frame with the same name as the variable containing the S&P 500 data in excessRet.ts. The forecasts are computed using

```
> ols.pred = predict(ols.fit,n.predict=3,newdata=sp500.new)
> class(ols.pred)
[1] "forecast"
> ols.pred
```

Predicted Values:

```
[1] -0.2924  0.0128  3.0646
```

The result of `predict` is an object of class "`forecast`" for which there are `print`, `summary` and `plot` methods. The `print` method shows just the forecasts. The `summary` method shows the forecasts and forecast standard errors (ignoring parameter estimation error)

```
> summary(ols.pred)
```

Predicted Values with Standard Errors:

```
              prediction std.err
1-step-ahead  -0.2924       0.0903
2-step-ahead   0.0128       0.0903
3-step-ahead   3.0646       0.0903
```

To view the forecasts and standard error band along with the historical data use

```
> plot(ols.pred, xold=excessRet.ts[,1], n.old=5, width=2)
```

The argument `xold` contains the historical data for the response variable, `n.old` determines how many historical observations to plot along with the forecasts and `width` specifies the multiplier for the forecast standard errors in the construction of the error bands. The created plot is illustrated in Figure 6.4.

6.4 Dynamic Regression

Often the time series regression model (6.1) contains lagged variables as regressors to capture dynamic effects. The general dynamic time series regression model contains lagged values of the response variable y_t and lagged values of the exogenous stationary regressors $x_{1t}, \ldots, x_{kt}$:

$$y_t = \alpha + \sum_{j=1}^{p} \phi_j y_{t-j} + \sum_{j=0}^{q_1} \beta_{1j} x_{1t-j} + \cdots + \sum_{j=0}^{q_k} \beta_{kj} x_{kt-j} + \varepsilon_t \qquad (6.8)$$

where the error term ε_t is assumed to be $WN(0, \sigma^2)$. The model (6.8) is called an *autoregressive distributed lag* (ADL) model and generalizes an AR(p) by including exogenous stationary regressors.

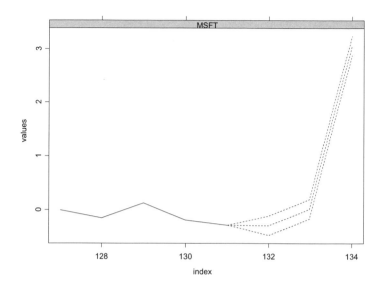

FIGURE 6.4. Conditional forecasts for the excess returns on Microsoft from the CAPM regression.

The main issues associated with the analysis and interpretation of the ADL model (6.8) can be illustrated using the following simple ADL model with a single exogenous variable x_t:

$$y_t = \alpha + \phi y_{t-1} + \beta_0 x_t + \beta_1 x_{t-1} + \varepsilon_t \qquad (6.9)$$

Since x_t is assumed to be stationary, and $\varepsilon_t \sim WN(0, \sigma^2)$, y_t behaves like an AR(1) process

$$y_t = \alpha + \phi y_{t-1} + w_t$$

where $w_t = \beta_0 x_t + \beta_1 x_{t-1} + \varepsilon_t$ is a composite error term. Therefore, the ADL model (6.9) is stationary provided $|\phi| < 1$. Given that y_t is stationary it has an infinite order moving average representation (impulse response function) in terms of the composite errors w_t

$$
\begin{aligned}
y_t &= \mu + \sum_{j=0}^{\infty} \psi_j w_{t-j} \\
&= \mu + w_t + \psi_1 w_{t-1} + \psi_2 w_{t-2} + \cdots
\end{aligned}
$$

where $\mu = 1/(1 - \phi)$ and $\psi_j = \phi^j$. Substituting $w_t = \beta_0 x_t + \beta_1 x_{t-1} + \varepsilon_t$ and $\psi_j = \phi^j$ into the above moving average representation gives

$$
\begin{aligned}
y_t &= \mu + (\beta_0 x_t + \beta_1 x_{t-1} + \varepsilon_t) + \phi(\beta_0 x_{t-1} + \beta_1 x_{t-2} + \varepsilon_{t-1}) \\
&\quad + \phi^2(\beta_0 x_{t-2} + \beta_1 x_{t-3} + \varepsilon_{t-2}) + \cdots \\
&= \mu + \beta_0 x_t + (\beta_1 + \phi\beta_0)x_{t-1} + \phi(\beta_1 + \phi\beta_0)x_{t-2} + \cdots \quad (6.10)\\
&\quad + \phi^{j-1}(\beta_1 + \phi\beta_0)x_{t-j} + \cdots + \varepsilon_t + \phi\varepsilon_{t-1} + \phi^2\varepsilon_{t-2} + \cdots
\end{aligned}
$$

Using (6.10), the interpretation of the coefficients in (6.9) becomes clearer. For example, the *immediate impact multiplier* is the impact of a change in x_t on y_t is

$$
\frac{\partial y_t}{\partial x_t} = \beta_0
$$

The first lag multiplier is the impact of a change in x_{t-1} on y_t

$$
\frac{\partial y_t}{\partial x_{t-1}} = \beta_1 + \phi\beta_0
$$

which incorporates a feedback effect $\phi\beta_0$ due to the lagged response variable in (6.9). The second lag multiplier is

$$
\frac{\partial y_t}{\partial x_{t-2}} = \phi(\beta_1 + \phi\beta_0)
$$

and is smaller in absolute value than the first lag multiplier since $|\phi| < 1$. In general, the kth lag multiplier is

$$
\frac{\partial y_t}{\partial x_{t-k}} = \phi^{k-1}(\beta_1 + \phi\beta_0)
$$

Notice that as $k \to \infty$, $\frac{\partial y_t}{\partial x_{t-k}} \to 0$ so that eventually the effect of a change in x_t on y_t dies out. The *long-run effect* of a change in x_t on y_t is defined as the cumulative sum of all the lag impact multipliers

$$
\begin{aligned}
\text{long-run effect} &= \frac{\partial y_t}{\partial x_t} + \frac{\partial y_t}{\partial x_{t-1}} + \frac{\partial y_t}{\partial x_{t-2}} + \cdots \\
&= \sum_{k=0}^{\infty} \phi^k(\beta_0 + \beta_1) \\
&= \frac{\beta_0 + \beta_1}{1 - \phi}
\end{aligned}
$$

The parameter ϕ on y_{t-1} determines the *speed of adjustment* between the immediate impact of x_t on y_t and the long-run impact. If $\phi = 0$, then the long-run impact is reached in one time period since $\frac{\partial y_t}{\partial x_{t-k}} = 0$ for $k > 1$. In contrast, if $\phi \approx 1$, then the long-run impact takes many periods. A parameter often reported is the *half-life* of the adjustment; that is, the lag at which one half of the adjustment to the long-run impact has been reached. In the simple ADL (6.9), it can be shown that the half-life is equal to $\ln(2)/\ln(\phi)$.

For the general ADL model (6.8), stationarity of y_t requires that all x_{it} be stationary and that the roots of the characteristic polynomial $\phi(z) = 1 - \phi_1 z - \cdots - \phi_p z^p = 0$ have modulus greater than one. The k immediate impact multipliers are the coefficients $\beta_{10}, \ldots, \beta_{k0}$ and the k long-run multipliers are

$$\frac{\sum_{j=0}^{q_2} \beta_{1j}}{1 - \phi_1 - \cdots - \phi_p}, \ldots, \frac{\sum_{j=0}^{q_k} \beta_{kj}}{1 - \phi_1 - \cdots - \phi_p}$$

The speed of adjustment to the long-run impacts is determined by the sum of the coefficients on the lagged responses $\phi_1 + \cdots + \phi_p$.

Example 34 *Estimating a simple dynamic CAPM regression for Microsoft*

Consider estimating a simple dynamic version of the CAPM regression

$$R_{it} - r_{ft} = \alpha + \phi(R_{it} - r_{ft}) + \beta_0(R_{Mt} - r_{ft}) + \beta_1(R_{Mt-1} - r_{ft-1}) + \varepsilon_{it}$$

using the monthly excess return data for Microsoft and the S&P 500 index. The "short-run beta" for Microsoft is β_0 and the "long-run beta" is $(\beta_0 + \beta_1)/(1 - \phi)$. The dynamic CAPM estimated using OLS is

```
> adl.fit = OLS(MSFT~SP500+ar(1)+tslag(SP500),
+ data=excessRet.ts)
```

In the regression formula, the lagged dependent variable (MSFT) is specified using the ar(1) term, and the lagged explanatory variable (SP500) is created using the S+FinMetrics function tslag. The dynamic regression results are

```
> summary(adl.fit)

Call:
OLS(formula = MSFT ~SP500 + ar(1) + tslag(SP500), data =
excessRet.ts)

Residuals:
     Min      1Q  Median      3Q     Max
 -0.3659 -0.0514  0.0059  0.0577  0.1957

Coefficients:
             Value Std. Error t value Pr(>|t|)
(Intercept) 0.0156  0.0083     1.8850  0.0617
      SP500 1.5021  0.2017     7.4474  0.0000
```

```
tslag(SP500) -0.0308  0.2453     -0.1257  0.9001
       lag1 -0.1107  0.0921      -1.2021  0.2316
```

Regression Diagnostics:

```
         R-Squared 0.3248
Adjusted R-Squared 0.3087
Durbin-Watson Stat 1.9132
```

Residual Diagnostics:
```
                Stat P-Value
Jarque-Bera 41.5581  0.0000
  Ljung-Box 10.5031  0.9716
```

```
Residual standard error: 0.0904 on 126 degrees of freedom
Time period: from Mar 1990 to Dec 2000
F-statistic: 20.2 on 3 and 126 degrees of freedom, the
p-value is 9.384e-011
```

The least squares estimates of dynamic CAPM parameters are $\hat{\alpha} = 0.016$, $\hat{\phi} = -0.111$, $\hat{\beta}_0 = 1.502$ and $\hat{\beta}_1 = -0.031$. The estimated "short-run beta" for Microsoft is 1.502 and the estimated "long-run beta" is[6]

```
> bhat = coef(adl.fit)
> lr.beta = (bhat[2]+bhat[3])/(1-bhat[4])
> lr.beta
 SP500
 1.325
```

Notice that the "long-run beta" is smaller than the "short-run beta". However, since the standard errors on the dynamic terms $\hat{\phi}$ and $\hat{\beta}_1$ are large relative to the estimated values, the data do not support the dynamic CAPM model.

6.4.1 Distributed Lags and Polynomial Distributed Lags

A special case of the general ADL model (6.8) is the distributed lag model

$$y_t = \alpha + \sum_{j=0}^{q} \beta_j x_{t-j} + \varepsilon_t \tag{6.11}$$

For simplicity, the model is shown with one exogenous variable x. The extension to multiple exogenous variables is straightforward. Given the

---

[6] Since the "long-run beta" is a nonlinear function of the least squares estimates, estimated standard errors for the "long-run beta" may be computed using the so-called "delta method". See Greene (2000) page 118.

results of the previous section, β_j is interpreted as the jth lag multiplier, and the long-run impact on y of a change in x is $\sum_{j=1}^{q} \beta_j$.

Determining the Lag Length

In many applications, the lag length q needs to be long to adequately capture the dynamics in the data. To determine the lag length, all models with $q \leq q_{max}$ are fit and the preferred model minimizes some model selection criterion like the Akaike (AIC) or Schwarz (BIC). For the distributed lag model, the AIC and BIC have the form

$$AIC(q) \quad = \quad \ln(\tilde{\sigma}^2(q)) + \frac{2}{T}q$$
$$BIC(q) \quad = \quad \ln(\tilde{\sigma}^2(q)) + \frac{\ln T}{T}q$$

where $\tilde{\sigma}^2(q)$ is the least squares estimate of σ^2 without a degrees of freedom correction. For objects of class "OLS", S+FinMetrics provides the extractor function IC to compute the AIC or BIC information criteria.

If the exogenous variable x_t is highly persistent, then lagged values $x_t, x_{t-1}, \ldots, x_{t-q}$ may be highly correlated and problems associated with near multicollinearity may occur in (6.11)[7]. In this case, the S+FinMetrics function collinearTest may be used to diagnose the extent of near multicollinearity in the data. The function collinearTest computes either the *condition number* for $\mathbf{X'X}$ or the *variance inflation statistics* associated with each variable.

Example 35 *Distributed lag model for U.S. real GDP growth*

The S+FinMetrics "timeSeries" policy.dat contains monthly data on U.S. real GDP and the Federal Funds rate. Consider estimating a distributed lag model with $q = 12$ for the growth rate in real GDP using the Federal Funds rate as an exogenous variable over the period January 1990 to March 1998:

```
> dl.fit = OLS(diff(log(GDP))~FFR+tslag(FFR,1:12),data=
+ policy.dat, start="Jan 1990",in.format="%m %Y",na.rm=T)
```

The AIC and BIC information criteria may be extracted using

```
> IC(dl.fit,type="AIC")
[1] -1271
> IC(dl.fit,type="BIC")
[1] -1235
```

---

[7]See Greene (2000) pages 255-259 for a discussion of the problems associated with near multicollinearity.

The model may be re-fit with different values of q and the preferred model is the one which produces the smallest value of the chosen information criterion.

The condition number and variance inflation statistics from the least square fit are

```
> collinearTest(dl.fit, method="cn")
[1] 311.2
> collinearTest(dl.fit, method="vif")
   FFR tslag(FFR, 1:12)lag1 tslag(FFR, 1:12)lag2
 111.8                278.7                    293

 tslag(FFR, 1:12)lag3 tslag(FFR, 1:12)lag4
               304.9                331.8

 tslag(FFR, 1:12)lag5 tslag(FFR, 1:12)lag6
               344.9                370.5

 tslag(FFR, 1:12)lag7 tslag(FFR, 1:12)lag8
                 369                  390

 tslag(FFR, 1:12)lag9 tslag(FFR, 1:12)lag10
               389.5                  410

 tslag(FFR, 1:12)lag11 tslag(FFR, 1:12)lag12
                424.5                  162.6
```

The large condition number and variance inflation statistics indicate that high correlation among the regressors is a potential problem.

6.4.2 Polynomial Distributed Lag Models

The unrestricted distributed lag model (6.11) may produce unsatisfactory results due to high correlation among the lagged variables. If the sample size is small and the lag length q is large then these problems are exacerbated. In these cases, one may want to restrict the behavior of the lag coefficients β_j in (6.11). One popular way to do this is to use the polynomial distributed lag (PDL) model[8]. The PDL model specifies that β_j follows a polynomial

$$\beta_j = \alpha_0 + \alpha_1 j + \alpha_2 j^2 + \cdots + \alpha_d j^d \tag{6.12}$$

for $j = 1, \ldots, q > d$. Usually, the order of the polynomial, d, is small. Whereas the general distributed lag model (6.11) has q lag parameters the PDL model has only $d + 1$ lag parameters. To see this more explicitly,

---

[8] The PDL model is also known as the Almon lag model.

the distributed lag model with p lags under the restriction (6.12) may be re-written as the linear regression with d variables

$$y_t = \alpha + \alpha_0 z_{0t} + \alpha_1 z_{1t} + \cdots + \alpha_d z_{dt} + \varepsilon_t \qquad (6.13)$$

where

$$z_{jt} = \sum_{i=1}^{q} i^j x_{t-i} \qquad (6.14)$$

Example 36 *PDL model for U.S. real GDP growth*

To estimate a PDL model for U.S. GDP growth using the Federal Funds rate with $d = 2$ and $q = 12$ use

```
> pdl.fit = OLS(diff(log(GDP))~pdl(FFR,d=2,q=12),
+ data=policy.dat, start="Jan 1990",
+ in.format="%m %Y", na.rm=T)
> pdl.fit

Call:
OLS(formula = diff(log(GDP)) ~pdl(FFR, d = 2, q = 12),
data = policy.dat, na.rm = T, start = "Jan 1990",
in.format = "%m %Y")

Coefficients:
 (Intercept) pdl(FFR, d = 2, q = 12)FFR.PDL0
  0.0006       -0.0070

 pdl(FFR, d = 2, q = 12)FFR.PDL1
  0.0031

 pdl(FFR, d = 2, q = 12)FFR.PDL2
 -0.0002

Degrees of freedom: 97 total; 93 residual
dropped 1 cases due to missing observations.
Time period: from Feb 1990 to Feb 1998
Residual standard error: 0.0003371
```

The S+FinMetrics function pdl used in the formula compute the regressors (6.14) for the PDL regression (6.13).

6.5   Heteroskedasticity and Autocorrelation Consistent Covariance Matrix Estimation

In the time series regression model, the efficiency of the least squares estimates and the validity of the usual formulas for the estimated coefficient standard errors and test statistics rely on validity of the underlying assumptions of the model outlined in the beginning of Section 6.2. In empirical applications using financial time series, it is often the case that the error terms ε_t have non constant variance (heteroskedasticity) as well as autocorrelation. As long as the regressors $\mathbf{x}_t$ are uncorrelated with the errors ε_t the least squares estimates of $\boldsymbol{\beta}$ will generally still be consistent and asymptotically normally distributed. However, they will not be efficient and the usual formula (6.3) for computing $\widehat{avar}(\hat{\boldsymbol{\beta}})$ will not be correct. As a result, any inference procedures based on (6.3) will also be incorrect. If the form of heteroskedasticity and autocorrelation is known, then efficient estimates may be computed using a *generalized least squares* procedure[9]. If the form of heteroskedasticity and autocorrelation is not known, it is possible to estimate $\widehat{avar}(\hat{\boldsymbol{\beta}})$ consistently so that valid standard errors and test statistics may be obtained. This section describes the construction of heteroskedasticity and autocorrelation consistent estimates of $\widehat{avar}(\hat{\boldsymbol{\beta}})$. First, the heteroskedasticity consistent estimate of $\widehat{avar}(\hat{\boldsymbol{\beta}})$ due to Eicker (1967) and White (1980) is discussed and then the heteroskedasticity and autocorrelation consistent estimate of $\widehat{avar}(\hat{\boldsymbol{\beta}})$ due to Newey and West (1987) is covered.

6.5.1   The Eicker-White Heteroskedasticity Consistent (HC) Covariance Matrix Estimate

A usual assumption of the time series regression model is that the errors ε_t are *conditionally homoskedastic*; i.e., $E[\varepsilon_t^2|\mathbf{X}] = \sigma^2 > 0$. In many situations it may be more appropriate to assume that the variance of ε_t is a function of $\mathbf{x}_t$ so that ε_t is *conditionally heteroskedastic*: $E[\varepsilon_t^2|\mathbf{x}_t] = \sigma^2 f(\mathbf{x}_t) > 0$. Formally, suppose the assumptions of the time series regression model hold but that $E[\varepsilon_t^2\mathbf{x}_t\mathbf{x}_t'] = \mathbf{S} \neq \sigma^2\boldsymbol{\Sigma}_{XX}$. This latter assumption allows the regression errors to be *conditionally heteroskedastic* and dependent on $\mathbf{x}_t$; i.e., $E[\varepsilon_t^2|\mathbf{x}_t] = \sigma^2 f(\mathbf{x}_t)$. In this case, it can be shown that the asymptotic variance matrix of the OLS estimate, $\hat{\boldsymbol{\beta}}$, is

$$avar(\hat{\boldsymbol{\beta}}) = T^{-1}\boldsymbol{\Sigma}_{XX}^{-1}\mathbf{S}\boldsymbol{\Sigma}_{XX}^{-1}. \qquad (6.15)$$

The above *generalized* OLS asymptotic variance matrix will not be equal to the usual OLS asymptotic matrix $\sigma^2\boldsymbol{\Sigma}_{XX}^{-1}$, and the usual estimate $\widehat{avar}(\hat{\boldsymbol{\beta}}) =$

---

[9] The S-PLUS function gls may be used to compute generalized least squares estimates using a variety of models for heteroskedasticity and autocorrelation.

$\hat{\sigma}^2(\mathbf{X'X})^{-1}$ will not be correct. Hence, in the presence of heteroskedasticity the usual OLS t-statistics, standard errors, Wald statistics cannot be trusted.

If the values of $f(\mathbf{x}_t)$ are known, then the *generalized* or *weighted least squares* (GLS) estimator

$$\hat{\beta}_{GLS} = (\mathbf{X'V(X)}^{-1}\mathbf{X})^{-1}\mathbf{X'V(X)y},$$

where $\mathbf{V(X)}$ is a $(T \times T)$ diagonal matrix with $f(\mathbf{x}_t)$ along the diagonal, is efficient.

In most circumstances $f(\mathbf{x}_t)$ is not known so that the efficient GLS estimator cannot be computed. If the OLS estimator is to be used, then a consistent estimate for the generalized OLS covariance matrix is needed for proper inference. A heteroskedasticity consistent (HC) estimate of $avar(\hat{\beta})$ due to Eicker (1967) and White (1980) is

$$\widehat{avar}_{HC}(\hat{\beta}) = (\mathbf{X'X})^{-1}\hat{\mathbf{S}}_{HC}(\mathbf{X'X})^{-1} \tag{6.16}$$

where

$$\hat{\mathbf{S}}_{HC} = \frac{1}{T-k}\sum_{t=1}^{T}\hat{\varepsilon}_t^2\mathbf{x}_t\mathbf{x}_t' \tag{6.17}$$

and $\hat{\varepsilon}_t$ is the OLS residual at time t.

The square root of the diagonal elements of $\widehat{avar}_{HC}(\hat{\beta})$ gives the Eicker-White *heteroskedasticity consistent standard errors* (HCSEs) for the least squares estimates of β_i. These are denoted $\widehat{SE}_{HC}(\hat{\beta}_i)$. Heteroskedasticity robust t-statistics and Wald statistics are computed in the usual way using (6.4) and (6.6) but with $\widehat{avar}_{HC}(\hat{\beta})$ and $\widehat{SE}_{HC}(\hat{\beta}_i)$ replacing $\widehat{avar}(\hat{\beta})$ and $\widehat{SE}(\hat{\beta}_i)$, respectively.

Example 37 *Heteroskedasticity robust inference for the CAPM*

Once a model has been fit using OLS, the HC estimate (6.16) may be extracted using vcov and $\widehat{SE}_{HC}(\hat{\beta}_i)$ may be computed using summary by specifying the optional argument correction="white" as follows

```
> ols.fit = OLS(MSFT~SP500, data=excessRet.ts)
> avar.HC = vcov(ols.fit, correction="white")
> summary(ols.fit, correction="white")

Call:
OLS(formula = MSFT ~SP500, data = excessRet.ts)

Residuals:
     Min       1Q  Median       3Q      Max
 -0.3835  -0.0566  0.0023   0.0604   0.1991
```

```
Coefficients:
            Value Std. Error  t value  Pr(>|t|)
(Intercept) 0.0128 0.0080      1.5937   0.1134
     SP500  1.5259 0.1920      7.9463   0.0000
```

```
Regression Diagnostics:

        R-Squared 0.3113
Adjusted R-Squared 0.3059
Durbin-Watson Stat 2.1171
```

```
Residual Diagnostics:
               Stat P-Value
Jarque-Bera 41.6842  0.0000
  Ljung-Box 11.9213  0.9417
```

```
Residual standard error: 0.09027 on 129 degrees of freedom
Time period: from Feb 1990 to Dec 2000
F-statistic: 58.3 on 1 and 129 degrees of freedom, the
p-value is 4.433e-012
```

Here, the HCSE values $\widehat{SE}_{HC}(\hat{\beta}_i)$ are almost identical to the usual OLS values $\widehat{SE}(\hat{\beta}_i)$ which suggests that the errors are not heteroskedastic.

6.5.2 Testing for Heteroskedasticity

If the error terms in the time series regression model are heteroskedastic, then the OLS estimates are consistent but not efficient and the usual formula (6.3) for computing $\widehat{avar}(\hat{\beta})$ is incorrect. As shown in the previous section, $\widehat{avar}_{HC}(\hat{\beta})$ given by (6.16) provides a consistent estimate of the generalized asymptotic variance (6.15). If the errors are not heteroskedastic, however, (6.15) is still consistent, but the usual formula (6.3) will generally give smaller standard errors and more powerful tests. Therefore, it is of interest to test for the presence of heteroskedasticity. If the errors are heteroskedastic and depend on some function of exogenous variables, then tests for heteroskedasticity may help determine which variables affect the error variance and how they might affect the variance. Finally, if the time series regression model is misspecified, e.g. some important variables have been omitted or the parameters are not constant over time, then often the errors will appear to be heteroskedastic. Hence, the presence of heteroskedasticity may also signal inadequacy of the estimated model. In this section, two common tests for heteroskedasticity are introduced. The first is Breusch and Pagan's (1979) LM test for heteroskedasticity caused by specified exogenous variables and the second is White's (1980) general test for unspecified heteroskedasticity.

Breusch-Pagan Test for Specific Heteroskedasticity

Suppose it is suspected that the variance of ε_t in (6.1) is functionally related to some known $(p \times 1)$ vector of exogenous variables $\mathbf{z}_t$, whose first element is unity, via the relation

$$E[\varepsilon_t | \mathbf{x}_t] = f(\mathbf{z}_t' \boldsymbol{\alpha})$$

where $f(\cdot)$ is an unknown positive function. Let $\hat{\varepsilon}_t$ denote the least squares residual from (6.1), and consider the *auxiliary regression*

$$\frac{\hat{\varepsilon}_t^2}{\bar{\sigma}^2} = \mathbf{z}_t' \boldsymbol{\alpha} + \text{ error} \tag{6.18}$$

where $\bar{\sigma}^2 = T^{-1} \sum_{t=1}^{T} \hat{\varepsilon}_t^2$. Since the first element of $\mathbf{z}_t$ is unity, the null hypothesis of homoskedasticity, $E[\varepsilon_t^2 | \mathbf{x}_t] = \sigma^2$, implies that all of the elements of $\boldsymbol{\alpha}$ except the first are equal to zero. Under the homoskedasticity null, Breusch and Pagan (1979) show that the test statistic

$$\frac{1}{2} RSS_{aux} \overset{A}{\sim} \chi^2(p-1)$$

where RSS_{aux} is the residual sum of squares from the auxiliary regression (6.18).

The Breusch-Pagan LM test is based on the assumption that the error terms are normally distributed. Koenker and Basset (1982) suggest a modification of the Breusch-Pagan LM test that is robust to non-normal errors and generally has more power than the Breusch-Pagan test when the errors are non-normal.

White's Test for General Heteroskedasticity

Suppose ε_t is generally heteroskedastic such that $E[\varepsilon_t^2 \mathbf{x}_t \mathbf{x}_t'] = \mathbf{S}$, where $\mathbf{S}$ is a $(k \times k)$ matrix. Recall, if ε_t is homoskedastic then $\mathbf{S} = \sigma^2 \boldsymbol{\Sigma}_{XX}$. Now, under general heteroskedasticity $\hat{\mathbf{S}}_{HC}$ in (6.17) is a consistent estimate of $\mathbf{S}$ and $\hat{\sigma}^2 (\mathbf{X}'\mathbf{X})^{-1}$ is a consistent estimate of $\sigma^2 \boldsymbol{\Sigma}_{XX}$ and $\mathbf{S} \neq \sigma^2 \boldsymbol{\Sigma}_{XX}$. However, under the null hypothesis of homoskedasticity, the difference between $\hat{\mathbf{S}}_{HC}$ and $\hat{\sigma}^2 (\mathbf{X}'\mathbf{X})^{-1}$ should go to zero as the sample size gets larger. White (1980) utilized this result to develop a very simple test for general heteroskedasticity. To describe this test, let $\boldsymbol{\psi}_t$ denote the $(m \times 1)$ vector of unique and nonconstant elements of the $(k \times k)$ matrix $\mathbf{x}_t \mathbf{x}_t'$. Let $\hat{\varepsilon}_t$ denote the least squares residual from (6.1) and form the auxiliary regression

$$\hat{\varepsilon}_t = \boldsymbol{\psi}_t' \boldsymbol{\gamma} + \text{ error} \tag{6.19}$$

Under the null hypothesis of homoskedasticity, White (1980) showed that

$$T \cdot R_{aux}^2 \sim \chi^2(m)$$

where R_{aux}^2 is the R^2 from the auxiliary regression (6.19).

Testing for Heteroskedasticity Using the S+FinMetrics Function
heteroTest

Once a model has been fit using OLS (or lm), the Breusch-Pagan, Koenker-Basset and White tests for heteroskedasticity may be computed using the S+FinMetrics function heteroTest. For example, consider the simple CAPM regression for Microsoft

```
> ols.fit = OLS(MSFT~SP500, data=excessRet.ts)
```

To apply the Breusch-Pagan LM test, a set of variables $\mathbf{z}_t$ for which $var(\varepsilon_t)$ is related must be identified. For illustrative purposes let $\mathbf{z}_t = (R_{Mt} - r_{ft}, (R_{Mt} - r_{ft})^2)'$. The LM may then be computed using

```
> z1 = as.matrix(seriesData(excessRet.ts[,"SP500"]))
> zmat = cbind(z1,z1^2)
> heteroTest(ols.fit, method="lm", regressors=zmat)
```

Test for Heteroskedasticity: Breusch-Pagan LM Test

```
 Null Hypothesis: data is homoskedastic
  Test Statistic: 0.152
Dist. under Null: chi-square with 2 degrees of freedom
         P-value: 0.9268
```

Coefficients:
```
  Intercept    SP500 SP500^2
      1.041   -1.320 -20.407
```

Degrees of freedom: 131 total; 128 residual
Residual standard error: 2.095

Notice that the regressors specified for the LM test must be in the form of a matrix. The high p-value of the test clearly signals that the null of homoskedasticity should not be rejected against the alternative that $var(\varepsilon_t)$ depends on $\mathbf{z}_t$. To compute the Koenker-Basset robust LM test, set the optional argument robust=T in the call to heteroTest.

The application of White's test for heteroskedasticity is more straightforward since $var(\varepsilon_t)$ is assumed to be functionally related to the variables used in the OLS fit:

```
> heteroTest(ols.fit, method="white")
```

Test for Heteroskedasticity: White General Test

```
 Null Hypothesis: data is homoskedastic
  Test Statistic: 0.152
Dist. under Null: chi-square with 2 degrees of freedom
```

```
P-value: 0.9268

Coefficients:
 Intercept   SP500 SP500^2
  0.0084    -0.0106 -0.1638

Degrees of freedom: 131 total; 128 residual
Residual standard error: 0.01681
```

Notice that in this particular example the LM test and White's test are identical.

6.5.3   The Newey-West Heteroskedasticity and Autocorrelation Consistent (HAC) Covariance Matrix Estimate

In some applications of time series regression, ε_t in (6.1) may be both conditionally heteroskedastic and serially correlated. In this case, the error covariance matrix $E[\varepsilon\varepsilon'|\mathbf{X}]$ is non-diagonal. Under certain assumptions about the nature of the error heteroskedasticity and serial correlation a consistent estimate of the generalized OLS covariance matrix can be computed. The most popular heteroskedasticity and autocorrelation consistent (HAC) covariance matrix estimate, due to Newey and West (1987), has the form

$$\widehat{avar}_{HAC}(\hat{\boldsymbol{\beta}}) = (\mathbf{X}'\mathbf{X})^{-1}\hat{\mathbf{S}}_{HAC}(\mathbf{X}'\mathbf{X})^{-1} \qquad (6.20)$$

where

$$\hat{\mathbf{S}}_{HAC} = \sum_{t=1}^{T}\hat{\varepsilon}_t^2\mathbf{x}_t\mathbf{x}_t' + \sum_{l=1}^{q}w_l\sum_{t=l+1}^{T}(\mathbf{x}_t\hat{\varepsilon}_t\hat{\varepsilon}_{t-l}\mathbf{x}_{t-l}' + \mathbf{x}_{t-l}\hat{\varepsilon}_{t-l}\hat{\varepsilon}_t\mathbf{x}_t') \qquad (6.21)$$

is a nonparametric long-run variance estimate, and w_l is the *Bartlett weight function*

$$w_l = 1 - \frac{l}{q+1}.$$

The Bartlett weight function, w_l, depends on a truncation parameter q that must grow with the sample size in order for the estimate to be consistent. Newey and West suggest choosing q to be the integer part of $4(T/100)^{2/9}$. In some cases, a *rectangular* weight function

$$w_l = \begin{cases} 1, & \text{for } l \leq q \\ 0, & \text{for } l > q \end{cases}$$

is used if it is known that autocovariances in (6.21) cut off at lag q. The square root of the diagonal elements of the HAC estimate (6.21) gives the *heteroskedasticity and autocorrelation consistent standard errors* (HAC-SEs) for the least squares estimates of β_i. These are denoted $\widehat{SE}_{HAC}(\hat{\beta}_i)$.

Heteroskedasticity robust t-statistics and Wald statistics are computed in the usual way using (6.4) and (6.6) but with $\widehat{avar}_{HAC}(\hat{\boldsymbol{\beta}})$ and $\widehat{SE}_{HAC}(\hat{\beta}_i)$ replacing $\widehat{avar}(\hat{\boldsymbol{\beta}})$ and $\widehat{SE}(\hat{\beta}_i)$, respectively.

Example 38 *Long horizon regressions of stock returns on dividend-price ratio*

There has been much interest recently in whether long-term stock returns are predictable by valuation ratios like dividend-to-price and earnings-to-price. See chapter 7 in Campbell, Lo and MacKinlay (1997) and chapter 20 in Cochrane (2001) for reviews of this literature. Predictability is investigated by regressing future multiperiod stock returns on current values of valuation ratios. To illustrate, let r_t denote the continuously compounded real annual total return on an asset in year t and and let $d_t - p_t$ denote the log dividend price ratio. The typical long-horizon regression has the form

$$r_{t+1} + \cdots + r_{t+K} = \alpha_K + \beta_K(d_t - p_t) + \varepsilon_{t+K}, \ t = 1, \ldots, T \qquad (6.22)$$

where $r_{t+1} + \cdots + r_{t+K}$ is the continuously compounded future K-year real total return. The dividend-price ratio predicts future returns if $\beta_K \neq 0$ at some horizon. Since the sampling frequency of the data is annual and the return horizon of the dependent variable is K years the dependent variable and error term in (6.22) will behave like an $MA(K-1)$ process. This serial correlation invalidates the usual formula for computing the estimated standard error of the least squares estimate of β_K. The HACSE, $\widehat{SE}_{HAC}(\hat{\beta}_K)$, however, will provide a consistent estimate.

The long-horizon regression (6.22) with $K = 10$ years is estimated using the annual stock price and dividend data on the S&P 500 composite index in the S+FinMetrics "timeSeries" object shiller.annual. The relevant data are constructed as

```
> colIds(shiller.annual)
[1] "price"          "dividend"      "earnings"
[4] "cpi"            "real.price"    "real.dividend"
[7] "real.earnings" "pe.10"
> # compute log of real data
> ln.p = log(shiller.annual[,"real.price"])
> colIds(ln.p) = "ln.p"
> ln.d = log(shiller.annual[,"real.dividend"])
> colIds(ln.d) = "ln.d"
> ln.dpratio = ln.d - ln.p
> colIds(ln.dpratio) = "ln.dpratio"
> # compute cc real total returns
> ln.r = diff(ln.p) + log(1+exp(ln.dpratio[-1,]))
> colIds(ln.r) = "ln.r"
> # create 10-year cc total returns
```

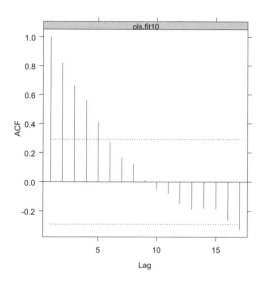

FIGURE 6.5. Residual ACF from regression of ten year real returns on dividend-price ratio.

```
> ln.r.10 = aggregateSeries(ln.r,moving=10,FUN=sum)
> colIds(ln.r.10) = "ln.r.10"
> stockdiv.ts = seriesMerge(ln.p,ln.d,ln.dpratio,
+ ln.r,ln.r.10,pos="union")
```

The continuously compounded real total return is computed as

$$r_t = \ln\left(\frac{P_t + D_t - P_{t-1}}{P_{t-1}}\right) = $$
$$\ln(P_t/P_{t-1}) + \ln(1 + \exp(\ln(D_t) - \ln(P_t)))$$

where P_t is the real price and D_t is the real dividend. Notice how the S-PLUS function aggregateSeries is used to compute the 10 year continuously compounded real total returns.

The long-horizon regression (6.22) using10 year real total return returns over the postwar period 1947 - 1995 is computed using

```
> ols.fit10 = OLS(ln.r.10~tslag(ln.dpratio),data=stockdiv.ts,
+ start="1947", end="1995", in.format="%Y", na.rm=T)
```

Figure 6.5 shows the residual ACF. There is clearly serial correlation in the residuals. The HACSEs are computed using summary with the optional argument correction="nw". By default, the Newey-West HAC covariance matrix is computed using a Bartlett kernel with automatic lag truncation

$q = 4(T/100)^{2/9}$. In the present context, the serial correlation is known to be of the form of an MA(9) process. Therefore, it is more appropriate to compute the Newey-West HAC covariance using a rectangular weight function with $q = 9$ which is accomplished by specifying bandwidth=9 and window="rectangular" in the call to summary:

```
> summary(ols.fit10, correction="nw", bandwidth=9,
+ window="rectangular")

Call:
OLS(formula = ln.r.10 ~tslag(ln.dpratio), data =
stockdiv.ts, na.rm = T, start = "1947", end =
"1995", in.format = "%Y")

Residuals:
     Min      1Q  Median      3Q     Max
 -0.6564 -0.2952  0.0030  0.1799  0.9997

Coefficients:
                    Value Std. Error t value Pr(>|t|)
       (Intercept) 5.7414 0.9633      5.9600  0.0000
tslag(ln.dpratio) 1.5604 0.3273      4.7668  0.0000

Regression Diagnostics:

        R-Squared 0.5012
Adjusted R-Squared 0.4896
Durbin-Watson Stat 0.2554

Residual Diagnostics:
                 Stat  P-Value
Jarque-Bera    1.7104   0.4252
  Ljung-Box 105.9256   0.0000

Residual standard error: 0.4116 on 43 degrees of freedom
Time period: from 1947 to 1991
F-statistic: 43.21 on 1 and 43 degrees of freedom, the
p-value is 5.359e-008
```

Notice the low DW statistic and the large value of the Ljung-Box statistic indicating serial correlation in the residuals. The regression results with the corrected standard errors indicate that future 10 year real total returns are highly predictable and positively related to the current dividend-price ratio. The predictability coefficient is $\hat{\beta}_{10} = 1.560$ with $\widehat{SE}_{HAC}(\hat{\beta}_{10}) = 0.416$ and $R^2 = 0.501$.

6.6   Recursive Least Squares Estimation

The time series regression model (6.1) assumes that the parameters of the model, $\boldsymbol{\beta}$, are constant over the estimation sample. A simple and intuitive way to investigate parameter constancy is to compute recursive estimates of $\boldsymbol{\beta}$; that is, to estimate the model

$$y_t = \boldsymbol{\beta}_t' \mathbf{x}_t + \varepsilon_t \tag{6.23}$$

by least squares recursively for $t = k+1, \ldots, T$ giving $T-k$ *recursive least squares* (RLS) estimates $(\hat{\boldsymbol{\beta}}_{k+1}, \ldots, \hat{\boldsymbol{\beta}}_T)$. If $\boldsymbol{\beta}$ is really constant then the recursive estimates $\hat{\boldsymbol{\beta}}_t$ should quickly settle down near a common value. If some of the elements in $\boldsymbol{\beta}$ are not constant then the corresponding RLS estimates should show instability. Hence, a simple graphical technique for uncovering parameter instability is to plot the RLS estimates $\hat{\beta}_{it}$ ($i = 0, \ldots, k$) and look for instability in the plots.

An alternative approach to investigate parameter instability is to compute estimates of the model's parameters over a fixed rolling window of a given length. Such rolling analysis is discussed in Chapter 9.

6.6.1   CUSUM and CUSUMSQ Tests for Parameter Stability

Brown, Durbin and Evans (1976) utilize the RLS estimates of (6.23) and propose two simple tests for parameter instability. These tests, know as the *CUSUM* and *CUSUMSQ* tests, are based on the standardized 1-step ahead recursive residuals

$$\hat{w}_t = \frac{\hat{\varepsilon}_t}{\hat{f}_t} = \frac{y_t - \hat{\boldsymbol{\beta}}_{t-1}' \mathbf{x}_t}{\hat{f}_t}$$

where $\hat{f}_t^2$ is an estimate of the recursive error variance

$$f_t^2 = \sigma^2 \left[1 + \mathbf{x}_t' (\mathbf{X}_{t-1}' \mathbf{X}_{t-1})^{-1} \mathbf{x}_t \right]$$

and $\mathbf{X}_t$ is the $(t \times k)$ matrix of observations on $\mathbf{x}_s$ using data from $s = 1, \ldots, t$.

The CUSUM test is based on the cumulated sum of the standardized recursive residuals

$$CUSUM_t = \sum_{j=k+1}^{t} \frac{\hat{w}_j}{\hat{\sigma}_w}$$

where $\hat{\sigma}_w$ is the sample standard deviation of $\hat{w}_j$. Under the null hypothesis that $\boldsymbol{\beta}$ in (6.1) is constant, $CUSUM_t$ has mean zero and variance that is proportional to $t-k-1$. Brown, Durbin and Evans (1976) show that approximate 95% confidence bands for $CUSUM_t$ are given by the two lines which connect the points $(k, \pm 0.948\sqrt{T-k-1})$ and $(T, \pm 0.948 \cdot 3\sqrt{T-k-1})$. If $CUSUM_t$ wanders outside of these bands, then the null of parameter stability may be rejected.

The CUSUMSQ test is based on the cumulative sum of the *squared* standardized recursive residuals and is given by

$$CUSUMSQ_t = \frac{\sum_{j=k+1}^{t} \hat{w}_j^2}{\sum_{j=k+1}^{T} \hat{w}_j^2}.$$

The distribution of $CUSUMSQ_t$ under the null of parameter stability is given in Brown, Durbin and Evans (1976) where it is shown that 95% confidence bands for $CUSUMSQ_t$ have the form $c \pm t/\sqrt{T-k-1}$. As with the $CUSUM_t$ statistic, if $CUSUMSQ_t$ wanders outside the confidence bands, then the null of parameter stability may be rejected.

6.6.2 Computing Recursive Least Squares Estimates Using the S+FinMetrics Function RLS

Efficient RLS estimation of the time series regression model (6.1) may be performed using the S+FinMetrics function RLS. The calling syntax of RLS is exactly the same as that of OLS so that any model that may be estimated using OLS may also be estimated using RLS. For example, to compute the RLS estimates of the CAPM regression for Microsoft use

```
> rls.fit = RLS(MSFT~SP500, data=excessRet.ts)
> class(rls.fit)
[1] "RLS"
```

RLS produces an object of class "RLS" for which there are coef, plot, print and residuals methods. The print method give a basic description of the RLS fit

```
> rls.fit

Call:
RLS(formula = MSFT ~SP500, data = excessRet.ts)
Time period: from Feb 1990 to Dec 2000

Coefficients:
          (Intercept)  SP500
     mean 0.0284       1.2975
std. dev. 0.0121       0.1531

Recursive Residuals Summary:
    mean std. dev.
 -0.0157  0.0893
```

Recursive Coefficients

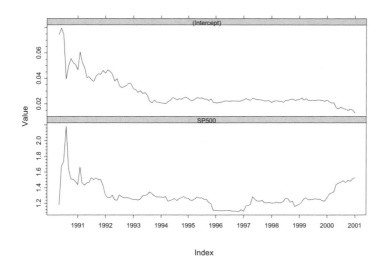

FIGURE 6.6. RLS coefficient estimates from the CAPM regression for Microsoft.

CUSUM of Residuals

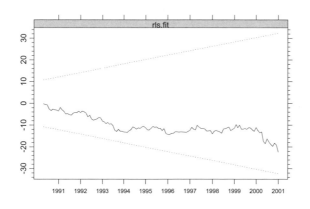

FIGURE 6.7. CUSUM of residuals from the CAPM regression for Microsoft.

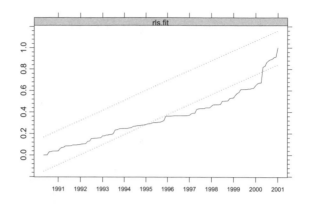

FIGURE 6.8. CUSUMSQ of residuals from CAPM regression for Microsoft.

The recursive intercept and slope estimates do not seem to vary too much. The `plot` method allows one to see the recursive coefficients, CUSUM and CUSUMSQ residuals

```
> plot(rls.fit)

Make a plot selection (or 0 to exit):

1: plot: All
2: plot: Coefficient Estimates
3: plot: CUSUM of Residuals
4: plot: CUSUM of Squared Residuals
Selection:
```

Figures 6.6, 6.7 and 6.8 show the plots from options 2, 3 and 4. The RLS estimates of α and β settle down in the middle of the sample but then the estimates of α decrease and the estimates of β increase. The $CUSUM_t$ statistics stay within the 95% confidence bands but the $CUSUMSQ_t$ statistics wander outside the bands. Hence, there is some evidence for instability in the CAPM coefficients.

6.7   References

[1] BREUSCH, T. AND A. PAGAN (1979). "A Simple Test for Heteroscedasticity and Random Coefficient Variation," *Econometrica*, 47, 1287-1294.

[2] BROWN, R., J. DURBIN AND J. EVANS (1976). "Techniques for Testing the Constancy of Regression Relationships over Time," *Journal of the Royal Statistical Society, Series B*, 37, 149-172.

[3] CAMPBELL, J. A. LO, C. MACKINLAY (1997). *The Econometrics of Financial Markets.* Princeton University Press, New Jersey.

[4] COCHRANE, J. (2001). *Asset Pricing.* Princeton University Press, New Jersey.

[5] EICKER, F. (1967). "Limit Theorems for Regression with Unequal and Dependent Errors," in L. LeCam and J. Neyman, eds., *Proceedings of the 5th Berkeley Symposium on Mathematical Statistics and Probability.* University of California Press, Berkeley.

[6] GREENE, W. (2000). *Econometric Analysis, Fifth Edition.* Prentice Hall, New Jersey.

[7] HAMILTON, J.D. (1994). *Time Series Analysis.* Princeton University Press, New Jersey.

[8] HAYASHI, F. (2000). *Econometrics.* Princeton University Press, New Jersey.

[9] JARQUE, C.M. AND A.K. BERA (1981). "Efficients Tests for Normality, Homoskedasticity and Serial Dependence of Regression Residuals," *Economics Letters*, 6, 255-259.

[10] KOENKER, R. AND G. BASSETT (1982). "Robust Tests for Heteroscedasticity Based on Regression Quantiles," *Econometrica*, 50, 43-61.

[11] MILLS, T.C. (1999). *The Econometrics Modelling of Financial Time Series, Second Edition.* Cambridge University Press, Cambridge.

[12] NEWEY, W.K. AND K.D. WEST (1987). "A Simple Positive Semidefinite Heteroskedasticity and Autocorrelation Consistent Covariance Matrix," *Econometrica*, 55, 703-708.

[13] WHITE, H. (1980). "A Heteroskedasticity Consistent Covariance Matrix Estimator and a Direct Test for Heteroskedasticity," *Econometrica*, 48, 817-838.

7
Univariate GARCH Modeling

7.1 Introduction

Previous chapters have concentrated on modeling and predicting the conditional mean, or the first order moment, of a univariate time series, and are rarely concerned with the conditional variance, or the second order moment, of a time series. However, it is well known that in financial markets large changes tend to be followed by large changes, and small changes tend to be followed by small changes. In other words, the financial markets are sometimes more volatile, and sometimes less active.

The volatile behavior in financial markets is usually referred to as the "volatility". Volatility has become a very important concept in different areas in financial theory and practice, such as risk management, portfolio selection, derivative pricing, etc. In statistical terms, volatility is usually measured by variance, or standard deviation. This chapter introduces the class of univariate *generalized autoregressive conditional heteroskedasticity* (GARCH) models developed by Engle (1982), Bollerslev (1986), Nelson (1991), and others, which are capable of modeling time varying volatility and capturing many of the stylized facts of the volatility behavior usually observed in financial time series. It will show how to formulate, estimate, evaluate and predict from various types of GARCH models, such as EGARCH, TGARCH, PGARCH, etc.

The outline of the chapter follows. Section 7.2 shows how to test for ARCH effects in a time series, then section 7.3 introduces the basic GARCH model and its properties. GARCH model estimation and diagnostics using

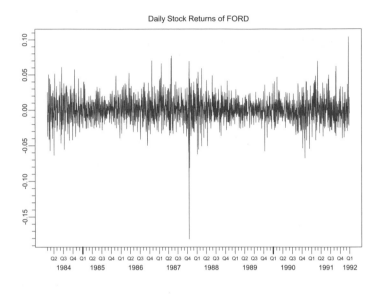

FIGURE 7.1. Daily Ford stock returns: `ford.s`.

the S+FinMetrics family of GARCH functions are illustrated in section 7.4. Section 7.5 extends the basic GARCH model to accommodate some well-known stylized facts of financial time series. Prediction and simulation from various GARCH models are treated at the end of the chapter.

The statistical properties of GARCH models are nicely summarized in Hamilton (1994), Tsay (2001) and the review papers by Bera and Higgins (1986), Bolerslev, Engle and Nelson (1994) and Diebold and Lopez (1996). Bollerslev, Chou and Kroner (1992) give a comprehensive survey of GARCH modeling in finance. Alexander (2001) provides many examples of the use of GARCH models in finance, and Engle (2001) and Engle and Patton (2001) discuss the usefulness of volatility modeling.

7.2   The Basic ARCH Model

Figure 7.1 plots a daily time series of Ford stock returns as contained in the "timeSeries" object `ford.s` in S+FinMetrics:

```
> class(ford.s)
[1] "timeSeries"
> plot(ford.s, reference.grid=F)
```

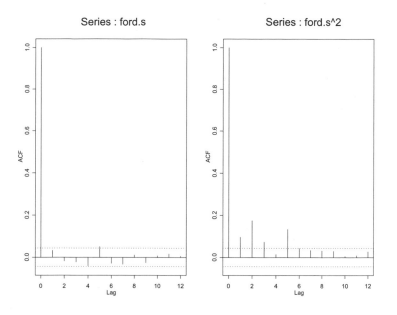

FIGURE 7.2. ACF of `ford.s` and `ford.s^2`.

Although there is little serial correlation in the time series `ford.s` itself, it seems that both large changes and small changes are clustered together, which is typical of many high frequency macroeconomic and financial time series. To confirm this conjecture, use the S-PLUS function `acf` to look at the autocorrelation plot of Ford returns and its squared returns:

```
> par(mfrow=c(1,2))
> tmp = acf(ford.s, lag=12)
> tmp = acf(ford.s^2, lag=12)
> par(mfrow=c(1,1))
```

The plots are shown in Figure 7.2. Obviously there is no autocorrelation in the return series itself, while the squared returns exhibit significant autocorrelation at least up to lag 5. Since the squared returns measure the second order moment of the original time series, this result indicates that the variance of `ford.s` conditional on its past history may change over time, or equivalently, the time series `ford.s` may exhibit *time varying conditional heteroskedasticity* or *volatility clustering*.

The serial correlation in squared returns, or conditional heteroskedasticity, can be modeled using a simple autoregressive (AR) process for squared residuals. For example, let y_t denote a stationary time series such as financial returns, then y_t can be expressed as its mean plus a white noise if there is no significant autocorrelation in y_t itself:

$$y_t = c + \epsilon_t \tag{7.1}$$

where c is the mean of y_t, and ϵ_t is i.i.d. with mean zero. To allow for volatility clustering or conditional heteroskedasticity, assume that $Var_{t-1}(\epsilon_t) = \sigma_t^2$ with $Var_{t-1}(\cdot)$ denoting the variance conditional on information at time $t-1$, and

$$\sigma_t^2 = a_0 + a_1\epsilon_{t-1}^2 + \cdots + a_p\epsilon_{t-p}^2. \tag{7.2}$$

since ϵ_t has a zero mean, $Var_{t-1}(\epsilon) = E_{t-1}(\epsilon_t^2) = \sigma_t^2$, the above equation can be rewritten as:

$$\epsilon_t^2 = a_0 + a_1\epsilon_{t-1}^2 + \cdots + a_p\epsilon_{t-p}^2 + u_t \tag{7.3}$$

where $u_t = \epsilon_t^2 - E_{t-1}(\epsilon_t^2)$ is a zero mean white noise process. The above equation represents an AR(p) process for ϵ_t^2, and the model in (7.1) and (7.2) is known as the **autoregressive conditional heteroskedasticity** (ARCH) model of Engle (1982), which is usually referred to as the ARCH(p) model.

An alternative formulation of the ARCH model is

$$
\begin{aligned}
y_t &= c + \epsilon_t \\
\varepsilon_t &= z_t \sigma_t \\
\sigma_t^2 &= a_0 + a_1\epsilon_{t-1}^2 + \cdots + a_p\epsilon_{t-p}^2
\end{aligned}
$$

where z_t is an *iid* random variable with a specified distribution. In the basic ARCH model z_t is assumed to be *iid* standard normal. The above representation is convenient for deriving properties of the model as well as for specifying the likelihood function for estimation.

Exercise 39 *Simulating an ARCH(p) model*

The S+FinMetrics function `simulate.garch` may be used to simulate observations from a variety of time-varying conditional heteroskedasticity models. For example, to simulate 250 observations from the ARCH(p) model (7.1)-(7.2) with $c = 0$, $p = 1$, $a_0 = 0.01$ and $a_1 = 0.8$ use

```
> sim.arch1 = simulate.garch(model=list(a.value=0.01, arch=0.8),
+ n=250, rseed=196)
> names(sim.arch1)
[1] "et"      "sigma.t"
```

The component `et` contains the ARCH errors ε_t and the component `sigma.t` contains the conditional standard deviations σ_t. These components are illustrated in Figure 7.3 created using

```
> par(mfrow=c(2,1))
> tsplot(sim.arch1$et,main="Simulated ARCH(1) errors",
```

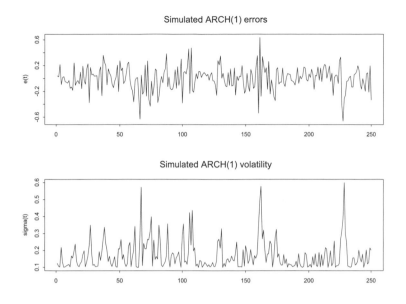

FIGURE 7.3. Simulated values of ε_t and σ_t from ARCH(1) process.

```
+ ylab="e(t)")
> tsplot(sim.arch1$sigma.t,main="Simulated ARCH(1) volatility",
+ ylab="sigma(t)")
```

Some summary statistics for the simulated data are

```
> summaryStats(sim.arch1$et)

Sample Quantiles:
     min       1Q median      3Q     max
 -0.6606 -0.1135 0.0112 0.1095 0.6357

Sample Moments:
      mean      std skewness kurtosis
 -0.003408 0.1846  -0.2515    4.041

Number of Observations:  250
```

Notice the somewhat high kurtosis value (relative to the kurtosis value of 3 for a normal distribution). Finally, Figure 7.4 shows the sample ACFs for ε_t^2 and σ_t^2. Both series exhibit almost identical serial correlation properties.

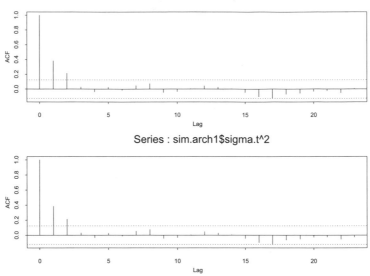

FIGURE 7.4. Sample ACFs for ε_t^2 and σ_t^2 from simulated ARCH(1) process.

7.2.1   Testing for ARCH Effects

Before estimating a full ARCH model for a financial time series, it is usually good practice to test for the presence of ARCH effects in the residuals. If there are no ARCH effects in the residuals, then the ARCH model is unnecessary and misspecified.

Since an ARCH model can be written as an AR model in terms of squared residuals as in (7.3), a simple Lagrange Multiplier (LM) test for ARCH effects can be constructed based on the auxiliary regression (7.3). Under the null hypothesis that there are no ARCH effects: $a_1 = a_2 = \cdots = a_p = 0$, the test statistic

$$LM = T \cdot R^2 \overset{A}{\sim} \chi^2(p)$$

where T is the sample size and R^2 is computed from the regression (7.3) using estimated residuals.[1]

The S+FinMetrics function archTest can be used to carry out the above test for ARCH effects. For example, to test for the presence of ARCH effects in ford.s, use the following command:

```
> archTest(ford.s, lag.n=12)
```

Test for ARCH Effects: LM Test

[1] We refer to Engle (1982) for details.

```
Null Hypothesis: no ARCH effects

Test Statistics:
                FORD
Test Stat 112.6884
  p.value   0.0000


Dist. under Null: chi-square with 12 degrees of freedom
    Total Observ.: 2000
```

In this case, the p-value is essentially zero, which is smaller than the conventional 5% level, so reject the null hypothesis that there are no ARCH effects. Note that `archTest` function takes a time series and an optional argument `lag.n` specifying the order of the ARCH effects. Since S-PLUS allows lazy evaluation, `lag` instead of `lag.n` could have been supplied as the optional argument.

7.3 The GARCH Model and Its Properties

If the LM test for ARCH effects is significant for a time series, one could proceed to estimate an ARCH model and obtain estimates of the time varying volatility σ_t based on past history. However, in practice it is often found that a large number of lags p, and thus a large number of parameters, is required to obtain a good model fit. A more parsimonious model proposed by Bollerslev (1986) replaces the AR model in (7.2) with the following formulation:

$$\sigma_t^2 = a_0 + \sum_{i=1}^{p} a_i \epsilon_{t-i}^2 + \sum_{j=1}^{q} b_j \sigma_{t-j}^2 \qquad (7.4)$$

where the coefficients a_i $(i = 0, \cdots, p)$ and b_j $(j = 1, \cdots, q)$ are all assumed to be positive to ensure that the conditional variance σ_t^2 is always positive.[2] The model in (7.4) together with (7.1) is known as the generalized ARCH or GARCH(p, q) model. When $q = 0$, the GARCH model reduces to the ARCH model.

Under the GARCH(p, q) model, the conditional variance of ϵ_t, σ_t^2, depends on the squared residuals in the previous p periods, and the conditional variance in the previous q periods. Usually a GARCH(1,1) model with only three parameters in the conditional variance equation is adequate to obtain a good model fit for financial time series.

---

[2] Positive coefficients are sufficient but not necessary conditions for the positivity of conditional variance. We refer to Nelson and Cao (1992) for the general conditions.

7.3.1 ARMA Representation of GARCH Model

Just as an ARCH model can be expressed as an AR model of squared residuals, a GARCH model can be expressed as an ARMA model of squared residuals. Consider the GARCH(1,1) model:

$$\sigma_t^2 = a_0 + a_1 \epsilon_{t-1}^2 + b_1 \sigma_{t-1}^2. \tag{7.5}$$

Since $E_{t-1}(\epsilon_t^2) = \sigma_t^2$, the above equation can be rewritten as:

$$\epsilon_t^2 = a_0 + (a_1 + b_1)\epsilon_{t-1}^2 + u_t - b_1 u_{t-1} \tag{7.6}$$

which is an ARMA(1,1) model with $u_t = \epsilon_t^2 - E_{t-1}(\epsilon_t^2)$ being the white noise disturbance term.

Given the ARMA representation of the GARCH model, many properties of the GARCH model follow easily from those of the corresponding ARMA process for ϵ_t^2. For example, for the GARCH(1,1) model to be stationary, requires that $a_1 + b_1 < 1$ as in (7.6). Assuming the stationarity of GARCH(1,1) model, the unconditional variance of ϵ_t can be shown to be $Var(\epsilon_t) = E(\epsilon_t^2) = a_0/(1 - a_1 - b_1)$, because from (7.6):

$$E(\epsilon_t^2) = a_0 + (a_1 + b_1)E(\epsilon_{t-1}^2)$$

and thus

$$E(\epsilon_t^2) = a_0 + (a_1 + b_1)E(\epsilon_t^2)$$

based on the assumption that ϵ_t^2 is stationary.

For the general GARCH(p, q) model (7.4), the squared residuals ε_t^2 behave like an ARMA($\max(p,q), q$) process. Covariance stationarity requires $\sum_{i=1}^{p} a_i + \sum_{j=1}^{q} b_j < 1$ and the unconditional variance of ε_t is

$$Var(\varepsilon_t) = \frac{a_0}{1 - \left(\sum_{i=1}^{p} a_i + \sum_{j=1}^{q} b_i\right)}. \tag{7.7}$$

7.3.2 GARCH Model and Stylized Facts

In practice, researchers have uncovered many so-called "stylized facts" about the volatility of financial time series; Bollerslev, Engle and Nelson (1994) give a complete account of these facts. Using the ARMA representation of GARCH models shows that the GARCH model is capable of explaining many of those stylized facts. This section will focus on three important ones: volatility clustering, fat tails, and volatility mean reversion. Other stylized facts are illustrated and explained in later sections.

Volatility Clustering

Consider the GARCH($1, 1$) model in (7.5). Usually the GARCH coefficient b_1 is found to be around 0.9 for many weekly or daily financial time series.

Given this value of b_1, it is obvious that large values of σ_{t-1}^2 will be followed by large values of σ_t^2, and small values of σ_{t-1}^2 will be followed by small values of σ_t^2. The same reasoning can be obtained from the ARMA representation in (7.6), where large/small changes in ϵ_{t-1}^2 will be followed by large/small changes in ϵ_t^2.

Fat Tails

It is well known that the distribution of many high frequency financial time series usually have fatter tails than a normal distribution. That is, large changes are more often to occur than a normal distribution would imply. Bollerslev (1986) gives the condition for the existence of the fourth order moment of a GARCH$(1,1)$ process. Assuming the fourth order moment exists, Bollerslev (1986) shows that the kurtosis implied by a GARCH$(1,1)$ process is greater than 3, the kurtosis of a normal distribution. He and Teräsvirta (1999a, 1999b) extend Bollerslev's results to general GARCH(p,q) models. Thus a GARCH model can replicate the fat tails usually observed in financial time series.

Volatility Mean Reversion

Although financial markets may experience excessive volatility from time to time, it appears that volatility will eventually settle down to a long run level. The previous subsection showed that the long run variance of ϵ_t for the stationary GARCH$(1,1)$ model is $a_0/(1-a_1-b_1)$. In this case, the volatility is always pulled toward this long run level by rewriting the ARMA representation in (7.6) as follows:

$$(\epsilon_t^2 - \frac{a_0}{1-a_1-b_1}) = (a_1+b_1)(\epsilon_{t-1}^2 - \frac{a_0}{1-a_1-b_1}) + u_t - b_1 u_{t-1}.$$

If the above equation is iterated k times, one can show that

$$(\epsilon_{t+k}^2 - \frac{a_0}{1-a_1-b_1}) = (a_1+b_1)^k(\epsilon_t^2 - \frac{a_0}{1-a_1-b_1}) + \eta_{t+k}$$

where η_t is a moving average process. Since $a_1+b_1 < 1$ for a stationary GARCH$(1,1)$ model, $(a_1+b_1)^k \to 0$ as $k \to \infty$. Although at time t there may be a large deviation between ϵ_t^2 and the long run variance, $\epsilon_{t+k}^2 - a_0/(1-a_1-b_1)$ will approach zero "on average" as k gets large, i.e., the volatility "mean reverts" to its long run level $a_0/(1-a_1-b_1)$. In contrast, if $a_1+b_1 > 1$ and the GARCH model is non-stationary, the volatility will eventually explode to infinity as $k \to \infty$. Similar arguments can be easily constructed for a GARCH(p,q) model.

7.4   GARCH Modeling Using S+FinMetrics

7.4.1   GARCH Model Estimation

This section illustrates how to estimate a GARCH model using functions in S+FinMetrics. Recall, the general GARCH(p, q) model has the form

$$y_t = c + \epsilon_t \tag{7.8}$$

$$\sigma_t^2 = a_0 + \sum_{i=1}^{p} a_i \epsilon_{t-i}^2 + \sum_{j=1}^{q} b_j \sigma_{t-j}^2 \tag{7.9}$$

for $t = 1, \cdots, T$, where $\sigma_t^2 = Var_{t-1}(\epsilon_t)$. Assuming that ϵ_t follows normal or Gaussian distribution conditional on past history, the prediction error decomposition of the log-likelihood function of the GARCH model conditional on initial values is:

$$\log L = -\frac{T}{2} \log(2\pi) - \frac{1}{2} \sum_{t=1}^{T} \log \sigma_t^2 - \sum_{t=1}^{T} \frac{\epsilon_t^2}{\sigma_t^2}. \tag{7.10}$$

The unknown model parameters c, a_i ($i = 0, \cdots, p$) and b_j ($j = 1, \cdots, q$) can be estimated using (conditional) maximum likelihood estimation (MLE). Details of the maximization are given in Hamilton (1994). Once the MLE estimates of the parameters are found, estimates of the time varying volatility σ_t ($t = 1, \ldots, T$) are also obtained as a side product.

For a univariate time series, S+FinMetrics provides the garch function for GARCH model estimation. For example, to fit a simple GARCH(1,1) model as in (7.8) and (7.9) to the "timeSeries" object ford.s, use the command:

```
> ford.mod11 = garch(ford.s~1, ~garch(1,1))
Iteration   0  Step Size =  1.00000  Likelihood =  2.62618
Iteration   0  Step Size =  2.00000  Likelihood =  2.61237
Iteration   1  Step Size =  1.00000  Likelihood =  2.62720
Iteration   1  Step Size =  2.00000  Likelihood =  2.62769
Iteration   1  Step Size =  4.00000  Likelihood =  2.59047
Iteration   2  Step Size =  1.00000  Likelihood =  2.62785
Iteration   2  Step Size =  2.00000  Likelihood =  2.62795
Iteration   2  Step Size =  4.00000  Likelihood =  2.62793
```

Convergence R-Square = 4.630129e-05 is less than tolerance = 0.000
Convergence reached.

In the above example, the garch function takes two arguments: the first argument is an S-PLUS formula which specifies the conditional mean equation (7.8), while the second argument is also an S-PLUS formula which specifies the conditional variance equation (7.9). The specification of the conditional mean formula is the same as usual S-PLUS formulas.[3] For the conditional variance formula, nothing needs to be specified on the left hand side, and the garch(1,1) term on the right hand side denotes the GARCH(1, 1) model. By default, the progress of the estimation is printed on screen. Those messages can be suppressed by setting the optional argument trace=F in the call to the garch function.

The object returned by garch function is of class "garch". Typing the name of the object at the command line invokes its print method:

```
> class(ford.mod11)
[1] "garch"
> ford.mod11

Call:
garch(formula.mean = ford.s ~ 1, formula.var =   ~ garch(1, 1))

Mean Equation: ford.s ~ 1

Conditional Variance Equation:   ~ garch(1, 1)

Coefficients:

        C 7.708e-04
        A 6.534e-06
  ARCH(1) 7.454e-02
 GARCH(1) 9.102e-01
```

The print method for a "garch" object shows the formulas for the conditional mean equation and conditional variance equation, together with the estimated model coefficients. Note that in the output C corresponds to the constant c in the conditional mean equation (7.8), A, ARCH(1) and GARCH(1) correspond to a_0, a_1 and b_1 in the conditional variance equation (7.9), respectively. Notice that the estimated GARCH(1) parameter is close to one and the ARCH(1) parameter is close to zero. The sum of these parameters is 0.985 which indicates a covariance stationary model with a high degree of persistence in the conditional variance. Use the S-PLUS function names to extract the component names for a "garch" object. For example:

```
> names(ford.mod11)
 [1] "residuals"  "sigma.t"     "df.residual" "coef"  "model"
 [6] "cond.dist"  "likelihood"  "opt.index"   "cov"   "prediction"
[11] "call"       "asymp.sd"    "series"
```

---

[3]Chapter 1 provides a review of the usage of S-PLUS formulas and modeling functions.

It should be clear what most of the components are and the on-line help file for the `garch` function provides details for these components. Of particular interest is the component `asymp.sd`, which gives an estimate of the unconditional standard deviation of the GARCH residuals provided the GARCH model is stationary. That is,

```
> ford.mod11$asymp.sd
[1] 0.02068
```

is an estimate of the square root of $a_0/(1 - \alpha_1 - b_1)$.

For most components that a user is interested in, S+FinMetrics provides methods for generic functions such as `coef`, `residuals`, and `vcov` for extracting those components. For example, the estimated coefficients can be extracted by calling the generic `coef` function:

```
> coef(ford.mod11)

        C 7.708418e-04
        A 6.534363e-06
  ARCH(1) 7.454134e-02
 GARCH(1) 9.101842e-01
```

Similarly, call the generic `vcov` function to obtain the covariance matrix of the estimated coefficients:

```
> vcov(ford.mod11)
                    C             A       ARCH(1)      GARCH(1)
       C  1.415744e-07 -1.212045e-13 -3.569911e-07  2.213101e-07
       A -1.212045e-13  3.046074e-12  2.553283e-09 -1.243965e-08
 ARCH(1) -3.569911e-07  2.553283e-09  2.875056e-05 -3.432774e-05
GARCH(1)  2.213101e-07 -1.243965e-08 -3.432774e-05  7.676607e-05
```

By default, the `vcov` method for "garch" objects uses the covariance matrix based on the outer product of gradients. However, for maximum likelihood estimation, there are three different ways of computing the covariance matrix of model parameters which are asymptotically equivalent if the underlying error distribution is Gaussian: one based on the outer product of gradients, one based on the numerical Hessian matrix, and one based on the asymptotic formula for *quasi-maximum likelihood estimation* (QMLE). These different covariance matrices can be obtained by setting the optional argument `method` to `"op"`, `"hessian"`, or `"qmle"`, respectively. For example, to obtain the covariance matrix of `ford.mod11` parameters based on QMLE formula, use the following command:

```
> vcov(ford.mod11, method="qmle")
                    C             A       ARCH(1)      GARCH(1)
       C  1.266714e-07 -7.543983e-11  5.676068e-07 -7.711838e-08
       A -7.543983e-11  2.698419e-11  1.375760e-07 -2.003637e-07
```

```
ARCH(1)   5.676068e-07  1.375760e-07  1.280160e-03 -1.467187e-03
GARCH(1) -7.711838e-08 -2.003637e-07 -1.467187e-03  1.841734e-03
```

This covariance matrix is sometimes referred to as the *robust* covariance matrix, because it is robust to possible misspecification of the error distribution, or the *sandwich* estimate, because of the form of the asymptotic formula (see Bollerslev and Wooldrige, 1992 or Davidson and MacKinnon, 1993).

The residuals method for a "garch" object takes an optional argument standardize, which can be used to obtain estimates of the standardized residuals ϵ_t/σ_t. For example:

```
> residuals(ford.mod11, standardize=T)
```

returns the standardized residuals of the fitted GARCH model ford.mod11. S+FinMetrics also provides another function sigma.t for extracting the fitted volatility series σ_t. Note that if the original data is a "timeSeries" object, the calendar information of the original data is also retained in the residual and volatility series.

7.4.2 GARCH Model Diagnostics

The previous subsection showed how to estimate a GARCH model using the S+FinMetrics function garch and how to extract various components of the fitted model. To assess the model fit, S+FinMetrics provides method functions for two generic functions: summary and plot, one for statistical summary information and the other for visual diagnostics of the model fit.

For example, to obtain a more detailed summary of ford.mod11, call the generic summary function:

```
> summary(ford.mod11)

Call:
garch(formula.mean = ford.s ~ 1, formula.var =  ~ garch(1, 1))

Mean Equation: ford.s ~ 1

Conditional Variance Equation:  ~ garch(1, 1)

Conditional Distribution:  gaussian

-----------------------------------------------------------------


Estimated Coefficients:
-----------------------------------------------------------------
           Value Std.Error t value  Pr(>|t|)
  C 7.708e-04 3.763e-04    2.049 2.031e-02
```

```
        A 6.534e-06 1.745e-06   3.744 9.313e-05
  ARCH(1) 7.454e-02 5.362e-03  13.902 0.000e+00
 GARCH(1) 9.102e-01 8.762e-03 103.883 0.000e+00


--------------------------------------------------------------


AIC(4) = -10503.79
BIC(4) = -10481.39

Normality Test:
--------------------------------------------------------------

 Jarque-Bera P-value Shapiro-Wilk P-value
       364.2       0       0.9915  0.9777

Ljung-Box test for standardized residuals:
--------------------------------------------------------------

 Statistic P-value Chi^2-d.f.
     14.82  0.2516         12

Ljung-Box test for squared standardized residuals:
--------------------------------------------------------------

 Statistic P-value Chi^2-d.f.
     14.04  0.2984         12

Lagrange multiplier test:
--------------------------------------------------------------

 Lag 1  Lag 2  Lag 3   Lag 4    Lag 5    Lag 6 Lag 7    Lag 8
 2.135 -1.085 -2.149 -0.1347 -0.9144 -0.2228 0.708 -0.2314

   Lag 9 Lag 10  Lag 11  Lag 12      C
 -0.6905 -1.131 -0.3081 -0.1018 0.9825

  TR^2 P-value F-stat P-value
 14.77  0.2545  1.352  0.2989
```

By default, the **summary** method shows the standard errors and p-values for the t-statistics for testing that the true coefficients are zero, together with various tests on the standardized residuals $\hat{\varepsilon}_t/\hat{\sigma}_t$ for assessing the model fit. The standard errors and p-values are computed using the default covariance estimate. To use robust or numerical Hessian based standard errors to compute the p-values, the **summary** method takes an optional argument **method** just like the vcov method does.

The various tests returned by the **summary** method can also be performed separately by using standard **S+FinMetrics** functions. For example, if the model is successful at modeling the serial correlation structure in the conditional mean and conditional variance, then there should be no autocorrelation left in the standardized residuals and squared standardized residuals. This can be checked by using the S+FinMetrics function autocorTest:

```
> autocorTest(residuals(ford.mod11, standardize=T), lag=12)

Test for Autocorrelation: Ljung-Box

Null Hypothesis: no autocorrelation

Test Statistics:

Test Stat 14.8161
  p.value  0.2516

Dist. under Null: chi-square with 12 degrees of freedom
    Total Observ.: 2000

> autocorTest(residuals(ford.mod11, standardize=T)^2, lag=12)

Test for Autocorrelation: Ljung-Box

Null Hypothesis: no autocorrelation

Test Statistics:

Test Stat 14.0361
  p.value  0.2984

Dist. under Null: chi-square with 12 degrees of freedom
    Total Observ.: 2000
```

In both cases, the tests are the same as those returned by the summary method, and the null hypothesis that there is no autocorrelation left cannot be rejected because the p-values in both cases are greater than the conventional 5% level. Note that lag was chosen to be 12 to match the results returned by the summary method.

Similarly, one can also apply the ARCH test on the standardized residuals to see if there are any ARCH effects left. For example, call archTest on the standardized residuals of ford.mod11 as follows:

```
> archTest(residuals(ford.mod11, standardize=T), lag=12)

Test for ARCH Effects: LM Test

Null Hypothesis: no ARCH effects
```

QQ-Plot of Standardized Residuals

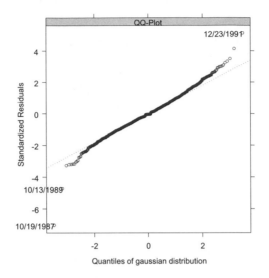

FIGURE 7.5. Normal QQ-plot of standardized residuals: `ford.mod11`.

```
Test Statistics:

Test Stat 14.7664
   p.value  0.2545

Dist. under Null: chi-square with 12 degrees of freedom
    Total Observ.: 2000
```

Again, the results match the Lagrange Multiplier test as returned by the summary method.

The basic garch model assumes a normal distribution for the errors ε_t. If the model is correctly specified then the estimated standardized residuals ε_t/σ_t should behave like a standard normal random variable. To evaluate the normality assumption, the summary method reports both the Jarque-Bera test and the Shapiro-Wilks test for the standardized residuals, which again can be performed separately using the S+FinMetrics function normalTest. However, in the above example, the Jarque-Bera test and the Shapiro-Wilks test lead to opposite conclusions, with one p-value close to zero and the other close to one.

To get a more decisive conclusion regarding the normality assumption, resort to the QQ-plot by calling the generic plot function on a "garch" object:

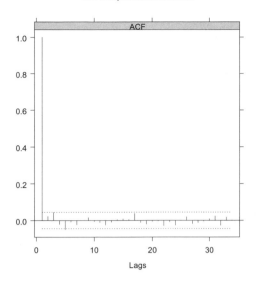

ACF of Squared Std. Residuals

FIGURE 7.6. ACF of squared standardized residuals: ford.mod11.

```
> plot(ford.mod11)

Make a plot selection (or 0 to exit):

1: plot: All
2: plot: Series and Conditional SD
3: plot: Series with 2 Conditional SD Superimposed
4: plot: ACF of the Observations
5: plot: ACF of Squared Observations
6: plot: Cross Correlation between Squared Series and Series
7: plot: Residuals
8: plot: Conditional Standard Deviations
9: plot: Standardized Residuals
10: plot: ACF of Standardized Residuals
11: plot: ACF of Squared Standardized Residuals
12: plot: Cross Correlation between Squared Std.Res and Std.
13: plot: QQ-Plot of Standardized Residuals
Selection:
```

By selecting 13, the QQ-plot of standardized residuals can be obtained as shown in Figure 7.5 In this case, there is significant deviation in both tails from the normal QQ-line, and thus it seems that the normality assumption for the residuals may not be appropriate. Section 7.5.6 will show how to

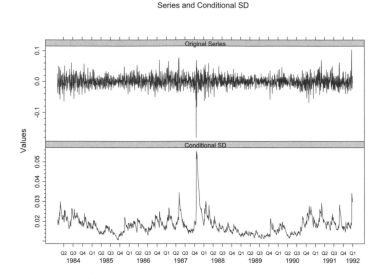

FIGURE 7.7. Daily Ford stock returns and conditional volatility.

use alternative distributions. Other plots can also be chosen to visualize the model fit. For example, choosing 11 generates the ACF plot of squared standardized residuals as shown in Figure 7.6, which shows that there is little autocorrelation left in the squared standardized residuals. Choosing 2 plots the original return series and the fitted volatility series as shown in Figure 7.7.

7.5   GARCH Model Extensions

In many cases, the basic GARCH model (7.4) provides a reasonably good model for analyzing financial time series and estimating conditional volatility. However, there are some aspects of the model which can be improved so that it can better capture the characteristics and dynamics of a particular time series. For example, the previous section showed that the normality assumption may not be appropriate for the time series `ford.s`. This section introduces several extensions to the basic GARCH model that make GARCH modeling more flexible and shows how to estimate those models using the `S+FinMetrics garch` function.

7.5.1 Asymmetric Leverage Effects and News Impact

In the basic GARCH model (7.9), since only squared residuals ϵ_{t-i}^2 enter the equation, the signs of the residuals or shocks have no effects on conditional volatility. However, a stylized fact of financial volatility is that bad news (negative shocks) tends to have a larger impact on volatility than good news (positive shocks). Black (1976) attributes this effect to the fact that bad news tends to drive down the stock price, thus increasing the leverage (i.e., the debt-equity ratio) of the stock and causing the stock to be more volatile. Based on this conjecture, the asymmetric news impact is usually referred to as the *leverage effect*. All the GARCH variants implemented in S+FinMetrics are capable of incorporating leverage effects. This subsection focuses on the EGARCH, TGARCH and PGARCH models.

EGARCH Model

Nelson (1991) proposed the following *exponential* GARCH (EGARCH) model to allow for leverage effects:

$$h_t = a_0 + \sum_{i=1}^{p} a_i \frac{|\epsilon_{t-i}| + \gamma_i \epsilon_{t-i}}{\sigma_{t-i}} + \sum_{j=1}^{q} b_j h_{t-j} \qquad (7.11)$$

where $h_t = \log \sigma_t^2$ or $\sigma_t^2 = e^{h_t}$. Note that when ϵ_{t-i} is positive or there is "good news", the total effect of ϵ_{t-i} is $(1+\gamma_i)|\epsilon_{t-i}|$; in contrast, when ϵ_{t-i} is negative or there is "bad news", the total effect of ϵ_{t-i} is $(1-\gamma_i)|\epsilon_{t-i}|$. Bad news can have a larger impact on volatility, and the value of γ_i would be expected to be negative.

The garch function can be used to fit an EGARCH model by specifying ~egarch(p,q) as the conditional variance formula. For example, to fit an EGARCH(1, 1) model with leverage effects using the daily Hewlett-Packard stock returns contained in the S+FinMetrics "timeSeries" object hp.s, use the following command:

```
> hp.egarch = garch(hp.s~1, ~egarch(1,1), leverage=T, trace=F)
> hp.egarch

Call:
garch(formula.mean = hp.s ~ 1, formula.var =  ~ egarch(1, 1),
      leverage = T, trace = F)

Mean Equation: hp.s ~ 1

Conditional Variance Equation:   ~ egarch(1, 1)

Coefficients:
```

```
        C   0.000313
        A  -1.037907
  ARCH(1)   0.227878
 GARCH(1)   0.886652
   LEV(1)  -0.133998
```

Note that the optional argument `trace=F` is set to suppress the iteration messages, and set `leverage=T` to impose leverage effects. In the output, the estimated γ_1 coefficient for the leverage effect is denoted by `LEV(1)` and is negative in this case. The t-statistic for testing $\gamma_1 = 0$ is

```
> coef(hp.egarch)[5]/sqrt(vcov(hp.egarch)[5,5])
[1] -2.159
```

Another advantage of the EGARCH model over the basic GARCH model is that the conditional variance σ_t^2 is guaranteed to be positive regardless of the values of the coefficients in (7.11), because the logarithm of σ_t^2 instead of σ_t^2 itself is modeled.

TGARCH Model

Another GARCH variant that is capable of modeling leverage effects is the *threshold* GARCH (TGARCH) model,[4] which has the following form:

$$\sigma_t^2 = a_0 + \sum_{i=1}^{p} a_i \epsilon_{t-i}^2 + \sum_{i=1}^{p} \gamma_i S_{t-i} \epsilon_{t-i}^2 + \sum_{j=1}^{q} b_j \sigma_{t-j}^2 \qquad (7.12)$$

where

$$S_{t-i} = \begin{cases} 1 & \text{if} \quad \epsilon_{t-i} < 0 \\ 0 & \text{if} \quad \epsilon_{t-i} \geq 0 \end{cases}$$

That is, depending on whether ϵ_{t-i} is above or below the threshold value of zero, ϵ_{t-i}^2 has different effects on the conditional variance σ_t^2: when ϵ_{t-i} is positive, the total effects are given by $a_i \epsilon_{t-i}^2$; when ϵ_{t-i} is negative, the total effects are given by $(a_i + \gamma_i) \epsilon_{t-i}^2$. So one would expect γ_i to be positive for bad news to have larger impacts. This model is also known as the GJR model because Glosten, Jagannathan and Runkle (1993) proposed essentially the same model.

Use the `garch` function to estimate a TGARCH model by specifying `~tgarch(p,q)` as the conditional variance formula. For example, to fit a TGARCH instead of an EGARCH model to `hp.s`, use the following command:

```
> hp.tgarch = garch(hp.s~1, ~tgarch(1,1), trace=F)
> hp.tgarch
```

---

[4] The original TGARCH model proposed by Zakoian (1991) models σ_t instead of σ_t^2.

```
Call:
garch(formula.mean = hp.s ~ 1, formula.var =  ~ tgarch(1, 1),
      trace = F)

Mean Equation: hp.s ~ 1

Conditional Variance Equation:  ~ tgarch(1, 1)

Coefficients:

        C 3.946e-04
        A 3.999e-05
  ARCH(1) 6.780e-02
 GARCH(1) 8.369e-01
 GAMMA(1) 3.306e-02
```

Note that when using the TGARCH model, the leverage effects are automatically imposed, so it is not necessary to set leverage=T. Also, the coefficient γ_1 for leverage effects is denoted by GAMMA(1) in the output to distinguish it from the EGARCH-type formulation of leverage effects. The estimated value of γ_1 is positive, indicating the presence of leverage effects, and is statistically different from zero at the 5% significance level since its t-statistic is greater than 2:

```
> coef(hp.tgarch)[5]/sqrt(vcov(hp.tgarch)[5,5])
[1] 2.5825
```

PGARCH Model

The basic GARCH model in S+FinMetrics is also extended to allow for leverage effects. This is made possible by treating the basic GARCH model as a special case of the *power* GARCH (PGARCH) model proposed by Ding, Granger and Engle (1993):

$$\sigma_t^d = a_0 + \sum_{i=1}^{p} a_i (|\epsilon_{t-i}| + \gamma_i \epsilon_{t-i})^d + \sum_{j=1}^{q} b_j \sigma_{t-j}^d \qquad (7.13)$$

where d is a positive exponent, and γ_i denotes the coefficient of leverage effects. Note that when $d = 2$, (7.13) reduces to the basic GARCH model with leverage effects. Ding, Granger and Engle (1993) show that the PGARCH model also includes many other GARCH variants as special cases.

To estimate a basic GARCH$(1, 1)$ model with leverage effects, specify ~garch(1,1) as the conditional variance formula and set the optional argument leverage=T:

```
> hp.garch = garch(hp.s~1, ~garch(1,1), leverage=T, trace=F)
> hp.garch
```

```
Call:
garch(formula.mean = hp.s ~ 1, formula.var =  ~ garch(1, 1),
      leverage = T, trace = F)
```

Mean Equation: hp.s ~ 1

Conditional Variance Equation: ~ garch(1, 1)

Coefficients:

```
        C   4.536e-04
        A   3.823e-05
  ARCH(1)   7.671e-02
 GARCH(1)   8.455e-01
   LEV(1)  -1.084e-01
```

The estimated value of γ_1 is negative and its t-statistic

```
> coef(hp.garch)[5]/sqrt(vcov(hp.garch)[5,5])
[1] -2.2987
```

is less than 2 so one can reject the null of no leverage effects. If ~pgarch(p,q) instead of ~garch(p,q) is used as the conditional variance formula, the garch function will estimate the PGARCH model (7.13) where the exponent d is also estimated by MLE.

One can fix the exponent d in PGARCH model at a value other than two. For example, a popular choice is to set $d = 1$ so that the GARCH model is robust to outliers. To fit such a model, simply use ~pgarch(p,q,d) as the conditional variance formula:

```
> hp.pgarch = garch(hp.s~1, ~pgarch(1,1,1), leverage=T, trace=F)
> hp.pgarch
```

```
Call:
garch(formula.mean = hp.s ~ 1, formula.var =  ~ pgarch(1, 1, 1),
      leverage = T, trace = F)
```

Mean Equation: hp.s ~ 1

Conditional Variance Equation: ~ pgarch(1, 1, 1)

Coefficients:

```
        C   0.0003312
        A   0.0015569
  ARCH(1)   0.0892505
```

GARCH(p,q)	$\bar{\sigma}^2 = a_0/[1 - \sum_{i=1}^{p} a_i(1 + \gamma_i^2) - \sum_{j=1}^{q} b_j]$
TGARCH(p,q)	$\bar{\sigma}^2 = a_0/[1 - \sum_{i=1}^{p}(a_i + \gamma_i/2) - \sum_{j=1}^{q} b_j]$
PGARCH$(p,q,1)$	$\bar{\sigma}^2 = a_0^2/[1 - \sum_{i=1}^{p} a_i\sqrt{2/\pi} - \sum_{j=1}^{q} b_j]^2$
EGARCH(p,q)	$\bar{\sigma}^2 = \exp\{(a_0 + \sum_{i=1}^{p} a_i\sqrt{2/\pi})/(1 - \sum_{j=1}^{q} b_j)\}$

TABLE 7.1. Unconditional variance of GARCH processes

```
GARCH(1)   0.8612378
  LEV(1)  -0.1499219
```

```
> coef(hp.pgarch)[5]/sqrt(vcov(hp.pgarch)[5,5])
[1] -2.2121
```

News Impact Curve

The above subsections have shown that GARCH, EGARCH, TGARCH and PGARCH models are all capable of modeling leverage effects. The choice of a particular model can be made by using a model selection criterion such as the Bayesian information criterion (BIC). Alternatively, Engle and Ng (1993) proposed that the *news impact curve* could also be used to compare these different models. Here is the definition of the news impact curve following Engle and Ng (1993):

The news impact curve is the functional relationship between conditional variance at time t and the shock term (error term) at time $t - 1$, holding constant the information dated $t - 2$ and earlier, and with all lagged conditional variance evaluated at the level of the unconditional variance.

To facilitate the comparison of news impact curves of different GARCH models, Table 7.1 summarizes the unconditional variance, $\bar{\sigma}^2$, of various GARCH models and Table 7.2 summarizes the news impact curves for models with $p = 1$ and $q = 1$.

For example, to compare the news impact curves implied by `hp.tgarch`, `hp.pgarch` and `hp.garch`, plot the corresponding news impact curves using the following commands:

```
> a0 = hp.tgarch$coef[2]
> a1 = hp.tgarch$coef[3]
> b1 = hp.tgarch$coef[4]
> g1 = hp.tgarch$coef[5]
> A = a0 + b1 * hp.tgarch$asymp.sd^2

> epsilon = seq(-0.21, 0.14, length=100)
```

GARCH(1,1)	$\sigma_t^2 = A + a_1(|\epsilon_{t-1}| + \gamma_1\epsilon_{t-1})^2$ $A = a_0 + b_1\bar{\sigma}^2$
TGARCH(1,1)	$\sigma_t^2 = A + (a_1 + \gamma_1 S_{t-1})\epsilon_{t-1}^2$ $A = a_0 + b_1\bar{\sigma}^2$
PGARCH(1,1,1)	$\sigma_t^2 = A + 2\sqrt{A}a_1(|\epsilon_{t-1}| + \gamma_1\epsilon_{t-1})$ $+a_1^2(|\epsilon_{t-1}| + \gamma_1\epsilon_{t-1})^2,\ A = (a_0 + b_1\bar{\sigma})^2$
EGARCH(1,1)	$\sigma_t^2 = A\exp\{a_1(|\epsilon_{t-1}| + \gamma_1\epsilon_{t-1})/\bar{\sigma}\}$ $A = \bar{\sigma}^{2b_1}\exp\{a_0\}$

TABLE 7.2. News impact curves of GARCH processes

```
> sigma2.t.TGARCH = A + (a1+g1*(epsilon < 0))*(epsilon^2)

> a0 = hp.pgarch$coef[2]
> a1 = hp.pgarch$coef[3]
> b1 = hp.pgarch$coef[4]
> g1 = hp.pgarch$coef[5]
> A = (a0 + b1 * hp.pgarch$asymp.sd)^2

> error = abs(epsilon) + g1*epsilon
> sigma2.t.PGARCH = A + 2*sqrt(A)*a1*error + (a1*error)^2

> a0 = hp.garch$coef[2]
> a1 = hp.garch$coef[3]
> b1 = hp.garch$coef[4]
> g1 = hp.garch$coef[5]
> A = a0 + b1 * hp.garch$asymp.sd^2

> error = abs(epsilon) + g1*epsilon
> sigma2.t.GARCH = A + a1*(error^2)

> matplot(cbind(epsilon, epsilon, epsilon), cbind(
  sigma2.t.TGARCH, sigma2.t.PGARCH, sigma2.t.GARCH), type="l")

> key(-0.05, 0.0045, lines=list(type="l", lty=1:3), text=
  list(c("TGARCH", "PGARCH", "GARCH")), border=1, adj=1)
```

In this plot, the range of ϵ_t is determined by the residuals from the fitted models. The resulting plot is shown in Figure 7.8. This plot shows that the news impact curves are all asymmetric because leverage effects are allowed in all three models, and negative shocks or bad news have larger impacts

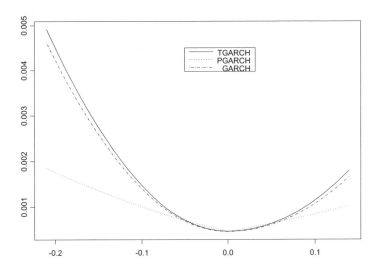

FIGURE 7.8. Camparison of news impact curves.

on volatility. The TGARCH model suggests larger impacts of shocks on volatility than the GARCH model with leverage effects, regardless of the size of the shock. Moreover, since the PGARCH model with $d = 1$ is more robust to extreme shocks, impacts of small shocks implied by the PGARCH model are larger compared to those from GARCH and TGARCH models, whereas impacts of large shocks implied by the PGARCH model are smaller compared to those from GARCH and TGARCH models.

7.5.2 Two Components Model

Section 7.3.2 illustrated that the GARCH model can be used to model mean reversion in conditional volatility; that is, the conditional volatility will always "mean revert" to its long run level if the GARCH model is stationary. Recall the mean reverting form of the basic GARCH(1, 1) model:

$$(\epsilon_t^2 - \bar{\sigma}^2) = (a_1 + b_1)(\epsilon_{t-1}^2 - \bar{\sigma}^2) + u_t - b_1 u_{t-1}$$

where $\bar{\sigma}^2 = a_0/(1 - a_1 - b_1)$ is the unconditional long run level of volatility. As previous examples have shown, the mean reverting rate $a_1 + b_1$ implied by most fitted models is usually very close to 1. For example, the `ford.mod11` object fitted in Section 7.4, has the following mean reverting rate:

```
> ford.mod11$coef[3] + ford.mod11$coef[4]
```

[1] 0.9847255

which is almost one. The half life of a volatility shock implied by this mean reverting rate is:[5]

```
> log(0.5)/log(ford.mod11$coef[3] + ford.mod11$coef[4])
[1] 45.03192
```

which amounts to more than two calendar months. So the fitted GARCH model implies that the conditional volatility is very persistent.

Engle and Lee (1999) suggest that the high persistence in volatility may be due to a time-varying long run volatility level. In particular, they suggest decomposing conditional variance into two components:

$$\sigma_t^2 = q_t + s_t \tag{7.14}$$

where q_t is a highly persistent long run component, and s_t is a transitory short run component.

S+FinMetrics supports a wide range of two component models by extending all the previously discussed GARCH variants to incorporate the two components form (7.14). The general form of the two components model is based on a modified version of Ding and Granger (1996):

$$\sigma_t^d = q_t^d + s_t^d \tag{7.15}$$

$$q_t^d = \alpha_1|\epsilon_{t-1}|^d + \beta_1 q_{t-1}^d \tag{7.16}$$

$$s_t^d = a_0 + \alpha_2|\epsilon_{t-1}|^d + \beta_2 s_{t-1}^d. \tag{7.17}$$

That is, the long run component q_t follows a highly persistent PGARCH$(1,1)$ model, and the transitory component s_t follows another PGARCH$(1,1)$ model. By expressing the above two PGARCH models using lag operator notation

$$q_t^d = (1 - \beta_1 L)^{-1}\alpha_1|\epsilon_{t-1}|^d$$

$$s_t^d = a_0 + (1 - \beta_2 L)^{-1}\alpha_2|\epsilon_{t-1}|^d$$

and then substituting them into (7.15), it can be shown that the reduced form of the two components model is:

$$\sigma_t^d = a_0 + (\alpha_1 + \alpha_2)|\epsilon_{t-1}|^d - (\alpha_1\beta_2 + \alpha_2\beta_1)|\epsilon_{t-2}|^d$$
$$+ (\beta_1 + \beta_2)\sigma_{t-1}^d - \beta_1\beta_2\sigma_{t-2}^d$$

which is in the form of a constrained PGARCH$(2,2)$ model. However, the two components model is not fully equivalent to the PGARCH$(2,2)$ model because not all PGARCH$(2,2)$ models have the component structure. In fact, since the two components model is a constrained version

---

[5] See Chapter 2 for the definition of half life.

of the PGARCH(2, 2) model, the estimation of a two components model
is often numerically more stable than the estimation of an unconstrained
PGARCH(2, 2) model.

Although the PGARCH(1, 1) model is used here as the component for the
two components model, S+FinMetrics actually allows any valid GARCH
variant as the component, and leverage effects are also allowed correspond-
ingly. For example, to fit a two components model using a GARCH component, EGARCH component, or PGARCH component, simply use the conditional variance formulas ~garch.2comp, ~egarch.2comp, ~pgarch.2comp(d),
respectively. Since a two components model reduces to a GARCH(2, 2)
model of the corresponding type, the orders of the ARCH and GARCH
terms need not be given in the formula specification. The only exception
is the PGARCH two components model, which can explicitly specify the
exponent d for the underlying PGARCH model. For example, to estimate
a two components PGARCH model with $d = 2$ using the daily Ford stock
returns ford.s, use the following command:

```
> ford.2comp = garch(ford.s~1, ~pgarch.2comp(2))
> summary(ford.2comp)
```

```
Call:
garch(formula.mean = ford.s ~ 1, formula.var =  ~ pgarch.2comp(2))

Mean Equation: ford.s ~ 1

Conditional Variance Equation:  ~ pgarch.2comp(2)

Conditional Distribution:  gaussian

------------------------------------------------------------

Estimated Coefficients:
------------------------------------------------------------
          Value Std.Error t value  Pr(>|t|)
       C 6.870e-04 3.795e-04   1.810 3.519e-02
       A 1.398e-06 5.877e-07   2.379 8.716e-03
ALPHA(1) 2.055e-02 6.228e-03   3.300 4.925e-04
ALPHA(2) 1.422e-01 2.532e-02   5.617 1.110e-08
 BETA(1) 9.664e-01 8.637e-03 111.883 0.000e+00
 BETA(2) 3.464e-01 1.091e-01   3.175 7.617e-04
```

The coefficients for the two components, α_1, β_1, α_2 and β_2, are identified by
ALPHA(1), BETA(1), ALPHA(2) and BETA(2) in the output. As expected, the
long run component associated with α_1 and β_1 is very persistent, whereas
the second component associated with α_2 and β_2 is not persistent at all.
Also, all the coefficients are highly significant.

In the above example, fixing $d = 2$ for the two components PGARCH model can be easily verified that the model is equivalent to a two components GARCH model. If the exponent d is not specified in the formula, it will be estimated by MLE. In addition, setting leverage=T when fitting a two components model, the coefficients for leverage effects will also be estimated, and the form of leverage effects is same as in (7.11) and (7.13). However, for the two components PGARCH model, S+FinMetrics also allows leverage effects to take the form as in the TGARCH model (7.12). The resulting model can be estimated by using ~two.comp(i,d) as the conditional variance formula, with $i = 2$ corresponding to the leverage effects as in (7.12), and $i = 1$ corresponding to the leverage effects as in (7.13). For example, the following model is essentially the two components TGARCH model:

```
> garch(ford.s~1, ~two.comp(2,2), leverage=T, trace=F)
```

```
Call:
garch(formula.mean = ford.s ~ 1, formula.var =   ~ two.comp(2, 2),
      leverage = T, trace = F)
```

Mean Equation: ford.s ~ 1

Conditional Variance Equation: ~ two.comp(2, 2)

Coefficients:

```
        C   5.371e-04
        A   1.368e-06
 ALPHA(1)   1.263e-02
 ALPHA(2)   1.154e-01
  BETA(1)   9.674e-01
  BETA(2)   2.998e-01
   LEV(1)   8.893e-02
   LEV(2)  -5.235e-02
```

7.5.3   GARCH-in-the-Mean Model

In financial investment, high risk is often expected to lead to high returns. Although modern capital asset pricing theory does not imply such a simple relationship, it does suggest there are some interactions between expected returns and risk as measured by volatility. Engle, Lilien and Robins (1987) propose to extend the basic GARCH model so that the conditional volatility can generate a *risk premium* which is part of the expected returns. This extended GARCH model is often referred to as *GARCH-in-the-mean* (GARCH-M) model.

$g(\sigma_t)$	Formula name
σ	sd.in.mean
σ^2	var.in.mean
$\ln(\sigma^2)$	logvar.in.mean

TABLE 7.3. Possible functions for $g(\sigma_t)$

The GARCH-M model extends the conditional mean equation (7.8) as follows:

$$y_t = c + \alpha g(\sigma_t) + \epsilon_t \tag{7.18}$$

where $g(\cdot)$ can be an arbitrary function of volatility σ_t. The garch function allows the GARCH-M specification in the conditional mean equation together with any valid conditional variance specification. However, the function $g(\sigma_t)$ must be one of the functions listed in Table 7.3, where the corresponding formula specifications are also given.

For example, to fit a GARCH-M model with $g(\sigma_t) = \sigma_t^2$ to Hewlett-Packard stock returns using a PGARCH$(1, 1, 1)$ model with leverage effects, use the following command:

```
> hp.gmean = garch(hp.s~var.in.mean, ~pgarch(1,1,1), leverage=T)
Iteration   0  Step Size =  1.00000  Likelihood =  2.40572
Iteration   0  Step Size =  2.00000  Likelihood =  2.40607
Iteration   0  Step Size =  4.00000  Likelihood =  2.38124
Iteration   1  Step Size =  1.00000  Likelihood =  2.40646
Iteration   1  Step Size =  2.00000  Likelihood =  2.40658
Iteration   1  Step Size =  4.00000  Likelihood =  2.40611
Iteration   2  Step Size =  1.00000  Likelihood =  2.40667
Iteration   2  Step Size =  2.00000  Likelihood =  2.40669
Iteration   2  Step Size =  4.00000  Likelihood =  2.40653

Convergence R-Square = 7.855063e-05 is less than tolerance = 0.0001
Convergence reached.
> summary(hp.gmean)

Call:
garch(formula.mean = hp.s ~ var.in.mean, formula.var =
      ~ pgarch(1, 1, 1), leverage = T)

Mean Equation: hp.s ~ var.in.mean

Conditional Variance Equation:   ~ pgarch(1, 1, 1)

Conditional Distribution:  gaussian
```

Estimated Coefficients:

```
---------------------------------------------------------------
              Value Std.Error t value  Pr(>|t|)
        C -0.001712 0.0013654  -1.254 1.050e-01
ARCH-IN-MEAN 4.373179 2.8699425   1.524 6.386e-02
        A  0.001648 0.0003027   5.444 2.920e-08
   ARCH(1)  0.093854 0.0096380   9.738 0.000e+00
  GARCH(1)  0.853787 0.0176007  48.509 0.000e+00
    LEV(1) -0.161515 0.0648241  -2.492 6.399e-03
```

The coefficient α in (7.18) is identified by ARCH-IN-MEAN in the output. In this case, the risk premium is positive which implies that high risk (volatility) leads to high expected returns. However, the p-value for the t-statistic is slightly larger than the conventional 5% level.

7.5.4   ARMA Terms and Exogenous Variables in Conditional Mean Equation

So far the conditional mean equation has been restricted to a constant when considering GARCH models, except for the GARCH-M model where volatility was allowed to enter the mean equation as an explanatory variable. The garch function in S+FinMetrics allows ARMA terms as well as exogenous explanatory variables in the conditional mean equation. The most general form for the conditional mean equation is

$$y_t = c + \sum_{i=1}^{r} \phi_i y_{t-i} + \sum_{j=1}^{s} \theta_j \epsilon_{t-j} + \sum_{l=1}^{L} \beta_l' \mathbf{x}_{t-l} + \epsilon_t \qquad (7.19)$$

where $\mathbf{x}_t$ is a $k \times 1$ vector of weakly exogenous variables, and β_l is the $k \times 1$ vector of coefficients. Note that distributed lags of the exogenous variables in $\mathbf{x}_t$ are also allowed. To include AR(r), MA(s), or ARMA(r, s) terms in the conditional mean, simply add ar(r), ma(s), or arma(r,s) to the conditional mean formula.

Example 40 *Single factor model with GARCH errors*

From the Capital Asset Pricing Model (CAPM), stock returns should be correlated with the returns on a market index, and the regression coefficient is usually referred to as the "market beta". S+FinMetrics comes with a "timeSeries" object nyse.s which represents daily returns on a value weighted New York Stock Exchange index and covers the same time period as ford.s. Use the S+FinMetrics function rvfPlot to generate a Trellis scatter plot of ford.s versus nyse.s:

```
> rvfPlot(ford.s, nyse.s, strip.text="Market Beta",
```

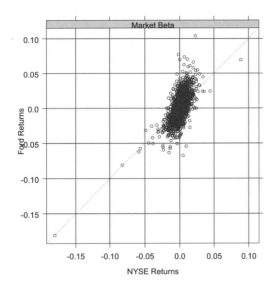

FIGURE 7.9. Daily Ford returns versus NYSE returns.

```
id.n=0, hgrid=T, vgrid=T,
xlab="NYSE Returns", ylab="Ford Returns")
```

The plot is shown in Figure 7.9, from which a clear linear relationship can be seen. To estimate the market beta for daily Ford returns allowing for a GARCH(1, 1) error, use the following command:

```
> ford.beta = garch(ford.s~ma(1)+seriesData(nyse.s),
  ~garch(1,1), trace=F)
> summary(ford.beta)

Call:
garch(formula.mean = ford.s ~ ma(1) + seriesData(nyse.s),
      formula.var = ~ garch(1, 1), trace = F)

Mean Equation: ford.s ~ ma(1) + seriesData(nyse.s)

Conditional Variance Equation:  ~ garch(1, 1)

Conditional Distribution:  gaussian

-----------------------------------------------------------------

Estimated Coefficients:
```

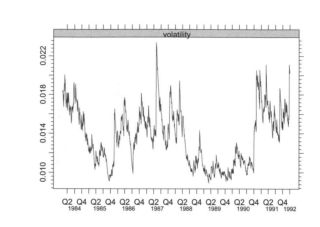

FIGURE 7.10. Idiosyncratic volatility of daily Ford returns.

```
-------------------------------------------------------------
                     Value  Std.Error   t value   Pr(>|t|)
            C    8.257e-05  3.063e-04    0.2695  3.938e-01
         MA(1)   4.448e-02  2.186e-02    2.0348  2.100e-02
seriesData(nyse.s) 1.234e+00 2.226e-02  55.4418  0.000e+00
            A    1.406e-06  5.027e-07    2.7971  2.603e-03
       ARCH(1)   3.699e-02  4.803e-03    7.7019  1.044e-14
      GARCH(1)   9.566e-01  6.025e-03  158.7691  0.000e+00
```

Note that an MA(1) term has also been added in the mean equation to allow
for first order serial correlation in the daily returns caused by the possible
bid-ask bounce often observed in daily stock prices. The above summary
shows that both the MA(1) coefficient and market beta are highly significant. The estimated volatility is shown in Figure 7.10, which is obtained
by choosing choice 8 from the plot method. Compare this with the estimated volatility without using nyse.s as shown in Figure 7.7: the estimated
volatility has the same pattern, but the magnitude of volatility has significantly decreased. Since the market effects are taken into consideration
here by using nyse.s as an explanatory variable, the resulting volatility
may be interpreted as the "idiosyncratic" volatility, while the volatility in
Figure 7.7 includes both the idiosyncratic component and the systematic
market component.

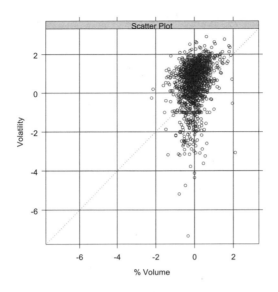

FIGURE 7.11. Log absolute returns versus changes in volume: Dell.

7.5.5 Exogenous Explanatory Variables in the Conditional Variance Equation

Adding explanatory variables into the conditional variance formula may have impacts on conditional volatility.[6] To illustrate, it is widely believed that trading volume affects the volatility. The S+FinMetrics object dell.s contains a time series of daily stock returns of Dell Computer Corporation, and dell.v contains daily trading volume of Dell stocks spanning the same time period. In the next example, use the percentage change in trading volume to forecast volatility.

Example 41 *Trading volume and volatility*

First, use the S+FinMetrics function getReturns to compute rates of changes in trading volume. Then look at the scatter plot of log absolute returns versus the changes in trading volume:

```
> log.abs.ret = log(abs(dell.s-mean(dell.s)))[-1]
> d.volume = getReturns(dell.v)
> rvfPlot(log.abs.ret, d.volume, strip="Scatter Plot",
          id.n=0, hgrid=T, vgrid=T,
```

---

[6] To guarantee that the conditional variance is always positive, one has to make sure that exogenous variables are positive unless an EGARCH type model is selected.

```
                xlab="% Volume", ylab="Volatility")
```

The resulting plot is shown in Figure 7.11. There seems to exist a fairly linear relationship between the changes in volume and the volatility as measured by the log absolute returns. Based on this observation, use the changes in volume as an explanatory variable in the EGARCH variance equation:

```
> dell.mod = garch(dell.s~1, ~egarch(1,1)+seriesData(d.volume),
  series.start=2)
> summary(dell.mod)

Call:
garch(formula.mean = dell.s ~ 1, formula.var =   ~ egarch(1, 1)
      + seriesData(d.volume), series.start = 2)

Mean Equation: dell.s ~ 1

Conditional Variance Equation:   ~ egarch(1, 1) +
      seriesData(d.volume)

Conditional Distribution:  gaussian
```

```
Estimated Coefficients:
```

	Value	Std.Error	t value	Pr(>|t|)
C	0.15678	0.06539	2.3977	8.321e-03
A	-0.02078	0.03927	-0.5293	2.984e-01
ARCH(1)	0.14882	0.03721	3.9992	3.364e-05
GARCH(1)	0.95140	0.01695	56.1226	0.000e+00
seriesData(d.volume)	1.39898	0.08431	16.5928	0.000e+00

The optional argument series.start=2 is used because the "timeSeries" d.volume has one less observation than the "timeSeries" dell.s. From the summary output, the coefficient on changes in volume is estimated to be 1.4 and is highly significant with a p-value essentially equal to zero. The estimated model implies a 1% change in trading volume causes about a 1.4% change in conditional variance.

7.5.6 Non-Gaussian Error Distributions

In all the examples illustrated so far, a normal error distribution has been exclusively used. However, given the well known fat tails in financial time series, it may be more desirable to use a distribution which has fatter tails than the normal distribution. The `garch` function in `S+FinMetrics` allows three fat-tailed error distributions for fitting GARCH models: the *Student-t distribution*; the *double exponential distribution*; and the *generalized error distribution*.

Student-t Distribution

If a random variable u_t has a Student-t distribution with ν degrees of freedom and a scale parameter s_t, the probability density function (PDF) of u_t is given by:

$$f(u_t) = \frac{\Gamma[(\nu+1)/2]}{(\pi\nu)^{1/2}\Gamma(\nu/2)} \frac{s_t^{-1/2}}{[1+u_t^2/(s_t\nu)]^{(\nu+1)/2}}$$

where $\Gamma(\cdot)$ is the gamma function. The variance of u_t is given by:

$$Var(u_t) = \frac{s_t\nu}{\nu-2}, \ v > 2.$$

If the error term ϵ_t in a GARCH model follows a Student-t distribution with ν degrees of freedom and $Var_{t-1}(\epsilon_t) = \sigma_t^2$, the scale parameter s_t should be chosen to be

$$s_t = \frac{\sigma_t^2(\nu-2)}{\nu}.$$

Thus the log-likelihood function of a GARCH model with Student-t distributed errors can be easily constructed based on the above PDF.

Generalized Error Distribution

Nelson (1991) proposed to use the *generalized error distribution* (GED) to capture the fat tails usually observed in the distribution of financial time series. If a random variable u_t has a GED with mean zero and unit variance, the PDF of u_t is given by:

$$f(u_t) = \frac{\nu \exp[-(1/2)|u_t/\lambda|^\nu]}{\lambda \cdot 2^{(\nu+1)/\nu}\Gamma(1/\nu)}$$

where

$$\lambda = \left[\frac{2^{-2/\nu}\Gamma(1/\nu)}{\Gamma(3/\nu)}\right]^{1/2}$$

and ν is a positive parameter governing the thickness of the tail behavior of the distribution. When $\nu = 2$ the above PDF reduces to the standard normal PDF; when $\nu < 2$, the density has thicker tails than the normal density; when $\nu > 2$, the density has thinner tails than the normal density.

When the tail thickness parameter $\nu = 1$, the PDF of GED reduces to the PDF of *double exponential distribution*:

$$f(u_t) = \frac{1}{\sqrt{2}}e^{-\sqrt{2}|u_t|}.$$

Based on the above PDF, the log-likelihood function of GARCH models with GED or double exponential distributed errors can be easily constructed. Refer to Hamilton (1994) for an example.

GARCH Estimation with Non-Gaussian Error Distributions

To estimate a GARCH model with the above three non-Gaussian error distributions using the garch function, simply set the optional argument cond.dist to "t" for the Student-t distribution, "ged" for the GED distribution, and "double.exp" for the double exponential distribution, respectively.

For example, to estimate a basic GARCH(1, 1) model with Student-t distribution using daily Ford stock returns ford.s, use the command:

```
> ford.mod11.t = garch(ford.s~1, ~garch(1,1), cond.dist="t")
Iteration    0  Step Size =  1.00000  Likelihood =   2.64592
Iteration    0  Step Size =  2.00000  Likelihood = -1.00000e+10
Iteration    1  Step Size =  1.00000  Likelihood =   2.64788
Iteration    1  Step Size =  2.00000  Likelihood =   2.64367
Iteration    2  Step Size =  1.00000  Likelihood =   2.64808
Iteration    2  Step Size =  2.00000  Likelihood =   2.64797

Convergence R-Square = 4.712394e-05 is less than tolerance = 0.0001
Convergence reached.
```

The distribution information is saved in the cond.dist component of the returned object:

```
> ford.mod11.t$cond.dist
$cond.dist:
[1] "t"

$dist.par:
[1] 7.793236

$dist.est:
[1] T
```

where the dist.par component contains the estimated degree of freedom ν for Student-t distribution. Calling the generic summary function on the returned object will also show the standard error of the estimate of ν.

To assess the goodness-of-fit of ford.mod11.t, generate the QQ-plot based on the estimated Student-t distribution by calling the plot function on ford.mod11.t, which is shown in Figure 7.12. Compare this with Figure 7.5 and the Student-t error distribution provides a much better fit than the normal error distribution.

QQ-Plot of Standardized Residuals

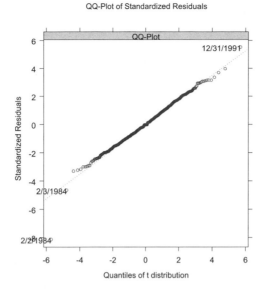

FIGURE 7.12. Student-t QQ-plot of standardized residuals: `ford.mod11.t`.

When using Student-t or GED distributions, the distribution parameter ν is estimated as part of the MLE procedure by default. One can also choose to fix ν at a certain value during the estimation. For example, to fix $\nu = 1$ for GED distribution, use the command:

```
> ford.mod11.dexp = garch(ford.s~1, ~garch(1,1),
+ cond.dist="ged", dist.par=1, dist.est=F)
```

where the optional argument `dist.par` is used to set the value, and `dist.est` is used to exclude the distribution parameter for MLE. It can be easily verified that this is equivalent to setting `cond.dist="double.exp"`.

7.6 GARCH Model Selection and Comparison

The previous sections have illustrated the variety of GARCH models available in `S+FinMetrics`. Obviously selecting the best model for a particular data set can be a daunting task. Model diagnostics based on standardized residuals and news impact curves for leverage effects can be used to compare the effectiveness of different aspects of GARCH models. In addition, since GARCH models can be treated as ARMA models for squared residuals, traditional model selection criteria such as Akaike information criterion (AIC) and Bayesian information criterion (BIC) can also be used for selecting models.

To facilitate the selection and comparison of different GARCH models, S+FinMetrics provides the function compare.mgarch to compare the fits of different "garch" objects.[7] For example, to compare the GARCH(1,1) fits of the "garch" objects ford.mod11 and ford.mod11.t, one fitted with the Gaussian distribution and the other with the Student-t distribution, use the following command:

```
> ford.compare = compare.mgarch(ford.mod11, ford.mod11.t)
> oldClass(ford.compare)
[1] "compare.garch"  "compare.mgarch"
> ford.compare
           ford.mod11 ford.mod11.t
       AIC     -10504       -10582
       BIC     -10481       -10554
Likelihood        5256         5296
```

The returned object ford.compare is an S version 3 object with class "compare.garch", which inherits from the class "compare.mgarch". The print method for this class of objects shows the AIC, BIC, and log-likelihood values of the fitted models. Since the BIC of ford.mod11.t is much smaller than that of ford.mod11, Student-t distribution seems to provide a much better fit than the normal distribution.

S+FinMetrics also provides a method for the generic plot function for objects inheriting from class "compare.mgarch". To see the arguments of the plot method, use the args function as usual:

```
> args(plot.compare.mgarch)
function(x, qq = F, hgrid = F, vgrid = F, lag.max = NULL,
        ci = 2, ...)
> plot(ford.compare)
```

The resulting plot is shown Figure 7.13. By default, the plot method compares the ACF of squared standardized residuals from the fitted models. This plot demonstrates that both models are successful at modeling conditional volatility. If the optional argument is set at qq=T, then a comparison of QQ-plots is generated:

```
> plot(ford.compare, qq=T, hgrid=T, vgrid=T)
```

which is shown in Figure 7.14. Note that since ford.mod11 is fitted using the normal distribution, the QQ-plot is based on normal assumption. In

---

[7]This is originally designed as a method function for the generic compare function for an S version 3 object. However, for S-PLUS 6 which is based on S version 4, the generic function compare does not work correctly when more than two objects are compared. So we suggest calling compare.mgarch directly.

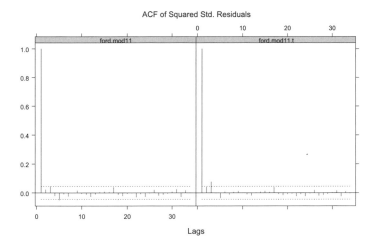

FIGURE 7.13. Comparison of ACF of squared std. residuals.

contrast, since `ford.mod11.t` is fitted using Student-t distribution, the QQ-plot is based on a Student-t distribution with degrees of freedom taken from the `cond.dist` component of the object.

7.6.1   Constrained GARCH Estimation

For a GARCH model, some model parameters can also be fixed at certain values to evaluate the fit of a particular model. Section 13.7 in Chapter 13 provides some examples.

7.7   GARCH Model Prediction

An important task of modeling conditional volatility is to generate accurate forecasts for both the future value of a financial time series as well as its conditional volatility. Since the conditional mean of the general GARCH model (7.19) assumes a traditional ARMA form, forecasts of future values of the underlying time series can be obtained following the traditional approach for ARMA prediction. However, by also allowing for a time varying conditional variance, GARCH models can generate accurate forecasts of future volatility, especially over short horizons. This section illustrates how to forecast volatility using GARCH models.

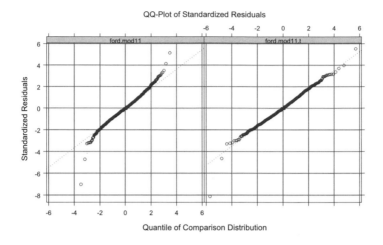

FIGURE 7.14. Comparison of QQ-plot of std. residuals.

For simplicity, consider the basic GARCH$(1, 1)$ model:

$$\sigma_t^2 = a_0 + a_1 \epsilon_{t-1}^2 + b_1 \sigma_{t-1}^2$$

which is estimated over the time period $t = 1, 2, \cdots, T$. To obtain $E_T[\sigma_{T+k}^2]$, the forecasts of future volatility σ_{T+k}^2, for $k > 0$, given information at time T. The above equation can easily obtain:

$$E_T[\sigma_{T+1}^2] = a_0 + a_1 E_T[\epsilon_T^2] + b_1 E_T[\sigma_T^2]$$
$$= a_0 + a_1 \epsilon_T^2 + b_1 \sigma_T^2$$

since it already has ϵ_T^2 and σ_T^2 after the estimation.[8] Now for $T + 2$

$$E_T[\sigma_{T+2}^2] = a_0 + a_1 E_T[\epsilon_{T+1}^2] + b_1 E_T[\sigma_{T+1}^2]$$
$$= a_0 + (a_1 + b_1) E_T[\sigma_{T+1}^2].$$

since $E_T[\varepsilon_{T+1}^2] = E_T[\sigma_{T+1}^2]$. The above derivation can be iterated to give the conditional volatility forecasting equation

$$E_T[\sigma_{T+k}^2] = a_0 \sum_{i=1}^{k-2} (a_1 + b_1)^i + (a_1 + b_1)^{k-1} E_T[\sigma_{T+1}^2] \qquad (7.20)$$

---

[8] We are a little bit loose with notations here because ϵ_T and σ_T^2 are actually the fitted values instead of the unobserved "true" values.

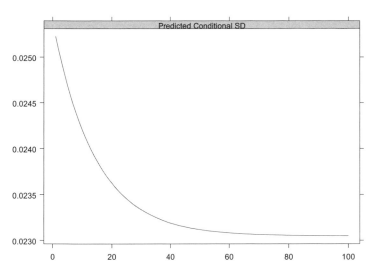

FIGURE 7.15. PGARCH forecasts of future volatility: `hp.pgarch`.

for $k \geq 2$. Notice that as $k \to \infty$, the volatility forecast in (7.20) approaches the unconditional variance $a_0/(1 - a_1 - b_1)$ if the GARCH process is stationary (i.e., if $\alpha_1 + b_1 < 1$).

The forecasting algorithm (7.20) produces forecasts for the conditional variance σ^2_{T+k}. The forecast for the conditional volatility, σ_{T+k}, is defined as the square root of the forecast for σ^2_{T+k}.

The `predict` method for "garch" objects in S+FinMetrics implements the forecasting procedure as described above for all the supported GARCH variants, allowing for leverage effects and the use of exogenous variables in both the conditional mean and the conditional variance. The forecasts can be easily obtained by calling the generic `predict` function on a fitted model object with the desired number of forecasting periods. For example, consider the PGARCH object `hp.pgarch` in Section 7.5.1. To obtain 10-step-ahead forecasts, simply use the command:

```
> hp.pgarch.pred = predict(hp.pgarch,10)
> class(hp.pgarch.pred)
[1] "predict.garch"
> names(hp.pgarch.pred)
[1] "series.pred" "sigma.pred"  "asymp.sd"
> hp.pgarch.pred
$series.pred:
 [1] 0.0003312 0.0003312 0.0003312 0.0003312 0.0003312
```

[6] 0.0003312 0.0003312 0.0003312 0.0003312 0.0003312

$sigma.pred:
 [1] 0.02523 0.02508 0.02494 0.02482 0.02470 0.02458 0.02448
 [8] 0.02438 0.02429 0.02421

$asymp.sd:
[1] 0.02305

attr(, "class"):
[1] "predict.garch"

The returned object hp.pgarch.pred is of class "predict.garch" for which there is only a plot method. Since the conditional mean was restricted to a constant in hp.pgarch, the forecasts of the future values contained in the component series.pred are simply the estimate of the mean. The component sigma.pred contains the forecasts of σ_t, and the component asymp.sd contains the estimate of the unconditional standard deviation if the estimated model is stationary. If a very large number of steps lie ahead, the forecasted volatility should approach the unconditional level. This can be easily verified for hp.pgarch as follows:

```
> plot(predict(hp.pgarch, 100))
```

where the plot method for the returned object can be directly invoked and the resulting plot is shown in Figure 7.15. Note that a plot of the forecasted series values can also be obtained. See the on-line help file for plot.predict.garch for details.

The forecasted volatility can be used together with forecasted series values to generate confidence intervals of the forecasted series values. In many cases, the forecasted volatility is of central interest, and confidence intervals for the forecasted volatility can be obtained as well. However, analytic formulas for confidence intervals of forecasted volatility are only known for some special cases (see Baillie and Bollerslev, 1992). The next section will show how a simulation-based method can be used to obtain confidence intervals for forecasted volatility from any of the GARCH variants available in S+FinMetrics.

7.8   GARCH Model Simulation

S+FinMetrics provides a method for the generic S-PLUS function simulate for objects of class "garch". This function, simulate.garch, allows observations as well as volatility to be simulated from a user-specified GARCH model or from the model contained in a fitted "garch" object. This section illustrates the use of `simulate` to create confidence intervals for volatility forecasts from a fitted GARCH model.

Example 42 *Simulation-based GARCH forecasts*

To obtain volatility forecasts from a fitted GARCH model, simply simulate from the last observation of the fitted model. This process can be repeated many times to obtain an "ensemble" of volatility forecasts. For example, suppose 100-step-ahead volatility forecasts need to be generated from `hp.pgarch`, take the residual term and fitted volatility of the last observation:[9]

```
> sigma.start = as.numeric(hp.pgarch$sigma.t[2000])
> eps.start = as.numeric(hp.pgarch$residuals[2000])
> eps.start = matrix(eps.start, 1, 1000)
> error = rbind(eps.start, matrix(rnorm(100*1000), 100))
```

Note that the first row of `error` contains the pre-sample values of ϵ_t to start off the simulation for each of the 1000 replications, whereas the rest of `error` are simply random variates with zero mean and unit variance which will be updated by the simulation procedure to result in GARCH errors. Now use these values to obtain the simulations as follows:

```
> set.seed(10)
> hp.sim.pred = simulate(hp.pgarch, n=100, n.rep=1000,
      sigma.start=sigma.start, etat=error)$sigma.t
```

The argument `n` specifies the desire to simulate 100 steps ahead, and `n.rep` specifies wanting to repeat this 1000 times. The simulation procedure returns both the simulated GARCH errors and volatility. Only take the simulated volatility contained in the `sigma.t` component; thus `hp.sim.pred` is a 100×1000 matrix with each column representing each simulation path. The simulation-based forecasts are simply the average of the 1000 simulation paths. 95% confidence intervals for the forecasts may be computed in two ways. They can be computed using the usual formula based on normally distributed forecasts; that is, mean forecast $\pm 2\cdot$ standard deviation of forecasts. Alternatively, the 95% confidence interval may be constructed from the 2.5% and 97.5% quantiles of the simulated forecasts. Use the following code to compute the forecasts and plot the 95% confidence interval based on the normal formula:

```
> vol.mean = rowMeans(hp.sim.pred)
> vol.stdev = rowStdevs(hp.sim.pred)
> vol.cf = cbind(vol.mean+2*vol.stdev, vol.mean-2*vol.stdev)
> tsplot(cbind(vol.mean, vol.cf))
```

---

[9]If the order of the fitted GARCH model is $m = \max(p, q)$, then m last observations are required.

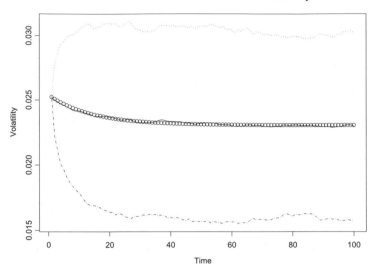

FIGURE 7.16. Simulation-based volatility forecasts: `hp.pgarch`.

```
> points(predict(hp.pgarch, 100)$sigma.pred, pch=1)
> title(main="Simulated Confidence Interval of Volatility",
    xlab="Time", ylab="Volatility")
```

The resulting plot is shown in Figure 7.16. Note that analytic forecasts are also added as points in the plot for comparison. The simulation-based forecasts agree with the analytic ones produced by the `predict` method.

In the above example, the "standardized" errors were generated by random sampling from the standard normal distribution. In practice, it may be desirable to generate standardized errors by bootstrapping from standardized residuals.

7.9   Conclusion

This chapter illustrated how to estimate and forecast from various GARCH models. The range of GARCH models supported by `S+FinMetrics` is very broad. Table 7.4   summarizes all the conditional variance formulas supported by the `garch` function.

Formula	Model
~garch(p,q)	GARCH(p,q) model
~egarch(p,q)	EGARCH(p,q) model
~tgarch(p,q)	TGARCH(p,q) model
~pgarch(p,q)	PGARCH(p,q) model with free exponent d
~pgarch(p,q,d)	PGARCH(p,q) model with fixed exponent d
~garch.2comp	GARCH TWO.COMP model
~egarch.2comp	EGARCH TWO.COMP model
~pgarch.2comp	PGARCH TWO.COMP model with free exponent d
~pgarch.2comp(d)	PGARCH TWO.COMP model with fixed exponent d
~two.comp(i)	PGARCH TWO.COMP model with choice of leverage effects
~two.comp(i,d)	PGARCH TWO.COMP model with choice of leverage effects and exponent d

TABLE 7.4. GARCH Formula Specifications

7.10   References

[1] ALEXANDER, C. (2001). *Market Models: A Guide to Financial Data Analysis*, John Wiley and Sons.

[2] BERA, A.K. AND M.L. HIGGINS (1995). "On ARCH Models: Properties, Estimation and Testing," *Journal of Economic Surveys*, 7, 305-362.

[3] BLACK, F. (1976). "Studies in Stock Price Volatility Changes", *Proceedings of the 1976 Business Meeting of the Business and Economics Statistics Section*, American Statistical Association, 177-181.

[4] BOLLERSLEV, T. (1986). "Generalized Autoregressive Conditional Heteroskedasticity", *Journal of Econometrics*, 31, 307-327.

[5] BOLLERSLEV, T., R.Y. CHU AND K.F. KRONER (1994). "ARCH Modeling in Finance: A Selective Review of the Theory and Empirical Evidence," *Journal of Econometrics*, 52, 5-59.

[6] BOLLERSLEV, T., ENGLE, R. F., AND NELSON, D. B. (1994). "ARCH Models", in R. F. Engle and D. L. McFadden (eds.) *Handbook of Econometrics*, Vol. 4, Elsevier Science B. V.

[7] BOLLERSLEV, T., AND WOOLDRIGE, J. M. (1992). "Quasi-maximum Likelihood Estimation and Inference in Dynamic Models with Time-varying Covariances", *Econometric Reviews*, 11, 143-172.

[8] DAVIDSON, R., MACKINNON, J. G. (1993). *Estimation and Inference in Econometrics*, Oxford University Press.

[9] DIEBOLD, F.X. AND J.A. LOPEZ (1996). "Modeling Volatility Dynamics," Chapter 11 in *Macroeconomics: Developments, Tensions and Prospects*, K. Hoover (ed.). Kluwer, Boston.

[10] DING, Z., AND GRANGER, C. W. J. (1996). "Modeling Volatility Persistence of Speculative Returns: A New Approach", *Journal of Econometrics*, 73, 185-215.

[11] DING, Z., GRANGER, C. W. J., AND ENGLE, R. F. (1993). "A Long Memory Property of Stock Market Returns and a New Model", *Journal of Empirical Finance*, 1, 83-106.

[12] ENGLE, R. F. (1982). "Autoregressive Conditional Heteroskedasticity with Estimates of the Variance of United Kingdom Inflation", *Econometrica*, 50 (4), 987-1007.

[13] ENGLE, R. F., AND LEE, G. J. (1999). "A Long-Run and Short-Run Component Model of Stock Return Volatility", in R. F. Engle and H. White (eds.), *Cointegration, Causality, and Forecasting*, Oxford University Press.

[14] ENGLE, R. F., LILIEN, D. M., AND ROBINS, R. P. (1987). "Estimating Time Varying Risk Premia in the Term-Structure: the ARCH-M Model", *Econometrica*, 55 (2), 391-407.

[15] ENGLE, R. F., AND NG, V. (1993). "Measuring and Testing the Impact of News on Volatility", *Journal of Finance*, 48 (5), 1749-1778.

[16] ENGLE, R.F. (2001). "GARCH 101: The Use of ARCH/GARCH Models in Applied Economics," *Journal of Economic Perspectives*, 15, 157-168.

[17] ENGLE, R.F. AND A.J. PATTON (2001). "What Good is a Volatility Model?," unpublished manuscript, Stern School of Business, New York University.

[18] GLOSTEN, L. R., JAGANNATHAN, R., AND RUNKLE, D. E. (1993). "On the Relation Between the Expected Value and the Volatility of the Nominal Excess Return on Stocks", *Journal of Finance*, 48 (5), 1779-1801.

[19] HAMILTON, J. D. (1994). *Time Series Analysis*. Princeton University Press.

[20] HE, C., TERÄSVIRTA, T. (1999a). "Properties of Moments of a Family of GARCH Processes", *Journal of Econometrics*, 92, 173-192.

[21] HE, C., TERÄSVIRTA, T. (1999b). "Fourth Moment Structure of the GARCH(p, q) Process", *Econometric Theory*, 15, 824-846.

[22] NELSON, D. B. (1991). "Conditional Heteroskedasticity in Asset Returns: a New Approach", *Econometrica*, 59 (2), 347-370.

[23] NELSON, D. B., AND CAO, C. Q. (1992). "Inequality Constraints in the Univariate GARCH Model", *Journal of Business and Economic Statistics*, 10 (2), 229-235.

[24] TSAY, R.S. (2001). *Analysis of Financial Time Series*, John Wiley & Sons, New York.

[25] ZAKOIAN, J. (1991). "Threshold Heteroskedasticity Model", unpublished manuscript, INSEE.

8
Long Memory Time Series Modeling

8.1 Introduction

Earlier chapters have demonstrated that many macroeconomic and financial time series like nominal and real interest rates, real exchange rates, exchange rate forward premiums, interest rate differentials and volatility measures are very persistent, i.e., that an unexpected shock to the underlying variable has long lasting effects. Persistence can occur in the first or higher order moments of a time series. The persistence in the first moment, or levels, of a time series can be confirmed by applying either unit root tests or stationarity tests to the levels, while the persistence in the volatility of the time series is usually exemplified by a highly persistent fitted GARCH model. Although traditional stationary ARMA processes often cannot capture the high degree of persistence in financial time series, the class of non-stationary unit root or $I(1)$ processes have some unappealing properties for financial economists. In the last twenty years, more applications have evolved using long memory processes, which lie halfway between traditional stationary $I(0)$ processes and the non-stationary $I(1)$ processes. There is substantial evidence that long memory processes can provide a good description of many highly persistent financial time series.

This chapter will cover the concept of long memory time series. Section 8.3 will explain various tests for long memory, or long range dependence, in a time series and show how to perform these tests using functions in S+FinMetrics module. In Section 8.4 will illustrate how to estimate the long memory parameter using R/S statistic and two periodogram-based method. Section 8.5 will extend the traditional ARIMA processes to fractional ARIMA (FARIMA) processes, which can be used to model the long range dependence and short run dynamics simultaneously. The semiparametric fractional autoregressive (SEMIFAR) process recently proposed by Beran and his coauthors will also be introduced. Section 8.6 will extend GARCH models to fractionally integrated GARCH models to allow for long memory in conditional volatility. Finally, section 8.7 will consider the prediction from long memory models such as FARIMA and FI-GARCH/FIEGARCH models. Beran (1994) gives an exhaustive treatment of statistical aspects of modeling with long memory processes, while Baillie (1996) provides a comprehensive survey of econometric analysis of long memory processes and applications in economics and finance.

8.2   Long Memory Time Series

To illustrate the long memory property in financial time series, consider the daily returns on the S&P500 index from January 4, 1928 to August 30, 1991 contained in the S+FinMetrics "timeSeries" object sp500. Since daily returns usually have a mean very close to zero, the absolute return is sometimes used as a measure of volatility. The sample autocorrelation function of the daily absolute returns can be plotted using the following commands:

```
> tmp = acf(abs(sp500), lag=200)
> sp500.ar = ar(abs(sp500))
> sp500.ar$order
[1] 37
> tmp.mod = list(ar=as.vector(sp500.ar$ar), sigma2=1, d=0)
> ar.acf = acf.FARIMA(tmp.mod, lag.max=200)
> lines(ar.acf$lags, ar.acf$acf/ar.acf$acf[1])
```

and the plot is shown in Figure 8.1. The autocorrelation of absolute returns is highly persistent and remains very significant at lag 200. In the above code fragment, the S-PLUS function ar is used to select the best fitting AR process using AIC, which turns out to be an AR(37) model. The S+FinMetrics function acf.FARIMA compares the theoretical autocorrelation function implied by the AR(37) process with the sample autocorrelation function. The following comments apply to this example:

1. Traditional stationary ARMA processes have short memory in the sense that the autocorrelation function decays exponentially. In the above example, the theoretical autocorrelation closely matches the sample autocorrelation at small lags. However, for large lags, the sample autocorrelation decays much more slowly than the theoretical autocorrelation.

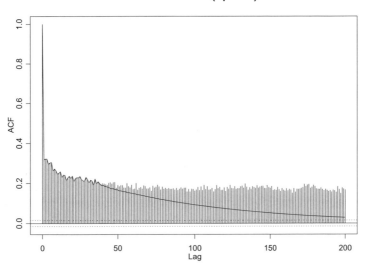

FIGURE 8.1. ACF of daily absolute returns of S&P500 index.

2. When the sample autocorrelation decays very slowly, traditional stationary ARMA processes usually result in an excessive number of parameters. In the above example, 37 autoregressive coefficients were found necessary to capture the dependence in the data.

Based on the above observations, a stationary process y_t has *long memory*, or *long range dependence*, if its autocorrelation function behaves like

$$\rho(k) \rightarrow C_\rho k^{-\alpha} \text{ as } k \rightarrow \infty \tag{8.1}$$

where C_ρ is a positive constant, and α is a real number between 0 and 1. Thus the autocorrelation function of a long memory process decays slowly at a *hyperbolic* rate. In fact, it decays so slowly that the autocorrelations are not summable:

$$\sum_{k=-\infty}^{\infty} \rho(k) = \infty.$$

For a stationary process, the autocorrelation function contains the same information as its spectral density. In particular, the spectral density is defined as:

$$f(\omega) = \frac{1}{2\pi} \sum_{k=-\infty}^{\infty} \rho(k) e^{ik\omega}$$

where ω is the Fourier frequency (c.f. Hamilton, 1994). From (8.1) it can be shown that

$$f(\omega) \to C_f \omega^{\alpha-1} \text{ as } \omega \to 0 \tag{8.2}$$

where C_f is a positive constant. So for a long memory process, its spectral density tends to infinity at zero frequency. Instead of using α, in practice use

$$H = 1 - \alpha/2 \in (0.5, 1), \tag{8.3}$$

which is known as the *Hurst coefficient* (see Hurst, 1951) to measure the long memory in y_t. The larger H is, the longer memory the stationary process has.

Based on the scaling property in (8.1) and the frequency domain property in (8.2), Granger and Joyeux (1980) and Hosking (1981) independently showed that a long memory process y_t can also be modeled parametrically by extending an integrated process to a *fractionally integrated process*. In particular, allow for fractional integration in a time series y_t as follows:

$$(1 - L)^d (y_t - \mu) = u_t \tag{8.4}$$

where L denotes the lag operator, d is the fractional integration or fractional difference parameter, μ is the expectation of y_t, and u_t is a stationary short-memory disturbance with zero mean.

In practice, when a time series is highly persistent or appears to be non-stationary, let $d = 1$ and difference the time series once to achieve stationarity. However, for some highly persistent economic and financial time series, it appears that an integer difference may be too much, which is indicated by the fact that the spectral density vanishes at zero frequency for the differenced time series. To allow for long memory and avoid taking an integer difference of y_t, allow d to be fractional. The *fractional difference filter* is defined as follows, for any real $d > -1$:

$$(1 - L)^d = \sum_{k=0}^{\infty} \binom{d}{k} (-1)^k L^k \tag{8.5}$$

with binomial coefficients:

$$\binom{d}{k} = \frac{d!}{k!(d-k)!} = \frac{\Gamma(d+1)}{\Gamma(k+1)\Gamma(d-k+1)}.$$

Notice that the fractional difference filter can be equivalently treated as an infinite order autoregressive filter.[1] It can be shown that when $|d| > 1/2$, y_t is non-stationary; when $0 < d < 1/2$, y_t is stationary and has long

---

[1] The S+FinMetrics function `FARIMA.d2ar` can be used to compute the autoregressive representation of the fractional difference filter.

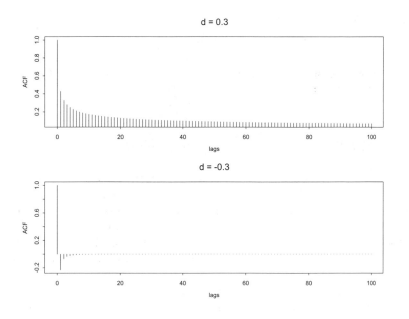

FIGURE 8.2. Autocorrelation of fractional integrated process.

memory; when $-1/2 < d < 0$, y_t is stationary and has short memory, and is sometimes referred to as *anti-persistent*.

When a fractionally integrated series y_t has long memory, it can also be shown that

$$d = H - 1/2, \qquad (8.6)$$

and thus d and H can be used interchangeably as the measure of long memory. Hosking (1981) showed that the scaling property in (8.1) and the frequency domain property in (8.2) are satisfied when $0 < d < 1/2$.

Example 43 *Theoretical ACF of fractionally integrated processes*

In this example, use the S+FinMetrics function acf.FARIMA to plot the theoretical autocorrelation function of a fractionally integrated process with a standard normal disturbance u_t, for $d = 0.3$ and $d = -0.3$, respectively:

```
> d.pos = acf.FARIMA(list(d=0.3, sigma2=1), 100)
> d.pos$acf = d.pos$acf / d.pos$acf[1]
> d.neg = acf.FARIMA(list(d=-0.3, sigma2=1), 100)
> d.neg$acf = d.neg$acf / d.neg$acf[1]

> par(mfrow=c(2,1))
> plot(d.pos$lags, d.pos$acf, type="h", main="d = 0.3",
+       xlab="lags", ylab="ACF")
```

```
> plot(d.neg$lags, d.neg$acf, type="h", main="d = -0.3",
+        xlab="lags", ylab="ACF")
> par(mfrow=c(1,1))
```

and the plot is shown in Figure 8.2. Notice that the signs of the ACF coefficients are determined by the sign of d.

8.3   Statistical Tests for Long Memory

Given the scaling property of the autocorrelation function, the frequency domain property and the fractionally integrated process representation of a long memory time series, various tests have been proposed to determine the existence of long memory in a time series. This section introduces the R/S statistic and GPH test. However, before getting into the details of those test statistics, it is important to note that the definition of long memory does not dictate the general behavior of the autocorrelation function or its spectral density. Instead, they only specify the asymptotic behavior when $k \to \infty$ or $\omega \to 0$. What this means is that for a long memory process, it is not necessary for the autocorrelation to remain significant at large lags as in the previous sp500 example, as long as the autocorrelation function decays slowly. Beran (1994) gives an example to illustrate this property.

8.3.1   R/S Statistic

The best-known test for long memory or long range dependence is probably the *rescaled range*, or *range over standard deviation*, or simply R/S statistic, which was originally proposed by Hurst (1951), and later refined by Mandelbrot and his coauthors. The R/S statistic is the range of partial sums of deviations of a time series from its mean, rescaled by its standard deviation. Specifically, consider a time series y_t, for $t = 1, \cdots, T$. The R/S statistic is defined as:

$$Q_T = \frac{1}{s_T} \left[\max_{1 \leq k \leq T} \sum_{j=1}^{k} (y_j - \bar{y}) - \min_{1 \leq k \leq T} \sum_{j=1}^{k} (y_j - \bar{y}) \right] \qquad (8.7)$$

where $\bar{y} = 1/T \sum_{i=1}^{T} y_i$ is the sample mean and $s_T = \sqrt{1/T \sum_{i=1}^{T} (y_i - \bar{y})^2}$ is the sample standard deviation. If y_t's are i.i.d. normal random variables, then

$$\frac{1}{\sqrt{T}} Q_T \Rightarrow V$$

where $\Rightarrow$ denotes weak convergence and V is the range of a Brownian bridge on the unit interval. Lo (1991) gives selected quantiles of V.

Lo (1991) pointed out that the R/S statistic is not robust to short range dependence. In particular, if y_t is autocorrelated (has short memory) then the limiting distribution of $Q_T/\sqrt{T}$ is V scaled by the square root of the long run variance of y_t. To allow for short range dependence in y_t, Lo (1991) modified the R/S statistic as follows:

$$\tilde{Q}_T = \frac{1}{\hat{\sigma}_T(q)} \left[\max_{1 \leq k \leq T} \sum_{j=1}^{k}(y_j - \bar{y}) - \min_{1 \leq k \leq T} \sum_{j=1}^{k}(y_j - \bar{y}) \right] \qquad (8.8)$$

where the sample standard deviation is replaced by the square root of the Newey-West estimate of the long run variance with bandwidth q.[2] Lo (1991) showed that if there is short memory but no long memory in y_t, $\tilde{Q}_T$ also converges to V, the range of a Brownian bridge.

The S+FinMetrics function rosTest can be used to test for long memory in a time series using the R/S statistic (8.7) or the modified R/S statistic (8.8). For example, to test for long memory in the absolute returns of S&P500 index, use the following command:

```
> rosTest(abs(sp500))

Test for Long Memory: Modified R/S Test

Null Hypothesis: no long-term dependence

Test Statistics:

 7.8823**

 *  : significant at 5% level
** : significant at 1% level

Total Observ.: 17054
   Bandwidth : 14
```

By default, Lo's modified R/S statistic is computed and the bandwidth q for obtaining the long run variance is chosen to be $[4(T/100)^{1/4}]$, where T is the sample size, and $[\cdot]$ denotes integer part of. In the above example, the modified R/S statistic is significant at 1% level of significance. A different bandwidth can be used by setting the optional argument bandwidth. If bandwidth is set to zero, then classical R/S statistic is returned:

```
> rosTest(abs(sp500), bandwidth=0)
```

---

[2] See Chapter 2 for the definition and estimation of long run variance and the online help file for the S+FinMetrics function asymp.var.

Test for Long Memory: R/S Test

Null Hypothesis: no long-term dependence

Test Statistics:

  17.821**

  * : significant at 5% level
  ** : significant at 1% level

 Total Observ.: 17054

which is also significant at 1% level of significance in this case.

8.3.2   GPH Test

Based on the fractionally integrated process representation of a long memory time series as in (8.4), Geweke and Porter-Hudak (1983) proposed a semi-nonparametric approach to testing for long memory. In particular, the *spectral density* of the fractionally integrated process y_t is given by:

$$f(\omega) = [4\sin^2(\frac{\omega}{2})]^{-d} f_u(\omega) \tag{8.9}$$

where ω is the Fourier frequency, and $f_u(\omega)$ is the spectral density corresponding to u_t. Note that the fractional difference parameter d can be estimated by the following regression:

$$\ln f(\omega_j) = \beta - d\ln[4\sin^2(\frac{\omega_j}{2})] + e_j, \tag{8.10}$$

for $j = 1, 2, \cdots, n_f(T)$. Geweke and Porter-Hudak (1993) showed that using a *periodogram* estimate of $f(\omega_j)$, the least squares estimate $\hat{d}$ using the above regression is normally distributed in large samples if $n_f(T) = T^\alpha$ with $0 < \alpha < 1$:

$$\hat{d} \sim N(d, \frac{\pi^2}{6\sum_{j=1}^{n_f}(U_j - \bar{U})^2})$$

where

$$U_j = \ln[4\sin^2(\frac{\omega_j}{2})]$$

and $\bar{U}$ is the sample mean of U_j, $j = 1, \cdots, n_f$. Under the null hypothesis of no long memory ($d = 0$), the t-statistic

$$t_{d=0} = \hat{d} \cdot \left(\frac{\pi^2}{6\sum_{j=1}^{n_f}(U_j - \bar{U})^2}\right)^{-1/2} \tag{8.11}$$

has a limiting standard normal distribution.

The S+FinMetrics function `gphTest` can be used to estimate d from (8.10) and compute the test statistic (8.11), which is usually referred to as the *GPH test*. The arguments taken by `gphTest` are:

```
> args(gphTest)
function(x, spans = 1, taper = 0.1, pad = 0, detrend = F,
        demean = T, alpha = 0.5, na.rm = F)
```

The optional arguments `spans`, `taper`, `pad`, `detrend` and `demean` are actually passed to the S-PLUS function `spec.pgram` to obtain a periodogram estimate.[3] The optional argument `alpha` is used to choose the number of frequencies $n_f(T)$. By default, $n_f(T) = T^\alpha$ with $\alpha = 0.5$. To illustrate the use of `gphTest`, consider estimating d and testing for long memory in the S&P 500 index absolute returns:

```
> gph.sp500 = gphTest(abs(sp500),taper=0)
> class(gph.sp500)
[1] "gphTest"
> names(gph.sp500)
[1] "d"        "n"        "na"        "n.freq"   "std.err"
```

The result of `gphTest` is an object of class "gphTest" for which there is only a `print` method:

```
> gph.sp500

Test for Long Memory: GPH Test

Null Hypothesis: d = 0

Test Statistics:

    d 0.4573
 stat 7.608**

  * : significant at 5% level
 ** : significant at 1% level

 Total Observ.: 17054
Number of Freq: 130
```

The estimated value of d from (8.10) is $\hat{d} = 0.457$, which suggests long memory, and the gph test statistic (8.11) is 7.608. Hence, the null of no long memory is rejected at the 1% significance level. The estimate of d is

---

[3] See *S-PLUS Guide to Statistics* for an introduction to the estimation of periodogram and the usage of `spec.pgram`.

close to the nonstationary range. In fact, a 95% confidence interval for d based on the asymptotic standard error

```
> gph.sp500$std.err
[1] 0.06011
```

is $[0.337, 0.578]$ and contains $d > 0.5$.

8.4   Estimation of Long Memory Parameter

The previous section introduced the R/S statistic and the log-periodogram regression to test for long memory in a time series. Cheung (1993) conducted a Monte Carlo comparison of these tests. Obtaining an estimate of the long memory parameter H or d is also of interest. The GPH test produces an estimate of d automatically. This section will show that the R/S statistic can also be used to obtain an estimate of the Hurst coefficient H. It will also introduce two periodogram-based methods for estimating the long memory parameter: the periodogram method and Whittle's method. In addition, the fractional difference parameter d can also be estimated by using a general FARIMA(p, d, q) model, which will be introduced in the next section. Taqqu, Teverovsky and Willinger (1995) and Taqqu and Teverovsky (1998) compared the performance of many different estimators of the long memory parameter, including the above mentioned methods.

8.4.1   R/S Analysis

Section 8.3.1 mentioned that when there is no long memory in a stationary time series, the R/S statistic converges to a random variable at rate $T^{1/2}$. However, when the stationary process y_t has long memory, Mandelbrot (1975) showed that the R/S statistic converges to a random variable at rate T^H, where H is the Hurst coefficient. Based on this result, the log-log plot of the R/S statistic versus the sample size used should scatter around a straight line with slope $1/2$ for a short memory time series. In contrast, for a long memory time series, the log-log plot should scatter around a straight line with slope equal to $H > 1/2$, provided the sample size is large enough.

  To use the above method to estimate the long memory parameter H, first compute the R/S statistic using k_1 consecutive observations in the sample, where k_1 should be large enough. Then increase the number of observations by a factor of f; that is, compute the R/S statistic using $k_i = fk_{i-1}$ consecutive observations for $i = 2, \cdots, s$. Note that to obtain the R/S statistic with k_i consecutive observations, one can actually divide the sample into $[T/k_i]$ blocks and obtain $[T/k_i]$ different values, where $[\cdot]$ denotes the integer part of a real number. Obviously, the larger k_i is, the

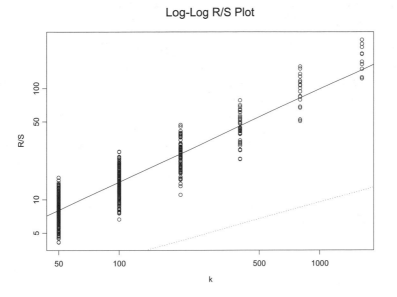

FIGURE 8.3. R/S estimate of long memory parameter.

smaller $[T/k_i]$ is. A line fit of all those R/S statistics versus k_i, $i = 1, \cdots, s$, on the log-log scale yields an estimate of the Hurst coefficient H.

The S+FinMetrics function d.ros implements the above procedure for estimating H. The arguments taken by d.ros are:

```
> args(d.ros)
function(x, minK = 4, k.ratio = 2, minNumPoints = 3,
        method = "ls", output = "d", plot = F, ...)
```

where minK specifies the value for k_1, k.ratio specifies the ratio factor f, and minNumPoints specifies the minimum requirement for $[T/k_s]$. For example, if minNumPoints=3, s must be such that one can divide T observations into three blocks with at least k_s observations in each block. The optional argument output specifies the type of output: if output="H", then the Hurst coefficient is returned; if output="d", then the fractional difference parameter d is returned. For example, to estimate the Hurst coefficient for absolute returns of S&P500 index using R/S statistic, use the following command:

```
> d.ros(abs(sp500), minK=50, k.ratio=2, minNumPoints=10,
+ output="H", plot=T)
[1] 0.8393
```

By setting plot=T, the log-log plot of R/S statistics versus k_i is generated, as shown in Figure 8.3: the solid line represents the fitted line, and the dotted line represents the case for no long memory. In this case, the solid line is far away from the dotted line, which is substantial evidence for long memory. The estimate of d using (8.6) is 0.3393.

The weakness of the above procedure is that for a particular sample, it is not clear what value of k_1 is "large enough". In addition, for large values of k_i, few values of the R/S statistic can be calculated unless the sample size is very large. To mitigate the latter problem, set the optional argument method="ll" when calling d.ros, which will direct the procedure to use the $L1$ method or least absolute deviation (LAD) method, for the line fit, and thus result in a robust estimate of the long memory parameter. For the S&P 500 absolute returns, the results using the $L1$ method are essentially the same as using the least squares method:

```
> d.ros(abs(sp500), minK=50, k.ratio=2, minNumPoints=10,
+ output="H", method="ll", plot=F)
[1] 0.8395
```

8.4.2 Periodogram Method

Section 8.3 demonstrates that for a long memory process, its spectral density approaches $C_f \omega^{1-2H}$ when the frequency ω approaches zero. Since the spectral density can be estimated by a periodogram, the log-log plot of periodogram versus the frequency should scatter around a straight line with slope $1 - 2H$ for frequencies close to zero. This method can also be used to obtain an estimate of the long memory parameter H, and it is usually referred to as the *periodogram method*.

The S+FinMetrics function d.pgram implements a procedure to estimate the long memory parameter using the periodogram method, which calls the S-PLUS function spec.pgram to obtain an estimate of periodogram. The arguments taken by d.pgram are:

```
> args(d.pgram)
function(x, spans = 1, taper = 0.1, pad = 0, detrend = F,
        demean = T, method = "ls", output = "d",
        lower.percentage = 0.1, minNumFreq = 10, plot = F, ...)
```

Similar to the gphTest function, the optional arguments spans, taper, pad, detrend and demean are passed to spec.pgram to obtain the periodogram estimate. The optional argument lower.percentage=0.1 specifies that only the lower 10% of the frequencies are used to estimate H. For example, to estimate the long memory parameter H of abs(sp500) with no tapering,use the following command:

```
> d.pgram(abs(sp500), taper=0, output="H", plot=F)
[1] 0.8741311
```

The implied estimate of d is then 0.3741.

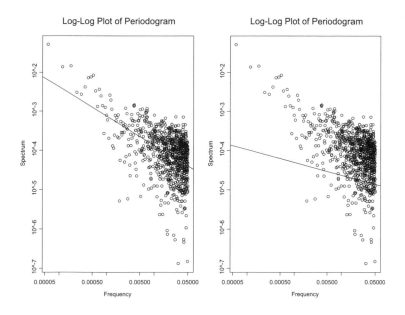

FIGURE 8.4. Periodogram estimates of long memory parameter using least squares and LAD.

Just like with the R/S estimate of the long memory parameter, it can be difficult to choose the value for `lower.percentage`. To obtain a more robust line fit, set the optional argument `method="l1"` when calling `d.pgram`, to use $L1$ method or LAD method instead of the default least squares fit. For example, to compare the least squares and $L1$ fits for `abs(sp500)` use

```
> par(mfrow=c(1,2))
> H.ls = d.pgram(abs(sp500),taper=0, output="d",plot=T)
> H.l1 = d.pgram(abs(sp500),taper=0, output="d",method="l1",
+ plot=T)
> H.ls
[1] 0.3741
> H.l1
[1] 0.1637
```

8.4.3 Whittle's Method

Whittle's method for estimating d is based on a frequency domain maximum likelihood estimation of a fractionally integrated process (8.4). It can be shown that the unknown parameters in (8.4) can be estimated by minimizing a discretized version of

$$Q(\theta) = \int_{-\pi}^{\pi} \frac{I(\omega)}{f(\theta; \omega)} d\omega$$

where θ is the vector of unknown parameters including the fractional difference parameter d, $I(\omega)$ is the periodogram of y_t, and $f(\theta, \omega)$ is the theoretical spectral density of y_t. Refer to Beran (1994) for the derivation of Whittle's method.

To use Whittle's method to estimate the fractional difference parameter d, use the S+FinMetrics function d.whittle. The syntax of d.whittle is similar to but more simple than that of d.pgram:

```
> args(d.whittle)
function(x, spans = 1, taper = 0.1, pad = 0, detrend = F,
         demean = T, output = "d")
```

where again the arguments spans, taper, pad, detrend and demean are passed to the S-PLUS function spec.pgram to obtain the periodogram. For example, to estimate the fractional difference parameter d of abs(sp500) with no tapering, use the command:

```
> d.whittle(abs(sp500), taper=0)
[1] 0.2145822
```

A caveat to using d.whittle is that although the Whittle's method is defined for a general fractionally integrated process y_t in (8.4), it is implemented assuming that u_t is a standard normal disturbance and thus y_t follows a FARIMA$(0, d, 0)$ process.

8.5   Estimation of FARIMA and SEMIFAR Models

Previous sections illustrated how to test for long memory and estimate the long memory parameter H or d. This section introduces the more flexible fractional ARIMA models, which are capable of modeling both the long memory and short run dynamics in a stationary time series. It will also introduce a semiparametric model for long memory, which allows a semiparametric estimation of a trend component.

Many empirical studies have found that there is strong evidence for long memory in financial volatility series, for example, see Lobato and Savin (1998) and Ray and Tsay (2000). Indeed, Andersen, Bollerslev, Diebold and Labys (1999) suggested to use FARIMA models to forecast daily volatility based on logarithmic realized volatility. This section will focus on modeling a volatility series for the examples.

8.5.1   Fractional ARIMA Models

The traditional approach to modeling an $I(0)$ time series y_t is to use the ARIMA model:

$$\phi(L)(1-L)^d(y_t - \mu) = \theta(L)\epsilon_t \tag{8.12}$$

where $\phi(L)$ and $\theta(L)$ are lag polynomials

$$\phi(L) = 1 - \sum_{i=1}^{p} \phi_i L^i$$

$$\theta(L) = 1 + \sum_{j=1}^{q} \theta_j L^j$$

with roots outside the unit circle, and ϵ_t is assumed to be an *iid* normal random variable with zero mean and variance σ^2.[4] This is usually referred to as the ARIMA(p, d, q) model. By allowing d to be a real number instead of a positive integer, the ARIMA model becomes the autoregressive fractionally integrated moving average (ARFIMA) model, or simply, fractional ARIMA (FARIMA) model[5].

For a stationary FARIMA model with $-1/2 < d < 1/2$, Sowell (1992) describes how to compute the exact maximum likelihood estimate (MLE). The S-PLUS function `arima.fracdiff` implements a very fast procedure based on the approximate MLE proposed by Haslett and Raftery (1989), and refer the reader to the *S-PLUS Guide to Statistics* for a discussion of this procedure.

However, for many economic and financial time series, the data usually seem to lie on the borderline separating stationarity from non-stationarity. As a result, one usually needs to decide whether or not to difference the original time series before estimating a stationary FARIMA model, and the inference of unknown FARIMA model parameters ignores this aspect of uncertainty in d. Beran (1995) extended the estimation of FARIMA models for any $d > -1/2$ by considering the following variation the FARIMA model:

$$\phi(L)(1-L)^\delta[(1-L)^m y_t - \mu] = \theta(L)\epsilon_t \tag{8.13}$$

where $-1/2 < \delta < 1/2$, and $\phi(L)$ and $\theta(L)$ are defined as above. The integer m is the number of times that y_t must be differenced to achieve stationarity, and thus the difference parameter is given by $d = \delta + m$. In the following discussions and in the S+FinMetrics module, restrict m to be either 0 or 1, which is usually sufficient for modeling economic and financial

---

[4] Note that the definition of the polynomial $\theta(L)$ is different from that of the ARIMA model defined in *S-PLUS Guide to Statistics*. In particular, the signs of θ_j are the opposite of those for ARIMA models.

[5] The S+FinMetrics module actually provides a convenience function FAR for estimating a FARIMA$(p, d, 0)$ model.

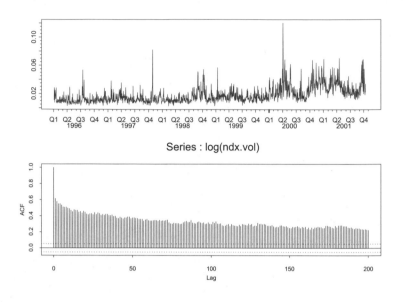

FIGURE 8.5. Garman-Klass volatility of daily NASDAQ-100 returns.

time series. Note that when $m = 0$, μ is the expectation of y_t; in contrast, when $m = 1$, μ is the slope of the linear trend component in y_t.

The S+FinMetrics function FARIMA implements a procedure (based on arima.fracdiff) to estimate the FARIMA model (8.13), and the standard errors of unknown parameters are computed using the asymptotic distribution derived by Beran (1995), which takes into account that m is also determined by data rather than by *a prior* decision.

To illustrate the usage of the FARIMA function, consider modeling the volatility of daily NASDAQ-100 index returns. In recent years, intra-day security prices have been employed to compute daily realized volatility, for example, see Andersen, Bollerslev, Diebold and Labys (2001a, 2001b). Since intra-day security prices can be hard to obtain, compute daily volatility based on the daily opening, highest, lowest, and closing prices, as proposed by Garman and Klass (1980) and implemented by the S+FinMetrics function TA.garmanKlass.

Example 44 *Long memory modeling of NASDAQ-100 index volatility*

The S+FinMetrics "timeSeries" ndx.dat contains the daily opening, highest, lowest and closing prices of NASDAQ-100 index from January 2, 1996 to October 12, 2001. First compute the volatility series using the Garman-Klass estimator and visualize its sample ACF:

```
> ndx.vol = TA.garmanKlass(ndx.dat[,"Open"], ndx.dat[,"High"],
```

```
+              ndx.dat[,"Low"], ndx.dat[,"Close"])
> par(mfrow=c(2,1))
> plot(ndx.vol, reference.grid=F)
> tmp = acf(log(ndx.vol), lag=200)
> par(mfrow=c(1,1))
```

The volatility series ndx.vol and the sample ACF of logarithmic volatility
are shown in Figure 8.5. The ACF decays very slowly and remains highly
significant at lag 200, which indicates that the series may exhibit long
memory.

First estimate a $\text{FARIMA}(0, d, 0)$ model for logarithmic volatility as follows:

```
> ndx.d = FARIMA(log(ndx.vol), p=0, q=0)
> class(ndx.d)
[1] "FARIMA"
> names(ndx.d)
 [1] "call"      "model"     "m"        "delta"
 [5] "n.used"    "BIC"       "loglike"  "residuals"
 [9] "fitted"    "x.name"    "cov"      "CI"
```

The result of FARIMA is an object of class "FARIMA", for which there are
print, summary, plot and predict methods as well as extractor functions
coef, fitted, residuals and vcov. The summary method gives

```
> summary(ndx.d)

Call:
FARIMA(x = log(ndx.vol), p = 0, q = 0)

Coefficients:
    Value Std. Error t value Pr(>|t|)
d  0.3534  0.0205   17.1964  0.0000

Information Criteria:
 log-likelihood      BIC
  -732.3           1471.9

Residual scale estimate: 0.4001

                  total residual
Degree of freedom:  1455      1453
Time period: from 01/04/1996 to 10/12/2001
```

The estimated model appears stationary and has long memory since $0 <
\hat{d} < 1/2$. Notice that m is estimated to be zero:

```
> ndx.d$m
```

```
[1] 0
```

To allow for long memory and short memory at the same time, use a FARIMA(p, d, q) model with $p \neq 0$ or $q \neq 0$. However, in practice, it is usually difficult to choose the appropriate value for p or q. The FARIMA function can choose the best fitting FARIMA model based on finding values of $p \leq p_{max}$ and $q \leq q_{max}$ which minimize the Bayesian Information Criterion (BIC). For example, to estimate all the FARIMA models with $0 \leq p \leq 2$ and $0 \leq q \leq 2$, use the optional arguments p.range and q.range as follows:

```
> ndx.bic = FARIMA(log(ndx.vol), p.range=c(0,2),
+ q.range=c(0,2), mmax=0)
p = 0   q = 0
p = 0   q = 1
p = 0   q = 2
p = 1   q = 0
p = 1   q = 1
p = 1   q = 2
p = 2   q = 0
p = 2   q = 1
p = 2   q = 2
```

In the above example, set mmax=0 to restrict m to be zero because the previous FARIMA$(0, d, 0)$ model fit suggests that the data may be stationary. A summary of the fitted model is

```
> summary(ndx.bic)

Call:
FARIMA(x = log(ndx.vol), p.range = c(0, 2), q.range = c(0, 2),
       mmax = 0)

Coefficients:
       Value Std. Error t value Pr(>|t|)
    d 0.4504  0.0287    15.6716  0.0000
MA(1) 0.2001  0.0359     5.5687  0.0000

Information Criteria:
 log-likelihood          BIC
   -717.9342       1450.4325

Residual scale estimate: 0.3963

                   total residual
Degree of freedom:  1454      1451
Time period: from 01/05/1996 to 10/12/2001
```

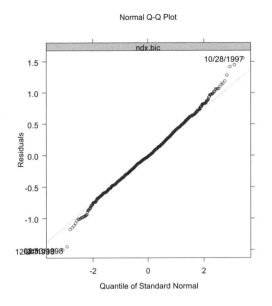

FIGURE 8.6. FARIMA residual QQ-plot of `log(ndx.vol)`.

```
BIC of all models estimated:
         q=0       q=1       q=2
p=0 1466.898 1450.432 1451.055
p=1 1457.319 1462.694 1455.590
p=2 1464.800 1457.243 1464.238
```

The BIC values for all the models considered are shown in the output. The model minimizing the BIC is a FARIMA$(0, d, 1)$ model. The estimates of d and the moving average coefficient are very significant, but the 95% Wald-type confidence interval of d includes $1/2$ and thus the non-stationary case.[6]

Further diagnostics of the model fit can be obtained by using the `plot` method:

```
> plot(ndx.bic)
```

```
Make a plot selection (or 0 to exit):
```

```
1: plot: all
```

_____
[6] Currently the standard error of the mean parameter is not available because `arima.fracdiff` concentrates out the mean and thus does not compute its standard error.

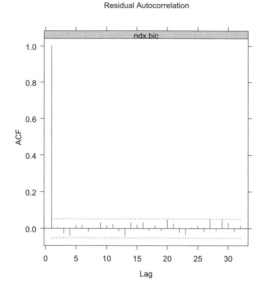

FIGURE 8.7. FARIMA residual ACF of log(ndx.vol).

```
2: plot: response vs fitted values
3: plot: response and fitted values
4: plot: normal QQ-plot of residuals
5: plot: residuals
6: plot: standardized residuals
7: plot: residual histogram
8: plot: residual ACF
9: plot: residual PACF
10: plot: residual^2 ACF
11: plot: residual^2 PACF
Selection:
```

For example, if 4 is chosen at the prompt the normal QQ-plot of the model residuals ϵ_t will be shown as in Figure 8.6. It seems that the normality assumption agrees well with the data. If 8 is chosen at the prompt, the ACF of model residuals will be shown as in Figure 8.7, and the FARIMA model is very successful at capturing the long memory in logarithmic volatility.

In the above example, m can also be allowed to be estimated:

```
> ndx.bic2 = FARIMA(log(ndx.vol),p.range=c(0,2),
+ q.range=c(0,2), mmax=1)
p = 0   q = 0
...
p = 2   q = 2
```

```
> ndx.bic2$m
[1] 1

> summary(ndx.bic2)

Call:
FARIMA(x = log(ndx.vol), p.range = c(0, 2), q.range =
c(0, 2), mmax = 1)

Coefficients:
        Value Std. Error t value Pr(>|t|)
    d  0.5161  0.1056     4.8864  0.0000
AR(1)  1.1387  0.3753     3.0340  0.0025
AR(2) -0.1561  0.3724    -0.4193  0.6751
MA(1)  1.4364  0.4416     3.2528  0.0012
MA(2) -0.4309  0.7574    -0.5689  0.5695

Information Criteria:
 log-likelihood     BIC
   -696.3        1429.0

Residual scale estimate: 0.3903

                 total residual
Degree of freedom:  1453     1447
Time period: from 01/08/1996 to 10/12/2001

BIC of all models estimated:
      q=0  q=1  q=2
p=0 1467 1450 1451
p=1 1457 1459 1456
p=2 1456 1454 1429
```

Here the best fitting model is a FARIMA$(2, 0.52, 2)$ model. However, the values of the AR and MA coefficients indicate an explosive model. The problem appears to be near canceling roots in the AR and MA polynomials. If the model is re-fitted with $p = q = 1$, the results make more sense:

```
> ndx.bic2 = FARIMA(log(ndx.vol), p=1, q=1, mmax=1)
> summary(ndx.bic2)

Call:
FARIMA(x = log(ndx.vol), p = 1, q = 1, mmax = 1)

Coefficients:
```

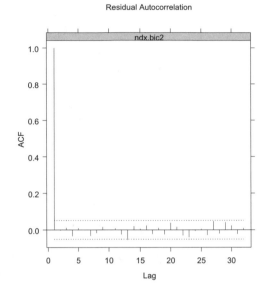

FIGURE 8.8. Residual ACF from FARIMA$(1, 0.51, 1)$ model fit to `log(ndx.vol)`.

```
        Value  Std. Error  t value  Pr(>|t|)
   d   0.5051    0.0436    11.5965   0.0000
AR(1)  0.2376    0.0687     3.4597   0.0006
MA(1)  0.4946    0.0367    13.4894   0.0000


Information Criteria:
 log-likelihood      BIC
  -712.7           1447.3

Residual scale estimate: 0.3948

                  total  residual
Degree of freedom:  1454      1450
Time period: from 01/05/1996 to 10/12/2001
```

Figure 8.8 gives the residual ACF from the above model. The long memory behavior has been well captured by the model. However, the fitted model has the undesirable property of being non-stationary.

8.5.2   SEMIFAR Model

The previous subsection demonstrated that for logarithmic volatility of NASDAQ-100 index returns, the FARIMA model chosen by BIC suggests that the underlying series may be non-stationary. In addition, from the time series plot in Figure 8.5, the volatility has become much larger since the middle of 2000. To allow for a possible deterministic trend in a time series, in addition to a stochastic trend, long memory and short memory components, Beran, Feng and Ocker (1998), Beran and Ocker (1999), and Beran and Ocker (2001) propose the **semi**parametric **f**ractional **a**uto**r**egressive (SEMIFAR) model. The SEMIFAR model is based on the following extension to the FARIMA$(p, d, 0)$ model (8.12):

$$\phi(L)(1 - L)^\delta[(1 - L)^m y_t - g(i_t)] = \epsilon_t \tag{8.14}$$

for $t = 1, \cdots, T$. The above equation is very similar to (8.13), except that the constant term μ is now replaced by $g(i_t)$, a smooth trend function on $[0, 1]$, with $i_t = t/T$. By using a nonparametric kernel estimate of $g(i_t)$, the S+FinMetrics function SEMIFAR implements a procedure to estimate the SEMIFAR model, and it uses BIC to choose the short memory autoregressive order p. Refer to Beran, Feng and Ocker (1998) for a detailed description of the algorithm.

Example 45 *Estimation of SEMIFAR model for NASDAQ-100 index volatility*

To obtain a SEMIFAR model of logarithmic volatility of NASDAQ-100 index returns, use the following command:

```
> ndx.semi = SEMIFAR(log(ndx.vol), p.range=c(0,2), trace=F)
> class(ndx.semi)
[1] "SEMIFAR"
```

Note that the optional argument trace=F is used to suppress the messages printed by the procedure. The result of SEMIFAR is an object of class "SEMIFAR" for which there are print, summary, plot and predict methods as well as extractor functions coef, residuals and vcov. The components of ndx.semi are

```
> names(ndx.semi)
 [1] "model"     "m"        "delta"     "BIC"
 [5] "loglike"   "trend"    "g.CI"      "bandwidth"
 [9] "Cf"        "nu"       "residuals" "cov"
[13] "CI"        "call"
```

The basic fit is

```
> ndx.semi

Call:
SEMIFAR(x = log(ndx.vol), p.range = c(0, 2), trace = F)

Difference:
```

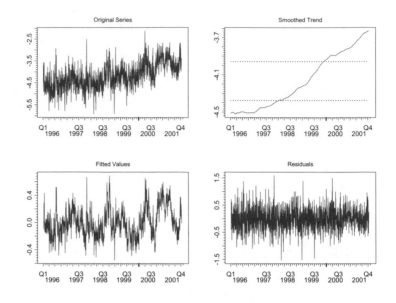

FIGURE 8.9. SEMIFAR decomposition of `log(ndx.vol)`.

```
0: estimates based on original series.

FAR coefficients:
     d
 0.2928


Residual scale estimate: 0.3946


                 total residual
Degree of freedom: 1453      1452
Time period: from 01/08/1996 to 10/12/2001
```

From the above output, after accounting for a smooth nonparametric trend component $g(i_t)$, the logarithmic volatility appears to be stationary and has long memory.

The estimated trend component can be visualized by calling the `plot` method of fitted model object:

```
> plot(ndx.semi)

Make a plot selection (or 0 to exit):

1: plot: all
2: plot: trend, fitted values, and residuals
```

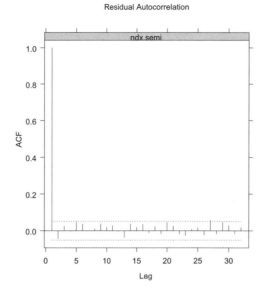

FIGURE 8.10. SEMIFAR residual ACF of `log(ndx.vol)`.

```
3: plot: normal QQ-plot of residuals
4: plot: standardized residuals
5: plot: residual histogram
6: plot: residual ACF
7: plot: residual PACF
8: plot: residual^2 ACF
9: plot: residual^2 PACF
Selection:
```

If 2 is selected at the prompt, a plot as in Figure 8.9 will be shown, which indicates the original time series, the estimated smooth trend component, the fitted values and model residuals. The smooth trend component is also plotted with a confidence band. If the trend falls outside the confidence band, it indicates that the trend component is significant. In this case, the trend in logarithmic volatility appears to be very significant, at least for the time period investigated. The model fit can also be checked by choosing 6 at the prompt, which will generate the ACF plot of residuals, as shown in Figure 8.10. Again, the SEMIFAR model seems to be very successful at modeling the long memory in the original time series.

Prediction from SEMIFAR models will be discussed in section 8.7.

8.6 Long Memory GARCH Models

8.6.1 FIGARCH and FIEGARCH Models

The previous section showed that the FARIMA or SEMIFAR model can be used directly to model the long memory behavior observed in the volatility of financial asset returns, given that a time series representing the volatility exists. However, sometimes a reliable estimate of volatility may be hard to obtain, or the user may want to model the dynamics of the asset returns together with its volatility. In those situations, the GARCH class models provide viable alternatives for volatility modeling.

Section 7.5.2 of Chapter 7 has illustrated that two components GARCH models can be used to capture the high persistence in volatility by allowing a highly persistent long run component and a short run transitory component in volatility. This subsection shows how GARCH models can be extended to allow directly for long memory and high persistence in volatility.

FIGARCH Model

Section 7.3 of Chapter 7 shows that a basic GARCH(1, 1) model can be written as an ARMA(1, 1) model in terms of squared residuals. In the same spirit, for the GARCH(p, q) model:

$$\sigma_t^2 = a + \sum_{i=1}^{p} a_i \epsilon_{t-i}^2 + \sum_{j=1}^{q} b_j \sigma_{t-j}^2$$

easily shows that it can be rewritten as follows:

$$\phi(L)\epsilon_t^2 = a + b(L)u_t \tag{8.15}$$

where

$$u_t = \epsilon_t^2 - \sigma_t^2$$
$$\phi(L) = 1 - \phi_1 L - \phi_2 L^2 - \cdots - \phi_m L^m$$
$$b(L) = 1 - b_1 L - b_2 L^2 - \cdots - b_q L^q$$

with $m = \max(p, q)$ and $\phi_i = a_i + b_i$. Obviously equation (8.15) represents an ARMA(m, q) process in terms of squared residuals ϵ_t^2 with u_t being a MDS disturbance term.

The high persistence in GARCH models suggests that the polynomial $\phi(z) = 0$ may have a unit root, in which case the GARCH model becomes the integrated GARCH (IGARCH) model. See Nelson (1990) for which the unconditional variance does not exist. To allow for high persistence and long memory in the conditional variance while avoiding the complications of IGARCH models, extend the ARMA(m, q) process in (8.15) to a

FARIMA(m, d, q) process as follows:

$$\phi(L)(1 - L)^d \epsilon_t^2 = a + b(L)u_t \qquad (8.16)$$

where all the roots of $\phi(z) = 0$ and $b(z) = 0$ lie outside the unit circle. When $d = 0$, this reduces to the usual GARCH model; when $d = 1$, this becomes the IGARCH model; when $0 < d < 1$, the *fractionally differenced squared residuals*, $(1 - L)^d \epsilon_t^2$, follow a stationary ARMA(m, q) process. The above FARIMA process for ϵ_t^2 can be rewritten in terms of the conditional variance σ_t^2:

$$b(L)\sigma_t^2 = a + [b(L) - \phi(L)(1 - L)^d]\epsilon_t^2. \qquad (8.17)$$

Baillie, Bollerslev and Mikkelsen (1996) refer to the above model as the fractionally integrated GARCH, or FIGARCH(m, d, q) model. When $0 < d < 1$, the coefficients in $\phi(L)$ and $b(L)$ capture the short run dynamics of volatility, while the fractional difference parameter d models the long run characteristics of volatility.

FIEGARCH

The FIEGARCH model directly extends the ARMA representation of squared residuals, which results from the GARCH model, to a fractionally integrated model. However, to guarantee that a general FIGARCH model is stationary and the conditional variance σ_t^2 is always positive, usually complicated and intractable restrictions have to be imposed on the model coefficients. For example, see Baillie, Bollerslev and Mikkelsen (1996) or Bollerslev and Mikkelsen (1996) for a discussion.

Noting that an EGARCH model can be represented as an ARMA process in terms of the logarithm of conditional variance and thus always guarantees that the conditional variance is positive, Bollerslev and Mikkelsen (1996) proposed the following fractionally integrated EGARCH (FIEGARCH) model:

$$\phi(L)(1 - L)^d \ln \sigma_t^2 = a + \sum_{j=1}^{q} (b_j |x_{t-j}| + \gamma_j x_{t-j}) \qquad (8.18)$$

where $\phi(L)$ is defined as earlier for the FIGARCH model, $\gamma_j \neq 0$ allows the existence of leverage effects, and x_t is the standardized residual:

$$x_t = \frac{\epsilon_t}{\sigma_t} \qquad (8.19)$$

Bollerslev and Mikkelsen (1996) showed that the FIEGARCH model is stationary if $0 < d < 1$.

8.6.2 Estimation of Long Memory GARCH Models

Given the iterative formulations of conditional variance as in (8.17) and (8.18), the FIGARCH and FIEGARCH model coefficients can be estimated using maximum likelihood estimation (MLE), if the residuals follow a conditional normal distribution. The S+FinMetrics function fgarch can be used to estimate the long memory FIGARCH or FIEGARCH model.

The syntax of fgarch is very similar to that of the garch function, except that ~figarch(m,q) is used as the FIGARCH conditional variance formula and ~fiegarch(m,q) as the FIEGARCH conditional variance formula. For example, to fit a FIGARCH$(1, d, 1)$ model to daily stock returns of Dell Computer contained in the S+FinMetrics "timeSeries" object dell.s, simply use the following command:

```
> dell.figarch = fgarch(dell.s~1, ~figarch(1,1))
Initializing model parameters.
Iteration No.    1: log-likelihood=-3282.303431
...
Iteration No.   10: log-likelihood=-3279.508705
Convergence in gradient.
> oldClass(dell.figarch)
[1] "fgarch" "garch"
```

The returned object is of class "fgarch", which inherits the "garch" class. Consequently, most of the method functions for a "garch" object (e.g. print, summary, plot, predict, coef, residuals, sigma.t, vcov)also work for a "fgarch" object. One exception is that currently there is no simulate method for "fgarch" objects. For example, the print method gives

```
> dell.figarch

Call:
fgarch(formula.mean = dell.s ~1, formula.var =  ~figarch(1, 1))

Mean Equation: dell.s ~1

Conditional Variance Equation:  ~figarch(1, 1)

Coefficients:

        C 0.4422
        A 0.6488
 GARCH(1) 0.6316
  ARCH(1) 0.4481
 fraction 0.2946
```

The estimate of d is 0.295, which indicates the existence of long memory. However, the sum ARCH(1) and GARCH(1) is greater than one which indicates a nonstationary model.

If the FIEGARCH model instead of FIGARCH model is desired, the optional argument `leverage` can be used to allow for leverage effects. For example,

```
> dell.fiegarch = fgarch(dell.s~1, ~fiegarch(1,1), leverage=T)
Initializing model parameters.
Iteration No.  1: log-likelihood=-3286.169656
...
Iteration No.  20: log-likelihood=-3274.244677
Convergence in gradient.

> summary(dell.fiegarch)

Call:
fgarch(formula.mean = dell.s ~1, formula.var =  ~fiegarch( 1, 1),
leverage = T)

Mean Equation: dell.s ~1

Conditional Variance Equation:  ~fiegarch(1, 1)


--------------------------------------------------------------

Estimated Coefficients:
--------------------------------------------------------------
          Value Std.Error t value    Pr(>|t|)
       C  0.39494   0.08981    4.397 5.946e-006
       A -0.06895   0.04237   -1.627 5.195e-002
GARCH(1)  0.65118   0.17820    3.654 1.343e-004
 ARCH(1)  0.15431   0.04578    3.370 3.867e-004
  LEV(1) -0.09436   0.02691   -3.507 2.346e-004
fraction  0.34737   0.11408    3.045 1.188e-003


--------------------------------------------------------------


AIC(6) = 6560.5
BIC(6) = 6591.3

Normality Test:
--------------------------------------------------------------
 Jarque-Bera  P-value Shapiro-Wilk P-value
       13.22 0.001348        0.9888  0.7888

Ljung-Box test for standardized residuals:
--------------------------------------------------------------
```

```
Statistic P-value Chi^2-d.f.
   13.13   0.3597          12
```

Ljung-Box test for squared standardized residuals:

```
Statistic P-value Chi^2-d.f.
   14.51   0.2696          12
```

Lagrange multiplier test:

```
 Lag 1  Lag 2  Lag 3  Lag 4  Lag 5  Lag 6    Lag 7  Lag 8
-0.925 0.6083 -1.581 0.2593 0.3943 0.6991 -0.03191 0.3339
```

```
Lag 9  Lag 10 Lag 11 Lag 12      C
1.959 -0.8794  2.422 0.1089 0.8896
```

```
TR^2 P-value F-stat P-value
15.1  0.2362  1.389  0.2797
```

In the above output, C corresponds to the constant term in the conditional mean equation, A corresponds to the constant term a, GARCH(1) corresponds to b_1, ARCH(1) corresponds to ϕ_1, LEV(1) corresponds to γ_1 and fraction corresponds to the fractional difference parameter d in the conditional variance equation (8.18). Notice that the leverage term is negative and significant, and the sum of ARCH(1) and GARCH(1) is now less than one. It appears that the FIEGARCH model fits the data better than the FIGARCH model.

Just like for "garch" objects, the generic plot function can be used visually to diagnose the model fit. Use compare.mgarch to compare multiple model fits. For example, consider comparing the above two FIGARCH, FIEGARCH with short memory GARCH and EGARCH models:

```
> dell.garch = garch(dell.s~1, ~garch(1,1), trace=F)
> dell.egarch = garch(dell.s~1, ~egarch(1,1),
+ leverage=T, trace=F)
> dell.comp = compare.mgarch(dell.garch,dell.egarch,
+ dell.figarch,dell.fiegarch)
> dell.comp
```
	dell.garch	dell.egarch	dell.figarch	dell.fiegarch
AIC	6564	6559	6569	6560
BIC	6585	6584	6595	6591
Likelihood	-3278	-3274	-3280	-3274

Here, the EGARCH and FIEGARCH models seem to provide better fits than the GARCH and FIGARCH models. The QQ-plots of standardized residuals for the four models can be compared using:

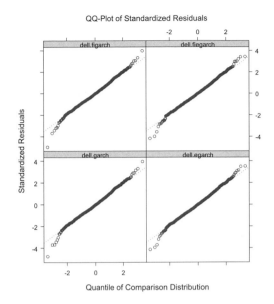

FIGURE 8.11. QQ-plot of standardized residuals from long memory GARCH models.

```
> plot(dell.comp, qq=T)
```

and the plot is shown in Figure 8.11, where the FIEGARCH model seems to provide a slightly better fit to the outliers in both tails.

8.6.3   Custom Estimation of Long Memory GARCH Models

ARMA Terms and Exogenous Variables

Just like with the `garch` function, the `fgarch` function also allows ARMA terms and exogenous variables in the conditional mean equation, as well as the conditional variance equation.

Example 46 *Trading volume and volatility (extended)*

The previous subsection shows that the fitted FIEGARCH model object `dell.fiegarch` suggests that there may be long memory in the volatility of Dell stocks. In Section 7.5 of Chapter 7, the changes in trading volume were used to explain the volatility of Dell stocks. If there is a 1% change in trading volume, it will cause about 1.4% change in conditional variance using an EGARCH model for volatility. In this example, the analysis using the FIEGARCH model instead of the EGARCH model is done again.

```
> dell.mod2 = fgarch(dell.s~1, ~fiegarch(1,1) +
```

```
+ seriesData(d.volume), series.start=2)
> summary(dell.mod2)

Call:
fgarch(formula.mean = dell.s ~ 1, formula.var = ~ fiegarch(1,1)
       + seriesData(d.volume), series.start = 2)

Mean Equation: dell.s ~ 1

Conditional Variance Equation:   ~ fiegarch(1, 1) +
        seriesData(d.volume)

----------------------------------------------------------------

Estimated Coefficients:
----------------------------------------------------------------
                        Value Std.Error  t value    Pr(>|t|)
                  C   0.14514   0.06245   2.3242 1.014e-002
                  A  -0.13640   0.03117  -4.3761 6.542e-006
           GARCH(1)   0.04123   0.10703   0.3852 3.501e-001
            ARCH(1)   0.16600   0.03809   4.3583 7.091e-006
seriesData(d.volume)  1.49123   0.07814  19.0849 0.000e+000
           fraction   0.80947   0.07523  10.7596 0.000e+000

...
```

First, compare the above output with dell.fiegarch, the FIEGARCH model fitted in the previous subsection. After controlling for the effects of trading volume, the GARCH coefficient has decreased significantly and become insignificant, while the fractional difference parameter has increased from 0.34 to 0.8. Second, compare this with the EGARCH model fit dell.mod in Chapter 7: after allowing for long memory, the GARCH coefficient decreased from 0.95 to 0.04, while the effects of trading volume remain almost the same.

Control of Model Estimation

For a "fgarch" object, all the model specific information is contained in the model component of the object. For example, view the model information of the fitted dell.figarch object as follows:

```
> dell.figarch$model

Mean Equation: dell.s ~ 1

Conditional Variance Equation:   ~ figarch(1, 1)
```

```
             Values
constant in mean 0.4422
 constant in var 0.6488
        GARCH(1) 0.6316
         ARCH(1) 0.4481
        fraction 0.2946
```

This model object can be edited to provide starting values for re-estimating the same model with the same or a different time series.[7] For example, to use this set of values as starting values for a FIGARCH model of the time series hp.s, use the following command:

```
> hp.figarch = fgarch(series=hp.s*100, model=dell.figarch$model)
Iteration No.   1: log-likelihood=-4419.644144
...
Iteration No.  10: log-likelihood=-4390.179116
Convergence in gradient.
> hp.figarch

Call:
fgarch(series = hp.s * 100, model = dell.figarch$model)

Mean Equation: dell.s ~ 1

Conditional Variance Equation:   ~ figarch(1, 1)

Coefficients:

       C 0.05776
       A 0.55897
GARCH(1) 0.49103
 ARCH(1) 0.40210
fraction 0.22533
```

Unlike the garch and mgarch functions which use the BHHH algorithm for MLE, the FIGARCH/FIEGARCH models are estimated using the BFGS algorithm (for example, see Press, Teukolsky, Vetterling, and Flannery, 1992 for details). Since daily financial returns are very small numbers, the algorithm can become badly scaled and may fail to converge. That is why in the above example the percentage returns are used to improve the convergence.

---

[7]However, unlike "garch" and "mgarch" objects, currently the coefficients cannot be fixed at certain values during the estimation of long memory GARCH models. See Section 13.7 in Chapter 13 for discussions related to "garch" and "mgarch" objects.

Other aspects of the BFGS algorithm can be controlled by passing the optional argument `control` to the `fgarch` function, where `control` must be set to an object returned by the `fgarch.control` function. For example, to change the convergence tolerance of gradient zeroing from the default value of `1e-5` to `1e-6` when fitting a FIGARCH model to `dell.s`, use the following command:

```
> fgarch(dell.s~1, ~figarch(1,1), control=
+ fgarch.control(tolg=1e-6))
```

The on-line help file for `fgarch.control` provides more details for the arguments accepted by the `fgarch.control` function.

Finally, introducing the FIGARCH/FIEGARCH models illustrated that both models are essentially an ARMA model fitted to the fractionally differenced squared residuals or fractionally differenced logarithmic conditional variance. The fractional difference operator is defined in (8.5), which involves an infinite order autoregressive filter. In practice, a very large number is usually chosen to approximate the fractional difference operator. Following Bollerslev and Mikkelsen (1996), the `fgarch` function sets the order to be 1000 by default. To change this number to another value, pass the optional argument `lag` to `fgarch.control`. For example, the command

```
> fgarch(dell.s~1, ~figarch(1,1), control=
+ fgarch.control(lag=500))
```

estimates a FIGARCH model using only 500 lags to approximate the fractional difference operator.

8.7   Prediction from Long Memory Models

S+FinMetrics long memory modeling functions such as FARIMA, SEMIFAR and `fgarch` all return objects for which there are corresponding `predict` methods. Therefore, predictions from those fitted model objects can be readily generated. This section gives an overview of how to predict from a long memory process. In particular, the truncation method and the best linear predictor will be introduced ,see Bhansali and Kokoszka (2001). How to predict from fitted model objects in S+FinMetrics module will be illustrated.

8.7.1   Prediction from FARIMA/SEMIFAR Models

To illustrate prediction from long memory processes, consider the FARIMA model in (8.12), which can be rewritten as:

$$\frac{\phi(L)(1-L)^d}{\theta(L)}(y_t - \mu) = \epsilon_t$$

The lag polynomial on the left hand side of the above equation can be expressed as an infinite order polynomial so that a FARIMA(p, d, q) model can be equivalently expressed as an AR(∞) model. Once the parameters of the FARIMA(p, d, q) model are known, one can solve for the parameters of the equivalent AR(∞) model. In practice, however, forecasting from the AR(∞) representation usually truncates the AR(∞) model to an AR(p) model with a very large value of p. This method is usually referred to as the *truncation method*.

In the truncation method, the AR(p) coefficients are the first p coefficients of the AR(∞) representation of the FARIMA(p, d, q) model. However, for any stationary process, choose to use p lagged values to predict future values:

$$\hat{y}_{T+1} = \psi_1 y_T + \cdots + \psi_p y_{T-p+1}$$

where ψ_i for $i = 1, \cdots, p$ are chosen to yield the best linear predictor of y_{T+1} in terms of $y_T, \cdots, y_{T-p+1}$ for any T. Note that although both the above method and the truncation method use an AR(p) model for prediction, the AR(p) coefficients in the truncation method do not necessarily correspond to best linear prediction coefficients ψ_i. Brockwell and Davis (1991) showed that the best linear prediction coefficients can be recursively computed using the Durbin-Levinson algorithm given the autocovariance function of the stationary process.[8]

The `predict` method for "FARIMA" objects in S+FinMetrics implements the Durbin-Levinson algorithm to compute the forecasts. The arguments taken by `predict.FARIMA` are:

```
> args(predict.FARIMA)
function(x, n.predict = 1, ar.approx = 50, kapprox = 100000,
         series = NULL)
```

where `n.predict` indicates the number of steps to predict ahead, `ar.approx` gives the order p of the AR representation used for prediction, `kapprox` is passed to `acf.FARIMA` to obtain the theoretical autocovariance function of the FARIMA model, and `series` can be used to pass the original time series used to fit the model. For example, to predict 100 steps ahead using an AR(100) representation from the fitted model object `ndx.bic`, use the following command:

```
> ndx.pred1 = predict(ndx.bic, n.predict=100, ar.approx=100)
> class(ndx.pred1)
```

---

[8] Although exact expressions of the autocovariance functions for FARIMA(p, d, q) models have been given by Sowell (1992), the derivation assumes that all the roots of the AR polynomial are distinct. The S+FinMetrics function `acf.FARIMA` implements a numerical quadrature procedure based on fast Fourier transform to approximate the autocovariance function of the FARIMA models, as proposed by Bhansali and Kokoszka (2001).

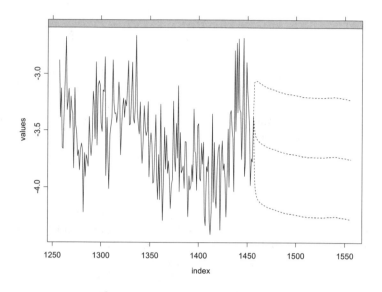

FIGURE 8.12. Predictions from a FARIMA model.

```
[1] "forecast"
```

The returned object has class "forecast" and has components

```
> names(ndx.pred1)
[1] "values"  "std.err" "coef"
```

where the values contains the predicted values, std.err contains the standard errors of the predictions, and coef contains the best linear prediction coefficients ψ_i $(i = 1, \ldots, p)$. The predictions and standard errors can be seen by calling the summary function on a "forecast" object. For example:

```
> summary(ndx.pred1)

Predicted Values with Standard Errors:

              prediction std.err
1-step-ahead  -3.4713     0.3965
2-step-ahead  -3.5407     0.4732
3-step-ahead  -3.5638     0.5023
4-step-ahead  -3.5792     0.5148
5-step-ahead  -3.5883     0.5204
...
```

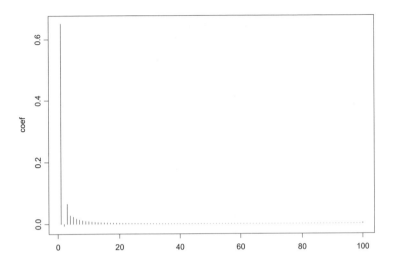

FIGURE 8.13. Best linear prediction coefficients.

A "forecast" object can be plotted together with the original data to visualize the predictions. For example, since ndx.bic was fitted using log(ndx.vol), the predictions can be visualized as follows:

```
> plot(ndx.pred1, log(ndx.vol), n.old=200)
```

where the optional argument n.old specifies the number of observations in the original data to be used in the plot. The plot is shown Figure 8.12. Also, the best linear prediction coefficients can also be visualized to see the effects of using more lags for prediction. For example:

```
> plot(ndx.pred1$coef, type="h", ylab="coef")
```

generates the coefficient plot shown in Figure 8.13. Adding lags beyond 30 should not change the predictions very much.

In S+FinMetrics, predictions from SEMIFAR models are computed in a similar fashion to predictions from FARIMA models, except that there is a choice to use a constant extrapolation or linear extrapolation for the trend component[9]

```
> args(predict.SEMIFAR)
function(x, n.predict = 1, ar.approx = 50, kapprox = 100000,
```

---

[9] We refer to Beran and Ocker (1999) for the details of predicting from a SEMIFAR model.

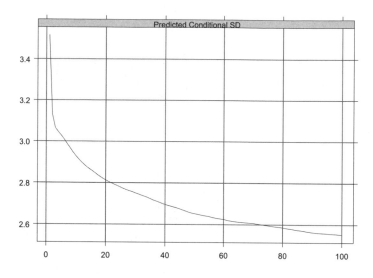

FIGURE 8.14. Predictions from FIGARCH model.

```
trend = "constant", series = NULL)
```

For example, to produce 100 steps ahead forecasts from the fitted model object `ndx.semi` using constant extrapolation, use the following command:

```
> ndx.pred2 = predict(ndx.semi, n.predict=100, trend="constant")
```

The returned object is also a "`forecast`" object, so the predictions can be visualized together with the original data

```
> plot(ndx.pred2, ndx.vol, n.old=200)
```

8.7.2 Prediction from FIGARCH/FIEGARCH Models

Predictions from the `S+FinMetrics` long memory GARCH models are computed using the truncation method because the user needs to generate forecasts for both the level and the volatility of the series at the same time. The arguments taken by the `predict` method are:

```
> args(predict.fgarch)
function(object, n.predict = 1, n.lag = 1000)
NULL
```

where `n.predcit` specifies the number of periods to predict ahead, and `n.lag` specifies the order p of the AR(p) representation used in the truncation method. For example, to use an AR(100) representation to predict 100 steps ahead from the fitted model object `dell.figarch`, use the following command:

```
> dell.pred3 = predict(dell.figarch, n.predict=100, n.lag=100)
> oldClass(dell.pred3)
[1] "predict.fgarch" "predict.garch"
```

The returned object is of class "`predict.fgarch`", which inherits from the class "`predict.garch`". So just like for a "`predict.garch`" object, use the generic `plot` function to visualize the volatility forecast:

```
> plot(dell.pred3, hgrid=T, vgrid=T)
```

and the plot is shown in Figure 8.14. The volatility predictions approach the long run level in a slowly decaying fashion for the long memory GARCH model[10].

8.8 References

[1] ANDERSEN, T., BOLLERSLEV, T., DIEBOLD, F. X., AND LABYS, P. (1999): "(Understanding, Optimizing, Using and Forecasting) Realized Volatility and Correlation", Manuscript, Northwestern University, Duke University and University of Pennsylvania.

[2] ANDERSEN, T., BOLLERSLEV, T., DIEBOLD, F. X., AND LABYS, P. (2001a): "The Distribution of Realized Exchange Rate Volatility", Journal of the American Statistical Association, 96, 42-55.

[3] ANDERSEN, T., BOLLERSLEV, T., DIEBOLD, F. X., AND LABYS, P. (2001b): "The Distribution of Realized Stock Return Volatility", Journal of Financial Economics, 61, 43-76.

[4] BAILLIE, R. T. (1996). "Long Memory Processes and Fractional Integration in Econometrics", Journal of Econometrics, 73, 5-59.

[5] BAILLIE, R. T., BOLLERSLEV, T., AND MIKKELSEN, H. O. (1996). "Fractionally Integrated Generalized Autoregressive Conditional Heteroskedasticity", Journal of Econometrics, 74, 3-30.

[6] BERAN, J. (1994). Statistics for Long Memory Processes, Chapman and Hall, New York.

[7] BERAN, J. (1995). "Maximum Likelihood Estimation of the Differencing Parameter for Invertible Short and Long Memory ARIMA Models", Journal of Royal Statistical Society Series B, 57(4), 659-672.

---

[10] Currently, standard errors are not available for the volatility predictions.

[8] BERAN, J., FENG, Y., AND OCKER, D. (1999). "SEMIFAR Models". Technical Report, 3/1999, SFB 475 University of Dortmund.

[9] BERAN, J., AND OCKER, D. (1999). "SEMIFAR Forecasts, with Applications to Foreign Exchange Rates", *Journal of Statistical Planning and Inference*, 80, 137-153.

[10] BERAN, J., AND OCKER, D. (2001). "Volatility of Stock Market Indices - An Analysis Based on SEMIFAR Models", *Journal of Business and Economic Statistics*, 19(1), 103-116.

[11] BHANSALI, R. J., AND KOKOSZKA, P. S. (2001). "Computation of the Forecast Coefficients for Multistep Prediction of Long-range Dependent Time Series", *International Journal of Forecasting*, forthcoming.

[12] BOLLERSLEV, T., AND MIKKELSEN, H. O. (1996). "Modeling and Pricing Long Memory in Stock Market Volatility", *Journal of Econometrics*, 73, 151-184.

[13] BROCKWELL, P. J., AND DAVIS, R. A. (1991). *Time Series: Theory and Methods*, Springer-Verlag.

[14] CHEUNG, Y.W. (1993). "Tests for Fractional Integration: A Monte Carlo Investigation", *Journal of Time Series Analysis*, 14, 331-345.

[15] GARMAN, M. B., AND KLASS, M. J. (1980). "On the Estimation of Security Price Volatility from Historical Data", *Journal of Business*, 53, 67-78.

[16] GEWEKE, J., AND PORTER-HUDAK, S. (1983). "The Estimation and Application of Long Memory Time Series Models", *Journal of Time Series Analysis*, 4, 221-237.

[17] GRANGER, C. W. J., AND JOYEUX, R. (1980). "An Introduction to Long-Memory Time Series Models and Fractional Differencing", *Journal of Time Series Analysis*, 1, 15-29.

[18] HAMILTON, J. D. (1994). *Time Series Analysis*. Princeton University Press.

[19] HASLETT, J., AND RAFTERY, A. E. (1989). "Space-time Modelling with Long-Memory Dependence: Assessing Ireland's Wind Power Resource", *Journal of Royal Statistical Society Series C*, 38, 1-21.

[20] HOSKING, J. R. M. (1981). "Fractional Differencing", *Biometrika*, 68, 165-176.

[21] HURST, H. E. (1951). "Long Term Storage Capacity of Reservoirs", *Transactions of the American Society of Civil Engineers*, 116, 770-799.

[22] LO, A. W. (1991). "Long Term Memory in Stock Market Prices", *Econometrica*, 59, 1279-1313.

[23] LOBATO, I. N., AND SAVIN, N. E. (1998). "Real and Spurious Long-Memory Properties of Stock-Market Data", *Journal of Business and Economic Statistics*, 16 (3), 261-268.

[24] MANDELBROT, B. B. (1975). "Limit Theorems on the Self-Normalized Range for Weakly and Strongly Dependent Processes", *Zeitschrift für Wahrscheinlichkeitstheorie und verwandte Gebiete*, 31, 271-285.

[25] PRESS, W. H., TEUKOLSKY, S. A., VETTERLING, W. T., AND FLANNERY, B. P. (1992). *Numerical Recipes in C: The Art of Scientific Computing*, Cambridge University Press.

[26] RAY, B. K., AND TSAY, R. S. (2000). "Long-Range Dependence in Daily Stock Volatilities", *Journal of Business and Economic Statistics*, 18, 254-262.

[27] SOWELL, F. (1992). "Maximum Likelihood Estimation of Stationary Univariate Fractionally Integrated Time Series Models", *Journal of Econometrics*, 53, 165-188.

[28] TAQQU, M. S., AND TEVEROVSKY, V. (1998). "On Estimating the Intensity of Long-Range Dependence in Finite and Infinite Variance Time Series", in R. J. Adler, R. E. Feldman and M. S. Taqqu (eds.): *A Practical Guide to Heavy Tails: Statistical Techniques and Applications*. Birkhaüser, Boston.

[29] TAQQU, M. S., TEVEROVSKY, V., WILLINGER, W. (1995). "Estimators for Long Range Dependence: An Empirical Study". *Fractals*, 3(4), 785-798.

9
Rolling Analysis of Time Series

9.1 Introduction

A rolling analysis of a time series model is often used to assess the model's stability over time. When analyzing financial time series data using a statistical model, a key assumption is that the parameters of the model are constant over time. However, the economic environment often changes considerably, and it may not be reasonable to assume that a model's parameters are constant. A common technique to assess the constancy of a model's parameters is to compute parameter estimates over a rolling window of a fixed size through the sample. If the parameters are truly constant over the entire sample, then the estimates over the rolling windows should not be too different. If the parameters change at some point during the sample, then the rolling estimates should capture this instability.

Rolling analysis is commonly used to backtest a statistical model on historical data to evaluate stability and predictive accuracy. Backtesting generally works in the following way. The historical data is initially split into an estimation sample and a prediction sample. The model is then fit using the estimation sample and h-step ahead predictions are made for the prediction sample. Since the data for which the predictions are made are observed h-step ahead prediction errors can be formed. The estimation sample is then rolled ahead a given increment and the estimation and prediction exercise is repeated until it is not possible to make any more h-step predictions. The statistical properties of the collection of h-step ahead prediction errors are then summarized and used to evaluate the adequacy of the statistical model.

Moving average methods are common in rolling analysis, and these methods lie at the heart of the technical analysis of financial time series. Moving averages typically use either equal weights for the observations or exponentially declining weights. One way to think of these simple moving average models is that they are a "poor man's" time varying parameter model. Sometimes simple moving average models are not adequate, however, and a general time varying parameter model is required. In these cases, the state space models discussed in Chapter 14 should be used.

This chapter describes various types of rolling analysis of financial time series using S-PLUS. Section 9.2 covers rolling descriptive statistics for univariate and bivariate time series with an emphasis on moving average techniques, and Section 9.3 gives a brief review of technical analysis using S+FinMetrics functions. Section 9.4 discusses rolling regression using the S+FinMetrics function rollOLS and illustrates how rollOLS may be used for backtesting regression models. Section 9.5 describes rolling analysis of general models using the S+FinMetrics function roll.

Rolling analysis of financial time series is widely used in practice but the technique is seldom discussed in textbook treatments of time series analysis. Notable exceptions are Alexander (2001) and Dacorogna et. al. (2001). Rolling analysis techniques in finance are generally discussed in the technical analysis literature, but the statistical properties of backtesting technical analysis are rarely addressed. A comprehensive treatment of technical analysis indicators is given in Colby and Meyers (1988) and a critical evaluation of technical analysis is provided in Bauer and Dahlquist (1999). The econometric literature on evaluating the predictive accuracy of models through backtesting has matured over the last decade. The main reference is Diebold and Mariano (1995).

9.2   Rolling Descriptive Statistics

9.2.1   Univariate Statistics

Consider the analysis of a univariate time series y_t over a sample from $t = 1, \ldots, T$. Whether the mean and variance (or standard deviation) parameters of the distribution of y_t are constant over the entire sample is of interest. To assess parameter constancy, let n denote the width of a sub-sample or window and define the *rolling* sample means, variances and standard deviations

$$\hat{\mu}_t(n) = \frac{1}{n} \sum_{i=0}^{n-1} y_{t-i} \qquad (9.1)$$

$$\hat{\sigma}_t^2(n) = \frac{1}{n-1} \sum_{i=0}^{n-1} (y_{t-i} - \hat{\mu}_t(n))^2 \qquad (9.2)$$

$$\hat{\sigma}_t(n) = \sqrt{\hat{\sigma}_t^2(n)} \qquad (9.3)$$

for windows $t = n, \ldots T$. The rolling mean and variance estimates at time t with window width n are the usual sample estimates using the most recent n observations. Provided the windows are rolled through the sample one observation at a time, there will be $T - n + 1$ rolling estimates of each parameter. The rolling mean $\hat{\mu}_t(n)$ is sometime called a n-period *simple moving average*.

Computing Rolling Descriptive Statistics Using the S-PLUS Function
aggregateSeries

Consider the monthly continuously compounded returns on Microsoft stock over the period February 1990 through January 2001 computed from the monthly closing prices in the S+FinMetrics "timeSeries" singleIndex.dat

```
> msft.ret = getReturns(singleIndex.dat[,"MSFT"])
> start(msft.ret)
[1] Feb 1990
> end(msft.ret)
[1] Jan 2001
> nrow(msft.ret)
[1] 132
```

24-month rolling mean and standard deviations may be computed easily using the S-PLUS function aggregateSeries[1]

```
> roll.mean = aggregateSeries(msft.ret,moving=24,adj=1,FUN=mean)
> roll.sd = aggregateSeries(msft.ret,moving=24,adj=1,FUN=stdev)
```

The arguments moving=24, adj=1 and FUN=mean(stdev) tell the S-PLUS function aggregateSeries to evaluate the mean (stdev) function on a rolling window of size 24 and to adjust the output positions to the end of each window. roll.mean and roll.sd are "timeSeries" objects containing 109 rolling estimates:

```
> class(roll.mean)
```

---

[1] aggregateSeries is the method function of the generic S-PLUS function aggregate for objects of class "timeSeries" and "signalSeries".

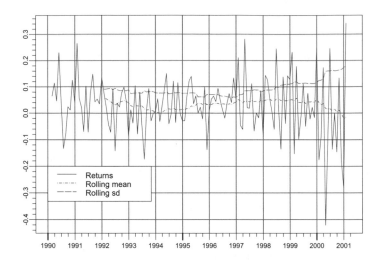

FIGURE 9.1. Monthly returns on Microsoft stock along with 24 month rolling means and standard deviations.

```
[1] "timeSeries"
> nrow(roll.mean)
[1] 109
> roll.mean[1:5]
 Positions        1
 Jan 1992   0.05671
 Feb 1992   0.05509
 Mar 1992   0.04859
 Apr 1992   0.04366
 May 1992   0.03795
```

The monthly returns along with the rolling means and standard deviations may be plotted together using

```
> plot(msft.ret,roll.mean,roll.sd,plot.args=list(lty=c(1,3,4)))
> legend(0,-0.2,legend=c("Returns","Rolling mean","Rolling sd"),
+ lty=c(1,3,4))
```

which is illustrated in Figure 9.1. The 24 month rolling estimates $\hat{\mu}_t(24)$ and $\hat{\sigma}_t(24)$ clearly vary over the sample. The rolling means start out around 2.5%, fall close to 0% in 1994, rise again to about 2.5% until 2000 and then fall below 0%. The rolling $\hat{\sigma}_t(24)$ values start out around 10%, fall slightly until 1997 and then begin to steadily rise for the rest of the sample. The end of sample value of $\hat{\sigma}_t(24)$ is almost twice as big as the beginning of sample value.

The moving average estimates (9.1) - (9.3) are one-sided backward looking estimates. The S-PLUS function `aggregateSeries` may also compute two-sided asymmetric moving averages by specifying a value between 0 and 1 for the optional argument `adj`. For example, to compute a 24 month symmetric two-sided simple moving average set `adj=0.5`

```
> roll.mean.5 = aggregateSeries(msft.ret,moving=24,adj=0.5,
+ FUN=mean)
> roll.mean.5[1:5]
 Positions     MSFT
 Feb 1991   0.056708
 Mar 1991   0.055095
 Apr 1991   0.048594
 May 1991   0.043658
 Jun 1991   0.037950
```

Instead of computing the rolling means and standard deviations in separate calls to `aggregateSeries`, they can be computed in a single call by supplying a user-written function to `aggregateSeries` that simply returns the mean and standard deviation. One such function is

```
> mean.sd = function (x) {
>      tmp1 = mean(x)
>      tmp2 = stdev(x)
>      ans = concat(tmp1,tmp2)
>      ans
> }
```

The call to `aggregateSeries` to compute the rolling means and standard deviations is then

```
> roll.mean.sd = aggregateSeries(msft.ret,moving=24,adj=1,
+ FUN=mean.sd,colnames=c("mean","sd"))
> roll.mean.sd[1:5,]
 Positions    mean       sd
 Jan 1992   0.05671  0.09122
 Feb 1992   0.05509  0.09140
 Mar 1992   0.04859  0.09252
 Apr 1992   0.04366  0.09575
 May 1992   0.03795  0.08792
```

Notice that the column names of `roll.mean.sd` are specified using optional argument `colnames=c("mean","sd")` in the call to `aggregateSeries`.

Standard error bands around the rolling estimates of μ and σ may be computed using the asymptotic formulas

$$\widehat{SE}(\hat{\mu}_t(n)) = \frac{\hat{\sigma}_t(n)}{\sqrt{n}}, \ \ \widehat{SE}(\hat{\sigma}_t(n)) = \frac{\hat{\sigma}_t(n)}{\sqrt{2n}}$$

Using the rolling estimates in roll.mean.sd, the S-PLUS commands to compute and plot the rolling estimates along with approximate 95% confidence bands are

```
> lower.mean = roll.mean.sd[,"mean"]-
+ 2*roll.mean.sd[,"sd"]/sqrt(24)
> upper.mean = roll.mean.sd[,"mean"]+
+ 2*roll.mean.sd[,"sd"]/sqrt(24)
> lower.sd = roll.mean.sd[,"sd"]-
+ 2*roll.mean.sd[,"sd"]/sqrt(2*24)
> upper.sd = roll.mean.sd[,"sd"]+
+ 2*roll.mean.sd[,"sd"]/sqrt(2*24)
> par(mfrow=c(2,1))
> plot(roll.mean.sd[,"mean"],lower.mean,upper.mean,
+ main="24 month rolling means",plot.args=list(lty=c(1,2,2)))
> plot(roll.mean.sd[,"sd"],lower.sd,upper.sd,
+ main="24 month rolling standard deviations",
+ plot.args=list(lty=c(1,2,2)))
```

Figure 9.2 shows the results. In general, the rolling $\hat{\sigma}_t(24)$ values are estimated much more precisely than the rolling $\hat{\mu}_t(24)$ values.

The rolling means, variances and standard deviations are not the only rolling descriptive statistics of interest, particularly for asset returns. For risk management purposes, one may be interested in extreme values. Therefore, one may want to compute rolling minima and maxima. These may be computed using aggregateSeries with FUN=min and FUN=max.

Computing Rolling Means, Variances, Maxima and Minima Using the S+FinMetrics Functions SMA, rollVar, rollMax and rollMin

The S-PLUS function aggregateSeries is extremely flexible but not efficient for computing rolling means, variances, maxima and minima. The S+FinMetrics functions SMA (simple moving average), rollVar, rollMax and rollMin implement efficient algorithms for computing rolling means, variances, maxima and minima. The arguments expected by these functions are

```
> args(SMA)
function(x, n = 9, trim = T, na.rm = F)
> args(rollVar)
function(x, n = 9, trim = T, unbiased = T, na.rm = F)
```

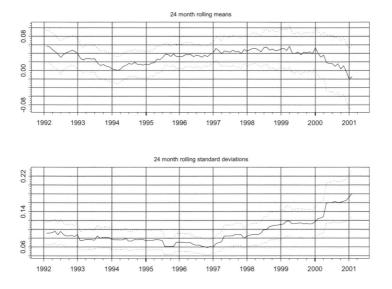

FIGURE 9.2. 24 month rolling estimates of $\hat{\mu}_t(24)$ and $\hat{\sigma}_t(24)$ for Microsoft with 95% confidence bands.

```
> args(rollMax)
function(x, n = 9, trim = T, na.rm = F)
> args(rollMin)
function(x, n = 9, trim = T, na.rm = F)
```

where x is a vector or univariate "timeSeries", n is the window width, trim determines if start-up values are trimmed from the output series and na.rm determines if missing values are to be removed. For rollVar, the option unbiased=T computes the unbiased variance estimator using $\frac{1}{n-1}$ as a divisor and unbiased=F computes the biased estimator using $\frac{1}{n}$.

To illustrate the use of SMA, rollVar, rollMax and rollMin 24 month rolling means, standard deviations, maxima and minima from the monthly returns on Microsoft are computed as

```
> roll2.mean = SMA(msft.ret,n=24)
> roll2.sd = sqrt(rollVar(msft.ret,n=24))
> roll.max = rollMax(msft.ret,n=24)
> roll.min = rollMin(msft.ret,n=24)
```

These estimates are identical to those computed using aggregateSeries, but the computation time required is much less. To compare the compu-

tation times in seconds within S-PLUS 6 for Windows the S-PLUS function
dos.time may be used[2]

```
> dos.time(SMA(msft.ret,n=24))
[1] 0.05
> dos.time(aggregateSeries(msft.ret,moving=24,adj=1,FUN=mean))
[1] 4.23
> dos.time(sqrt(rollVar(msft.ret,n=24)))
[1] 0.06
> dos.time(aggregateSeries(msft.ret,moving=24,adj=1,FUN=stdev))
[1] 6.76
```

Example 47 *Computing rolling standard deviations from high frequency returns*

Rolling estimates of σ^2 and σ based on high frequency continuously compounded return data are often computed assuming the mean return is zero

$$\hat{\sigma}_t^2(n) = \frac{1}{n}\sum_{i=1}^{n} r_{t-i}^2$$

In this case the rolling estimates of σ^2 may be computed using the computationally efficient S+FinMetrics function SMA. For example, consider computing rolling estimates of σ based on the daily continuously compounded returns for Microsoft over the 10 year period from January 1991 through January 2001. The squared return data is computed from the daily closing price data in the S+FinMetrics "timeSeries" object DowJones30

```
> msft.ret2.d = getReturns(DowJones30[,"MSFT"],
+ type="continuous")^2
```

Rolling estimates of σ based on 25, 50 and 100 day windows are computed using SMA

```
> roll.sd.25 = sqrt(SMA(msft.ret2.d,n=25))
> roll.sd.50 = sqrt(SMA(msft.ret2.d,n=50))
> roll.sd.100 = sqrt(SMA(msft.ret2.d,n=100))
```

The rolling estimates $\hat{\sigma}_t(n)$ are illustrated in Figure 9.3 created using

```
> plot(roll.sd.25,roll.sd.50,roll.sd.100,
+ plot.args=(list(lty=c(1,3,4))))
> legend(0,0.055,legend=c("n=25","n=50","n=100"),
+ lty=c(1,3,4))
```

---

[2]The computations are carried out using S-PLUS 6 Professional Release 2 on a Dell Inspiron 3500 400MHz Pentium II with 96MB RAM.

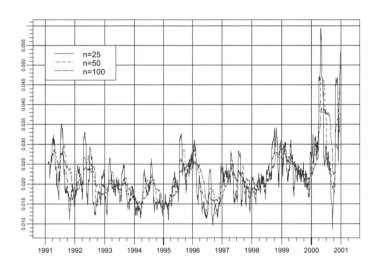

FIGURE 9.3. 25, 50 and 100 day rolling estimates of σ for the daily returns on Microsoft stock.

There is considerable variation in the rolling estimates of daily σ, and there appears to be a seasonal pattern with higher volatility in the summer months and lower volatility in the winter months.

9.2.2   Bivariate Statistics

Consider now the analysis of two univariate time series y_{1t} and y_{2t} over the sample from $t = 1, \ldots, T$. To assess if the covariance and correlation between y_{1t} and y_{2t} is constant over the entire sample the n-period rolling sample covariances and correlations

$$\hat{\sigma}_{12,t}(n) = \frac{1}{n-1} \sum_{i=0}^{n-1} (y_{1t-i} - \hat{\mu}_{1t}(n))(y_{2t-i} - \hat{\mu}_{2t}(n))$$

$$\hat{\rho}_{12,t}(n) = \frac{\hat{\sigma}_{12,t}(n)}{\hat{\sigma}_{1t}(n)\hat{\sigma}_{2t}(n)}$$

may be computed.

Example 48 *24 month rolling correlations between the returns on Microsoft and the S&P 500 index*

Consider the monthly continuously compounded returns on Microsoft stock and S&P 500 index over the period February 1990 through January 2001 computed from the monthly closing prices in the S+FinMetrics "timeSeries" object singleIndex.dat

```
> ret.ts = getReturns(singleIndex.dat,type="continuous")
> colIds(ret.ts)
[1] "MSFT"  "SP500"
```

The 24-month rolling correlations between the returns on Microsoft and S&P 500 index may be computed using the S-PLUS function aggregateSeries with a user specified function to compute the correlations. One such function is

```
> cor.coef = function(x) cor(x)[1,2]
```

The 24-month rolling correlations are then computed as

```
> smpl = positions(ret.ts)>=start(roll.cor)
> roll.cor = aggregateSeries(ret.ts,moving=24,together=T,
+ adj=1,FUN=cor.coef)
>   roll.cor[1:5]
 Positions        1
 Jan 1992  0.6549
 Feb 1992  0.6535
 Mar 1992  0.6595
 Apr 1992  0.6209
 May 1992  0.5479
```

In the call to aggregateSeries the argument together=T passes all of the columns of ret.ts to the function cor.coef instead of passing each column separately. The monthly returns on Microsoft and the S&P 500 index along with the rolling correlations are illustrated in Figure 9.4 which is created by

```
> par(mfrow=c(2,1))
> plot(ret.ts[smpl,],main="Returns on Microsoft and
+ S&P 500 index",
+ plot.args=list(lty=c(1,3)))
> legend(0,-0.2,legend=c("Microsoft","S&P 500"),
+ lty=c(1,3))
> plot(roll.cor,main="24-month rolling correlations")
```

At the beginning of the sample, the correlation between Microsoft and the S&P 500 is fairly high at 0.6. The rolling correlation declines steadily, hits

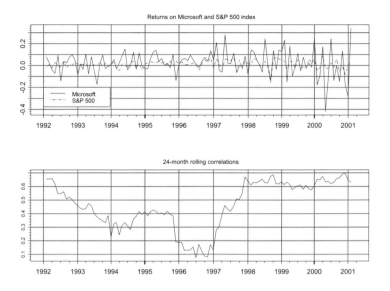

FIGURE 9.4. Returns on Microsoft and the S&P 500 index along with 24-month rolling correlations.

a low of about 0.1 at the beginning of 1997, then increases quickly to 0.6 and stabilizes at this value through the end of the sample[3].

9.2.3 Exponentially Weighted Moving Averages

The rolling descriptive statistics described in the previous sections are based on equally weighted moving averages of an observed time series y_t. Equally weighted moving averages are useful for uncovering periods of instability but may produce misleading results if used for short-term forecasting. This is because equally weighted averages are sensitive (not robust) to extreme values. To illustrate, consider $T = 100$ observations from a simulated time series $y_t \sim GWN(0, 1)$ with an outlier inserted at $t = 20$: i.e., $y_{20} = 10$. The data and rolling values $\hat{\mu}_t(10)$ and $\hat{\sigma}_t(10)$ are illustrated in Figure 9.5. Notice how the outlier at $t = 20$ inflates the rolling estimates $\hat{\mu}_t(10)$ and $\hat{\sigma}_t(10)$ for 9 periods.

---

[3] Approximate standard errors for the rolling correlations may be computed using

$$\widehat{SE}(\hat{\rho}_t(n)) = \sqrt{\frac{1 - \hat{\rho}_t(n)^2}{n}}$$

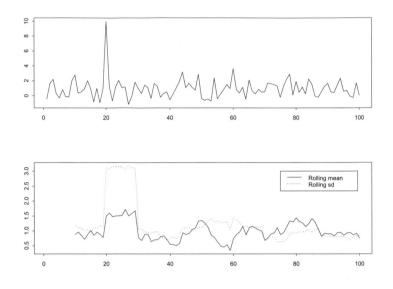

FIGURE 9.5. Effect of an outlier on equally weighted rolling estimates of μ and σ.

To mitigate the effects of extreme observations on moving average estimates the observations in a rolling window can be weighted differently. A common weighting scheme that puts more weight on the most recent observations is based on exponentially declining weights and the resulting weighted moving average is called an *exponentially weighted moving average* (EWMA). An n-period EWMA of a time series y_t is defined as

$$\tilde{\mu}_t(n) = \sum_{i=0}^{n-1} w_i \cdot y_{t-i}, \quad w_i = \frac{\lambda^{i-1}}{\sum_{i=0}^{n-1} \lambda^{i-1}}$$

where $0 < \lambda < 1$ is the decay parameter. As $n \rightarrow \infty$, $\lambda^n \rightarrow 0$, $w_n \rightarrow 0$, and the EWMA converges to

$$\tilde{\mu}_t(\lambda) = (1 - \lambda) \sum_{i=0}^{\infty} \lambda^i y_{t-i} \tag{9.4}$$

so the EWMA may be defined independently of the window width n. The EWMA in (9.4) may be efficiently computed using the recursion

$$\tilde{\mu}_t(\lambda) = (1 - \lambda)y_t + \lambda\tilde{\mu}_{t-1}(\lambda) \tag{9.5}$$

From (9.5), it is clear that the closer λ is to one the more weight is put on the the previous period's estimate relative to the current period's observation.

Therefore, λ may be interpreted as a persistence parameter. The recursive formula (9.5) requires a starting value $\mu_0(\lambda)$. Common choices are the first observation and the average over a local window.

EWMA estimates of descriptive statistics for continuously compounded asset returns are usually computed using high frequency data with the assumption that the mean returns are zero. Accordingly, the EWMA estimates of σ^2 and σ_{12} are

$$\tilde{\sigma}_t^2(\lambda) = (1-\lambda)r_t^2 + \lambda\tilde{\sigma}_{t-1}^2(\lambda) \qquad (9.6)$$
$$\tilde{\sigma}_{12,t}(\lambda) = (1-\lambda)r_{1t}r_{2t} + \lambda\tilde{\sigma}_{12,t-1}(\lambda)$$

where r_t denotes the continuously compounded return on an asset. The EWMA estimate of volatility (9.6) is in the form of a IGARCH(1,1) model without an constant term.

Computing EWMA Estimates Using the S+FinMetrics Function EWMA

EWMA estimates based on (9.5) may be efficiently computed using the S+FinMetrics function EWMA. The arguments expected by EWMA are

```
> args(EWMA)
function(x, n = 9, lambda = (n - 1)/(n + 1), start =
"average", na.rm = F)
```

where x is the data input, n is a window width, lambda is the decay parameter and start specifies the starting value for the recursion (9.5). The implied default value for λ is 0.8. Valid choices for start are "average" and "first". The use of EWMA is illustrated with the following examples.

Example 49 *Outlier example*

Consider again the outlier example data shown in Figure 9.5. EWMA estimates of μ for $\lambda = 0.95$, 0.75 and 0.5 are computed and plotted in Figure 9.6 using

```
> ewma95.mean = EWMA(e,lambda=0.95)
> ewma75.mean = EWMA(e,lambda=0.75)
> ewma50.mean = EWMA(e,lambda=0.5)
> tsplot(ewma95.mean,ewma75.mean,ewma50.mean)
> legend(60,4,legend=c("lamda=0.95","lamda=0.75",
+ "lamda=0.50"),lty=1:3)
```

Notice that the EWMA estimates with $\lambda = 0.95$, which put the most weight on recent observations, are only minimally affected by the one-time outlier whereas the EWMA estimates with $\lambda = 0.75$ and 0.5 increase sharply at the date of the outlier.

Example 50 *EWMA estimates of standard deviations and correlations from high frequency data*

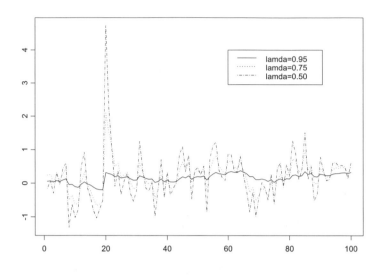

FIGURE 9.6. EWMA estimates of μ for outlier example data.

EWMA estimates of asset return standard deviations computed from high frequency data are commonly used as local or short-term estimates of volatility. Similarly, EWMA estimates of pairwise return correlations are often used to infer local interactions between assets. Indeed, J.P. Morgan's RiskMetrics® methodology is based on EWMA estimates of volatility and correlation. To illustrate, consider computing EWMA estimates of volatility and correlation with $\lambda = 0.95$ using daily closing price data on Microsoft and IBM stock over the five year period 1996-2000:

```
> smpl = (positions(DowJones30) >= timeDate("1/1/1996"))
> msft.ret.d = getReturns(DowJones30[smpl,"MSFT"])
> ibm.ret.d = getReturns(DowJones30[smpl,"IBM"])
> msft.ewma95.sd = sqrt(EWMA(msft.ret.d^2,lambda=0.95))
> ibm.ewma95.sd = sqrt(EWMA(ibm.ret.d^2,lambda=0.95))
> cov.ewma95 = EWMA(msft.ret.d*ibm.ret.d,lambda=0.95)
> cor.ewma95 = cov.ewma95/(msft.ewma95.sd*ibm.ewma95.sd)
> par(mfrow=c(2,1))
> plot(msft.ewma95.sd,ibm.ewma95.sd,
+ main="Rolling EWMA SD values",
+ plot.args=list(lty=c(1,3)))
> legend(0,0.055,legend=c("Microsoft","IBM"),lty=c(1,3))
> plot(cor.ewma95,main="Rolling EWMA correlation values")
```

Figure 9.7 shows the EWMA estimates of volatility and correlation. Daily

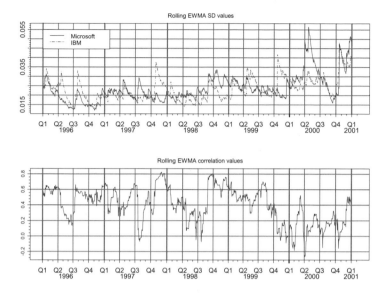

FIGURE 9.7. EWMA estimates of daily volatility and correlation with $\lambda = 0.95$.

volatility for Microsoft and IBM varies considerably, exhibiting apparent seasonality and an increasing trend. The daily correlations fluctuate around 0.5 for the first part of the sample and then drop to about 0.1 at the end of the sample.

9.2.4 Moving Average Methods for Irregularly Spaced High Frequency Data

The use of moving average and rolling methods on irregularly spaced or *inhomogeneous* high frequency time series data requires care. The moving average tools discussed so far are designed to work on regularly spaced or *homogeneous* time series data. Two approaches have been used to apply moving average methods to irregularly spaced data. The first approach converts the irregularly spaced data to regularly spaced data and then applies the tools for appropriate for regularly spaced data. The second approach, pioneered by Zumbach and Müller (2001), utilizes moving average methods specifically designed for irregularly spaced data.

Converting Inhomogeneous Time Series to Homogeneous Time Series

To illustrate the conversion of a inhomogeneous time series to a homogeneous time series, consider the transactions level data on 3M corporation stock for December 1999 in the S+FinMetrics data frame highFreq3M.df. As in Chapter 2, a "timeSeries" object may be created using

```
> td = timeDate(julian=(highFreq3M.df$trade.day-1),
+ ms=highFreq3M.df$trade.time*1000,
+ in.origin=c(month=12,day=1,year=1999),zone="GMT")
> hf3M.ts = timeSeries(pos=td,data=highFreq3M.df)
> hf3M.ts[1:20,]
           Positions trade.day trade.time trade.price
 12/1/99 9:33:32 AM 1           34412       94.69
 12/1/99 9:33:34 AM 1           34414       94.69
 12/1/99 9:33:34 AM 1           34414       94.69
 ...
 12/1/99 9:34:45 AM 1           34485       94.69
 12/1/99 9:34:47 AM 1           34487       94.63
 ...
```

The trade time is measured in second from midnight. Notice that many of the first trades took place at the same price and that there are instances of multiple transactions at the same time. The analysis is limited to the first three trading days of December

```
> smpl = positions(hf3M.ts) < timeDate("12/4/1999")
> hf3M.ts = hf3M.ts[smpl,]
```

The data in hf3M.ts may be made homogeneous by use of an interpolation method to align the irregularly spaced time sequence and associated data to a regularly spaced time sequence. For example, consider creating a homogeneous time series of five minute observations. Since the data in hf3M.ts may not be recorded at all five minute intervals, some interpolation scheme must be used to create the data. Two common interpolation schemes are: *previous tick interpolation*, and *linear interpolation*. The former method uses the most recent values, and the latter method uses observations bracketing the desired time. The S-PLUS functions align may be used to perform these interpolation schemes.

The function align takes a "timeSeries" and a "timeDate" vector of new positions to align to. An easy way to create a "timeDate" sequence of five minute observations covering the trading hours for 3M stock is to use the S-PLUS function aggregateSeries as follows:

```
> tmp = aggregateSeries(hf3M.ts,by="minutes",k.by=5,FUN=mean)
```

The positions slot of "timeSeries" tmp contains the desired five minute "timeDate" sequence:

```
> positions(tmp[1:4])
 [1] 12/1/99 9:30:00 AM  12/1/99 9:35:00 AM
 [3] 12/1/99 9:40:00 AM  12/1/99 9:45:00 AM
```

To align the 3M price data to the five minute time sequence using previous tick interpolation use

```
> hf3M.5min = align(hf3M.ts[,"trade.price"], positions(tmp),
+ how="before")
> hf3M.5min[1:5,]
          Positions trade.price
 12/1/99 9:30:00 AM     NA
 12/1/99 9:35:00 AM 94.63
 12/1/99 9:40:00 AM 94.75
 12/1/99 9:45:00 AM 94.50
 12/1/99 9:50:00 AM 94.31
```

To align the price data using linear interpolation use

```
> hf3M.5min = align(hf3M.ts[,"trade.price"], positions(tmp),
+ how="interp")
> hf3M.5min[1:5,]
          Positions trade.price
 12/1/99 9:30:00 AM     NA
 12/1/99 9:35:00 AM 94.65
 12/1/99 9:40:00 AM 94.75
 12/1/99 9:45:00 AM 94.42
 12/1/99 9:50:00 AM 94.26
```

The usual methods for the analysis of homogeneous data may now be performed on the newly created data. For example, to compute and plot an EWMA of price with $\lambda = 0.9$ use

```
> hf3M.5min.ewma = EWMA(hf3M.5min,lambda=0.9,na.rm=T)
> plot(hf3M.5min.ewma)
```

The resulting plot is shown in Figure 9.8.

Inhomogeneous Moving Average Operators

Zumbach and Müller (2001) present a general framework for analyzing inhomogeneous time series. A detailed exposition of this framework is beyond the scope of this book. Only a brief description of the most fundamental inhomogeneous time series operators is presented and reader is referred to Zumbach and Müller (2001) or Dacorogna et. al. (2001) for technical details and further examples.

Zumbach and Müller (2001) distinguish between *microscopic* and *macroscopic* operations on inhomogeneous time series. A microscopic operation depends on the actual sampling times of the time series, whereas a macroscopic operator extracts an average over a specified range. Macroscopic operations on high frequency inhomogeneous time series are advantageous because they are essentially immune to small variations in the individual

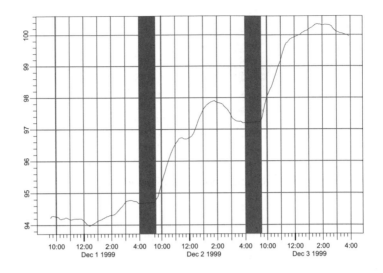

FIGURE 9.8. EWMA of five minute prices on 3M stock.

data observations and are better behaved and more robust than microscopic operations. The S+FinMetrics functions for analyzing inhomogeneous time series are based on a subset of the macroscopic operators discussed in Zumbach and Müller (2001). These functions are summarized in Table 9.1.

In general, given a continuous time signal $z(t)$, a macroscopic operator Ω can be defined as a *convolution* with a causal kernel $\omega(\cdot)$:

$$\Omega(t) = \int_0^t w(t-s)z(s)ds \qquad (9.7)$$

for $t > 0$. Note that for a causal kernel $\omega(t) = 0$ for any $t < 0$, since future information cannot be utilized. In addition, it is usually required that

$$\int_0^\infty \omega(t)dt = 1$$

so that the operator can be interpreted as a weighted moving average of the signal $z(t)$. For example, the exponential moving average (EMA) operator is defined with an exponential kernel:

$$\omega(t) = \frac{e^{-t/\tau}}{\tau} \qquad (9.8)$$

and it is easy to verify that

$$\int_0^\infty \frac{e^{-t/\tau}}{\tau} = 1$$

Function	Description
iEMA	Inhomogeneous EWMA
iMA	Inhomogeneous moving average
iMNorm	Inhomogeneous moving norm
iMVar	Inhomogeneous moving variance
iMSD	Inhomogeneous moving SD
iMSkewness	Inhomogeneous moving skewness
iMKurtosis	Inhomogeneous moving kurtosis
iMCor	Inhomogeneous moving correlation
iDiff	Inhomogeneous moving difference
iEMA.kernel	Kernel function for iEMA
iMA.kernel	Kernel function for iMA

TABLE 9.1. S+FinMetrics inhomogeneous time series function

The parameter τ can be shown to be the *range* of the EMA kernel.[4]

In reality, a time series signal is usually observed at discrete times. In addition, financial transactions level data are usually observed on irregular intervals. For the EMA operator, Zumbach and Müller suggest to use the following iterative formula to compute a discrete time approximation to (9.7):[5]

$$\text{EMA}(t_n; \tau) = \mu \text{EMA}(t_{n-1}; \tau) + (1-\mu)z(t_n) + (\mu - \nu)[z(t_n) - z(t_{n-1})] \quad (9.9)$$

where

$$\mu = e^{-\alpha}, \nu = (1 - \mu)/\alpha$$

and

$$\alpha = (t_n - t_{n-1}).$$

Note that when α is very small, $e^\alpha \approx 1 + \alpha$ and it can be shown that $\mu \approx \nu$. In this case, the above formula reduces to the same iteration for evenly spaced EWMA operator.

Using the basic EMA operator, different operators can be constructed. For example, Zumbach and Müller suggest that the basic EMA operator can be iterated a finite number of times to obtain an operator with a different kernel, denoted $\text{EMA}(\tau, k)$. The $\text{EMA}(\tau, k)$ operator can be summed to obtain the analog of the moving average (MA) operator for inhomogeneous time series:

$$\text{MA}(\tau, k) = \frac{1}{k} \sum_{i=1}^{k} \text{EMA}(s, i)$$

where $s = 2\tau/(k + 1)$ so that the range of $\text{MA}(\tau, k)$ is equal to τ, independent of k.

---

[4] The range is defined as the first moment of the kernel, i.e., $\int_0^\infty \omega(t)t\,dt$.

[5] This formula is actually obtained by assuming linear interpolation between points. If previous tick interpolation is used, then $\nu = 1$.

The S+FinMetrics functions iEMA.kernel and iMA.kernel can be used to plot the kernel functions for EMA and MA operators, while iEMA and iMA can be used to compute the EMA and MA operator for inhomogeneous time series. For example, the following code plots the $EMA(\tau, k)$ and $MA(\tau, k)$ kernel functions for $\tau = 1$ and $k = 1, 2, \cdots, 10$:

```
> par(mfrow=c(2,1))
> knl = iEMA.kernel(1, 1)
> plot(knl, type="l", main="EMA Kernel")
> for(i in 2:10) {
>   knl = iEMA.kernel(1, i)
>   lines(knl, lty=i)
> }

> knl = iMA.kernel(1, 1)
> plot(knl, type="l", main="MA Kernel")
> for(i in 2:10) {
>   knl = iMA.kernel(1, i)
>   lines(knl, lty=i)
> }
> par(mfrow=c(1,1))
```

and the resulting plot is shown in Figure 9.9. From the figure, it can be seen that when $k = 1$, $EMA(\tau, k)$ and $MA(\tau, 1)$ are equivalent by definition. However, as k gets larger, the kernel function of $EMA(\tau, k)$ becomes flatter, while the kernel function of $MA(\tau, 1)$ becomes more like a rectangle. In fact, Zumbach and Müller show that the range of $EMA(\tau, k)$ is $k\tau$, while the range of $MA(\tau, 1)$ becomes a constant for $t \leq 2\tau$ as $k \to \infty$. As a result, to obtain an MA operator with window width equal to 9 (which corresponds to a range of 8, i.e., using 8 observations in the past), one sets $\tau = 4$ and k to a large number:

```
> iMA(1:100, 4, iter=10)
 [1]  1.000  1.084  1.305  1.662  2.150  2.761  3.481
 [8]  4.289  5.166  6.091  7.047  8.024  9.011 10.005
[15] 11.002 12.001 13.000 14.000 15.000 16.000 17.000
[22] 18.000 19.000 20.000 21.000 22.000 23.000 24.000
[29] 25.000 26.000 27.000 28.000 29.000 30.000 31.000
[36] 32.000 33.000 34.000 35.000 36.000 37.000 38.000
[43] 39.000 40.000 41.000 42.000 43.000 44.000 45.000
[50] 46.000 47.000 48.000 49.000 50.000 51.000 52.000
[57] 53.000 54.000 55.000 56.000 57.000 58.000 59.000
[64] 60.000 61.000 62.000 63.000 64.000 65.000 66.000
[71] 67.000 68.000 69.000 70.000 71.000 72.000 73.000
[78] 74.000 75.000 76.000 77.000 78.000 79.000 80.000
[85] 81.000 82.000 83.000 84.000 85.000 86.000 87.000
```

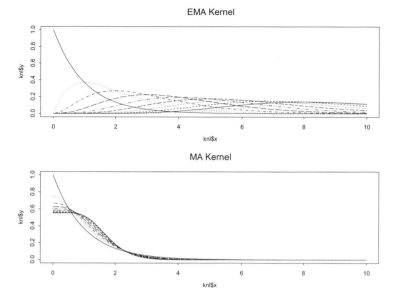

FIGURE 9.9. Kernel function for EMA and MA operators for inhomogeneous time series.

```
[92]  88.000  89.000  90.000  91.000  92.000  93.000  94.000
[99]  95.000  96.000
```

The S+FinMetrics iMA function requires at least two arguments: the first is the input series, and the second specifies the value for τ. In the above example, the optional argument iter is used to specify the number of iterations k; in addition, since the input series is not a "timeSeries" object, iMA treats it as evenly spaced and τ is in units of observations. If the input series is a "timeSeries" object, then τ should be specified in units of "business days". To illustrate the usage of iMA in this case, first create a "timeSeries" object representing the transaction price data from hf3M.ts created earlier[6]:

```
> smpl2 = positions(hf3M.ts) < timeDate("12/02/1999")
> hf3m.1min = aggregateSeries(hf3M.ts[smpl2,"trade.price"],
+ by="minutes", FUN=mean)
> hf3m.1min[103:110]
              Positions trade.price
12/1/1999 11:28:00 AM 94.25000
```

---

[6] The S-PLUS function aggregateSeries is used to eliminate multiple transactions that occur at the same time. Currently, the S+FinMetrics inhomogeneous time series functions do not work if there are multiple observations with the same time stamp.

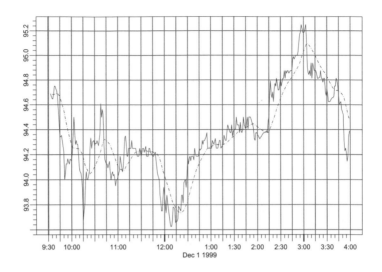

FIGURE 9.10. 20 minute moving average computed from iMA for 3M stock prices.

```
12/1/1999 11:30:00 AM 94.18750
12/1/1999 11:32:00 AM 94.25000
12/1/1999 11:33:00 AM 94.25000
12/1/1999 11:34:00 AM 94.21875
12/1/1999 11:36:00 AM 94.26563
12/1/1999 11:37:00 AM 94.18750
12/1/1999 11:39:00 AM 94.18750
```

Note that the data is not evenly spaced. To obtain a 20 minute moving average of hf3m.1min, set $\tau = 10/(6.5*60)$ because there are 6.5 hours for the default trading hours (from 9:30 AM to 4:00 PM):

```
> hf3m.ma = iMA(hf3m.1min, 10/(6.5*60), iter=10)
> plot(seriesMerge(hf3m.1min, hf3m.ma),
+ plot.args=list(lty=c(1,3)))
```

The original data and the 20 minutes moving average hf3m.ma are plotted together in Figure 9.10.

9.2.5 Rolling Analysis of Miscellaneous Functions

The standard analysis tools for time series require the data to be stationary. Rolling analysis of descriptive statistics can give an indication of structural change or instability in the moments of a time series. Level shifts and

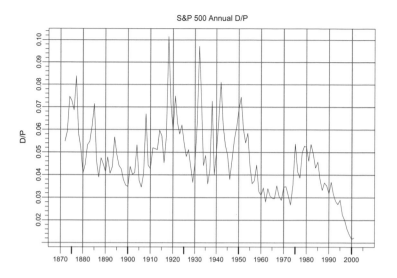

FIGURE 9.11. S & P 500 annual dividend/price ratio.

variance changes can usually be detected by rolling analyses. The S-PLUS function aggregateSeries may be used to perform rolling analysis with a variety of functions to uncover periods of instability and nonstationarity. The following example illustrates the use of aggregateSeries with the S+FinMetrics function unitroot to determine periods of unitroot nonstationarity of a time series.

Example 51 *Rolling unit root tests applied to annual dividend/price ratio*

Predictive regressions of asset returns on valuation ratios like dividend/price or earnings/price require the valuation ratios to be stationary or, more generally, $I(0)$, for the regressions to be statistically valid. Since asset returns are $I(0)$, if valuation ratios are $I(1)$ then the predictive regressions are unbalanced and the results will be nonsensical. To illustrate, consider the annual dividend-price (D/P) ratio on S&P 500 index taken from the S+FinMetrics "timeSeries" shiller.annual

```
> dp.ratio = shiller.annual[,"dp.ratio"]
> plot(dp.ratio,main="S&P 500 Annual D/P",ylab="D/P")
```

shown in Figure 9.11. For most of the sample the annual D/P looks to be $I(0)$ with mean near 5%. However, there are long periods when the ratio stays above or below 5% suggesting periods of non-mean reverting (nonstationary) behavior. Also, there is a clear drop in the ratio at the end of the sample suggesting a fundamental change in the mean. Rolling unit root tests may be used to uncover periods of nonstationary behavior in D/P. To compute rolling ADF t-tests and normalized bias statistics using the S-PLUS function `aggregateSeries` create the following function `adf.tests`

```
> adf.tests = function(x, trend = "c", lags = 3)
> {
>      tmp1 = unitroot(x,trend=trend,lags=lags,statistic="t")
>      tmp2 = unitroot(x,trend=trend,lags=lags,statistic="n")
>      ans = concat(tmp1$sval,tmp2$sval)
>      ans
> }
```

The function `adf.tests` takes a time series x, passes it to the S+FinMetrics function `unitroot` twice and returns the ADF t-statistic and normalized bias statistic. Three lags are chosen for the tests based on a full sample analysis using the Ng-Perron backward selection procedure. Rolling unit root tests using a window of 50 years are then computed using the function `aggregateSeries`:

```
> roll.adf = aggregateSeries(dp.ratio,moving=50,adj=1,
+ FUN=adf.tests,colnames=c("t.test","norm.bias"))
```

The object `roll.adf` is a "`timeSeries`" containing the rolling unit root tests

```
> roll.adf[1:3,]
 Positions t.test norm.bias
 Dec 1920  -1.840 -13.24
 Dec 1921  -2.168 -15.24
 Dec 1922  -2.270 -16.03
```

Figure 9.12 is created using

```
> cvt.05 = qunitroot(0.05,trend="c",n.sample=50)
> cvn.05 = qunitroot(0.05,trend="c",statistic="n",
+ n.sample=50)
> par(mfrow=c(2,1))
> plot(roll.adf[,"t.test"], reference.grid=F,
+ main="Rolling ADF t-statistics")
> abline(h=cvt.05)
> plot(roll.adf[,"norm.bias"], reference.grid=F,
+ main="Rolling ADF normalized bias")
> abline(h=cvn.05)
```

and shows the rolling unit root tests along with 5% critical values. The results indicate that D/P is stationary mainly in the middle of the sample and becomes nonstationary toward the end of the sample. However, some

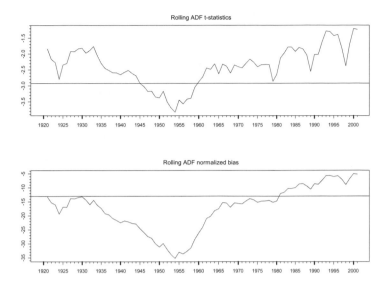

FIGURE 9.12. 50 year rolling ADF t-statistics and normalized bias statistics for the S&P 500 dividend-price ratio.

care must be used when interpreting the significance of the rolling unit root tests. The 5% critical values shown in the figures are appropriate for evaluating a single test and not a sequence of rolling tests. Critical values appropriate for rolling unit root tests are given in Banerjee, Lumsdaine and Stock (1992).

9.3   Technical Analysis Indicators

Technical analysis is, perhaps, the most widely used method for analyzing financial time series. Many of the most commonly used technical indicators are based on moving average techniques so it is appropriate to include a discussion of them here. A comprehensive survey of technical analysis is beyond the scope of this book. Useful references are Colby and Meyers (1988) and Bauer and Dahlquist (1999). The S+FinMetrics technical analysis indicators are implemented using the definitions in Colby and Meyers (1988). Broadly, the main technical indicators can be classified into four categories: price indicators, momentum indicators and oscillators, volatility indicators and volume indicators.

Function	Description
TA.Bollinger	Bollinger band
TA.medprice	Median price
TA.typicalPrice	Typical price
TA.wclose	Weighted close

TABLE 9.2. S+FinMetrics price indicators

9.3.1 Price Indicators

The S+FinMetrics price indicator functions are summarized in Table 9.2. To illustrate the use of these functions, consider the calculation of the typical daily price, which is defined to be the average of the highest, lowest and closing prices during the day, using the S+FinMetrics function TA.typicalPrice. The arguments expected by TA.typicalPrice are

```
> args(TA.typicalPrice)
function(high, low, close)
```

In order to compute this indicator, a data set with high, low and close prices is required. To compute the typical price for the Dow Jone Industrial Average over the period January 1, 1990 to February 20, 1990 using the S-PLUS "timeSeries" djia, use

```
> smpl = positions(djia) >= timeDate("1/1/1990")
> dj = djia[smpl,]
> tp.dj = TA.typicalPrice(dj[,"high"],
+ dj[,"low"],dj[,"close"])
> class(tp.dj)
[1] "timeSeries"
```

The typical price along with the high, low, open and close prices may be plotted together using

```
> plot.out = plot(dj[,1:4],plot.type="hloc")
> lines.render(positions(tp.dj),seriesData(tp.dj),
+ x.scale=plot.out$scale)
```

and the resulting plot is shown in Figure 9.13.

9.3.2 Momentum Indicators and Oscillators

The S+FinMetrics *momentum indicator and oscillator functions* are summarized in Table 9.3. For example, consider the popular *moving average convergence divergence* (MACD) indicator. This is an oscillator that represents the difference between two exponential moving averages. A signal line is computed as the exponential moving average of MACD. When the oscillator crosses above the signal line, it indicates a buy signal; when

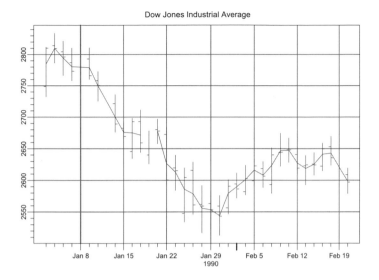

FIGURE 9.13. Typical price along with high, low, open and close prices for the Dow Jones Industrial Average.

the oscillator crosses below the signal line, it indicates a sell signal. The S+FinMetrics function TA.macd computes the MACD and has arguments

```
> args(TA.macd)
function(x, n.short = 12, n.long = 26, n.signal = 9, start
= "average", na.rm = F)
```

where x is a price series, n.short is a positive integer specifying the number of periods to be used for calculating the short window EWMA, n.long is a positive integer specifying the number of periods to be used for the calculating the long window EWMA, and n.signal is a positive integer

Function	Description
TA.accel	Acceleration
TA.momentum	Momentum
TA.macd	Moving average convergence divergence
TA.roc	Price rate of change
TA.rsi	Relative strength index
TA.stochastic	Stochastic Oscillator
TA.williamsr	Williams' %R
TA.williamsad	Williams' accumulation distribution

TABLE 9.3. S+FinMetrics momentum indicators

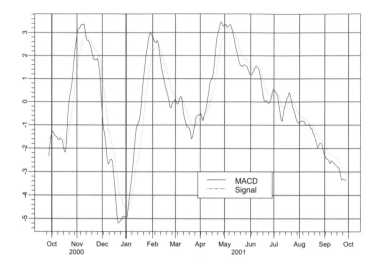

FIGURE 9.14. MACD and signal for daily closing prices on Microsoft stock.

Function	Description
TA.adoscillator	accumulation/distribution oscillator
TA.chaikinv	Chaikin's volatility
TA.garmanKlass	Garman-Klass estimator of volatility

TABLE 9.4. S+FinMetrics volatility indicator functions

giving the number of periods for the signal line. To compute and plot the MACD using daily closing prices on Microsoft use

```
> msft.macd = TA.macd(msft.dat[,"Close"])
> colIds(msft.macd) = c("MACD","Signal")
> plot(msft.macd,plot.args=list(lty=c(1:3)))
> legend(0.5,-3,legend=colIds(msft.macd),
+ lty=c(1,3))
```

Figure 9.14 shows the plot of the MACD and signal.

9.3.3   Volatility Indicators

The S+FinMetrics *volatility indicator functions* are summarized in Table 9.4. These functions compute estimates of volatility based on high, low, open and close information. For example, consider Chaikin's volatility indicator computed using the S+FinMetrics function TA.chaikin. It com-

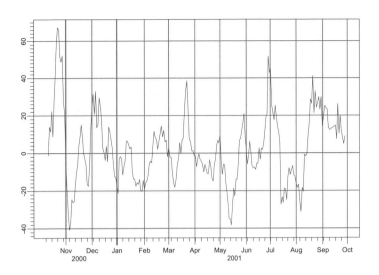

FIGURE 9.15. Chainkin's volatility estimate using the daily prices on Microsoft stock.

pares the spread between a security's high and low prices and quantifies volatility as a widening of the range between the high and low price. Let h_t and l_t represent the highest and lowest price for period t, respectively. Chaikin's volatility is calculated as the percentage change in the EWMA of $r_t = h_t - l_t$:

$$\frac{r_t - r_{t-nc}}{r_{t-nc}} \cdot 100$$

where nc is a positive number specifying the number of periods to use for computing the percentage change. To compute and plot Chaikin's volatility with $nc = 10$ and a ten day EWMA for the daily high and low price for Microsoft stock use

```
> msft.cv = TA.chaikinv(msft.dat[,"High"],
+ msft.dat[,"Low"],n.range=10,n.change=10)
> plot(msft.cv)
```

Figure 9.15 shows the estimated Chaikin volatility.

9.3.4 Volume Indicators

The S+FinMetrics *volume indicator functions* are summarized in Table 9.5. These indicators relate price movements with volume movements. To illustrate, consider the S+FinMetrics function TA.adi which computes the

Function	Description
TA.adi	Accumulation/distribution indicator
TA.chaikino	Chaikin oscillator
TA.nvi	Negative volume index
TA.pvi	Positive volume index
TA.obv	On balance volume
TA.pvtrend	Price-volume trend

TABLE 9.5. S+FinMetrics volume indicator functions

accumulations/distribution (A/D) indicator. This indicator associates price changes with volume as follows. Let c_t denote the closing price, h_t the highest price, l_t the lowest price, and v_t the trading volume for time t. The A/D indicator is the cumulative sum

$$AD_t = \sum_{i=1}^{t} \frac{c_i - l_i - (h_i - c_i)}{h_i - l_i} \cdot v_i$$

When AD_t moves up, it indicates that the security is being accumulated; when it moves down it indicates that the security is being distributed. To compute and plot the A/D indicator for Microsoft stock use

```
> msft.adi = TA.adi(msft.dat[,"High"],msft.dat[,"Low"],
+ msft.dat[,"Close"],msft.dat[,"Volume"])
> plot(msft.adi)
```

The resulting plot is shown in Figure 9.16.

9.4   Rolling Regression

For the linear regression model, rolling analysis may be used to assess the stability of the model's parameters and to provide a simple "poor man's" time varying parameter model. For a window of width $n < T$, the *rolling linear regression model* may be expressed as

$$\mathbf{y}_t(n) = \mathbf{X}_t(n)\boldsymbol{\beta}_t(n) + \boldsymbol{\varepsilon}_t(n), \; t = n, \ldots, T \tag{9.10}$$

where $\mathbf{y}_t(n)$ is an $(n \times 1)$ vector of observations on the response, $\mathbf{X}_t(n)$ is an $(n \times k)$ matrix of explanatory variables, $\boldsymbol{\beta}_t(n)$ is an $(k \times 1)$ vector of regression parameters and $\boldsymbol{\varepsilon}_t(n)$ is an $(n \times 1)$ vector of error terms. The n observations in $\mathbf{y}_t(n)$ and $\mathbf{X}_t(n)$ are the n most recent values from times $t - n + 1$ to t. It is assumed that $n > k$. The rolling least squares estimates

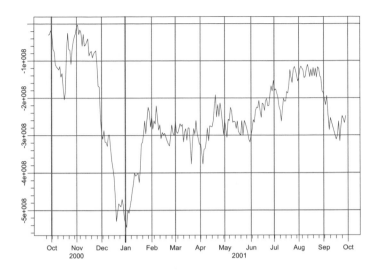

FIGURE 9.16. Accumulation/distribution indicator for Microsoft stock.

are

$$
\begin{aligned}
\hat{\boldsymbol{\beta}}_t(n) &= \left[\mathbf{X}_t(n)'\mathbf{X}_t(n)\right]^{-1}\mathbf{X}_t(n)'\mathbf{y}_t(n) \\
\hat{\sigma}_t^2(n) &= \frac{1}{n-k}\hat{\boldsymbol{\varepsilon}}_t(n)'\hat{\boldsymbol{\varepsilon}}_t(n) \\
&= \frac{1}{n-k}\left[\mathbf{y}_t(n)-\mathbf{X}_t(n)\hat{\boldsymbol{\beta}}_t(n)\right]'\left[\mathbf{y}_t(n)-\mathbf{X}_t(n)\hat{\boldsymbol{\beta}}_t(n)\right] \\
\widehat{avar}(\hat{\boldsymbol{\beta}}_t(n)) &= \hat{\sigma}_t^2(n)\cdot\left[\mathbf{X}_t(n)'\mathbf{X}_t(n)\right]^{-1}
\end{aligned}
$$

9.4.1 Estimating Rolling Regressions Using the S+FinMetrics Function rollOLS

The S+FinMetrics function rollOLS may be used to estimate general rolling regression models. rollOLS is based on the S+FinMetrics regression function OLS and implements efficient block updating algorithms for fast computation of rolling estimates. The arguments expected by rollOLS are

```
> args(rollOLS)
function(formula, data, subset, na.rm = F, method = "fit",
contrasts = NULL, start = NULL, end = NULL, width =
NULL, incr = 1, tau = 1e-010, trace = T, ...)
```

which are similar to those used by OLS. In particular, AR may be used in formulas to allow for lagged dependent variables and tslag and pdl may be used to allow for lagged independent variables. The argument width determines the rolling window width and the argument incr determines the increment size by which the windows are rolled through the sample. The output of rollOLS is an object of class "rollOLS" for which there are print, summary, plot and predict methods and extractor function coefficients. The use of rollOLS is illustrated with the following example.

Example 52 *Rolling estimation of CAPM for Microsoft*

Consider the estimation of the capital asset pricing model (CAPM) for an asset using rolling regression on the excess returns market model

$$r_t - r_{ft} = \alpha + \beta(r_{Mt} - r_{ft}) + \varepsilon_t, \ \varepsilon_t \sim WN(0, \sigma^2) \tag{9.11}$$

where r_t denotes the monthly return on an asset, r_{ft} denotes the 30 day T-bill rate, and r_{Mt} denotes the monthly return on a market portfolio proxy. The coefficient β measures the magnitude of market risk, and the CAPM imposes the restriction that $\alpha = 0$. Positive values of α indicate an average excess return above that predicted by the CAPM and negative values indicate an average return below that predicted by the CAPM. Rolling regression can be used to assess the stability of the CAPM regression over time and to uncover periods of time where an asset may have been overpriced or underpriced relative to the CAPM.

The monthly excess return data on Microsoft stock and S&P 500 index over the ten year period February 1990 through December 2000 are in the S+FinMetrics "timeSeries" object excessReturns.ts.

```
> colIds(excessReturns.ts)
[1] "MSFT"   "SP500"
> start(excessReturns.ts)
[1] Feb 1990
> end(excessReturns.ts)
[1] Dec 2000
```

The full sample CAPM estimates using the S+FinMetrics function OLS are

```
> ols.fit = OLS(MSFT~SP500,data=excessReturns.ts)
> summary(ols.fit)

Call:
OLS(formula = MSFT ~SP500, data = excessReturns.ts)

Residuals:
     Min      1Q  Median      3Q     Max
 -0.3101 -0.0620 -0.0024  0.0581  0.2260
```

```
Coefficients:
            Value Std. Error  t value Pr(>|t|)
(Intercept) 0.0175 0.0081      2.1654  0.0322
    SP500 1.5677 0.2015        7.7788  0.0000
```

```
Regression Diagnostics:

        R-Squared 0.3193
Adjusted R-Squared 0.3140
Durbin-Watson Stat 2.1891
```

```
Residual standard error: 0.09095 on 129 degrees of freedom
Time period: from Feb 1990 to Dec 2000
F-statistic: 60.51 on 1 and 129 degrees of freedom, the p-va
lue is 2.055e-012
```

The estimated full sample β for Microsoft is 1.57, which indicates that Microsoft was riskier than the market. Also, the full sample estimate of α is significantly different from zero so, on average, the returns on Microsoft are larger than predicted by the CAPM.

Consider now the 24-month rolling regression estimates incremented by 1 month computed using rollOLS

```
> roll.fit = rollOLS(MSFT~SP500, data=excessReturns.ts,
+ width=24,incr=1)
Rolling Window #1: Total Rows = 24
Rolling Window #2: Total Rows = 25
Rolling Window #3: Total Rows = 26
...
Rolling Window #108: Total Rows = 131
```

To suppress the printing of the window count, specify trace=F in the call to rollOLS. The returned object roll.fit is of class "rollOLS" and has components

```
> names(roll.fit)
 [1] "width"      "incr"      "nwin"      "contrasts" "rdf"
 [6] "coef"       "stddev"    "sigma"     "terms"     "call"
[11] "positions"
```

The components coef, stddev and sigma give the estimated coefficients, standard errors, and residual standard deviations for each of the nwin regressions. The positions component gives the start and end date of the estimation sample.

The print method, invoked by typing the object's name, gives a brief report of the fit

```
> roll.fit

Call:
rollOLS(formula = MSFT ~SP500, data = excessReturns.ts,
width = 24, incr = 1)

Rolling Windows:
 number width increment
    108    24          1
Time period: from Feb 1990 to Dec 2000

Coefficients:
          (Intercept)  SP500
     mean 0.0221       1.2193
std. dev. 0.0120       0.4549

Coefficient Standard Deviations:
          (Intercept)  SP500
     mean 0.0177       0.5057
std. dev. 0.0034       0.1107

Residual Scale Estimate:
   mean std. dev.
 0.0827 0.0168
```

Regression estimates are computed for 108 rolling windows. The mean and standard deviation are computed for the estimates and for the estimated coefficient standard errors. The average and standard deviation of the $\hat{\alpha}$ values are 0.0221 and 0.0120, respectively, and the average and standard deviation of the $SE(\hat{\alpha})$ values are 0.0177 and 0.0034, respectively. Hence, most of the $\hat{\alpha}$ values appear to be not significantly different from zero as predicted by the CAPM. The average and standard deviation of the $\hat{\beta}$ values are 1.2193 and 0.4549, respectively. The $\hat{\beta}$ values are quite variable and indicate that amount of market risk in Microsoft is not constant over time.

The rolling coefficient estimates for each rolling regression may be viewed using summary

```
> summary(roll.fit)

Call:
rollOLS(formula = MSFT ~ SP500, data = excessReturns.ts,
width = 24, incr = 1)

Rolling Windows:
 number width increment
```

```
      108     24          1
Time period: from Feb 1990 to Dec 2000

Coefficient: (Intercept)
          Value Std. Error t value Pr(>|t|)
Jan 1992 0.05075    0.01551   3.271 0.003492
Feb 1992 0.04897    0.01559   3.141 0.004751
Mar 1992 0.04471    0.01561   2.863 0.009035
...
Coefficient: SP500
          Value Std. Error t value  Pr(>|t|)
Jan 1992 1.3545    0.3322    4.077 0.0004993
Feb 1992 1.3535    0.3337    4.056 0.0005260
Mar 1992 1.3735    0.3332    4.123 0.0004472
...
```

or by using the coef extractor function. Notice that the first 24-month rolling estimates are computed for January 1992, which is 24 months after the sample start date of February 1990. The rolling estimates, however, are best viewed graphically using plot

```
> plot(roll.fit)

Make a plot selection (or 0 to exit):

1: plot: All
2: plot: Coef Estimates
3: plot: Coef Estimates with Confidence Intervals
4: plot: Residual Scale Estimates
Selection:
```

Plot selections 3 and 4 are illustrated in Figures 9.17 and 9.18. From the graphs of the rolling estimate it is clear that $\hat{\alpha}$ is significantly positive only at the very beginning of the sample. The $\hat{\beta}$ values are near unity for most windows and increase sharply at the end of the sample. However, the large standard errors make it difficult to determine if β is really changing over time. The residual scale estimates, $\hat{\sigma}$, increase sharply after 1999. This implies that the magnitude of the non-market risk in Microsoft increased after 1999.

In rollOLS, the optional argument incr sets the number of observations between the rolling blocks of data of length determined by width. Therefore, rolling regressions may be computed for arbitrary overlapping and non-overlapping blocks of data. For example, consider computing the CAPM estimates for Microsoft over the two non-overlapping but adjacent subsamples, February 1990 - June 1995 and July 1996 - November 2000 using rollOLS:

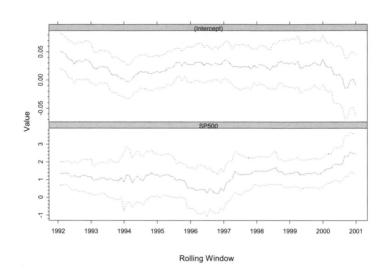

FIGURE 9.17. Rolling regression estimates of CAPM coefficients $\hat{\alpha}$ and $\hat{\beta}$ for Microsoft.

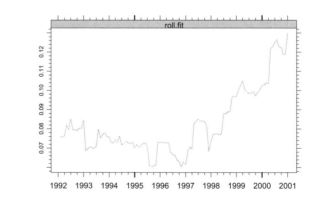

FIGURE 9.18. Rolling regression estimates of CAPM residual standard error for Microsoft.

```
> roll.fit2 = rollOLS(MSFT~SP500, data=excessReturns.ts,
+ width=65, incr=65)
Rolling Window #1: Total Rows = 65
Rolling Window #2: Total Rows = 130
> summary(roll.fit2)

Call:
rollOLS(formula = MSFT ~SP500, data = excessReturns.ts,
width = 65, incr = 65)

Rolling Windows:
 number width increment
    2    65        65
Time period: from Feb 1990 to Dec 2000

Coefficient: (Intercept)
            Value Std. Error t value Pr(>|t|)
Jun 1995 0.02765   0.009185  3.0100 0.003755
Nov 2000 0.01106   0.012880  0.8585 0.393851

Coefficient: SP500
          Value Std. Error t value    Pr(>|t|)
Jun 1995 1.339     0.2712   4.937 6.125e-006
Nov 2000 1.702     0.2813   6.050 8.739e-008
```

9.4.2 Rolling Predictions and Backtesting

Rolling regressions may be used to evaluate a model's predictive performance based on historical data using a technique commonly referred to as *backtesting*. To illustrate, consider the rolling regression model (9.10). The "out-of-sample" predictive performance of (9.10) is based on the rolling h-step predictions and prediction errors

$$\hat{y}_{t+h|t} \quad = \quad \mathbf{x}'_{t+h}\hat{\boldsymbol{\beta}}_t(n), \tag{9.12}$$

$$\hat{\varepsilon}_{t+h|t} \quad = \quad y_{t+h} - \hat{y}_{t+h|t} = y_{t+h} - \mathbf{x}'_{t+h}\hat{\boldsymbol{\beta}}_t(n) \tag{9.13}$$

The predictions are "out-of-sample" because $\hat{\boldsymbol{\beta}}_t(n)$ only uses data up to time t, whereas the predictions are for observations at times $t + h$ for $h > 0$. The rolling predictions are adaptive since $\hat{\boldsymbol{\beta}}_t(n)$ is updated when t is increased. When $h = 1$ there are $T - n$ rolling 1-step predictions $\{\hat{y}_{n+1|n}, \hat{y}_{n+2|n+1}, \ldots, \hat{y}_{T|T-1}\}$, when $h = 2$ there are $T - n - 1$ rolling 2-step predictions $\{\hat{y}_{n+2|n}, \hat{y}_{n+3|n+1}, \ldots, \hat{y}_{T|T-2}\}$ and so on.

Forecast Evaluation Statistics

The rolling forecasts (9.12) may be evaluated by examining the properties of the rolling forecast errors (9.13). Common evaluation statistics are

$$ME \quad = \quad \frac{1}{T-n-h+1} \sum_{t=n}^{T-h} \hat{\varepsilon}_{t+h|t} \tag{9.14}$$

$$MSE(h) \quad = \quad \frac{1}{T-n-h+1} \sum_{t=n}^{T-h} \hat{\varepsilon}_{t+h|t}^2 \tag{9.15}$$

$$RMSE(h) \quad = \quad \sqrt{(MSE(h))}$$

$$MAE(h) \quad = \quad \frac{1}{T-n-h+1} \sum_{t=n}^{T-h} |\hat{\varepsilon}_{t+h|t}|$$

$$MAPE(h) \quad = \quad \frac{1}{T-n-h+1} \sum_{t=n}^{T-h} \left| \frac{\hat{\varepsilon}_{t+h|t}}{y_{t+h}} \right|$$

The first measure evaluates the bias of the forecasts, and the other measures evaluate bias and precision.

Example 53 *Backtesting the CAPM*

Consider again the estimation of the CAPM (9.11) for Microsoft using rolling regression. The rolling regression information is contained in the "rollOLS" object roll.fit. The rolling h-step predictions (9.12) may be computed using the generic predict method. For example, the rolling 1-step forecasts are computed as

```
> roll.pred = predict(roll.fit,n.step=1)
> class(roll.pred)
[1] "listof"
> names(roll.pred)
[1] "1-Step-Ahead Forecasts"
```

The argument n.step determines the step length of the predictions. The object roll.pred is of class "listof" whose list component is a "timeSeries" object containing the rolling 1-step predictions:

```
> roll.pred[[1]]
 Positions             1
 Feb 1992    0.05994784
 Mar 1992    0.01481398
 ...
 Dec 2000   -0.00049354
```

The prediction errors (9.13) are then computed as

```
ehat.1step = excessReturns.ts[,"MSFT"]-roll.pred[[1]]
```

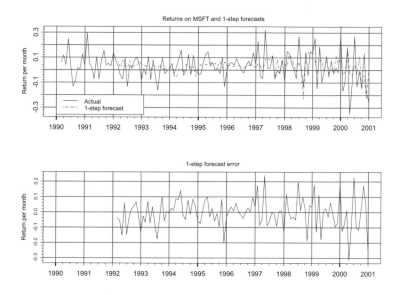

FIGURE 9.19. Monthly returns on Microsoft, 1-step rolling forecasts and forecast errors.

The monthly returns on Microsoft, 1-step forecasts and 1-step forecast errors are shown in Figure 9.19 created by

```
> par(mfrow=c(2,1))
> plot(excessReturns.ts[,"MSFT"], roll.pred[[1]],
+ main="Returns on MSFT and 1-step forecasts",
+ plot.args=list(lty=c(1,3)))
> legend(0, -0.2, legend=c("Actual","1-step forecast"),
+ lty=c(1,3))
> plot(ehat.1step,main="1-step forecast error")
```

The forecast evaluation statistics (9.14) may be computed as

```
> me.1step = mean(ehat.1step)
> mse.1step = as.numeric(var(ehat.1step))
> rmse.1step = sqrt(mse.1step)
> mae.1step = mean(abs(ehat.1step))
> mape.1step = mean(abs(ehat.1step/excessReturns.ts[,"MSFT"]),
+ na.rm=T)
```

To compute just the 2-step forecasts, specify n.step=2 in the call to predict. To compute the 1-step and 2-step forecasts specify n.step=1:2

```
> roll.pred.12 = predict(roll.fit,n.steps=1:2)
```

```
> names(roll.pred.12)
[1] "1-Step-Ahead Forecasts" "2-Step-Ahead Forecasts"

> roll.pred.12[[1]]
 Positions              1
 Feb 1992    0.05994784
 Mar 1992    0.01481398
 ...
 Dec 2000   -0.00049354

> roll.pred.12[[2]]
 Positions              1
 Mar 1992    0.0165764
 Apr 1992    0.0823867
 ...
 Dec 2000   -0.0025076
```

Since the 1-step and 2-step predictions are components of the list object
roll.pred.12, the S-PLUS function lapply may be used to simplify the
computation of the forecast errors and evaluation statistics. To illustrate,
supplying the user-defined function

```
> make.ehat = function(x,y) {
+     ans = y - x
+     ans[!is.na(ans),]
+ }
```

to lapply creates a "named" object containing the 1-step and 2-step forecasts errors as components:

```
> ehat.list = lapply(roll.pred.12, make.ehat,
+ excessReturns.ts[,"MSFT"])
> names(ehat.list)
[1] "1-Step-Ahead Forecasts" "2-Step-Ahead Forecasts"
```

The forecast evaluation statistics (9.14) may be computed for each component of ehat.list using lapply with the following user-defined function

```
> make.errorStats = function(x){
+     me = mean(x)
+     mse = as.numeric(var(x))
+     rmse = sqrt(mse)
+     mae = mean(abs(x))
+     ans = list(ME=me,MSE=mse,RMSE=rmse,MAE=mae)
+     ans
+ }

> errorStat.list = lapply(ehat.list,make.errorStats)
```

```
> unlist(errorStat.list)
1-Step-Ahead Forecasts.ME 1-Step-Ahead Forecasts.MSE
             -0.006165                    0.009283

1-Step-Ahead Forecasts.RMSE 1-Step-Ahead Forecasts.MAE
              0.09635                     0.07207

2-Step-Ahead Forecasts.ME 2-Step-Ahead Forecasts.MSE
             -0.007269                    0.009194

2-Step-Ahead Forecasts.RMSE 2-Step-Ahead Forecasts.MAE
              0.09589                     0.07187
```

The S-PLUS function `sapply` may be used instead of `lapply` to summarize the forecast error evaluation statistics:

```
> sapply(ehat.list,make.errorStats)
       1-Step-Ahead Forecasts 2-Step-Ahead Forecasts
[1,] -0.006165                 -0.007269
[2,] 0.009283                  0.009194
[3,] 0.09635                   0.09589
[4,] 0.07207                   0.07187
```

Comparing Predictive Accuracy

Backtesting is often used to compare the forecasting accuracy of two or more competing models. Typically, the forecast evaluation statistics (9.14) are computed for each model, and the model that produces the smallest set of statistics is judged to be the better model. Recently, Diebold and Mariano (1995) proposed a simple procedure using rolling h-step forecast errors for statistically determining if one model's forecast is more accurate than another's. Let $\hat{\varepsilon}^1_{t+h|t}$ and $\hat{\varepsilon}^2_{t+h|t}$ denote the h-step forecast errors from two competing models, and let N denote the number of h-step forecasts. The accuracy of each forecast is measured by a particular forecast evaluation or *loss function*

$$L(\hat{\varepsilon}^i_{t+h|t}), \ i = 1, 2$$

Two popular loss functions are the *squared error loss* $L(\hat{\varepsilon}^i_{t+h|t}) = \left(\hat{\varepsilon}^i_{t+h|t}\right)^2$ and *absolute error loss* $L(\hat{\varepsilon}^i_{t+h|t}) = \left|\hat{\varepsilon}^i_{t+h|t}\right|$. To determine if one model forecasts better than another Diebold and Mariano (1995) suggest computing the loss differential

$$d_t = L(\hat{\varepsilon}^1_{t+h|t}) - L(\hat{\varepsilon}^2_{t+h|t})$$

and testing the null hypothesis of equal forecasting accuracy

$$H_0 : E[d_t] = 0$$

The Diebold-Mariano test statistic is the simple ratio

$$DM = \frac{\bar{d}}{\widehat{lrv}(\bar{d})^{1/2}} \qquad (9.16)$$

where

$$\bar{d} = \frac{1}{N} \sum_{t=1}^{N} d_t$$

is the average loss differential, and $\widehat{lrv}(\bar{d})$ is a consistent estimate of the long-run asymptotic variance of $\bar{d}$. Diebold and Mariano suggest computing $\widehat{lrv}(\bar{d})$ using the Newey-West nonparametric estimator with a rectangular weight function and a lag truncation parameter equal to the forecast step length, h, less one. Diebold and Mariano show that under the null hypothesis of equal predictive accuracy the DM statistic is asymptotically distributed $N(0,1)$.

Example 54 *Backtesting regression models for predicting asset returns*

To illustrate model comparison and evaluation by backtesting, consider the problem of predicting the annual real return on S&P 500 index using two different valuation ratios. The regression model is of the form

$$r_t = \alpha + \beta x_{t-1} + \varepsilon_t \qquad (9.17)$$

where r_t denotes the natural logarithm of the annual real total return on S&P 500 index and x_t denotes the natural logarithm of a valuation ratio. The first valuation ratio considered is the dividend/price ratio and the second ratio is the earning/price ratio. The data are constructed from the S+FinMetrics "timeSeries" shiller.annual as follows:

```
> colIds(shiller.annual)
 [1] "price"          "dividend"      "earnings"
 [4] "cpi"            "real.price"    "real.dividend"
 [7] "real.earnings"  "pe.10"         "dp.ratio"
[10] "dp.yield"
> # compute log of real data
> ln.p = log(shiller.annual[,"real.price"])
> colIds(ln.p) = "ln.p"
> ln.dpratio = log(dp.ratio)
> colIds(ln.dpratio) = "ln.dpratio"
> ln.epratio = -log(shiller.annual[,"pe.10"])
> ln.epratio = ln.epratio[!is.na(ln.epratio),]
> colIds(ln.epratio) = "ln.epratio"
> # compute cc real total returns - see CLM pg. 261
> ln.r = diff(ln.p) + log(1+exp(ln.dpratio[-1,]))
> colIds(ln.r) = "ln.r"
```

```
> stock.ts = seriesMerge(ln.p,ln.d,ln.dpratio,
+ ln.epratio,ln.r,pos=positions(ln.epratio))
> start(stock.ts)
[1] Dec 1881
> end(stock.ts)
[1] Dec 2000
```

Rolling regression estimates of (9.17) with the two valuation ratios using a 50 year window incremented by 1 year are computed as

```
> roll.dp.fit = rollOLS(ln.r~tslag(ln.dpratio),data=stock.ts,
+ width=50,incr=1)
Rolling Window #1: Total Rows = 50
Rolling Window #2: Total Rows = 51
...
> roll.ep.fit = rollOLS(ln.r~tslag(ln.epratio),data=stock.ts,
+ width=50,incr=1)
Rolling Window #1: Total Rows = 50
Rolling Window #2: Total Rows = 51
...
Rolling Window #70: Total Rows = 119
```

Figures 9.20 and 9.21 show the rolling coefficient estimates from the two models along with standard error bands. The rolling estimates of β for the two models are similar. For both models, the strongest evidence for return predictability occurs between 1960 and 1990. The value of β for the earning/price model appears to be different from zero during more periods than the value of β for the dividend/price model.

The rolling h-step predictions for $h = 1, \ldots, 5$ and prediction errors are

```
> roll.dp.pred = predict(roll.dp.fit,n.steps=1:5)
> roll.ep.pred = predict(roll.ep.fit,n.steps=1:5)
> ehat.dp.list = lapply(roll.dp.pred,make.ehat,
+ stock.ts[,"ln.r"])
> ehat.ep.list = lapply(roll.ep.pred,make.ehat,
+ stock.ts[,"ln.r"])
```

The forecast evaluation statistics are

```
> errorStats.dp.list = lapply(ehat.dp.list,make.errorStats)
> errorStats.ep.list = lapply(ehat.ep.list,make.errorStats)
> tmp = cbind(unlist(errorStats.dp.list),
+ unlist(errorStats.ep.list))
> colIds(tmp) = c("D/P","E/P")
> tmp
numeric matrix: 20 rows, 2 columns.
                                D/P      E/P
   1-Step-Ahead Forecasts.ME 0.03767 0.01979
```

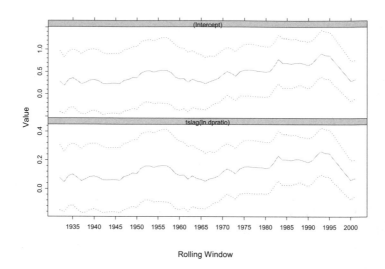

FIGURE 9.20. 50 year rolling regression estimates of (9.17) using dividend/price ratio.

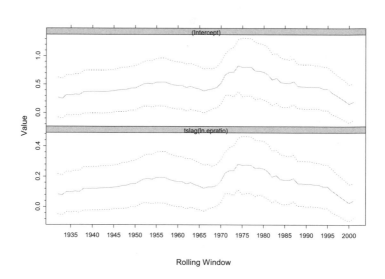

FIGURE 9.21. 50 year rolling regression estimates of (9.17) using earning/price.

```
 1-Step-Ahead Forecasts.MSE  0.03150 0.03139
 1-Step-Ahead Forecasts.RMSE 0.17749 0.17718
 1-Step-Ahead Forecasts.MAE  0.14900 0.14556
 2-Step-Ahead Forecasts.ME   0.04424 0.02334
 2-Step-Ahead Forecasts.MSE  0.03223 0.03205
2-Step-Ahead Forecasts.RMSE  0.17952 0.17903
 2-Step-Ahead Forecasts.MAE  0.15206 0.14804
 3-Step-Ahead Forecasts.ME   0.04335 0.02054
 3-Step-Ahead Forecasts.MSE  0.03203 0.03180
3-Step-Ahead Forecasts.RMSE  0.17898 0.17832
 3-Step-Ahead Forecasts.MAE  0.14993 0.14731
 4-Step-Ahead Forecasts.ME   0.04811 0.02397
 4-Step-Ahead Forecasts.MSE  0.03292 0.03248
 4-Step-Ahead Forecasts.RMSE 0.18143 0.18022
 4-Step-Ahead Forecasts.MAE  0.15206 0.14855
                                D/P     E/P
 5-Step-Ahead Forecasts.ME   0.04707 0.02143
 5-Step-Ahead Forecasts.MSE  0.03339 0.03255
5-Step-Ahead Forecasts.RMSE  0.18272 0.18043
 5-Step-Ahead Forecasts.MAE  0.15281 0.14825
```

The forecast evaluation statistics are generally smaller for the model using
the earning/price ratio. The Diebold-Mariano statistics based on squared
error and absolute error loss functions may be computed using

```
> for (i in 1:5) {
+    d.mse[,i] = ehat.dp.list[[i]]^2 - ehat.ep.list[[i]]^2
+    DM.mse[i] = mean(d.mse[,i])/sqrt(asymp.var(d.mse[,i],
+      bandwidth=i-1,window="rectangular"))
+    d.mae[,i] = abs(ehat.dp.list[[i]]) - abs(ehat.ep.list[[i]])
+    DM.mae[i] = mean(d.mae[,i])/sqrt(asymp.var(d.mae[,i],
+      bandwidth=i-1,window="rectangular"))
+ }
> names(DM.mse) = names(ehat.dp.list)
> names(DM.mae) = names(ehat.dp.list)
> cbind(DM.mse,DM.mae)
                        DM.mse  DM.mae
1-Step-Ahead Forecasts 0.07983 0.07987
2-Step-Ahead Forecasts 0.09038 0.08509
3-Step-Ahead Forecasts 0.07063 0.05150
4-Step-Ahead Forecasts 0.08035 0.06331
5-Step-Ahead Forecasts 0.07564 0.06306
```

Since the DM statistics are asymptotically standard normal, one cannot
reject the null hypothesis of equal predictive accuracy at any reasonable

significance level based on the 1-step through 5-step forecast errors for the two models.

9.5 Rolling Analysis of General Models Using the S+FinMetrics Function roll

The S-PLUS aggregateSeries function is appropriate for rolling analysis of simple functions and the S+FinMetrics function rollOLS handles rolling regression. The S+FinMetrics function roll is designed to perform rolling analysis of general S-PLUS modeling functions that take a formula argument describing the relationship between a response and explanatory variables and where the data, usually a data frame or "timeSeries" object with a data frame in the data slot, is supplied explicitly in a data argument. The arguments expected by roll are

```
> args(roll)
function(FUN, data, width, incr = 1, start = NULL, end =
NULL, na.rm = F, save.list = NULL, arg.data =
"data", trace = T, ...)
```

where FUN is the S-PLUS modeling function to be applied to each rolling window, data is the data argument to FUN which must be either a data frame or a "timeSeries" with a data frame in the data slot, width specifies the width of the rolling window and incr determines the increment size by which the windows are rolled through the sample. The argument save.list specifies the components of the object returned by FUN to save in the object returned by roll. If FUN requires more arguments in addition to data, for example a formula relating a response to a set of explanatory variables, then these arguments should be supplied in place of .... The use of roll is illustrated with the following examples.

Example 55 *Rolling regression*

In this example, the 24-month rolling regression estimation of the CAPM for Microsoft using the "timeSeries" excessReturns.ts is repeated using the S+FinMetrics function roll with FUN=OLS. OLS requires a formula argument for model specification and a data frame or "timeSeries" in data argument. The 24 month rolling CAPM estimates using roll are

```
> roll.fit = roll(FUN=OLS, data=excessReturns.ts,
+ width=24, incr=1, formula=MSFT~SP500)
Rolling Window #1: Total Rows = 24
Rolling Window #2: Total Rows = 25
...
Rolling Window #108: Total Rows = 131
```

```
> class(roll.fit)
[1] "roll"
```

The return `roll.fit` is an object of class "roll" for which there are no specific method functions. Since the `data` argument `excessReturns.ts` is a "timeSeries", the default components of `roll.fit` are the positions of the rolling windows and "timeSeries" objects containing the components that are produced by `OLS` for each of the windows:

```
> names(roll.fit)
 [1] "R"          "coef"      "df.resid"  "fitted"
 [5] "residuals"  "assign"    "contrasts" "ar.order"
 [9] "terms"      "call"      "positions"
> class(roll.fit$coef)
[1] "timeSeries"
> nrow(roll.fit$coef)
[1] 108
> class(roll.fit$residuals)
[1] "timeSeries"
> nrow(roll.fit$residuals)
[1] 108
```

The first column of the "timeSeries" `roll.fit$coef` contains the rolling intercept estimates, and the second column contains the rolling slope estimates.

```
> roll.fit$coef[1:2,]
 Positions       1       2
 Jan 1992   0.05075 1.354
 Feb 1992   0.04897 1.353
```

The rows of the "timeSeries" `roll.fit$residuals` contain the residuals for the OLS fit on each 24-month window

```
> roll.fit$residuals[1:2,]
 Positions        1        2        3        4          5
 Jan 1992   0.007267 0.04021 0.03550 0.085707  0.004596
 Feb 1992   0.042014 0.03726 0.08757 0.006368 -0.164498

 ...

        24
  0.05834
 -0.03393
```

If only some of the components of `OLS` are needed for each rolling window, these components may be specified in the optional argument `save.list`. For example, to retain only the components `coef` and `residuals` over the rolling windows specify save.list=c("coef","residuals") in the call to roll:

```
> roll.fit = roll(FUN=OLS, data=excessReturns.ts,
+ width=24, incr=1, formula=MSFT~SP500,
+ save.list=c("coef","residuals"), trace=F)
> names(roll.fit)
[1] "coef"      "residuals" "call"      "positions"
```

9.6 References

[1] ALEXANDER, C. (2001). *Market Models: A Guide to Financial Data Analysis*, John Wiley and Sons.

[2] BAUER, R.J. AND J.R. DAHLQUIST (1999). *Techincal Market Indicators: Analysis & Performance.* John Wiley & Sons, New York.

[3] BANERJEE, A. R. LUMSDAINE AND J.H. STOCK (1992). "Recursive and Sequential Tests of the Unit Root and Trend Break Hypothesis: Theory and International Evidence," *Journal of Business and Economic Statistics*, 10(3), 271-288.

[4] COLBY, R.W. AND T.A MEYERS (1988). *The Encyclopedia of Technical Market Indicators.* Irwin.

[5] DACOROGNA, M.M., R. GENÇAY, U.A. MÜLLER, R.B. OLSEN, AND O.V. PICTET (2001). *An Introduction to High-Frequency Finance.* Academic Press, San Diego.

[6] DIEBOLD, F.X. AND R.S. MARIANO (1995). "Comparing Predictive Accuracy," *Journal of Business and Economic Statistics*, 13, 253-263.

[7] SHILLER, R. (1998). *Irrational Exuberance.* Princeton University Press, New Jersey.

[8] ZUMBACH, G.O., AND U.A. MÜLLER (2001). "Operators on Inhomogeneous Time Series," *International Journal of Theoretical and Applied Finance*, 4, 147-178.

10
Systems of Regression Equations

10.1 Introduction

The previous chapters dealt with models for univariate financial time series. In many applications, it is desirable to model the joint behavior of multiple time series because of possible efficiency gains to the joint estimation of a system of time series models. For example, there may be complex interactions between the variables and/or the error structure across models. Univariate models cannot capture these interactions whereas multivariate models can. Furthermore, many equilibrium models for asset returns, like the capital asset pricing model (CAPM) or the arbitrage price model (APT), imply parameter restrictions that are common to the model representation of all assets. Hence, the testing of equilibrium asset pricing models requires the testing of cross equation parameter constraints, and the proper estimation of these models would impose these cross equation restrictions.

This chapter introduces methods for modeling and analyzing systems of linear and nonlinear regression equations. Section 10.2 describes Zellner's seemingly unrelated regression (SUR) system of regression equations that may be linked through common regressors, correlated error terms, or cross equation parameter restrictions. Section 10.3 describes the specification and estimation of linear SUR models and gives examples using the S+FinMetrics function SUR. Section 10.4 describes the specification and estimation of nonlinear SUR models and gives examples using the S+FinMetrics function NLSUR.

The SUR model was developed by Theil (1961) and Zellner (1962) and is described in most econometric textbooks. The nonlinear SUR model was developed by Gallant (1974). Greene (2000) gives a general overview of linear and nonlinear SUR models and Srivastava and Giles (1987) provides a thorough treatment. Burmeister and McElroy (1986) and Campbell, Lo and MacKinlay (1997) describe the estimation and testing of systems of asset pricing models using SUR and nonlinear SUR models.

10.2   Systems of Regression Equations

Many applications in economics and finance involve a *system of linear regression equations* of the form

$$
\begin{aligned}
\mathbf{y}_1 &= \mathbf{X}_1\boldsymbol{\beta}_1 + \boldsymbol{\varepsilon}_1 \\
\mathbf{y}_2 &= \mathbf{X}_2\boldsymbol{\beta}_2 + \boldsymbol{\varepsilon}_2 \\
&\vdots \\
\mathbf{y}_M &= \mathbf{X}_M\boldsymbol{\beta}_M + \boldsymbol{\varepsilon}_M
\end{aligned}
\tag{10.1}
$$

where $\mathbf{y}_i$ is a $(T \times 1)$ vector of dependent variables, $\mathbf{X}_i$ is a $(T \times k_i)$ matrix of explanatory variables and $\boldsymbol{\varepsilon}_i$ is a $(T \times 1)$ vector of errors for equations $i = 1, ..., M$. It is assumed that each $\mathbf{X}_i$ is exogenous, i.e., uncorrelated with $\boldsymbol{\varepsilon}_i$. Depending on the application, each $\mathbf{X}_i$ may be distinct or there may be common regressors across equations. The equations in (10.1) are potentially linked either through the covariance structure of the errors or through cross equation restrictions on the elements of $\boldsymbol{\beta}_i$ $(i = 1, ..., M)$, and estimation of the entire system generally produces more efficient estimates than the estimation of each equation individually.

Economic theory often implies a *system of nonlinear regression equations* of the form

$$
\begin{aligned}
\mathbf{y}_1 &= \mathbf{f}_1(\boldsymbol{\beta}_1, \mathbf{X}_1) + \boldsymbol{\varepsilon}_1 \\
\mathbf{y}_2 &= \mathbf{f}_2(\boldsymbol{\beta}_2, \mathbf{X}_2) + \boldsymbol{\varepsilon}_2 \\
&\vdots \\
\mathbf{y}_M &= \mathbf{f}_M(\boldsymbol{\beta}_M, \mathbf{X}_M) + \boldsymbol{\varepsilon}_M
\end{aligned}
$$

where $\mathbf{f}_i(\boldsymbol{\beta}_i, \mathbf{X}_i)$ is a $(T \times 1)$ vector containing the nonlinear function values $f_i(\boldsymbol{\beta}_i, \mathbf{x}_{it})$ for equations $i = 1, \ldots, M$. The functions f_i may be the same or different across equations, the error structures may be linked, and there may be cross equation restrictions on the elements of $\boldsymbol{\beta}_i$ $(i = 1, ..., M)$.

Some common applications in finance are illustrated below.

Example 56 *Exchange rate regressions*

Consider the system of M exchange rate regressions

$$\Delta s_{i,t+k} = \alpha_i + \gamma_i(f_{i,t}^k - s_{i,t}) + \varepsilon_{i,t+k}, \ i = 1, \ldots, M \qquad (10.2)$$

where $s_{i,t+k}$ represents the natural log of the spot exchange exchange rate for currency i (relative, say, to the U.S. dollar) at time $t + k$ and $f_{i,t}^k$ denotes the natural log of the forward exchange rate at time t for a forward contract in currency i that will deliver at time $t + k$. In terms of the previous notation for the system of linear regression equations, $y_{it} = s_{i,t+k}$, $\mathbf{x}_{it} = (1, f_{i,t}^k - s_{i,t})'$ and $\boldsymbol{\beta}_i = (\alpha_i, \gamma_i)'$, the only common regressor in the system is a vector of ones. The error terms, $\varepsilon_{i,t+k}$, are likely to be correlated contemporaneously across equations due to common random shocks affecting all exchange rates. That is, $E[\boldsymbol{\varepsilon}_i \boldsymbol{\varepsilon}_j'] = \sigma_{ij} \mathbf{I}_T$ where $E[\varepsilon_{it}\varepsilon_{js}] = \sigma_{ij}$ for $t = s$ and 0 otherwise. In the present context, this across equation correlation can be used to increase the efficiency of the parameter estimates for each equation.

Example 57 *The capital asset pricing model with a risk-free asset*

Consider the excess return single index model regression

$$R_{it} - r_{ft} = \alpha_i + \beta_i(R_{Mt} - r_{ft}) + \varepsilon_{it}, \ i = 1, \ldots, M$$

where R_{it} denotes the return on asset i at time t, r_{ft} denotes the return on a risk-free asset, R_{Mt} denotes the return on an proxy for the "market portfolio" and ε_{it} denotes the residual return not explained by the "market" for asset i. In terms of the previous notation for the system of regression equations, $y_{it} = R_{it} - r_{ft}, \mathbf{x}_{it} = (1, R_{Mt} - r_{ft})'$, and $\boldsymbol{\beta}_i = (\alpha_i, \beta_i)'$ so that all regression equations share the same regressors. It is likely that the residual returns, ε_{it}, are contemporaneously correlated across assets due to common shocks not related to the "market". That is, $E[\boldsymbol{\varepsilon}_i \boldsymbol{\varepsilon}_j'] = \sigma_{ij} \mathbf{I}_T$ where $E[\varepsilon_{it}\varepsilon_{js}] = \sigma_{ij}$ for $t = s$ and 0 otherwise. However, unless there are across equation restrictions on $\boldsymbol{\beta}_i$, the fact that $\mathbf{x}_{it}$ is the same for each equation means that there will be no efficiency gain in estimating the parameters from exploiting the across equation error correlation. The capital asset pricing model (CAPM) imposes the restriction $\alpha_i = 0$ for all assets i so that $E[R_{it}] - r_{ft} = \beta_i(E[R_{Mt} - r_{ft})$. Testing the CAPM therefore involves a joint test of many cross equation zero restrictions.

Example 58 *The capital asset pricing model without a risk-free asset*

The CAPM formulation above assumes the existence of a risk-free asset. If there is no risk-free asset, then Black (1972) showed that the CAPM takes the form

$$E[R_{it}^{\text{real}}] - \gamma = \beta_i(E[R_{Mt}^{\text{real}}] - \gamma)$$

where R_{it}^{real} denotes the real return on asset i, R_{Mt}^{real} denotes the real return on the market, and γ denotes the unobservable return on a zero-beta portfolio. The Black form of the CAPM may be estimated from the system of nonlinear regression equations

$$R_{it}^{\text{real}} = (1 - \beta_i)\gamma + \beta_i R_{Mt}^{\text{real}} + \varepsilon_{it}, \ i = 1, \ldots, M \tag{10.3}$$

In terms of the above notation for systems of nonlinear regression equations, Black's restricted CAPM has $y_{it} = R_{it}^{\text{real}}$, $\mathbf{x}_{it} = (1, R_{Mt}^{\text{real}})'$, $\boldsymbol{\beta}_i = (\gamma, \beta_i)'$ and $f_i(\boldsymbol{\beta}_i, \mathbf{x}_{it}) = (1 - \beta_i)\gamma + \beta_i R_{Mt}^{\text{real}}$. Notice that the parameter γ is common across all equations. The Black form of the CAPM may be tested by estimating the unrestricted system

$$R_{it}^{\text{real}} = \alpha_i + \beta_i R_{Mt}^{\text{real}} + \varepsilon_{it}, \ i = 1, \ldots, M \tag{10.4}$$

and testing the M nonlinear cross equation restrictions $\alpha_i = (1 - \beta_i)\gamma$.

10.3   Linear Seemingly Unrelated Regressions

The *seemingly unrelated regression* (SUR) model due to Theil (1961) and Zellner (1962) is the unrestricted system of M linear regression equations

$$\mathbf{y}_i = \mathbf{X}_i \boldsymbol{\beta}_i + \boldsymbol{\varepsilon}_i, \ i = 1, \ldots, M \tag{10.5}$$

where $\mathbf{y}_i$ is $(T \times 1)$, $\mathbf{X}_i$ is $(T \times k_i)$, $\boldsymbol{\beta}_i$ is $(k \times 1)$ and $\boldsymbol{\varepsilon}_i$ is $(T \times 1)$. The error terms are assumed to be contemporaneously correlated across equations but temporally uncorrelated: $E[\varepsilon_{it}\varepsilon_{js}] = \sigma_{ij}$ for $t = s$; 0 otherwise.

The M equations may be stacked to form the *giant regression* model

$$\begin{pmatrix} \mathbf{y}_1 \\ \vdots \\ \mathbf{y}_M \end{pmatrix} = \begin{pmatrix} \mathbf{X}_1 & 0 & 0 \\ 0 & \ddots & 0 \\ 0 & 0 & \mathbf{X}_M \end{pmatrix} \begin{pmatrix} \boldsymbol{\beta}_1 \\ \vdots \\ \boldsymbol{\beta}_M \end{pmatrix} + \begin{pmatrix} \boldsymbol{\varepsilon}_1 \\ \vdots \\ \boldsymbol{\varepsilon}_M \end{pmatrix}$$

or

$$\underline{\mathbf{y}} = \underline{\mathbf{X}}\boldsymbol{\beta} + \underline{\boldsymbol{\varepsilon}} \tag{10.6}$$

where $\underline{\mathbf{y}}$ is $(MT \times 1)$, $\underline{\mathbf{X}}$ is $(MT \times K)$, $\boldsymbol{\beta}$ is $(K \times 1)$ and $\underline{\boldsymbol{\varepsilon}}$ is $(MT \times 1)$. Here $K = \sum_{i=1}^{M} k_i$ is the total number of regressors across all equations. The error term in the giant regression has non-diagonal covariance matrix

$$\mathbf{V} = E[\underline{\boldsymbol{\varepsilon}}\,\underline{\boldsymbol{\varepsilon}}'] = \boldsymbol{\Sigma} \otimes \mathbf{I}_T \tag{10.7}$$

where the $(M \times M)$ matrix $\boldsymbol{\Sigma}$ has elements σ_{ij}.

10.3.1   Estimation

Since $\mathbf{V}$ is not diagonal, least squares estimation of $\boldsymbol{\beta}$ in the giant regression (10.6) is not efficient. The *generalized least squares* (GLS) estimator of $\boldsymbol{\beta}$,

$$\begin{aligned} \hat{\boldsymbol{\beta}}_{GLS} &= (\underline{\mathbf{X}}'\mathbf{V}^{-1}\underline{\mathbf{X}})^{-1}\underline{\mathbf{X}}'\mathbf{V}^{-1}\underline{\mathbf{y}} \\ &= (\underline{\mathbf{X}}'(\boldsymbol{\Sigma}^{-1} \otimes \mathbf{I}_T)\underline{\mathbf{X}})^{-1}\underline{\mathbf{X}}'(\boldsymbol{\Sigma}^{-1} \otimes \mathbf{I}_T)\underline{\mathbf{y}} \end{aligned} \tag{10.8}$$

is efficient.

It can be shown, e.g. Greene (2000) chapter 15, that if $\mathbf{X}_i = \mathbf{X}$ for all equations $i = 1, ..., M$ (i.e., all equations have the same regressors), or if the error covariance matrix $\mathbf{V}$ is diagonal and there are no cross equation restrictions on the values of $\boldsymbol{\beta}_i$ then least squares estimation of (10.5) equation by equation produces the GLS estimator (10.8).

Feasible GLS Estimation

The GLS estimator of $\boldsymbol{\beta}$ is usually not feasible since the covariance matrix $\boldsymbol{\Sigma}$, and hence $\mathbf{V}$, is generally not known. However, in the SUR model the elements of $\boldsymbol{\Sigma}$ can be consistently estimated by equation least squares of (10.5),

$$
\begin{aligned}
\hat{\sigma}_{ij} &= T^{-1}\hat{\boldsymbol{\varepsilon}}_i'\hat{\boldsymbol{\varepsilon}}_j \\
&= T^{-1}(\mathbf{y}_i - \mathbf{X}_i\hat{\boldsymbol{\beta}}_i)'(\mathbf{y}_j - \mathbf{X}_j\hat{\boldsymbol{\beta}}_j),
\end{aligned}
$$

producing $\hat{\boldsymbol{\Sigma}}$. The *feasible generalized least squares* estimator (FGLS) is

$$
\hat{\boldsymbol{\beta}}_{FGLS} = (\underline{\mathbf{X}}'(\hat{\boldsymbol{\Sigma}}^{-1} \otimes \mathbf{I}_T)\underline{\mathbf{X}})^{-1}\underline{\mathbf{X}}'(\hat{\boldsymbol{\Sigma}}^{-1} \otimes \mathbf{I}_T)\underline{\mathbf{y}} \tag{10.9}
$$

and its asymptotic variance is consistently estimated by

$$
\widehat{avar}(\hat{\boldsymbol{\beta}}_{FGLS}) = (\underline{\mathbf{X}}'(\hat{\boldsymbol{\Sigma}}^{-1} \otimes \mathbf{I}_T)\underline{\mathbf{X}})^{-1}
$$

The FGLS estimator (10.9) is asymptotically equivalent to the GLS estimator (10.8).

Tests of linear hypotheses of the form $\mathbf{R}\boldsymbol{\beta} = \mathbf{r}$, which may incorporate cross equation linear restrictions, may be computed in the usual way with the Wald statistic

$$
Wald = (\mathbf{R}\hat{\boldsymbol{\beta}}_{FGLS} - \mathbf{r})'\left[\mathbf{R}\widehat{avar}(\hat{\boldsymbol{\beta}}_{FGLS})\mathbf{R}'\right]^{-1}(\mathbf{R}\hat{\boldsymbol{\beta}}_{FGLS} - \mathbf{r}) \tag{10.10}
$$

which is asymptotically distributed chi-square with degrees of freedom equal to the number of restrictions being tested under the null.

Iterated Feasible GLS Estimation

The estimate of $\boldsymbol{\Sigma}$ in FGLS estimation uses the inefficient least squares estimate of $\boldsymbol{\beta}_i$. The *iterated* FGLS estimator repeats the construction of the FGLS estimator using an updated estimator of $\boldsymbol{\Sigma}$ based on the FGLS estimator (10.9). That is, at each iteration updated estimates of σ_{ij} are computed as

$$
\hat{\sigma}_{ij,FGLS} = T^{-1}(\mathbf{y}_i - \mathbf{X}_i\hat{\boldsymbol{\beta}}_{i,FGLS})'(\mathbf{y}_j - \mathbf{X}_j\hat{\boldsymbol{\beta}}_{j,FGLS})
$$

and the resulting updated estimator of $\boldsymbol{\Sigma}$ is used to recompute the FGLS estimator. This process is iterated until $\hat{\boldsymbol{\beta}}_{FGLS}$ no longer changes. If the error terms for each equation are Gaussian, it can be shown that the iterated FGLS estimator of $\boldsymbol{\beta}$ is the maximum likelihood estimator (MLE). It should be noted, however, that iteration does not improve the asymptotic properties of the FGLS estimator.

Maximum Likelihood Estimation

Although the MLE of $\boldsymbol{\beta}$ may be obtained by iterating the FGLS estimator, it is often computationally more efficient to compute the MLE directly. To conveniently express the likelihood function for the SUR model it is necessary to re-express the SUR model by grouping the data horizontally by observations instead of vertically by equations. The SUR model expressed this way is given by

$$\mathbf{y}_t' = \mathbf{x}_t'\boldsymbol{\Pi} + \boldsymbol{\varepsilon}_t', \ t = 1, \ldots, T$$

where $\mathbf{y}_t' = (y_{1t}, y_{2t}, \ldots, y_{Mt})$ is $(1 \times M)$ vector of dependent variables, $\mathbf{x}_t' = (x_{1t}, x_{2t}, \ldots, x_{Kt})$ is the $(1 \times K)$ vector containing all of the unique explanatory variables, $\boldsymbol{\Pi} = [\boldsymbol{\pi}_1, \boldsymbol{\pi}_2, \ldots, \boldsymbol{\pi}_M]$ is a $(K \times M)$ matrix where the $(K \times 1)$ vector $\boldsymbol{\pi}_i$ contains the coefficients on $\mathbf{x}_t'$ for the ith equation, and $\boldsymbol{\varepsilon}_t' = (\varepsilon_{1t}, \varepsilon_{2t}, \ldots, \varepsilon_{Mt})$ is a $(1 \times M)$ vector of error terms with covariance matrix $\boldsymbol{\Sigma}$. Note that since the ith equation may not have all of the variables as regressors so that some of the values in $\boldsymbol{\pi}_i$ may be equal to zero.

The log-likelihood function for a sample of size T is

$$\ln L(\boldsymbol{\beta}, \boldsymbol{\Sigma}) = -\frac{MT}{2} \ln(2\pi) - \frac{T}{2} \ln|\boldsymbol{\Sigma}| - \frac{1}{2} \sum_{t=1}^{T} \boldsymbol{\varepsilon}_t'\boldsymbol{\Sigma}^{-1}\boldsymbol{\varepsilon}_t$$

where $\boldsymbol{\beta}$ represents the appropriate non-zero elements of $\boldsymbol{\Pi}$. The log-likelihood function may be concentrated with respect to $\boldsymbol{\Sigma}$ giving

$$\ln L(\boldsymbol{\beta}) = -\frac{MT}{2} (\ln(2\pi) + 1) - \frac{T}{2} \ln (|\boldsymbol{\Sigma}(\boldsymbol{\beta})|) \qquad (10.11)$$

where

$$\boldsymbol{\Sigma}(\boldsymbol{\beta}) = T^{-1} \sum_{t=1}^{T} \boldsymbol{\varepsilon}_t\boldsymbol{\varepsilon}_t' \qquad (10.12)$$

is the MLE for $\boldsymbol{\Sigma}$ given $\boldsymbol{\beta}$. Hence, the MLE for $\boldsymbol{\beta}$ solves

$$\min_{\boldsymbol{\beta}} \frac{1}{2} \ln (|\boldsymbol{\Sigma}(\boldsymbol{\beta})|) .$$

and the resulting estimator $\hat{\boldsymbol{\beta}}_{mle}$ is equivalent to the iterated feasible GLS estimator.

Likelihood Ratio Tests

The form of the concentrated log-likelihood function (10.11), implies that likelihood ratio (LR) tests for hypotheses about elements of $\boldsymbol{\beta}$ have the simple form

$$LR = T \left(\ln \left(|\boldsymbol{\Sigma}(\tilde{\boldsymbol{\beta}}_{mle})| \right) - \ln \left(|\boldsymbol{\Sigma}(\hat{\boldsymbol{\beta}}_{mle})| \right) \right) \qquad (10.13)$$

where $\tilde{\boldsymbol{\beta}}_{mle}$ denotes the MLE imposing the restrictions under the null being tested and $\hat{\boldsymbol{\beta}}_{mle}$ denotes the unrestricted MLE. The LR statistic (10.13) is asymptotically distributed chi-square with degrees of freedom equal to the number of restrictions being tested under the null.

10.3.2   Analysis of SUR Models with the S+FinMetrics Function SUR

The S+FinMetrics function SUR may be used for the estimation of linear SUR models without cross equation restrictions. The arguments for SUR are

```
> args(SUR)
function(formulas, data, subset, na.rm = F, start = NULL, end
= NULL, method = "fit", contrasts = NULL, df = 1,
tol = 1e-006, iterate = F, trace = T, ...)
```

Generally, the two specified arguments are formulas, which is a list containing the formulas for each equation in the SUR model, and data, which must be either a data frame, or a "timeSeries" object with a data frame in the data slot. Formulas are specified in the usual way with the response variables on the left hand side of the ~ character and explanatory variables on the right hand side. If the variables in formulas can be directly accessed, e.g. through an attached data frame, then the data argument may be skipped. The default fitting method is one-step (not iterated) feasible GLS as in (10.9). To specify iterated feasible GLS set the optional argument iterate=T. In this case, the trace option controls printing of the iteration count and the tol option specifies the numerical tolerance of the convergence criterion.

SUR produces an object of class "SUR" for which there are print, summary and plot methods as well as extractor functions residuals, fitted.values (or fitted), coef, and vcov[1]. The use of SUR is illustrated using the following examples.

Example 59 *Testing efficiency in foreign exchange markets*

---

[1] Currently, AR terms are not supported in formulas and there is no predict method.

Consider estimating the system of exchange rate regressions (10.2) using monthly data on six currencies relative to the US dollar over the period August 1978 through June 1996. The data are in the "timeSeries" object surex1.ts, which is constructed from the data in the "timeSeries" lexrates.dat. The variables in surex1.ts are

```
> collds(surex1.ts)
 [1] "USCN.FP.lag1" "USCNS.diff"  "USDM.FP.lag1" "USDMS.diff"
 [5] "USFR.FP.lag1" "USFRS.diff"  "USIL.FP.lag1" "USILS.diff"
 [9] "USJY.FP.lag1" "USJYS.diff"  "USUK.FP.lag1" "USUKS.diff"
```

The variables with extensions .FP.lag1 are one month forward premia, $f_{i,t}^1 - s_{i,t}$, and variables with extensions .diff are future returns on spot currency, $\Delta s_{i,t+1}$. The list of formulas for the regressions in the system (10.2) is created using

```
> formula.list = list(USCNS.diff~USCN.FP.lag1,
+ USDMS.diff~USDM.FP.lag1,
+ USFRS.diff~USFR.FP.lag1,
+ USILS.diff~USIL.FP.lag1,
+ USJYS.diff~USJY.FP.lag1,
+ USUKS.diff~USUK.FP.lag1)
```

The command to compute the feasible GLS estimator of the SUR system over the period August 1978 through June 1996 is

```
> sur.fit = SUR(formula.list, data=surex1.ts,
+ start="Aug 1978", in.format="%m %Y")
> class(sur.fit)
[1] "SUR"
```

As usual, the print method is invoked by typing the name of the object and gives basic output:

```
> sur.fit

Seemingly Unrelated Regression:

Eq. 1: USCNS.diff ~USCN.FP.lag1

Coefficients:
 (Intercept) USCN.FP.lag1
 -0.0031     -1.6626


Degrees of freedom: 215 total; 213 residual
Time period: from Aug 1978 to Jun 1996
Residual scale estimate: 0.0135
```

Eq. 2: USDMS.diff ~USDM.FP.lag1

Coefficients:
 (Intercept) USDM.FP.lag1
 0.0006   0.5096

Degrees of freedom: 215 total; 213 residual
Time period: from Aug 1978 to Jun 1996
Residual scale estimate: 0.0358

...

Eq. 6: USUKS.diff ~USUK.FP.lag1

Coefficients:
 (Intercept) USUK.FP.lag1
 -0.0035   -1.2963

Degrees of freedom: 215 total; 213 residual
Time period: from Aug 1978 to Jun 1996
Residual scale estimate: 0.0344

Log determinant of residual covariance: -47.935

In the above output, the log determinant of residual covariance is the quantity $\ln\left(|\Sigma(\hat{\boldsymbol{\beta}}_{FGLS})|\right)$. The forward rate is an unbiased predictor of the future spot rate if the coefficient on the forward premium is equal to 1. The results above suggest that unbiasedness holds only for the US/France exchange rate.

The summary method provides more detailed information about the fit including estimated standard errors of coefficients and fit measures for each equation

> summary(sur.fit)
Seemingly Unrelated Regression:

Eq. 1: USCNS.diff ~USCN.FP.lag1

Coefficients:
               Value Std. Error t value Pr(>|t|)
 (Intercept) -0.0031 0.0012   -2.5943 0.0101
USCN.FP.lag1 -1.6626 0.5883   -2.8263 0.0052

Regression Diagnostics:

```
        R-Squared 0.0300
Adjusted R-Squared 0.0254
Durbin-Watson Stat 2.2161

Degrees of freedom: 215 total; 213 residual
Time period: from Aug 1978 to Jun 1996
Residual scale estimate: 0.0135


   ...


Eq. 6: USUKS.diff ~USUK.FP.lag1

Coefficients:
              Value Std. Error t value Pr(>|t|)
 (Intercept) -0.0035  0.0027    -1.3256  0.1864
USUK.FP.lag1 -1.2963  0.6317    -2.0519  0.0414

Regression Diagnostics:

        R-Squared 0.0253
Adjusted R-Squared 0.0207
Durbin-Watson Stat 1.9062

Degrees of freedom: 215 total; 213 residual
Time period: from Aug 1978 to Jun 1996
Residual scale estimate: 0.0344

Log determinant of residual covariance: -47.935
```

Graphical summaries of each equation are provided by the plot method which produces a menu of plot choices:

```
> plot(sur.fit)

Make a plot selection (or 0 to exit):

1: plot: All
2: plot: Response and Fitted Values
3: plot: Residuals
4: plot: Normal QQplot of Residuals
5: plot: ACF of Residuals
6: plot: PACF of Residuals
7: plot: ACF of Squared Residuals
8: plot: PACF of Squared Residuals
Selection:
```

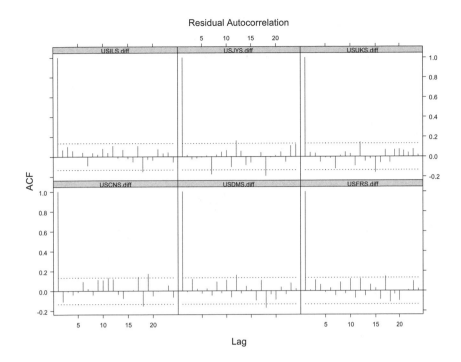

FIGURE 10.1. Residual ACF plots from SUR fit to exchange rate data.

Plot choices 2-8 create multi-panel plots, one panel for each equation, using Trellis graphics. For example, Figure 10.1 shows the ACF of Residuals plot for the exchange rate data.

The above results are based on the non-iterated feasible GLS estimator (10.9). The iterated estimator is computed using

```
> sur.fit2 = SUR(formula.list, data=surex1.ts,
+ start="Aug 1978", in.format="%m %Y", iterate=T)
Iteration 1
Iteration 2
Iteration 3
Iteration 4
Iteration 5
Iteration 6
Iteration 7
Iteration 8
```

which converges after eight iterations. The non-iterated and iterated estimators may be easily compared using the coef extractor function:

```
> cbind(coef(sur.fit),coef(sur.fit2))
```

```
                       [,1]          [,2]
   (Intercept) -0.00312063 -0.00312126
  USCN.FP.lag1 -1.66255897 -1.66303965
   (Intercept)  0.00058398  0.00035783
  USDM.FP.lag1  0.50956590  0.65014949
   (Intercept)  0.00133327  0.00135930
  USFR.FP.lag1  1.01512081  1.02834484
   (Intercept) -0.00058789 -0.00083921
  USIL.FP.lag1  0.46173993  0.40852433
   (Intercept)  0.00778918  0.00744485
  USJY.FP.lag1 -1.76416190 -1.63952144
   (Intercept) -0.00354947 -0.00334026
  USUK.FP.lag1 -1.29625869 -1.19508947
```

There is not much difference between the two estimators.

The SUR estimator is more efficient than least squares equation-by-equation in this example provided the error terms across equations are correlated. The residual correlation matrix of the SUR fit (10.12) may be computed using

```
> sd.vals = sqrt(diag(sur.fit$Sigma))
> cor.mat = sur.fit$Sigma/outer(sd.vals,sd.vals)
> cor.mat
            USCNS.diff USDMS.diff USFRS.diff USILS.diff
USCNS.diff     1.00000    0.20187    0.19421    0.27727
USDMS.diff     0.20187    1.00000    0.97209    0.85884
USFRS.diff     0.19421    0.97209    1.00000    0.85090
USILS.diff     0.27727    0.85884    0.85090    1.00000
USJYS.diff     0.12692    0.61779    0.61443    0.50835
USUKS.diff     0.31868    0.71424    0.70830    0.72274

            USJYS.diff USUKS.diff
USCNS.diff     0.12692    0.31868
USDMS.diff     0.61779    0.71424
USFRS.diff     0.61443    0.70830
USILS.diff     0.50835    0.72274
USJYS.diff     1.00000    0.53242
USUKS.diff     0.53242    1.00000
```

Many of the estimated correlations are large so there appears to be an efficiency benefit to using SUR.

The forward rate unbiasedness implies that $\gamma_i = 1$ in (10.2) for $i = 1, \ldots, 6$. A formal test of the unbiasedness hypothesis for all six currencies simultaneously may be done using the Wald statistic (10.10) or the LR statistic (10.13). For the LR statistic, the iterated FGLS estimate should be used. The S-PLUS commands to compute the Wald statistic are

```
> bigR = matrix(0,6,12)
> bigR[1,2] = bigR[2,4] = bigR[3,6] = bigR[4,8] =
+ bigR[5,10] = bigR[6,12] = 1
> rr = rep(1,6)
> bHat = as.vector(coef(sur.fit))
> avar = bigR%*%vcov(sur.fit)%*%t(bigR)
> Wald = t((bigR%*%bHat-rr))%*%solve(avar)%*%(bigR%*%bHat-rr)
> Wald
        [,1]
[1,] 47.206
> 1-pchisq(Wald,6)
[1] 1.7025e-008
```

The data clearly reject the unbiased hypothesis. To compute the LR statistic (10.13), the restricted model with $\gamma_i = 1$ for $i = 1, \ldots, 6$ must first be computed. The restricted model takes the form

$$\Delta s_{i,t+k} - (f_{i,t}^k - s_{i,t}) = \alpha_i + \varepsilon_{i,t+k}$$

The S-PLUS commands to compute the restricted model are

```
> formula.list = list((USCNS.diff-USCN.FP.lag1)~1,
+ (USDMS.diff-USDM.FP.lag1)~1,
+ (USFRS.diff-USFR.FP.lag1)~1,
+ (USILS.diff-USIL.FP.lag1)~1,
+ (USJYS.diff-USJY.FP.lag1)~1,
+ (USUKS.diff-USUK.FP.lag1)~1)
> sur.fit2r = SUR(formula.list, data=surex1.ts,
+ start="Aug 1978", in.format="%m %Y", iterate=T)
Iteration 1
Iteration 2
> sur.fit2r

Seemingly Unrelated Regression:

Eq. 1: (USCNS.diff - USCN.FP.lag1) ~1

Coefficients:
 (Intercept)
 0.0004

Degrees of freedom: 215 total; 214 residual
Time period: from Aug 1978 to Jun 1996
Residual scale estimate: 0.014

...
```

```
Eq. 6: (USUKS.diff - USUK.FP.lag1) ~1

Coefficients:
 (Intercept)
 0.0012

Degrees of freedom: 215 total; 214 residual
Time period: from Aug 1978 to Jun 1996
Residual scale estimate: 0.0353
```

```
Log determinant of residual covariance: -47.61
```

The LR statistic (10.13) may then be computed using

```
> nobs = nrow(residuals(sur.fit2r))
> LR = nobs*(determinant(sur.fit2r$Sigma,log=T)$modulus-
+ determinant(sur.fit2$Sigma,log=T)$modulus)
> as.numeric(LR)
[1] 70.09
> 1-pchisq(LR,6)
[1] 3.912e-013
```

The LR statistic also confirms the rejection of the unbiasedness hypothesis.

10.4   Nonlinear Seemingly Unrelated Regression Models

The nonlinear SUR model is the system of M nonlinear regression equations

$$\mathbf{y}_i = \mathbf{f}_i(\boldsymbol{\beta}_i, \mathbf{X}_i) + \boldsymbol{\varepsilon}_i, \ i = 1, \ldots, M$$

where $\mathbf{y}_i$ is a $(T \times 1)$ vector of response variables, $\mathbf{f}_i(\boldsymbol{\beta}_i, \mathbf{X}_i)$ is a $(T \times 1)$ vector containing the nonlinear function values $f_i(\boldsymbol{\beta}_i, \mathbf{x}_{it})$, $\mathbf{X}_i$ is a $(T \times k_i)$ matrix of explanatory variables, and $\boldsymbol{\beta}_i$ is a $(k_i \times 1)$ vector of parameters. As with the linear SUR model, some of the explanatory variables in each $\mathbf{X}_i$ may be common across equations and some of the parameters in each $\boldsymbol{\beta}_i$ may also be common across equations. Without loss of generality, let $\mathbf{X}$ denote the $(T \times K)$ matrix of unique variables and let $\boldsymbol{\beta}$ denote the $(Q \times 1)$ vector of unique parameters,[2] and rewrite the nonlinear SUR system as

$$\mathbf{y}_i = \mathbf{f}_i(\boldsymbol{\beta}, \mathbf{X}) + \boldsymbol{\varepsilon}_i, \ i = 1, \ldots, M$$

---

[2] In nonlinear models the number of parameters does not have to be equal to the number of variables.

The assumptions about the $(MT \times 1)$ system error vector $\underline{\varepsilon} = (\varepsilon'_1 \ldots, \varepsilon'_M)'$ are the same as in the linear SUR model. That is, the covariance matrix of $\underline{\varepsilon}$ is given by (10.7).

The estimation of nonlinear SUR models is detailed in Greene (2000) chapter 15 and only a brief description is given here. The nonlinear FGLS estimator of β solves

$$\min_{\beta} \sum_{i=1}^{M} \sum_{j=1}^{M} \hat{\sigma}^{ij} (\mathbf{y}_i - \mathbf{f}_i(\beta, \mathbf{X}))' (\mathbf{y}_j - \mathbf{f}_j(\beta, \mathbf{X})) \qquad (10.14)$$

where σ^{ij} denotes the ijth element of Σ^{-1}. The nonlinear FGLS estimator utilizes initial estimates of σ^{ij} based on minimizing (10.14) with $\hat{\sigma}^{ij} = 1$. The iterated FGLS estimator minimizes (10.14) utilizing updated estimates of σ^{ij}. Assuming standard regularity conditions on the functions f_i the FGLS and iterated FGLS estimators are consistent and asymptotically normally distributed with asymptotic covariance matrix given by the inverse of the empirical Hessian matrix of (10.14).

10.4.1 Analysis of Nonlinear SUR Models with the S+FinMetrics Function NLSUR

The S+FinMetrics function NLSUR may be used to estimate general nonlinear SUR models as well as linear SUR models with parameter restrictions. The arguments for NLSUR are

```
> args(NLSUR)
function(formulas, data, na.rm = F, coef = NULL, start = NULL,
end = NULL, control = NULL, ...)
```

The usage of NLSUR is similar to that of SUR. The argument formulas contains a list of nonlinear model formulas for each equation in the SUR model. Nonlinear formulas are specified with the response on the left hand side of the ~ character and the nonlinear regression function specified on the right hand side. The K parameters of the nonlinear regression functions in the SUR model are specified explicitly by user specified coefficient values. For example, consider a "timeSeries" specified in the data argument with variables y1, y2, y3, x1 and suppose the nonlinear SUR model has three equations

$$
\begin{aligned}
y_{1t} &= \beta_{10} + \beta_{11} x_{1t}^{\beta} + \varepsilon_{1t} \\
y_{2t} &= \beta_{20} + \beta_{21} x_{1t}^{\beta} + \varepsilon_{2t} \\
y_{3t} &= \beta_{30} + \beta_{31} x_{1t}^{\beta} + \varepsilon_{3t}
\end{aligned}
$$

The vector of $K = 7$ parameters of the SUR system are

$$\beta = (\beta_{10}, \beta_{11}, \beta_{20}, \beta_{21}, \beta_{30}, \beta_{31}, \beta)'$$

Notice that the parameter β is common across the three equations. The formulas for the three equations above could be specified in a list as

```
> formula.list = list(y1~b10+b11*x1^b,
+ y2~b20+b21*x1^b,
+ y3~b30+b31*x1^b)
```

Notice that the user-specified coefficients b10, b11, b20, b21, b30, b31, b match the values in the parameter vector β. The common parameter β across equations is given by the user specified coefficient b. Starting values for the coefficients may be specified in the named object coef. The parameter coefficients specified in the formulas argument must match the named elements in coef. For example, the starting values $\beta_{10} = \beta_{20} = \beta_{30} = 0, \beta_{11} = \beta_{21} = \beta_{31} = 1$ and $\beta = 0.5$ may be specified using

```
> start.vals = c(0,1,0,1,0,1,0.5)
> names(start.vals) = c("b10","b11","b20","b21","b30",
+ "b31","b")
```

Finally, the argument control is a list variable containing control parameters for the nonlinear optimization. These control parameters are the same as those used for the S-PLUS function nlregb. See the online help for nlregb.control for details.

NLSUR produces an object of class "NLSUR", that inherits from the class "SUR", for which there are print, summary and plot methods as well as extractor functions residuals, fitted, coef and vcov. The use of NLSUR is illustrated with the following examples.

Example 60 *Black CAPM model*

Consider estimating and testing the Black form of the CAPM (10.3) using monthly data on 16 assets over the five year period January 1983 through December 1987. The real return data are in the "timeSeries" black.ts which is constructed from the nominal return data in the "timeSeries" berndt.dat and the consumer price data in the "timeSeries" CPI.dat. The variables in black.ts are

```
> colIds(black.ts)
 [1] "BOISE"   "CITCRP"  "CONED"   "CONTIL"  "DATGEN"  "DEC"
 [7] "DELTA"   "GENMIL"  "GERBER"  "IBM"     "MARKET"  "MOBIL"
[13] "PANAM"   "PSNH"    "TANDY"   "TEXACO"  "WEYER"
```

The variable MARKET is a value weighted index of all stocks on the NYSE and AMEX. The system (10.3) imposes $M = 16$ nonlinear cross equation restrictions on the intercept parameters: $\alpha_i = (1 - \beta_i)\gamma$. As a result, the parameter vector β has $K = 17$ elements: $\beta = (\gamma, \beta_1, \ldots, \beta_{16})'$. A list of formulas for the 16 nonlinear regressions imposing the cross equation restrictions $\alpha_i = (1 - \beta_i)\gamma$ is

```
> formula.list = list(BOISE~(1-b1)*g + b1*MARKET,
+ CITCRP~(1-b2)*g + b2*MARKET,
+ CONED~(1-b3)*g + b3*MARKET,
+ CONTIL~(1-b4)*g + b4*MARKET,
+ DATGEN~(1-b5)*g + b5*MARKET,
+ DEC~(1-b6)*g + b6*MARKET,
+ DELTA~(1-b7)*g + b7*MARKET,
+ GENMIL~(1-b8)*g + b8*MARKET,
+ GERBER~(1-b9)*g + b9*MARKET,
+ IBM~(1-b10)*g + b10*MARKET,
+ MOBIL~(1-b11)*g + b11*MARKET,
+ PANAM~(1-b12)*g + b12*MARKET,
+ PSNH~(1-b13)*g + b13*MARKET,
+ TANDY~(1-b14)*g + b14*MARKET,
+ TEXACO~(1-b15)*g + b15*MARKET,
+ WEYER~(1-b16)*g + b16*MARKET)
```

The user specified coefficients g, b1, ..., b16 represent the elements of the parameter vector β, and the cross equation restrictions are imposed by expressing each intercept coefficient as the function (1-bi)*g for $i = 1, \ldots, 16$. The starting values $\gamma = 0$ and $\beta_i = 1$ $(i = 1, \ldots 16)$ for the estimation may be specified using

```
> start.vals = c(0,rep(1,16))
> names(start.vals) = c("g",paste("b",1:16,sep=""))
```

The FGLS nonlinear SUR estimator is computed using NLSUR

```
> nlsur.fit = NLSUR(formula.list,data=black.ts,
+ coef=start.vals,start="Jan 1983",in.format="%m %Y")
> class(nlsur.fit)
[1] "NLSUR"
```

The components of an "NLSUR" object are

```
> names(nlsur.fit)
 [1] "coef"       "objective"  "message"    "grad.norm"
 [5] "iterations" "r.evals"    "j.evals"    "scale"
 [9] "cov"        "call"       "parm.list"  "X.k"
[13] "residuals"  "fitted"     "Sigma"
```

The message component indicates that the nonlinear optimization converged:

```
> nlsur.fit$message
[1] "RELATIVE FUNCTION CONVERGENCE"
```

Since "NLSUR" objects inherit from "SUR" objects the print, summary and plot methods for "NLSUR" objects are identical to those for "SUR" objects. The print method gives basic fit information:

```
> nlsur.fit
```

Nonlinear Seemingly Unrelated Regression:

Eq. 1: BOISE ~(1 - b1) * g + b1 * MARKET

Coefficients:
```
    b1      g
 1.0120 0.0085
```

Degrees of freedom: 60 total; 58 residual
Time period: from Jan 1983 to Dec 1987
Residual scale estimate: 0.065

Eq. 2: CITCRP ~(1 - b2) * g + b2 * MARKET

Coefficients:
```
    b2      g
 1.0699 0.0085
```

Degrees of freedom: 60 total; 58 residual
Time period: from Jan 1983 to Dec 1987
Residual scale estimate: 0.0581

...

Eq. 16: WEYER ~(1 - b16) * g + b16 * MARKET

Coefficients:
```
   b16      g
 1.0044 0.0085
```

Degrees of freedom: 60 total; 58 residual
Time period: from Jan 1983 to Dec 1987
Residual scale estimate: 0.0574

Log determinant of residual covariance: -85.29

The estimated coefficients and their standard errors may be extracted using coef and vcov:

```
> std.ers = sqrt(diag(vcov(nlsur.fit)))
> cbind(coef(nlsur.fit),std.ers)
numeric matrix: 17 rows, 2 columns.
              std.ers
  g 0.008477 0.004642
```

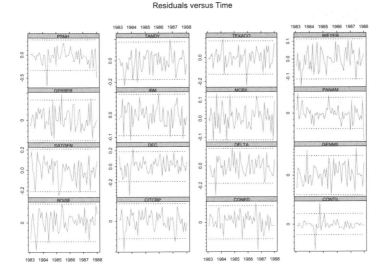

Residuals versus Time

FIGURE 10.2. Estimated residuals from nonlinear SUR fit to Black's form of the CAPM.

```
 b1  1.012043  0.134400
 b2  1.069874  0.119842
 b3  0.028169  0.104461
 b4  1.479293  0.361368
 b5  1.133384  0.218596
 b6  1.099063  0.195965
 b7  0.704410  0.182686
 b8  0.547502  0.127458
 b9  0.960858  0.157903
b10  0.649761  0.096975
b11  0.741609  0.121843
b12  0.715984  0.265048
b13  0.205356  0.348101
b14  1.054715  0.185498
b15  0.574735  0.145838
b16  1.004     0.1186
```

More detailed information about the fit may be viewed using `summary`, and a graphical analysis of the fit may be created using `plot`. For example, Figure 10.2 shows the residuals from the 16 nonlinear equations.

The nonlinear restrictions implied by the Black form of the CAPM may be tested using a LR statistic. The unrestricted model (10.4) is specified using the formula list

```
> formula.list = list(BOISE~a1+b1*MARKET,
+ CITCRP~a2+b2*MARKET,
+ CONED~a3+b3*MARKET,
+ CONTIL~a4+b4*MARKET,
+ DATGEN~a5+b5*MARKET,
+ DEC~a6+b6*MARKET,
+ DELTA~a7+b7*MARKET,
+ GENMIL~a8+b8*MARKET,
+ GERBER~a9+b9*MARKET,
+ IBM~a10+b10*MARKET,
+ MOBIL~a11+b11*MARKET,
+ PANAM~a12+b12*MARKET,
+ PSNH~a13+b13*MARKET,
+ TANDY~a14+b14*MARKET,
+ TEXACO~a15+b15*MARKET,
+ WEYER~a16+b16*MARKET)
```

and is estimated using NLSUR with the starting values $\alpha_i = 0$ and $\beta_i = 1$ $(i = 1, \ldots, 16)$:

```
> start.vals = c(rep(0,16),rep(1,16))
> names(start.vals) =
+ c(paste("a",1:16,sep=""),paste("b",1:16,sep=""))
> nlsur.fit2 = NLSUR(formula.list,data=black.ts,
+ coef=start.vals,start="Jan 1983",in.format="%m %Y")
```

The LR statistic for testing the $M = 16$ nonlinear cross equation restrictions $\alpha_i = (1 - \beta_i)\gamma$ is computed using

```
> nobs = nrow(residuals(nlsur.fit2))
> LR = nobs*(determinant(nlsur.fit$Sigma,log=T)$modulus-
+ determinant(nlsur.fit2$Sigma,log=T)$modulus)
> as.numeric(LR)
[1] 15.86
> 1-pchisq(LR,16)
[1] 0.4625
```

The p-value of the test is 0.4627, and so the Black CAPM restrictions are not rejected at any reasonable significance level.

Example 61 *Estimation of exchange rate system with cross equation parameter restrictions*

Consider estimating the system of exchange rates (10.2), using the data described in the previous section, imposing the cross equation restriction that $\gamma_1 = \cdots = \gamma_M = \gamma$. The list of formulas for this restricted system may be constructed as

```
> formula.list = list(USCNS.diff~a1+g*USCN.FP.lag1,
+ USDMS.diff~a2+g*USDM.FP.lag1,
+ USFRS.diff~a3+g*USFR.FP.lag1,
+ USILS.diff~a4+g*USIL.FP.lag1,
+ USJYS.diff~a5+g*USJY.FP.lag1,
+ USUKS.diff~a6+g*USUK.FP.lag1)
```

Notice that the common parameter β is captured by the user-specified coefficient g. The starting values are chosen to be $\alpha_1 = \cdots = \alpha_6 = 0$ and $\gamma = 1$ and are specified using

```
> start.vals = c(rep(0,6),1)
> names(start.vals) = c(paste("a",1:6,sep=""),"g")
```

The FGLS estimator is computed using NLSUR

```
> nlsur.fit = NLSUR(formula.list, data=surex1.ts,
+ coef=start.vals, start="Aug 1978", in.format="%m %Y")
> nlsur.fit

Nonlinear Seemingly Unrelated Regression:

Eq. 1: USCNS.diff ~a1 + g * USCN.FP.lag1

Coefficients:
     a1      g
 -0.0005  0.3467

Degrees of freedom: 215 total; 213 residual
Time period: from Aug 1978 to Jun 1996
Residual scale estimate: 0.0138


...


Eq. 6: USUKS.diff ~a6 + g * USUK.FP.lag1

Coefficients:
     a6      g
 -0.0002  0.3467

Degrees of freedom: 215 total; 213 residual
Time period: from Aug 1978 to Jun 1996
Residual scale estimate: 0.035
```

```
Log determinant of residual covariance: -47.679
```

The estimate of the common parameter γ is 0.3467, and its asymptotic standard error is

```
> sqrt(diag(vcov(nlsur.fit)))[7]
[1] 0.16472
```

Hence, the data indicate that the common value of γ is less than 1. The LR statistic, however, rejects the common parameter restriction

```
> nobs = nrow(residuals(nlsur.fit))
> LR = nobs*(determinant(nlsur.fit$Sigma,log=T)$modulus
+ -determinant(sur.fit2$Sigma,log=T)$modulus)
> as.numeric(LR)
[1] 55.65
> 1 - pchisq(LR,6)
[1] 3.433e-010
```

10.5 References

[1] BLACK, F. (1972). "Capital Market Equilibrium with Restricted Borrowing," *Journal of Business*, 44, 444-454.

[2] BURMEISTER, E. AND M.B. MCELROY (1988). "Arbitrage Pricing Theory as a Restricted Nonlinear Multivariate Regression Model: ITNLSUR Estimates," *Journal of Business and Economic Statistics*, January.

[3] CAMPBELL, J. A. LO AND C. MACKINLAY (1997). *The Econometrics of Financial Markets*. Princeton University Press, New Jersey.

[4] GALLANT, R.A. (1974). "Seemingly Unrelated Nonlinear Regressions," *Journal of Econometrics*, 3, 35-50.

[5] GREENE, W. (2000). *Econometric Analysis*, Fourth Edition. Prentice Hall, New Jersey.

[6] SRIVASTAVA, V.K. AND D.E.A. GILES (1987). *Seemingly Unrelated Regression Models: Estimation and Inference*. Marcel Dekker, New York.

[7] THEIL, H. (1961). *Economic Forecasts and Policy*. North Holland, Amsterdam.

[8] ZELLNER, A. (1962). "An Efficient Method of Estimating Seemingly Unrelated Regressions and Tests of Aggregation Bias," *Journal of the American Statistical Association*, 57, 500-509.

11

Vector Autoregressive Models for Multivariate Time Series

11.1 Introduction

The *vector autoregression* (VAR) *model* is one of the most successful, flexible, and easy to use models for the analysis of multivariate time series. It is a natural extension of the univariate autoregressive model to dynamic multivariate time series. The VAR model has proven to be especially useful for describing the dynamic behavior of economic and financial time series and for forecasting. It often provides superior forecasts to those from univariate time series models and elaborate theory-based simultaneous equations models. Forecasts from VAR models are quite flexible because they can be made conditional on the potential future paths of specified variables in the model.

In addition to data description and forecasting, the VAR model is also used for structural inference and policy analysis. In structural analysis, certain assumptions about the causal structure of the data under investigation are imposed, and the resulting causal impacts of unexpected shocks or innovations to specified variables on the variables in the model are summarized. These causal impacts are usually summarized with impulse response functions and forecast error variance decompositions.

This chapter focuses on the analysis of covariance stationary multivariate time series using VAR models. The following chapter describes the analysis of nonstationary multivariate time series using VAR models that incorporate cointegration relationships.

This chapter is organized as follows. Section 11.2 describes specification, estimation and inference in VAR models and introduces the S+FinMetrics function VAR. Section 11.3 covers forecasting from VAR model. The discussion covers traditional forecasting algorithms as well as simulation-based forecasting algorithms that can impose certain types of conditioning information. Section 11.4 summarizes the types of structural analysis typically performed using VAR models. These analyses include Granger-causality tests, the computation of impulse response functions, and forecast error variance decompositions. Section 11.5 gives an extended example of VAR modeling. The chapter concludes with a brief discussion of Bayesian VAR models.

This chapter provides a relatively non-technical survey of VAR models. VAR models in economics were made popular by Sims (1980). The definitive technical reference for VAR models is Lütkepohl (1991), and updated surveys of VAR techniques are given in Watson (1994) and Lütkepohl (1999) and Waggoner and Zha (1999). Applications of VAR models to financial data are given in Hamilton (1994), Campbell, Lo and MacKinlay (1997), Cuthbertson (1996), Mills (1999) and Tsay (2001).

11.2   The Stationary Vector Autoregression Model

Let $\mathbf{Y}_t = (y_{1t}, y_{2t}, \ldots, y_{nt})'$ denote an $(n \times 1)$ vector of time series variables. The basic p-lag *vector autoregressive* (VAR(p)) model has the form

$$\mathbf{Y}_t = \mathbf{c} + \mathbf{\Pi}_1 \mathbf{Y}_{t-1} + \mathbf{\Pi}_2 \mathbf{Y}_{t-2} + \cdots + \mathbf{\Pi}_p \mathbf{Y}_{t-p} + \boldsymbol{\varepsilon}_t, \ t = 1, \ldots, T \quad (11.1)$$

where $\mathbf{\Pi}_i$ are $(n \times n)$ coefficient matrices and $\boldsymbol{\varepsilon}_t$ is an $(n \times 1)$ unobservable zero mean white noise vector process (serially uncorrelated or independent) with time invariant covariance matrix $\mathbf{\Sigma}$. For example, a bivariate VAR(2) model equation by equation has the form

$$\begin{pmatrix} y_{1t} \\ y_{2t} \end{pmatrix} = \begin{pmatrix} c_1 \\ c_2 \end{pmatrix} + \begin{pmatrix} \pi_{11}^1 & \pi_{12}^1 \\ \pi_{21}^1 & \pi_{22}^1 \end{pmatrix} \begin{pmatrix} y_{1t-1} \\ y_{2t-1} \end{pmatrix} \quad (11.2)$$

$$+ \begin{pmatrix} \pi_{11}^2 & \pi_{12}^2 \\ \pi_{21}^2 & \pi_{22}^2 \end{pmatrix} \begin{pmatrix} y_{1t-2} \\ y_{2t-2} \end{pmatrix} + \begin{pmatrix} \varepsilon_{1t} \\ \varepsilon_{2t} \end{pmatrix} \quad (11.3)$$

or

$$y_{1t} = c_1 + \pi_{11}^1 y_{1t-1} + \pi_{12}^1 y_{2t-1} + \pi_{11}^2 y_{1t-2} + \pi_{12}^2 y_{2t-2} + \varepsilon_{1t}$$

$$y_{2t} = c_2 + \pi_{21}^1 y_{1t-1} + \pi_{22}^1 y_{2t-1} + \pi_{21}^2 y_{1t-1} + \pi_{22}^2 y_{2t-1} + \varepsilon_{2t}$$

where $cov(\varepsilon_{1t}, \varepsilon_{2s}) = \sigma_{12}$ for $t = s$; 0 otherwise. Notice that each equation has the same regressors – lagged values of y_{1t} and y_{2t}. Hence, the VAR(p) model is just a *seemingly unrelated regression* (SUR) model with lagged variables and deterministic terms as common regressors.

In lag operator notation, the VAR(p) is written as

$$\mathbf{\Pi}(L)\mathbf{Y}_t = \mathbf{c} + \boldsymbol{\varepsilon}_t$$

where $\mathbf{\Pi}(L) = \mathbf{I}_n - \mathbf{\Pi}_1 L - \ldots - \mathbf{\Pi}_p L^p$. The VAR($p$) is stable if the roots of

$$\det\left(\mathbf{I}_n - \mathbf{\Pi}_1 z - \cdots - \mathbf{\Pi}_p z^p\right) = 0$$

lie outside the complex unit circle (have modulus greater than one), or, equivalently, if the eigenvalues of the companion matrix

$$\mathbf{F} = \begin{pmatrix} \mathbf{\Pi}_1 & \mathbf{\Pi}_2 & \cdots & \mathbf{\Pi}_n \\ \mathbf{I}_n & \mathbf{0} & \cdots & \mathbf{0} \\ \mathbf{0} & \ddots & \mathbf{0} & \vdots \\ \mathbf{0} & \mathbf{0} & \mathbf{I}_n & \mathbf{0} \end{pmatrix}$$

have modulus less than one. Assuming that the process has been initialized in the infinite past, then a stable VAR(p) process is stationary and ergodic with time invariant means, variances, and autocovariances.

If $\mathbf{Y}_t$ in (11.1) is covariance stationary, then the unconditional mean is given by

$$\boldsymbol{\mu} = (\mathbf{I}_n - \mathbf{\Pi}_1 - \cdots - \mathbf{\Pi}_p)^{-1}\mathbf{c}$$

The *mean-adjusted* form of the VAR(p) is then

$$\mathbf{Y}_t - \boldsymbol{\mu} = \mathbf{\Pi}_1(\mathbf{Y}_{t-1} - \boldsymbol{\mu}) + \mathbf{\Pi}_2(\mathbf{Y}_{t-2} - \boldsymbol{\mu}) + \cdots + \mathbf{\Pi}_p(\mathbf{Y}_{t-p} - \boldsymbol{\mu}) + \boldsymbol{\varepsilon}_t$$

The basic VAR(p) model may be too restrictive to represent sufficiently the main characteristics of the data. In particular, other deterministic terms such as a linear time trend or seasonal dummy variables may be required to represent the data properly. Additionally, stochastic exogenous variables may be required as well. The general form of the VAR(p) model with deterministic terms and exogenous variables is given by

$$\mathbf{Y}_t = \mathbf{\Pi}_1\mathbf{Y}_{t-1} + \mathbf{\Pi}_2\mathbf{Y}_{t-2} + \cdots + \mathbf{\Pi}_p\mathbf{Y}_{t-p} + \mathbf{\Phi}\mathbf{D}_t + \mathbf{G}\mathbf{X}_t + \boldsymbol{\varepsilon}_t \qquad (11.4)$$

where $\mathbf{D}_t$ represents an $(l \times 1)$ matrix of deterministic components, $\mathbf{X}_t$ represents an $(m \times 1)$ matrix of exogenous variables, and $\mathbf{\Phi}$ and $\mathbf{G}$ are parameter matrices.

Example 62 *Simulating a stationary VAR(1) model using S-PLUS*

A stationary VAR model may be easily simulated in S-PLUS using the S+FinMetrics function `simulate.VAR`. The commands to simulate $T = 250$ observations from a bivariate VAR(1) model

$$\begin{aligned} y_{1t} &= -0.7 + 0.7y_{1t-1} + 0.2y_{2t-1} + \varepsilon_{1t} \\ y_{2t} &= 1.3 + 0.2y_{1t-1} + 0.7y_{2t-1} + \varepsilon_{2t} \end{aligned}$$

with

$$\mathbf{\Pi}_1 = \begin{pmatrix} 0.7 & 0.2 \\ 0.2 & 0.7 \end{pmatrix}, \ \mathbf{c} = \begin{pmatrix} -0.7 \\ 1.3 \end{pmatrix}, \ \boldsymbol{\mu} = \begin{pmatrix} 1 \\ 5 \end{pmatrix}, \ \boldsymbol{\Sigma} = \begin{pmatrix} 1 & 0.5 \\ 0.5 & 1 \end{pmatrix}$$

and normally distributed errors are

```
> pi1 = matrix(c(0.7,0.2,0.2,0.7),2,2)
> mu.vec = c(1,5)
> c.vec = as.vector((diag(2)-pi1)%*%mu.vec)
> cov.mat = matrix(c(1,0.5,0.5,1),2,2)
> var1.mod = list(const=c.vec,ar=pi1,Sigma=cov.mat)
> set.seed(301)
> y.var = simulate.VAR(var1.mod,n=250,
+ y0=t(as.matrix(mu.vec)))
> dimnames(y.var) = list(NULL,c("y1","y2"))
```

The simulated data are shown in Figure 11.1. The VAR is stationary since the eigenvalues of $\mathbf{\Pi}_1$ are less than one:

```
> eigen(pi1,only.values=T)
$values:
[1] 0.9 0.5

$vectors:
NULL
```

Notice that the intercept values are quite different from the mean values of y_1 and y_2:

```
> c.vec
[1] -0.7  1.3
> colMeans(y.var)
      y1     y2
 0.8037  4.751
```

11.2.1 Estimation

Consider the basic VAR(p) model (11.1). Assume that the VAR(p) model is covariance stationary, and there are no restrictions on the parameters of the model. In SUR notation, each equation in the VAR(p) may be written as

$$\mathbf{y}_i = \mathbf{Z}\boldsymbol{\pi}_i + \mathbf{e}_i, \ i = 1, \dots, n$$

where $\mathbf{y}_i$ is a $(T \times 1)$ vector of observations on the ith equation, $\mathbf{Z}$ is a $(T \times k)$ matrix with t^{th} row given by $\mathbf{Z}'_t = (1, \mathbf{Y}'_{t-1}, \dots, \mathbf{Y}'_{t-p})$, $k = np + 1$, $\boldsymbol{\pi}_i$ is a $(k \times 1)$ vector of parameters and $\mathbf{e}_i$ is a $(T \times 1)$ error with covariance matrix $\sigma_i^2 \mathbf{I}_T$. Since the VAR(p) is in the form of a SUR model

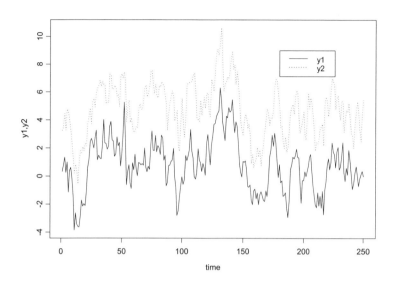

FIGURE 11.1. Simulated stationary VAR(1) model.

where each equation has the same explanatory variables, each equation may
be estimated separately by ordinary least squares without losing efficiency
relative to generalized least squares. Let $\hat{\mathbf{\Pi}} = [\hat{\boldsymbol{\pi}}_1, \ldots, \hat{\boldsymbol{\pi}}_n]$ denote the $(k \times n)$
matrix of least squares coefficients for the n equations.

Let $vec(\hat{\mathbf{\Pi}})$ denote the operator that stacks the columns of the $(n \times k)$
matrix $\hat{\mathbf{\Pi}}$ into a long $(nk \times 1)$ vector. That is,

$$vec(\hat{\mathbf{\Pi}}) = \begin{pmatrix} \hat{\boldsymbol{\pi}}_1 \\ \vdots \\ \hat{\boldsymbol{\pi}}_n \end{pmatrix}$$

Under standard assumptions regarding the behavior of stationary and ergodic VAR models (see Hamilton (1994) or Lütkepohl (1991)) $vec(\hat{\mathbf{\Pi}})$ is
consistent and asymptotically normally distributed with asymptotic covariance matrix

$$\widehat{avar}(vec(\hat{\mathbf{\Pi}})) = \hat{\boldsymbol{\Sigma}} \otimes (\mathbf{Z}'\mathbf{Z})^{-1}$$

where

$$\hat{\boldsymbol{\Sigma}} = \frac{1}{T-k} \sum_{t=1}^{T} \hat{\boldsymbol{\varepsilon}}_t \hat{\boldsymbol{\varepsilon}}_t'$$

and $\hat{\boldsymbol{\varepsilon}}_t = \mathbf{Y}_t - \hat{\mathbf{\Pi}}'\mathbf{Z}_t$ is the multivariate least squares residual from (11.1) at
time t.

11.2.2 Inference on Coefficients

The ith element of $vec(\hat{\Pi})$, $\hat{\pi}_i$, is asymptotically normally distributed with standard error given by the square root of ith diagonal element of $\hat{\Sigma} \otimes (\mathbf{Z}'\mathbf{Z})^{-1}$. Hence, asymptotically valid t-tests on individual coefficients may be constructed in the usual way. More general linear hypotheses of the form $\mathbf{R} \cdot vec(\mathbf{\Pi}) = \mathbf{r}$ involving coefficients across different equations of the VAR may be tested using the Wald statistic

$$Wald = (\mathbf{R} \cdot vec(\hat{\Pi}) - \mathbf{r})' \left\{ \mathbf{R} \left[\widehat{avar}(vec(\hat{\Pi})) \right] \mathbf{R}' \right\}^{-1} (\mathbf{R} \cdot vec(\hat{\Pi}) - \mathbf{r}) \quad (11.5)$$

Under the null, (11.5) has a limiting $\chi^2(q)$ distribution where $q = rank(\mathbf{R})$ gives the number of linear restrictions.

11.2.3 Lag Length Selection

The lag length for the VAR(p) model may be determined using model selection criteria. The general approach is to fit VAR(p) models with orders $p = 0, ..., p_{max}$ and choose the value of p which minimizes some model selection criteria. Model selection criteria for VAR(p) models have the form

$$IC(p) = \ln |\tilde{\Sigma}(p)| + c_T \cdot \varphi(n, p)$$

where $\tilde{\Sigma}(p) = T^{-1} \sum_{t=1}^{T} \hat{\varepsilon}_t \hat{\varepsilon}_t'$ is the residual covariance matrix *without a degrees of freedom correction* from a VAR(p) model, c_T is a sequence indexed by the sample size T, and $\varphi(n, p)$ is a penalty function which penalizes large VAR(p) models. The three most common information criteria are the Akaike (AIC), Schwarz-Bayesian (BIC) and Hannan-Quinn (HQ):

$$\begin{aligned}
AIC(p) &= \ln |\tilde{\Sigma}(p)| + \frac{2}{T} pn^2 \\
BIC(p) &= \ln |\tilde{\Sigma}(p)| + \frac{\ln T}{T} pn^2 \\
HQ(p) &= \ln |\tilde{\Sigma}(p)| + \frac{2 \ln \ln T}{T} pn^2
\end{aligned}$$

The AIC criterion asymptotically overestimates the order with positive probability, whereas the BIC and HQ criteria estimate the order consistently under fairly general conditions if the true order p is less than or equal to p_{max}. For more information on the use of model selection criteria in VAR models see Lütkepohl (1991) chapter four.

11.2.4 Estimating VAR Models Using the S+FinMetrics Function VAR

The S+FinMetrics function VAR is designed to fit and analyze VAR models as described in the previous section. VAR produces an object of class "VAR" for which there are `print`, `summary`, `plot` and `predict` methods as well as extractor functions `coefficients`, `residuals`, `fitted` and `vcov`. The calling syntax of `VAR` is a bit complicated because it is designed to handle multivariate data in matrices, data frames as well as "`timeSeries`" objects. The use of `VAR` is illustrated with the following example.

Example 63 *Bivariate VAR model for exchange rates*

This example considers a bivariate VAR model for $\mathbf{Y}_t = (\Delta s_t, fp_t)'$, where s_t is the logarithm of the monthly spot exchange rate between the US and Canada, $fp_t = f_t - s_t = i_t^{US} - i_t^{CA}$ is the forward premium or interest rate differential, and f_t is the natural logarithm of the 30-day forward exchange rate. The data over the 20 year period March 1976 through June 1996 is in the S+FinMetrics "`timeSeries`" `lexrates.dat`. The data for the VAR model are computed as

```
> dspot = diff(lexrates.dat[,"USCNS"])
> fp = lexrates.dat[,"USCNF"]-lexrates.dat[,"USCNS"]
> uscn.ts = seriesMerge(dspot,fp)
> colIds(uscn.ts) = c("dspot","fp")
> uscn.ts@title = "US/CN Exchange Rate Data"
> par(mfrow=c(2,1))
> plot(uscn.ts[,"dspot"],main="1st difference of US/CA spot
+ exchange rate")
> plot(uscn.ts[,"fp"],main="US/CN interest rate
+ differential")
```

Figure 11.2 illustrates the monthly return Δs_t and the forward premium fp_t over the period March 1976 through June 1996. Both series appear to be $I(0)$ (which can be confirmed using the S+FinMetrics functions `unitroot` or `stationaryTest`) with Δs_t much more volatile than fp_t. fp_t also appears to be heteroskedastic.

Specifying and Estimating the VAR(p) Model

To estimate a VAR(1) model for $\mathbf{Y}_t$ use

```
> var1.fit = VAR(cbind(dspot,fp)~ar(1),data=uscn.ts)
```

Note that the VAR model is specified using an S-PLUS formula, with the multivariate response on the left hand side of the ~ operator and the built-in AR term specifying the lag length of the model on the right hand side. The optional `data` argument accepts a data frame or "`timeSeries`" object with variable names matching those used in specifying the formula. If the data are in a "`timeSeries`" object or in an unattached data frame ("`timeSeries`" objects cannot be attached) then the `data` argument must be used. If the data are in a matrix then the `data` argument may be omitted. For example,

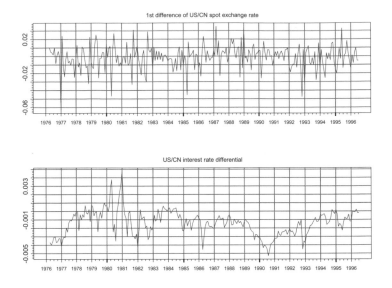

FIGURE 11.2. US/CN forward premium and spot rate.

```
> uscn.mat = as.matrix(seriesData(uscn.ts))
> var2.fit = VAR(uscn.mat~ar(1))
```

If the data are in a "timeSeries" object then the start and end options may be used to specify the estimation sample. For example, to estimate the VAR(1) over the sub-period January 1980 through January 1990

```
> var3.fit = VAR(cbind(dspot,fp)~ar(1), data=uscn.ts,
+ start="Jan 1980", end="Jan 1990", in.format="%m %Y")
```

may be used. The use of in.format="%m %Y" sets the format for the date strings specified in the start and end options to match the input format of the dates in the positions slot of uscn.ts.

The VAR model may be estimated with the lag length p determined using a specified information criterion. For example, to estimate the VAR for the exchange rate data with p set by minimizing the BIC with a maximum lag $p_{\max} = 4$ use

```
> var4.fit = VAR(uscn.ts,max.ar=4, criterion="BIC")
> var4.fit$info
    ar(1) ar(2) ar(3) ar(4)
BIC -4028 -4013 -3994 -3973
```

When a formula is not specified and only a data frame, "timeSeries" or matrix is supplied that contains the variables for the VAR model, VAR fits all VAR(p) models with lag lengths p less than or equal to the value given to `max.ar`, and the lag length is determined as the one which minimizes the information criterion specified by the `criterion` option. The default criterion is BIC but other valid choices are `logL`, `AIC` and `HQ`. In the computation of the information criteria, a common sample based on `max.ar` is used. Once the lag length is determined, the VAR is re-estimated using the appropriate sample. In the above example, the BIC values were computed using the sample based on `max.ar=4` and $p = 1$ minimizes BIC. The VAR(1) model was automatically re-estimated using the sample size appropriate for $p = 1$.

Print and Summary Methods

The function `VAR` produces an object of class "VAR" with the following components.

```
> class(var1.fit)
[1] "VAR"
> names(var1.fit)
 [1] "R"         "coef"      "fitted"    "residuals"
 [5] "Sigma"     "df.resid"  "rank"      "call"
 [9] "ar.order"  "n.na"      "terms"     "Y0"
```

To see the estimated coefficients of the model use the `print` method:

```
> var1.fit

Call:
VAR(formula = cbind(dspot, fp) ~ar(1), data = uscn.ts)

Coefficients:
                dspot       fp
(Intercept) -0.0036  -0.0003
 dspot.lag1 -0.1254   0.0079
    fp.lag1 -1.4833   0.7938

Std. Errors of Residuals:
  dspot       fp
 0.0137  0.0009

Information Criteria:
  logL    AIC    BIC     HQ
  2058  -4104  -4083  -4096

                  total  residual
Degree of freedom:    243       240
Time period: from Apr 1976 to Jun 1996
```

The first column under the label "Coefficients:" gives the estimated coefficients for the Δs_t equation, and the second column gives the estimated coefficients for the fp_t equation:

$$\Delta s_t = -0.0036 - 0.1254 \cdot \Delta s_{t-1} - 1.4833 \cdot fp_{t-1}$$
$$fp_t = -0.0003 + 0.0079 \cdot \Delta s_{t-1} + 0.7938 \cdot fp_{t-1}$$

Since uscn.ts is a "timeSeries" object, the estimation time period is also displayed.

The summary method gives more detailed information about the fitted VAR:

```
> summary(var1.fit)

Call:
VAR(formula = cbind(dspot, fp) ~ar(1), data = uscn.ts)

Coefficients:
                dspot       fp
(Intercept)   -0.0036   -0.0003
  (std.err)    0.0012    0.0001
  (t.stat)    -2.9234   -3.2885

dspot.lag1    -0.1254    0.0079
  (std.err)    0.0637    0.0042
  (t.stat)    -1.9700    1.8867

  fp.lag1     -1.4833    0.7938
  (std.err)    0.5980    0.0395
  (t.stat)    -2.4805   20.1049

Regression Diagnostics:
                  dspot      fp
    R-squared 0.0365 0.6275
Adj. R-squared 0.0285 0.6244
  Resid. Scale 0.0137 0.0009

Information Criteria:
  logL   AIC   BIC    HQ
  2058 -4104 -4083 -4096

                  total residual
Degree of freedom:    243      240
Time period: from Apr 1976 to Jun 1996
```

In addition to the coefficient standard errors and t-statistics, summary also displays R^2 measures for each equation (which are valid because each equation is estimated by least squares). The summary output shows that the coefficients on Δs_{t-1} and fp_{t-1} in both equations are statistically significant at the 10% level and that the fit for the fp_t equation is much better than the fit for the Δs_t equation.

As an aside, note that the S+FinMetrics function OLS may also be used to estimate each equation in a VAR model. For example, one way to compute the equation for Δs_t using OLS is

```
> dspot.fit = OLS(dspot~ar(1)+tslag(fp),data=uscn.ts)
> dspot.fit

Call:
OLS(formula = dspot ~ar(1) + tslag(fp), data = uscn.ts)

Coefficients:
 (Intercept) tslag(fp)     lag1
  -0.0036      -1.4833    -0.1254

Degrees of freedom: 243 total; 240 residual
Time period: from Apr 1976 to Jun 1996
Residual standard error: 0.01373
```

Graphical Diagnostics

The plot method for "VAR" objects may be used to graphically evaluate the fitted VAR. By default, the plot method produces a menu of plot options:

```
> plot(var1.fit)

Make a plot selection (or 0 to exit):

1: plot: All
2: plot: Response and Fitted Values
3: plot: Residuals
4: plot: Normal QQplot of Residuals
5: plot: ACF of Residuals
6: plot: PACF of Residuals
7: plot: ACF of Squared Residuals
8: plot: PACF of Squared Residuals
Selection:
```

Alternatively, plot.VAR may be called directly. The function plot.VAR has arguments

```
> args(plot.VAR)
function(x, ask = T, which.plots = NULL, hgrid = F, vgrid
= F, ...)
```

Response and Fitted Values

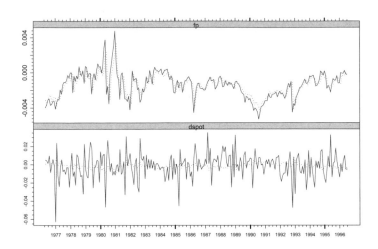

FIGURE 11.3. Response and fitted values from VAR(1) model for US/CN exchange rate data.

To create all seven plots without using the menu, set ask=F. To create the Residuals plot without using the menu, set which.plot=2. The optional arguments hgrid and vgrid control printing of horizontal and vertical grid lines on the plots.

Figures 11.3 and 11.4 give the Response and Fitted Values and Residuals plots for the VAR(1) fit to the exchange rate data. The equation for fp_t fits much better than the equation for Δs_t. The residuals for both equations look fairly random, but the residuals for the fp_t equation appear to be heteroskedastic. The qq-plot (not shown) indicates that the residuals for the Δs_t equation are highly non-normal.

Extractor Functions

The residuals and fitted values for each equation of the VAR may be extracted using the generic extractor functions residuals and fitted:

```
> var1.resid = resid(var1.fit)
> var1.fitted = fitted(var.fit)
> var1.resid[1:3,]
 Positions      dspot            fp
 Apr 1976   0.0044324   -0.00084150
 May 1976   0.0024350   -0.00026493
 Jun 1976   0.0004157    0.00002435
```

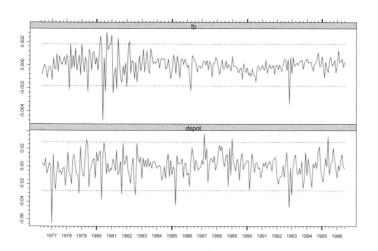

FIGURE 11.4. Residuals from VAR(1) model fit to US/CN exchange rate data.

Notice that since the data are in a "timeSeries" object, the extracted residuals and fitted values are also "timeSeries" objects.

The coefficients of the VAR model may be extracted using the generic coef function:

```
> coef(var1.fit)
                    dspot              fp
(Intercept)  -0.003595149  -0.0002670108
 dspot.lag1  -0.125397056   0.0079292865
    fp.lag1  -1.483324622   0.7937959055
```

Notice that coef produces the (3×2) matrix $\hat{\Pi}$ whose columns give the estimated coefficients for each equation in the VAR(1).

To test stability of the VAR, extract the matrix Π_1 and compute its eigenvalues

```
> PI1 = t(coef(var1.fit)[2:3,])
> abs(eigen(PI1,only.values=T)$values)
[1] 0.7808 0.1124
```

Since the modulus of the two eigenvalues of Π_1 are less than 1, the VAR(1) is stable.

Testing Linear Hypotheses

Now, consider testing the hypothesis that $\mathbf{\Pi}_1 = \mathbf{0}$ (i.e., $\mathbf{Y}_{t-1}$ does not help to explain $\mathbf{Y}_t$) using the Wald statistic (11.5). In terms of the columns of $vec(\mathbf{\Pi})$ the restrictions are $\pi_1 = (c_1, 0, 0)'$ and $\pi_2 = (c_2, 0, 0)$ and may be expressed as $\mathbf{R}vec(\mathbf{\Pi}) = \mathbf{r}$ with

$$\mathbf{R} = \begin{pmatrix} 0 & 1 & 0 & 0 & 0 & 0 \\ 0 & 0 & 1 & 0 & 0 & 0 \\ 0 & 0 & 0 & 0 & 1 & 0 \\ 0 & 0 & 0 & 0 & 0 & 1 \end{pmatrix}, \mathbf{r} = \begin{pmatrix} 0 \\ 0 \\ 0 \\ 0 \end{pmatrix}$$

The Wald statistic is easily constructed as follows

```
> R = matrix(c(0,1,0,0,0,0,
+ 0,0,1,0,0,0,
+ 0,0,0,0,1,0,
+ 0,0,0,0,0,1),
+ 4,6,byrow=T)
> vecPi = as.vector(var.coef)
> avar = R%*%vcov(var1.fit)%*%t(R)
> wald = t(R%*%vecPi)%*%solve(avar)%*%(R%*%vecPi)
> wald
        [,1]
[1,] 417.1
> 1-pchisq(wald,4)
[1] 0
```

Since the p-value for the Wald statistic based on the $\chi^2(4)$ distribution is essentially zero, the hypothesis that $\mathbf{\Pi}_1 = \mathbf{0}$ should be rejected at any reasonable significance level.

11.3   Forecasting

Forecasting is one of the main objectives of multivariate time series analysis. Forecasting from a VAR model is similar to forecasting from a univariate AR model and the following gives a brief description.

11.3.1   Traditional Forecasting Algorithm

Consider first the problem of forecasting future values of $\mathbf{Y}_t$ when the parameters $\mathbf{\Pi}$ of the VAR(p) process are assumed to be known and there are no deterministic terms or exogenous variables. The best linear predictor, in terms of minimum mean squared error (MSE), of $\mathbf{Y}_{t+1}$ or 1-step forecast based on information available at time T is

$$\mathbf{Y}_{T+1|T} = \mathbf{c} + \mathbf{\Pi}_1 \mathbf{Y}_T + \cdots + \mathbf{\Pi}_p \mathbf{Y}_{T-p+1}$$

Forecasts for longer horizons h (h-step forecasts) may be obtained using the *chain-rule of forecasting* as

$$\mathbf{Y}_{T+h|T} = \mathbf{c} + \mathbf{\Pi}_1 \mathbf{Y}_{T+h-1|T} + \cdots + \mathbf{\Pi}_p \mathbf{Y}_{T+h-p|T}$$

where $\mathbf{Y}_{T+j|T} = \mathbf{Y}_{T+j}$ for $j \leq 0$. The h-step forecast errors may be expressed as

$$\mathbf{Y}_{T+h} - \mathbf{Y}_{T+h|T} = \sum_{s=0}^{h-1} \mathbf{\Psi}_s \boldsymbol{\varepsilon}_{T+h-s}$$

where the matrices $\mathbf{\Psi}_s$ are determined by recursive substitution

$$\mathbf{\Psi}_s = \sum_{j=1}^{p-1} \mathbf{\Psi}_{s-j} \mathbf{\Pi}_j \tag{11.6}$$

with $\mathbf{\Psi}_0 = \mathbf{I}_n$ and $\mathbf{\Pi}_j = 0$ for $j > p$.[1] The forecasts are unbiased since all of the forecast errors have expectation zero and the MSE matrix for $\mathbf{Y}_{t+h|T}$ is

$$
\begin{aligned}
\mathbf{\Sigma}(h) &= MSE\left(\mathbf{Y}_{T+h} - \mathbf{Y}_{T+h|T}\right) \\
&= \sum_{s=0}^{h-1} \mathbf{\Psi}_s \mathbf{\Sigma} \mathbf{\Psi}_s' \tag{11.7}
\end{aligned}
$$

Now consider forecasting $\mathbf{Y}_{T+h}$ when the parameters of the VAR(p) process are estimated using multivariate least squares. The best linear predictor of $\mathbf{Y}_{T+h}$ is now

$$\hat{\mathbf{Y}}_{T+h|T} = \hat{\mathbf{\Pi}}_1 \hat{\mathbf{Y}}_{T+h-1|T} + \cdots + \hat{\mathbf{\Pi}}_p \hat{\mathbf{Y}}_{T+h-p|T} \tag{11.8}$$

where $\hat{\mathbf{\Pi}}_j$ are the estimated parameter matrices. The h-step forecast error is now

$$\mathbf{Y}_{T+h} - \hat{\mathbf{Y}}_{T+h|T} = \sum_{s=0}^{h-1} \mathbf{\Psi}_s \boldsymbol{\varepsilon}_{T+h-s} + \left(\mathbf{Y}_{T+h} - \hat{\mathbf{Y}}_{T+h|T}\right) \tag{11.9}$$

and the term $\left(\mathbf{Y}_{T+h} - \hat{\mathbf{Y}}_{T+h|T}\right)$ captures the part of the forecast error due to estimating the parameters of the VAR. The MSE matrix of the h-step forecast is then

$$\hat{\mathbf{\Sigma}}(h) = \mathbf{\Sigma}(h) + MSE\left(\mathbf{Y}_{T+h} - \hat{\mathbf{Y}}_{T+h|T}\right)$$

---

[1] The S+FinMetrics fucntion VAR.ar2ma computes the $\mathbf{\Psi}_s$ matrices given the $\mathbf{\Pi}_j$ matrices using (11.6).

In practice, the second term $MSE\left(\mathbf{Y}_{T+h} - \hat{\mathbf{Y}}_{T+h|T}\right)$ is often ignored and $\hat{\mathbf{\Sigma}}(h)$ is computed using (11.7) as

$$\hat{\mathbf{\Sigma}}(h) = \sum_{s=0}^{h-1} \hat{\mathbf{\Psi}}_s \hat{\mathbf{\Sigma}} \hat{\mathbf{\Psi}}_s' \tag{11.10}$$

with $\hat{\mathbf{\Psi}}_s = \sum_{j=1}^{s} \hat{\mathbf{\Psi}}_{s-j} \hat{\mathbf{\Pi}}_j$. Lütkepohl (1991, chapter 3) gives an approximation to $MSE\left(\mathbf{Y}_{T+h} - \hat{\mathbf{Y}}_{T+h|T}\right)$ which may be interpreted as a finite sample correction to (11.10).

Asymptotic $(1-\alpha)\cdot 100\%$ confidence intervals for the individual elements of $\hat{\mathbf{Y}}_{T+h|T}$ are then computed as

$$\left[\hat{y}_{k,T+h|T} - c_{1-\alpha/2}\hat{\sigma}_k(h), \ \hat{y}_{k,T+h|T} + c_{1-\alpha/2}\hat{\sigma}_k(h)\right]$$

where $c_{1-\alpha/2}$ is the $(1-\alpha/2)$ quantile of the standard normal distribution and $\hat{\sigma}_k(h)$ denotes the square root of the diagonal element of $\hat{\mathbf{\Sigma}}(h)$.

Example 64 *Forecasting exchange rates from a bivariate VAR*

Consider computing h-step forecasts, $h = 1, \ldots, 12$, along with estimated forecast standard errors from the bivariate VAR(1) model for exchange rates. Forecasts and forecast standard errors from the fitted VAR may be computed using the generic S-PLUS `predict` method

```
> uscn.pred = predict(var1.fit,n.predict=12)
```

The `predict` function recognizes `var1.fit` as a "VAR" object, and calls the appropriate method function `predict.VAR`. Alternatively, `predict.VAR` can be applied directly on an object inheriting from class "VAR". See the online help for explanations of the arguments to `predict.VAR`.

The output of `predict.VAR` is an object of class "forecast" for which there are `print`, `summary` and `plot` methods. To see just the forecasts, the `print` method will suffice:

```
> uscn.pred
```

```
Predicted Values:

                dspot      fp
1-step-ahead  -0.0027  -0.0005
2-step-ahead  -0.0026  -0.0006
3-step-ahead  -0.0023  -0.0008
4-step-ahead  -0.0021  -0.0009
5-step-ahead  -0.0020  -0.0010
6-step-ahead  -0.0018  -0.0011
7-step-ahead  -0.0017  -0.0011
```

```
 8-step-ahead -0.0017 -0.0012
 9-step-ahead -0.0016 -0.0012
10-step-ahead -0.0016 -0.0013
11-step-ahead -0.0015 -0.0013
12-step-ahead -0.0015 -0.0013
```

The forecasts and their standard errors can be shown using summary:

```
> summary(uscn.pred)

Predicted Values with Standard Errors:

                 dspot       fp
1-step-ahead   -0.0027  -0.0005
  (std.err)     0.0137   0.0009
2-step-ahead   -0.0026  -0.0006
  (std.err)     0.0139   0.0012

...

12-step-ahead  -0.0015  -0.0013
   (std.err)    0.0140   0.0015
```

Lütkepohl's finite sample correction to the forecast standard errors computed from asymptotic theory may be obtained by using the optional argument fs.correction=T in the call to predict.VAR.

The forecasts can also be plotted together with the original data using the generic plot function as follows:

```
> plot(uscn.pred,uscn.ts,n.old=12)
```

where the n.old optional argument specifies the number of observations to plot from uscn.ts. If n.old is not specified, all the observations in uscn.ts will be plotted together with uscn.pred. Figure 11.5 shows the forecasts produced from the VAR(1) fit to the US/CN exchange rate data[2]. At the beginning of the forecast horizon the spot return is below its estimated mean value, and the forward premium is above its mean values. The spot return forecasts start off negative and grow slowly toward the mean, and the forward premium forecasts decline sharply toward the mean. The forecast standard errors for both sets of forecasts, however, are fairly large.

---

[2] Notice that the dates associated with the forecasts are not shown. This is the result of "timeDate" objects not having a well defined frequency from which to extrapolate dates.

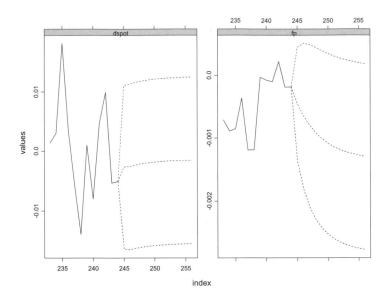

FIGURE 11.5. Predicted values from VAR(1) model fit to US/CN exchange rate data.

11.3.2 Simulation-Based Forecasting

The previous subsection showed how to generate multivariate forecasts from a fitted VAR model, using the chain-rule of forecasting (11.8). Since the multivariate forecast errors (11.9) are asymptotically normally distributed with covariance matrix (11.10), the forecasts of $\mathbf{Y}_{t+h}$ can be simulated by generating multivariate normal random variables with mean zero and covariance matrix (11.10). These simulation-based forecasts can be obtained by setting the optional argument `method` to `"mc"` in the call to `predict.VAR`.

When `method="mc"`, the multivariate normal random variables are actually generated as a vector of standard normal random variables scaled by the Cholesky factor of the covariance matrix (11.10). Instead of using standard normal random variables, one could also use the standardized residuals from the fitted VAR model. Simulation-based forecasts based on this approach are obtained by setting the optional argument method to `"bootstrap"` in the call to `predict.VAR`.

Example 65 *Simulation-based forecasts of exchange rate data from bivariate VAR*

The h-step forecasts ($h = 1, \ldots, 12$) for Δs_{t+h} and fp_{t+h} using the Monte Carlo simulation method are

```
> uscn.pred.MC = predict(var1.fit,n.predict=12,method="mc")
> summary(uscn.pred.MC)
```

```
Predicted Values with Standard Errors:

                 dspot       fp
 1-step-ahead  -0.0032  -0.0005
    (std.err)   0.0133   0.0009
 2-step-ahead  -0.0026  -0.0006
    (std.err)   0.0133   0.0012
...
12-step-ahead  -0.0013  -0.0013
    (std.err)   0.0139   0.0015
```

The Monte Carlo forecasts and forecast standard errors for fp_{t+h} are almost identical to those computed using the chain-rule of forecasting. The Monte Carlo forecasts for Δs_{t+h} are slightly different and the forecast standard errors are slightly larger than the corresponding values computed from the chain-rule.

The h-step forecasts computed from the bootstrap simulation method are

```
> uscn.pred.boot = predict(var1.fit,n.predict=12,
+ method="bootstrap")
> summary(uscn.pred.boot)
```

```
Predicted Values with Standard Errors:

                 dspot       fp
 1-step-ahead  -0.0020  -0.0005
    (std.err)   0.0138   0.0009
 2-step-ahead  -0.0023  -0.0007
    (std.err)   0.0140   0.0012
...
12-step-ahead  -0.0023  -0.0013
    (std.err)   0.0145   0.0015
```

As with the Monte Carlo forecasts, the bootstrap forecasts and forecast standard errors for fp_{t+h} are almost identical to those computed using the chain-rule of forecasting. The bootstrap forecasts for Δs_{t+h} are slightly different from the chain-rule and Monte Carlo forecasts. In particular, the bootstrap forecast standard errors are larger than corresponding values from the chain-rule and Monte Carlo methods.

The simulation-based forecasts described above are different from the traditional simulation-based approach taken in VAR literature, e.g., see

Runkle (1987). The traditional approach is implemented using the following procedure:

1. Obtain VAR coefficient estimates Π and residuals ε_t.

2. Simulate the fitted VAR model by Monte Carlo simulation or by bootstrapping the fitted residuals $\hat{\varepsilon}_t$.

3. Obtain new estimates of Π and forecasts of $\mathbf{Y}_{t+h}$ based on the simulated data.

The above procedure is repeated many times to obtain simulation-based forecasts as well as their confidence intervals. To illustrate this approach, generate 12-step ahead forecasts from the fitted VAR object `var1.fit` by Monte Carlo simulation using the S+FinMetrics function `simulate.VAR` as follows:

```
> set.seed(10)
> n.pred=12
> n.sim=100
> sim.pred = array(0,c(n.sim, n.pred, 2))
> y0 = seriesData(var1.fit$Y0)
> for (i in 1:n.sim) {
+     dat = simulate.VAR(var1.fit,n=243)
+     dat = rbind(y0,dat)
+     mod = VAR(dat~ar(1))
+     sim.pred[i,,] = predict(mod,n.pred)$values
+ }
```

The simulation-based forecasts are obtained by averaging the simulated forecasts:

```
> colMeans(sim.pred)
             [,1]         [,2]
 [1,] -0.0017917 -0.0012316
 [2,] -0.0017546 -0.0012508
 [3,] -0.0017035 -0.0012643
 [4,] -0.0016800 -0.0012741
 [5,] -0.0016587 -0.0012814
 [6,] -0.0016441 -0.0012866
 [7,] -0.0016332 -0.0012904
 [8,] -0.0016253 -0.0012932
 [9,] -0.0016195 -0.0012953
[10,] -0.0016153 -0.0012967
[11,] -0.0016122 -0.0012978
[12,] -0.0016099 -0.0012986
```

Comparing these forecasts with those in `uscn.pred` computed earlier, one can see that for the first few forecasts, these simulated forecasts are slightly different from the asymptotic forecasts. However, at larger steps, they approach the long run stable values of the asymptotic forecasts.

Conditional Forecasting

The forecasts algorithms considered up to now are unconditional multivariate forecasts. However, sometimes it is desirable to obtain forecasts of some variables in the system conditional on some knowledge of the future path of other variables in the system. For example, when forecasting multivariate macroeconomic variables using quarterly data from a VAR model, it may happen that some of the future values of certain variables in the VAR model are known, because data on these variables are released earlier than data on the other variables. By incorporating the knowledge of the future path of certain variables, in principle it should be possible to obtain more reliable forecasts of the other variables in the system. Another use of conditional forecasting is the generation of forecasts conditional on different "policy" scenarios. These scenario-based conditional forecasts allow one to answer the question: if something happens to some variables in the system in the future, how will it affect forecasts of other variables in the future?

S+FinMetrics provides a generic function cpredict for computing conditional forecasts, which has a method cpredict.VAR for "VAR" objects. The algorithms in cpredict.VAR are based on the conditional forecasting algorithms described in Waggoner and Zha (1999). Waggoner and Zha classify conditional information into "hard" conditions and "soft conditions". The hard conditions restrict the future values of certain variables at fixed values, while the soft conditions restrict the future values of certain variables in specified ranges. The arguments taken by cpredict.VAR are:

```
> args(cpredict.VAR)
function(object, n.predict = 1, newdata = NULL, olddata = NULL,
method = "mc", unbiased = T, variables.conditioned =
NULL, steps.conditioned = NULL, upper = NULL, lower =
NULL, middle = NULL, seed = 100, n.sim - 1000)
```

Like most predict methods in S-PLUS, the first argument must be a fitted model object, while the second argument, n.predict, specifies the number of steps to predict ahead. The arguments newdata and olddata can usually be safely ignored, unless exogenous variables were used in fitting the model.

With classical forecasts that ignore the uncertainty in coefficient estimates, hard conditional forecasts can be obtained in closed form as shown by Doan, Litterman and Sims (1984), and Waggoner and Zha (1999). To obtain hard conditional forecasts, the argument middle is used to specify fixed values of certain variables at certain steps. For example, to fix the 1-step ahead forecast of dspot in var1.fit at -0.005 and generate other predictions for 2-step ahead forecasts, use the following command:

```
> cpredict(var1.fit, n.predict=2, middle=-0.005,
```

```
+ variables="dspot", steps=1)
```

Predicted Values:

```
                 dspot       fp
1-step-ahead  -0.0050  -0.0005
2-step-ahead  -0.0023  -0.0007
```

In the call to cpredict, the optional argument variables is used to specify the restricted variables, and steps to specify the restricted steps.

To specify a soft condition, the optional arguments upper and lower are used to specify the upper bound and lower bound, respectively, of a soft condition. Since closed form results are not available for soft conditional forecasts, either Monte Carlo simulation or bootstrap methods are used to obtain the actual forecasts. The simulations follow a similar procedure implemented in the function predict.VAR, except that a reject/accept method to sample from the distribution conditional on the soft conditions is used. For example, to restrict the range of the first 2-step ahead forecasts of dspot to be $(-0.004, -0.001)$ use:

```
> cpredict(var1.fit, n.predict=2, lower=c(-0.004, -0.004),
+ upper=c(-0.001, -0.001), variables="dspot",
+ steps=c(1,2))
```

Predicted Values:

```
                 dspot       fp
1-step-ahead  -0.0027  -0.0003
2-step-ahead  -0.0029  -0.0005
```

11.4   Structural Analysis

The general VAR(p) model has many parameters, and they may be difficult to interpret due to complex interactions and feedback between the variables in the model. As a result, the dynamic properties of a VAR(p) are often summarized using various types of *structural analysis*. The three main types of structural analysis summaries are (1) *Granger causality tests*; (2) *impulse response functions*; and (3) *forecast error variance decompositions*. The following sections give brief descriptions of these summary measures.

11.4.1   Granger Causality

One of the main uses of VAR models is forecasting. The structure of the VAR model provides information about a variable's or a group of variables' forecasting ability for other variables. The following intuitive notion of a variable's forecasting ability is due to Granger (1969). If a variable, or group of variables, y_1 is found to be helpful for predicting another variable, or group of variables, y_2 then y_1 is said to *Granger-cause* y_2; otherwise it is said to *fail to Granger-cause* y_2. Formally, y_1 fails to Granger-cause y_2 if for all $s > 0$ the MSE of a forecast of $y_{2,t+s}$ based on $(y_{2,t}, y_{2,t-1}, \ldots)$ is the same as the MSE of a forecast of $y_{2,t+s}$ based on $(y_{2,t}, y_{2,t-1}, \ldots)$ and $(y_{1,t}, y_{1,t-1}, \ldots)$. Clearly, the notion of Granger causality does not imply true causality. It only implies forecasting ability.

Bivariate VAR Models

In a bivariate VAR(p) model for $\mathbf{Y}_t = (y_{1t}, y_{2t})'$, y_2 fails to Granger-cause y_1 if all of the p VAR coefficient matrices $\mathbf{\Pi}_1, \ldots, \mathbf{\Pi}_p$ are lower triangular. That is, the VAR(p) model has the form

$$
\begin{pmatrix} y_{1t} \\ y_{2t} \end{pmatrix} = \begin{pmatrix} c_1 \\ c_2 \end{pmatrix} + \begin{pmatrix} \pi_{11}^1 & 0 \\ \pi_{21}^1 & \pi_{22}^1 \end{pmatrix} \begin{pmatrix} y_{1t-1} \\ y_{2t-1} \end{pmatrix} + \cdots
$$
$$
+ \begin{pmatrix} \pi_{11}^p & 0 \\ \pi_{21}^p & \pi_{22}^p \end{pmatrix} \begin{pmatrix} y_{1t-p} \\ y_{2t-p} \end{pmatrix} + \begin{pmatrix} \varepsilon_{1t} \\ \varepsilon_{2t} \end{pmatrix}
$$

so that all of the coefficients on lagged values of y_2 are zero in the equation for y_1. Similarly, y_1 fails to Granger-cause y_2 if all of the coefficients on lagged values of y_1 are zero in the equation for y_2. The p linear coefficient restrictions implied by Granger non-causality may be tested using the Wald statistic (11.5). Notice that if y_2 fails to Granger-cause y_1 and y_1 fails to Granger-cause y_2, then the VAR coefficient matrices $\mathbf{\Pi}_1, \ldots, \mathbf{\Pi}_p$ are diagonal.

General VAR Models

Testing for Granger non-causality in general n variable VAR(p) models follows the same logic used for bivariate models. For example, consider a VAR(p) model with $n = 3$ and $\mathbf{Y}_t = (y_{1t}, y_{2t}, y_{3t})'$. In this model, y_2 does not Granger-cause y_1 if all of the coefficients on lagged values of y_2 are zero in the equation for y_1. Similarly, y_3 does not Granger-cause y_1 if all of the coefficients on lagged values of y_3 are zero in the equation for y_1. These simple linear restrictions may be tested using the Wald statistic (11.5). The reader is encouraged to consult Lütkepohl (1991) or Hamilton (1994) for more details and examples.

Example 66 *Testing for Granger causality in bivariate VAR(2) model for exchange rates*

Consider testing for Granger causality in a bivariate VAR(2) model for $\mathbf{Y}_t = (\Delta s_t, fp_t)'$. Using the notation of (11.2), fp_t does not Granger cause Δs_t if $\pi_{12}^1 = 0$ and $\pi_{12}^2 = 0$. Similarly, Δs_t does not Granger cause fp_t if

$\pi_{21}^1 = 0$ and $\pi_{21}^2 = 0$. These hypotheses are easily tested using the Wald statistic (11.5). The restriction matrix $\mathbf{R}$ for the hypothesis that fp_t does not Granger cause Δs_t is

$$\mathbf{R} = \begin{pmatrix} 0 & 0 & 1 & 0 & 0 & 0 & 0 & 0 & 0 & 0 \\ 0 & 0 & 0 & 0 & 1 & 0 & 0 & 0 & 0 & 0 \end{pmatrix}$$

and the matrix for the hypothesis that Δs_t does not Granger cause fp_t is

$$\mathbf{R} = \begin{pmatrix} 0 & 0 & 0 & 0 & 0 & 0 & 1 & 0 & 0 & 0 \\ 0 & 0 & 0 & 0 & 0 & 0 & 0 & 0 & 1 & 0 \end{pmatrix}$$

The S-PLUS commands to compute and evaluate these Granger causality Wald statistics are

```
> # H0: fp does not Granger cause dspot
> R = matrix(c(0,0,1,0,0,0,0,0,0,0,
+ 0,0,0,0,0,1,0,0,0,0),
+ 2,10,byrow=T)
> vecPi = as.vector(coef(var2.fit))
> avar = R%*%vcov(var2.fit)%*%t(R)
> wald = t(R%*%vecPi)%*%solve(avar)%*%(R%*%vecPi)
> wald
        [,1]
[1,] 14.5
> 1-pchisq(wald,2)
[1] 0.0007113

> R = matrix(c(0,0,0,0,0,0,1,0,0,0,
+ 0,0,0,0,0,0,0,0,1,0),
+ 2,10,byrow=T)
> vecPi = as.vector(coef(var2.fit))
> avar = R%*%vcov(var2.fit)%*%t(R)
> wald = t(R%*%vecPi)%*%solve(avar)%*%(R%*%vecPi)
> wald
        [,1]
[1,] 6.157
> 1-pchisq(wald,2)
[1] 0.04604
```

The p-values for the Wald tests indicate a strong rejection of the null that fp_t does not Granger cause Δs_t but only a weak rejection of the null that Δs_t does not Granger cause fp_t. Hence, lagged values of fp_t appear to be useful for forecasting future values of Δs_t and lagged values of Δs_t appear to be useful for forecasting future values of fp_t.

11.4.2 Impulse Response Functions

Any covariance stationary VAR(p) process has a Wold representation of the form

$$\mathbf{Y}_t = \boldsymbol{\mu} + \boldsymbol{\varepsilon}_t + \boldsymbol{\Psi}_1 \boldsymbol{\varepsilon}_{t-1} + \boldsymbol{\Psi}_2 \boldsymbol{\varepsilon}_{t-2} + \cdots \qquad (11.11)$$

where the ($n \times n$) moving average matrices $\boldsymbol{\Psi}_s$ are determined recursively using (11.6). It is tempting to interpret the (i, j)-th element, ψ_{ij}^s, of the matrix $\boldsymbol{\Psi}_s$ as the dynamic multiplier or impulse response

$$\frac{\partial y_{i,t+s}}{\partial \varepsilon_{j,t}} = \frac{\partial y_{i,t}}{\partial \varepsilon_{j,t-s}} = \psi_{ij}^s, \; i,j = 1, \ldots, n$$

However, this interpretation is only possible if $var(\boldsymbol{\varepsilon}_t) = \boldsymbol{\Sigma}$ is a diagonal matrix so that the elements of $\boldsymbol{\varepsilon}_t$ are uncorrelated. One way to make the errors uncorrelated is to follow Sims (1980) and estimate the *triangular structural* VAR(p) model

$$
\begin{aligned}
y_{1t} &= c_1 + \boldsymbol{\gamma}_{11}' \mathbf{Y}_{t-1} + \cdots + \boldsymbol{\gamma}_{1p}' \mathbf{Y}_{t-p} + \eta_{1t} \qquad (11.12) \\
y_{2t} &= c_1 + \beta_{21} y_{1t} + \boldsymbol{\gamma}_{21}' \mathbf{Y}_{t-1} + \cdots + \boldsymbol{\gamma}_{2p}' \mathbf{Y}_{t-p} + \eta_{2t} \\
y_{3t} &= c_1 + \beta_{31} y_{1t} + \beta_{32} y_{2t} + \boldsymbol{\gamma}_{31}' \mathbf{Y}_{t-1} + \cdots + \boldsymbol{\gamma}_{3p}' \mathbf{Y}_{t-p} + \eta_{3t} \\
&\;\;\vdots \\
y_{nt} &= c_1 + \beta_{n1} y_{1t} + \cdots + \beta_{n,n-1} y_{n-1,t} + \boldsymbol{\gamma}_{n1}' \mathbf{Y}_{t-1} + \cdots + \boldsymbol{\gamma}_{np}' \mathbf{Y}_{t-p} + \eta_{nt}
\end{aligned}
$$

In matrix form, the triangular structural VAR(p) model is

$$\mathbf{B}\mathbf{Y}_t = \mathbf{c} + \boldsymbol{\Gamma}_1 \mathbf{Y}_{t-1} + \boldsymbol{\Gamma}_2 \mathbf{Y}_{t-2} + \cdots + \boldsymbol{\Gamma}_p \mathbf{Y}_{t-p} + \boldsymbol{\eta}_t \qquad (11.13)$$

where

$$\mathbf{B} = \begin{pmatrix} 1 & 0 & \cdots & 0 \\ -\beta_{21} & 1 & 0 & 0 \\ \vdots & \vdots & \ddots & \vdots \\ -\beta_{n1} & -\beta_{n2} & \cdots & 1 \end{pmatrix} \qquad (11.14)$$

is a lower triangular matrix with $1's$ along the diagonal. The algebra of least squares will ensure that the estimated covariance matrix of the error vector $\boldsymbol{\eta}_t$ is diagonal. The uncorrelated/orthogonal errors $\boldsymbol{\eta}_t$ are referred to as *structural* errors.

The triangular structural model (11.12) imposes the *recursive causal ordering*

$$y_1 \rightarrow y_2 \rightarrow \cdots \rightarrow y_n \qquad (11.15)$$

The ordering (11.15) means that the contemporaneous values of the variables to the left of the arrow $\rightarrow$ affect the contemporaneous values of the variables to the right of the arrow but not vice-versa. These contemporaneous effects are captured by the coefficients β_{ij} in (11.12). For example, the ordering $y_1 \to y_2 \to y_3$ imposes the restrictions: y_{1t} affects y_{2t} and y_{3t} but y_{2t} and y_{3t} do not affect y_1; y_{2t} affects y_{3t} but y_{3t} does not affect y_{2t}. Similarly, the ordering $y_2 \to y_3 \to y_1$ imposes the restrictions: y_{2t} affects y_{3t} and y_{1t} but y_{3t} and y_{1t} do not affect y_2; y_{3t} affects y_{1t} but y_{1t} does not affect y_{3t}. For a VAR(p) with n variables there are $n!$ possible recursive causal orderings. Which ordering to use in practice depends on the context and whether prior theory can be used to justify a particular ordering. Results from alternative orderings can always be compared to determine the sensitivity of results to the imposed ordering.

Once a recursive ordering has been established, the Wold representation of $\mathbf{Y}_t$ based on the orthogonal errors $\boldsymbol{\eta}_t$ is given by

$$\mathbf{Y}_t = \boldsymbol{\mu} + \boldsymbol{\Theta}_0 \boldsymbol{\eta}_t + \boldsymbol{\Theta}_1 \boldsymbol{\eta}_{t-1} + \boldsymbol{\Theta}_2 \boldsymbol{\eta}_{t-2} + \cdots \tag{11.16}$$

where $\boldsymbol{\Theta}_0 = \mathbf{B}^{-1}$ is a lower triangular matrix. The impulse responses to the orthogonal shocks η_{jt} are

$$\frac{\partial y_{i,t+s}}{\partial \eta_{j,t}} = \frac{\partial y_{i,t}}{\partial \eta_{j,t-s}} = \theta_{ij}^s, \ i,j = 1,\ldots,n; s > 0 \tag{11.17}$$

where θ_{ij}^s is the (i,j) th element of $\boldsymbol{\Theta}_s$. A plot of θ_{ij}^s against s is called the *orthogonal impulse response function* (IRF) of y_i with respect to η_j. With n variables there are n^2 possible impulse response functions.

In practice, the orthogonal IRF (11.17) based on the triangular VAR(p) (11.12) may be computed directly from the parameters of the non triangular VAR(p) (11.1) as follows. First, decompose the residual covariance matrix $\boldsymbol{\Sigma}$ as

$$\boldsymbol{\Sigma} = \mathbf{ADA}'$$

where $\mathbf{A}$ is an invertible lower triangular matrix with $1's$ along the diagonal and $\mathbf{D}$ is a diagonal matrix with positive diagonal elements. Next, define the structural errors as

$$\boldsymbol{\eta}_t = \mathbf{A}^{-1}\boldsymbol{\varepsilon}_t$$

These structural errors are orthogonal by construction since $var(\boldsymbol{\eta}_t) = \mathbf{A}^{-1}\boldsymbol{\Sigma}\mathbf{A}^{-1\prime} = \mathbf{A}^{-1}\mathbf{ADA}'\mathbf{A}^{-1\prime} = \mathbf{D}$. Finally, re-express the Wold representation (11.11) as

$$\begin{aligned}\mathbf{Y}_t &= \boldsymbol{\mu} + \mathbf{AA}^{-1}\boldsymbol{\varepsilon}_t + \boldsymbol{\Psi}_1\mathbf{AA}^{-1}\boldsymbol{\varepsilon}_{t-1} + \boldsymbol{\Psi}_2\mathbf{AA}^{-1}\boldsymbol{\varepsilon}_{t-2} + \cdots \\ &= \boldsymbol{\mu} + \boldsymbol{\Theta}_0\boldsymbol{\eta}_t + + \boldsymbol{\Theta}_1\boldsymbol{\eta}_{t-1} + \boldsymbol{\Theta}_2\boldsymbol{\eta}_{t-2}\end{aligned}$$

where $\boldsymbol{\Theta}_j = \boldsymbol{\Psi}_j\mathbf{A}$. Notice that the structural B matrix in (11.13) is equal to $\mathbf{A}^{-1}$.

Computing the Orthogonal Impulse Response Function Using the S+FinMetrics Function impRes

The orthogonal impulse response function (11.17) from a triangular structural VAR model (11.13) may be computed using the S+FinMetrics function impRes. The function impRes has arguments

```
> args(impRes)
function(x, period = NULL, std.err = "none", plot = F,
unbiased = T, order = NULL, ...)
```

where x is an object of class "VAR" and period specifies the number of responses to compute. By default, no standard errors for the responses are computed. To compute asymptotic standard errors for the responses, specify std.err="asymptotic". To create a panel plot of all the response functions, specify plot=T. The default recursive causal ordering is based on the ordering of the variables in $\mathbf{Y}_t$ when the VAR model is fit. The optional argument order may be used to specify a different recursive causal ordering for the computation of the impulse responses. The argument order accepts a character vector of variable names whose order defines the recursive causal ordering. The output of impRes is an object of class "impDecomp" for which there are print, summary and plot methods. The following example illustrates the use of impRes.

Example 67 *IRF from VAR(1) for exchange rates*

Consider again the VAR(1) model for $\mathbf{Y}_t = (\Delta s_t, fp_t)'$. For the impulse response analysis, the initial ordering of the variables imposes the assumption that structural shocks to fp_t have no contemporaneous effect on Δs_t but structural shocks to Δs_t do have a contemporaneous effect on fp_t. To compute the four impulse response functions

$$\frac{\partial \Delta s_{t+h}}{\partial \eta_{1t}}, \ \frac{\partial \Delta s_{t+h}}{\partial \eta_{2t}}, \ \frac{\partial fp_{t+h}}{\partial \eta_{1t}}, \ \frac{\partial fp_{t+h}}{\partial \eta_{2t}}$$

for $h = 1, \dots, 12$ we use S+FinMetrics function impRes. The first twelve impulse responses from the VAR(1) model for exchange rates are computed using

```
> uscn.irf = impRes(var1.fit, period=12, std.err="asymptotic")
```

The print method shows the impulse response values without standard errors:

```
> uscn.irf

Impulse Response Function:
(with responses in rows, and innovations in columns)

, , lag.0
         dspot       fp
dspot   0.0136   0.0000
   fp   0.0000   0.0009

, , lag.1
```

```
          dspot        fp
dspot  -0.0018  -0.0013
   fp   0.0001   0.0007


, , lag.2
          dspot        fp
dspot   0.0000  -0.0009
   fp   0.0001   0.0006


...


, , lag.11
          dspot        fp
dspot   0.0000  -0.0001
   fp   0.0000   0.0001
```

The **summary** method will display the responses with standard errors and t-statistics. The **plot** method will produce a four panel Trellis graphics plot of the impulse responses

```
> plot(uscn.irf)
```

A plot of the impulse responses can also be created in the initial call to impRes by using the optional argument plot=T.

Figure 11.6 shows the impulse response functions along with asymptotic standard errors. The top row shows the responses of Δs_t to the structural shocks, and the bottom row shows the responses of fp_t to the structural shocks. In response to the first structural shock, η_{1t}, Δs_t initially increases but then drops quickly to zero after 2 months. Similarly, fp_t initially increases, reaches its peak response in 2 months and then gradually drops off to zero after about a year. In response to the second shock, η_{2t}, by assumption Δs_t has no initial response. At one month, a sharp drop occurs in Δs_t followed by a gradual return to zero after about a year. In contrast, fp_t initially increases and then gradually drops to zero after about a year.

The orthogonal impulse responses in Figure 11.6 are based on the recursive causal ordering $\Delta s_t \rightarrow fp_t$. It must always be kept in mind that this ordering identifies the orthogonal structural shocks η_{1t} and η_{2t}. If the ordering is reversed, then a different set of structural shocks will be identified, and these may give very different impulse response functions. To compute the orthogonal impulse responses using the alternative ordering $fp_t \rightarrow \Delta s_t$ specify order=c("fp","dspot") in the call to impRes:

```
> uscn.irf2 = impRes(var1.fit,period=12,std.err="asymptotic",
+ order=c("fp","dspot"),plot=T)
```

These impulse responses are presented in Figure 11.7 and are almost identical to those computed using the ordering $\Delta s_t \rightarrow fp_t$. The reason for this

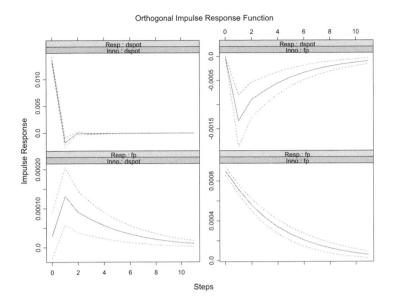

FIGURE 11.6. Impulse response function from VAR(1) model fit to US/CN exchange rate data with Δs_t ordered first.

response is that the reduced form VAR residuals $\hat{\varepsilon}_{1t}$ and $\hat{\varepsilon}_{2t}$ are almost uncorrelated. To see this, the residual correlation matrix may be computed using

```
> sd.vals = sqrt(diag(var1.fit$Sigma))
> cor.mat = var1.fit$Sigma/outer(sd.vals,sd.vals)
> cor.mat
         dspot        fp
dspot 1.000000 0.033048
   fp 0.033048 1.000000
```

Because of the near orthogonality in the reduced form VAR errors, the error in the Δs_t equation may be interpreted as an orthogonal shock to the exchange rate and the error in the fp_t equation may be interpreted as an orthogonal shock to the forward premium.

11.4.3 Forecast Error Variance Decompositions

The *forecast error variance decomposition* (FEVD) answers the question: what portion of the variance of the forecast error in predicting $y_{i,T+h}$ is due to the structural shock η_j? Using the orthogonal shocks $\boldsymbol{\eta}_t$ the h-step ahead forecast error vector, with known VAR coefficients, may be expressed

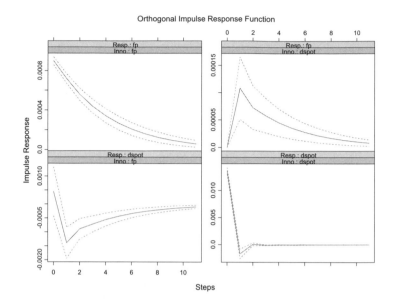

FIGURE 11.7. Impulse response function from VAR(1) model fit to US/CN exchange rate with fp_t ordered first.

as

$$\mathbf{Y}_{T+h} - \mathbf{Y}_{T+h|T} = \sum_{s=0}^{h-1} \mathbf{\Theta}_s \boldsymbol{\eta}_{T+h-s}$$

For a particular variable $y_{i,T+h}$, this forecast error has the form

$$y_{i,T+h} - y_{i,T+h|T} = \sum_{s=0}^{h-1} \theta_{i1}^s \eta_{1,T+h-s} + \cdots + \sum_{s=0}^{h-1} \theta_{in}^s \eta_{n,T+h-s}$$

Since the structural errors are orthogonal, the variance of the h-step forecast error is

$$var(y_{i,T+h} - y_{i,T+h|T}) = \sigma_{\eta_1}^2 \sum_{s=0}^{h-1} \left(\theta_{i1}^s\right)^2 + \cdots + \sigma_{\eta_n}^2 \sum_{s=0}^{h-1} \left(\theta_{in}^s\right)^2$$

where $\sigma_{\eta j}^2 = var(\eta_{jt})$. The portion of $var(y_{i,T+h} - y_{i,T+h|T})$ due to shock η_j is then

$$FEVD_{i,j}(h) = \frac{\sigma_{\eta_j}^2 \sum_{s=0}^{h-1} \left(\theta_{ij}^s\right)^2}{\sigma_{\eta_1}^2 \sum_{s=0}^{h-1} \left(\theta_{i1}^s\right)^2 + \cdots + \sigma_{\eta_n}^2 \sum_{s=0}^{h-1} \left(\theta_{in}^s\right)^2}, \quad i,j = 1,\ldots,n$$

$$(11.18)$$

In a VAR with n variables there will be n^2 $FEVD_{i,j}(h)$ values. It must be kept in mind that the FEVD in (11.18) depends on the recursive causal ordering used to identify the structural shocks $\boldsymbol{\eta}_t$ and is not unique. Different causal orderings will produce different FEVD values.

Computing the FEVD Using the S+FinMetrics Function fevDec

Once a VAR model has been fit, the S+FinMetrics function fevDec may be used to compute the orthogonal FEVD. The function fevDec has arguments

```
> args(fevDec)
function(x, period = NULL, std.err = "none", plot = F,
unbiased = F, order = NULL, ...)
```

where x is an object of class "VAR" and period specifies the number of responses to compute. By default, no standard errors for the responses are computed and no plot is created. To compute asymptotic standard errors for the responses, specify std.err="asymptotic" and to plot the decompositions, specify plot=T. The default recursive causal ordering is based on the ordering of the variables in $\mathbf{Y}_t$ when the VAR model is fit. The optional argument order may be used to specify a different recursive causal ordering for the computation of the FEVD. The argument order accepts a text string vector of variable names whose order defines the recursive causal ordering. The output of fevDec is an object of class "impDecomp" for which there are print, summary and plot methods. The use of fevDec is illustrated with the following example.

Example 68 *FEVD from VAR(1) for exchange rates*

The orthogonal FEVD of the forecast errors from the VAR(1) model fit to the US/CN exchange rate data using the recursive causal ordering $\Delta s_t \rightarrow fp_t$ is computed using

```
> uscn.fevd = fevDec(var1.fit,period=12,
+ std.err="asymptotic")
> uscn.fevd


Forecast Error Variance Decomposition:
(with responses in rows, and innovations in columns)

, , 1-step-ahead
        dspot      fp
dspot 1.0000 0.0000
   fp 0.0011 0.9989

, , 2-step-ahead
        dspot      fp
```

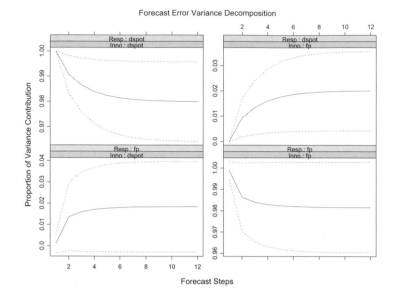

FIGURE 11.8. Orthogonal FEVDs computed from VAR(1) model fit to US/CN exchange rate data using the recursive causal ordering with Δs_t first.

```
dspot 0.9907 0.0093
   fp 0.0136 0.9864
```

...

```
, , 12-step-ahead
      dspot      fp
dspot 0.9800 0.0200
   fp 0.0184 0.9816
```

The summary method adds standard errors to the above output if they are computed in the call to fevDec. The plot method produces a four panel Trellis graphics plot of the decompositions:

```
> plot(uscn.fevd)
```

The FEVDs in Figure 11.8 show that most of the variance of the forecast errors for Δs_{t+s} at all horizons s is due to the orthogonal Δs_t innovations. Similarly, most of the variance of the forecast errors for fp_{t+s} is due to the orthogonal fp_t innovations.

The FEVDs using the alternative recursive causal ordering $fp_t \rightarrow \Delta s_t$ are computed using

```
> uscn.fevd2 = fevDec(var1.fit,period=12,
```

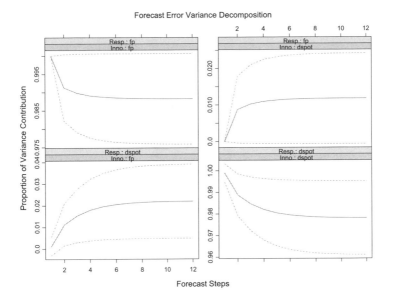

FIGURE 11.9. Orthogonal FEVDs from VAR(1) model fit to US/CN exchange rate data using recursive causal ordering with fp_t first.

```
+ std.err="asymptotic",order=c("fp","dspot"),plot=T)
```

and are illustrated in Figure 11.9. Since the residual covariance matrix is almost diagonal (see analysis of IRF above), the FEVDs computed using the alternative ordering are almost identical to those computed with the initial ordering.

11.5   An Extended Example

In this example the causal relations and dynamic interactions among monthly real stock returns, real interest rates, real industrial production growth and the inflation rate is investigated using a VAR model. The analysis is similar to that of Lee (1992). The variables are in the S+FinMetrics "timeSeries" object varex.ts

```
> colIds(varex.ts)
[1] "MARKET.REAL" "RF.REAL" "INF" "IPG"
```

Details about the data are in the documentation slot of varex.ts

```
> varex.ts@documentation
```

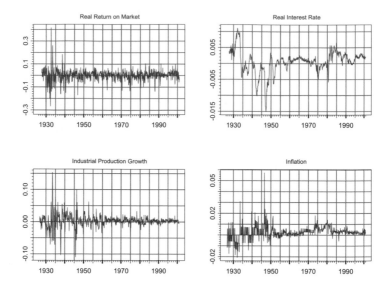

FIGURE 11.10. Monthly data on stock returns, interest rates, output growth and inflation.

To be comparable to the results in Lee (1992), the analysis is conducted over the postwar period January 1947 through December 1987

```
> smpl = (positions(varex.ts) >= timeDate("1/1/1947") &
+ positions(varex.ts) < timeDate("1/1/1988"))
```

The data over this period is displayed in Figure 11.10. All variables appear to be $I(0)$, but the real T-bill rate and the inflation rate appear to be highly persistent.

To begin the analysis, autocorrelations and cross correlations at leads and lags are computed using

```
> varex.acf = acf(varex.ts[smpl,])
```

and are illustrated in Figure 11.11. The real return on the market shows a significant positive first lag autocorrelation, and inflation appears to lead the real market return with a negative sign. The real T-bill rate is highly positively autocorrelated, and inflation appears to lead the real T-bill rate strongly with a negative sign. Inflation is also highly positively autocorrelated and, interestingly, the real T-bill rate appears to lead inflation with a positive sign. Finally, industrial production growth is slightly positively autocorrelated, and the real market return appears to lead industrial production growth with a positive sign.

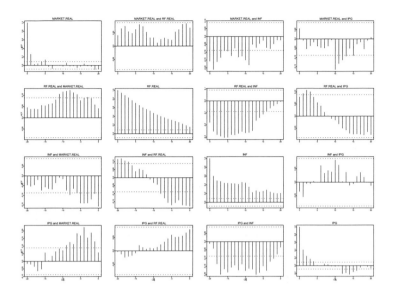

FIGURE 11.11. Autocorrelations and cross correlations at leads and lags of data in VAR model.

The VAR(p) model is fit with the lag length selected by minimizing the AIC and a maximum lag length of 6 months:

```
> varAIC.fit = VAR(varex.ts,max.ar=6,criterion="AIC",
+ start="Jan 1947",end="Dec 1987",
+ in.format="%m %Y")
```

The lag length selected by minimizing AIC is $p = 2$:

```
> varAIC.fit$info
     ar(1)  ar(2)  ar(3)  ar(4)  ar(5)  ar(6)
AIC -14832 -14863 -14853 -14861 -14855 -14862
> varAIC.fit$ar.order
[1] 2
```

The results of the VAR(2) fit are

```
> summary(varAIC.out)

Call:
VAR(data = varex.ts, start = "Jan 1947", end = "Dec 1987",
max.ar = 6, criterion = "AIC", in.format = "%m %Y")

Coefficients:
```

	MARKET.REAL	RF.REAL	INF	IPG
(Intercept)	0.0074	0.0002	0.0010	0.0019
(std.err)	0.0023	0.0001	0.0002	0.0007
(t.stat)	3.1490	4.6400	4.6669	2.5819
MARKET.REAL.lag1	0.2450	0.0001	0.0072	0.0280
(std.err)	0.0470	0.0011	0.0042	0.0146
(t.stat)	5.2082	0.0483	1.7092	1.9148
RF.REAL.lag1	0.8146	0.8790	0.5538	0.3772
(std.err)	2.0648	0.0470	0.1854	0.6419
(t.stat)	0.3945	18.6861	2.9867	0.5877
INF.lag1	-1.5020	-0.0710	0.4616	-0.0722
(std.err)	0.4932	0.0112	0.0443	0.1533
(t.stat)	-3.0451	-6.3147	10.4227	-0.4710

	MARKET.REAL	RF.REAL	INF	IPG
IPG.lag1	-0.0003	0.0031	-0.0143	0.3454
(std.err)	0.1452	0.0033	0.0130	0.0452
(t.stat)	-0.0018	0.9252	-1.0993	7.6501
MARKET.REAL.lag2	-0.0500	0.0022	-0.0066	0.0395
(std.err)	0.0466	0.0011	0.0042	0.0145
(t.stat)	-1.0727	2.0592	-1.5816	2.7276
RF.REAL.lag2	-0.3481	0.0393	-0.5855	-0.3289
(std.err)	1.9845	0.0452	0.1782	0.6169
(t.stat)	-0.1754	0.8699	-3.2859	-0.5331
INF.lag2	-0.0602	0.0079	0.2476	-0.0370
(std.err)	0.5305	0.0121	0.0476	0.1649
(t.stat)	-0.1135	0.6517	5.1964	-0.2245

	MARKET.REAL	RF.REAL	INF	IPG
IPG.lag2	-0.1919	0.0028	0.0154	0.0941
(std.err)	0.1443	0.0033	0.0130	0.0449
(t.stat)	-1.3297	0.8432	1.1868	2.0968

Regression Diagnostics:

	MARKET.REAL	RF.REAL	INF	IPG
R-squared	0.1031	0.9299	0.4109	0.2037
Adj. R-squared	0.0882	0.9287	0.4011	0.1905
Resid. Scale	0.0334	0.0008	0.0030	0.0104

Information Criteria:
```
  logL    AIC     BIC     HQ
  7503  -14935  -14784  -14875
```

```
                total residual
Degree of freedom:   489       480
Time period: from Mar 1947 to Nov 1987
```

The signs of the statistically significant coefficient estimates corroborate the informal analysis of the multivariate autocorrelations and cross lag autocorrelations. In particular, the real market return is positively related to its own lag but negatively related to the first lag of inflation. The real T-bill rate is positively related to its own lag, negatively related to the first lag of inflation, and positively related to the first lag of the real market return. Industrial production growth is positively related to its own lag and positively related to the first two lags of the real market return. Judging from the coefficients it appears that inflation Granger causes the real market return and the real T-bill rate, the real T-bill rate Granger causes inflation, and the real market return Granger causes the real T-bill rate and industrial production growth. These observations are confirmed with formal tests for Granger non-causality. For example, the Wald statistic for testing the null hypothesis that the real market return does not Granger-cause industrial production growth is

```
> bigR = matrix(0,2,36)
> bigR[1,29]=bigR[2,33]=1
> vecPi = as.vector(coef(varAIC.fit))
> avar = bigR%*%vcov(varAIC.fit)%*%t(bigR)
> wald = t(bigR%*%vecPi)%*%solve(avar)%*%(bigR%*%vecPi)
> as.numeric(wald)
[1] 13.82
> 1-pchisq(wald,2)
[1] 0.0009969
```

The 24-period IRF using the recursive causal ordering MARKET.REAL → RF.REAL → IPG → INF is computed using

```
> varAIC.irf = impRes(varAIC.fit,period=24,
+ order=c("MARKET.REAL","RF.REAL","IPG","INF"),
+ std.err="asymptotic",plot=T)
```

and is illustrated in Figure 11.12. The responses of MARKET.REAL to unexpected orthogonal shocks to the other variables are given in the first row of the figure. Most notable is the strong negative response of MARKET.REAL to an unexpected increase in inflation. Notice that it takes about ten months for the effect of the shock to dissipate. The responses of RF.REAL to the orthogonal shocks is given in the second row of the figure. RF.REAL also

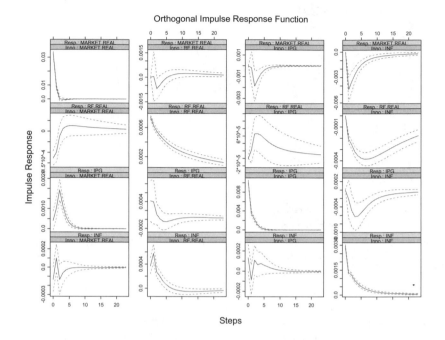

FIGURE 11.12. IRF using the recursive causal ordering `MARKET.REAL` → `RF.REAL` → `IPG` → `INF`.

reacts negatively to an inflation shock and the effect of the shock is felt for about two years. The responses of `IPG` to the orthogonal shocks is given in the third row of the figure. Industrial production growth responds positively to an unexpected shock to `MARKET.REAL` and negatively to shocks to `RF.REAL` and `INF`. These effects, however, are generally short term. Finally, the fourth row gives the responses of `INF` to the orthogonal shocks. Inflation responds positively to a shock to the real T-bill rate, but this effect is short-lived.

The 24 month FEVD computed using the recursive causal ordering as specified by `MARKET.REAL` → `RF.REAL` → `IPG` → `INF`,

```
> varAIC.fevd = fevDec(varAIC.out,period=24,
> order=c("MARKET.REAL","RF.REAL","IPG","INF"),
> std.err="asymptotic",plot=T)
```

is illustrated in Figure 11.13. The first row gives the variance decompositions for `MARKET.REAL` and shows that most of the variance of the forecast errors is due to own shocks. The second row gives the decompositions for `RF.REAL`. At short horizons, most of the variance is attributable to own shocks but at long horizons inflation shocks account for almost half the vari-

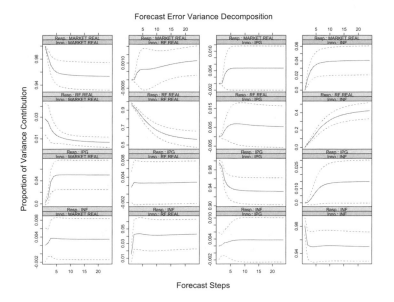

FIGURE 11.13. FEVDs using the recursive causal ordering `MARKET.REAL` →
`RF.REAL` → `IPG` → `INF`.

ance. The third row gives the variance decompositions for `IPG`. Most of the
variance is due to own shocks and a small fraction is due to `MARKET.REAL`
shocks. Finally, the fourth row shows that the forecast error variance of
`INF` is due mostly to its own shocks.

The IRFs and FEVDs computed above depend on the imposed recursive
causal ordering. However, in this example, the ordering of the variables will
have little effect on the IRFs and FEVDs because the errors in the reduced
form VAR are nearly uncorrelated:

```
> sd.vals = sqrt(diag(varAIC.out$Sigma))
> cor.mat = varAIC.out$Sigma/outer(sd.vals,sd.vals)
> cor.mat
            MARKET.REAL   RF.REAL       INF      IPG
MARKET.REAL     1.00000  -0.16855  -0.04518  0.03916
    RF.REAL    -0.16855   1.00000   0.13046  0.03318
        INF    -0.04518   0.13046   1.00000  0.04732
        IPG     0.03916   0.03318   0.04732  1.00000
```

11.6   Bayesian Vector Autoregression

VAR models with many variables and long lags contain many parameters. Unrestricted estimation of these models reqires lots of data and often the estimated parameters are not very precise, the results are hard to interpret, and forecasts may appear more precise than they really are because standard error bands do not account for parameter uncertainty. The estimates and forecasts can be improved if one has prior information about the structure of the model or the possible values of the parameters or functions of the parameters. In a classical framework, it is difficult to incorporate non-sample information into the estimation. Nonsample information is easy to incorporate in a Bayesian framework. A Bayesian framework also naturally incorporates parameter uncertainty into common measures of precision. This section briefly describes the Bayesian VAR modeling tools in S+FinMetrics and illustrates these tools with an example. Details of underlying Bayesian methods are given in Sims and Zha (1998) and Zha (1998).

11.6.1   An Example of a Bayesian VAR Model

S+FinMetrics comes with a "timeSeries" object policy.dat, which contains six U.S. macroeconomic variables:

```
> colIds(policy.dat)
[1] "CP"  "M2"  "FFR" "GDP" "CPI" "U"
```

which represent IMF's index of world commodity prices, M2 money stock, federal funds rate, real GDP, consumer price index for urban consumers, and civilian unemployment rate. The data set contains monthly observations from January 1959 to March 1998. Tao Zha and his co-authors have analyzed this data set in a number of papers, for example see Zha (1998). To use the same time period as in Zha (1998), create a subset of the data:

```
> zpolicy.dat = policy.dat[1:264,]
> zpolicy.mat = as.matrix(seriesData(zpolicy.dat))
```

which contains monthly observations from January 1959 to December 1980.

Estimating a Bayesian VAR Model

To estimate a Bayesian vector autoregression model, use the S+FinMetrics function BVAR. For macroeconomic modeling, it is usually found that many trending macroeconomic variables have a unit root, and in some cases, they may also have a cointegrating relationship (as described in the next chapter). To incorporate these types of prior beliefs into the model, use the unit.root.dummy and coint.dummy optional arguments to the BVAR function, which add some dummy observations to the beginning of the data to reflect these beliefs:

```
> zpolicy.bar13 = BVAR(zpolicy.mat~ar(13), unit.root=T,
+ coint=T)
> class(zpolicy.bar13)
[1] "BVAR"
```

The returned object is of class "BVAR", which inherits from "VAR", so many method functions for "VAR" objects work similarly for "BVAR" objects, such as the extractor functions, impulse response functions, and forecast error variance decomposition functions.

The Bayesian VAR models are controlled through a set of hyper parameters, which can be specified using the optional argument control, which is usually a list returned by the function BVAR.control. For example, the tightness of the belief in the unit root prior and cointegration prior is specified by mu5 and mu6, respectively. To see what default values are used for these hyper parameters, use

```
> args(BVAR.control)
function(L0 = 0.9, L1 = 0.1, L2 = 1, L3 = 1, L4 = 0.05,
        mu5 = 5, mu6 = 5)
```

For the meanings of these hyper parameters, see the online help file for BVAR.control.

Adding Exogenous Variables to the Model

Other exogenous variables can be added to the estimation formula, just as for OLS and VAR functions. The BVAR function and related functions will automatically take that into consideration and return the coefficient estimates for those variables.

Unconditional Forecasts

To forecast from a fitted Bayesian VAR model, use the generic predict function, which automatically calls the method function predict.BVAR for an object inheriting from class "BVAR". For example, to compute 12-step ahead forecasts use

```
> zpolicy.bpred = predict(zpolicy.bar13,n.predict=12)
> class(zpolicy.bpred)
[1] "forecast"
> names(zpolicy.bpred)
[1] "values"  "std.err" "draws"
> zpolicy.bpred


Predicted Values:

                  CP     M2     FFR    GDP    CPI      U
1-step-ahead  4.6354 7.3794 0.1964 8.4561 4.4714 0.0725
```

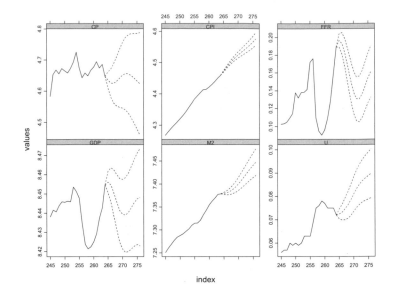

FIGURE 11.14. Forecasts from Bayesian VAR model.

```
 2-step-ahead  4.6257  7.3808  0.1930  8.4546  4.4842  0.0732
 3-step-ahead  4.6247  7.3834  0.1823  8.4505  4.4960  0.0746
 4-step-ahead  4.6310  7.3876  0.1670  8.4458  4.5065  0.0763
 5-step-ahead  4.6409  7.3931  0.1515  8.4414  4.5160  0.0785
 6-step-ahead  4.6503  7.3998  0.1384  8.4394  4.5244  0.0810
 7-step-ahead  4.6561  7.4075  0.1309  8.4390  4.5321  0.0833
 8-step-ahead  4.6552  7.4159  0.1307  8.4403  4.5397  0.0852
 9-step-ahead  4.6496  7.4242  0.1362  8.4428  4.5475  0.0867
10-step-ahead  4.6415  7.4323  0.1451  8.4453  4.5561  0.0879
11-step-ahead  4.6321  7.4402  0.1546  8.4473  4.5655  0.0889
12-step-ahead  4.6232  7.4476  0.1618  8.4482  4.5753  0.0899
```

The forecasts can also be plotted along with the original data using

```
> plot(zpolicy.bpred, zpolicy.mat, n.old=20)
```

The resulting plot is shown in Figure 11.14. The Bayesian forecasts usually have wider error bands than classical forecasts, because they take into account the uncertainty in the coefficient estimates. To ignore the uncertainty in coefficient estimates, one can call the classical VAR `predict` method function, `predict.VAR`, directly instead of the generic `predict` function.

The forecasts from Bayesian VAR models are of class "`forecast`", and are computed using Monte Carlo integration. By default, 1000 simulation draws are used. To change the number of simulation draws and random seed, specify the **n.sim** and **seed** optional arguments, respectively. For forecasts from Bayesian VAR models, there is one more component in the returned object: **draws**, which contains all the simulated forecasts. This can be used to assess other statistical properties of the forecasts.

11.6.2 Conditional Forecasts

As mentioned earlier, conditional forecasts from classical VAR models ignore the uncertainty in estimated coefficients. In contrast, conditional forecasts from Bayesian VAR models take into account the uncertainty associated with estimated coefficients. To perform conditional forecasts from a fitted Bayesian VAR model, use the generic **cpredict** function. For example, if it is known that **FFR** in January 1981 is between 0.185 and 0.195, one can incorporate this (soft condition) information into the forecasts using:

```
> zpolicy.spred = cpredict(zpolicy.bar13, 12, steps=1,
+ variables="FFR", upper=0.195, lower=0.185)
> zpolicy.spred
```

Predicted Values:

	CP	M2	FFR	GDP	CPI	U
1-step-ahead	4.6374	7.3797	0.1910	8.4554	4.4714	0.0729
2-step-ahead	4.6286	7.3816	0.1855	8.4540	4.4840	0.0736
3-step-ahead	4.6279	7.3850	0.1743	8.4498	4.4954	0.0752
4-step-ahead	4.6349	7.3899	0.1587	8.4452	4.5057	0.0768
5-step-ahead	4.6447	7.3960	0.1443	8.4414	4.5149	0.0791
6-step-ahead	4.6525	7.4033	0.1324	8.4406	4.5231	0.0814
7-step-ahead	4.6549	7.4114	0.1270	8.4412	4.5307	0.0835
8-step-ahead	4.6523	7.4201	0.1283	8.4428	4.5383	0.0851
9-step-ahead	4.6453	7.4284	0.1349	8.4457	4.5461	0.0864
10-step-ahead	4.6389	7.4365	0.1432	8.4482	4.5547	0.0876
11-step-ahead	4.6317	7.4444	0.1516	8.4501	4.5641	0.0885
12-step-ahead	4.6264	7.4519	0.1572	8.4511	4.5741	0.0896

For conditional forecasts with soft conditions, a Monte Carlo integration with acceptance/rejection method is used. By default, 1000 simulation draws are used. However, it may occur that only a small number of draws satisfy the soft conditions if the intervals are very tight. To see how many draws satisfied the soft conditions and thus are used for inference, simply check the dimension of the **draws** component of the returned object (see the on-line help file for **forecast.object** for details):

```
> dim(zpolicy.spred$draws)
[1] 372  72
```

In this case, only 372 out of 1000 simulation draws satisfied the conditions. To continue simulating from the posterior moment distribution, use the same command as before, with seed set to the current value of .Random.seed:

```
> zpolicy.spred2 = cpredict(zpolicy.bar13, 12, steps=1,
+ variables="FFR", upper=0.195, lower=0.185, seed=.Random.seed)
> dim(zpolicy.spred2$draws)
[1] 389  72
```

Note that the draws in zpolicy.spred2 can be combined with the draws in zpolicy.spred to obtain an updated and more accurate estimate of conditional forecasts.

To ignore the coefficient uncertainty for the conditional forecasts, call the classical method function cpredict.VAR directly on a fitted Bayesian VAR object. The technique introduced above can also be used for classical prediction with soft conditions.

11.7 References

[1] CAMPBELL, J. A. LO AND C. MACKINLAY (1997). *The Econometrics of Financial Markets*. Princeton University Press, New Jersey.

[2] CULBERTSON, K. (1996). *Quantitative Financial Economics: Stocks, Bonds and Foreign Exchange*. John Wiley and Sons, Chichester.

[3] DOAN, T. A., LITTERMAN, R. B., AND SIMS, C. A. (1984). "Forecasting and Conditional Projection Using Realistic Prior Distributions", *Econometric Reviews*, 3, 1-100.

[4] GRANGER, C.W.J. (1969). "Investigating Causal Relations by Econometric Models and Cross Spectral Methods," *Econometrica*, 37, 424-438.

[5] HAMILTON, J.D. (1994). *Time Series Analysis*. Princeton University Press, Princeton.

[6] LEE, B.-S. (1992). "Causal Relations Among Stock Returns, Interest Rates, Real Activity, and Inflation," *Journal of Finance*, 47, 1591-1603.

[7] LUTKEPOHL, H. (1991). *Introduction to Multiple Time Series Analysis*. Springer-Verlag, Berlin.

[8] LUTKEPOHL, H. (1999). "Vector Autoregressions," unpublished manuscript, Institut für Statistik und Ökonometrie, Humboldt-Universität zu Berlin.

[9] MILLS, T.C. (1999). *The Econometric Modeling of Financial Time Series, Second Edition.* Cambridge University Press, Cambridge.

[10] RUNKLE, D. E. (1987). "Vector Autoregressions and Reality," *Journal of Business and Economic Statistics*, 5 (4), 437-442.

[11] SIMS, C.A. (1980). "Macroeconomics and Reality," *Econometrica*, 48, 1-48.

[12] SIMS, C. A., AND ZHA, T. (1998). "Bayesian Methods for Dynamic Multivariate Models", *International Economic Review*, 39 (4), 949-968

[13] STOCK, J.H. AND M.W. WATSON (2001). "Vector Autoregressions," *Journal of Economic Perspectives*, 15, 101-115.

[14] TSAY, R. (2001). *Analysis of Financial Time Series.* John Wiley & Sons. New York.

[15] WATSON, M. (1994). "Vector Autoregressions and Cointegration," in *Handbook of Econometrics, Volume IV.* R.F. Engle and D. McFadden (eds.). Elsevier Science Ltd., Amsterdam.

[16] WAGGONER, D. F., AND ZHA, T. (1999). "Conditional Forecasts in Dynamic Multivariate Models," *Review of Economics and Statistics*, 81 (4), 639-651.

[17] ZHA, T. (1998). "Dynamic Multivariate Model for Use in Formulating Policy", *Economic Review*, Federal Reserve Bank of Atlanta, First Quarter, 1998.

12
Cointegration

12.1 Introduction

The regression theory of Chapter 6 and the VAR models discussed in the previous chapter are appropriate for modeling $I(0)$ data, like asset returns or growth rates of macroeconomic time series. Economic theory often implies equilibrium relationships between the levels of time series variables that are best described as being $I(1)$. Similarly, arbitrage arguments imply that the $I(1)$ prices of certain financial time series are linked. This chapter introduces the statistical concept of cointegration that is required to make sense of regression models and VAR models with $I(1)$ data.

The chapter is organized as follows. Section 12.2 gives an overview of the concepts of spurious regression and cointegration, and introduces the error correction model as a practical tool for utilizing cointegration with financial time series. Section 12.3 discusses residual-based tests for cointegration. Section 12.4 covers regression-based estimation of cointegrating vectors and error correction models. In Section 12.5, the connection between VAR models and cointegration is made, and Johansen's maximum likelihood methodology for cointegration modeling is outlined. Some technical details of the Johansen methodology are provided in the appendix to this chapter.

Excellent textbook treatments of the statistical theory of cointegration are given in Hamilton (1994), Johansen (1995) and Hayashi (2000). Applications of cointegration to finance may be found in Campbell, Lo and

MacKinlay (1997), Mills (1999), Alexander (2001), Cochrane (2001) and Tsay (2001).

12.2 Spurious Regression and Cointegration

12.2.1 Spurious Regression

The time series regression model discussed in Chapter 6 required all variables to be $I(0)$. In this case, the usual statistical results for the linear regression model hold. If some or all of the variables in the regression are $I(1)$ then the usual statistical results may or may not hold[1]. One important case in which the usual statistical results do not hold is *spurious regression* when all the regressors are $I(1)$ and not cointegrated. The following example illustrates.

Example 69 *An illustration of spurious regression using simulated data*

Consider two independent and not cointegrated $I(1)$ processes y_{1t} and y_{2t} such that

$$y_{it} = y_{it-1} + \varepsilon_{it}, \text{ where } \varepsilon_{it} \sim GWN(0,1), \ i = 1, 2$$

Following Granger and Newbold (1974), 250 observations for each series are simulated and plotted in Figure 12.1 using

```
> set.seed(458)
> e1 = rnorm(250)
> e2 = rnorm(250)
> y1 = cumsum(e1)
> y2 = cumsum(e2)
> tsplot(y1, y2, lty=c(1,3))
> legend(0, 15, c("y1","y2"), lty=c(1,3))
```

The data in the graph resemble stock prices or exchange rates. A visual inspection of the data suggests that the levels of the two series are positively related. Regressing y_{1t} on y_{2t} reinforces this observation:

```
> summary(OLS(y1~y2))

Call:
OLS(formula = y1 ~y2)
```

---

[1] A systematic technical analysis of the linear regression model with $I(1)$ and $I(0)$ variables is given in Sims, Stock and Watson (1990). Hamilton (1994) gives a nice summary of these results and Stock and Watson (1989) provides useful intuition and examples.

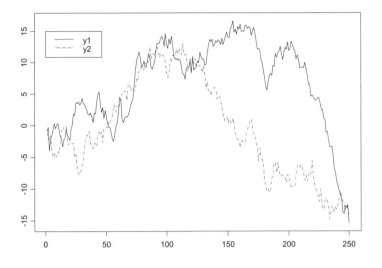

FIGURE 12.1. Two simulated independent $I(1)$ processes.

```
Residuals:
     Min        1Q   Median       3Q      Max
 -16.360    -4.352   -0.128    4.979   10.763


Coefficients:
              Value Std. Error t value Pr(>|t|)
(Intercept)  6.7445     0.3943   17.1033   0.0000
        y2   0.4083     0.0508    8.0352   0.0000


Regression Diagnostics:

         R-Squared 0.2066
Adjusted R-Squared 0.2034
Durbin-Watson Stat 0.0328


Residual standard error: 6.217 on 248 degrees of freedom
F-statistic: 64.56 on 1 and 248 degrees of freedom, the p-value
is 3.797e-014
```

The estimated slope coefficient is 0.408 with a large t-statistic of 8.035 and the regression R^2 is moderate at 0.201. The only suspicious statistic is the very low Durbin-Watson statistic suggesting strong residual autocorrelation. These statistics are representative of the spurious regression phenomenon with $I(1)$ that are not cointegrated. If Δy_{1t} is regressed on Δy_{2t} the correct relationship between the two series is revealed

```
> summary(OLS(diff(y1)~diff(y2)))

Call:
OLS(formula = diff(y1) ~diff(y2))

Residuals:
     Min      1Q  Median      3Q     Max
  -3.6632 -0.7706 -0.0074  0.6983  2.7184

Coefficients:
             Value Std. Error t value Pr(>|t|)
(Intercept) -0.0565  0.0669   -0.8447  0.3991
   diff(y2)  0.0275  0.0642    0.4290  0.6683

Regression Diagnostics:

        R-Squared  0.0007
Adjusted R-Squared -0.0033
Durbin-Watson Stat  1.9356

Residual standard error: 1.055 on 247 degrees of freedom
F-statistic: 0.184 on 1 and 247 degrees of freedom, the p-value
is 0.6683
```

Similar results to those above occur if $cov(\varepsilon_{1t}, \varepsilon_{2t}) \neq 0$. The levels regression remains spurious (no real long-run common movement in levels), but the differences regression will reflect the non-zero contemporaneous correlation between Δy_{1t} and Δy_{2t}.

Statistical Implications of Spurious Regression

Let $\mathbf{Y}_t = (y_{1t}, \ldots, y_{nt})'$ denote an $(n \times 1)$ vector of $I(1)$ time series that are not cointegrated. Using the partition $\mathbf{Y}_t = (y_{1t}, \mathbf{Y}'_{2t})'$, consider the least squares regression of y_{1t} on $\mathbf{Y}_{2t}$ giving the fitted model

$$y_{1t} = \hat{\boldsymbol{\beta}}'_2 \mathbf{Y}_{2t} + \hat{u}_t \tag{12.1}$$

Since y_{1t} is not cointegrated with $\mathbf{Y}_{2t}$ (12.1) is a *spurious regression* and the true value of $\boldsymbol{\beta}_2$ is zero. The following results about the behavior of $\hat{\boldsymbol{\beta}}_2$ in the spurious regression (12.1) are due to Phillips (1986):

- $\hat{\boldsymbol{\beta}}_2$ does not converge in probability to zero but instead converges in distribution to a non-normal random variable not necessarily centered at zero. This is the spurious regression phenomenon.

- The usual OLS t-statistics for testing that the elements of $\boldsymbol{\beta}_2$ are zero diverge to $\pm\infty$ as $T \to \infty$. Hence, with a large enough sample it will appear that $\mathbf{Y}_t$ is cointegrated when it is not if the usual asymptotic normal inference is used.

- The usual R^2 from the regression converges to unity as $T \to \infty$ so that the model will appear to fit well even though it is misspecified.

- Regression with $I(1)$ data only makes sense when the data are cointegrated.

12.2.2   Cointegration

Let $\mathbf{Y}_t = (y_{1t}, \ldots, y_{nt})'$ denote an $(n \times 1)$ vector of $I(1)$ time series. $\mathbf{Y}_t$ is *cointegrated* if there exists an $(n \times 1)$ vector $\boldsymbol{\beta} = (\beta_1, \ldots, \beta_n)'$ such that

$$\boldsymbol{\beta}' \mathbf{Y}_t = \beta_1 y_{1t} + \cdots + \beta_n y_{nt} \sim I(0) \tag{12.2}$$

In words, the nonstationary time series in $\mathbf{Y}_t$ are cointegrated if there is a linear combination of them that is stationary or $I(0)$. If some elements of $\boldsymbol{\beta}$ are equal to zero then only the subset of the time series in $\mathbf{Y}_t$ with non-zero coefficients is cointegrated. The linear combination $\boldsymbol{\beta}' \mathbf{Y}_t$ is often motivated by economic theory and referred to as a *long-run equilibrium* relationship. The intuition is that $I(1)$ time series with a long-run equilibrium relationship cannot drift too far apart from the equilibrium because economic forces will act to restore the equilibrium relationship.

Normalization

The cointegration vector $\boldsymbol{\beta}$ in (12.2) is not unique since for any scalar c the linear combination $c\boldsymbol{\beta}' \mathbf{Y}_t = \boldsymbol{\beta}^{*'} \mathbf{Y}_t \sim I(0)$. Hence, some *normalization* assumption is required to uniquely identify $\boldsymbol{\beta}$. A typical normalization is

$$\boldsymbol{\beta} = (1, -\beta_2, \ldots, -\beta_n)'$$

so that the cointegration relationship may be expressed as

$$\boldsymbol{\beta}' \mathbf{Y}_t = y_{1t} - \beta_2 y_{2t} - \cdots - \beta_n y_{nt} \sim I(0)$$

or

$$y_{1t} = \beta_2 y_{2t} + \cdots + \beta_n y_{nt} + u_t \tag{12.3}$$

where $u_t \sim I(0)$. In (12.3), the error term u_t is often referred to as the *disequilibrium error* or the *cointegrating residual*. In long-run equilibrium, the disequilibrium error u_t is zero and the long-run equilibrium relationship is

$$y_{1t} = \beta_2 y_{2t} + \cdots + \beta_n y_{nt}$$

Multiple Cointegrating Relationships

If the $(n \times 1)$ vector $\mathbf{Y}_t$ is cointegrated there may be $0 < r < n$ linearly independent cointegrating vectors. For example, let $n = 3$ and suppose there are $r = 2$ cointegrating vectors $\boldsymbol{\beta}_1 = (\beta_{11}, \beta_{12}, \beta_{13})'$ and $\boldsymbol{\beta}_2 = (\beta_{21}, \beta_{22}, \beta_{23})'$. Then $\boldsymbol{\beta}_1' \mathbf{Y}_t = \beta_{11} y_{1t} + \beta_{12} y_{2t} + \beta_{13} y_{3t} \sim I(0)$, $\boldsymbol{\beta}_2' \mathbf{Y}_t = \beta_{21} y_{1t} + \beta_{22} y_{2t} + \beta_{23} y_{3t} \sim I(0)$ and the (3×2) matrix

$$\mathbf{B}' = \left(\begin{array}{c} \boldsymbol{\beta}_1' \\ \boldsymbol{\beta}_2' \end{array} \right) = \left(\begin{array}{ccc} \beta_{11} & \beta_{12} & \beta_{13} \\ \beta_{21} & \beta_{22} & \beta_{33} \end{array} \right)$$

forms a *basis* for the space of cointegrating vectors. The linearly independent vectors $\boldsymbol{\beta}_1$ and $\boldsymbol{\beta}_2$ in the cointegrating basis $\mathbf{B}$ are not unique unless some normalization assumptions are made. Furthermore, any linear combination of $\boldsymbol{\beta}_1$ and $\boldsymbol{\beta}_2$, e.g. $\boldsymbol{\beta}_3 = c_1 \boldsymbol{\beta}_1 + c_2 \boldsymbol{\beta}_2$ where c_1 and c_2 are constants, is also a cointegrating vector.

Examples of Cointegration and Common Trends in Economics and Finance

Cointegration naturally arises in economics and finance. In economics, cointegration is most often associated with economic theories that imply equilibrium relationships between time series variables. The permanent income model implies cointegration between consumption and income, with consumption being the common trend. Money demand models imply cointegration between money, income, prices and interest rates. Growth theory models imply cointegration between income, consumption and investment, with productivity being the common trend. Purchasing power parity implies cointegration between the nominal exchange rate and foreign and domestic prices. Covered interest rate parity implies cointegration between forward and spot exchange rates. The Fisher equation implies cointegration between nominal interest rates and inflation. The expectations hypothesis of the term structure implies cointegration between nominal interest rates at different maturities. The equilibrium relationships implied by these economic theories are referred to as *long-run equilibrium* relationships, because the economic forces that act in response to deviations from equilibriium may take a long time to restore equilibrium. As a result, cointegration is modeled using long spans of low frequency time series data measured monthly, quarterly or annually.

In finance, cointegration may be a high frequency relationship or a low frequency relationship. Cointegration at a high frequency is motivated by arbitrage arguments. The *Law of One Price* implies that identical assets must sell for the same price to avoid arbitrage opportunities. This implies cointegration between the prices of the same asset trading on different markets, for example. Similar arbitrage arguments imply cointegration between spot and futures prices, and spot and forward prices, and bid and ask prices. Here the terminology long-run equilibrium relationship is somewhat misleading because the economic forces acting to eliminate arbitrage opportunities work very quickly. Cointegration is appropriately modeled using short spans of high frequency data in seconds, minutes, hours or days. Cointegration at a low frequency is motivated by economic equilibrium theories linking assets prices or expected returns to fundamentals. For example, the present value model of stock prices states that a stock's price is an expected discounted present value of its expected future dividends or earnings. This links the behavior of stock prices at low frequencies to the behavior of dividends or earnings. In this case, cointegration is modeled using low frequency data and is used to explain the long-run behavior of stock prices or expected returns.

12.2.3 Cointegration and Common Trends

If the $(n \times 1)$ vector time series $\mathbf{Y}_t$ is cointegrated with $0 < r < n$ cointegrating vectors then there are $n - r$ *common $I(1)$ stochastic trends*. To illustrate the duality between cointegration and common trends, let $\mathbf{Y}_t = (y_{1t}, y_{2t})' \sim I(1)$ and $\boldsymbol{\varepsilon}_t = (\varepsilon_{1t}, \varepsilon_{2t}, \varepsilon_{3t})' \sim I(0)$ and suppose that $\mathbf{Y}_t$ is cointegrated with cointegrating vector $\boldsymbol{\beta} = (1, -\beta_2)'$. This cointegration relationship may be represented as

$$y_{1t} = \beta_2 \sum_{s=1}^{t} \varepsilon_{1s} + \varepsilon_{3t}$$

$$y_{2t} = \sum_{s=1}^{t} \varepsilon_{1s} + \varepsilon_{2t}$$

The common stochastic trend is $\sum_{s=1}^{t} \varepsilon_{1s}$. Notice that the cointegrating relationship annihilates the common stochastic trend:

$$\boldsymbol{\beta}'\mathbf{Y}_t = \beta_2 \sum_{s=1}^{t} \varepsilon_{1s} + \varepsilon_{3t} - \beta_2 \left(\sum_{s=1}^{t} \varepsilon_{1s} + \varepsilon_{2t} \right) = \varepsilon_{3t} - \beta_2 \varepsilon_{2t} \sim I(0).$$

12.2.4 Simulating Cointegrated Systems

Cointegrated systems may be conveniently simulated using Phillips' (1991) *triangular representation*. For example, consider a bivariate cointegrated system for $\mathbf{Y}_t = (y_{1t}, y_{2t})'$ with cointegrating vector $\boldsymbol{\beta} = (1, -\beta_2)'$. A triangular representation has the form

$$y_{1t} = \beta_2 y_{2t} + u_t, \text{ where } u_t \sim I(0) \tag{12.4}$$

$$y_{2t} = y_{2t-1} + v_t, \text{ where } v_t \sim I(0) \tag{12.5}$$

The first equation describes the long-run equilibrium relationship with an $I(0)$ disequilibrium error u_t. The second equation specifies y_{2t} as the common stochastic trend with innovation v_t:

$$y_{2t} = y_{20} + \sum_{j=1}^{t} v_j.$$

In general, the innovations u_t and v_t may be contemporaneously and serially correlated. The time series structure of these innovations characterizes the short-run dynamics of the cointegrated system. The system (12.4)-(12.5) with $\beta_2 = 1$, for example, might be used to model the behavior of the logarithm of spot and forward prices, spot and futures prices or stock prices and dividends.

Example 70 *Simulated bivariate cointegrated system*

Consider simulating $T = 250$ observations from the system (12.4)-(12.5) using $\beta = (1, -1)'$, $u_t = 0.75u_{t-1} + \varepsilon_t$, $\varepsilon_t \sim iid$ $N(0, (0.5)^2)$ and $v_t \sim iid$ $N(0, (0.5)^2)$. The S-PLUS code is

```
> set.seed(432)
> e = rmvnorm(250, mean=rep(0,2), sd=c(0.5,0.5))
> u.ar1 = arima.sim(model=list(ar=0.75), innov=e[,1])
> y2 = cumsum(e[,2])
> y1 = y2 + u.ar1
> par(mfrow=c(2,1))
> tsplot(y1, y2, lty=c(1,3),
+ main="Simulated bivariate cointegrated system",
+ sub="1 cointegrating vector, 1 common trend")
> legend(0, 7, legend=c("y1","y2"), lty=c(1,3))
> tsplot(u.ar1, main="Cointegrating residual")
```

Figure 12.2 shows the simulated data for y_{1t} and y_{2t} along with the cointegrating residual $u_t = y_{1t} - y_{2t}$. Since y_{1t} and y_{2t} share a common stochastic trend they follow each other closely. The impulse response function for u_t may be used to determine the speed of adjustment to long-run equilibrium. Since u_t is an AR(1) with $\phi = 0.75$ the half life of a shock is $\ln(0.5)/\ln(0.75) = 2.4$ time periods.

Next, consider a trivariate cointegrated system for $\mathbf{Y}_t = (y_{1t}, y_{2t}, y_{3t})'$. With a trivariate system there may be one or two cointegrating vectors. With one cointegrating vector there are two common stochastic trends and with two cointegrating vectors there is one common trend. A triangular representation with one cointegrating vector $\beta = (1, -\beta_2, -\beta_3)'$ and two

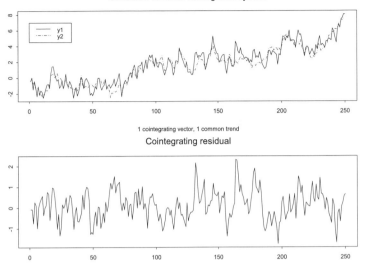

FIGURE 12.2. Simulated bivariate cointegrated system with $\boldsymbol{\beta} = (1, -1)'$.

stochastic trends is

$$
\begin{align}
y_{1t} &= \beta_2 y_{2t} + \beta_3 y_{3t} + u_t, \text{ where } u_t \sim I(0) \tag{12.6} \\
y_{2t} &= y_{2t-1} + v_t, \text{ where } v_t \sim I(0) \tag{12.7} \\
y_{3t} &= y_{3t-1} + w_t, \text{ where } w_t \sim I(0) \tag{12.8}
\end{align}
$$

The first equation describes the long-run equilibrium and the second and third equations specify the common stochastic trends. An example of a trivariate cointegrated system with one cointegrating vector is a system of nominal exchange rates, home country price indices and foreign country price indices. A cointegrating vector $\boldsymbol{\beta} = (1, -1, -1)'$ implies that the real exchange rate is stationary.

Example 71 *Simulated trivariate cointegrated system with 1 cointegrating vector*

The S-PLUS code for simulating $T = 250$ observation from (12.6)-(12.8) with $\boldsymbol{\beta} = (1, -0.5, -0.5)'$, $u_t = 0.75 u_{t-1} + \varepsilon_t$, $\varepsilon_t \sim iid\ N(0, (0.5)^2)$, $v_t \sim iid\ N(0, (0.5)^2)$ and $w_t \sim iid\ N(0, (0.5)^2)$ is

```
> set.seed(573)
> e = rmvnorm(250, mean=rep(0,3), sd=c(0.5,0.5,0.5))
> u1.ar1 = arima.sim(model=list(ar=0.75), innov=e[,1])
> y2 = cumsum(e[,2])
```

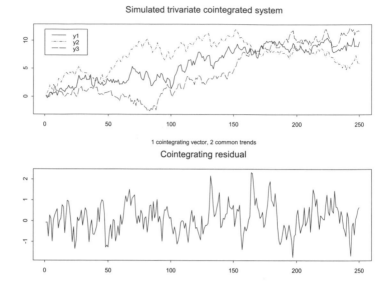

FIGURE 12.3. Simulated trivariate cointegrated system with one cointegrating vector $\beta = (1, -0.5, -0.5)'$ and two stochastic trends.

```
> y3 = cumsum(e[,3])
> y1 = 0.5*y2 + 0.5*y3 + u1.ar1
> par(mfrow=c(2,1))
> tsplot(y1, y2, y3, lty=c(1,3,4),
+ main="Simulated trivariate cointegrated system",
+ sub="1 cointegrating vector, 2 common trends")
> legend(0, 12, legend=c("y1","y2","y3"), lty=c(1,3,4))
> tsplot(u.ar1, main="Cointegrating residual")
```

Figure 12.3 illustrates the simulated data. Here, y_{2t} and y_{3t} are the two independent common trends and $y_{1t} = 0.5y_{2t} + 0.5y_{3t} + u_t$ is the average of the two trends plus an AR(1) residual.

Finally, consider a trivariate cointegrated system with two cointegrating vectors and one common stochastic trend. A triangular representation for this system with cointegrating vectors $\beta_1 = (1, 0, -\beta_{13})'$ and $\beta_2 = (0, 1, -\beta_{23})'$ is

$$y_{1t} = \beta_{13}y_{3t} + u_t, \text{ where } u_t \sim I(0) \tag{12.9}$$

$$y_{2t} = \beta_{23}y_{3t} + v_t, \text{ where } v_t \sim I(0) \tag{12.10}$$

$$y_{3t} = y_{3t-1} + w_t, \text{ where } w_t \sim I(0) \tag{12.11}$$

Here the first two equations describe two long-run equilibrium relations and the third equation gives the common stochastic trend. An example in finance of such a system is the term structure of interest rates where y_3 represents the short rate and y_1 and y_2 represent two different long rates. The cointegrating relationships would indicate that the spreads between the long and short rates are stationary.

Example 72 *Simulated trivariate cointegrated system with 2 cointegrating vectors*

The S-PLUS code for simulating $T = 250$ observation from (12.9)-(12.11) with $\beta_1 = (1, 0, -1)'$, $\beta_2 = (0, 1, -1)'$, $u_t = 0.75u_{t-1} + \varepsilon_t$, $\varepsilon_t \sim iid$ $N(0, (0.5)^2)$, $v_t = 0.75v_{t-1} + \eta_t$, $\eta_t \sim iid$ $N(0, (0.5)^2)$ and $w_t \sim iid$ $N(0, (0.5)^2)$ is

```
> set.seed(573)
> e = rmvnorm(250,mean=rep(0,3), sd=c(0.5,0.5,0.5))
> u.ar1 = arima.sim(model=list(ar=0.75), innov=e[,1])
> v.ar1 = arima.sim(model=list(ar=0.75), innov=e[,2])
> y3 = cumsum(e[,3])
> y1 = y3 + u.ar1
> y2 = y3 + v.ar1
> par(mfrow=c(2,1))
> tsplot(y1, y2, y3, lty=c(1,3,4),
+ main="Simulated trivariate cointegrated system",
+ sub="2 cointegrating vectors, 1 common trend")
> legend(0, 10, legend=c("y1","y2","y3"), lty=c(1,3,4))
> tsplot(u.ar1, v.ar1, lty=c(1,3),
+ main="Cointegrated residuals")
> legend(0, -1, legend=c("u","v"), lty=c(1,3))
```

12.2.5 Cointegration and Error Correction Models

Consider a bivariate $I(1)$ vector $\mathbf{Y}_t = (y_{1t}, y_{2t})'$ and assume that $\mathbf{Y}_t$ is cointegrated with cointegrating vector $\boldsymbol{\beta} = (1, -\beta_2)'$ so that $\boldsymbol{\beta}'\mathbf{Y}_t = y_{1t} - \beta_2 y_{2t}$ is $I(0)$. In an extremely influential and important paper, Engle and Granger (1987) showed that cointegration implies the existence of an *error correction model* (ECM) of the form

$$\Delta y_{1t} = c_1 + \alpha_1(y_{1t-1} - \beta_2 y_{2t-1}) \qquad (12.12)$$
$$+ \sum_j \psi_{11}^j \Delta y_{1t-j} + \sum_j \psi_{12}^j \Delta y_{2t-j} + \varepsilon_{1t}$$

$$\Delta y_{2t} = c_2 + \alpha_2(y_{1t-1} - \beta_2 y_{2t-1}) \qquad (12.13)$$
$$+ \sum_j \psi_{21}^j \Delta y_{1t-j} + \sum_j \psi_{22}^2 \Delta y_{2t-j} + \varepsilon_{2t}$$

that describes the dynamic behavior of y_{1t} and y_{2t}. The ECM links the long-run equilibrium relationship implied by cointegration with the short-

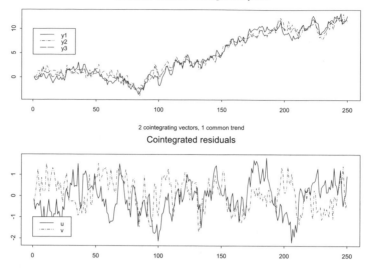

FIGURE 12.4. Simulated trivatiate cointegrated system with two cointegrating vectors $\boldsymbol{\beta}_1 = (1, 0, -1)'$, $\boldsymbol{\beta}_2 = (0, 1, -1)'$ and one common trend.

run dynamic adjustment mechanism that describes how the variables react when they move out of long-run equilibrium. This ECM makes the concept of cointegration useful for modeling financial time series.

Example 73 *Bivariate ECM for stock prices and dividends*

As an example of an ECM, let s_t denote the log of stock prices and d_t denote the log of dividends and assume that $\mathbf{Y}_t = (s_t, d_t)'$ is $I(1)$. If the log dividend-price ratio is $I(0)$ then the logs of stock prices and dividends are cointegrated with $\boldsymbol{\beta} = (1, -1)'$. That is, the long-run equilibrium is

$$d_t = s_t + \mu + u_t$$

where μ is the mean of the log dividend-price ratio, and u_t is an $I(0)$ random variable representing the dynamic behavior of the log dividend-price ratio (disequilibrium error). Suppose the ECM has the form

$$
\begin{aligned}
\Delta s_t &= c_s + \alpha_s(d_{t-1} - s_{t-1} - \mu) + \varepsilon_{st} \\
\Delta d_t &= c_d + \alpha_d(d_{t-1} - s_{t-1} - \mu) + \varepsilon_{dt}
\end{aligned}
$$

where $c_s > 0$ and $c_d > 0$. The first equation relates the growth rate of dividends to the lagged disequilibrium error $d_{t-1} - s_{t-1} - \mu$, and the second equation relates the growth rate of stock prices to the lagged disequilibrium as well. The reactions of s_t and d_t to the disequilibrium error are captured by the *adjustment coefficients* α_s and α_d.

Consider the special case of (12.12)-(12.13) where $\alpha_d = 0$ and $\alpha_s = 0.5$. The VECM equations become

$$
\begin{aligned}
\Delta s_t &= c_s + 0.5(d_{t-1} - s_{t-1} - \mu) + \varepsilon_{st}, \\
\Delta d_t &= c_d + \varepsilon_{dt}.
\end{aligned}
$$

so that only s_t responds to the lagged disequilibrium error. Notice that $E[\Delta s_t | \mathbf{Y}_{t-1}] = c_s + 0.5(d_{t-1} - s_{t-1} - \mu)$ and $E[\Delta d_t | \mathbf{Y}_{t-1}] = c_d$. Consider three situations:

1. $d_{t-1} - s_{t-1} - \mu = 0$. Then $E[\Delta s_t | \mathbf{Y}_{t-1}] = c_s$ and $E[\Delta d_t | \mathbf{Y}_{t-1}] = c_d$, so that c_s and c_d represent the growth rates of stock prices and dividends in long-run equilibrium.

2. $d_{t-1} - s_{t-1} - \mu > 0$. Then $E[\Delta s_t | \mathbf{Y}_{t-1}] = c_s + 0.5(d_{t-1} - s_{t-1} - \mu) > c_s$. Here the dividend yield has increased above its long-run mean (positive disequilibrium error) and the ECM predicts that s_t will grow faster than its long-run rate to restore the dividend yield to its long-run mean. Notice that the magnitude of the adjustment coefficient $\alpha_s = 0.5$ controls the speed at which s_t responds to the disequilibrium error.

3. $d_{t-1} - s_{t-1} - \mu < 0$. Then $E[\Delta s_t | \mathbf{Y}_{t-1}] = c_s + 0.5(d_{t-1} - s_{t-1} - \mu) < c_s$. Here the dividend yield has decreased below its long-run mean (negative disequilibrium error) and the ECM predicts that s_t will grow more slowly than its long-run rate to restore the dividend yield to its long-run mean.

In Case 1, there is no expected adjustment since the model was in long-run equilibrium in the previous period. In Case 2, the model was above long-run equilibrium last period so the expected adjustment in s_t is downward toward equilibrium. In Case 3, the model was below long-run equilibrium last period and so the expected adjustment is upward toward the equilibrium. This discussion illustrates why the model is called an error correction model. When the variables are out of long-run equilibrium, there are economic forces, captured by the adjustment coefficients, that push the model back to long-run equilibrium. The speed of adjustment toward equilibrium is determined by the magnitude of α_s. In the present example, $\alpha_s = 0.5$ which implies that roughly one half of the disequilibrium error is corrected in one time period. If $\alpha_s = 1$ then the entire disequilibrium is corrected in one period. If $\alpha_s = 1.5$ then the correction overshoots the long-run equilibrium.

12.3   Residual-Based Tests for Cointegration

Let the $(n \times 1)$ vector $\mathbf{Y}_t$ be $I(1)$. Recall, $\mathbf{Y}_t$ is cointegrated with $0 < r < n$ cointegrating vectors if there exists an $(r \times n)$ matrix $\mathbf{B}'$ such that

$$\mathbf{B}'\mathbf{Y}_t = \begin{pmatrix} \boldsymbol{\beta}_1'\mathbf{Y}_t \\ \vdots \\ \boldsymbol{\beta}_r'\mathbf{Y}_t \end{pmatrix} = \begin{pmatrix} u_{1t} \\ \vdots \\ u_{rt} \end{pmatrix} \sim I(0)$$

Testing for cointegration may be thought of as testing for the existence of long-run equilibria among the elements of $\mathbf{Y}_t$. Cointegration tests cover two situations:

- There is at most one cointegrating vector

- There are possibly $0 \leq r < n$ cointegrating vectors.

The first case was originally considered by Engle and Granger (1986) and they developed a simple two-step residual-based testing procedure based on regression techniques. The second case was originally considered by Johansen (1988) who developed a sophisticated sequential procedure for determining the existence of cointegration and for determining the number of cointegrating relationships based on maximum likelihood techniques. This section explains Engle and Granger's two-step procedure. Johansen's more general procedure will be discussed later on.

Engle and Granger's two-step procedure for determining if the $(n \times 1)$ vector $\boldsymbol{\beta}$ is a cointegrating vector is as follows:

- Form the cointegrating residual $\boldsymbol{\beta}'\mathbf{Y}_t = u_t$

- Perform a unit root test on u_t to determine if it is $I(0)$.

The null hypothesis in the Engle-Granger procedure is no-cointegration and the alternative is cointegration. There are two cases to consider. In the first case, the proposed cointegrating vector $\boldsymbol{\beta}$ is pre-specified (not estimated). For example, economic theory may imply specific values for the elements in $\boldsymbol{\beta}$ such as $\boldsymbol{\beta} = (1, -1)'$. The cointegrating residual is then readily constructed using the prespecified cointegrating vector. In the second case, the proposed cointegrating vector is estimated from the data and an estimate of the cointegrating residual $\hat{\boldsymbol{\beta}}'\mathbf{Y}_t = \hat{u}_t$ is formed. Tests for cointegration using a pre-specified cointegrating vector are generally much more powerful than tests employing an estimated vector.

12.3.1   Testing for Cointegration When the Cointegrating Vector Is Pre-specified

Let $\mathbf{Y}_t$ denote an $(n \times 1)$ vector of $I(1)$ time series, let $\boldsymbol{\beta}$ denote an $(n \times 1)$ prespecified cointegrating vector and let $u_t = \boldsymbol{\beta}'\mathbf{Y}_t$ denote the prespecified

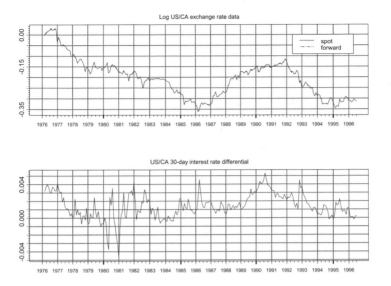

FIGURE 12.5. Log of US/CA spot and 30-day exchange rates and 30-day interest rate differential.

cointegrating residual. The hypotheses to be tested are

$$H_0 \quad : \quad u_t = \boldsymbol{\beta}' \mathbf{Y}_t \sim I(1) \text{ (no cointegration)} \qquad (12.14)$$

$$H_1 \quad : \quad u_t = \boldsymbol{\beta}' \mathbf{Y}_t \sim I(0) \text{ (cointegration)}$$

Any unit root test statistic may be used to evaluate the above hypotheses. The most popular choices are the ADF and PP statistics. Cointegration is found if the unit root test rejects the no-cointegration null. It should be kept in mind, however, that the cointegrating residual may include deterministic terms (constant or trend) and the unit root tests should account for these terms accordingly. See chapter four for details about the application of unit root tests.

Example 74 *Testing for cointegration between spot and forward exchange rates using a known cointegrating vector*

In international finance, the covered interest rate parity arbitrage relationship states that the difference between the logarithm of spot and forward exchange rates is equal to the difference between nominal domestic and foreign interest rates. It seems reasonable to believe that interest rate spreads are $I(0)$ which implies that spot and forward rates are cointegrated with cointegrating vector $\boldsymbol{\beta} = (1, -1)'$. To illustrate, consider the log monthly spot, s_t, and 30 day forward, f_t, exchange rates between the

US and Canada over the period February 1976 through June 1996 taken from the S+FinMetrics "timeSeries" object lexrates.dat

```
> uscn.s = lexrates.dat[,"USCNS"]
> uscn.s@title = "Log of US/CA spot exchange rate"
> uscn.f = lexrates.dat[,"USCNF"]
> uscn.f@title = "Log of US/CA 30-day forward exchange rate"
> u = uscn.s - uscn.f
> colIds(u) = "USCNID"
> u@title = "US/CA 30-day interest rate differential"
```

The interest rate differential is constructed using the pre-specified cointe-grating vector $\beta = (1, -1)'$ as $u_t = s_t - f_t$. The spot and forward exchange rates and interest rate differential are illustrated in Figure 12.5. Visually, the spot and forward exchange rates clearly share a common trend and the interest rate differential appears to be $I(0)$. In addition, there is no clear deterministic trend behavior in the exchange rates. The S+FinMetrics function unitroot may be used to test the null hypothesis that s_t and f_t are not cointegrated ($u_t \sim I(1)$). The ADF t-test based on 11 lags and a constant in the test regression leads to the rejection at the 5% level of the hypothesis that s_t and f_t are not cointegrated with cointegrating vector $\beta = (1, -1)'$:

```
> unitroot(u, trend="c", method="adf", lags=11)

Test for Unit Root: Augmented DF Test

Null Hypothesis: there is a unit root
   Type of Test: t-test
 Test Statistic: -2.881
        P-value: 0.04914

Coefficients:
    lag1    lag2    lag3    lag4    lag5    lag6    lag7
 -0.1464 -0.1171 -0.0702 -0.1008 -0.1234 -0.1940  0.0128

    lag8    lag9   lag10   lag11 constant
 -0.1235  0.0550  0.2106 -0.1382  0.0002

Degrees of freedom: 234 total; 222 residual
Time period: from Jan 1977 to Jun 1996
Residual standard error: 8.595e-4
```

12.3.2 Testing for Cointegration When the Cointegrating Vector Is Estimated

Let $\mathbf{Y}_t$ denote an $(n \times 1)$ vector of $I(1)$ time series and let $\boldsymbol{\beta}$ denote an $(n \times 1)$ unknown cointegrating vector. The hypotheses to be tested are given in (12.14). Since $\boldsymbol{\beta}$ is unknown, to use the Engle-Granger procedure it must be first estimated from the data. Before $\boldsymbol{\beta}$ can be estimated some normalization assumption must be made to uniquely identify it. A common normalization is to specify the first element in $\mathbf{Y}_t$ as the dependent variable and the rest as the explanatory variables. Then $\mathbf{Y}_t = (y_{1t}, \mathbf{Y}_{2t}')'$ where $\mathbf{Y}_{2t} = (y_{2t}, \ldots, y_{nt})'$ is an $((n-1) \times 1)$ vector and the cointegrating vector is normalized as $\boldsymbol{\beta} = (1, -\boldsymbol{\beta}_2')'$. Engle and Granger propose estimating the normalized cointegrating vector $\boldsymbol{\beta}_2$ by least squares from the regression

$$y_{1t} = c + \boldsymbol{\beta}_2' \mathbf{Y}_{2t} + u_t \tag{12.15}$$

and testing the no-cointegration hypothesis (12.14) with a unit root test using the estimated cointegrating residual

$$\hat{u}_t = y_{1t} - \hat{c} - \hat{\boldsymbol{\beta}}_2 \mathbf{Y}_{2t} \tag{12.16}$$

where $\hat{c}$ and $\hat{\boldsymbol{\beta}}_2$ are the least squares estimates of c and $\boldsymbol{\beta}_2$. The unit root test regression in this case is without deterministic terms (constant or constant and trend). Phillips and Ouliaris (1990) show that ADF and PP unit root tests (t-tests and normalized bias) applied to the estimated cointegrating residual (12.16) *do not* have the usual Dickey-Fuller distributions under the null hypothesis (12.14) of no-cointegration. Instead, due to the spurious regression phenomenon under the null hypothesis (12.14), the distribution of the ADF and PP unit root tests have asymptotic distributions that are functions of Wiener processes that depend on the deterministic terms in the regression (12.15) used to estimate $\boldsymbol{\beta}_2$ *and* the number of variables, $n-1$, in $\mathbf{Y}_{2t}$. These distributions are known as the *Phillips-Ouliaris* (PO) distributions, and are described in Phillips and Ouliaris (1990). To further complicate matters, Hansen (1992) showed the appropriate PO distributions of the ADF and PP unit root tests applied to the residuals (12.16) also depend on the trend behavior of y_{1t} and $\mathbf{Y}_{2t}$ as follows:

Case I: $\mathbf{Y}_{2t}$ and y_{1t} are both $I(1)$ without drift. The ADF and PP unit root test statistics follow the PO distributions, adjusted for a constant, with dimension parameter $n-1$.

Case II: $\mathbf{Y}_{2t}$ is $I(1)$ with drift and y_{1t} may or may not be $I(1)$ with drift. The ADF and PP unit root test statistics follow the PO distributions, adjusted for a constant and trend, with dimension parameter $n-2$. If $n-2 = 0$ then the ADF and PP unit root test statistics follow the DF distributions adjusted for a constant and trend.

Case III: $\mathbf{Y}_{2t}$ is $I(1)$ without drift and y_{1t} is $I(1)$ with drift. In this case, $\boldsymbol{\beta}_2$ should be estimated from the regression

$$y_{1t} = c + \delta t + \boldsymbol{\beta}'_2 \mathbf{Y}_{2t} + u_t \tag{12.17}$$

The resulting ADF and PP unit root test statistics on the residuals from (12.17) follow the PO distributions, adjusted for a constant and trend, with dimension parameter $n - 1$.

Computing Quantiles and P-values from the Phillips-Ouliaris Distributions Using the S+FinMetrics Functions pcoint and qcoint

The S+FinMetrics functions qcoint and pcoint, based on the response surface methodology of MacKinnon (1996), may be used to compute quantiles and p-values from the PO distributions. For example, to compute the 10%, 5% and 1% quantiles from the PO distribution for the ADF t-statistic, adjusted for a constant, with $n - 1 = 3$ and a sample size $T = 100$ use

```
> qcoint(c(0.1,0.05,0.01), n.sample=100, n.series=4,
+ trend="c", statistic="t")
[1] -3.8945 -4.2095 -4.8274
```

Notice that the argument n.series represents the total number of variables n. To adjust the PO distributions for a constant and trend set trend="ct". To compute the PO distribution for the ADF normalized bias statistic set statistic="n". The quantiles from the PO distributions can be very different from the quantiles from the DF distributions, especially if $n - 1$ is large. To illustrate, the 10%, 5% and 1% quantiles from the DF distribution for the ADF t-statistic with a sample size $T = 100$ are

```
> qunitroot(c(0.1,0.05,0.01), n.sample=100,
+ trend="c", statistic="t")
[1] -2.5824 -2.8906 -3.4970
```

The following examples illustrate testing for cointegration using an estimated cointegrating vector.

Example 75 *Testing for cointegration between spot and forward exchange rates using an estimated cointegrating vector*

Consider testing for cointegration between spot and forward exchange rates assuming the cointegrating vector is not known using the same data as in the previous example. Let $\mathbf{Y}_t = (s_t, f_t)'$ and normalize the cointegrating vector on s_t so that $\boldsymbol{\beta} = (1, -\beta_2)'$. The normalized cointegrating coefficient β_2 is estimated by least squares from the regression

$$s_t = c + \beta_2 f_t + u_t$$

giving the estimated cointegrating residual $\hat{u}_t = s_t - \hat{c} - \hat{\beta}_2 f_t$. The OLS function in S+FinMetrics is used to estimate the above regression:

```
> uscn.ts = seriesMerge(uscn.s,uscn.f)
> ols.fit = OLS(USCNS~USCNF,data=uscn.ts)
> ols.fit

Call:
OLS(formula = USCNS ~USCNF, data = uscn.ts)

Coefficients:
 (Intercept)   USCNF
   0.0023      1.0041

Degrees of freedom: 245 total; 243 residual
Time period: from Feb 1976 to Jun 1996
Residual standard error: 0.001444
```

The estimated value of β_2 is 1.004 and is almost identical to the value $\beta_2 = 1$ implied by covered interest parity. The estimated cointegrating residual $\hat{u}_t$ is extracted from the least squres fit using

```
> u.hat = residuals(ols.fit)
```

Next, the no-cointegration hypothesis (12.14) is tested using the ADF and PP t-tests. Because the mean of $\hat{u}_t$ is zero, the unitroot test regressions are estimated without a constant or trend. The ADF t-statistic is computed using 11 lags, as in the previous example, and the PP t-statistic is computed using an automatic lag truncation parameter:

```
> adf.fit = unitroot(u.hat,trend="nc",method="adf",lags=11)
> adf.tstat = adf.fit$sval
> adf.tstat
    lag1
 -2.721

> pp.fit = unitroot(u.hat,trend="nc",method="pp")
> pp.tstat = pp.fit$sval
> pp.tstat
    lag1
 -5.416
```

The ADF t-statistic is -2.721 whereas the PP t-statistic is -5.416. Since s_t and f_t are both $I(1)$ without drift, the 10%, 5% and 1% quantiles from the approrpiate Phillips-Ouliaris distribution for the ADF t-statistic is

```
> qcoint(c(0.10,0.05,0.01),n.sample=nrow(uscn.s),n.series=2,
+ trend="c",statistic="t")
[1] -3.062 -3.361 -3.942
```

The no-cointegration null hypothesis is not rejected at the 10% level using the ADF t-statistic but is rejected at the 1% level using the PP t-statistic. The p-values for the ADF and PP t-statistics are

```
> pcoint(adf.tstat, n.sample=nrow(uscn.s), n.series=2,
+ trend="c", statistic="t")
[1] 0.1957
```

```
> pcoint(pp.tstat, n.sample=nrow(uscn.s), n.series=2,
+ trend="c", statistic="t")
[1] 0.00003925
```

12.4   Regression-Based Estimates of Cointegrating Vectors and Error Correction Models

12.4.1   Least Square Estimator

Least squares may be used to consistently estimate a normalized cointegrating vector. However, the asymptotic behavior of the least squares estimator is non-standard. The following results about the behavior of $\hat{\beta}_2$ if $\mathbf{Y}_t$ is cointegrated are due to Stock (1987) and Phillips (1991):

- $T(\hat{\beta}_2 - \beta_2)$ converges in distribution to a non-normal random variable not necessarily centered at zero.

- The least squares estimate $\hat{\beta}_2$ is consistent for β_2 and converges to β_2 at rate T instead of the usual rate $T^{1/2}$. That is, $\hat{\beta}_2$ is *super consistent*.

- $\hat{\beta}_2$ is consistent even if Y_{2t} is correlated with u_t so that there is no asymptotic simultaneity bias.

- In general, the asymptotic distribution of $T(\hat{\beta}_2 - \beta_2)$ is asymptotically biased and non-normal. The usual OLS formula for computing $\widehat{avar}(\hat{\beta}_2)$ is incorrect and so the usual OLS standard errors are not correct.

- Even though the asymptotic bias goes to zero as T gets large $\hat{\beta}_2$ may be substantially biased in small samples. The least squres estimator is also not efficient.

The above results indicate that the least squares estimator of the cointegrating vector β_2 could be improved upon. A simple improvement is suggested by Stock and Watson (1993).

12.4.2 Stock and Watson's Efficient Lead/Lag Estimator

Stock and Watson (1993) provide a very simple method for obtaining an asymptotically efficient (equivalent to maximum likelihood) estimator for the normalized cointegrating vector $\boldsymbol{\beta}_2$ as well as a valid formula for computing its asymptotic variance[2].

Let $\mathbf{Y}_t = (y_{1t}, \mathbf{Y}'_{2t})'$ where $\mathbf{Y}_{2t} = (y_{2t}, \ldots, y_{nt})'$ is an $((n-1) \times 1)$ vector and let the cointegrating vector be normalized as $\boldsymbol{\beta} = (1, -\boldsymbol{\beta}'_2)'$. Stock and Watson's efficient estimation procedure is:

- Augment the cointegrating regression of y_{1t} on $\mathbf{Y}_{2t}$ with appropriate deterministic terms $\mathbf{D}_t$ with p leads and lags of $\Delta \mathbf{Y}_{2t}$

$$
\begin{aligned}
y_{1t} &= \boldsymbol{\gamma}'\mathbf{D}_t + \boldsymbol{\beta}'_2 \mathbf{Y}_{2t} + \sum_{j=-p}^{p} \boldsymbol{\psi}'_j \Delta \mathbf{Y}_{2t-j} + u_t \qquad (12.18) \\
&= \boldsymbol{\gamma}'\mathbf{D}_t + \boldsymbol{\beta}'_2 \mathbf{Y}_{2t} + \boldsymbol{\psi}'_{j+p}\Delta \mathbf{Y}_{2t+p} + \cdots + \boldsymbol{\psi}'_{j+1}\Delta \mathbf{Y}_{2t+1} \\
&\quad + \boldsymbol{\psi}'_0 \Delta \mathbf{Y}_{2t} + \boldsymbol{\psi}'_{j-1}\Delta \mathbf{Y}_{2t-1} + \cdots + \boldsymbol{\psi}'_{j-p}\Delta \mathbf{Y}_{2t-p} + u_t
\end{aligned}
$$

- Estimate the augmented regression by least squares. The resulting estimator of $\boldsymbol{\beta}_2$ is called the *dynamic OLS* estimator and is denoted $\hat{\boldsymbol{\beta}}_{2,DOLS}$. It will be consistent, asymptotically normally distributed and efficient (equivalent to MLE) under certain assumptions (see Stock and Watson (1993))

- Asymptotically valid standard errors for the individual elements of $\hat{\boldsymbol{\beta}}_{2,DOLS}$ are given by the OLS standard errors from (12.18) multiplied by the ratio

$$
\left(\frac{\hat{\sigma}_u^2}{\widehat{lrv}(u_t)} \right)^{1/2}
$$

where $\hat{\sigma}_u^2$ is the OLS estimate of $var(u_t)$ and $\widehat{lrv}(u_t)$ is any consistent estimate of the long-run variance of u_t using the residuals $\hat{u}_t$ from (12.18). Alternatively, the Newey-West HAC standard errors may also be used.

Example 76 *DOLS estimation of cointegrating vector using exchange rate data*[3]

Let s_t denote the log of the monthly spot exchange rate between two currencies at time t and let f_t^k denote the log of the forward exchange rate at time t for delivery of foreign currency at time $t + k$. Under rational

---

[2] Hamilton (1994) chapter 19, and Hayashi (2000) chapter 10, give nice discussions of the Stock and Watson procedure.

[3] This example is based on Zivot (2000).

expectations and risk neutrality f_t^k is an unbiased predictor of s_{t+k}, the spot exchange rate at time $t + k$. That is

$$s_{t+k} = f_t^k + \varepsilon_{t+k}$$

where ε_{t+k} is a white noise error term. This is known as the *forward rate unbiasedness hypothesis* (FRUH). Assuming that s_t and f_t^k are $I(1)$ the FRUH implies that s_{t+k} and f_t^k are cointegrated with cointegrating vector $\boldsymbol{\beta} = (1, -1)'$. To illustrate, consider again the log monthly spot, s_t, and one month forward, f_t^1, exchange rates between the US and Canada over the period February 1976 through June 1996 taken from the S+FinMetrics "timeSeries" object lexrates.dat. The cointegrating vector between s_{t+1} and f_t^1 is estimated using least squares and Stock and Watson's dynamic OLS estimator computed from (12.18) with $y_{1t} = s_{t+1}$, $\mathbf{D}_t = 1$, $\mathbf{Y}_{2t} = f_t^1$ and $p = 3$. The data for the DOLS regression equation (12.18) are constucted as

```
> uscn.df = diff(uscn.f)
> collds(uscn.df) = "D.USCNF"
> uscn.df.lags = tslag(uscn.df,-3:3,trim=T)
> uscn.ts = seriesMerge(uscn.s,uscn.f,uscn.df.lags)
> collds(uscn.ts)
[1] "USCNS"         "USCNF"         "D.USCNF.lead3"
[4] "D.USCNF.lead2" "D.USCNF.lead1" "D.USCNF.lag0"
[7] "D.USCNF.lag1"  "D.USCNF.lag2"  "D.USCNF.lag3"
```

The least squares estimator of the normalized cointegrating coefficient β_2 computed using the S+FinMetrics function OLS is

```
> summary(OLS(tslag(USCNS,-1)~USCNF,data=uscn.ts,na.rm=T))


Call:
OLS(formula = tslag(USCNS, -1) ~USCNF, data = uscn.ts,
na.rm = T)


Residuals:
    Min      1Q  Median      3Q     Max
 -0.0541 -0.0072  0.0006  0.0097  0.0343


Coefficients:
               Value Std. Error  t value Pr(>|t|)
(Intercept) -0.0048     0.0025  -1.9614   0.0510
      USCNF  0.9767     0.0110  88.6166   0.0000


Regression Diagnostics:

        R-Squared 0.9709
```

```
Adjusted R-Squared 0.9708
Durbin-Watson Stat 2.1610
```

```
Residual standard error: 0.01425 on 235 degrees of freedom
Time period: from Jun 1976 to Feb 1996
F-statistic: 7853 on 1 and 235 degrees of freedom,
the p-value is 0
```

Notice that in the regression formula, `tslag(USCN,-1)` computes s_{t+1}. The least squares estimate of β_2 is 0.977 with an estimated standard error of 0.011 indicating that f_t^1 underpredicts s_{t+1}. However, the usual formula for computing the estimated standard error is incorrect and should not be trusted.

The DOLS estimator of β_2 based on (12.18) is computed using

```
> dols.fit = OLS(tslag(USCNS,-1)~USCNF +
+ D.USCNF.lead3+D.USCNF.lead2+D.USCNF.lead1 +
+ D.USCNF.lag0+D.USCNF.lag1+D.USCNF.lag2+D.USCNF.lag3,
+ data=uscn.ts,na.rm=T)
```

The Newey-West HAC standard errors for the estimated coefficients are computed using `summary` with `correction="nw"`

```
> summary(dols.fit,correction="nw")
```

```
Call:
OLS(formula = tslag(USCNS, -1) ~USCNF + D.USCNF.lead3 +
D.USCNF.lead2 + D.USCNF.lead1 + D.USCNF.lag0 +
D.USCNF.lag1 + D.USCNF.lag2 + D.USCNF.lag3, data =
uscn.ts, na.rm = T)
```

```
Residuals:
      Min     1Q  Median     3Q     Max
  -0.0061 -0.0008  0.0000  0.0009  0.0039
```

```
Coefficients:
                Value Std. Error   t value  Pr(>|t|)
 (Intercept)  0.0023    0.0005     4.3948    0.0000
       USCNF  1.0040    0.0019   531.8862    0.0000
D.USCNF.lead3  0.0114    0.0063     1.8043    0.0725
D.USCNF.lead2  0.0227    0.0068     3.3226    0.0010
D.USCNF.lead1  1.0145    0.0090   112.4060    0.0000
 D.USCNF.lag0  0.0005    0.0073     0.0719    0.9427
 D.USCNF.lag1 -0.0042    0.0061    -0.6856    0.4937
 D.USCNF.lag2 -0.0056    0.0061    -0.9269    0.3549
 D.USCNF.lag3 -0.0014    0.0045    -0.3091    0.7575
```

Regression Diagnostics:

```
        R-Squared 0.9997
Adjusted R-Squared 0.9997
Durbin-Watson Stat 0.4461
```

Residual standard error: 0.001425 on 228 degrees of freedom
Time period: from Jun 1976 to Feb 1996
F-statistic: 101000 on 8 and 228 degrees of freedom,
the p-value is 0

The DOLS estimator of β_2 is 1.004 with a very small estimated standard error of 0.0019 and indicates that f_t^1 is essentially an unbiased predictor of the future spot rate s_{t+1}.

12.4.3   Estimating Error Correction Models by Least Squares

Consider a bivariate $I(1)$ vector $\mathbf{Y}_t = (y_{1t}, y_{2t})'$ and assume that $\mathbf{Y}_t$ is cointegrated with cointegrating vector $\boldsymbol{\beta} = (1, -\beta_2)'$ so that $\boldsymbol{\beta}'\mathbf{Y}_t = y_{1t} - \beta_2 y_{2t}$ is $I(0)$. Suppose one has a consistent estimate $\hat{\beta}_2$ (by OLS or DOLS) of the cointegrating coefficient and is interested in estimating the corresponding error correction model (12.12) - (12.13) for Δy_{1t} and Δy_{2t}. Because $\hat{\beta}_2$ is super consistent it may be treated as known in the ECM, so that the estimated disequilibrium error $y_{1t} - \hat{\beta}_2 y_{2t}$ may be treated like the known disequilibrium error $y_{1t} - \beta_2 y_{2t}$. Since all variables in the ECM are $I(0)$, the two regression equations may be consistently estimated using ordinary least squares (OLS). Alternatively, the ECM system may be estimated by seemingly unrelated regressions (SUR) to increase efficiency if the number of lags in the two equations are different.

Example 77 *Estimation of error correction model for exchange rate data*

Consider again the monthly log spot rate, s_t, and log forward rate, f_t, data between the U.S. and Canada. Earlier it was shown that s_t and f_t are cointegrated with an estimated cointegrating coefficient $\hat{\beta}_2 = 1.004$. Now consider estimating an ECM of the form (12.12) - (12.13) by least squares using the estimated disequilibrium error $s_t - 1.004 \cdot f_t$. In order to estimate the ECM, the number of lags of Δs_t and Δf_t needs to be determined. This may be done using test statistics for the significance of the lagged terms or model selection criteria like AIC or BIC. An initial estimation using one lag of Δs_t and Δf_t may be performed using

```
> u.hat = uscn.s - 1.004*uscn.f
> colIds(u.hat) = "U.HAT"
> uscn.ds = diff(uscn.s)
> colIds(uscn.ds) = "D.USCNS"
```

```
> uscn.df = diff(uscn.f)
> collds(uscn.df) = "D.USCNF"
> uscn.ts = seriesMerge(uscn.s,uscn.f,uscn.ds,uscn.df,u.hat)
> ecm.s.fit = OLS(D.USCNS~tslag(U.HAT)+tslag(D.USCNS)
+ +tslag(D.USCNF),data=uscn.ts,na.rm=T)
> ecm.f.fit = OLS(D.USCNF~tslag(U.HAT)+tslag(D.USCNS)+
+ tslag(D.USCNF),data=uscn.ts,na.rm=T)
```

The estimated coefficients from the fitted ECM are

```
> ecm.s.fit

Call:
OLS(formula = D.USCNS ~tslag(U.HAT) + tslag(D.USCNS) + tslag(
D.USCNF), data = uscn.ts, na.rm = T)

Coefficients:
 (Intercept) tslag(U.HAT) tslag(D.USCNS) tslag(D.USCNF)
 -0.0050       1.5621         1.2683         -1.3877

Degrees of freedom: 243 total; 239 residual
Time period: from Apr 1976 to Jun 1996
Residual standard error: 0.013605

> ecm.f.fit

Call:
OLS(formula = D.USCNF ~tslag(U.HAT) + tslag(D.USCNS) + tslag(
D.USCNF), data = uscn.ts, na.rm = T)

Coefficients:
 (Intercept) tslag(U.HAT) tslag(D.USCNS) tslag(D.USCNF)
 -0.0054       1.7547         1.3595         -1.4702

Degrees of freedom: 243 total; 239 residual
Time period: from Apr 1976 to Jun 1996
Residual standard error: 0.013646
```

12.5 VAR Models and Cointegration

The Granger representation theorem links cointegration to error correction models. In a series of important papers and in a marvelous textbook, Soren Johansen firmly roots cointegration and error correction models in a vector autoregression framework. This section outlines Johansen's approach to cointegration modeling.

12.5.1   The Cointegrated VAR

Consider the levels VAR(p) model for the $(n \times 1)$ vector $\mathbf{Y}_t$

$$\mathbf{Y}_t = \mathbf{\Phi D}_t + \mathbf{\Pi}_1 \mathbf{Y}_{t-1} + \cdots + \mathbf{\Pi}_p \mathbf{Y}_{t-p} + \boldsymbol{\varepsilon}_t, \ t = 1, \ldots, T, \qquad (12.19)$$

where $\mathbf{D}_t$ contains deterministic terms (constant, trend, seasonal dummies etc.). Recall, the VAR(p) model is stable if

$$\det(\mathbf{I}_n - \mathbf{\Pi}_1 z - \cdots - \mathbf{\Pi}_p z^p) = 0 \qquad (12.20)$$

has all roots outside the complex unit circle. If (12.20) has a root on the unit circle then some or all of the variables in $\mathbf{Y}_t$ are $I(1)$ and they may also be cointegrated. Recall, $\mathbf{Y}_t$ is cointegrated if there exists some linear combination of the variables in $\mathbf{Y}_t$ that is $I(0)$. Suppose $\mathbf{Y}_t$ is $I(1)$ and possibly cointegrated. Then the VAR representation (12.19) is not the most suitable representation for analysis because the cointegrating relations are not explicitly apparent. The cointegrating relations become apparent if the levels VAR (12.19) is transformed to the *vector error correction model* (VECM)

$$\Delta \mathbf{Y}_t = \mathbf{\Phi D}_t + \mathbf{\Pi y}_{t-1} + \mathbf{\Gamma}_1 \Delta \mathbf{y}_{t-1} + \cdots + \mathbf{\Gamma}_{p-1} \Delta \mathbf{y}_{t-p+1} + \boldsymbol{\varepsilon}_t \qquad (12.21)$$

where $\mathbf{\Pi} = \mathbf{\Pi}_1 + \cdots + \mathbf{\Pi}_p - \mathbf{I}_n$ and $\mathbf{\Gamma}_k = -\sum_{j=k+1}^{p} \mathbf{\Pi}_j, \ k = 1, \ldots, p-1$. The matrix $\mathbf{\Pi}$ is called the *long-run impact matrix* and $\mathbf{\Gamma}_k$ are the *short-run impact matrices*. Notice that the VAR parameters $\mathbf{\Pi}_i$ may be recovered from the VECM parameters $\mathbf{\Pi}$ and $\mathbf{\Gamma}_k$ via

$$\begin{aligned} \mathbf{\Pi}_1 &= \mathbf{\Gamma}_1 + \mathbf{\Pi} + \mathbf{I}_n, & (12.22) \\ \mathbf{\Pi}_k &= \mathbf{\Gamma}_k - \mathbf{\Gamma}_{k-1}, \ k = 2, \ldots, p. \end{aligned}$$

In the VECM (12.21), $\Delta \mathbf{Y}_t$ and its lags are $I(0)$. The term $\mathbf{\Pi Y}_{t-1}$ is the only one which includes potential $I(1)$ variables and for $\Delta \mathbf{Y}_t$ to be $I(0)$ it must be the case that $\mathbf{\Pi Y}_{t-1}$ is also $I(0)$. Therefore, $\mathbf{\Pi Y}_{t-1}$ must contain the cointegrating relations if they exit. If the VAR(p) process has unit roots then from (12.20) it is clear that $\mathbf{\Pi}$ is a singular matrix. If $\mathbf{\Pi}$ is singular then it has *reduced rank*; that is $rank(\mathbf{\Pi}) = r < n$. There are two cases to consider:

1. $rank(\mathbf{\Pi}) = 0$. This implies that $\mathbf{\Pi} = \mathbf{0}$ and $\mathbf{Y}_t$ is $I(1)$ and not cointegrated. The VECM (12.21) reduces to a VAR($p-1$) in first differences

$$\Delta \mathbf{Y}_t = \mathbf{\Phi D}_t + \mathbf{\Gamma}_1 \Delta \mathbf{Y}_{t-1} + \cdots + \mathbf{\Gamma}_{p-1} \Delta \mathbf{Y}_{t-p+1} + \boldsymbol{\varepsilon}_t.$$

2. $0 < rank(\mathbf{\Pi}) = r < n$. This implies that $\mathbf{Y}_t$ is $I(1)$ with r linearly independent cointegrating vectors and $n-r$ common stochastic trends

(unit roots)[4]. Since $\boldsymbol{\Pi}$ has rank r it can be written as the product

$$\underset{(n \times n)}{\boldsymbol{\Pi}} = \underset{(n \times r)}{\boldsymbol{\alpha}} \underset{(r \times n)}{\boldsymbol{\beta}'}$$

where $\boldsymbol{\alpha}$ and $\boldsymbol{\beta}$ are $(n \times r)$ matrices with $rank(\boldsymbol{\alpha}) = rank(\boldsymbol{\beta}) = r$. The rows of $\boldsymbol{\beta}'$ form a basis for the r cointegrating vectors and the elements of $\boldsymbol{\alpha}$ distribute the impact of the cointegrating vectors to the evolution of $\Delta \mathbf{Y}_t$. The VECM (12.21) becomes

$$\Delta \mathbf{Y}_t = \boldsymbol{\Phi} \mathbf{D}_t + \boldsymbol{\alpha} \boldsymbol{\beta}' \mathbf{Y}_{t-1} + \boldsymbol{\Gamma}_1 \Delta \mathbf{Y}_{t-1} + \cdots + \boldsymbol{\Gamma}_{p-1} \Delta \mathbf{Y}_{t-p+1} + \boldsymbol{\varepsilon}_t, \tag{12.23}$$

where $\boldsymbol{\beta}' \mathbf{Y}_{t-1} \sim I(0)$ since $\boldsymbol{\beta}'$ is a matrix of cointegrating vectors.

It is important to recognize that the factorization $\boldsymbol{\Pi} = \boldsymbol{\alpha} \boldsymbol{\beta}'$ is not unique since for any $r \times r$ nonsingular matrix $\mathbf{H}$ we have

$$\boldsymbol{\alpha} \boldsymbol{\beta}' = \boldsymbol{\alpha} \mathbf{H} \mathbf{H}^{-1} \boldsymbol{\beta}' = (\mathbf{a} \mathbf{H})(\boldsymbol{\beta} \mathbf{H}^{-1'})' = \mathbf{a}^* \boldsymbol{\beta}^{*'}.$$

Hence the factorization $\boldsymbol{\Pi} = \boldsymbol{\alpha} \boldsymbol{\beta}'$ only identifies the space spanned by the cointegrating relations. To obtain unique values of $\boldsymbol{\alpha}$ and $\boldsymbol{\beta}'$ requires further restrictions on the model.

Example 78 *A bivariate cointegrated VAR(1) model*

Consider the bivariate VAR(1) model for $\mathbf{Y}_t = (y_{1t}, y_{2t})'$

$$\mathbf{Y}_t = \boldsymbol{\Pi}_1 \mathbf{Y}_{t-1} + \boldsymbol{\epsilon}_t.$$

The VECM is

$$\Delta \mathbf{Y}_t = \boldsymbol{\Pi} \mathbf{Y}_{t-1} + \boldsymbol{\varepsilon}_t$$

where $\boldsymbol{\Pi} = \boldsymbol{\Pi}_1 - \mathbf{I}_2$. Assuming $\mathbf{Y}_t$ is cointegrated there exists a 2×1 vector $\boldsymbol{\beta} = (\beta_1, \beta_2)'$ such that $\boldsymbol{\beta}' \mathbf{Y}_t = \beta_1 y_{1t} + \beta_2 y_{2t}$ is $I(0)$. Using the normalization $\beta_1 = 1$ and $\beta_2 = -\beta$ the cointegrating relation becomes $\boldsymbol{\beta}' \mathbf{Y}_t = y_{1t} - \beta y_{2t}$. This normalization suggests the stochastic long-run equilibrium relation

$$y_{1t} = \beta y_{2t} + u_t$$

where u_t is $I(0)$ and represents the stochastic deviations from the long-run equilibrium $y_{1t} = \beta y_{2t}$.

Since $\mathbf{Y}_t$ is cointegrated with one cointegrating vector, $rank(\boldsymbol{\Pi}) = 1$ and can be decomposed as

$$\boldsymbol{\Pi} = \boldsymbol{\alpha} \boldsymbol{\beta}' = \begin{pmatrix} \alpha_1 \\ \alpha_2 \end{pmatrix} \begin{pmatrix} 1 & -\beta \end{pmatrix} = \begin{pmatrix} \alpha_1 & -\alpha_1 \beta \\ \alpha_2 & -\alpha_2 \beta \end{pmatrix}.$$

---

[4] To see that $\mathbf{Y}_t$ has $n - r$ common stochastic trends we have to look at the Beveridge-Nelson decomposition of the moving average representation of $\Delta \mathbf{Y}_t$.

The elements in the vector $\boldsymbol{\alpha}$ are interpreted as *speed of adjustment* coefficients. The cointegrated VECM for $\Delta \mathbf{Y}_t$ may be rewritten as

$$\Delta \mathbf{Y}_t = \boldsymbol{\alpha}\boldsymbol{\beta}'\mathbf{Y}_{t-1} + \boldsymbol{\varepsilon}_t. \tag{12.24}$$

Writing the VECM equation by equation gives

$$\begin{aligned}
\Delta y_{1t} &= \alpha_1(y_{1t-1} - \beta y_{2t-1}) + \varepsilon_{1t}, \\
\Delta y_{2t} &= \alpha_2(y_{1t-1} - \beta y_{2t-1}) + \varepsilon_{2t}.
\end{aligned}$$

The first equation relates the change in y_{1t} to the lagged disequilibrium error $\boldsymbol{\beta}'\mathbf{Y}_{t-1} = (y_{1t-1} - \beta y_{2t-1})$ and the second equation relates the change in Δy_{2t} to the lagged disequilibrium error as well. Notice that the reactions of y_1 and y_2 to the disequilibrium errors are captured by the adjustment coefficients α_1 and α_2.

The stability conditions for the bivariate VECM are related to the stability conditions for the disequilibrium error $\boldsymbol{\beta}'\mathbf{Y}_t$. By pre-multiplying (12.24) by $\boldsymbol{\beta}'$, it is straightforward to show that $\boldsymbol{\beta}'\mathbf{Y}_t$ follows an AR(1) process

$$\boldsymbol{\beta}'\mathbf{Y}_t = (1 + \boldsymbol{\beta}'\boldsymbol{\alpha})\boldsymbol{\beta}'\mathbf{Y}_{t-1} + \boldsymbol{\beta}'\boldsymbol{\varepsilon}_t$$

or

$$u_t = \phi u_{t-1} + v_t$$

where $u_t = \boldsymbol{\beta}'\mathbf{Y}_t$, $\phi = 1 + \boldsymbol{\beta}'\boldsymbol{\alpha} = 1 + (\alpha_1 - \beta\alpha_2)$ and $v_t = \boldsymbol{\beta}'\boldsymbol{\varepsilon}_t = u_{1t} - \beta u_{2t}$. The AR(1) model for u_t is stable as long as $|\phi| = |1 + (\alpha_1 - \beta\alpha_2)| < 1$. For example, suppose $\beta = 1$. Then the stability condition is $|\phi| = |1 + (\alpha_1 - \alpha_2)| < 1$ which is satisfied if $\alpha_1 - \alpha_2 < 0$ and $\alpha_1 - \alpha_2 > -2$. If $\alpha_2 = 0$ then $-2 < \alpha_1 < 0$ is the required stability condition.

12.5.2   Johansen's Methodology for Modeling Cointegration

The basic steps in Johansen's methodology are:

- Specify and estimate a VAR(p) model for $\mathbf{Y}_t$.

- Construct likelihood ratio tests for the rank of $\boldsymbol{\Pi}$ to determine the number of cointegrating vectors.

- If necessary, impose normalization and identifying restrictions on the cointegrating vectors.

- Given the normalized cointegrating vectors estimate the resulting cointegrated VECM by maximum likelihood.

12.5.3 Specification of Deterministic Terms

Following Johansen (1995), the deterministic terms in (12.23) are restricted
to the form

$$\boldsymbol{\Phi}\mathbf{D}_t = \boldsymbol{\mu}_t = \boldsymbol{\mu}_0 + \boldsymbol{\mu}_1 t$$

If the deterministic terms are unrestricted then the time series in $\mathbf{Y}_t$ may
exhibit quadratic trends and there may be a linear trend term in the cointegrating relationships. Restricted versions of the trend parameters $\boldsymbol{\mu}_0$ and
$\boldsymbol{\mu}_1$ limit the trending nature of the series in $\mathbf{Y}_t$. The trend behavior of $\mathbf{Y}_t$
can be classified into five cases:

1. Model $H_2(r)$: $\boldsymbol{\mu}_t = 0$ (no constant). The restricted VECM is

$$\Delta\mathbf{Y}_t = \boldsymbol{\alpha}\boldsymbol{\beta}'\mathbf{Y}_{t-1} + \boldsymbol{\Gamma}_1\Delta\mathbf{Y}_{t-1} + \cdots + \boldsymbol{\Gamma}_{p-1}\Delta\mathbf{Y}_{t-p+1} + \boldsymbol{\varepsilon}_t,$$

   and all the series in $\mathbf{Y}_t$ are $I(1)$ without drift and the cointegrating
   relations $\boldsymbol{\beta}'\mathbf{Y}_t$ have mean zero.

2. Model $H_1^*(r)$: $\boldsymbol{\mu}_t = \boldsymbol{\mu}_0 = \boldsymbol{\alpha}\boldsymbol{\rho}_0$ (restricted constant). The restricted
   VECM is

$$\Delta\mathbf{Y}_t = \boldsymbol{\alpha}(\boldsymbol{\beta}'\mathbf{Y}_{t-1} + \boldsymbol{\rho}_0) + \boldsymbol{\Gamma}_1\Delta\mathbf{Y}_{t-1} + \cdots + \boldsymbol{\Gamma}_{p-1}\Delta\mathbf{Y}_{t-p+1} + \boldsymbol{\varepsilon}_t,$$

   the series in $\mathbf{Y}_t$ are $I(1)$ without drift and the cointegrating relations
   $\boldsymbol{\beta}'\mathbf{Y}_t$ have non-zero means $\boldsymbol{\rho}_0$.

3. Model $H_1(r)$: $\boldsymbol{\mu}_t = \boldsymbol{\mu}_0$ (unrestricted constant). The restricted VECM
   is

$$\Delta\mathbf{Y}_t = \boldsymbol{\mu}_0 + \boldsymbol{\alpha}\boldsymbol{\beta}'\mathbf{Y}_{t-1} + \boldsymbol{\Gamma}_1\Delta\mathbf{Y}_{t-1} + \cdots + \boldsymbol{\Gamma}_{p-1}\Delta\mathbf{Y}_{t-p+1} + \boldsymbol{\varepsilon}_t$$

   the series in $\mathbf{Y}_t$ are $I(1)$ with drift vector $\boldsymbol{\mu}_0$ and the cointegrating
   relations $\boldsymbol{\beta}'\mathbf{Y}_t$ may have a non-zero mean.

4. Model $H^*(r)$: $\boldsymbol{\mu}_t = \boldsymbol{\mu}_0 + \boldsymbol{\alpha}\boldsymbol{\rho}_1 t$ (restricted trend). The restricted VECM
   is

$$\begin{aligned}
\Delta\mathbf{Y}_t &= \boldsymbol{\mu}_0 + \boldsymbol{\alpha}(\boldsymbol{\beta}'\mathbf{Y}_{t-1} + \boldsymbol{\rho}_1 t) \\
&+ \boldsymbol{\Gamma}_1\Delta\mathbf{Y}_{t-1} + \cdots + \boldsymbol{\Gamma}_{p-1}\Delta\mathbf{Y}_{t-p+1} + \boldsymbol{\varepsilon}_t
\end{aligned}$$

   the series in $\mathbf{Y}_t$ are $I(1)$ with drift vector $\boldsymbol{\mu}_0$ and the cointegrating
   relations $\boldsymbol{\beta}'\mathbf{Y}_t$ have a linear trend term $\boldsymbol{\rho}_1 t$.

5. Model $H(r)$: $\boldsymbol{\mu}_t = \boldsymbol{\mu}_0 + \boldsymbol{\mu}_1 t$ (unrestricted constant and trend). The unrestricted VECM is

$$\Delta\mathbf{Y}_t = \boldsymbol{\mu}_0 + \boldsymbol{\mu}_1 t + \boldsymbol{\alpha}\boldsymbol{\beta}'\mathbf{Y}_{t-1} + \boldsymbol{\Gamma}_1\Delta\mathbf{Y}_{t-1} + \cdots + \boldsymbol{\Gamma}_{p-1}\Delta\mathbf{Y}_{t-p+1} + \boldsymbol{\varepsilon}_t,$$

   the series in $\mathbf{Y}_t$ are $I(1)$ with a linear trend (quadratic trend in levels)
   and the cointegrating relations $\boldsymbol{\beta}'\mathbf{Y}_t$ have a linear trend.

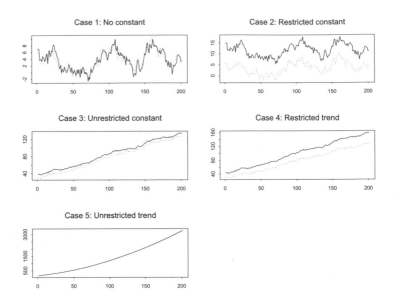

FIGURE 12.6. Simulated $\mathbf{Y}_t$ from bivariate cointegrated VECM for five trend cases.

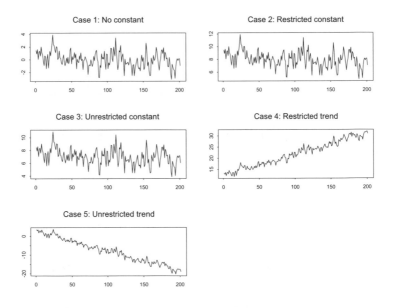

FIGURE 12.7. Simulated $\boldsymbol{\beta}'\mathbf{Y}_t$ from bivariate cointegrated VECM for five trend cases.

Simulated data from the five trend cases for a bivariate cointegrated VAR(1) model are illustrated in Figures 12.6 and 12.7. Case I is not really relevant for empirical work. The restricted contstant Case II is appropriate for non-trending $I(1)$ data like interest rates and exchange rates. The unrestriced constant Case III is appropriate for trending $I(1)$ data like asset prices, macroeconomic aggregates (real GDP, consumption, employment etc). The restricted trend case IV is also appropriate for trending $I(1)$ as in Case III. However, notice the deterministic trend in the cointegrating residual in Case IV as opposed to the stationary residual in case III. Finally, the unrestricted trend Case V is appropriate for $I(1)$ data with a quadratic trend. An example might be nominal price data during times of extreme inflation.

12.5.4 Likelihood Ratio Tests for the Number of Cointegrating Vectors

The unrestricted cointegrated VECM (12.23) is denoted $H(r)$. The $I(1)$ model $H(r)$ can be formulated as the condition that the rank of $\mathbf{\Pi}$ is less than or equal to r. This creates a nested set of models

$$H(0) \subset \cdots \subset H(r) \subset \cdots \subset H(n)$$

where $H(0)$ represents the non-cointegrated VAR model with $\mathbf{\Pi} = \mathbf{0}$ and $H(n)$ represents an unrestricted stationary VAR(p) model. This nested formulation is convenient for developing a sequential procedure to test for the number r of cointegrating relationships.

Since the rank of the long-run impact matrix $\mathbf{\Pi}$ gives the number of cointegrating relationships in $\mathbf{Y}_t$, Johansen formulates likelihood ratio (LR) statistics for the number of cointegrating relationships as LR statistics for determining the rank of $\mathbf{\Pi}$. These tests are based on the estimated eigenvalues $\hat{\lambda}_1 > \hat{\lambda}_2 > \cdots > \hat{\lambda}_n$ of the matrix $\mathbf{\Pi}$[5]. These eigenvalues also happen to equal the squared *canonical correlations* between $\Delta \mathbf{Y}_t$ and $\mathbf{Y}_{t-1}$ corrected for lagged $\Delta \mathbf{Y}_t$ and $\mathbf{D}_t$ and so lie between 0 and 1. Recall, the rank of $\mathbf{\Pi}$ is equal to the number of non-zero eigenvalues of $\mathbf{\Pi}$.

Johansen's Trace Statistic

Johansen's LR statistic tests the nested hypotheses

$$H_0(r) : r = r_0 \text{ vs. } H_1(r_0) : r > r_0$$

The LR statistic, called the *trace statistic*, is given by

$$LR_{trace}(r_0) = -T \sum_{i=r_0+1}^{n} \ln(1 - \hat{\lambda}_i)$$

---

[5] The calculation of the eigenvalues $\hat{\lambda}_i$ $(i = 1, \ldots, n)$ is described in the appendix.

If $rank(\Pi) = r_0$ then $\hat{\lambda}_{r_0+1}, \ldots, \hat{\lambda}_n$ should all be close to zero and $LR_{trace}(r_0)$ should be small. In contrast, if $rank(\mathbf{\Pi}) > r_0$ then some of $\hat{\lambda}_{r_0+1}, \ldots, \hat{\lambda}_n$ will be nonzero (but less than 1) and $LR_{trace}(r_0)$ should be large. The asymptotic null distribution of $LR_{trace}(r_0)$ is not chi-square but instead is a multivariate version of the Dickey-Fuller unit root distribution which depends on the dimension $n - r_0$ and the specification of the deterministic terms. Critical values for this distribution are tabulated in Osterwald-Lenum (1992) for the five trend cases discussed in the previous section for $n - r_0 = 1, \ldots, 10$.

Sequential Procedure for Determining the Number of Cointegrating Vectors

Johansen proposes a sequential testing procedure that consistently determines the number of cointegrating vectors. First test $H_0(r_0 = 0)$ against $H_1(r_0 > 0)$. If this null is not rejected then it is concluded that there are no cointegrating vectors among the n variables in Y_t. If $H_0(r_0 = 0)$ is rejected then it is concluded that there is at least one cointegrating vector and proceed to test $H_0(r_0 = 1)$ against $H_1(r_0 > 1)$. If this null is not rejected then it is concluded that there is only one cointegrating vector. If the null is rejected then it is concluded that there is at least two cointegrating vectors. The sequential procedure is continued until the null is not rejected.

Johansen's Maximum Eigenvalue Statistic

Johansen also derives a LR statistic for the hypotheses

$$H_0(r_0) : r = r_0 \text{ vs. } H_1(r_0) : r_0 = r_0 + 1$$

The LR statistic, called the maximum eigenvalue statistic, is given by

$$LR_{\max}(r_0) = -T \ln(1 - \hat{\lambda}_{r_0+1})$$

As with the trace statistic, the asymptotic null distribution of $LR_{\max}(r_0)$ is not chi-square but instead is a complicated function of Brownian motion, which depends on the dimension $n - r_0$ and the specification of the deterministic terms. Critical values for this distribution are tabulated in Osterwald-Lenum (1992) for the five trend cases discussed in the previous section for $n - r_0 = 1, \ldots, 10$.

Finite Sample Correction to LR Tests

Reinsel and Ahn (1992) and Reimars (1992) have suggested that the LR tests perform better in finite samples if the factor $T - np$ is used instead of T in the construction of the LR tests.

12.5.5   Testing for the Number of Cointegrating Vectors Using the *S+FinMetrics* Function `coint`

The Johansen LR tests for determining the number of cointegrating vectors in multivariate time series may be computed using the S+FinMetrics function coint. The function coint has arguments

```
> args(coint)
function(Y, X = NULL, lags = 1, trend = "c", save.VECM = T)
```

where Y is a matrix, data frame or "timeSeries" containing the $I(1)$ variables in $\mathbf{Y}_t$, X is a numeric object representing exogenous variables to be added to the VECM, lags denotes the number of lags in the VECM (one less than the number of lags in the VAR representation), trend determines the trend case specification, and save.VECM determines if the VECM information is to be saved. The result of coint is an object of class "coint" for which there are print and summary methods. The use of coint is illustrated with the following examples.

Example 79 *Exchange rate data*

   Consider testing for the number of cointegrating relations among the logarithms of the monthly spot and forward exchange rates in the "timeSeries" uscn.ts examined earlier. The first step is to determine the number of lags to use in the VECM. Using the S+FinMetrics function VAR, the lag length that minimizes the AIC with a maximum lag of 6 is $p = 2$:

```
> uscn.ts = seriesMerge(uscn.s, uscn.f)
> var.fit = VAR(uscn.ts,max.ar=6,criterion="AIC")
> var.fit$ar.order
[1] 2
```

The lag length for the VECM is then $p-1 = 1$. Since the monthly exchange rate data are not trending, the Johansen LR tests are computed assuming the restricted constant case II:

```
> coint.rc = coint(uscn.ts,trend="rc",lags=1)
> class(coint.rc)
[1] "coint"
> coint.rc

Call:
coint(Y = uscn.ts, lags = 1, trend = "rc")

Trend Specification:
H1*(r): Restricted constant

Trace tests significant at the 5% level are flagged by ' +'.
```

```
Trace tests significant at the 1% level are flagged by '++'.
Max Eigenvalue tests significant at the 5% level are flagged
by ' *'.
Max Eigenvalue tests significant at the 1% level are flagged
by '**'.


Tests for Cointegration Rank:
          Eigenvalue Trace Stat  95% CV   99% CV Max Stat
H(0)++**  0.0970      32.4687   19.9600 24.6000 24.8012
H(1)      0.0311       7.6675    9.2400 12.9700  7.6675


          95% CV  99% CV
H(0)++** 15.6700 20.2000
H(1)      9.2400 12.9700
```

Recall, the number of cointegrating vectors is equal to the number of non-zero eigenvalues of $\mathbf{\Pi}$. The two estimated eigenvalues are 0.0970 and 0.0311. The first row in the table gives $LR_{trace}(0)$ and $LR_{\max}(0)$ for testing the null of $r_0 = 0$ cointegrating vectors as well as the 95% and 99% quantiles of the appropriate asymptotic distributions taken from the tables in Osterwald-Lenum (1992). Both the trace and maximum eigenvalue statistics reject the $r_0 = 0$ null at the 1% level. The second row in the table gives $LR_{trace}(1)$ and $LR_{\max}(1)$ for testing the null of $r_0 = 1$. Neither statistic rejects the null that $r_0 = 1$.

The **summary** method gives the same output as **print** as well as the un-normalized cointegrating vectors, adjustment coefficients and the estimate of $\mathbf{\Pi}$.

12.5.6 Maximum Likelihood Estimation of the Cointegrated VECM

If it is found that $rank(\mathbf{\Pi}) = r$, $0 < r < n$, then the cointegrated VECM (12.23) becomes a reduced rank multivariate regression. The details of the maximum likelihood estimation of (12.23) under the reduced rank restriction $rank(\mathbf{\Pi}) = r$ is briefly outlined in the Appendix to this chapter. There it is shown that

$$\hat{\beta}_{mle} = (\hat{\mathbf{v}}_1, \ldots, \hat{\mathbf{v}}_r), \tag{12.25}$$

where $\hat{\mathbf{v}}_i$ are the eigenvectors associated with the eigenvalues $\hat{\lambda}_i$, and that the MLEs of the remaining parameters are obtained by multivariate least squares estimation of (12.23) with β replaced by $\hat{\beta}_{mle}$.

Normalized Estimates

Recall, the factorization $\mathbf{\Pi} = \alpha\beta'$ is not unique and so the columns of $\hat{\beta}_{mle}$ in (12.25) may be interpreted as linear combinations of the underlying cointegrating relations. For interpretations, it is often convenient to normalize or identify the cointegrating vectors by choosing a specific coordinate system in which to express the variables. One arbitrary way to do this, suggested by Johansen, is to solve for the triangular representation of the cointegrated system. The details of this normalization process is given in the appendix. The resulting normalized cointegrating vector is denoted $\hat{\beta}_{c,mle}$. The normalization of the MLE for β to $\hat{\beta}_{c,mle}$ will affect the MLE of α but not the MLEs of the other parameters in the VECM.

It must be emphasized that it is not possible to estimate the individual elements of β without a specific normalization or identification scheme and that the normalization based on Phillips' triangular representation is arbitrary and the resulting normalized cointegrating vectors (12.28) may not have any economic meaning. Only in the case $r = 1$ can a unique cointegrating vector be found after normalization.

Example 80 *Unnormalzed MLEs for exchange rate, term structure and stock index data*

The unnormalized cointegrating vector assuming $r_0 = 1$ may also be extracted directly from the "coint" object:

```
> coint.rc$coint.vectors[1,]
     USCNS    USCNF Intercept*
 -739.0541 743.314    2.023532
```

Notice in the case of a restricted constant, the last coefficient in $\hat{\beta}_{mle}$ is an estimate of the restricted constant. Normalizing on USCNS by dividing each element in $\hat{\beta}_{mle}$ by -739.0541 gives

```
> coint.rc$coint.vectors[1,]/
+ as.numeric(-coint.rc$coint.vectors[1,1])
 USCNS     USCNF   Intercept*
   -1 1.005764 0.002738003
```

The normalized MLEs, $\hat{\beta}_{c,mle} = (-1, 1.006)'$ and $\hat{\mu}_c = 0.0027$ are almost identical to the least squares estimates $\hat{\beta} = (1, -1.004)'$ and $\hat{\mu} = 0.0023$ found earlier.

Asymptotic Distributions

Let $\hat{\beta}_{c,mle}$ denote the MLE of the normalized cointegrating matrix β_c. Johansen (1995) shows that $T(vec(\hat{\beta}_{c,mle}) - vec(\beta_c))$ is asymptotically (mixed) normally distributed and that a consistent estimate of the asymptotic covariance of $\hat{\beta}_{c,mle}$ is given by

$$\widehat{avar}(vec(\hat{\beta}_{c,mle})) =$$

$$T^{-1}(\mathbf{I}_n - \hat{\beta}_{c,mle}\mathbf{c}')\mathbf{S}_{11}^{-1}(\mathbf{I}_n - \hat{\beta}_{c,mle}\mathbf{c}')' \otimes \left(\hat{\alpha}'_{c,mle}\hat{\mathbf{\Omega}}^{-1}\hat{\alpha}_{c,mle}\right)^{-1} \quad (12.26)$$

Notice that this result implies that $\hat{\boldsymbol{\beta}}_{c,mle} \overset{p}{\to} \boldsymbol{\beta}_c$ at rate T instead of the usual rate $T^{1/2}$. Hence, like the least squares estimator, $\hat{\boldsymbol{\beta}}_{c,mle}$ is *super consistent*. However, unlike the least squares estimator, asymptotically valid standard errors may be compute using the square root of the diagonal elements of (12.26).

12.5.7 Maximum Likelihood Estimation of the Cointegrated VECM Using the *S+FinMetrics* Function *VECM*

Once the number of cointegrating vectors is determined from the `coint` function, the maximum likelihood estimates of the full VECM may be obtained using the S+FinMetrics function VECM. The arguments expected by VECM are

```
> args(VECM)
function(test, coint.rank = 1, unbiased = T, levels = F)
```

where `test` is a "coint" object, usually produced by a call to the function `coint`, and `coint.rank` is the rank of $\mathbf{\Pi}$ (number of cointegrating vectors). The optional argument `levels` determines if the VECM is to be fit to the levels $\mathbf{Y}_t$ or to the first differences $\Delta\mathbf{Y}_t$, and determines if forecasts are to be computed for the levels or the first differences. The result of VECM is an object of class "VECM", which inherits from "VAR" for which there are print, summary, plot, cpredict and predict methods and extractor functions coef, fitted, residuals and vcov. Since "VECM" objects inherit from "VAR" objects, most of the method and extractor functions for "VECM" objects work similarly to those for "VAR" objects. The use of VECM is illustrated with the following example.

Example 81 *Maximum likelihood estimation of the VECM for exchange rate data*

Using the "coint" object `coint.rc` computed from the VAR(2) model with a restricted constant, the VECM(1) with a restricted constant for the exchange rate data is computed using

```
> vecm.fit = VECM(coint.rc)
> class(vecm.fit)
[1] "VECM"
> inherits(vecm.fit,"VAR")
[1] T
```

The print method gives the basic output

```
> vecm.fit
```

Call:

```
VECM(test = coint.rc)

Cointegrating Vectors:
          coint.1
   USCNS  1.0000
   USCNF -1.0058
Intercept* -0.0027

VECM Coefficients:
            USCNS    USCNF
  coint.1  1.7771   1.9610
USCNS.lag1  1.1696   1.2627
USCNF.lag1 -1.2832  -1.3679

Std. Errors of Residuals:
  USCNS   USCNF
 0.0135  0.0136

Information Criteria:
    logL     AIC     BIC      HQ
 2060.2  -4114.4 -4103.9 -4110.1

                  total residual
Degree of freedom:   243       240
Time period: from Apr 1976 to Jun 1996
```

The print method output is similar to that created by the VAR function.
The output labeled Cointegrating Vectors: gives the estimated cointegrating vector coefficients normalized on the first variable in the specification of the VECM. To see standard errors for the estimated coefficients use
the summary method

```
> summary(vecm.fit)

Call:
VECM(test = coint.rc)

Cointegrating Vectors:
          coint.1
          1.0000

    USCNF    -1.0058
 (std.err)    0.0031
 (t.stat) -326.6389

Intercept*   -0.0027
```

```
(std.err)      0.0007
(t.stat)     -3.9758


VECM Coefficients:
             USCNS    USCNF
   coint.1  1.7771   1.9610
 (std.err)  0.6448   0.6464
 (t.stat)   2.7561   3.0335

USCNS.lag1  1.1696   1.2627
 (std.err)  0.9812   0.9836
 (t.stat)   1.1921   1.2837

USCNF.lag1 -1.2832  -1.3679
 (std.err)  0.9725   0.9749
 (t.stat)  -1.3194  -1.4030


Regression Diagnostics:
                  USCNS   USCNF
      R-squared  0.0617  0.0689
 Adj. R-squared  0.0538  0.0612
   Resid. Scale  0.0135  0.0136


Information Criteria:
    logL     AIC      BIC       HQ
  2060.2 -4114.4  -4103.9  -4110.1


                    total residual
Degree of freedom:     243       240
Time period: from Apr 1976 to Jun 1996
```

The VECM fit may be inspected graphically using the generic **plot** method

```
> plot(vecm.fit)

Make a plot selection (or 0 to exit):

1: plot: All
2: plot: Response and Fitted Values
3: plot: Residuals
4: plot: Normal QQplot of Residuals
5: plot: ACF of Residuals
6: plot: PACF of Residuals
7: plot: ACF of Squared Residuals
```

Cointegrating Residuals

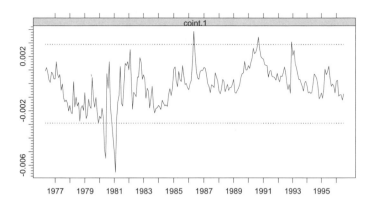

FIGURE 12.8. Cointegrating residual from maximum likelihood estimation of VECM(1) for exchange rate data.

```
8: plot: PACF of Squared Residuals
9: plot: Cointegrating Residuals
10: plot: ACF of Cointegrating Residuals
11: plot: PACF of Cointegrating Residuals
12: plot: ACF of Squared Cointegrating Residuals
13: plot: PACF of Squared Cointegrating Residuals
Selection:
```

The first eight plot options are the same as those created for a "VAR" object. The remaining plot options allow a graphical inspection of the cointegrating residual. For example, plot option 9 is illustrated in Figure 12.8. The estimated cointegrating residual appears to be $I(0)$.

12.5.8 Forecasting from the VECM

Forecasts from a VECM are computed by first transforming the VECM to a VAR using (12.22), and then using the forecasting algorithms for VAR models described in the previous chapter. For VECM models, one may forecast the changes in the variables, $\Delta \mathbf{Y}_t$, or the levels of the variables $\mathbf{Y}_t$. The generic S+FinMetrics functions predict and cpredict are used to compute unconditional and conditional forecasts from a "VECM" object. The following example illustrates the use of the **predict** method to compute forecasts for the differences and levels of the exchange rate data.

Example 82 *Forecasts from VECM fit to exchange rate data*

The "VECM" object **vecm.fit** was produced with the optional argument **levels=F**. Consequently, the **predict** method will produce forecasts for the changes in s_t and f_t. To compute h-step forecasts for Δs_t and Δf_t for $h = 1, \ldots, 12$ use

```
> vecm.fcst = predict(vecm.fit,n.predict=12)
> class(vecm.fcst)
[1] "forecast"
```

To see the forecast and forecast standard errors use

```
> summary(vecm.fcst)
```

Predicted Values with Standard Errors:

```
                 USCNS    USCNF
 1-step-ahead  -0.0105  -0.0110
    (std.err)   0.0136   0.0136
 2-step-ahead  -0.0130  -0.0139
    (std.err)   0.0183   0.0183
 ...
12-step-ahead  -0.0237  -0.0260
    (std.err)   0.0435   0.0432
```

By default, the forecasts are computed using the chain-rule of forecasting. To compute simulation-based forecasts use **method = "mc"** or **method = "bootstrap"** in the call to **predict**.

To see the forecasts with standard error bands along the original data use

```
> plot(vecm.fcst, xold=diff(uscn.ts), n.old=12)
```

Since the forecasts are of the first differenced data, the data passed to **xold** must be first differenced. The resulting plot is shown in Figure 12.9.

To compute forecasts for the levels s_t and f_t, re-fit the VECM with the optional argument **levels=T**

```
> vecm.fit.level = VECM(coint.rc, levels=T)
```

and then call the **predict** method as before

```
> vecm.fcst.level = predict(vecm.fit.level, n.predict=12)
> summary(vecm.fcst.level)
```

Predicted Values with Standard Errors:

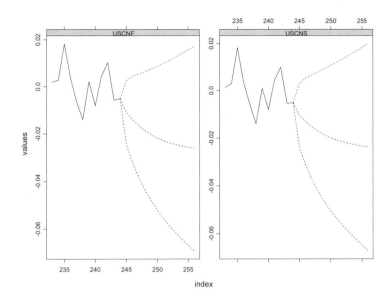

FIGURE 12.9. VECM forecasts of first differences of exchange rate data.

```
                 USCNS     USCNF
1-step-ahead  -0.3150   -0.3154
   (std.err)   0.0136    0.0136
2-step-ahead  -0.3157   -0.3161
   (std.err)   0.0183    0.0183
...
12-step-ahead -0.3185   -0.3193
   (std.err)   0.0435    0.0432
```

To plot the forecasts use

```
> plot(vecm.fcst.level, xold=uscn.ts, n.old=12)
```

The resulting plot is shown in Figure 12.10.

12.6 Appendix: Maximum Likelihood Estimation of a Cointegrated VECM

The following brief discussion of maximum likelihood estimation of the cointegrated VECM (12.23) follows Hamilton (1994) and Johansen (1995). For simplicity, assume the absence of deterministic terms.

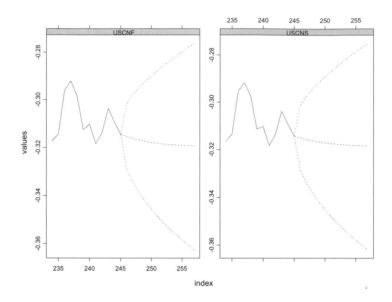

FIGURE 12.10. VECM forecasts of levels of exchange rate data.

- Concentrate the likelihood function with respect to the error covariance matrix and short-run dynamics by estimating the regressions

$$\Delta \mathbf{Y}_t = \hat{\boldsymbol{\Gamma}}_1 \Delta \mathbf{Y}_{t-1} + \cdots \hat{\boldsymbol{\Gamma}}_{p-1} \Delta \mathbf{Y}_{t-p+1} + \hat{\mathbf{U}}_t$$
$$\mathbf{Y}_t = \hat{\boldsymbol{\Phi}}_1 \Delta \mathbf{Y}_{t-1} + \cdots \hat{\boldsymbol{\Phi}}_{p-1} \Delta \mathbf{Y}_{t-p+1} + \hat{\mathbf{V}}_t$$

- Form the sample covariance matrices

$$\mathbf{S}_{00} = \frac{1}{T} \sum_{t=1}^{T} \hat{\mathbf{U}}_t \hat{\mathbf{U}}_t', \ \mathbf{S}_{01} = \frac{1}{T} \sum_{t=1}^{T} \hat{\mathbf{U}}_t \hat{\mathbf{V}}_t', \ \mathbf{S}_{11} = \frac{1}{T} \sum_{t=1}^{T} \hat{\mathbf{V}}_t \hat{\mathbf{V}}_t'$$

- Solve the eigenvalue problem

$$|\lambda \mathbf{S}_{11} - \mathbf{S}_{10} \mathbf{S}_{00}^{-1} \mathbf{S}_{01}| = 0$$

giving ordered eigenvalues[6] $\hat{\lambda}_1 > \hat{\lambda}_2 > \cdots > \hat{\lambda}_n$ and associated eigenvectors $\hat{\mathbf{v}}_1, \hat{\mathbf{v}}_2, \ldots, \hat{\mathbf{v}}_n$ that satisfy

$$\hat{\lambda}_i \mathbf{S}_{11} \hat{\mathbf{v}}_i = \mathbf{S}_{10} \mathbf{S}_{00}^{-1} \mathbf{S}_{01}, \ i = 1, \ldots, n$$
$$\hat{\mathbf{V}} \mathbf{S}_{11} \hat{\mathbf{V}} = \mathbf{I}_n$$

---

[6] These eigenvalues are the squared canonical correlations between $\mathbf{Y}_t$ and $\Delta \mathbf{Y}_t$ corrected for $\Delta \mathbf{Y}_{t-1}, \ldots, \Delta \mathbf{Y}_{t-p+1}$. Johansen (1995) describes how to solve for the eigenvalues.

where $\hat{\mathbf{V}} = [\hat{\mathbf{v}}_1, \ldots, \hat{\mathbf{v}}_n]$

- The unnormalized MLE for the $(n \times r)$ matrix $\boldsymbol{\beta}$ based on $0 < r < n$ cointegrating vectors is given by the first r eigenvectors

$$\hat{\boldsymbol{\beta}}_{mle} = (\hat{\mathbf{v}}_1, \ldots, \hat{\mathbf{v}}_r)$$

- Form the normalized estimator $\hat{\boldsymbol{\beta}}_{c,mle}$ by imposing the appropriate normalizing and identifying restrictions. The MLE for the normalized estimator of α may be computed as

$$\hat{\boldsymbol{\alpha}}_{c,mle} = \mathbf{S}_{01}\hat{\boldsymbol{\beta}}_{c,mle}$$

- The maximum likelihood estimators for the remaining parameters may be obtained by multivariate least squares of the VECM with $\boldsymbol{\beta}$ replaced by $\hat{\boldsymbol{\beta}}_{c,mle}$

$$\Delta\mathbf{Y}_t = \boldsymbol{\alpha}_c\hat{\boldsymbol{\beta}}'_{c,mle}\mathbf{Y}_{t-1} + \boldsymbol{\Gamma}_1\Delta\mathbf{Y}_{t-1} + \cdots + \boldsymbol{\Gamma}_{p-1}\Delta\mathbf{Y}_{t-p+1} + \boldsymbol{\varepsilon}_t$$

- The maximized value of the likelihood function based on r cointegrating vectors used in the construction of LR tests for the number of cointegrating vectors is

$$L_{max}^{-2/T} \propto |\mathbf{S}_{00}| \prod_{i=1}^{r}(1 - \hat{\lambda}_i)$$

- Estimates of the orthogonal complements of $\boldsymbol{\alpha}_c$ and $\boldsymbol{\beta}_c$ are given by

$$\hat{\boldsymbol{\alpha}}_{c,\perp} = \mathbf{S}_{00}^{-1}\mathbf{S}_{11}(\hat{\mathbf{v}}_{r+1}, \ldots, \hat{\mathbf{v}}_n)$$
$$\hat{\boldsymbol{\beta}}_{c,\perp} = \mathbf{S}_{11}(\hat{\mathbf{v}}_{r+1}, \ldots, \hat{\mathbf{v}}_n)$$

Let $\mathbf{c}$ be any $(n \times r)$ matrix such that $\boldsymbol{\beta}'\mathbf{c}$ has full rank. Then $\boldsymbol{\beta}$ may be normalized as

$$\boldsymbol{\beta}_c = \boldsymbol{\beta}(\mathbf{c}'\boldsymbol{\beta})^{-1}$$

satisfying $\mathbf{c}'\boldsymbol{\beta}_c = \mathbf{I}_r$ provided $|\mathbf{c}'\boldsymbol{\beta}| \neq \mathbf{0}$. Johansen suggests setting

$$\mathbf{c} = (\mathbf{I}_r \vdots \mathbf{0})' \tag{12.27}$$

This choice of $\mathbf{c}$ corresponds to solving the cointegrating relations $\boldsymbol{\beta}'\mathbf{Y}_t$ for the first r variables. To see this, let $\mathbf{Y}_t = (\mathbf{Y}'_{1t}, \mathbf{Y}'_{2t})'$, where $\mathbf{Y}_{1t}$ contains the first r variables and $\mathbf{Y}_{2t}$ contains the remaining $n-r$ variables, and let $\boldsymbol{\beta}' = (-\boldsymbol{\beta}_1 \vdots \boldsymbol{\beta}_2)$, where $\boldsymbol{\beta}_1$ is $(r \times r)$ and $\boldsymbol{\beta}_2$ is $(r \times (n-r))$. Then $\boldsymbol{\beta}'\mathbf{c} = -\boldsymbol{\beta}_1$ and

$$\boldsymbol{\beta}_c = \begin{pmatrix} \mathbf{I}_r \\ -\boldsymbol{\beta}_1^{-1}\boldsymbol{\beta}_2 \end{pmatrix} \tag{12.28}$$

provided $\boldsymbol{\beta}_1$ has full rank r.

Some examples will help clarify the normalization scheme described above. First, suppose there is only one cointegrating vector so that $r = 1$. Let the $(n \times 1)$ vector $\boldsymbol{\beta} = (-\beta_1, \beta_2, \ldots, \beta_n)'$ and define $\mathbf{c} = (1, 0, \ldots, 0)'$ so that $\boldsymbol{\beta}'\mathbf{c} = -\beta_1$ and $\boldsymbol{\beta}_c = (1, -\beta_2/\beta_1, \ldots, -\beta_n/\beta_1)'$ is the normalized cointegrating vector. Notice that this normalization requires $\beta_1 \neq 0$. Next, suppose there are two cointegrating vectors, $r = 2$, and let

$$
\boldsymbol{\beta}' = \begin{pmatrix} -\beta_{11} & -\beta_{12} & \beta_{13} & \cdots & \beta_{1n} \\ -\beta_{21} & -\beta_{22} & \beta_{23} & \cdots & \beta_{2n} \end{pmatrix} = \begin{pmatrix} -\boldsymbol{\beta}_1 \vdots \boldsymbol{\beta}_2 \end{pmatrix}
$$

$$
\mathbf{c}' = \begin{pmatrix} 1 & 0 & 0 & \cdots & 0 \\ 0 & 1 & 0 & \cdots & 0 \end{pmatrix} = (\mathbf{I}_2 \vdots \mathbf{0})
$$

such that $\boldsymbol{\beta}_1$ has full rank. Then $\boldsymbol{\beta}'\mathbf{c} = -\boldsymbol{\beta}_1$ and

$$
\boldsymbol{\beta}'_c = \begin{pmatrix} 1 & 0 & \beta_{13}^* & \cdots & \beta_{1n}^* \\ 0 & 1 & \beta_{23}^* & \cdots & \beta_{2n}^* \end{pmatrix} = (\mathbf{I}_2 \vdots \boldsymbol{\beta}^*)
$$

where $\boldsymbol{\beta}^* = -\boldsymbol{\beta}_1^{-1}\boldsymbol{\beta}_2$. The rows of $\boldsymbol{\beta}'_c$ are the normalized cointegrating vectors.

12.7   References

[1] ALEXANDER, C. (2001). *Market Models: A Guide to Financial Data Analysis*, John Wiley and Sons.

[2] COCHRANE, J. (2001). *Asset Pricing*. Princeton University Press, New Jersey.

[3] ENGLE, R.F. AND C.W.J. GRANGER (1987). "Co-Integration and Error Correction: Representation, Estimation and Testing," *Econometrica*, 55, 251-276.

[4] GRANGER, C.W.J. AND P.E. NEWBOLD (1974). "Spurious Regression in Econometrics," *Journal of Econometrics*, 2, 111-120.

[5] HAMILTON, J.D. (1994). *Time Series Analysis*, Princeton Unversity Press, New Jersey.

[6] HANSEN, B.E. (1992). "Efficient Estimation and Testing of Cointegrating Vectors in the Presence of Deterministic Trends," *Journal of Econometrics*, 53, 87-121.

[7] HAYASHI, F. (2000). *Econometrics*, Princeton University Press, New Jersey.

[8] JOHANSEN, S. (1988). "Statistical Analysis of Cointegration Vectors," *Journal of Economic Dynamics and Control*, 12, 231-254.

[9] JOHANSEN, S. (1995). *Likelihood Based Inference in Cointegrated Vector Error Correction Models*, Oxford University Press, Oxford.

[10] MACKINNON, J. (1996). "Numerical Distribution Functions for Unit Root and Cointegration Tests," *Journal of Applied Econometrics*, 11, 601-618.

[11] MILLS, T. (1999). *The Econometric Analysis of Financial Time Series*, Cambridge University Press, Cambridge.

[12] OSTERWALD-LENUM, M. (1992). "A Note with Quantiles of the Asymptotic Distribution of the Maximum Likelihood Cointegration Rank Statistics," *Oxford Bulletin of Economics and Statistics*,54, 461-472.

[13] PHILLIPS, P.C.B. (1986). "Understanding Spurious Regression in Econometrics," *Journal of Econometrics*, 33, 311-340.

[14] PHILLIPS, P.C.B. (1991). "Optimal Inference in Cointegrated Systems," *Econometrica*, 59, 283-306.

[15] PHILLIPS, P.C.B. AND S. OULIARIS (1990). "Asymptotic Properties of Residual Based Tests for Cointegration," *Econometrica*, 58, 73-93.

[16] REIMARS, H.-E. (1992). "Comparisons of Tests for Multivariate Cointegration," *Statistical Papers*, 33, 335-359.

[17] REINSEL, G.C. AND S.K. AHN (1992). "Vector Autoregression Models with Unit Roots and Reduced Rank Structure: Estimation, Likelihood Ratio Test, and Forecasting," *Journal of Time Series Analysis*, 13, 353-375.

[18] SIMS, C.A., J.H. STOCK AND M.W. WATSON (1990). "Inference in Linear Time Series Models with Some Unit Roots," *Econometrica*, 58, 113-144.

[19] STOCK, J.H. (1987). "Asymptotic Properties of Least Squares Estimation of Cointegrating Vectors," *Econometrica*, 55, 1035-1056.

[20] STOCK, J.H. AND M.W. WATSON (1989). "Variable Trends in Economic Time Series," *Journal of Economic Perspectives*, Vol. 2(3), 147-174.

[21] STOCK, J.H. AND M.W. WATSON (1993). "A Simple Estimator of Cointegrating Vectors in Higher Order Integrated Systems," *Econometrica*, 61, 783-820.

[22] TSAY, R. (2001). *The Analysis of Financial Time Series,* John Wiley & Sons, New York.

[23] ZIVOT, E. (2000). "Cointegration and Forward and Spot Exchange Rate Regressions," *Journal of International Money and Finance,* 19, 785-812.

13
Multivariate GARCH Modeling

13.1 Introduction

When modeling multivariate economic and financial time series using vector autoregressive (VAR) models, squared residuals often exhibit significant serial correlation. For univariate time series, Chapter 7 indicates that the time series may be conditionally heteroskedastic, and GARCH models have been proved to be very successful at modeling the serial correlation in the second order moment of the underlying time series.

This chapter extends the univariate GARCH models to the multivariate context and shows how multivariate GARCH models can be used to model conditional heteroskedasticity in multivariate time series. In particular, it will focus on modeling and predicting the time varying volatility and volatility co-movement of multivariate time series. The multivariate GARCH models in S+FinMetrics are so general that they actually include the vector ARMA (VARMA) model as a special case.

To motivate multivariate GARCH models, Section 13.2 first introduces an exponentially weighted covariance estimate and shows how to estimate the optimal weight using the mgarch function in S+FinMetrics. Section 13.3 modifies exponentially weighted covariance estimates to obtain the popular diagonal VEC (DVEC) model. Section 13.4 illustrates how to use the mgarch function to estimate a multivariate GARCH model such as the DVEC model. Section 13.5 introduces some alternative formulations of multivariate GARCH models. Section 13.6 focuses on how to predict from multivariate GARCH models supported by S+FinMetrics. Sec-

Multivariate Series : hp.ibm^2

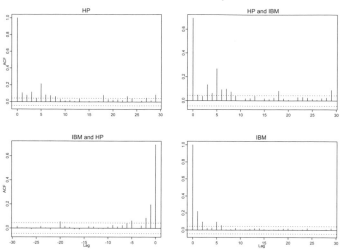

FIGURE 13.1. ACF of multivariate hp.ibm^2.

tion 13.7 gives a detailed explanation of the structure of "garch.model" and "mgarch.model" objects and shows how to use them to fine-tune or constrain a GARCH model, univariate or multivariate. Finally, section 13.8 illustrates how to simulate from selected multivariate GARCH models.

13.2 Exponentially Weighted Covariance Estimate

S+FinMetrics module comes with two "timeSeries" objects, hp.s and ibm.s, which represent daily stock returns of Hewlett-Packard and International Business Machine for the same time period. Chapter 7 shows that these financial return series usually exhibit little serial correlation, but squared returns are usually autocorrelated. In multivariate context, cross-correlations of the levels as well as the volatility of the time series are also of interest. Cross-correlation in the levels can be modeled using vector autoregression (VAR) as shown in the previous chapter. This chapter focuses on cross-correlation, or co-movement, of the volatility.

Just as in the univariate context, the existence of cross-correlation can be diagnosed using the S-PLUS function acf, which also takes a multivariate time series as an argument, to produce both autocorrelation and cross-correlation plots:

```
> hp.ibm = seriesMerge(hp.s, ibm.s)
```

```
> tmp = acf(hp.ibm^2)
```

Use the S-PLUS function seriesMerge, which is specifically designed for "timeSeries" objects, to create a multivariate time series. The plot is shown in Figure 13.1. Both the autocorrelation and cross-correlation of the second order moments are significant at least up to lag 5, which indicates that the covariance matrix of hp.ibm may be time varying and serially correlated.

Now let $\mathbf{y}_t$ be a $k \times 1$ vector of multivariate time series:

$$\mathbf{y}_t = \mathbf{c} + \boldsymbol{\epsilon}_t, \text{ for } t = 1, 2, \cdots, T \tag{13.1}$$

where $\mathbf{c}$ is the $k \times 1$ mean vector, and $\boldsymbol{\epsilon}_t$ is $k \times 1$ vector of white noise with zero mean. The sample covariance matrix is given by:

$$\boldsymbol{\Sigma} = \frac{1}{T-1} \sum_{t=1}^{T} (\mathbf{y}_t - \bar{\mathbf{y}})(\mathbf{y}_t - \bar{\mathbf{y}})'$$

where $\bar{\mathbf{y}}$ is the $k \times 1$ vector of sample mean. In the above calculation, the same weight $1/(T-1)$ is applied to the outer product of "demeaned" multivariate time series. To allow for time varying covariance matrix, in practice an *ad hoc* approach uses exponentially decreasing weights as follows:[1]

$$\boldsymbol{\Sigma}_t = \lambda \boldsymbol{\epsilon}_{t-1}\boldsymbol{\epsilon}'_{t-1} + \lambda^2 \boldsymbol{\epsilon}_{t-2}\boldsymbol{\epsilon}'_{t-2} + \cdots$$
$$= \sum_{i=1}^{\infty} \lambda^i \boldsymbol{\epsilon}_{t-i}\boldsymbol{\epsilon}'_{t-i}$$

where $0 < \lambda < 1$ so that smaller weights are placed on observations further back into the past history. Since

$$\lambda + \lambda^2 + \cdots = \frac{\lambda}{1-\lambda}$$

the weights are usually scaled so that they sum up to one:

$$\boldsymbol{\Sigma}_t = (1 - \lambda) \sum_{i=1}^{\infty} \lambda^{i-1} \boldsymbol{\epsilon}_{t-i}\boldsymbol{\epsilon}'_{t-i}. \tag{13.2}$$

The above equation can be easily rewritten to obtain the following recursive form for exponentially weighted covariance matrix:

$$\boldsymbol{\Sigma}_t = (1 - \lambda)\boldsymbol{\epsilon}_{t-1}\boldsymbol{\epsilon}'_{t-1} + \lambda\boldsymbol{\Sigma}_{t-1} \tag{13.3}$$

which will be referred to as the EWMA model of time varying covariance. From the above equation, given λ and an initial estimate $\boldsymbol{\Sigma}_1$, the time varying exponentially weighted covariance matrices can be computed easily.

---

[1] This approach has recently been justified and exhaustively investigated by Foster and Nelson (1996), and Andreou and Ghysels (2002). Fleming, Kirby and Ostdiek (2001) applied this method for constructing portfolios.

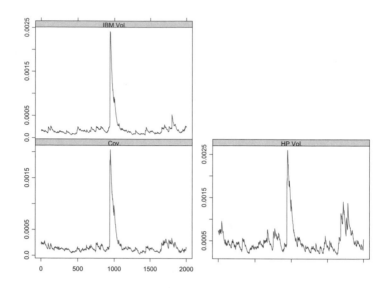

FIGURE 13.2. Exponentially weighted covariance estimate.

The S+FinMetrics function EWMA.cov can be used to compute the exponentially weighted covariance matrix. For example, to obtain the time varying covariance estimate of hp.ibm, use the following command:

```
> hp.ibm.cov = EWMA.cov(hp.ibm, lambda=0.9672375)
> seriesPlot(cbind(hp.ibm.cov[,1,1], hp.ibm.cov[,2,2],
+ hp.ibm.cov[,1,2]), one.plot=F,
+ strip.text=c("HP Vol.", "IBM Vol.", "Cov."))
```

The returned object hp.ibm.cov is an array of dimension $2000 \times 2 \times 2$ representing the time varying covariance matrices, since there are 2000 observations in hp.ibm. Then use the S+FinMetrics function seriesPlot to obtain a Trellis multivariate plot of the time varying covariance matrix as shown in Figure 13.2, where the large spikes in the middle correspond to the 1987 stock market crash.

In practice, the value of λ is usually chosen in an *ad hoc* way as typified by the RiskMetrics proposal. However, if one assumes that ϵ_t in (13.1) follows a multivariate normal distribution with zero mean, and $\Sigma_t = \text{Cov}_{t-1}(\epsilon_t)$ is treated as the covariance of ϵ_t conditional on the past history, then the log-likelihood function of the observed time series can be written as:

$$\log L = -\frac{kT}{2}\log(2\pi) - \frac{1}{2}\sum_{t=1}^{T}|\Sigma_t| - \frac{1}{2}\sum_{t=1}^{T}(\mathbf{y}_t - \mathbf{c})'\Sigma_t^{-1}(\mathbf{y}_t - \mathbf{c}). \quad (13.4)$$

Since Σ_t can be recursively calculated as in (13.3), the log-likelihood function can also be easily evaluated. Thus the mean vector **c** and λ can be treated as unknown model parameters and estimated using quasi-maximum likelihood estimation (MLE), given the initial value Σ_1.

The mgarch function in S+FinMetrics actually allows the estimation of the above EWMA model using either (13.3) or an exact form of (13.2) with limited past history. The syntax of mgarch is very much similar to that of garch function. For example, to estimate the EWMA model as in (13.3), use the following command:

```
> hp.ibm.ewma = mgarch(hp.ibm~1, ~ewma1, trace=F)
> hp.ibm.ewma
```

```
Call:
mgarch(formula.mean = hp.ibm ~ 1, formula.var =  ~ ewma1,
        trace = F)
```

```
Mean Equation: hp.ibm ~ 1
```

```
Conditional Variance Equation:   ~ ewma1
```

```
Coefficients:
```

```
  C(1) 0.0005202
  C(2) 0.0004732
ALPHA 0.0327625
```

where the conditional variance formula is specified by ~ewma1. In the output, C(1) and C(2) correspond to the 2×1 vector of **c** in (13.1), and ALPHA corresponds to $1 - \lambda$ in (13.3). This is why lambda=0.9672375 is set in the earlier EWMA.cov example.

The EWMA model with an exact form of (13.2) can also be estimated by specifying ~ewma2 as the conditional variance formula. However, in that case, the coefficient labeled by ALPHA actually corresponds to λ in (13.2):

```
> mgarch(hp.ibm~1, ~ewma2, trace=F)
```

```
Call:
mgarch(formula.mean = hp.ibm ~ 1, formula.var =  ~ ewma2,
        trace = F)
```

```
Mean Equation: hp.ibm ~ 1
```

```
Conditional Variance Equation:   ~ ewma2
```

```
Coefficients:
```

```
C(1) 0.0007369
C(2) 0.0002603
ALPHA 0.9730018
```

13.3 Diagonal VEC Model

In the univariate context, the EWMA model introduced in the previous section reduces to:

$$\Sigma_t = (1 - \lambda)\epsilon_{t-1}^2 + \lambda\Sigma_{t-1}$$

which is simply a GARCH$(1,1)$ model with $a_1 = 1 - \lambda$, $b_1 = \lambda$ and thus $a_1 + b_1 = 1$. Since $a_1 + b_1$ corresponds to the AR(1) coefficient in the ARMA representation of GARCH models (see Section 7.3 in Chapter 7), the condition $a_1 + b_1 = 1$ implies that the GARCH model is not stationary in the weak sense.[2] Engle and Bollerslev (1986) termed this model the integrated GARCH (IGARCH) model in the univariate context.[3] Given the non-stationarity of IGARCH and EWMA models, they are sometimes not favored for modeling volatility.

To preserve the intuition behind EWMA models while allowing for a flexible and stationary model for time varying covariance, generalize the EWMA model as follows:

$$\mathbf{\Sigma}_t = \mathbf{A}_0 + \sum_{i=1}^{p} \mathbf{A}_i \otimes (\boldsymbol{\epsilon}_{t-i}\boldsymbol{\epsilon}_{t-i}') + \sum_{j=1}^{q} \mathbf{B}_j \otimes \mathbf{\Sigma}_{t-j} \qquad (13.5)$$

where the symbol $\otimes$ stands for Hadamard product, i.e., element-by-element multiplication, and all the coefficient matrices have dimension $k \times k$. This model is first proposed by Bollerslev, Engle and Wooldridge (1988), and they called it the diagonal VEC, or DVEC(p, q) model.

---

[2] Unlike the unit root time series, a GARCH model may be strongly stationary, even when it is not weakly stationary. See Nelson (1990) and Bougerol and Picard (1992) for technical proof.

[3] In fact, the mgarch function can be called with a univariate time series using ~ewma1 as the conditional variance formula to estimate such an IGARCH model.

To appreciate the intuition behind DVEC model, consider the bivariate DVEC$(1, 1)$ model:

$$
\begin{bmatrix} \boldsymbol{\Sigma}_t^{(11)} \\ \boldsymbol{\Sigma}_t^{(21)} & \boldsymbol{\Sigma}_t^{(22)} \end{bmatrix} = \begin{bmatrix} \mathbf{A}_0^{(11)} \\ \mathbf{A}_0^{(21)} & \mathbf{A}_0^{(22)} \end{bmatrix}
$$
$$
+ \begin{bmatrix} \mathbf{A}_1^{(11)} \\ \mathbf{A}_1^{(21)} & \mathbf{A}_1^{(22)} \end{bmatrix} \begin{bmatrix} \varepsilon_{t-1}^{(1)}\varepsilon_{t-1}^{(1)} \\ \varepsilon_{t-1}^{(2)}\varepsilon_{t-1}^{(1)} & \varepsilon_{t-1}^{(2)}\varepsilon_{t-1}^{(2)} \end{bmatrix}
$$
$$
+ \begin{bmatrix} \mathbf{B}_1^{(11)} \\ \mathbf{B}_1^{(21)} & \mathbf{B}_1^{(22)} \end{bmatrix} \begin{bmatrix} \boldsymbol{\Sigma}_{t-1}^{(11)} \\ \boldsymbol{\Sigma}_{t-1}^{(21)} & \boldsymbol{\Sigma}_{t-1}^{(22)} \end{bmatrix}
$$

where only the lower triangular part of the system is considered, with $\mathbf{X}^{(ij)}$ denoting the (i, j)-th element of matrix $\mathbf{X}$, and $\boldsymbol{\epsilon}^{(i)}$ the i-th element of vector $\boldsymbol{\epsilon}$. The above matrix notation can be rewritten as follows:[4]

$$
\boldsymbol{\Sigma}_t^{(11)} = \mathbf{A}_0^{(11)} + \mathbf{A}_1^{(11)}\boldsymbol{\epsilon}_{t-1}^{(1)}\boldsymbol{\epsilon}_{t-1}^{(1)} + \mathbf{B}_1^{(11)}\boldsymbol{\Sigma}_{t-1}^{(11)}
$$
$$
\boldsymbol{\Sigma}_t^{(21)} = \mathbf{A}_0^{(21)} + \mathbf{A}_1^{(21)}\boldsymbol{\epsilon}_{t-1}^{(2)}\boldsymbol{\epsilon}_{t-1}^{(1)} + \mathbf{B}_1^{(21)}\boldsymbol{\Sigma}_{t-1}^{(21)}
$$
$$
\boldsymbol{\Sigma}_t^{(22)} = \mathbf{A}_0^{(22)} + \mathbf{A}_1^{(22)}\boldsymbol{\epsilon}_{t-1}^{(2)}\boldsymbol{\epsilon}_{t-1}^{(2)} + \mathbf{B}_1^{(22)}\boldsymbol{\Sigma}_{t-1}^{(22)}
$$

so the (i, j)-th element of the time varying covariance matrix only depends on its own lagged element and the corresponding cross-product of errors. As a result, the volatility of each series follows a GARCH process, while the covariance process can also be treated as a GARCH model in terms of the cross-moment of the errors.

Since a covariance matrix must be symmetric, in practice it suffices to treat $\boldsymbol{\Sigma}_t$ as symmetric and only consider the lower triangular part of the system. A covariance matrix must be also positive semi-definite (PSD). However, $\boldsymbol{\Sigma}_t$ in the DVEC model cannot be guaranteed to be PSD, which is considered a weakness of the DVEC model. Section 13.5 will introduce other formulations of multivariate GARCH models that guarantee the time varying covariance matrix to be PSD.

13.4 Multivariate GARCH Modeling in S+FinMetrics

13.4.1 Multivariate GARCH Model Estimation

Section 13.2 showed that the mgarch function in S+FinMetrics can be used to estimate a multivariate GARCH model such as the EWMA model. It

---

[4] If these equations are written using matrix notation with a vector on the left hand side, then the coefficient matrices become diagonal matrices; thus this model is referred to as the diagonal VEC model.

can also be used to fit other types of multivariate GARCH models such
as the DVEC model by using a different conditional variance formula. For
example, to fit a DVEC(1, 1) model to the bivariate time series hp.ibm,
use the following command:

```
> hp.ibm.dvec = mgarch(hp.ibm~1, ~dvec(1,1), trace=F)
> class(hp.ibm.dvec)
[1] "mgarch"
> hp.ibm.dvec

Call:
mgarch(formula.mean = hp.ibm ~ 1, formula.var =   ~ dvec(1, 1),
        trace = F)

Mean Equation: hp.ibm ~ 1

Conditional Variance Equation:   ~ dvec(1, 1)

Coefficients:

           C(1) 7.018e-04
           C(2) 2.932e-04
        A(1, 1) 3.889e-05
        A(2, 1) 1.322e-05
        A(2, 2) 2.877e-05
  ARCH(1; 1, 1) 6.226e-02
  ARCH(1; 2, 1) 3.394e-02
  ARCH(1; 2, 2) 1.049e-01
 GARCH(1; 1, 1) 8.568e-01
 GARCH(1; 2, 1) 8.783e-01
 GARCH(1; 2, 2) 7.421e-01
```

The returned object is of class "mgarch". Similar to "garch" objects, the
print method shows the conditional mean equation, conditional variance
equation, together with the estimated model coefficients. In the output,
C(i) corresponds to the i-th element of c in (13.1), while A(i,j) corresponds to the (i, j)-th element of $\mathbf{A}_0$, ARCH(i;j,k) corresponds to the
(j, k)-th element of $\mathbf{A}_i$, and GARCH(j;i,k) corresponds to the (i, k)-th element of $\mathbf{B}_j$ in (13.5).

As usual, use the S-PLUS function names to find out the component
names of an "mgarch" object:

```
> names(hp.ibm.dvec)
 [1] "residuals"    "sigma.t"        "df.residual"  "coef"
 [5] "model"        "cond.dist"      "likelihood"   "opt.index"
 [9] "cov"          "std.residuals"  "R.t"          "S.t"
```

[13] "prediction" "call"   "series"

These components are similar to those of "garch" objects, and the on-line help file for mgarch provides details for them. For most components that a user is interested in, S+FinMetrics provides methods for generic functions such as coef, residuals, and vcov for extracting those components. For example, extract the estimated coefficients by calling the generic coef function:

```
> coef(hp.ibm.dvec)
```

```
        C(1)  7.017567e-04
        C(2)  2.932253e-04
     A(1, 1)  3.888696e-05
     A(2, 1)  1.322108e-05
     A(2, 2)  2.876733e-05
 ARCH(1; 1, 1)  6.225657e-02
 ARCH(1; 2, 1)  3.393546e-02
 ARCH(1; 2, 2)  1.048581e-01
GARCH(1; 1, 1)  8.567934e-01
GARCH(1; 2, 1)  8.783100e-01
GARCH(1; 2, 2)  7.421328e-01
```

Note that since only the lower triangular part of the system is considered for DVEC models, only that part of the coefficient matrices are shown here.

Similarly, call the generic vcov function to obtain the covariance matrix of the estimated coefficients. By default, the covariance matrix based on the outer product of gradients is returned. Just like in the univariate case, the covariance matrix based on the inverse of numerical Hessian and the robust covariance matrix can be obtained by setting the optional argument method to "op" and "qmle", respectively. For example, to obtain the robust standard error of the estimated coefficients, use the command:

```
> sqrt(diag(vcov(hp.ibm.dvec, method="qmle")))
 [1] 0.00048803101 0.00030789132 0.00003531643 0.00001088806
 [5] 0.00001685943 0.03070917257 0.02983075055 0.06630322823
 [9] 0.10170075535 0.09285527451 0.13273539264
```

Similar to the method functions for "garch" objects, residuals and sigma.t can be used to extract the model residuals and estimated volatility, respectively. If the original multivariate data is a "timeSeries" object, the extracted model residuals and conditional volatility will also be "timeSeries" objects with the same dimension. Note that in the multivariate case, the standardized residuals are computed as $\Sigma_t^{-1/2}\epsilon_t$, where $\Sigma_t^{1/2}$ is the Cholesky factor of Σ_t. To obtain the standardized residuals, set the optional argument standardize=T when calling the residuals function:

```
> residuals(hp.ibm.dvec, standardize=T)
```

The `sigma.t` function only extracts the conditional standard deviation of each series, and ignores the conditional covariance term. To obtain the conditional covariance or conditional correlation term, extract the `S.t` and `R.t` component, respectively. Both `S.t` and `R.t` are three dimensional arrays with dimension $T \times k \times k$.

13.4.2 Multivariate GARCH Model Diagnostics

The previous subsection showed how to estimate a multivariate GARCH model in S+FinMetrics, and how to extract various components of the fitted model. To assess the model fit, S+FinMetrics provides method functions for two generic functions: `summary` and `plot`, one for statistical summary and the other for visual diagnostics of the model fit.

For example, to obtain more detailed summary of `hp.ibm.dvec`, call the generic `summary` function:

```
> summary(hp.ibm.dvec)

Call:
mgarch(formula.mean = hp.ibm ~ 1, formula.var =  ~ dvec(1, 1),
       trace = F)

Mean Equation: hp.ibm ~ 1

Conditional Variance Equation:  ~ dvec(1, 1)

Conditional Distribution:  gaussian

-----------------------------------------------------------------

Estimated Coefficients:
-----------------------------------------------------------------
                  Value Std.Error t value  Pr(>|t|)
       C(1) 7.018e-04 4.630e-04   1.516 6.489e-02
       C(2) 2.932e-04 2.870e-04   1.022 1.536e-01
    A(1, 1) 3.889e-05 6.175e-06   6.297 1.860e-10
    A(2, 1) 1.322e-05 2.461e-06   5.372 4.345e-08
    A(2, 2) 2.877e-05 4.302e-06   6.687 1.469e-11
 ARCH(1; 1, 1) 6.226e-02 8.690e-03   7.164 5.498e-13
 ARCH(1; 2, 1) 3.394e-02 6.848e-03   4.955 3.916e-07
 ARCH(1; 2, 2) 1.049e-01 9.212e-03  11.382 0.000e+00
GARCH(1; 1, 1) 8.568e-01 1.762e-02  48.625 0.000e+00
GARCH(1; 2, 1) 8.783e-01 1.885e-02  46.589 0.000e+00
GARCH(1; 2, 2) 7.421e-01 2.966e-02  25.019 0.000e+00
```

AIC(11) = -21886.25
BIC(11) = -21824.64

Normality Test:

      Jarque-Bera P-value Shapiro-Wilk P-value
HP   755.8   0   0.9891 0.7105
IBM   2606.3   0   0.9697 0.0000

Ljung-Box test for standardized residuals:

      Statistic P-value Chi^2-d.f.
HP   18.57 0.09952   12
IBM   11.76 0.46511   12

Ljung-Box test for squared standardized residuals:

      Statistic P-value Chi^2-d.f.
HP   11.43 0.4925   12
IBM   4.44 0.9741   12

Lagrange multiplier test:

        Lag 1   Lag 2   Lag 3 Lag 4 Lag 5   Lag 6   Lag 7
HP -0.1990 0.2496 -0.7004 2.594 0.1039 -0.1167 -0.2286
IBM -0.7769 -0.9883 -0.5770 -1.198 0.4664 -0.2077 -0.4439

        Lag 8   Lag 9 Lag 10 Lag 11   Lag 12   C
HP   0.09018 -0.7877 -0.1279 -0.9280 -0.03133 1.8549
IBM -0.26423 -0.5352 -0.6724 0.1852 0.02102 -0.0729

        TR^2 P-value F-stat P-value
HP 11.914 0.4526 1.090 0.4779
IBM 4.522 0.9721 0.412 0.9947

By default, the summary method shows the standard errors and P-values of estimated coefficients, together with various tests on the standardized residuals for assessing the model fit. The standard errors and P-values are computed using the default covariance estimate. To use robust or numerical Hessian based standard errors to compute the P-values, the summary method takes an optional argument method just like the vcov method does.

All the tests performed on the standardized residuals can also be performed independently by using standard S+FinMetrics functions. In general, if the model is successful at modeling the serial correlation in the time series and the time varying aspect of covariance matrix, there should be no serial correlation left in both the first order and second order moments of standardized residuals. For example, to check that there is no serial correlation left in squared standardized residuals, use the following command:

```
> autocorTest(residuals(hp.ibm.dvec, standardize=T)^2, lag=12)


Test for Autocorrelation: Ljung-Box


Null Hypothesis: no autocorrelation


Test Statistics:
                HP      IBM
Test Stat 11.4299   4.4404
  p.value  0.4925   0.9741


Dist. under Null: chi-square with 12 degrees of freedom
    Total Observ.: 2000
```

which is the same as the test results returned by the **summary** method. Since the P-values for both series are much greater than the conventional 5% level, the null hypothesis that there is no autocorrelation left cannot be rejected.

Similarly, the LM test for ARCH effects can be performed on the multivariate standardized residuals:

```
> archTest(residuals(hp.ibm.dvec, standardize=T), lag=12)


Test for ARCH Effects: LM Test


Null Hypothesis: no ARCH effects


Test Statistics:
                HP      IBM
Test Stat 11.9136   4.5219
  p.value  0.4526   0.9721


Dist. under Null: chi-square with 12 degrees of freedom
    Total Observ.: 2000
```

which is also the same as the LM test returned by the **summary** method. The P-values for LM tests are very close to those of the autocorrelation tests, which confirms that the DVEC model is very successful at modeling the time varying aspect of covariance matrix.

Note the above tests are applied to each series separately, and they do not check the serial correlation of the cross-moment. Hence those tests are not really multivariate tests. However, the `autocorTest` function does have an option to produce a *multivariate portmanteau test* as proposed by Hosking (1980), which is a multivariate extension of the univariate Ljung-Box test. For example, to produce the multivariate test of squared standardized residuals, use the command:

```
> autocorTest(residuals(hp.ibm.dvec, standardize=T)^2,
+ lag=12, bycol=F)

Multivariate Portmanteau Test: Ljung-Box Type

Null Hypothesis: no serial correlation

Test Statistics:

Test Stat 42.4585
  p.value  0.6985

Dist. under Null: chi-square with 48 degrees of freedom
   Total Observ.: 2000
```

where the optional argument `bycol` is set to `FALSE` to use the Hosking's test. The `autocorTest` function sets `bycol` to `TRUE` by default, and thus tests the multivariate series column by column.

The goodness-of-fit of a multivariate GARCH model can also be assessed by calling the generic `plot` function on a fitted "mgarch" object. For example:

```
> plot(hp.ibm.dvec)

Make a plot selection (or 0 to exit):

1: plot: All
2: plot: Original Observations
3: plot: ACF of Observations
4: plot: ACF of Squared Observations
5: plot: Residuals
6: plot: Conditional SD
7: plot: Standardized Residuals
8: plot: ACF of Standardized Residuals
9: plot: ACF of Squared Standardized Residuals
10: plot: QQ-Plots of Standardized Residuals
Selection:
```

By selecting 9 the ACF of squared standardized residuals can be obtained, which is shown in Figure 13.3. After fitting the DVEC model, there is essentially little serial correlation left in the second order moments of the

ACF of Squared Std. Residuals

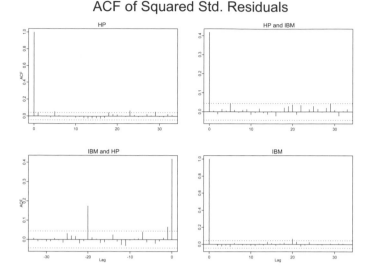

FIGURE 13.3. ACF of squared standardized residuals.

residuals. Normal QQ-plot of standardized residuals can be obtained by selecting 10, which is shown in Figure 13.4. There is significant deviation in the tails from the normal QQ-line for both residuals, which is also confirmed by the normality tests in the **summary** output shown earlier. Thus it seems that the normality assumption for the residuals may not be appropriate. Section 13.5.5 will show how to use alternative distributions in multivariate GARCH models.

Other plots can also be chosen to visualize the model fit. For example, choosing 6 plots the estimated conditional standard deviation as shown in Figure 13.5. For the bivariate time series `hp.ibm`, the time varying cross-correlation, which is contained in the `R.t` component of the fitted object, is also of interest. Since `R.t` is a three-dimensional array, use the following command to generate a time series of the conditional cross-correlation:

```
> hp.ibm.cross = hp.ibm.dvec$R.t[,1,2]
> hp.ibm.cross = timeSeries(hp.ibm.cross, pos=positions(hp.ibm))
> seriesPlot(hp.ibm.cross, strip="Conditional Cross Corr.")
```

The plot is shown in Figure 13.6. Although the conditional cross correlation between `hp.s` and `ibm.s` usually fluctuates around 0.5, it can suddenly drop down to 0.3 and then go back to 0.5 very quickly.

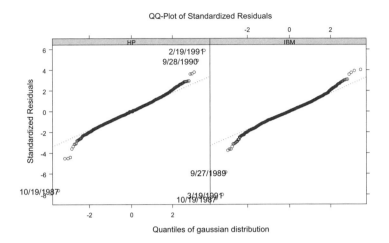

FIGURE 13.4. QQ-plot of standardized residuals.

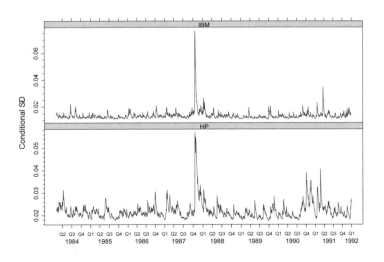

FIGURE 13.5. Multivariate conditional volatility: hp.ibm.

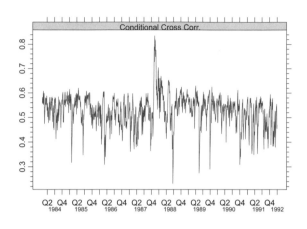

FIGURE 13.6. Conditional cross correlation: `hp.ibm`.

13.5   Multivariate GARCH Model Extensions

13.5.1   Matrix-Diagonal Models

Although the DVEC model provided a good model fit for the bivariate time series `hp.ibm`, the time varying covariance matrices are not guaranteed to be PSD given the formulation as in (13.5). Note that a sufficient condition for $\boldsymbol{\Sigma}_t$ to be PSD is that $\mathbf{A}_0$, $\mathbf{A}_i$ (for $i = 1, \cdots, p$) and $\mathbf{B}_j$ (for $j = 1, \cdots, q$) are all PSD. Based on this observation, Ding (1994) and Bollerslev, Engle and Nelson (1994) proposed to estimate the Cholesky factors of the coefficient matrices:

$$\boldsymbol{\Sigma}_t = \mathbf{A}_0\mathbf{A}_0' + \sum_{i=1}^p (\mathbf{A}_i\mathbf{A}_i') \otimes (\boldsymbol{\epsilon}_{t-i}\boldsymbol{\epsilon}_{t-i}') + \sum_{j=1}^q (\mathbf{B}_j\mathbf{B}_j') \otimes \boldsymbol{\Sigma}_{t-j} \qquad (13.6)$$

where $\mathbf{A}_0$, $\mathbf{A}_i$ (for $i = 1, \cdots, p$) and $\mathbf{B}_j$ (for $j = 1, \cdots, q$) are all lower triangular matrices. This model will be referred to as the *matrix-diagonal* model.

The matrix-diagonal models can be further simplified by restricting $\mathbf{A}_i$ and $\mathbf{B}_j$ to be a vector, which results in:

$$\boldsymbol{\Sigma}_t = \mathbf{A}_0\mathbf{A}_0' + \sum_{i=1}^p (\mathbf{a}_i\mathbf{a}_i') \otimes (\boldsymbol{\epsilon}_{t-i}\boldsymbol{\epsilon}_{t-i}') + \sum_{j=1}^q (\mathbf{b}_j\mathbf{b}_j') \otimes \boldsymbol{\Sigma}_{t-j} \qquad (13.7)$$

where $\mathbf{a}_i$ and $\mathbf{b}_j$ are $k \times 1$ vectors. Even simpler, use the following formulation:

$$\boldsymbol{\Sigma}_t = \mathbf{A}_0 \mathbf{A}_0' + \sum_{i=1}^{p} a_i \otimes (\boldsymbol{\epsilon}_{t-i} \boldsymbol{\epsilon}_{t-i}') + \sum_{j=1}^{q} b_j \otimes \boldsymbol{\Sigma}_{t-j} \qquad (13.8)$$

where a_i and b_j are positive scalars. It is easy to show that all the formulations given in (13.6), (13.7), and (13.8) guarantee that the time varying covariance matrix $\boldsymbol{\Sigma}_t$ is PSD. However, the simpler the model is, the more stringent restrictions are placed on the dynamics of the model.

The mgarch function in S+FinMetrics allows the estimation of all the above modifications of the DVEC model by using ~dvec.type.type(p,q) as the conditional variance formula, where type can be mat for the (13.6) formulation, vec for the (13.7) formulation, or scalar for the (13.8) formulation, and the first type refers to the type of $\mathbf{A}_i$, the second type refers to the type of $\mathbf{B}_j$. Hence, one can use mgarch to estimate a multivariate GARCH model with different formulations for $\mathbf{A}_i$ and $\mathbf{B}_j$. For example, to estimate a multivariate GARCH model with the following covariance matrix formulation:

$$\boldsymbol{\Sigma}_t = \mathbf{A}_0 \mathbf{A}_0' + \mathbf{A}_1 \mathbf{A}_1' \otimes (\boldsymbol{\epsilon}_{t-i} \boldsymbol{\epsilon}_{t-i}') + b_1 \otimes \boldsymbol{\Sigma}_{t-j} \qquad (13.9)$$

with $\mathbf{A}_0$ and $\mathbf{A}_1$ being lower triangular matrices and b_1 just a scalar, use the following conditional variance formula:

```
> mgarch(hp.ibm~1, ~dvec.mat.scalar(1,1), trace=F)

Call:
mgarch(formula.mean = hp.ibm ~ 1, formula.var =
       ~ dvec.mat.scalar(1, 1), trace = F)

Mean Equation: hp.ibm ~ 1

Conditional Variance Equation:   ~ dvec.mat.scalar(1, 1)

Coefficients:
           C(1)  0.0007500
           C(2)  0.0003268
        A(1, 1)  0.0099384
        A(2, 1)  0.0037295
        A(2, 2)  0.0044583
   ARCH(1; 1, 1)  0.3215890
   ARCH(1; 2, 1)  0.1984259
   ARCH(1; 2, 2)  0.2958904
        GARCH(1)  0.6968114
```

Note that in the output the GARCH(1) coefficient corresponds to b_1, while ARCH(1;i,j) corresponds to the (i, j)-th element of $\mathbf{A}_1$ in (13.9).

13.5.2 BEKK Models

Although the DVEC model can be modified in various ways to ensure the time varying covariance matrices are PSD, the dynamics allowed in the conditional covariance matrix are still somewhat restricted. In particular, the conditional variance and covariance are only dependent on their own lagged element and the corresponding cross-product of shocks or error terms. For example, consider the bivariate time series hp.ibm. If there is a shock to hp.s in the current period, it will affect the conditional volatility of hp.s and the conditional correlation between hp.s and ibm.s in the next period. However, it will not directly affect the volatility of ibm.s.

The BEKK model, as formalized by Engle and Kroner (1995), provides an alternative formulation of the conditional variance equation:

$$\Sigma_t = \mathbf{A}_0 \mathbf{A}_0' + \sum_{i=1}^{p} \mathbf{A}_i (\epsilon_{t-i} \epsilon_{t-i}') \mathbf{A}_i' + \sum_{j=1}^{q} \mathbf{B}_j \Sigma_{t-j} \mathbf{B}_j'$$

where $\mathbf{A}_0$ is a lower triangular matrix, but $\mathbf{A}_i$ $(i = 1, \cdots, p)$ and $\mathbf{B}_j$ $(j = 1, \cdots, q)$ are unrestricted square matrices. It is easy to show that Σ_t is guaranteed to be symmetric and PSD in the above formulation. Furthermore, the dynamics allowed in the BEKK model are richer than the DVEC model, which can be illustrated by considering the $(2, 2)$ element of Σ_t in the BEKK$(1, 1)$ model:

$$\Sigma_t^{(22)} = \mathbf{A}_0^{(22)} \mathbf{A}_0^{(22)} + [\mathbf{A}_1^{(21)} \epsilon_{t-1}^{(1)} + \mathbf{A}_1^{(22)} \epsilon_{t-1}^{(2)}]^2 +$$
$$[\mathbf{B}_1^{(21)} \mathbf{B}_1^{(21)} \Sigma_{t-1}^{(11)} + 2\mathbf{B}_1^{(21)} \mathbf{B}_1^{(22)} \Sigma_{t-1}^{(21)} + \mathbf{B}_1^{(22)} \mathbf{B}_1^{(22)} \Sigma_{t-1}^{(22)}]$$

where both $\epsilon_{t-1}^{(1)}$ and $\epsilon_{t-1}^{(2)}$ enter the equation. In addition, $\Sigma_{t-1}^{(11)}$, the volatility of the first series, also has direct impacts on $\Sigma_t^{(22)}$, the volatility of the second series. However, for the bivariate BEKK$(1, 1)$ model, flexibility is achieved at the cost of two extra parameters, i.e., $\mathbf{A}_1^{(12)}$ and $\mathbf{B}_1^{(12)}$, which are not needed for the DVEC$(1, 1)$ model. In general, a BEKK(p, q) model requires $k(k - 1)(p + q)/2$ more parameters than a DVEC model of the same order.

One can fit a BEKK model by using ~bekk(p,q) as the conditional variance formula. For example, to fit a BEKK$(1, 1)$ model to the bivariate time series hp.ibm, use the following command:

```
> hp.ibm.bekk = mgarch(hp.ibm~1, ~bekk(1,1))
> hp.ibm.bekk
```

```
Call:
mgarch(formula.mean = hp.ibm ~ 1, formula.var =   ~ bekk(1, 1))

Mean Equation: hp.ibm ~ 1

Conditional Variance Equation:   ~ bekk(1, 1)

Coefficients:

          C(1)    0.0007782
          C(2)    0.0002870
       A(1, 1)    0.0077678
       A(2, 1)   -0.0035790
       A(2, 2)    0.0046844
 ARCH(1; 1, 1)    0.2054901
 ARCH(1; 2, 1)   -0.0287318
 ARCH(1; 1, 2)   -0.0734735
 ARCH(1; 2, 2)    0.4169672
GARCH(1; 1, 1)    0.8078184
GARCH(1; 2, 1)    0.1277266
GARCH(1; 1, 2)    0.2867068
GARCH(1; 2, 2)    0.6954790
```

Note that in the output, the coefficient matrix $\mathbf{A}_1$ (the ARCH(1;i,j) coefficients) and $\mathbf{B}_1$ (the GARCH(1;i,j)) are not restricted.

Compare the conditional correlations between hp.s and ibm.s implied by the DVEC model and BEKK model as follows:

```
> seriesPlot(cbind(hp.ibm.dvec$R.t[,1,2], hp.ibm.bekk$R.t[,1,2]),
+ strip=c("DVEC Corr.", "BEKK Corr."), one.plot=F,
+ layout=c(1,2,1))
```

The plot is shown in Figure 13.7, from which one can see that the conditional correlation implied by the BEKK model is more volatile than that implied by the DVEC model.

13.5.3 Univariate GARCH-based Models

For BEKK model, DVEC model and its modifications, the conditional covariance matrix is modeled directly. This approach can result in a large number of parameters since the covariance terms need to be modeled separately. Another approach in multivariate GARCH modeling is to transform the multivariate time series into uncorrelated time series and then apply the univariate GARCH models in Chapter 7 to each of those uncorrelated series. This subsection introduces three types of multivariate GARCH models in this fashion.

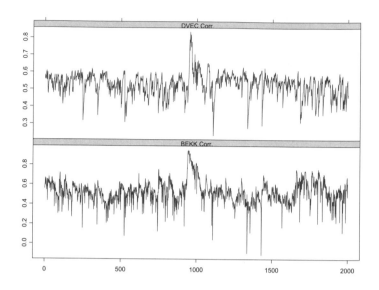

FIGURE 13.7. Comparison of conditional correlation: `hp.ibm`.

Constant Conditional Correlation Model

In general, a $k \times k$ covariance matrix $\boldsymbol{\Sigma}$ can be decomposed into the following form:

$$\boldsymbol{\Sigma} = \boldsymbol{\Delta R \Delta}$$

where $\mathbf{R}$ is the correlation matrix, $\boldsymbol{\Delta}$ is a diagonal matrix with the vector $(\sigma_1, \cdots, \sigma_k)$ on the diagonal, and σ_i is the standard deviation of the i-th series. Based on the observation that the correlation matrix of foreign exchange rate returns is usually constant over time, Bollerslev (1990) suggested modelling the time varying covariance matrix as follows:

$$\boldsymbol{\Sigma}_t = \boldsymbol{\Delta}_t \mathbf{R} \boldsymbol{\Delta}_t$$

where $\mathbf{R}$ is the constant conditional correlation matrix, and $\boldsymbol{\Delta}_t$ is the following diagonal matrix:

$$\boldsymbol{\Delta}_t = \begin{bmatrix} \sigma_{1t} & & \\ & \ddots & \\ & & \sigma_{kt} \end{bmatrix}$$

with σ_{it} following any univariate GARCH process, for $i = 1, \cdots, k$. This model is usually referred to as the *constant conditional correlation* (CCC) model.

The mgarch function can be used to estimate a CCC model with a GARCH(p, q) model for each series, by specifying ~ccc(p,q) as the conditional variance formula. In addition, a more general formula such as ~ccc.type(p,q) can also be used, where type can be any of the GARCH variants supported by the garch function.[5] For example, to use a two components model for each series when fitting a CCC model to the bivariate time series hp.ibm, use the following conditional variance formula:

```
> mgarch(hp.ibm~1, ~ccc.two.comp(1,1), trace=F)
```

```
Call:
mgarch(formula.mean = hp.ibm ~ 1, formula.var =
        ~ ccc.two.comp(1, 1), trace = F)
```

```
Mean Equation: hp.ibm ~ 1
```

```
Conditional Variance Equation:    ~ ccc.two.comp(1, 1)
```

```
Coefficients:

          C(1)  4.907e-04
          C(2)  1.844e-04
       A(1, 1)  8.722e-05
       A(2, 2)  6.579e-05
  ARCH(1; 1, 1) 8.102e-03
  ARCH(1; 2, 2) 9.621e-03
  ARCH(2; 1, 1) 9.669e-02
  ARCH(2; 2, 2) 9.582e-02
 GARCH(1; 1, 1) 9.699e-01
 GARCH(1; 2, 2) 9.654e-01
 GARCH(2; 1, 1) 7.365e-01
 GARCH(2; 2, 2) 7.271e-01
```

```
Conditional Constant Correlation Matrix:
          HP     IBM
 HP 1.0000 0.5582
IBM 0.5582 1.0000
```

When fitting a CCC model, mgarch function allows several alternatives for the estimation of the constant conditional correlation matrix $\mathbf{R}$ by setting the optional argument cccor.choice:

1. cccor.choice=0: The sample correlation matrix is used, and no further MLE estimation of $\mathbf{R}$ is carried out.

---

[5] See Section 7.9 in Chapter 7 for a summary of those specifications.

2. cccor.choice=1: The sample correlation matrix is used as the initial estimate, and the final estimate of **R** is obtained as part of the MLE method. This is the default value.

3. cccor.choice=2: The user supplies an initial correlation matrix estimate, and the final estimate of **R** is obtained as part of the MLE method. In this case, the user needs to supply the initial estimate with the optional argument cccor.value.

A potentially important use of the last choice is to obtain robustness toward multivariate outliers by using a robust initial covariance matrix estimate. The covRob function in S-PLUS robust library provides several robust covariance and correlation estimates.

Principal Component Model

In principal component analysis, it is well known that for any covariance matrix $\mathbf{\Sigma}$, one can always find an orthogonal matrix $\mathbf{\Lambda}$ and a diagonal matrix $\mathbf{\Delta}$ such that

$$\mathbf{\Lambda}\mathbf{\Delta}\mathbf{\Lambda}' = \mathbf{\Sigma}$$

where $\mathbf{\Lambda}$ is usually normalized so that $\mathbf{\Lambda}\mathbf{\Lambda}' = \mathbf{I}$ with $\mathbf{I}$ being an identity matrix. It can be shown that the diagonal elements of $\mathbf{\Delta}$ are the eigenvalues of $\mathbf{\Sigma}$, while the columns of $\mathbf{\Lambda}$ correspond to the eigenvectors of $\mathbf{\Sigma}$. Based on this result, the principal components of $\mathbf{y}_t$, which are defined as $\mathbf{z}_t = \mathbf{\Lambda}'\mathbf{y}_t$, have a diagonal covariance matrix. Ding (1994) describes the principal component GARCH model, which essentially models each principal component in $\mathbf{z}_t$ as a univariate GARCH model. This model is also proposed by Alexander (1998).

The mgarch function can be used to estimate a principal component model with a GARCH(p, q) model for principal component, by specifying ~prcomp(p,q) as the conditional variance formula. Similar to the CCC model, a more general formula such as ~prcomp.type(p,q) can also be used, where type can be any of the GARCH variants supported by the garch function. For example, to use a PGARCH($1, 1, 1$) model for each series when fitting the principal component model to the bivariate time series hp.ibm, use the following conditional variance formula:

```
> mgarch(hp.ibm~1, ~prcomp.pgarch(1,1,1), trace=F)

Call:
mgarch(formula.mean = hp.ibm ~ 1, formula.var =
        ~ prcomp.pgarch(1, 1, 1), trace = F)

Mean Equation: hp.ibm ~ 1

Conditional Variance Equation:    ~ prcomp.pgarch(1, 1, 1)
```

Coefficients:

```
        C(1)  -3.519e-04
        C(2)  -1.614e-05
     A(1, 1)   1.848e-03
     A(2, 2)   3.565e-04
 ARCH(1; 1, 1)  1.100e-01
 ARCH(1; 2, 2)  5.992e-02
GARCH(1; 1, 1)  8.380e-01
GARCH(1; 2, 2)  9.222e-01
```

Eigenvectors: (orthonormal transform matrix):

```
        HP      IBM
 HP -0.9054   0.4245
IBM -0.4245  -0.9054
```

Eigenvalues:
[1] 0.0006002 0.0001222

Pure Diagonal Model

Sometimes, the user may want to fit the same type of GARCH model to a large number of time series. The `mgarch` function also allows this type of univariate GARCH-based estimation, which totally ignores the correlation of the multivariate time series. For this purpose, any univariate GARCH specification can be used directly with the `mgarch` function. For example, to estimate a TGARCH$(1, 1)$ model to both `hp.s` and `ibm.s` at the same time, use the following command:

```
> mgarch(hp.ibm~1, ~egarch(1,1), leverage=T, trace=F)
```

Call:
```
mgarch(formula.mean = hp.ibm ~ 1, formula.var = ~ egarch(1, 1),
       leverage = T, trace = F)
```

Mean Equation: hp.ibm ~ 1

Conditional Variance Equation: ~ egarch(1, 1)

Coefficients:

```
        C(1)   0.0004561
        C(2)   0.0001810
     A(1, 1)  -0.7959068
     A(2, 2)  -0.9192535
```

```
 ARCH(1; 1, 1)    0.1618657
 ARCH(1; 2, 2)    0.1350345
GARCH(1; 1, 1)    0.9124564
GARCH(1; 2, 2)    0.9066042
  LEV(1; 1, 1)    0.0243099
  LEV(1; 2, 2)   -0.1743824
```

Although the optional argument `leverage` can be used with any univariate GARCH-based models for `mgarch` function, it is ignored for BEKK, DVEC and its modifications.

13.5.4   ARMA Terms and Exogenous Variables

All the multivariate GARCH models considered so far have been restricted to a constant mean assumption. However, the `mgarch` function actually allows a more general model with a vector ARMA (VARMA) structure and optional inclusion of weakly exogenous variables in the conditional mean:

$$\mathbf{y}_t = \mathbf{c} + \sum_{i=1}^{r} \mathbf{\Phi}_i \mathbf{y}_{t-i} + \sum_{l=0}^{L} \boldsymbol{\beta}_l \mathbf{x}_{t-l} + \boldsymbol{\epsilon}_t + \sum_{j=1}^{s} \mathbf{\Theta}_j \boldsymbol{\epsilon}_{t-j} \qquad (13.10)$$

where $\mathbf{\Phi}_i$ are $k \times k$ autoregressive coefficient matrix, $\mathbf{\Theta}_j$ are $k \times k$ moving average coefficient matrix, $\mathbf{x}_t$ is the $m \times 1$ vector of weakly exogenous variables, and $\boldsymbol{\beta}_l$ is $k \times m$ coefficients of $\mathbf{x}_{t-l}$. Note that a distributed lag structure of $\mathbf{x}_t$ is allowed in the above equation by setting L to be a positive integer.

To include an $AR(r)$, $MA(s)$, or $ARMA(r, s)$ term in the conditional mean, the user can simply add an `ar(r)`, `ma(s)`, or `arma(r,s)` term to the conditional mean formula. However, by default, $\mathbf{\Phi}_i$ and $\mathbf{\Theta}_j$ are restricted to be diagonal matrices for parsimonious reasons. This behavior can be changed by setting the optional argument `armaType` of the `mgarch` function. In particular, if `armaType="lower"`, then $\mathbf{\Phi}_i$ and $\mathbf{\Theta}_j$ are restricted to be lower triangular matrices; if `armaType="full"`, then $\mathbf{\Phi}_i$ and $\mathbf{\Theta}_j$ are not restricted. When weakly exogenous variables $\mathbf{x}_t$ are used, the optional argument `xlag` can be set to a positive integer to use a distributed lag structure.

Example 83 *Single factor model with multivariate GARCH errors*

Section 7.5 of Chapter 7 developed a single factor model with GARCH errors. Here that example is extended to multivariate context using the bivariate time series `hp.ibm`. The univariate example used daily returns on the value weighted New York Stock Exchange index as the "market returns" to estimate the "market beta". In practice, this market beta can be biased due to the serial correlation in the market returns. Hence, both

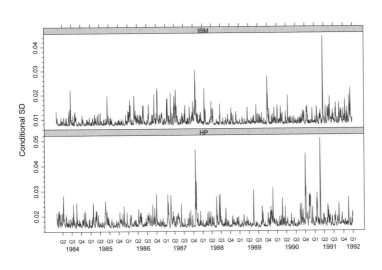

FIGURE 13.8. Idiosyncratic volatility of bivariate `hp.ibm`.

`nyse.s` and its first lag as regressors are included in the conditional mean equation, and the $DVEC(1, 1)$ model is used in the conditional variance:

```
> hp.ibm.beta = mgarch(hp.ibm~seriesData(nyse.s), ~dvec(1,1),
+ xlag=1)
> summary(hp.ibm.beta)

Call:
mgarch(formula.mean = hp.ibm ~ seriesData(nyse.s),
        formula.var = ~ dvec(1, 1), xlag = 1)

Mean Equation: hp.ibm ~ seriesData(nyse.s)

Conditional Variance Equation:   ~ dvec(1, 1)

Conditional Distribution:  gaussian

-----------------------------------------------------------

Estimated Coefficients:
-----------------------------------------------------------
                Value Std.Error  t value  Pr(>|t|)
        C(1)  7.860e-05 3.714e-04   0.2116 4.162e-01
```

```
           C(2) -3.343e-04 1.947e-04  -1.7166 4.311e-02
     X(0; 1, 1)  1.491e+00 2.867e-02  52.0032 0.000e+00
     X(0; 2, 1)  1.112e+00 1.751e-02  63.4896 0.000e+00
     X(1; 1, 1) -1.497e-01 3.233e-02  -4.6297 1.949e-06
     X(1; 2, 1) -1.802e-01 1.898e-02  -9.4945 0.000e+00
       A(1, 1)   1.028e-04 1.420e-05   7.2413 3.160e-13
       A(2, 1)   6.166e-06 4.520e-06   1.3642 8.633e-02
       A(2, 2)   3.117e-05 3.226e-06   9.6600 0.000e+00
  ARCH(1; 1, 1)  1.230e-01 1.812e-02   6.7878 7.482e-12
  ARCH(1; 2, 1)  5.030e-03 1.530e-02   0.3288 3.712e-01
  ARCH(1; 2, 2)  2.567e-01 2.155e-02  11.9125 0.000e+00
 GARCH(1; 1, 1)  5.494e-01 5.543e-02   9.9112 0.000e+00
 GARCH(1; 2, 1)  7.904e-01 1.483e-01   5.3285 5.511e-08
 GARCH(1; 2, 2)  4.261e-01 4.432e-02   9.6126 0.000e+00
```

. . .

In the above output, the coefficient matrix β_0 of nyse.s is denoted by
X(0;i,j) and β_1 of the first lag of nyse.s is denoted by X(1;i,j). All
those coefficients are very significant. Now compare the GARCH(1;i,j) coefficients with those of hp.ibm.dvec; after taking account of the market
effects, the persistence in the GARCH volatilities has dropped quite a bit.
The estimated conditional volatility can also be plotted as shown in Figure 13.8. Compare this with Figure 13.5: since the market effects are already
taken into account in the above single factor model, the volatility in Figure 13.8 can be treated as the "idiosyncratic" volatility, while Figure 13.5
also includes the systematic market component.

Weakly exogenous variables are also allowed in the conditional variance
equation for multivariate GARCH models. For example, for the DVEC(p, q)
model, the general conditional variance equation is:

$$\Sigma_t = \mathbf{A}_0 + \sum_{i=1}^{p} \mathbf{A}_i \otimes (\epsilon_{t-i}\epsilon'_{t-i}) + \sum_{j=1}^{q} \mathbf{B}_j \otimes \Sigma_{t-j} + \mathbf{D} \cdot \mathbf{Z}_t \cdot \mathbf{D}' \quad (13.11)$$

where $\mathbf{Z}_t$ is a diagonal matrix with the $m \times 1$ weakly exogenous variable
$(Z_{t1}, \cdots, Z_{tm})$ on the diagonal, and $\mathbf{D}$ is $k \times m$ coefficient matrix. Note that
using this formulation, the regressor effects are guaranteed to be positive
semi-definite as long as the regressors $\mathbf{Z}_t$ are non-negative.

Example 84 *Monday and Friday effects of volatility*

There is a conjecture that the volatility in stock markets may be higher
on Mondays and Fridays. To investigate if this conjecture holds for the
bivariate time series hp.ibm, build a dummy variable for those observations
falling on a Monday or a Friday:

```
> weekdaysVec = as.integer(weekdays(positions(hp.ibm)))
```

```
> MonFriDummy = (weekdaysVec == 2 | weekdaysVec == 6)
```

Note that the integer representation of Monday in S-PLUS is two because Sunday is represented as one. Now add `MonFriDummy` as an exogenous variable in the conditional variance formula:

```
> hp.ibm.dummy = mgarch(hp.ibm~1, ~dvec(1,1)+MonFriDummy)
> summary(hp.ibm.dummy)

Call:
mgarch(formula.mean = hp.ibm ~ 1, formula.var =  ~ dvec(1, 1)
       + MonFriDummy)

Mean Equation: hp.ibm ~ 1

Conditional Variance Equation:  ~ dvec(1, 1) + MonFriDummy

Conditional Distribution:  gaussian

 -----------------------------------------------------------

Estimated Coefficients:
 -----------------------------------------------------------
                 Value Std.Error  t value   Pr(>|t|)
     C(1)    6.953e-04 4.696e-04   1.4806  6.943e-02
     C(2)    2.659e-04 2.849e-04   0.9333  1.754e-01
   A(1, 1)   3.369e-05 8.612e-06   3.9124  4.723e-05
   A(2, 1)   7.384e-06 5.682e-06   1.2997  9.693e-02
   A(2, 2)   2.011e-05 5.214e-06   3.8565  5.934e-05
 ARCH(1; 1, 1) 6.400e-02 8.952e-03  7.1494  6.088e-13
 ARCH(1; 2, 1) 3.546e-02 7.029e-03  5.0443  2.482e-07
 ARCH(1; 2, 2) 1.076e-01 1.004e-02 10.7141  0.000e+00
GARCH(1; 1, 1) 8.600e-01 1.716e-02 50.1061  0.000e+00
GARCH(1; 2, 1) 8.805e-01 1.816e-02 48.4743  0.000e+00
GARCH(1; 2, 2) 7.472e-01 2.855e-02 26.1706  0.000e+00
   Z(1,1)    3.139e-03 2.440e-03   1.2865  9.921e-02
   Z(2,1)    4.426e-03 1.074e-03   4.1215  1.959e-05

. . .
```

In the above output, $Z(1,1)$ denotes the coefficient of the dummy variable for `hp.s`, the P-value of which is higher than the conventional 5% level, and $Z(2,1)$ denotes the coefficient for `ibm.s`, the P-value of which is very close to zero. So it seems that for IBM stocks, the volatility tends to be slightly higher on Mondays and Fridays.

13.5.5 Multivariate Conditional t-Distribution

In all the multivariate GARCH models fitted so far, it has been assumed that the residuals ϵ_t follow a conditional multivariate normal distribution. The mgarch function also allows the residuals to follow a multivariate Student-t distribution.

If a k-dimensional random variable $\mathbf{u}_t$ follows a multivariate Student-t distribution with ν degrees of freedom and the scale matrix $\mathbf{S}_t$, the probability density function (PDF) of $\mathbf{u}_t$ is given by:

$$f(\mathbf{u}_t) = \frac{\Gamma[(\nu+k)/2]}{(\pi\nu)^{k/2}\Gamma(\nu/2)} \frac{|\mathbf{S}_t|^{-1/2}}{[1 + \mathbf{u}_t'\mathbf{S}_t^{-1}\mathbf{u}_t/\nu]^{(\nu+k)/2}} \tag{13.12}$$

where $\Gamma(\cdot)$ is the gamma function. The covariance matrix of $\mathbf{u}_t$ is given by:

$$\mathrm{Cov}(\mathbf{u}_t) = \frac{\nu}{\nu-2}\mathbf{S}_t.$$

If the error term ϵ_t is assumed in multivariate GARCH models follows a conditional multivariate Student-t distribution with ν degrees of freedom and $\mathrm{Cov}(\epsilon_t) = \Sigma_t$, obviously the scale matrix $\mathbf{S}_t$ should be chosen so that

$$\mathbf{S}_t = \frac{\nu-2}{\nu}\Sigma_t.$$

By substituting the above relationship into (13.12), the user can easily derive the log-likelihood function for multivariate GARCH models with conditional multivariate Student-t distributed errors. The unknown model parameters can also be routinely estimated using maximum likelihood estimation.

To use multivariate Student-t distribution with the mgarch function to estimate a multivariate GARCH model, simply set the optional argument cond.dist to "t". For example:

```
> hp.ibm.dvec.t = mgarch(hp.ibm~1, ~dvec(1,1), cond.dist="t")
```

The estimated degree of freedom ν is contained in the cond.dist component of the returned object:

```
> hp.ibm.dvec.t$cond.dist
$cond.dist:
[1] "t"

$dist.par:
[1] 6.697768

$dist.est:
[1] T
```

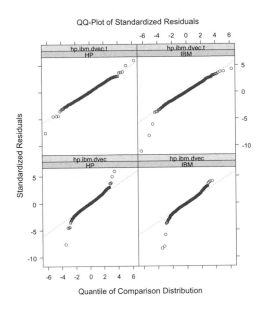

FIGURE 13.9. Comparison of QQ-plot using normal and Student-t distributions.

Compare this model with the one fitted using multivariate normal distribution:

```
> hp.ibm.comp = compare.mgarch(hp.ibm.dvec, hp.ibm.dvec.t)
> hp.ibm.comp
            hp.ibm.dvec hp.ibm.dvec.t
      AIC      -21886       -22231
      BIC      -21825       -22164
Likelihood      10954        11128
> plot(hp.ibm.comp, qq=T)
```

Obviously, the multivariate Student-t distribution provides a much better fit. This can also be confirmed by comparing the QQ-plot of standardized residuals, which is shown in Figure 13.9.

13.6 Multivariate GARCH Prediction

Predictions from multivariate GARCH models can be generated in a similar fashion to predictions from univariate GARCH models. Indeed, for the univariate GARCH-based models, such as CCC model and principal component model, the predictions are generated from the underlying univariate GARCH models and then converted to the scale of the original multivariate time series by using the appropriate transformation. This section focuses on predicting from DVEC model, because predicting from BEKK model can be performed similarly.

For multivariate GARCH models, predictions can be generated for both the levels of the original multivariate time series and its conditional covariance matrix. Predictions of the levels are obtained just as for vector autoregressive (VAR) models. Compared with VAR models, the predictions of the conditional covariance matrix from multivariate GARCH models can be used to construct more reliable confidence intervals for predictions of the levels.

To illustrate the prediction of conditional covariance matrix for multivariate GARCH models, consider the conditional variance equation for the DVEC(1,1) model:

$$\mathbf{\Sigma}_t = \mathbf{A}_0 + \mathbf{A}_1 \otimes (\epsilon_{t-1}\epsilon'_{t-1}) + \mathbf{B}_1 \otimes \Sigma_{t-1}$$

which is estimated over the time period $t = 1, 2, \cdots, T$. To obtain $E_T(\mathbf{\Sigma}_{T+k})$, use the forecasts of conditional covariance matrix at time $T + k$ for $k > 0$, given information at time T. For one-step-ahead prediction, it is easy to obtain:

$$E_T(\mathbf{\Sigma}_{T+1}) = \mathbf{A}_0 + \mathbf{A}_1 \otimes E_T(\epsilon_T\epsilon'_T) + \mathbf{B}_1 \otimes E_T(\mathbf{\Sigma}_T)$$
$$= \mathbf{A}_0 + \mathbf{A}_1 \otimes (\epsilon_T\epsilon'_T) + \mathbf{B}_1 \otimes \mathbf{\Sigma}_T$$

since an estimate of ϵ_T and $\mathbf{\Sigma}_T$ already exists after estimating the DVEC model. When $k = 2$, it can be shown that

$$E_T(\mathbf{\Sigma}_{T+2}) = \mathbf{A}_0 + \mathbf{A}_1 \otimes E_T(\epsilon_{T+1}\epsilon'_{T+1}) + \mathbf{B}_1 \otimes E_T(\mathbf{\Sigma}_{T+1})$$
$$= \mathbf{A}_0 + (\mathbf{A}_1 + \mathbf{B}_1) \otimes E_T(\mathbf{\Sigma}_{T+1}).$$

where $E_T(\mathbf{\Sigma}_{T+1})$ is obtained in the previous step. This procedure can be iterated to obtain $E_T(\mathbf{\Sigma}_{T+k})$ for $k > 2$.

The predict method for "mgarch" objects in S+FinMetrics implements the forecasting procedure for all the multivariate GARCH models supported by the mgarch function. The forecasts can be easily obtained by calling the generic predict function for an "mgarch" object with the desired number of forecasting periods. For example, to obtain 10-step-ahead forecasts from the BEKK model object hp.ibm.bekk fitted in Section 13.5, use the following command:

```
> hp.ibm.pred = predict(hp.ibm.bekk, 10)
> class(hp.ibm.pred)
[1] "predict.mgarch"
> names(hp.ibm.pred)
[1] "series.pred" "sigma.pred"  "R.pred"
```

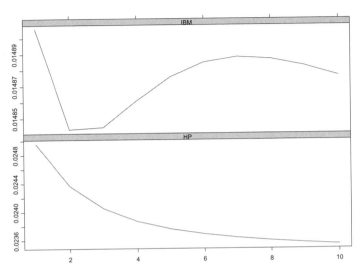

FIGURE 13.10. BEKK prediction of conditional standard deviations.

The returned object `hp.ibm.pred` is of class "`predict.mgarch`", and has three components: `series.pred` represents the forecasts of the levels of the time series, `sigma.pred` represents the forecasts of the conditional standard deviations, and `R.pred` represents the forecasts of the conditional correlation matrix. Note that the `sigma.pred` and `R.pred` components can be used together to obtain the forecasts of the conditional covariance matrix.

S+FinMetrics also implements a `plot` method for "`predict.mgarch`" objects, so that the multivariate forecasts can be visualized directly. For example, if the user calls the generic `plot` function directly on `hp.ibm.pred`:

```
> plot(hp.ibm.pred)
```

```
Make a plot selection (or 0 to exit):
```

```
1: plot: All
2: plot: Predicted Conditional Mean
3: plot: Predicted Conditional SD
Selection:
```

Selecting 3 will generate the plot of predicted conditional standard deviations, as shown in Figure 13.10, the confidence interval of the volatility forecasts should be obtained as well. Section 13.8 shows how to obtain a confidence interval using simulation-based forecasts.

13.7 Custom Estimation of GARCH Models

13.7.1 GARCH Model Objects

For both "garch" and "mgarch" objects, there is a model component which contains all the necessary model specific information about the fitted univariate or multivariate GARCH model. For example, for the univariate "garch" object ford.mod11 fitted in Section 7.4 of Chapter 7:

```
> class(ford.mod11$model)
[1] "garch.model"
> ford.mod11$model

Mean Equation: ford.s ~ 1

Conditional Variance Equation:   ~ garch(1, 1)

 ------------ Constants in mean ------------

      value which
 0.0007708     1

 ---------- Constants in variance ----------

      value which
 6.534e-06     1

 ------------------ ARCH ------------------

          value which
 lag 1 0.07454     1

 ------------------ GARCH ------------------

          value which
 lag 1 0.9102      1
```

So the model component of a "garch" object is of class "garch.model". Similarly, for the "mgarch" object hp.ibm.dvec fitted in this chapter:

```
> class(hp.ibm.dvec$model)
[1] "mgarch.model"
> hp.ibm.dvec$model

Mean Equation: hp.ibm ~ 1

Conditional Variance Equation:   ~ dvec(1, 1)
```

```
------------ Constants in mean ------------

          value which
v1 0.0007017567     T
v2 0.0002932253     T

---------- Constants in variance ----------

        v1.value      v2.value *** v1.which v2.which
v1 3.888696e-05 1.322108e-05 ***        T        T
v2 1.322108e-05 2.876733e-05 ***        T        T

------------------ ARCH ------------------

Lag 1
       v1.value    v2.value *** v1.which v2.which
v1 0.06225657 0.03393546 ***        T        T
v2 0.03393546 0.10485809 ***        T        T

------------------ GARCH ------------------

Lag 1
     v1.value   v2.value *** v1.which v2.which
v1 0.8567934 0.8783100 ***        T        T
v2 0.8783100 0.7421328 ***        T        T
```

So the model component of an "mgarch" object is of class "mgarch.model",
which has similar structures to a "garch.model" object. This section will
focus on "mgarch.model" objects, though all the things illustrated can also
be applied to "garch.model" objects.

Since an "mgarch.model" object contains all the necessary information
about a fitted GARCH model, this object can be saved or edited for many
purposes.[6] The names of the components of an "mgarch.model" object can
be obtained using the S-PLUS function names:

```
> names(hp.ibm.dvec$model)
[1] "c.which" "c.value" "MA"      "AR"      "arch"    "garch"
[7] "a.which" "a.value" "info"
```

---

[6] In the first release of S+GARCH module, there was a revise function which provides
a graphical user interface for editing this object. However, the function was broken as
the graphical user interface of S-PLUS went through several evolutions. Currently there
is no revise function in S+FinMetrics module.

The component c.value contains the value of the constant terms in the conditional mean equation, while the component a.value contains the value of the constant terms in the conditional variance equation. The MA, AR, arch and garch components are lists themselves. For example:

```
> hp.ibm.dvec$model$arch
$order:
[1] 1

$value:
$lag.1:
           [,1]        [,2]
[1,] 0.06225657 0.03393546
[2,] 0.03393546 0.10485809


$which:
$lag.1:
     [,1] [,2]
[1,]   T    T
[2,]   T    T
```

Note that for each of the model coefficients, there is a corresponding which component that specifies if the coefficient is free to be estimated by MLE. If the which component is 1 or TRUE, then the corresponding coefficient is free to be estimated; otherwise, the corresponding coefficient is fixed at that value during MLE. The next subsection shows how these values can be edited for different purposes.

13.7.2 Revision of GARCH Model Estimation

For both univariate and multivariate GARCH models, the unknown model parameters are estimated using the BHHH algorithm (for example, see Bollerslev, 1986). Both garch and mgarch functions take an optional argument control, which can be used to control certain numerical aspects of the BHHH algorithm. The defaults for those settings are provided in the on-line help file for bhhh.control.

Like many other nonlinear optimization algorithms, the BHHH algorithm performs local optimization in the sense that the optimal solution it finds may well be just a local optimum instead of the global optimum. To make sure that the global optimum has indeed been reached, start the algorithm using a few different starting values and see if they all lead to the same optimum. For this purpose, edit the model component of a fitted "garch" or "mgarch" object and use it as a new starting value.

Example 85 *Restarting multivariate GARCH estimation*

```
> bekk.mod = hp.ibm.bekk$model
> bekk.mod$a.value[2,1] = 0
> hp.ibm.bekk2 = mgarch(series=hp.ibm, model=bekk.mod)
```

Note that when a model object is supplied directly to the mgarch (or garch) function, the series argument must be used to supply the data. The user can easily verify that hp.ibm.bekk2 reached a smaller log-likelihood value, so the original fit hp.ibm.bekk seems to be better.

Example 86 *Constraining multivariate GARCH estimation*

For some GARCH models, the user may want to fix certain parameters at certain values during maximum likelihood estimation. For example, most daily financial security returns seem to fluctuate around a zero mean. In this example, fix the constant terms in the conditional mean equation of hp.ibm.bekk to zero and re-estimate the model:

```
> bekk.mod = hp.ibm.bekk$model
> bekk.mod$c.value = rep(0,2)
> bekk.mod$c.which = rep(F,2)
> hp.ibm.bekk3 = mgarch(series=hp.ibm, model=bekk.mod)
> LR.stat = -2*(hp.ibm.bekk3$likelihood-
+ hp.ibm.bekk$likelihood)
```

Note that since the log-likelihood value of the fitted model is returned, a likelihood ratio (LR) test of the restrictions imposed in the above example can easily be performed.

The "garch.model" or "mgarch.model" object can be used for simulation. For example, simulation from fitted univariate GARCH models actually uses this component. The next section illustrates this usage for multivariate GARCH models.

13.8   Multivariate GARCH Model Simulation

S+FinMetrics provides a method of the generic function simulate for objects of class "mgarch". The method function, simulate.mgarch, can take a fitted "mgarch" object, or an "mgarch.model object, or simply a user specified list. This section illustrates how to create confidence intervals for the predictions of conditional standard deviations using simulations.

Example 87 *Simulation-based multivariate GARCH forecasts*

The function simulate.mgarch only supports those multivariate GARCH models of order $(1,1)$, which should be enough for most applications. To simulate a multivariate GARCH process directly from a fitted "mgarch" object such as hp.ibm.bekk, call the generic function simulate as follows:

```
> hp.ibm.sim = simulate(hp.ibm.bekk, n=10)
```

where $n = 10$ specifies the length of the simulated time series. Since all the model specific information is contained in the `model` component of an "mgarch" object, which is an "mgarch.model" object as shown in the previous section, an "mgarch.model can also pass directly to the function `simulate.mgarch`. The following code example simulates 100 steps ahead from the end of estimation period in `hp.ibm.bekk`, and replicates the simulation 200 times:

```
> eps.start = residuals(hp.ibm.bekk)[2000,]@data
> V.start = hp.ibm.bekk$S.t[2000, , ]
> n.rep = 200
> hp.ibm.sim = array(0, c(100, 2, n.rep))

> set.seed(10)
> for (i in 1:n.rep) {
+    eps.pred = rbind(eps.start, rmvnorm(100))
+    tmp = simulate(hp.ibm.bekk, n=100, n.start=0,
+          etat=eps.pred, V.start=V.start)$V.t
+    hp.ibm.sim[, , i] = matrix(tmp, byrow=T, nrow=100)[,c(1,4)]
+ }

> hp.ibm.sim = sqrt(hp.ibm.sim)
> hp.ibm.simpred = rowMeans(hp.ibm.sim, dims=2)
> hp.ibm.simstde = rowStdevs(hp.ibm.sim, dims=2)
```

Note that to simulate the multivariate GARCH process using the last observation in the sample as the starting value, set `n.start=0` and `V.start` to the last estimated conditional covariance matrix. Similarly, the last estimated residual vector is used as the starting value in `eps.pred`, which is otherwise standard normal random variables. All the simulated conditional standard deviations are saved in `hp.ibm.sim`, which is a three dimensional array. The simulation-based forecasts of conditional standard deviations are computed as the average of `hp.ibm.sim`, and saved in the object `hp.ibm.simpred`, while `hp.ibm.simstde` contains the standard errors of those forecasts.

Finally, use the following code to plot confidence intervals around the simulation-based forecasts:

```
> par(mfrow=c(2,1))
> ci.upper = hp.ibm.simpred + 2*hp.ibm.simstde
> ci.lower = hp.ibm.simpred - 2*hp.ibm.simstde

> tsplot(cbind(hp.ibm.simpred[,1], ci.upper[,1], ci.lower[,1]))
> title("Forecasted HP Volatility", xlab="Time", ylab="SD")
```

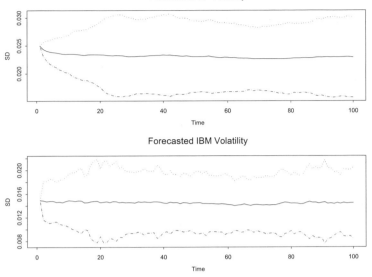

FIGURE 13.11. Simulation-based forecasts of BEKK model.

```
> tsplot(cbind(hp.ibm.simpred[,2], ci.upper[,2], ci.lower[,2]))
> title("Forecasted IBM Volatility", xlab="Time", ylab="SD")
> par(mfrow=c(1,1))
```

The plot shown in Figure 13.11 only used 200 replications, so the confidence intervals are a little rough. If more replications are used, the confidence intervals should be relatively smooth.

13.9   References

[1] ALEXANDER, C. O. (1998). "Volatility and Correlation: Methods, Models and Applications", in C. O. Alexander (ed.) *Risk Management and Analysis: Measuring and Modeling Financial Risk*, Wiley.

[2] ANDREOU, E., AND GHYSELS, E. (2002). "Rolling Volatility Estimators: Some new Theoretical, Simulation and Empirical Results", *Journal of Business and Economic Statistics*, 20 (3), 363-376.

[3] BOLLERSLEV, T. (1986). "Generalized Autoregressive Conditional Heteroskedasticity", *Journal of Econometrics*, 31, 307-327.

[4] BOLLERSLEV, T. (1990). "Modeling the Coherence in Short-run Nominal Exchange Rates: a Multivariate Generalized ARCH Model", *Review of Economics and Statistics*, 72, 498-505.

[5] BOLLERSLEV, T., ENGLE, R. F., AND NELSON, D. B. (1994). "ARCH Models", in R. F. Engle and D. L. McFadden (eds.) *Handbook of Econometrics*, Vol. 4, Elsevier Science B. V.

[6] BOLLERSLEV, T., ENGLE, R. F., AND WOOLDRIDGE, J. M. (1988). "A Capital-Asset Pricing Model with Time-Varying Covariances", *Journal of Political Economy*, 96, 116-131.

[7] BOUGEROL, P., AND PICARD, N. (1992). "Stationarity of GARCH Processes and of Some Nonnegative Time Series", *Journal of Econometrics*, 52, 115-127.

[8] DING, Z. (1994). "Time Series Analysis of Speculative Returns", *Ph.D. Thesis*, Department of Economics, University of California, San Diego.

[9] ENGLE, R. F., AND BOLLERSLEV, T. (1986). "Modeling the Persistence of Conditional Variances", *Econometric Reviews*, 5, 1-50.

[10] ENGLE, R. F., AND KRONER, K. F. (1995). "Multivariate Simultaneous Generalized ARCH", *Econometric Theory*, 11, 122-150.

[11] FLEMING, J., KIRBY, C., AND OSTDIEK, B. (2001). "The Economic Value of Volatility Timing", *Journal of Finance*, 56, 329-352.

[12] FOSTER, D. P., AND NELSON, D. B. (1996). "Continuous Record Asymptotics for Rolling Sample Variance Estimators", *Econometrica*, 64, 139-174.

[13] HOSKING, J. R. M. (1980). "The Multivariate Portmanteau Statistic", *Journal of the American Statistical Association*, 75, 602-608.

[14] NELSON, D. B. (1990). "Stationarity and Persistence in the GARCH (1,1) Model", *Econometric Theory*, 6, 318-334.

14
State Space Models

14.1 Introduction

The state space modeling tools in S+FinMetrics are based on the algorithms in *SsfPack* 3.0 developed by Siem Jan Koopman and described in Koopman, Shephard and Doornik (1999, 2001)[1]. *SsfPack* is a suite of C routines for carrying out computations involving the statistical analysis of univariate and multivariate models in state space form. The routines allow for a variety of state space forms from simple time invariant models to complicated time-varying models. Functions are available to put standard models like ARMA and spline models in state space form. General routines are available for filtering, smoothing, simulation smoothing, likelihood evaluation, forecasting and signal extraction. Full details of the statistical analysis is provided in Durbin and Koopman (2001). This chapter gives an overview of state space modeling and the reader is referred to the papers by Koopman, Shephard and Doornik for technical details on the algorithms used in the S+FinMetrics/SsfPack functions.

This chapter is organized as follows. Section 14.2 describes the general state space model and state space representation required for the S+FinMetrics/SsfPack state space functions. Subsections describe the various S+FinMetrics/SsfPack functions for putting common time series models into state space form. The process of simulating observations from a given state space model is also covered. Section 14.3 summarizes the main

---

[1]Information about *Ssfpack* can be found at http://www.ssfpack.com.

algorithms used for the analysis of state space models. These include the Kalman filter, Kalman smoother, moment smoothing, disturbance smoothing and forecasting. Estimation of the unknown parameters in a state space model is described in Section 14.4. The chapter concludes with a short discussion of simulation smoothing.

Textbook treatments of state space models are given in Harvey (1989, 1993), Hamilton (1994), West and Harrison (1997), and Kim and Nelson (1999). Interesting applications of state space models in finance are given in Engle and Watson (1987), Bomhoff (1994), Duan and Simonato (1999), and Harvey, Ruiz and Shephard (1994), Carmona (2001) and Chan (2002).

14.2 State Space Representation

Many dynamic time series models in economics and finance may be represented in *state space form*. Some common examples are ARMA models, time-varying regression models, dynamic linear models with unobserved components, discrete versions of continuous time diffusion processes, stochastic volatility models, non-parametric and spline regressions. The linear Gaussian *state space model* may be represented as the system of equations

$$
\underset{m\times 1}{\boldsymbol{\alpha}_{t+1}} = \underset{m\times 1}{\mathbf{d}_t} + \underset{m\times m}{\mathbf{T}_t} \cdot \underset{m\times 1}{\boldsymbol{\alpha}_t} + \underset{m\times r}{\mathbf{H}_t} \cdot \underset{r\times 1}{\boldsymbol{\eta}_t} \tag{14.1}
$$

$$
\underset{N\times 1}{\boldsymbol{\theta}_t} = \underset{N\times 1}{\mathbf{c}_t} + \underset{N\times m}{\mathbf{Z}_t} \cdot \underset{m\times 1}{\boldsymbol{\alpha}_t} \tag{14.2}
$$

$$
\underset{N\times 1}{\mathbf{y}_t} = \underset{N\times 1}{\boldsymbol{\theta}_t} + \underset{N\times N}{\mathbf{G}_t} \cdot \underset{N\times 1}{\boldsymbol{\varepsilon}_t} \tag{14.3}
$$

where $t = 1, \ldots, n$ and

$$
\boldsymbol{\alpha}_1 \sim N(\mathbf{a}, \mathbf{P}), \tag{14.4}
$$

$$
\boldsymbol{\eta}_t \sim iid\ N(0, \mathbf{I}_r) \tag{14.5}
$$

$$
\boldsymbol{\varepsilon}_t \sim iid\ N(\mathbf{0}, \mathbf{I}_N) \tag{14.6}
$$

and it is assumed that

$$
E[\boldsymbol{\varepsilon}_t \boldsymbol{\eta}_t'] = \mathbf{0}
$$

In (14.4), $\mathbf{a}$ and $\mathbf{P}$ are fixed and known but that can be generalized. The *state vector* $\boldsymbol{\alpha}_t$ contains unobserved stochastic processes and unknown fixed effects and the *transition equation* (14.1) describes the evolution of the state vector over time using a first order Markov structure. The *measurement equation* (14.3) describes the vector of observations $\mathbf{y}_t$ in terms of the state vector $\boldsymbol{\alpha}_t$ through the signal $\boldsymbol{\theta}_t$ and a vector of disturbances $\boldsymbol{\varepsilon}_t$. It is assumed that the innovations in the transition equation and the innovations in the measurement equation are independent, but this assumption can be relaxed. The deterministic matrices $\mathbf{T}_t, \mathbf{Z}_t, \mathbf{H}_t, \mathbf{G}_t$ are called *system matrices* and are usually sparse selection matrices. The vectors $\mathbf{d}_t$ and $\mathbf{c}_t$ contain fixed components and may be used to incorporate known effects or known patterns into the model; otherwise they are equal to zero.

The state space model (14.1)-(14.6) may be compactly expressed as

$$
\begin{pmatrix} \boldsymbol{\alpha}_{t+1} \\ \mathbf{y}_t \end{pmatrix} = \underset{(m+N)\times 1}{\boldsymbol{\delta}_t} + \underset{(m+N)\times m}{\boldsymbol{\Phi}_t} \cdot \underset{m\times 1}{\boldsymbol{\alpha}_t} + \underset{(m+N)\times 1}{\mathbf{u}_t}, \qquad (14.7)
$$

$$
\boldsymbol{\alpha}_1 \sim N(\mathbf{a}, \mathbf{P}) \qquad (14.8)
$$

$$
\mathbf{u}_t \sim iid\ N(\mathbf{0}, \boldsymbol{\Omega}_t) \qquad (14.9)
$$

where

$$
\boldsymbol{\delta}_t = \begin{pmatrix} \mathbf{d}_t \\ \mathbf{c}_t \end{pmatrix}, \boldsymbol{\Phi}_t = \begin{pmatrix} \mathbf{T}_t \\ \mathbf{Z}_t \end{pmatrix}, \mathbf{u}_t = \begin{pmatrix} \mathbf{H}_t \boldsymbol{\eta}_t \\ \mathbf{G}_t \boldsymbol{\varepsilon}_t \end{pmatrix}, \boldsymbol{\Omega}_t = \begin{pmatrix} \mathbf{H}_t \mathbf{H}_t' & \mathbf{0} \\ \mathbf{0} & \mathbf{G}_t \mathbf{G}_t' \end{pmatrix}
$$

The initial value parameters are summarized in the $(m+1) \times m$ matrix

$$
\boldsymbol{\Sigma} = \begin{pmatrix} \mathbf{P} \\ \mathbf{a}' \end{pmatrix} \qquad (14.10)
$$

For multivariate models, i.e. $N > 1$, it is assumed that the $N \times N$ matrix $\mathbf{G}_t \mathbf{G}_t'$ is diagonal. In general, the system matrices in (14.7) are time varying.

14.2.1 *Initial Conditions*

The variance matrix $\mathbf{P}$ of the initial state vector $\boldsymbol{\alpha}_1$ is assumed to be of the form

$$
\mathbf{P} = \mathbf{P}_* + \kappa \mathbf{P}_\infty \qquad (14.11)
$$

where $\mathbf{P}_\infty$ and $\mathbf{P}_*$ are symmetric $m \times m$ matrices with ranks r_∞ and r_*, respectively, and κ is a large scalar value, e.g. $\kappa = 10^6$. The matrix $\mathbf{P}_*$ captures the covariance structure of the stationary components in the initial state vector, and the matrix $\mathbf{P}_\infty$ is used to specify the initial variance matrix for nonstationary components. When the ith diagonal element of $\mathbf{P}_\infty$ is negative, the corresponding ith column and row of $\mathbf{P}_*$ are assumed to be zero, and the corresponding row and column of $\mathbf{P}_\infty$ will be taken into consideration. When some elements of state vector are nonstationary, the S+FinMetrics/SsfPack algorithms implement an "exact diffuse prior" approach as described in Durbin and Koopman (2001) and Koopman, Shephard and Doornik (2001).

14.2.2 *State Space Representation in S+FinMetrics/SsfPack*

State space models in S+FinMetrics/SsfPack utilize the compact representation (14.7) with initial value information (14.10). The following examples describe the specification of a state space model for use in the S+FinMetrics/SsfPack state space modeling functions.

Example 88 *State space representation of the local level model*

Consider the following simple model for the stochastic evolution of the logarithm of an asset price y_t

$$
\begin{align}
\alpha_{t+1} &= \alpha_t + \eta_t^*, \; \eta_t^* \sim iid \; N(0, \sigma_\eta^2) \tag{14.12}\\
y_t &= \alpha_t + \varepsilon_t^*, \; \varepsilon_t^* \sim iid \; N(0, \sigma_\varepsilon^2) \tag{14.13}\\
\alpha_1 &\sim N(a, P) \tag{14.14}
\end{align}
$$

where it is assumed that $E[\varepsilon_t^* \eta_t^*] = 0$. In the above model, the observed asset price y_t is the sum of two unobserved components, α_t and ε_t^*. The component α_t is the state variable and represents the fundamental value (signal) of the asset. The transition equation (14.12) shows that the fundamental values evolve according to a random walk. The component ε_t^* represents random deviations (noise) from the fundamental value that are assumed to be independent from the innovations to α_t. The strength of the signal in the fundamental value relative to the random deviation is measured by the signal-to-noise ratio of variances $q = \sigma_\eta^2 / \sigma_\varepsilon^2$. The model (14.12)-(14.14) is called the *random walk plus noise model, signal plus noise model* or the *local level model.*[2]

The state space form (14.7) of the local level model has time invariant parameters

$$
\boldsymbol{\delta} = \begin{pmatrix} 0 \\ 0 \end{pmatrix}, \boldsymbol{\Phi} = \begin{pmatrix} 1 \\ 1 \end{pmatrix}, \boldsymbol{\Omega} = \begin{pmatrix} \sigma_\eta^2 & 0 \\ 0 & \sigma_\varepsilon^2 \end{pmatrix} \tag{14.15}
$$

with errors $\sigma_\eta \eta_t = \eta_t^*$ and $\sigma_\varepsilon \varepsilon_t = \varepsilon_t^*$. Since the state variable α_t is $I(1)$, the unconditional distribution of the initial state α_1 doesn't have finite variance. In this case, it is customary to set $a = E[\alpha_1] = 0$ and $P = var(\alpha_1)$ to some large positive number, e.g. $P = 10^7$, in (14.14) to reflect that no prior information is available. Using (14.11), the initial variance is specified with $P_* = 0$ and $P_\infty = 1$. Therefore, the initial state matrix (14.10) for the local level model has the form

$$
\boldsymbol{\Sigma} = \begin{pmatrix} -1 \\ 0 \end{pmatrix} \tag{14.16}
$$

where -1 implies that $P_\infty = 1$.

In S+FinMetrics/SsfPack, a state space model is specified by creating either a list variable with components giving the minimum components necessary for describing a particular state space form or by creating an "ssf" object. To illustrate, consider creating a list variable containing the state space parameters in (14.15)-(14.16), with $\sigma_\eta = 0.5$ and $\sigma_\varepsilon = 1$

---

[2] A detailed technical analysis of this model is given in Durbin and Koopman (2001), chapter 2.

State space parameter	List component name
δ	mDelta
Φ	mPhi
Ω	mOmega
Σ	mSigma

TABLE 14.1. State space form list components

```
> sigma.e = 1
> sigma.n = 0.5
> a1 = 0
> P1 = -1
> ssf.ll.list = list(mPhi=as.matrix(c(1,1)),
+ mOmega=diag(c(sigma.n^2,sigma.e^2)),
+ mSigma=as.matrix(c(P1,a1)))
> ssf.ll.list
$mPhi:
      [,1]
[1,]    1
[2,]    1

$mOmega:
      [,1] [,2]
[1,] 0.25    0
[2,] 0.00    1

$mSigma:
      [,1]
[1,]   -1
[2,]    0
```

In the list variable **ssf.ll.list**, the component names match the state space form parameters in (14.7) and (14.10). This naming convention, summarized in Table 14.1, must be used for the specification of any valid state space model. Also, notice the use of the coercion function **as.matrix**. This ensures that the dimensions of the state space parameters are correctly specified.

An "ssf" object may be created from the list variable **ssf.ll.list** using the S+FinMetrics/SsfPack function CheckSsf:

```
> ssf.ll = CheckSsf(ssf.ll.list)
> class(ssf.ll)
[1] "ssf"
> names(ssf.ll)
 [1] "mDelta"  "mPhi"    "mOmega"  "mSigma"  "mJPhi"
 [6] "mJOmega" "mJDelta" "mX"      "cT"      "cX"
```

```
[11] "cY"        "cSt"
> ssf.ll
$mPhi:
      [,1]
[1,]    1
[2,]    1

$mOmega:
      [,1] [,2]
[1,] 0.25    0
[2,] 0.00    1

$mSigma:
      [,1]
[1,]    -1
[2,]     0

$mDelta:
      [,1]
[1,]     0
[2,]     0

$mJPhi:
[1] 0

$mJOmega:
[1] 0

$mJDelta:
[1] 0

$mX:
[1] 0

$cT:
[1] 0

$cX:
[1] 0

$cY:
[1] 1

$cSt:
[1] 1
```

```
attr(, "class"):
[1] "ssf"
```

The function `CheckSsf` takes a list variable with a minimum state space form, coerces the components to matrix objects and returns the full parameterization of a state space model used in many of the S+FinMetrics/SsfPack state space modeling functions. See the online help for `CheckSsf` for descriptions of the components of an "ssf" object.

Example 89 *State space representation of a time varying parameter regression model*

Consider the Capital Asset Pricing Model (CAPM) with time varying intercept and slope

$$r_t = \alpha_t + \beta_t r_{M,t} + \nu_t, \ \nu_t \sim GWN(0, \sigma_\nu^2) \tag{14.17}$$

$$\alpha_{t+1} = \alpha_t + \xi_t, \ \xi_t \sim GWN(0, \sigma_\xi^2) \tag{14.18}$$

$$\beta_{t+1} = \beta_t + \varsigma_t, \ \varsigma_t \sim GWN(0, \sigma_\varsigma^2) \tag{14.19}$$

where r_t denotes the return on an asset in excess of the risk free rate, and $r_{M,t}$ denotes the excess return on a market index. In this model, both the abnormal excess return α_t and asset risk β_t are allowed to vary over time following a random walk specification. Let $\boldsymbol{\alpha}_t = (\alpha_t, \beta_t)'$, $y_t = r_t$, $\mathbf{x}_t = (1, r_{M,t})'$, $\mathbf{H}_t = diag(\sigma_\xi, \sigma_\varsigma)'$ and $G_t = \sigma_\nu$. Then the state space form (14.7) of (14.17) - (14.19) is

$$\left(\begin{array}{c} \boldsymbol{\alpha}_{t+1} \\ y_t \end{array} \right) = \left(\begin{array}{c} \mathbf{I}_2 \\ \mathbf{x}_t' \end{array} \right) \boldsymbol{\alpha}_t + \left(\begin{array}{c} \mathbf{H}\boldsymbol{\eta}_t \\ G\varepsilon_t \end{array} \right)$$

and has parameters

$$\boldsymbol{\Phi}_t = \left(\begin{array}{c} \mathbf{I}_2 \\ \mathbf{x}_t' \end{array} \right), \ \boldsymbol{\Omega} = \left(\begin{array}{ccc} \sigma_\xi^2 & 0 & 0 \\ 0 & \sigma_\varsigma^2 & 0 \\ 0 & 0 & \sigma_\nu^2 \end{array} \right) \tag{14.20}$$

Since $\boldsymbol{\alpha}_t$ is $I(1)$ the initial state vector $\boldsymbol{\alpha}_1$ doesn't have finite variance so it is customary to set $\mathbf{a} = \mathbf{0}$ and $\mathbf{P} = \kappa \mathbf{I}_2$ where κ is large. Using (14.11), the initial variance is specified with $\mathbf{P}_* = \mathbf{0}$ and $\mathbf{P}_\infty = \mathbf{I}_2$. Therefore, the initial state matrix (14.10) for the time varying CAPM has the form

$$\boldsymbol{\Sigma} = \left(\begin{array}{cc} -1 & 0 \\ 0 & -1 \\ 0 & 0 \end{array} \right)$$

The state space parameter matrix $\boldsymbol{\Phi}_t$ in (14.20) has a time varying system element $\mathbf{Z}_t = \mathbf{x}_t'$. In S+FinMetrics/SsfPack, the specification of this time varying element in $\mathbf{\Phi}_t$ requires an index matrix $\mathbf{J}_\Phi$ and a data matrix $\mathbf{X}$ to which the indices in $\mathbf{J}_\Phi$ refer. The index matrix $\mathbf{J}_\Phi$ must have the same dimension as $\mathbf{\Phi}_t$. The elements of $\mathbf{J}_\Phi$ are all set to -1 except the elements for which the corresponding elements of $\mathbf{\Phi}_t$ are time varying. The non-negative index value indicates the column of the data matrix $\mathbf{X}$ which contains the time varying values.

The specification of the state space form for the time varying CAPM requires values for the variances σ_ξ^2, σ_ς^2, and σ_ν^2 as well as a data matrix $\mathbf{X}$ whose rows correspond with $\mathbf{Z}_t = \mathbf{x}_t' = (1, r_{M,t})$. For example, let $\sigma_\xi^2 = (0.01)^2$, $\sigma_\varsigma^2 = (0.05)^2$ and $\sigma_\nu^2 = (0.1)^2$ and construct the data matrix $\mathbf{X}$ using the excess return data in the S+FinMetrics "timeSeries" excessReturns.ts

```
> X.mat = cbind(1,
+ as.matrix(seriesData(excessReturns.ts[,"SP500"])))
```

The state space form may be created using

```
> Phi.t = rbind(diag(2),rep(0,2))
> Omega = diag(c((.01)^2,(.05)^2,(.1)^2))
> J.Phi = matrix(-1,3,2)
> J.Phi[3,1] = 1
> J.Phi[3,2] = 2
> Sigma = -Phi.t
> ssf.tvp.capm = list(mPhi=Phi.t,
+ mOmega=Omega,
+ mJPhi=J.Phi,
+ mSigma=Sigma,
+ mX=X.mat)
> ssf.tvp.capm
$mPhi:
      [,1] [,2]
[1,]    1    0
[2,]    0    1
[3,]    0    0

$mOmega:
        [,1]    [,2] [,3]
[1,] 0.0001 0.0000 0.00
[2,] 0.0000 0.0025 0.00
[3,] 0.0000 0.0000 0.01

$mJPhi:
      [,1] [,2]
[1,]   -1   -1
[2,]   -1   -1
```

Parameter index matrix	List component name
$\mathbf{J}_\delta$	mJDelta
$\mathbf{J}_\Phi$	mJPhi
$\mathbf{J}_\Omega$	mJOmega
Time varying component data matrix	List component name
$\mathbf{X}$	mX

TABLE 14.2. S+FinMetrics time varying state space components

```
[3,]    1    2

$mSigma:
      [,1] [,2]
[1,]   -1    0
[2,]    0   -1
[3,]    0    0


$mX:
numeric matrix: 131 rows, 2 columns.
         SP500
  1 1   0.002803
  2 1   0.017566
...
131 1 -0.0007548
```

Notice in the specification of $\mathbf{\Phi}_t$ the values associated with $\mathbf{x}'_t$ in the third row are set to zero. In the index matrix $\mathbf{J}_\Phi$, the (3,1) element is 1 and the (3,2) element is 2 indicating that the data for the first and second columns of $\mathbf{x}'_t$ come from the first and second columns of the component mX, respectively.

In the general state space model (14.7), it is possible that all of the system matrices δ_t, $\mathbf{\Phi}_t$ and $\mathbf{\Omega}_t$ have time varying elements. The corresponding index matrices $\mathbf{J}_\delta$, $\mathbf{J}_\Phi$ and $\mathbf{J}_\Omega$ indicate which elements of the matrices δ_t, $\mathbf{\Phi}_t$ and $\mathbf{\Omega}_t$ are time varying and the data matrix $\mathbf{X}$ contains the time varying components. The naming convention for these components is summarized in Table 14.2.

14.2.3 Missing Values

The S+FinMetrics/SsfPack state space modeling functions can handle missing values in the vector of response variables $\mathbf{y}_t$ in (14.3). Missing values are not allowed in the state space system matrices $\mathbf{\Phi}_t$, $\mathbf{\Omega}_t$, $\mathbf{\Sigma}$ and δ_t. Missing values are represented by NA in S-PLUS.

In the S+FinMetrics/SsfPack state space functions, the observation vector $\mathbf{y}_t$ with missing values will be be reduced to the vector $\mathbf{y}_t^\dagger$ without missing values and the measurement equation will be adjusted accordingly.

For example, the measurement equation $\mathbf{y}_t = \mathbf{c}_t + \mathbf{Z}_t\boldsymbol{\alpha}_t + \mathbf{G}_t\boldsymbol{\varepsilon}_t$ with

$$
\mathbf{y}_t = \begin{pmatrix} 5 \\ NA \\ 3 \\ NA \end{pmatrix}, \quad \mathbf{c}_t = \begin{pmatrix} 1 \\ 2 \\ 3 \\ 4 \end{pmatrix}, \quad \mathbf{Z}_t = \begin{pmatrix} Z_{1,t} \\ Z_{2,t} \\ Z_{3,t} \\ Z_{4,t} \end{pmatrix}, \quad \mathbf{G}_t = \begin{pmatrix} G_{1,t} \\ G_{2,t} \\ G_{3,t} \\ G_{4,t} \end{pmatrix}
$$

reduces to the measurement equation $\mathbf{y}_t^\dagger = \mathbf{c}_t^\dagger + \mathbf{Z}_t^\dagger\boldsymbol{\alpha}_t + \mathbf{G}_t^\dagger\boldsymbol{\varepsilon}_t$ with

$$
\mathbf{y}_t^\dagger = \begin{pmatrix} 5 \\ 3 \end{pmatrix}, \quad \mathbf{c}_t^\dagger = \begin{pmatrix} 1 \\ 3 \end{pmatrix}, \quad \mathbf{Z}_t^\dagger = \begin{pmatrix} Z_{1,t} \\ Z_{3,t} \end{pmatrix}, \quad \mathbf{G}_t^\dagger = \begin{pmatrix} G_{1,t} \\ G_{3,t} \end{pmatrix}
$$

The *SsfPack* algorithms in S+FinMetrics automatically replace the observation vector $\mathbf{y}_t$ with $\mathbf{y}_t^\dagger$ when missing values are encountered and the system matrices are adjusted accordingly.

14.2.4 *S+FinMetrics/SsfPack Functions for Specifying the State Space Form for Some Common Time Series Models*

S+FinMetrics/SsfPack has functions for the creation of the state space representation of some common time series models. These functions and models are described in the following sub-sections.

ARMA Models

Following Harvey (1993, Section 4.4), the ARMA(p, q) model with zero mean[3]

$$
y_t = \phi_1 y_{t-1} + \cdots + \phi_p y_{t-p} + \xi_t + \theta_1\xi_{t-1} + \cdots + \theta_q\xi_{t-q} \tag{14.21}
$$

may be put in state space form with transition and measurement equations

$$
\begin{aligned}
\boldsymbol{\alpha}_{t+1} &= \mathbf{T}\boldsymbol{\alpha}_t + \mathbf{H}\xi_t, \ \xi_t \sim N(0, \sigma_\varepsilon^2) \\
y_t &= \mathbf{Z}\boldsymbol{\alpha}_t
\end{aligned}
$$

and time invariant system matrices

$$
\mathbf{T} = \begin{pmatrix} \phi_1 & 1 & 0 & \cdots & 0 \\ \phi_2 & 0 & 1 & & 0 \\ \vdots & & & \ddots & \vdots \\ \phi_{m-1} & 0 & 0 & & 1 \\ \phi_m & 0 & 0 & \cdots & \end{pmatrix}, \quad \mathbf{H} = \begin{pmatrix} 1 \\ \theta_1 \\ \vdots \\ \theta_{m-1} \\ \theta_m \end{pmatrix}, \tag{14.22}
$$

$$
\mathbf{Z} = \begin{pmatrix} 1 & 0 & \cdots & 0 & 0 \end{pmatrix}
$$

---

[3] Note that the MA coefficients are specified with positive signs, which is the opposite of how the MA coefficients are specified for models estimated by the S-PLUS function `arima.mle`.

where $\mathbf{d}, \mathbf{c}$ and $\mathbf{G}$ of the state space form (14.1)-(14.3) are all zero and $m = \max(p, q+1)$. The state vector $\boldsymbol{\alpha}_t$ has the form

$$
\boldsymbol{\alpha}_t = \begin{pmatrix} y_t \\ \phi_2 y_{t-1} + \cdots + \phi_p y_{t-m+1} + \theta_1 \xi_t + \cdots + \theta_{m-1} \xi_{t-m+2} \\ \phi_3 y_{t-1} + \cdots + \phi_p y_{t-m+2} + \theta_2 \xi_t + \cdots + \theta_{m-1} \xi_{t-m+3} \\ \vdots \\ \phi_m y_{t-1} + \theta_{m-1} \xi_t \end{pmatrix} \quad (14.23)
$$

In compact state space form (14.7), the model is

$$
\begin{pmatrix} \boldsymbol{\alpha}_{t+1} \\ y_t \end{pmatrix} = \begin{pmatrix} \mathbf{T} \\ \mathbf{Z} \end{pmatrix} \boldsymbol{\alpha}_t + \begin{pmatrix} \mathbf{H} \\ 0 \end{pmatrix} \xi_t
$$
$$
= \boldsymbol{\Phi} \boldsymbol{\alpha}_t + \mathbf{u}_t
$$

and

$$
\Omega = \begin{pmatrix} \sigma_\xi^2 \mathbf{H} \mathbf{H}' & 0 \\ 0 & 0 \end{pmatrix}
$$

If y_t is stationary then $\boldsymbol{\alpha}_t \sim N(0, \mathbf{V})$ is the unconditional distribution of the state vector, and the covariance matrix $\mathbf{V}$ satisfies $\mathbf{V} = \mathbf{T} \mathbf{V} \mathbf{T}' + \sigma_\xi^2 \mathbf{H} \mathbf{H}'$, which can be solved for the elements of $\mathbf{V}$. The initial value parameters are then

$$
\boldsymbol{\Sigma} = \begin{pmatrix} \mathbf{V} \\ \mathbf{0}' \end{pmatrix}
$$

The S+FinMetrics/SsfPack function GetSsfArma creates the state space system matrices for any univariate stationary and invertible ARMA model. The arguments expected by GetSsfArma are

```
> args(GetSsfArma)
function(ar = NULL, ma = NULL, sigma = 1, model = NULL)
```

where ar is the vector of p AR coefficients, ma is the vector of q MA coefficients, sigma is the innovation standard deviation σ_ξ, and model is a list with components giving the AR, MA and innovation standard deviation. If the arguments ar, ma, and sigma are specified, then model is ignored. The function GetSsfArma returns a list containing the system matrices $\boldsymbol{\Phi}$, $\boldsymbol{\Omega}$ and the initial value parameters $\boldsymbol{\Sigma}$.

Example 90 *AR(1) and ARMA(2,1)*

Consider the AR(1) model

$$
y_t = 0.75 y_{t-1} + \xi_t, \ \xi_t \sim GWN(0, (0.5)^2)
$$

The state space form may be computed using

```
> ssf.ar1 = GetSsfArma(ar=0.75,sigma=.5)
> ssf.ar1
$mPhi:
      [,1]
[1,]  0.75
[2,]  1.00

$mOmega:
      [,1] [,2]
[1,]  0.25    0
[2,]  0.00    0

$mSigma:
        [,1]
[1,]  0.5714
[2,]  0.0000
```

In the component `mSigma`, the unconditional variance of the initial state α_1 is computed as $var(\alpha_1) = (0.5)^2/(1 - 0.75^2) = 0.5714$.

Next, consider the ARMA(2,1) model

$$y_t = 0.6y_{t-1} + 0.2y_{t-2} + \varepsilon_t - 0.2\varepsilon_{t-1}, \ \varepsilon_t \sim GWN(0, 0.9)$$

The state space system matrices may be computed using

```
> arma21.mod = list(ar=c(0.6,0.2),ma=c(-0.2),sigma=sqrt(0.9))
> ssf.arma21 = GetSsfArma(model=arma21.mod)
> ssf.arma21
$mPhi:
      [,1] [,2]
[1,]   0.6    1
[2,]   0.2    0
[3,]   1.0    0

$mOmega:
        [,1]     [,2] [,3]
[1,]    0.90  -0.180     0
[2,]   -0.18   0.036     0
[3,]    0.00   0.000     0

$mSigma:
          [,1]      [,2]
[1,]   1.58571   0.01286
[2,]   0.01286   0.09943
[3,]   0.00000   0.00000
```

The unconditional variance of the initial state vector $\boldsymbol{\alpha}_1 = (\alpha_{11}, \alpha_{12})'$ is in the top 2×2 block of mSigma and is

$$var(\boldsymbol{\alpha}_1) = \begin{pmatrix} 1.586 & 0.013 \\ 0.013 & 0.099 \end{pmatrix}.$$

Structural Time Series Models

The basic univariate unobserved components *structural time series model* (STSM) for a time series y_t has the form

$$y_t = \mu_t + \gamma_t + \psi_t + \xi_t \qquad (14.24)$$

where μ_t represents the unobserved *trend* component, γ_t represents the unobserved *seasonal* component, ψ_t represents the unobserved *cycle* component, and ξ_t represents the unobserved *irregular* component.

The nonstationary trend component μ_t has the form of a *local linear trend*:

$$\mu_{t+1} = \mu_t + \beta_t + \eta_t, \ \eta_t \sim GWN(0, \sigma_\eta^2) \qquad (14.25)$$

$$\beta_t = \beta_t + \varsigma_t, \ \varsigma_t \sim GWN(0, \sigma_\varsigma^2) \qquad (14.26)$$

with $\mu_1 \sim N(0, \kappa)$ and $\beta_1 \sim N(0, \kappa)$ where k is a large number, e.g. $k = 10^6$. If $\sigma_\varsigma^2 = 0$ then μ_t follows a random walk with drift β_1. If both $\sigma_\varsigma^2 = 0$ and $\sigma_\eta^2 = 0$ then μ_t follows a linear deterministic trend.

The stochastic seasonal component γ_t has the form

$$S(L)\gamma_t = \omega_t, \ \omega_t \sim GWN(0, \sigma_\omega^2) \qquad (14.27)$$

$$S(L) = 1 + L + \cdots + L^{s-1}$$

where s gives the number of seasons. When $\sigma_\omega^2 = 0$, the seasonal component becomes fixed.

The stochastic cycle component ψ_t is specified as

$$\begin{pmatrix} \psi_{t+1} \\ \psi_{t+1}^* \end{pmatrix} = \rho \begin{pmatrix} \cos \lambda_c & \sin \lambda_c \\ -\sin \lambda_c & \cos \lambda_c \end{pmatrix} \begin{pmatrix} \psi_t \\ \psi_t^* \end{pmatrix} + \begin{pmatrix} \chi_t \\ \chi_t^* \end{pmatrix}, \qquad (14.28)$$

$$\begin{pmatrix} \chi_t \\ \chi_t^* \end{pmatrix} \sim GWN \left(\begin{pmatrix} 0 \\ 0 \end{pmatrix}, \sigma_\psi^2 (1 - \rho^2) \mathbf{I}_2 \right)$$

where $\psi_0 \sim N(0, \sigma_\psi^2)$, $\psi_0^* \sim N(0, \sigma_\psi^2)$ and $cov(\psi_0, \psi_0^*) = 0$. The parameter $\rho \in (0, 1]$ is interpreted as a damping factor. The frequency of the cycle is $\lambda_c = 2\pi/c$ and c is the period. When $\rho = 1$ the cycle reduces to a deterministic sine-cosine wave.

The S+FinMetrics/SsfPack function GetSsfStsm creates the state space system matrices for the univariate structural time series model (14.24). The arguments expected by GetSsfStsm are

Argument	STSM parameter
irregular	σ_η
level	σ_ξ
slope	σ_ς
seasonalDummy	s
seasonalTrig	σ_ω, s
seasonalHS	σ_ω, s
cycle0	$\sigma_\psi, \lambda_c, \rho$
$\vdots$	$\vdots$
cycle9	$\sigma_\psi, \lambda_c, \rho$

TABLE 14.3. Arguments to the S+FinMetrics function GetSsfStsm

```
> args(GetSsfStsm)
function(irregular = 1, level = 0.1, slope = NULL,
    seasonalDummy = NULL, seasonalTrig = NULL, seasonalHS
    = NULL, cycle0 = NULL, cycle1 = NULL, cycle2 = NULL,
    cycle3 = NULL, cycle4 = NULL, cycle5 = NULL, cycle6 =
    NULL, cycle7 = NULL, cycle8 = NULL, cycle9 = NULL)
```

These arguments are explained in Table 14.3.

Example 91 *Local level model*

The state space for the local level model (14.12)-(14.14) may be constructed using

```
> ssf.stsm = GetSsfStsm(irregular=1, level=0.5)
> class(ssf.stsm)
[1] "list"
> ssf.stsm
$mPhi:
     [,1]
[1,]    1
[2,]    1

$mOmega:
     [,1] [,2]
[1,] 0.25    0
[2,] 0.00    1

$mSigma:
     [,1]
[1,]   -1
[2,]    0
```

The arguments `irregular=1` and `level=0.5` specify $\sigma_\varepsilon = 1$ and $\sigma_\eta = 1$ in (14.13) and (14.14), respectively.

Regression Models

The linear regression model

$$y_t = \mathbf{x}_t'\boldsymbol{\beta} + \xi_t, \ \ \xi_t \sim GWN(0, \sigma_\xi^2),$$

where $\mathbf{x}_t$ is a $k \times 1$ data matrix and $\boldsymbol{\beta}$ is a $k \times 1$ fixed parameter vector, may be put in the state space

$$\begin{pmatrix} \boldsymbol{\alpha}_{t+1} \\ y_t \end{pmatrix} = \begin{pmatrix} \mathbf{I}_k \\ \mathbf{x}_t' \end{pmatrix} \boldsymbol{\alpha}_t + \begin{pmatrix} \mathbf{0} \\ \sigma_\xi \varepsilon_t \end{pmatrix} \tag{14.29}$$

The state vector satisfies $\boldsymbol{\alpha}_{t+1} = \boldsymbol{\alpha}_t = \boldsymbol{\beta}$. The state space system matrices are $\mathbf{T}_t = \mathbf{I}_k$, $\mathbf{Z}_t = \mathbf{x}_t'$, $\mathbf{G}_t = \sigma_\xi$ and $\mathbf{H}_t = 0$. The coefficient vector $\boldsymbol{\beta}$ is fixed and unknown so that the initial conditions are $\boldsymbol{\alpha}_1 \sim N(\mathbf{0}, \kappa \mathbf{I}_k)$ where κ is large. An advantage of analyzing the linear regression model in state space form is that recursive least squares estimates of the regression coefficient vector $\boldsymbol{\beta}$ are readily computed. Another advantage is that it is straightforward to allow some or all of the regression coefficients to be time varying.

The linear regression model with time varying parameters may be introduced by setting $\mathbf{H}_t$ not equal to zero in (14.29). For example, to allow all regressors to evolve as random walks set

$$\mathbf{H}_t = \begin{pmatrix} \sigma_{\beta_1} \\ \vdots \\ \sigma_{\beta_k} \end{pmatrix}$$

so that the state equation becomes

$$\boldsymbol{\alpha}_{t+1} = \boldsymbol{\alpha}_t + \mathbf{H}_t \boldsymbol{\eta}_t \tag{14.30}$$

More explicitly, since $\alpha_{i,t+1} = \alpha_{i,t} = \beta_{i,t}$ the state equation (14.30) implies

$$\beta_{i,t+1} = \beta_{i,t} + \sigma_{\beta_i} \cdot \eta_{i,t}, \ \ i = 1, \ldots, k$$

If $\sigma_{\beta_i} = 0$ then β_i is constant.

The S+FinMetrics/SsfPack function `GetSsfReg` creates the state space system matrices for the linear regression model. The arguments expected by `GetSsfReg` are

```
> args(GetSsfReg)
function(mX)
```

where `mX` is a rectangular data object which represents the regressors in the model. The function `GetSsfReg` returns a list with components describing the minimal state space representation of the linear regression model.

Example 92 *Time trend regression model*

Consider the time trend regression model

$$y_t = \mu + \delta t + \xi_t, \ \xi_t \sim GWN(0, \sigma_\xi^2)$$

The state space form for a sample of size $n = 10$ is computed using

```
> ssf.reg = GetSsfReg(cbind(1,1:10))
> class(ssf.reg)
[1] "list"
> names(ssf.reg)
[1] "mPhi"   "mOmega" "mSigma" "mJPhi"   "mX"
> ssf.reg
$mPhi:
      [,1] [,2]
[1,]    1    0
[2,]    0    1
[3,]    0    0

$mOmega:
      [,1] [,2] [,3]
[1,]    0    0    0
[2,]    0    0    0
[3,]    0    0    1

$mSigma:
      [,1] [,2]
[1,]   -1    0
[2,]    0   -1
[3,]    0    0

$mJPhi:
      [,1] [,2]
[1,]   -1   -1
[2,]   -1   -1
[3,]    1    2

$mX:
      [,1] [,2]
[1,]    1    1
[2,]    1    2
[3,]    1    3
[4,]    1    4
[5,]    1    5
[6,]    1    6
```

```
 [7,]    1    7
 [8,]    1    8
 [9,]    1    9
[10,]    1   10
```

Since the system matrix $\mathbf{Z}_t = \mathbf{x}'_t$, the parameter $\mathbf{\Phi}_t$ is time varying and the index matrix $\mathbf{J}_\Phi$, represented by the component mJPhi, determines the association between the time varying data in $\mathbf{Z}_t$ and the data supplied in the component mX.

To specify a time trend regression with a time varying slope of the form

$$\delta_{t+1} = \delta_t + \zeta_t, \ \zeta_t \sim GWN(0, \sigma_\zeta^2) \tag{14.31}$$

one needs to specify a non-zero value for σ_ζ^2 in $\mathbf{\Omega}_t$. For example, if $\sigma_\zeta^2 = 0.5$ then

```
> ssf.reg.tvp = ssf.reg
> ssf.reg.tvp$mOmega[2,2] = 0.5
> ssf.reg.tvp$mOmega
     [,1] [,2] [,3]
[1,]    0  0.0    0
[2,]    0  0.5    0
[3,]    0  0.0    1
```

modifies the state space form for the time trend regression to allow a time varying slope of the form (14.31).

Regression Models with ARMA Errors

The ARMA(p, q) models created with GetSsfArma do not have deterministic terms (e.g., constant, trend, seasonal dummies) or exogenous regressors and are therefore limited. The general ARMA(p, q) model with exogenous regressors has the form

$$y_t = \mathbf{x}'_t \boldsymbol{\beta} + \xi_t$$

where ξ_t follows an ARMA(p, q) process of the form (14.21). Let $\boldsymbol{\alpha}_t$ be defined as in (14.23) and let

$$\boldsymbol{\alpha}^*_t = \begin{pmatrix} \boldsymbol{\alpha}_t \\ \boldsymbol{\beta}_t \end{pmatrix} \tag{14.32}$$

where $\boldsymbol{\beta}_t = \boldsymbol{\beta}$. Writing the state equation implied by (14.32) as $\boldsymbol{\alpha}^*_{t+1} = \mathbf{T}^* \boldsymbol{\alpha}^*_t + \mathbf{H}^* \boldsymbol{\eta}_t$ and let

$$\mathbf{T}^* = \begin{bmatrix} \mathbf{T} & 0 \\ 0 & \mathbf{I}_k \end{bmatrix}, \ \mathbf{H}^* = \begin{bmatrix} \mathbf{H} \\ 0 \end{bmatrix},$$

$$\mathbf{Z}^*_t = (1 \quad 0 \quad \cdots \quad 0 \quad \mathbf{x}'_t)$$

where **T** and **H** are defined in (14.23). Then the state space form of the regression model with ARMA errors is

$$
\begin{pmatrix} \boldsymbol{\alpha}_{t+1} \\ y_t \end{pmatrix} = \begin{pmatrix} \mathbf{T}^* \\ \mathbf{Z}_t^* \end{pmatrix} \boldsymbol{\alpha}_t^* + \begin{pmatrix} \mathbf{H}^* \boldsymbol{\eta}_t \\ 0 \end{pmatrix}
$$

The S+FinMetrics/SsfPack function GetSsfRegArma creates the state space system matrices for the linear regression model with ARMA errors. The arguments expected by GetSsfRegArma are

```
> args(GetSsfRegArma)
function(mX, ar = NULL, ma = NULL, sigma = 1, model = NULL)
```

where mX is a rectangular data object which represents the regressors in the model, and the remaining arguments are the same as those for GetSsfArma. The function GetSsfRegArma returns a list with components describing the minimal state space representation of the linear regression model.

Example 93 *Time trend regression with AR(2) errors*

The state space form of the time trend regression with AR(2) errors

$$
\begin{aligned}
y_t &= \mu + \delta t + \xi_t, \\
\xi_t &= \phi_1 \xi_{t-1} + \phi_2 \xi_{t-2} + \nu_t, \ \nu_t \sim GWN(0, \sigma_\xi^2)
\end{aligned}
$$

may be computed using

```
> ssf.reg.ar2 = GetSsfRegArma(cbind(1,1:10),
+ ar=c(1.25,-0.5))
> ssf.reg.ar2
$mPhi:
        [,1] [,2] [,3] [,4]
[1,]   1.25    1    0    0
[2,]  -0.50    0    0    0
[3,]   0.00    0    1    0
[4,]   0.00    0    0    1
[5,]   1.00    0    0    0

$mOmega:
        [,1] [,2] [,3] [,4] [,5]
[1,]     1    0    0    0    0
[2,]     0    0    0    0    0
[3,]     0    0    0    0    0
[4,]     0    0    0    0    0
[5,]     0    0    0    0    0

$mSigma:
        [,1]    [,2] [,3] [,4]
```

```
[1,]   4.364 -1.818     0     0
[2,]  -1.818  1.091     0     0
[3,]   0.000  0.000    -1     0
[4,]   0.000  0.000     0    -1
[5,]   0.000  0.000     0     0
```

$mJPhi:
```
        [,1] [,2] [,3] [,4]
[1,]     -1   -1   -1   -1
[2,]     -1   -1   -1   -1
[3,]     -1   -1   -1   -1
[4,]     -1   -1   -1   -1
[5,]     -1   -1    1    2
```

$mX:
```
        [,1] [,2]
 [1,]     1    1
 [2,]     1    2
...
[10,]     1   10
```

Nonparametric Cubic Spline Model

Suppose the continuous time process $y(t)$ is observed at discrete time points $t_1, \ldots, t_n$. Define $\delta_i = t_i - t_{i-1} \geq 0$ as the time duration between observations. The goal of the *nonparametric cubic spline model* is to estimate a smooth signal $\mu(t)$ from $y(t)$ using

$$y(t) = \mu(t) + \varepsilon(t)$$

where $\varepsilon(t)$ is a stationary error. The signal $\mu(t)$ is extracted by minimizing

$$\sum_{i=1}^{n} (y(t_i) - \mu(t_i))^2 + q^{-1} \int \left(\frac{\partial^2 \mu(t)}{\partial t^2} \right)^2 dt$$

where the second term is a penalty term that forces $\mu(t)$ to be "smooth"[4], and q may be interpreted as a signal-to-noise ratio. The resulting function $\mu(t)$ may be expressed as the structural time series model

$$\begin{aligned} \mu(t_{i+1}) &= \mu(t_i) + \delta_i \beta(t_i) + \eta(t_i) \\ \beta(t_{i+1}) &= \beta(t_i) + \varsigma(t_i) \end{aligned} \qquad (14.33)$$

---

[4]This process can be interpreted as an interpolation technique and is similar to the technique used in the S+FinMetrics functions interpNA and hpfilter. See also the smoothing spline method described in chapter sixteen.

where

$$\begin{pmatrix} \eta(t_i) \\ \varsigma(t_i) \end{pmatrix} \sim N\left[\begin{pmatrix} 0 \\ 0 \end{pmatrix}, \sigma_\varsigma^2 \delta_i \begin{pmatrix} \frac{1}{3}\delta_i^2 & \frac{1}{2}\delta_i \\ \frac{1}{2}\delta_i & 1 \end{pmatrix}\right]$$

Combining (14.33) with the measurement equation

$$y(t_i) = \mu(t_i) + \varepsilon(t_i)$$

where $\varepsilon(t_i) \sim N(0, \sigma_\varepsilon^2)$ and is independent of $\eta(t_i)$ and $\varsigma(t_i)$, gives the state space form for the nonparametric cubic spline model. The state space system matrices are

$$\Phi_t = \begin{pmatrix} 1 & \delta_i \\ 0 & 1 \\ 1 & 0 \end{pmatrix}, \quad \Omega_t = \begin{pmatrix} \frac{q\delta_t^2}{3} & \frac{q\delta_t^2}{2} & 0 \\ \frac{q\delta_t^2}{2} & q\delta_t & 0 \\ 0 & 0 & 1 \end{pmatrix}$$

When the observations are equally spaced, δ_i is constant and the above system matrices are time invariant.

The S+FinMetrics/SsfPack function GetSsfSpline creates the state space system matrices for the nonparametric cubic spline model. The arguments expected by GetSsfSpline are

```
> args(GetSsfSpline)
function(snr = 1, delta = 0)
```

where snr is the signal-to-noise ratio q, and delta is a numeric vector containing the time durations δ_i $(i = 1, \ldots, n)$. If delta=0 then δ_i is assumed to be equal to unity and the time invariant form of the model is created. The function GetSsfSpline returns a list with components describing the minimal state space representation of the nonparametric cubic spline model.

Example 94 *State space form of non-parametric cubic spline model*

The default non-parametric cubic spline model with $\delta_t = 1$ is created using

```
> GetSsfSpline()
$mPhi:
      [,1] [,2]
[1,]    1    1
[2,]    0    1
[3,]    1    0

$mOmega:
        [,1]  [,2] [,3]
[1,] 0.3333   0.5    0
[2,] 0.5000   1.0    0
```

```
[3,] 0.0000  0.0     1
```

```
$mSigma:
     [,1] [,2]
[1,]   -1    0
[2,]    0   -1
[3,]    0    0
```

```
$mJPhi:
NULL
```

```
$mJOmega:
NULL
```

```
$mX:
NULL
```

For unequally spaced observations

```
> t.vals = c(2,3,5,9,12,17,20,23,25)
> delta.t = diff(t.vals)
```

and $q = 0.2$, the state space form is

```
> GetSsfSpline(snr=0.2,delta=delta.t)
$mPhi:
     [,1] [,2]
[1,]    1    1
[2,]    0    1
[3,]    1    0
```

```
$mOmega:
         [,1] [,2] [,3]
[1,] 0.06667  0.1    0
[2,] 0.10000  0.2    0
[3,] 0.00000  0.0    1
```

```
$mSigma:
     [,1] [,2]
[1,]   -1    0
[2,]    0   -1
[3,]    0    0
```

```
$mJPhi:
     [,1] [,2]
[1,]   -1    1
[2,]   -1   -1
```

```
[3,]    -1    -1
```

$mJOmega:

```
      [,1] [,2] [,3]
[1,]    4    3   -1
[2,]    3    2   -1
[3,]   -1   -1   -1
```

$mX:

```
          [,1]    [,2]   [,3] [,4] [,5] [,6] [,7]   [,8]
[1,] 1.00000 2.0000 4.000   3.0 5.000   3.0  3.0 2.0000
[2,] 0.20000 0.4000 0.800   0.6 1.000   0.6  0.6 0.4000
[3,] 0.10000 0.4000 1.600   0.9 2.500   0.9  0.9 0.4000
[4,] 0.06667 0.5333 4.267   1.8 8.333   1.8  1.8 0.5333
```

14.2.5 Simulating Observations from the State Space Model

Once a state space model has been specified, it is often interesting to draw simulated values from the model. The S+FinMetrics/SsfPack function SsfSim may be used for such a purpose. The arguments expected from SsfSim are

```
> args(SsfSim)
function(ssf, n = 100, mRan = NULL, a1 = NULL)
```

where ssf represents either a list with components giving a minimal state space form or a valid "ssf" object, n is the number of simulated observations, mRan is user-specified matrix of disturbances, and a1 is the initial state vector. The use of SsfSim is illustrated with the following examples.

Example 95 *Simulating observations from the local level model*

To generate 250 observations on the state variable α_{t+1} and observations y_t in the local level model (14.12) - (14.14) use

```
> set.seed(112)
> ll.sim = SsfSim(ssf.ll.list,n=250)
> class(ll.sim)
[1] "matrix"
> colIds(ll.sim)
[1] "state"     "response"
```

The function SsfSim returns a matrix containing the simulated state variables α_{t+1} and observations y_t. These values are illustrated in Figure 14.1 created using

```
> tsplot(ll.sim)
> legend(0,4,legend=c("State","Response"),lty=1:2)
```

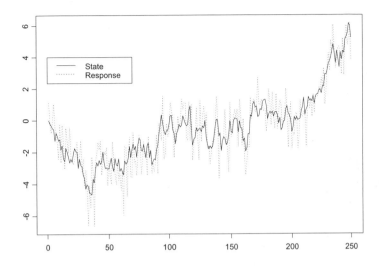

FIGURE 14.1. Simulated values from local level model created using the S+FinMetrics function SsfSim.

Example 96 *Simulating observations from CAPM with time varying parameters*

When simulating observations from a state space form with a data matrix component mX using the function SsfSim, the number of simulated values must match the number of rows of mX. The state space form for the CAPM with time varying parameters created earlier uses a data matrix mX with $n = 131$ observations

```
> nrow(ssf.tvp.capm$mX)
[1] 131
```

The state variables are the time varying intercept α_{t+1} and the time varying β_{t+1}. Natural initial values for these parameters are $\alpha_1 = 0$ and $\beta_1 = 1$. Using these initial values, $n = 131$ observations are generated from the CAPM with time varying parameters using

```
> set.seed(444)
> tvp.sim = SsfSim(ssf.tvp.capm,n=nrow(X.mat),a1=c(0,1))
> colIds(tvp.sim)
[1] "state.1"  "state.2"  "response"
```

The simulated state and response variables are illustrated in Figure 14.2 created using

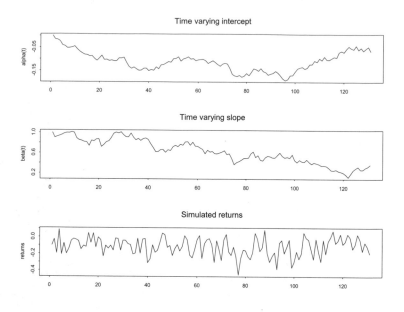

FIGURE 14.2. Simulated state and response values from the CAPM with time varying parameters state space form ssf.tvp.

```
> par(mfrow=c(3,1))
> tsplot(tvp.sim[,"state.1"],main="Time varying intercept",
+ ylab="alpha(t)")
> tsplot(tvp.sim[,"state.2"],main="Time varying slope",
+ ylab="beta(t)")
> tsplot(tvp.sim[,"response"],main="Simulated returns",
+ ylab="returns")
```

14.3 Algorithms

14.3.1 Kalman Filter

The Kalman filter is a recursive algorithm for the evaluation of moments of the normally distributed state vector $\boldsymbol{\alpha}_{t+1}$ conditional on the observed data $\mathbf{Y}_t = (y_1, \ldots, y_t)$. To describe the algorithm, let $\mathbf{a}_t = E[\boldsymbol{\alpha}_t | \mathbf{Y}_{t-1}]$ denote the conditional mean of $\boldsymbol{\alpha}_t$ based on information available at time $t-1$ and let $\mathbf{P}_t = var(\boldsymbol{\alpha}_t | \mathbf{Y}_{t-1})$ denote the conditional variance of $\boldsymbol{\alpha}_t$.

The *filtering* or *updating* equations of the Kalman filter compute $\mathbf{a}_{t|t} = E[\boldsymbol{\alpha}_t | \mathbf{Y}_t]$ and $\mathbf{P}_{t|t} = var(\boldsymbol{\alpha}_t | \mathbf{Y}_t)$ using

$$\mathbf{a}_{t|t} = \mathbf{a}_t + \mathbf{K}_t \mathbf{v}_t \tag{14.34}$$

$$\mathbf{P}_{t|t} = \mathbf{P}_t - \mathbf{P}_t \mathbf{Z}'_t \mathbf{K}'_t \tag{14.35}$$

where

$$\mathbf{v}_t = \mathbf{y}_t - \mathbf{c}_t - \mathbf{Z}_t \mathbf{a}_t \tag{14.36}$$

$$\mathbf{F}_t = \mathbf{Z}_t \mathbf{P}_t \mathbf{Z}'_t + \mathbf{G}_t \mathbf{G}'_t \tag{14.37}$$

$$\mathbf{K}_t = \mathbf{P}_t \mathbf{Z}'_t \mathbf{F}_t^{-1} \tag{14.38}$$

The variable $\mathbf{v}_t$ is the *measurement equation innovation* or prediction error, $\mathbf{F}_t = var(\mathbf{v}_t)$ and $\mathbf{K}_t$ is the *Kalman gain* matrix.

The *prediction* equations of the Kalman filter compute $\mathbf{a}_{t+1}$ and $\mathbf{P}_{t+1}$ using

$$\mathbf{a}_{t+1} = \mathbf{T}_t \mathbf{a}_{t|t} \tag{14.39}$$

$$\mathbf{P}_{t+1} = \mathbf{T}_t \mathbf{P}_{t|t} \mathbf{T}'_t + \mathbf{H}_t \mathbf{H}'_t \tag{14.40}$$

In the Kalman filter recursions, if there are missing values in $\mathbf{y}_t$ then $\mathbf{v}_t = \mathbf{0}$, $\mathbf{F}_t^{-1} = \mathbf{0}$ and $\mathbf{K}_t = \mathbf{0}$. This allows out-of-sample forecasts of $\boldsymbol{\alpha}_t$ and $\mathbf{y}_t$ to be computed from the updating and prediction equations.

14.3.2 Kalman Smoother

The Kalman filtering algorithm is a forward recursion which computes one-step ahead estimates $\mathbf{a}_{t+1}$ and $\mathbf{P}_{t+1}$ based on $\mathbf{Y}_t$ for $t = 1, \dots, n$. The *Kalman smoothing* algorithm is a backward recursion which computes the mean and variance of specific conditional distributions based on the full data set $\mathbf{Y}_n = (y_1, \dots, y_n)$. The *smoothing equations* are

$$\mathbf{r}_t^* = \mathbf{T}'_t \mathbf{r}_t, \ \mathbf{N}_t^* = \mathbf{T}_t \mathbf{N}_t \mathbf{T}'_t, \ \mathbf{K}_t^* = \mathbf{N}_t^* \mathbf{K}_t \tag{14.41}$$
$$\mathbf{e}_t = \mathbf{F}_t^{-1} \mathbf{v}_t - \mathbf{K}'_t \mathbf{r}_t^*, \ \mathbf{D}_t = \mathbf{F}_t^{-1} + \mathbf{K}_t \mathbf{K}_t^{*\prime}$$

and the *backwards updating equations* are

$$\mathbf{r}_{t-1} = \mathbf{Z}'_t \mathbf{e}_t + \mathbf{r}_t^*, \ \mathbf{N}_{t-1} = \mathbf{Z}'_t \mathbf{D}_t \mathbf{Z}_t - < \mathbf{K}_t^* \mathbf{Z}_t > + \mathbf{N}_t^* \tag{14.42}$$

for $t = n, \dots, 1$ with initializations $\mathbf{r}_n = 0$ and $\mathbf{N}_n = 0$. For any square matrix $\mathbf{A}$, the operator $< \mathbf{A} > = \mathbf{A} + \mathbf{A}'$. The values $\mathbf{r}_t$ are called *state smoothing residuals* and the values $\mathbf{e}_t$ are called *response smoothing residuals*. The recursions (14.41) and (14.42) are somewhat non-standard. Durbin and Koopman (2001) show how they may be re-expressed in more standard form.

14.3.3   Smoothed State and Response Estimates

The smoothed estimates of the state vector $\boldsymbol{\alpha}_t$ and its variance matrix are denoted $\hat{\boldsymbol{\alpha}}_t = E[\boldsymbol{\alpha}_t|\mathbf{Y}_n]$ and $var(\hat{\boldsymbol{\alpha}}_t|\mathbf{Y}_n)$, respectively. The smoothed estimate $\hat{\boldsymbol{\alpha}}_t$ is the optimal estimate of $\boldsymbol{\alpha}_t$ using all available information $\mathbf{Y}_n$, whereas the filtered estimate $\hat{\mathbf{a}}_{t|t}$ is the optimal estimate only using information available at time $t, \mathbf{Y}_t$. The computation of $\hat{\boldsymbol{\alpha}}_t$ and its variance from the Kalman smoother algorithm is described in Durbin and Koopman (2001).

The smoothed estimate of the response $\mathbf{y}_t$ and its variance are computed using

$$
\begin{aligned}
\hat{\mathbf{y}}_t &= \hat{\boldsymbol{\theta}}_t = E[\boldsymbol{\theta}_t|\mathbf{Y}_n] = \mathbf{c}_t + \mathbf{Z}_t \hat{\boldsymbol{\alpha}}_t \\
var(\hat{\mathbf{y}}_t|\mathbf{Y}_n) &= \mathbf{Z}_t var(\hat{\boldsymbol{\alpha}}_t|\mathbf{Y}_n)\mathbf{Z}_t'
\end{aligned}
$$

14.3.4   Smoothed Disturbance Estimates

The smoothed disturbance estimates are the estimates of the measurement equations innovations $\boldsymbol{\varepsilon}_t$ and transition equation innovations $\boldsymbol{\eta}_t$ based on all available information $\mathbf{Y}_n$, and are denoted $\hat{\boldsymbol{\varepsilon}}_t = E[\boldsymbol{\varepsilon}_t|\mathbf{Y}_n]$ and $\hat{\boldsymbol{\eta}}_t = E[\boldsymbol{\eta}_t|\mathbf{Y}_n]$, respectively. The computation of $\hat{\boldsymbol{\varepsilon}}_t$ and $\hat{\boldsymbol{\eta}}_t$ from the Kalman smoother algorithm is described in Durbin and Koopman (2001). These smoothed disturbance estimates are useful for parameter estimation by maximum likelihood and for diagnostic checking. See chapter seven in Durbin and Koopman (2001) for details.

14.3.5   Forecasting

The Kalman filter prediction equations (14.39) - (14.40) produces one-step ahead predictions of the state vector, $\mathbf{a}_{t+1} = E[\boldsymbol{\alpha}_{t+1}|\mathbf{Y}_t]$, along with prediction variance matrices $\mathbf{P}_{t+1}$. Out of sample predictions, together with associated mean square errors, can be computed from the Kalman filter prediction equations by extending the data set $\mathbf{y}_1, \ldots, \mathbf{y}_n$ with a set of missing values. When y_τ is missing, the Kalman filter reduces to the prediction step described above. As a result, a sequence of m missing values at the end of the sample will produce a set of h-step ahead forecasts for $h = 1, \ldots, m$.

14.3.6   S+FinMetrics/SsfPack Implementation of State Space Modeling Algorithms

The S+FinMetrics/SsfPack function KalmanFil implements the Kalman filter forward recursions in a computationally efficient way, see Koopman, Shephard and Doornik (2001). It produces an object of class "KalmanFil" for which there are print and plot methods. The S+FinMetrics/SsfPack function `KalmanSmo` computes the Kalman smoother backwards recursions, and produces an object of class "KalmanSmo" for which there are `print` and `plot` methods. The functions `KalmanFil` and `KalmanSmo` are primarily used by other S+FinMetrics/SsfPack state space functions that require the output from the Kalman filter and Kalman smoother.

Filtered and smoothed estimates of $\boldsymbol{\alpha}_t$ and $\mathbf{y}_t$, with estimated variances, as well as smoothed estimates of $\boldsymbol{\varepsilon}_t$ and $\boldsymbol{\eta}_t$, with estimated variances, are computed using the S+FinMetrics/SsfPack function `SsfMomentEst`. The result of `SsfMomentEst` is an object of class "SsfMomentEst" for which there is only a `plot` method. The function `SsfMomentEst` may also be used to compute out-of-sample forecasts and forecast variances of $\boldsymbol{\alpha}_t$ and y_t.

The use of the S+FinMetrics/SsfPack functions for implementing the state space algorithms are illustrated with the following examples.

Example 97 *State space algorithms applied to local level model*

Consider the simulated data for the local level model (14.12) - (14.14) in the object `ll.sim` computed earlier. The response variable y_t is extracted using

```
> y.ll = ll.sim[,"response"]
```

Kalman Filter

The Kalman filter recursions for the simulated data from the local level model are obtained using the S+FinMetrics/SsfPack function `KalmanFil` with the optional argument `task="STFIL"` (which stands for state filtering)

```
> KalmanFil.ll = KalmanFil(y.ll,ssf.ll,task="STFIL")
> class(KalmanFil.ll)
[1] "KalmanFil"
```

The function `KalmanFil` takes as input a vector of response data and either a list describing the minimal state space form or a valid "ssf" object. The result of `KalmanFil` is an object of class "KalmanFil" with components

```
> names(KalmanFil.ll)
 [1] "mOut"          "innov"          "std.innov"
 [4] "mGain"         "loglike"        "loglike.conc"
 [7] "dVar"          "mEst"           "mOffP"
[10] "task"          "err"            "call"
```

A complete explanation of the components of a "KalmanFil" object is given in the online help for `KalmanFil`. These components are mainly used by other S+FinMetrics/SsfPack functions and are only briefly discussed here. The component `mOut` contains the basic Kalman filter output.

```
> KalmanFil.ll$mOut
numeric matrix: 250 rows, 3 columns.
```

```
          [,1]    [,2]    [,3]
  [1,]   0.00000 1.0000 0.0000
  [2,]  -1.28697 0.5556 0.4444
...
[250,]  -1.6371 0.3904 0.6096
```

The first column of mOut contains the prediction errors v_t, the second column contains the Kalman gains, K_t, and the last column contains the inverses of the prediction error variances, F_t^{-1}. Since task="STFIL" the filtered estimates $a_{t|t}$ and $y_{t|t} = Z_t a_{t|t}$ are in the component mEst

```
> KalmanFil.ll$mEst
numeric matrix:  250 rows, 4 columns.
          [,1]     [,2]    [,3]    [,4]
  [1,]   1.10889  1.10889 1.0000  1.0000
  [2,]   0.39390  0.39390 0.5556  0.5556
...
[250,]  4.839 4.839 0.3904 0.3904
```

The plot method allows for a graphical analysis of the Kalman filter output

```
> plot(KalmanFil.ll)

Make a plot selection (or 0 to exit):

1: plot: all
2: plot: innovations
3: plot: standardized innovations
4: plot: innovation histogram
5: plot: normal QQ-plot of innovations
6: plot: innovation ACF
Selection:
```

The standardized innovations v_t/F_t are illustrated in Figure 14.3.

Kalman Smoother

The Kalman smoother backwards recursions for the simulated data from the local level model are obtained using the S+FinMetrics/SsfPack function KalmanSmo

```
> KalmanSmo.ll = KalmanSmo(KalmanFil.ll,ssf.ll)
> class(KalmanSmo.ll)
[1] "KalmanSmo"
```

The function KalmanSmo takes as input an object of class "KalmanFil" and an associated list variable containing the state space form used to produce the "KalmanFil" object. The result of KalmanSmo is an object of class "KalmanSmo" with components

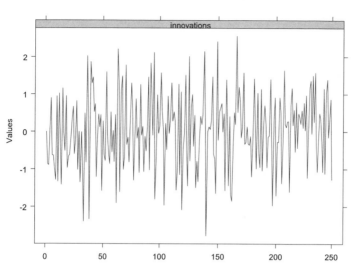

FIGURE 14.3. Standardized innovations from Kalman filter applied to simulated data from local level model.

```
> names(KalmanSmo.ll)
[1] "state.residuals"      "response.residuals"
[3] "state.variance"       "response.variance"
[5] "aux.residuals"        "scores"
[7] "call"
```

The component `state.residuals` contains the smoothing residuals from the state equation, `response.residuals` contains the smoothing residuals from the measurement equation. The corresponding variances of these residuals are in the components `state.variance` and `response.variance`. A multi-panel timeplot of the standardized residuals in the component `aux.residuals`, illustrated in Figure 14.4, is created with the `plot` method

```
> plot(KalmanSmo.ll,layout=c(1,2))
```

Filtered and Smoothed Moment Estimates

Filtered and smoothed estimates of α_t and y_t with corresponding estimates of variances may be computed using the `S+FinMetrics/SsfPack` function `SsfMomentEst`. To compute filtered estimates, call `SsfMomentEst` with the argument `task="STFIL"` (which stands for state filtering)

```
> FilteredEst.ll = SsfMomentEst(y.ll,ssf.ll,task="STFIL")
> class(FilteredEst.ll)
```

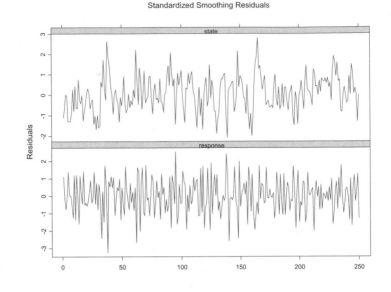

FIGURE 14.4. Standardized smoothing residuals from Kalman smoother recursions computed from simulated data from local level model.

```
[1] "SsfMomentEst"
> names(FilteredEst.ll)
[1] "state.moment"      "state.variance"
[3] "response.moment"   "response.variance"
[5] "task"
```

The function SsfMomentEst takes as input a vector of response data and either a list describing the minimal state space form or a valid "ssf" object. The result of SsfMomentEst is an object of class "SsfMomentEst" for which there is only a plot method. The filtered estimates $a_{t|t}$ and $y_{t|t} = c_t + Z_t a_{t|t}$ are in the components state.moment and response.moment, respectively, and the corresponding filtered variance estimates are in the components state.variance and response.variance. From the measurement equation (14.13) in the local level model, $a_{t|t} = y_{t|t}$

```
> FilteredEst.ll$state.moment[1:5]
[1]   1.1089   0.3939  -0.1389  -0.1141   0.3461
> FilteredEst.ll$response.moment[1:5]
[1]   1.1089   0.3939  -0.1389  -0.1141   0.3461
```

The plot method creates a multi-panel timeplot, illustrated in Figure 14.5, of the estimates of α_t and y_t

```
> plot(FilteredEst.ll,layout=c(1,2))
```

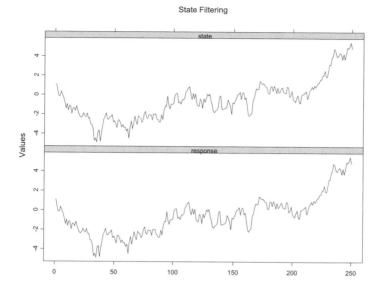

FIGURE 14.5. Filtered estimates of α_t and y_t computed from simulated data from local level model.

A plot of the filtered state estimates with 95% confidence intervals may be created using

```
> upper.state = FilteredEst.ll$state.moment +
+ 2*sqrt(FilteredEst.ll$state.variance)
> lower.state = FilteredEst.ll$state.moment -
+ 2*sqrt(FilteredEst.ll$state.variance)
> tsplot(FilteredEst.ll$state.moment,upper.state,lower.state,
+ lty=c(1,2,2),ylab="filtered state")
```

and is shown in Figure 14.6.

The smoothed estimates $\hat{\alpha}_t$ and $\hat{y}_t$ along with estimated variances may be computed using SsfMomentEst with task="STSMO" (state smoothing)

```
> SmoothedEst.ll = SsfMomentEst(y.ll,ssf.ll.list,task="STSMO")
```

In the local level model, $\hat{\alpha}_t = \hat{y}_t$

```
> SmoothedEst.ll$state.moment[1:5]
[1]   0.24281   0.02629 -0.13914 -0.13925 -0.15455
> SmoothedEst.ll$response.moment[1:5]
[1]   0.24281   0.02629 -0.13914 -0.13925 -0.15455
```

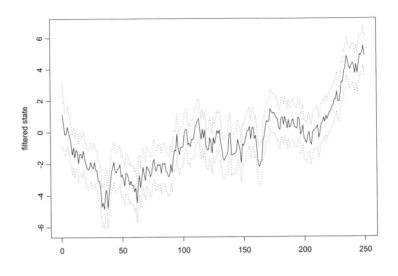

FIGURE 14.6. Filtered estimates of α_t with 95% confidence intervals computed from simulated values from local level model.

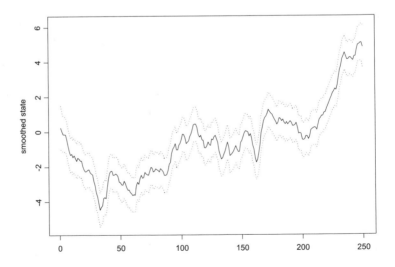

FIGURE 14.7. Smoothed estimates of α_t with 95% confidence intervals computed from simulated values from local level model.

The smoothed state estimates with 95% confidence bands are illustrated in Figure 14.7. Compared to the filtered state estimates, the smoothed estimates are "smoother" and the confidence bands are slightly smaller.

Smoothed estimates of α_t and y_t without estimated variances may be obtained using the S+FinMetrics/SsfPack function SsfCondDens with the argument task="STSMO" (which stands for state smoothing)

```
> smoothedEst.ll = SsfCondDens(y.ll,ssf.ll.list,task="STSMO")
> class(smoothedEst.ll)
[1] "SsfCondDens"
> names(smoothedEst.ll)
[1] "state"    "response" "task"
```

The object smoothedEst.ll is of class "SsfCondDens" with components state, giving the smoothed state estimates $\hat{\alpha}_t$, response, which gives the smoothed response estimates $\hat{y}_t$, and task, naming the task performed. The smoothed estimates $\hat{y}_t$ and $\hat{\alpha}_t$ may be visualized using the plot method for "SsfCondDens" objects

```
> plot(smoothedEst.ll)
```

The resulting plot has the same format at the plot shown in Figure 14.5.

Smoothed Disturbance Estimates

The smoothed disturbance estimates $\hat{\varepsilon}_t$ and $\hat{\eta}_t$ may be computed using SsfMomentEst with the optional argument task="DSSMO" (which stands for disturbance smoothing)

```
> disturbEst.ll = SsfMomentEst(y.ll,ssf.ll,task="DSSMO")
> names(disturbEst.ll)
[1] "state.moment"      "state.variance"
[3] "response.moment"   "response.variance"
[5] "task"
```

The estimates $\hat{\eta}_t$ are in the component state.moment, and the estimates $\hat{\varepsilon}_t$ are in the component response.moment. These estimates may be visualized using the plot method.

Koopman, Shephard and Doornik (1999) point out that, in the local level model, the standardized smoothed disturbances

$$\frac{\hat{\eta}_t}{\sqrt{\widehat{var}(\hat{\eta}_t)}}, \quad \frac{\hat{\varepsilon}_t}{\sqrt{\widehat{var}(\hat{\varepsilon}_t)}} \tag{14.43}$$

may be interpreted as t-statistics for impulse intervention variables in the transition and measurement equations, respectively. Consequently, large values of (14.43) indicate outliers and/or structural breaks in the local level model.

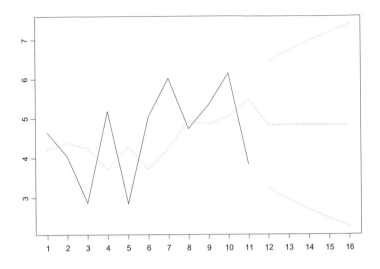

FIGURE 14.8. Actual values, h-step forecasts and 95% confidence intervals for y_t from local level model.

Forecasting

To produce out-of-sample h-step ahead forecasts $y_{t+h|t}$ for $h = 1, \ldots, 5$ a sequence of 5 missing values is appended to the end of the response vector y.ll

```
> y.ll.new = c(y.ll,rep(NA,5))
```

The forecast values and mean squared errors are computed using the function SsfMomentEst with the argument task="STPRED"

```
> PredictedEst.ll = SsfMomentEst(y.ll.new,ssf.ll,task="STPRED")
> y.ll.fcst = PredictedEst.ll$response.moment
> fcst.var = PredictedEst.ll$response.variance
```

The actual values, forecasts and 95% confidence bands are illustrated in Figure 14.8 created by

```
> upper = y.ll.fcst + 2*sqrt(fcst.var)
> lower = y.ll.fcst - 2*sqrt(fcst.var)
> upper[1:250] = lower[1:250] = NA
> tsplot(y.ll.new[240:255],y.ll.fcst[240:255],
+ upper[240:255],lower[240:255],lty=c(1,2,2,2))
```

14.4   Estimation of State Space Models

14.4.1   Prediction Error Decomposition of Log-Likelihood

The *prediction error decomposition* of the log-likelihood function for the unknown parameters φ of a state space model may be conveniently computed using the output of the Kalman filter

$$\ln L(\varphi|Y_n) = \sum_{t=1}^{n} \ln f(\mathbf{y}_t|\mathbf{Y}_{t-1};\varphi) \tag{14.44}$$

$$= -\frac{nN}{2}\ln(2\pi) - \frac{1}{2}\sum_{t=1}^{n}\left(\ln|\mathbf{F}_t| + \mathbf{v}_t'\mathbf{F}_t^{-1}\mathbf{v}_t\right)$$

where $f(\mathbf{y}_t|\mathbf{Y}_{t-1};\varphi)$ is a conditional Gaussian density implied by the state space model (14.1) - (14.6). The vector of prediction errors $\mathbf{v}_t$ and prediction error variance matrices $\mathbf{F}_t$ are computed from the Kalman filter recursions.

A useful diagnostic is the estimated variance of the standardized prediction errors for a given value of φ:

$$\hat{\sigma}^2(\varphi) = \frac{1}{Nn}\sum_{t=1}^{n}\mathbf{v}_t'\mathbf{F}_t^{-1}\mathbf{v}_t \tag{14.45}$$

As mentioned by Koopman, Shephard and Doornik (1999), it is helpful to choose starting values for φ such that $\hat{\sigma}^2(\varphi_{start}) \approx 1$. For well specified models, $\hat{\sigma}^2(\hat{\varphi}_{mle})$ should be very close to unity.

Concentrated Log-likelihood

In some models, e.g. ARMA models, it is possible to solve explicitly for one scale factor and concentrate it out of the log-likelihood function (14.44). The resulting log-likelihood function is called the *concentrated log-likelihood* or *profile log-likelihood* and is denoted $\ln L^c(\varphi|\mathbf{Y}_n)$. Following Koopman, Shephard and Doornik (1999), let σ denote such a scale factor, and let

$$\mathbf{y}_t = \boldsymbol{\theta}_t + \mathbf{G}_t^c \boldsymbol{\varepsilon}_t^c$$

with $\boldsymbol{\varepsilon}_t^c \sim iid\ N(0,\sigma^2\mathbf{I})$ denote the scaled version of the measurement equation (14.3). The state space form (14.1) - (14.3) applies but with $\mathbf{G}_t = \sigma\mathbf{G}_t^c$ and $\mathbf{H}_t = \sigma\mathbf{H}_t^c$. This formulation implies that one non-zero element of $\sigma\mathbf{G}_t^c$ or $\sigma\mathbf{H}_t^c$ is kept fixed, usually at unity, which reduces the dimension of the parameter vector φ by one. The solution for σ^2 from (14.44) is given by

$$\tilde{\sigma}^2(\varphi) = \frac{1}{Nn}\sum_{t=1}^{n}\mathbf{v}_t'(F_t^c)^{-1}\mathbf{v}_t$$

and the resulting concentrated log-likelihood function is

$$\ln L^c(\varphi|\mathbf{Y}_n) = -\frac{nN}{2}\ln(2\pi) - \frac{nN}{2}\ln\left(\sigma^2(\varphi) + 1\right) - \frac{1}{2}\sum_{t=1}^{n}\ln|\mathbf{F}_t^c| \quad (14.46)$$

14.4.2 Fitting State Space Models Using the S+FinMetrics/SsfPack Function SsfFit

The S+FinMetrics/SsfPack function SsfFit may be used to compute MLEs of the unknown parameters in the state space model (14.1)-(14.6) from the prediction error decomposition of the log-likelihood function (14.44). The arguments expected by SsfFit are

```
> args(SsfFit)
function(parm, data, FUN, conc = F, scale = 1, gradient =
NULL, hessian = NULL, lower = - Inf, upper = Inf,
trace = T, control = NULL, ...)
```

where parm is a vector containing the starting values of the unknown parameters φ, data is a rectangular object containing the response variables y_t, and FUN is a character string giving the name of the function which takes parm together with the optional arguments in ... and produces an "ssf" object representing the state space form. The remaining arguments control aspects of the S-PLUS optimization algorithm nlminb. An advantage of using nlminb is that box constraints may be imposed on the parameters of the log-likelihood function using the optional arguments lower and upper. See the online help for nlminb for details. A disadvantage of using nlminb is that the value of the Hessian evaluated at the MLEs is returned only if an analytic formula is supplied to compute the Hessian. The use of SsfFit is illustrated with the following examples.

Example 98 *Exact maximum likelihood estimation of AR(1) model*

Consider estimating by exact maximum likelihood the AR(1) model discussed earlier. First, $n = 250$ observations are simulated from the model

```
> ssf.ar1 = GetSsfArma(ar=0.75,sigma=.5)
> set.seed(598)
> sim.ssf.ar1 = SsfSim(ssf.ar1,n=250)
> y.ar1 = sim.ssf.ar1[,"response"]
```

Least squares estimation of the AR(1) model, which is equivalent to conditional MLE, gives

```
> OLS(y.ar1~tslag(y.ar1)-1)
```

```
Call:
OLS(formula = y.ar1 ~tslag(y.ar1) - 1)
```

```
Coefficients:
 tslag(y.ar1)
 0.7739
```

```
Degrees of freedom: 249 total; 248 residual
Residual standard error: 0.4921
```

The S+FinMetrics/SsfPack function SsfFit requires as input a function which takes the unknown parameters $\varphi = (\phi, \sigma^2)'$ and produces the state space form for the AR(1). One such function is

```
> ar1.mod = function(parm) {
+    phi = parm[1]
+    sigma2 = parm[2]
+    ssf.mod = GetSsfArma(ar=phi,sigma=sqrt(sigma2))
+    CheckSsf(ssf.mod)
+ }
```

In addition, starting values for φ are required. Somewhat arbitrary starting values are

```
> ar1.start = c(0.5,1)
> names(ar1.start) = c("phi","sigma2")
```

The prediction error decomposition of the log-likelihood function evaluated at the starting values $\varphi = (0.5, 1)'$ may be computed using the S+FinMetrics/SsfPack function KalmanFil with task="KFLIK"

```
> KalmanFil(y.ar1,ar1.mod(ar1.start),task="KFLIK")
```

```
Call:
KalmanFil(mY = y.ar1, ssf = ar1.mod(ar1.start), task =
"KFLIK")
```

```
Log-likelihood:  -265.5222
Prediction error variance:  0.2851
Sample observations: 250
```

```
Standardized Innovations:
    Mean Std.Error
 -0.0238  0.5345
```

Notice that the standardized prediction error variance (14.45) is 0.285, far below unity, which indicates that the starting values are not very good.

The MLEs for $\varphi = (\phi, \sigma^2)'$ using SsfFit are computed as

```
> ar1.mle = SsfFit(ar1.start,y.ar1,"ar1.mod",
+ lower=c(-.999,0),upper=c(0.999,Inf))
```

```
Iteration  0 : objective =   265.5
Iteration  1 : objective =   282.9
...
Iteration  18 : objective =   176.9
RELATIVE FUNCTION CONVERGENCE
```

In the call to SsfFit, the stationarity condition $-1 < \phi < 1$ and the positive variance condition $\sigma^2 > 0$ is imposed in the estimation. The result of SsfFit is a list with components

```
> names(ar1.mle)
 [1] "parameters" "objective"  "message"    "grad.norm"
 [5] "iterations" "f.evals"    "g.evals"    "hessian"
 [9] "scale"      "aux"        "call"
```

The exact MLEs for $\varphi = (\phi, \sigma^2)'$ are

```
> ar1.mle$parameters
    phi sigma2
 0.7708 0.2403
```

and the MLE for σ is

```
> sqrt(ar1.mle$parameters["sigma2"])
 sigma2
 0.4902
```

These values are very close to the least squares estimates. A summary of the log-likelihood evaluated at the MLEs is

```
> KalmanFil(y.ar1,ar1.mod(ar1.mle$parameters),
+ task="KFLIK")

Call:
KalmanFil(mY = y.ar1, ssf = ar1.mod(ar1.mle$parameters),
task = "KFLIK")

Log-likelihood:  -176.9359
Prediction error variance:  1
Sample observations: 250

Standardized Innovations:
    Mean Std.Error
 -0.0213   1.0018
```

Notice that the estimated variance of the standardized prediction errors is equal to 1.

An alternative function to compute the state space form of the AR(1) is

```
> ar1.mod2 = function(parm) {
```

```
+    phi = parm[1]
+    sigma2 = exp(parm[2])
+    ssf.mod = GetSsfArma(ar=phi,sigma=sqrt(sigma2))
+    CheckSsf(ssf.mod)
+ }
```

In the above model, a positive value for σ^2 is guaranteed by parameterizing the log-likelihood in terms $\gamma = \ln(\sigma^2)$ instead of σ^2. By the invariance property of maximum likelihood estimation, $\hat{\sigma}^2_{mle} = \exp(\hat{\gamma}_{mle})$ where $\hat{\gamma}_{mle}$ is the MLE for γ. The MLEs for $\varphi = (\phi, \theta)'$ are computed using

```
> ar1.start = c(0.5,0)
> names(ar1.start) = c("phi","ln(sigma2)")
> ar1.mle = SsfFit(ar1.start,y.ar1,"ar1.mod2")
Iteration  0 : objective =   265.5
Iteration  1 : objective =   194.9
...
Iteration  8 : objective =   176.9
RELATIVE FUNCTION CONVERGENCE
> ar1.mle$parameters
      phi ln(sigma2)
  0.7708     -1.426
```

The MLE for ϕ is identical to the one computed earlier. The MLEs for σ^2 and σ are

```
> exp(ar1.mle$parameters["ln(sigma2)"])
 ln(sigma2)
     0.2403
> sqrt(exp(ar1.mle$parameters["ln(sigma2)"]))
 ln(sigma2)
     0.4902
```

and exactly match the previous MLEs.

In the AR(1) model, the variance parameter σ^2 can be analytically concentrated out of the log-likelihood. To maximize the resulting concentrated log-likelihood function (14.46), use SsfFit with the optional argument conc=T and the starting value for σ^2 equal to unity:

```
> ar1.start = c(0.5,1)
> names(ar1.start) = c("phi","sigma2")
> ar1.cmle = SsfFit(ar1.start,y.ar1,"ar1.mod",conc=T)
Iteration  0 : objective =   198
Iteration  1 : objective =   1e+010
Iteration  2 : objective =   177.2
Iteration  3 : objective =   176.9
Iteration  4 : objective =   176.9
Iteration  5 : objective =   176.9
```

```
RELATIVE FUNCTION CONVERGENCE
> ar1.cmle$parameters
    phi sigma2
 0.7708      1
```

The value of the log-likelihood and the MLE for ϕ are the same as found previously. The MLE for σ^2 may be recovered by running the Kalman filter and computing the variance of the prediction errors:

```
> ar1.KF = KalmanFil(y.ar1,ar1.mod(ar1.cmle$parameters),
+ task="KFLIK")
> ar1.KF$dVar
[1] 0.2403
```

Example 99 *Maximum likelihood estimation of CAPM with time varying parameters*

Consider estimating the CAPM with time varying coefficients (14.17) - (14.19) using monthly data on Microsoft and the S&P 500 index over the period February, 1990 through December, 2000 contained in the **S+FinMetrics** "timeSeries" excessReturns.ts. The parameters of the model are the variances of the innovations to the transition and measurement equations; $\sigma_\xi^2, \sigma_\varsigma^2$ and σ_ν^2. Since these variances must be positive the log-likelihood is parameterized using $\varphi = (\ln(\sigma_\xi^2), \ln(\sigma_\varsigma^2), \ln(\sigma_\nu^2))'$. Since the state space form for the CAPM with time varying coefficients requires a data matrix **X** containing the excess returns on the S&P 500 index, the function SsfFit requires as input a function which takes both φ and **X** and returns the appropriate state space form. One such function is

```
> tvp.mod = function(parm,mX=NULL) {
+    parm = exp(parm)
+    Phi.t = rbind(diag(2),rep(0,2))
+    Omega = diag(parm)
+    J.Phi = matrix(-1,3,2)
+    J.Phi[3,1] = 1
+    J.Phi[3,2] = 2
+    Sigma = -Phi.t
+    ssf.tvp = list(mPhi=Phi.t,
+    mOmega=Omega,
+    mJPhi=J.Phi,
+    mSigma=Sigma,
+    mX=mX)
+    CheckSsf(ssf.tvp)
}
```

Starting values for φ are specified as

```
> tvp.start = c(0,0,0)
```

```
> names(tvp.start) = c("ln(s2.alpha)","ln(s2.beta)","ln(s2.y)")
```

The MLEs for φ are computed using

```
> y.capm = as.matrix(seriesData(excessReturns.ts[,"MSFT"]))
> X.mat = cbind(1,
+ as.matrix(seriesData(excessReturns.ts[,"SP500"])))
> tvp.mle = SsfFit(tvp.start,y.capm,"tvp.mod",mX=X.mat)
Iteration  0 : objective =   183.2
Iteration  1 : objective =   138.4
...
Iteration  18 : objective =  -124.5
RELATIVE FUNCTION CONVERGENCE
> tvp.mle$parameters
 ln(s2.alpha) ln(s2.beta) ln(s2.y)
      -11.57      -5.314   -4.855
```

The MLEs for the associated standard deviations are then

```
> sigma.mle = sqrt(exp(tvp.mle$parameters))
> names(sigma.mle) = c("s.alpha","s.beta","s.y")
> sigma.mle
  s.alpha  s.beta      s.y
 0.003078 0.07015 0.08825
```

The smoothed estimates of the time varying parameters α_t and β_t as well as the expected returns may be extracted and plotted using

```
> smoothedEst.tvp = SsfCondDens(y.capm,
+ tvp.mod(tvp.mle$parameters,mX=X.mat),
+ task="STSMO")
> plot(smoothedEst.tvp,strip.text=c("alpha(t)",
+ "beta(t)","Expected returns"),main="Smoothed Estimates")
```

These estimates are illustrated in Figure 14.9. Notice the increase in $\hat{\beta}_t$ and decrease in $\hat{\alpha}_t$ over the sample.

14.5 Simulation Smoothing

The simulation of state and response vectors α_t and y_t or disturbance vectors η_t and ε_t conditional on the observations Y_n is called *simulation smoothing*. Simulation smoothing is useful for evaluating the appropriateness of a proposed state space model and for the Bayesian analysis of state space models using Markov chain Monte Carlo (MCMC) techniques. The S+FinMetrics/SsfPack function SimSmoDraw generates random draws from the distributions of the state and response variables or from the dis-

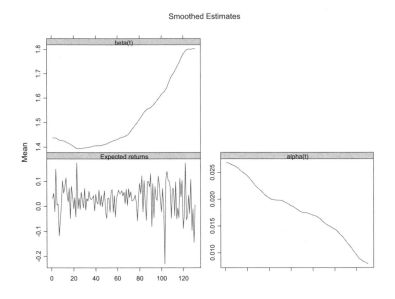

FIGURE 14.9. Smoothed estimates of α_t and β_t from CAPM with time varying parameter fit to the monthly excess returns on Microsoft.

tributions of the state and response disturbances. The arguments expected by SimSmoDraw are

```
> args(SimSmoDraw)
function(kf, ssf, task = "DSSIM", mRan = NULL, a1 = NULL)
```

where kf is a "KalmanFil" object, ssf is a list which either contains the minimal necessary components for a state space form or is a valid "ssf" object and task determines whether the state smoothing ("STSIM") or disturbance smoothing ("DSSIM") is performed.

Example 100 *Simulation smoothing from the local level model*

Simulated state and response values from the local level model may be generated using

```
> KalmanFil.ll = KalmanFil(y.ll,ssf.ll,task="STSIM")
> ll.state.sim = SimSmoDraw(KalmanFil.ll,ssf.ll,
+ task="STSIM")
> class(ll.state.sim)
[1] "SimSmoDraw"
> names(ll.state.sim)
[1] "state"    "response" "task"
```

The resulting simulated values may be visualized using

```
> plot(ll.state.sim,layout=c(1,2))
```

To simulate disturbances from the state and response equations, set
task="DSSIM" in the calls to KalmanFil and SimSmoDraw.

14.6   References

[1] BOMHOFF, E. J. (1994). *Financial Forecasting for Business and Economics*. Academic Press, San Diego.

[2] CARMONA, R. (2001). *Statistical Analysis of Financial Data, with an implementation in Splus*. Textbook under review.

[3] CHAN, N.H. (2002). *Time Series: Applicatios to Finance*. John Wiley & Sons, New York.

[4] DURBIN, J. AND S.J. KOOPMAN (2001). *Time Series Analysis by State Space Methods*. Oxford University Press, Oxford.

[5] DUAN, J.-C. AND J.-G. SIMONATO (1999). "Estimating Exponential-Affine Term Structure Models by Kalman Filter," Review of Quantitative Finance and Accounting, 13, 111-135.

[6] HAMILTON, J.D. (1994). *Time Series Analysis*. Princeton University Press, Princeton.

[7] HARVEY, A. C. (1989). *Forecasting, Structural Time Series Models and the Kalman Filter*. Cambridge University Press, Cambridge.

[8] HARVEY, A.C. (1993). *Time Series Models*, 2nd edition. MIT Press, Cambridge.

[9] HARVEY, A.C., E. RUIZ AND N. SHEPHARD (1994). "Multivariate Stochastic Variance Models," *Review of Economic Studies*, 61, 247-264.

[10] KIM, C.-J., AND C.R. NELSON (1999). *State-Space Models with Regime Switching*. MIT Press, Cambridge.

[11] KOOPMAN, S.J., N. SHEPHARD, AND J.A. DOORNIK (1999). "Statistical Algorithms for State Space Models Using SsfPack 2.2," *Econometrics Journal*, 2, 113-166.

[12] KOOPMAN, S.J., N. SHEPHARD, AND J.A. DOORNIK (2001). "Ssf-Pack 3.0beta: Statistical Algorithms for Models in State Space," unpublished manuscript, Free University, Amsterdam.

[13] ENGLE, R.F. AND M.W. WATSON (1987). "The Kalman Filter: Applications to Forecasting and Rational Expectations Models," in T.F. Bewley (ed.) *Advances in Econometrics: Fifth World Congress, Volume I.* Cambridge University Press, Cambridge.

[14] WEST, M. AND J. HARRISON (1997). *Bayesian Forecasting and Dynamic Models*, 2nd edition. Springer-Verlag, New York.

15
Factor Models for Asset Returns

15.1 Introduction

Multifactor models can be used to predict returns, generate estimates of abnormal return, and estimate the variability and covariability of returns. This chapter focuses on the use of multifactor models to describe the covariance structure of returns[1]. Asset return covariance matrices are key inputs to portfolio optimization routines used for asset allocation and active asset management. A factor model decomposes an asset's return into factors common to all assets and an asset specific factor. Often the common factors are interpreted as capturing fundamental risk components, and the factor model isolates an asset's sensitivities to these risk factors. The three main types of multifactor models for asset returns are: (1) *macroeconomic* factor models; (2) *fundamental* factor models; and (3) *statistical* factor models. Macroeconomic factor models use observable economic time series like interest rates and inflation as measures of pervasive or common factors in asset returns. Fundamental factor models use observable firm or asset specific attributes such as firm size, dividend yield, and industry classification to determine common factors in asset returns. Statistical factor models treat the common factors as unobservable or latent factors. Estimation of multifactor models is type-specific, and this chapter summarizes

---

[1] A recent review of factor models for this purpose is given in Chan, Karceski and Lakonishok (1998).

the econometric issues associated with estimating each type of factor model and gives illustrations using S-PLUS.

This chapter is organized as follows. Section two presents the general factor model specification. Section three describes the macroeconomic factor model. Examples using Sharpe's single index model as well as a general macroeconomic model are given. Section four surveys the fundamental factor model and provides illustrations of an industry factor model and a Fama-French type model. Statistical factor models estimated using factor analysis and principal components analysis are covered in Section five. Particular emphasis is given to techniques appropriate for the case in which the number of assets is greater than the number of time periods.

Connor (1995) gives an overview of three types of factor models for asset returns and compares their explanatory power. Campbell, Lo and MacKinlay (1997) and Grinold and Kahn (2000) survey the econometric specification of these models. Johnson and Wichern (1998) provides an excellent treatment of statistical factor models. Good textbook discussions of statistical factor models with applications in finance are given in Alexander (2001) and Tsay (2001).

15.2   Factor Model Specification

Each of the three types of multifactor models for asset returns has the general form

$$
\begin{aligned}
R_{it} &= \alpha_i + \beta_{1i} f_{1t} + \beta_{2i} f_{2t} + \cdots + \beta_{Ki} f_{Kt} + \varepsilon_{it} \qquad (15.1) \\
&= \alpha_i + \boldsymbol{\beta}_i' \mathbf{f}_t + \varepsilon_{it}
\end{aligned}
$$

where R_{it} is the return (real or in excess of the risk-free rate) on asset i $(i = 1, \ldots, N)$ in time period t $(t = 1, \ldots, T)$, α_i is the intercept, f_{kt} is the kth *common factor* $(k = 1, \ldots, K)$, β_{ki} is the *factor loading* or *factor beta* for asset i on the kth factor, and ε_{it} is the asset *specific factor*. In the multifactor model, it is assumed that the factor realizations, $\mathbf{f}_t$, are $I(0)$ with unconditional moments

$$
\begin{aligned}
E[\mathbf{f}_t] &= \boldsymbol{\mu}_f \\
cov(\mathbf{f}_t) &= E[(\mathbf{f}_t - \boldsymbol{\mu}_f)(\mathbf{f}_t - \boldsymbol{\mu}_f)'] = \boldsymbol{\Omega}_f
\end{aligned}
$$

and that the asset specific error terms, ε_{it}, are uncorrelated with each of the common factors, f_{kt}, so that

$$
cov(f_{kt}, \varepsilon_{it}) = 0, \text{ for all } k, \ i \text{ and } t.
$$

It is also assumed that the error terms ε_{it} are serially uncorrelated and contemporaneously uncorrelated across assets

$$
\begin{aligned}
cov(\varepsilon_{it}, \varepsilon_{js}) &= \sigma_i^2 \text{ for all } i = j \text{ and } t = s \\
&= 0, \text{ otherwise}
\end{aligned}
$$

In applications, it is often the case that the number of assets, N, is substantially larger than the number of time periods, T. In what follows a subscript t represents time and a subscript i represents asset so that $\mathbf{R}_t$ represents an $(N \times 1)$ vector of assets at time t and $\mathbf{R}_i$ represents a $(T \times 1)$ vector of returns on asset i.

The multifactor model (15.1) may be rewritten as a *cross-sectional* regression model at time t by stacking the equations for each asset to give

$$\underset{(N\times 1)}{\mathbf{R}_t} = \underset{(N\times 1)}{\boldsymbol{\alpha}} + \underset{(N\times K)}{\mathbf{B}}\ \underset{(K\times 1)}{\mathbf{f}_t} + \underset{(N\times 1)}{\boldsymbol{\varepsilon}_t}\ ,\ t = 1,\ldots,T \quad (15.2)$$

$$E[\boldsymbol{\varepsilon}_t \boldsymbol{\varepsilon}_t'|\mathbf{f}_t] = \mathbf{D}$$

where $\mathbf{B}$ is the $(N \times K)$ matrix of factor betas, $\mathbf{f}_t$ is the $(K \times 1)$ vector of factor realizations for time period t, and $\boldsymbol{\varepsilon}_t$ is the $(N \times 1)$ vector of asset specific error terms with $(N \times N)$ diagonal covariance matrix $\mathbf{D}$. Given the assumption of the multifactor model, the $(N \times N)$ covariance matrix of asset returns has the form

$$cov(\mathbf{R}_t) = \boldsymbol{\Omega} = \mathbf{B}\boldsymbol{\Omega}_f\mathbf{B}' + \mathbf{D}$$

The multifactor model (15.1) may also be rewritten as a *time-series* regression model for asset i by stacking observations for a given asset i to give

$$\underset{(T\times 1)}{\mathbf{R}_i} = \underset{(T\times 1)(1\times 1)}{\mathbf{1}_T\ \alpha_i} + \underset{(T\times K)(K\times 1)}{\mathbf{F}\ \boldsymbol{\beta}_i} + \underset{(T\times 1)}{\boldsymbol{\varepsilon}_i}\ ,\ i = 1,\ldots,N \quad (15.3)$$

$$E[\boldsymbol{\varepsilon}_i\boldsymbol{\varepsilon}_i'] = \sigma_i^2\mathbf{I}_T$$

where $\mathbf{1}_T$ is a $(T \times 1)$ vector of ones, $\mathbf{F}$ is a $(T \times K)$ matrix of factor realizations (the tth row of $\mathbf{F}$ is $\mathbf{f}_t'$), $\boldsymbol{\beta}_i$ is a $(K \times 1)$ vector of factor loadings, and $\boldsymbol{\varepsilon}_i$ is a $(T \times 1)$ vector of error terms with covariance matrix $\sigma_i^2\mathbf{I}_T$.

Finally, collecting data from $t = 1,\ldots,T$ allows the model (15.2) to be expressed in matrix form as the multivariate regression

$$\underset{(N\times T)}{\mathbf{R}} = \underset{(N\times 1)}{\boldsymbol{\alpha}} + \underset{(N\times K)(K\times T)}{\mathbf{B}\ \mathbf{F}} + \underset{(N\times T)}{\mathbf{E}} \quad (15.4)$$

15.3 Macroeconomic Factor Models for Returns

In a *macroeconomic factor model*, the factor realizations $\mathbf{f}_t$ in (15.1) are observed macroeconomic variables that are assumed to be uncorrelated with the asset specific error terms ε_{it}. The two most common macroeconomic factor models are Sharpe's (1970) single factor model and Chen, Roll and Ross's (1986) multifactor model. Once the macroeconomic factors are specified and constructed the econometric problem is then to estimate the factor betas, β_{ki}, residual variances, σ_i^2, and factor covariance, $\boldsymbol{\Omega}_f$, using time series regression techniques.

15.3.1 Sharpe's Single Index Model

The most famous macroeconomic factor model is *Sharpe's single factor model* or market model

$$R_{it} = \alpha_i + \beta_i R_{Mt} + \varepsilon_{it}, \ i = 1, \ldots, N; t = 1, \ldots, T \quad (15.5)$$

where R_{Mt} denotes the return or excess return (relative to the risk-free rate) on a market index (typically a value weighted index like the S&P 500 index) in time period t. The market index is meant to capture economy-wide or market risk, and the error term captures non-market firm specific risk. The multifactor model (15.1) reduces to (15.5) if $f_{1t} = R_{Mt}$, $\beta_{ik} = 0$ $(i = 1, \ldots, N; k = 2, \ldots, K)$. The covariance matrix of assets from the single factor model is

$$\Omega = \sigma_M^2 \beta\beta' + \mathbf{D} \quad (15.6)$$

where $\sigma_M^2 = var(R_{Mt})$, $\beta = (\beta_1, \ldots, \beta_N)'$ and $\mathbf{D}$ is a diagonal matrix with $\sigma_i^2 = var(\varepsilon_{it})$ along the diagonal.

Because R_{Mt} is observable, the parameters β_i and σ_i^2 of the single factor model (15.5) for each asset can be estimated using time series regression giving

$$\mathbf{R}_i = \widehat{\alpha}_i \mathbf{1} + \mathbf{R}_M \widehat{\beta}_i + \widehat{\varepsilon}_i, \ i = 1, \ldots, N$$
$$\widehat{\sigma}_i^2 = \frac{1}{T-2} \widehat{\varepsilon}_i' \widehat{\varepsilon}_i$$

The variance of the market index is estimated using the time series sample variance

$$\widehat{\sigma}_M^2 = \frac{1}{T-1} \sum_{t=1}^{T} (R_{Mt} - \overline{R}_M)^2$$
$$\overline{R}_M = \frac{1}{T} \sum_{t=1}^{T} R_{Mt}$$

The estimated single factor model covariance is then

$$\widehat{\Omega} = \widehat{\sigma}_M^2 \widehat{\beta}\widehat{\beta}' + \widehat{\mathbf{D}},$$

where $\widehat{\mathbf{D}}$ has $\widehat{\sigma}_i^2$ along the diagonal.

Remarks

1. Computational efficiency may be obtained by using multivariate regression[2]. The coefficients α_i and β_i and the residual variances σ_i^2

---

[2] Since R_M is the regressor for each asset, multivariate OLS estimates are numerically equivalent to multivariate GLS estimates that take into account the across equation correlation between the errors in each equation.

may be computed in one step in the multivariate regression model

$$\mathbf{R}_T = \mathbf{X}\boldsymbol{\Gamma}' + \mathbf{E}_T$$

where $\mathbf{R}_T$ is a $(T \times N)$ matrix of asset returns, $\mathbf{X} = [\mathbf{1} : \mathbf{R}_M]$ is a $(T \times 2)$ matrix, $\boldsymbol{\Gamma}' = [\boldsymbol{\alpha} : \boldsymbol{\beta}]'$ is a $(2 \times N)$ matrix of coefficients and $\mathbf{E}_T$ is a $(T \times N)$ matrix of errors. The multivariate OLS estimator of $\boldsymbol{\Gamma}'$ is

$$\widehat{\boldsymbol{\Gamma}}' = (\mathbf{X}'\mathbf{X})^{-1}\mathbf{X}'\mathbf{R}_T.$$

The estimate of the residual covariance matrix is

$$\widehat{\boldsymbol{\Sigma}} = \frac{1}{T-2}\widehat{\mathbf{E}}'_T\widehat{\mathbf{E}}_T$$

where $\widehat{\mathbf{E}}_T = \mathbf{R}_T - \mathbf{X}\widehat{\boldsymbol{\Gamma}}'$ is the multivariate least squares residual matrix. The diagonal elements of $\widehat{\boldsymbol{\Sigma}}$ are the diagonal elements of $\widehat{\mathbf{D}}$.

2. The R^2 from the time series regression is a measure of the proportion of "market" risk, and $1 - R^2$ is a measure of asset specific risk. Additionally, $\widehat{\sigma}_i$ is a measure of the typical size of asset specific risk.

3. Robust regression techniques can be used to estimate β_i and σ_i^2. Also, a robust estimate of σ_M^2 could be computed.

4. In practice, the estimated value of β_i is often adjusted toward unity. Adjusted β_i values are discussed in chapter seven of Elton and Gruber (1997).

5. The single factor covariance matrix (15.6) is constant over time. This may not be a good assumption. There are several ways to allow (15.6) to vary over time. For example, assume that β_i is constant and that σ_i^2 and σ_M^2 are conditionally time varying. That is, $\sigma_i^2 = \sigma_{it}^2$ and $\sigma_M^2 = \sigma_{Mt}^2$. To capture conditional heteroskedasticity, GARCH models may be used for σ_{it}^2 and σ_{Mt}^2. One may also use exponential weights in computing the sample variances of σ_i^2 and σ_M^2. Alternatively, one may assume that β_i is not constant over time.

Example 101 *Estimation of Sharpe's single factor model using S-PLUS*

The single factor model parameters and the return covariance matrix (15.6) may be efficiently estimated using the matrix functions in S-PLUS. To illustrate, consider estimating the single factor model using the monthly return data over the period January 1978 through December 1987 in the "timeSeries" berndt.dat. The variables in berndt.dat are

```
> colIds(berndt.dat)
 [1] "CITCRP" "CONED"  "CONTIL" "DATGEN" "DEC"    "DELTA"
 [7] "GENMIL" "GERBER" "IBM"    "MARKET" "MOBIL"  "PANAM"
[13] "PSNH"   "TANDY"  "TEXACO" "WEYER"  "RKFREE"
```

See the online help for berndt.dat for a description of these variables. The
return data on the assets and the market index are extracted using:

```
> returns = as.matrix(seriesData(berndt.dat[, c(-10, -17)]))
> market = as.vector(seriesData(berndt.dat)[,10])
```

The single factor model parameters may be estimated by multivariate regression using

```
> n.obs = nrow(returns)
> X.mat = cbind(rep(1,n.obs),market)
> G.hat = solve(X.mat,returns)
> beta.hat = G.hat[2,]
> E.hat = returns - X.mat%*%G.hat
> diagD.hat = diag(crossprod(E.hat)/(n.obs-2))
> names(diagD.hat) = colIds(G.hat)
> r.square = 1 - (n.obs-2)*diagD.hat/diag(var(returns,SumSquares=T))
```

The second row of G.hat contains the estimated β_i values, and the vector
diagD.hat contains the estimated residual variances σ_i^2:

```
> t(rbind(beta.hat,sqrt(diagD.hat),r.square))
          beta.hat              r.square
CITCRP 0.667776 0.067163 0.317769
 CONED 0.091021 0.050096 0.015316
CONTIL 0.738357 0.142597 0.112158
DATGEN 1.028160 0.106880 0.303631
   DEC 0.843053 0.081018 0.337829
 DELTA 0.489461 0.090289 0.121627
GENMIL 0.267765 0.062676 0.079188
GERBER 0.624807 0.076966 0.236938
   IBM 0.453024 0.050461 0.275235
 MOBIL 0.713515 0.064072 0.368818
 PANAM 0.730140 0.122507 0.143372
  PSNH 0.212632 0.108961 0.017627
 TANDY 1.055494 0.105649 0.319860
TEXACO 0.613277 0.068076 0.276615
 WEYER 0.816867 0.064448 0.430829
```

The β_i and R^2 values are illustrated graphically in Figure 15.1. The assets
most sensitive to the market factor (those with highest β_i values) are the
technology and forest sector stocks DATGEN, DEC, TANDY and WEYER. Those
least sensitive are the utility stocks CONED and PSNH. These stocks also have
the lowest R^2 values.

The single factor covariance matrix (15.6) and corresponding correlation
matrix are computed using

```
> cov.si = var(market)*(beta.hat%o%beta.hat) +
```

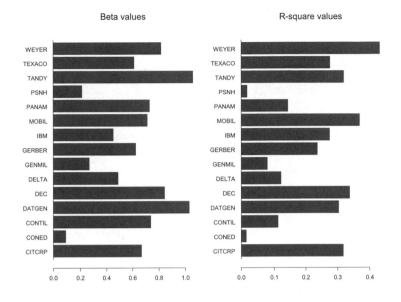

FIGURE 15.1. Estimated β_i and R^2 values from single index model for Berndt data.

```
+ diag(diagD.hat)
> sd = sqrt(diag(cov.si))
> cor.si = cov.si/outer(sd,sd)
```

Since all estimated β_i values are positive, all of the values in the single factor covariance (15.6) will be positive. To illustrate, some of the single factor correlations are displayed below

```
> print(cor.si,digits=1,width=2)
        CITCRP CONED CONTIL DATGEN  DEC DELTA GENMIL GERBER
CITCRP    1.00  0.07   0.19   0.31 0.33  0.20   0.16   0.27
 CONED    0.07  1.00   0.04   0.07 0.07  0.04   0.03   0.06
CONTIL    0.19  0.04   1.00   0.18 0.19  0.12   0.09   0.16
DATGEN    0.31  0.07   0.18   1.00 0.32  0.19   0.15   0.27
   DEC    0.33  0.07   0.19   0.32 1.00  0.20   0.16   0.28
 DELTA    0.20  0.04   0.12   0.19 0.20  1.00   0.10   0.17
GENMIL    0.16  0.03   0.09   0.15 0.16  0.10   1.00   0.14
GERBER    0.27  0.06   0.16   0.27 0.28  0.17   0.14   1.00
   IBM    0.29  0.06   0.17   0.29 0.30  0.18   0.15   0.25
 MOBIL    0.34  0.07   0.20   0.33 0.35  0.21   0.17   0.29
 PANAM    0.21  0.05   0.13   0.21 0.22  0.13   0.11   0.18
  PSNH    0.07  0.02   0.04   0.07 0.08  0.05   0.04   0.06
 TANDY    0.32  0.07   0.19   0.31 0.33  0.20   0.16   0.27
```

```
TEXACO   0.29  0.06    0.17    0.29 0.30  0.18    0.15    0.25
 WEYER   0.37  0.08    0.22    0.36 0.38  0.23    0.18    0.32
...
```

These correlations may be compared with the sample correlations

```
> print(cor(returns),digits=1,width=2)
          CITCRP  CONED CONTIL DATGEN  DEC DELTA GENMIL
CITCRP     1.0   0.269    0.5   0.53 0.49  0.40  0.473
 CONED     0.3   1.000    0.1   0.10 0.11  0.09  0.329
CONTIL     0.5   0.105    1.0   0.26 0.23  0.17  0.206
DATGEN     0.5   0.096    0.3   1.00 0.58  0.33  0.280
   DEC     0.5   0.108    0.2   0.58 1.00  0.43  0.212
 DELTA     0.4   0.092    0.2   0.33 0.43  1.00  0.373
GENMIL     0.5   0.329    0.2   0.28 0.21  0.37  1.000
GERBER     0.4   0.171    0.4   0.14 0.16  0.19  0.350
   IBM     0.4   0.091    0.3   0.49 0.44  0.34  0.170
 MOBIL     0.3   0.003    0.2   0.32 0.41  0.13  0.047
 PANAM     0.3   0.163    0.1   0.29 0.27  0.39  0.207
  PSNH     0.1   0.112    0.1   0.08 0.04  0.03  0.059
 TANDY     0.5   0.102    0.2   0.51 0.49  0.46  0.400
TEXACO     0.3  -0.106    0.2   0.32 0.25  0.13  0.002
 WEYER     0.5   0.158    0.2   0.48 0.59  0.49  0.357
...
```

Another way to compare the single index covariance matrix to the sample covariance is to compute the global minimum variance portfolio. The global minimum variance portfolio is the portfolio w that solves

$$\min_{w} \ \sigma_{p,w}^2 = \mathbf{w}'\boldsymbol{\Omega}\mathbf{w} \ \text{s.t.} \ \mathbf{w}'\mathbf{1} = 1$$

and is given by

$$\mathbf{w} = \frac{\boldsymbol{\Omega}^{-1}\mathbf{1}}{\mathbf{1}'\boldsymbol{\Omega}^{-1}\mathbf{1}}$$

The global minimum variance portfolios based on the single index covariance and the sample covariance are

```
> w.gmin.si = solve(cov.si)%*%rep(1,nrow(cov.si))
> w.gmin.si = w.gmin.si/sum(w.gmin.si)
> t(w.gmin.si)
numeric matrix: 1 rows, 15 columns.
        CITCRP  CONED    CONTIL    DATGEN        DEC DELTA
[1,]  0.04379 0.3757  0.005229  -0.02348  -0.004413 0.0525

        GENMIL  GERBER      IBM   MOBIL     PANAM    PSNH
[1,]   0.1819 0.04272  0.1866 0.03372  0.007792 0.06618
```

```
          TANDY   TEXACO    WEYER
[1,] -0.02719 0.05782 0.001173
```

```
> w.gmin.sample = solve(var(returns))%*%rep(1,nrow(cov.si))
> w.gmin.sample = w.gmin.sample/sum(w.gmin.sample)
> t(w.gmin.sample)
numeric matrix: 1 rows, 15 columns.
          CITCRP  CONED    CONTIL   DATGEN       DEC    DELTA
[1,] -0.06035 0.3763 -0.002152 -0.06558 0.03626 0.03155
```

```
     GENMIL   GERBER    IBM   MOBIL   PANAM    PSNH
[1,] 0.1977 -0.02966 0.2846 0.02257 0.01071 0.07517
```

```
        TANDY TEXACO    WEYER
[1,] -0.01868 0.1996 -0.05804
```

15.3.2   The General Multifactor Model

The general macroeconomic multifactor model specifies K observable macro-variables as the factor realizations $\mathbf{f}_t$ in (15.1). The paper by Chen, Roll and Ross (1986) provides a description of the most commonly used macro-economic factors. Typically, the macroeconomic factors are standardized to have mean zero and a common scale. The factors must also be transformed to be *stationary* (not trending). Sometimes the factors are made orthogonal but this in not necessary.

The general form of the covariance matrix for the macroeconomic factor model is

$$\Omega = \mathbf{B}\Omega_f\mathbf{B}' + \mathbf{D}$$

where $\mathbf{B} = [\boldsymbol{\beta}_1, \boldsymbol{\beta}_2, \cdots, \boldsymbol{\beta}_N]'$, $\Omega_f = E[(\mathbf{f}_t - \boldsymbol{\mu}_f)(\mathbf{f}_t - \boldsymbol{\mu}_f)']$ is the covariance matrix of the observed factors and $\mathbf{D}$ is a diagonal matrix with $\sigma_i^2 - var(\varepsilon_{it})$ along the diagonal.

Because the factor realizations are observable, the parameter matrices $\mathbf{B}$ and $\mathbf{D}$ of the model may be estimated using time series regression giving

$$\mathbf{R}_i = \widehat{\alpha}_i\mathbf{1} + \mathbf{F}\widehat{\boldsymbol{\beta}}_i + \widehat{\boldsymbol{\varepsilon}}_i, \; i = 1, \ldots, N$$

$$\widehat{\sigma}_i^2 = \frac{1}{T - K - 1}\widehat{\boldsymbol{\varepsilon}}_i'\widehat{\boldsymbol{\varepsilon}}_i$$

The covariance matrix of the factor realizations may be estimated using the time series sample covariance matrix

$$\widehat{\Omega}_f = \frac{1}{T - 1}\sum_{t=1}^{T}(\mathbf{f}_t - \overline{\mathbf{f}})(\mathbf{f}_t - \overline{\mathbf{f}})'$$

$$\overline{\mathbf{f}} = \frac{1}{T}\sum_{t=1}^{T}\mathbf{f}_t$$

The estimated multifactor model covariance matrix is then

$$\widehat{\Omega} = \widehat{\mathbf{B}}\widehat{\Omega}_f\widehat{\mathbf{B}}' + \widehat{\mathbf{D}} \tag{15.7}$$

Remarks

1. As with the single factor model, robust regression may be used to compute $\boldsymbol{\beta}_i$ and σ_i^2. A robust covariance matrix estimator may also be used to compute and estimate of Ω_f.

Example 102 *Estimating a general macroeconomic factor model using S-PLUS*

As explained in Chen, Roll and Ross (1986), the macroeconomic factors should be constructed as surprise variables so that the returns on assets will respond to unexpected changes in economy-wide factors. To illustrate the construction of a macroeconomic factor model with macroeconomic surprise variables, consider a simple factor model for the monthly returns in the "timeSeries" returns, constructed earlier, using as factors the surprise to inflation and the surprise to industrial production growth. Monthly observations on inflation and industrial production growth are constructed from the S+FinMetrics "timeSeries" CPI.dat and IP.dat as follows

```
> infl = getReturns(CPI.dat)
> ipg = getReturns(IP.dat)
```

In general, to compute surprise variables, one must first explain the expected behavior and then define the surprise to be the difference between what is observed and what is expected. A common way to compute the expected behavior is to use a VAR model. For simplicity, consider a VAR(6) model for inflation and industrial production growth fit over the period July 1977 through December 1987

```
> factor.ts = seriesMerge(ipg,infl)
> var6.fit = VAR(cbind(CPI,IP)~ar(6),data=factor.ts,
> start="July 1977",end="Jan 1988",in.format="%m %Y")
```

The start date of July 1977 allows for six initial values so that the first fitted value is for January 1978. The factor surprises are constructed as the residuals from the VAR(6) fit:

```
> factor.surprise = residuals(var6.fit)
```

The factor betas and R^2 values for the fifteen assets in the "timeSeries" returns are computed using

```
> factor.surprise = as.matrix(seriesData(factor.surprise))
> n.obs = nrow(returns)
> X.mat = cbind(rep(1,n.obs),factor.surprise)
```

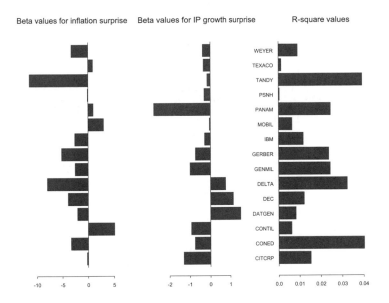

FIGURE 15.2. Estimated macroeconomic factor model for Berndt data.

```
> G.hat = solve(X.mat,returns)
> beta.hat = t(G.hat[2:3,])
> E.hat = returns - X.mat%*%G.hat
> diagD.hat = diag(crossprod(E.hat)/(n.obs-3))
> names(diagD.hat) = colIds(G.hat)
> r.square = 1 - (n.obs-2)*diagD.hat/diag(var(returns,SumSquares=T))
```

These results are illustrated graphically in Figure 15.2 created by

```
> par(mfrow=c(1,3))
> barplot(beta.hat[,1],names=names(beta.hat),horiz=T,
+ main="Beta values for inflation surprise")
> barplot(beta.hat[,2],names=names(beta.hat),horiz=T,
+ main="Beta values for IP growth surprise")
> barplot(r.square,names=names(r.square),horiz=T,
+ main="R-square values")
```

Most stocks have negative loadings on the inflation surprise factor. Notice the very low R^2 values indicating that the factor surprises do not explain much of the variability in the monthly asset returns.

The estimated factor model covariance using (15.7) is

```
> cov.macro = beta.hat%*%var(factor.surprise)%*%t(beta.hat) +
+ diag(diagD.hat)
```

and the corresponding correlation matrix is

```
> sd = sqrt(diag(cov.macro))
> cor.macro = cov.macro/outer(sd,sd)
> print(cor.macro,digits=1,width=2)
           CITCRP   CONED   CONTIL DATGEN     DEC   DELTA GENMIL   GERBER
CITCRP     1.000   0.0181   0.0035 -0.010  -0.008 -0.0019  0.017   0.0115
 CONED     0.018   1.0000  -0.0056 -0.007   0.002  0.0214  0.030   0.0300
CONTIL     0.004  -0.0056   1.0000 -0.005  -0.008 -0.0134 -0.002  -0.0062
DATGEN    -0.010  -0.0069  -0.0052  1.000   0.009  0.0081 -0.008  -0.0030
   DEC    -0.008   0.0017  -0.0083  0.009   1.000  0.0164 -0.002   0.0042
 DELTA    -0.002   0.0214  -0.0134  0.008   0.016  1.0000  0.011   0.0200
GENMIL     0.017   0.0301  -0.0017 -0.008  -0.002  0.0114  1.000   0.0218
GERBER     0.011   0.0300  -0.0062 -0.003   0.004  0.0200  0.022   1.0000
   IBM     0.007   0.0208  -0.0049 -0.001   0.004  0.0150  0.015   0.0164
 MOBIL    -0.002  -0.0128   0.0053 -0.002  -0.006 -0.0137 -0.008  -0.0109
 PANAM     0.019   0.0195   0.0061 -0.013  -0.012 -0.0066  0.019   0.0115
  PSNH     0.003   0.0033   0.0005 -0.002  -0.001 -0.0001  0.003   0.0021
 TANDY     0.007   0.0335  -0.0121  0.003   0.013  0.0325  0.022   0.0280
TEXACO     0.003   0.0002   0.0027 -0.003  -0.004 -0.0051  0.001  -0.0008
 WEYER     0.007   0.0183  -0.0042 -0.001   0.003  0.0131  0.013   0.014
...
```

The macroeconomic factor model global minimum variance portfolio is

```
> w.gmin.macro = solve(cov.macro)%*%rep(1,nrow(cov.macro))
> w.gmin.macro = w.gmin.macro/sum(w.gmin.macro)
> t(w.gmin.macro)
numeric matrix: 1 rows, 15 columns.
        CITCRP   CONED   CONTIL   DATGEN      DEC    DELTA GENMIL
[1,]   0.06958  0.1776  0.02309  0.03196  0.04976  0.04766 0.1049

        GERBER     IBM    MOBIL    PANAM     PSNH    TANDY
[1,]   0.05463  0.1318  0.08186  0.02469  0.04019  0.02282

        TEXACO    WEYER
[1,]   0.07759  0.06185
```

15.4 Fundamental Factor Model

Fundamental factor models use observable asset specific characteristics (fundamentals) like industry classification, market capitalization, style classification (value, growth) etc. to determine the common risk factors. In practice, fundamental factor models are estimated in two ways. The first way was pioneered by Bar Rosenberg, founder of BARRA Inc., and is discussed at length in Grinold and Kahn (2000). In this approach, hereafter referred to as the "BARRA" approach, the observable asset specific fundamentals (or some transformation of them) are treated as the factor betas, $\boldsymbol{\beta}_i$, which are time invariant[3]. The factor realizations at time t, $\mathbf{f}_t$, however, are unobservable. The econometric problem is then to estimate the factor realizations at time t given the factor betas. This is done by running T cross-section regressions. The second way was introduced by Eugene Fama and Kenneth French (1992) and is referred to as the "Fama-French" approach. For a given observed asset specific characteristic, e.g. size, they determined factor realizations using a two step process. First they sorted the cross-section of assets based on the values of the asset specific characteristic. Then they formed a hedge portfolio which is long in the top quintile of the sorted assets and short in the bottom quintile of the sorted assets. The observed return on this hedge portfolio at time t is the observed factor realization for the asset specific characteristic. This process is repeated for each asset specific characteristic. Then, given the observed factor realizations for $t = 1, \ldots, T$ the factor betas for each asset are estimated using N time series regressions.

15.4.1 BARRA-type Single Factor Model

Consider a single factor model in the form of a cross-sectional regression at time t

$$\underset{(N\times 1)}{\mathbf{R}_t} = \underset{(N\times 1)(1\times 1)}{\boldsymbol{\beta} \ f_t} + \underset{(N\times 1)}{\boldsymbol{\varepsilon}_t} \ , t = 1, \ldots, T$$

where $\boldsymbol{\beta}$ is a vector of observed values of an asset specific attribute (e.g., market capitalization, industry classification, style classification) and f_t is an unobserved factor realization. It is assumed that

$$\begin{aligned}
var(f_t) &= \sigma_f^2 \\
cov(f_t, \varepsilon_{it}) &= 0, \text{ for all } i, t \\
var(\varepsilon_{it}) &= \sigma_i^2, i = 1, \ldots, N.
\end{aligned}$$

In the above model the factor realization f_t is the parameter to be estimated for each time period $t = 1, \ldots, T$. Since the error term ε_t is heteroskedastic, efficient estimation of f_t is done by weighted least squares (WLS) (assuming the asset specific variances σ_i^2 are known)

$$\hat{f}_{t,wls} = (\boldsymbol{\beta}'\mathbf{D}^{-1}\boldsymbol{\beta})^{-1}\boldsymbol{\beta}'\mathbf{D}^{-1}\mathbf{R}_t, \ t = 1, \ldots, T \qquad (15.8)$$

where $\mathbf{D}$ is a diagonal matrix with σ_i^2 along the diagonal. The above WLS estimate of f_t is infeasible since σ_i^2 is not known. However, σ_i^2 may be

---

[3] See Sheikh (1995) for a description of the BARRA fundamental factor model for U.S. equities.

consistently estimated and a feasible WLS estimate may be computed. How σ_i^2 may be consistently estimated and how a feasible WLS estimate may be computed is illustrated below.

The WLS estimate of f_t in (15.8) has an interesting interpretation as the return on a portfolio $\mathbf{h} = (h_1, \ldots, h_N)'$ that solves

$$\min_{\mathbf{h}} \frac{1}{2} \mathbf{h}' \mathbf{D} \mathbf{h} \text{ subject to } \mathbf{h}' \boldsymbol{\beta} = 1$$

The portfolio $\mathbf{h}$ minimizes asset return residual variance subject to having unit exposure to the attribute β and is given by

$$\mathbf{h}' = (\boldsymbol{\beta}' \mathbf{D}^{-1} \boldsymbol{\beta})^{-1} \boldsymbol{\beta}' \mathbf{D}^{-1}$$

The estimated factor realization is then the portfolio return

$$\hat{f}_{t,wls} = \mathbf{h}' \mathbf{R}_t$$

When the portfolio $\mathbf{h}$ is normalized such that $\sum_i^N h_i = 1$, it is referred to as a *factor mimicking portfolio*.

15.4.2 BARRA-type Industry Factor Model

As an example of a fundamental factor model with K factors, consider a stylized BARRA-type industry factor model with K mutually exclusive industries. The factor sensitivities β_{ik} in (15.1) for each asset are time invariant and of the form

$$\begin{aligned}
\beta_{ik} &= 1 \text{ if asset } i \text{ is in industry } k \\
&= 0, \text{ otherwise}
\end{aligned}$$

and f_{kt} represents the factor realization for the kth industry in time period t. Notice that factor betas are simply dummy variables indicating whether a given asset is in a particular industry. Hence, the industry factor betas do not have to be estimated from the data. The factor realizations, however, are not initially observable. As will become apparent, the estimated value of f_{kt} will be equal to the weighted average excess return in time period t of the firms operating in industry k. This weighted average excess return at time t can be easily estimated using a cross-section regression over all asset returns at time t.

The industry factor model with K industries is summarized as

$$\begin{aligned}
R_{it} &= \beta_{i1} f_{1t} + \cdots + \beta_{iK} f_{Kt} + \varepsilon_{it}, \ i = 1, \ldots, N; t = 1, \ldots, T \\
var(\varepsilon_{it}) &= \sigma_i^2, \ i = 1, \ldots, N \\
cov(\varepsilon_{it}, f_{jt}) &= 0, \ j = 1, \ldots, K; \ i = 1, \ldots, N \\
cov(f_{it}, f_{jt}) &= \sigma_{ij}^f, \ i, j = 1, \ldots, K
\end{aligned}$$

where $\beta_{ik} = 1$ if asset i is in industry k $(k = 1, \ldots, K)$ and is zero otherwise[4]. It is assumed that there are N_k firms in the kth industry such $\sum_{k=1}^{K} N_k = N$.

Least Squares Estimation of the Factor Realizations

The factor realizations $f_{1t}, \ldots, f_{Kt}$ for $t = 1, \ldots, T$, can be estimated from the observed cross-section of returns at time period t as follows. Consider the cross-section regression at time t

$$
\begin{aligned}
\mathbf{R}_t &= \boldsymbol{\beta}_1 f_{1t} + \cdots + \boldsymbol{\beta}_K f_{Kt} + \varepsilon_t, & (15.9) \\
&= \mathbf{B}\mathbf{f}_t + \varepsilon_t \\
E[\varepsilon_t \varepsilon_t'] &= \mathbf{D},\ cov(\mathbf{f}_t) = \Omega_f
\end{aligned}
$$

where $\mathbf{R}_t$ is an $(N \times 1)$ vector of returns, $\mathbf{B} = [\boldsymbol{\beta}_1, \ldots, \boldsymbol{\beta}_K]$ is a $(N \times K)$ matrix of zeros and ones reflecting the industry factor sensitivities for each asset, $\mathbf{f}_t = (f_{1t}, \ldots, f_{Kt})'$ is a $(K \times 1)$ vector of unobserved factor realizations, ε_t is an $(N \times 1)$ error term, and $\mathbf{D}$ is a diagonal matrix with σ_i^2 along the diagonal. Note that the error term is heteroskedastic across assets. Since the industries are mutually exclusive it follows that

$$
\boldsymbol{\beta}_j' \boldsymbol{\beta}_k = N_k \text{ for } j = k, \ 0 \text{ otherwise} \tag{15.10}
$$

An unbiased but inefficient estimate of the factor realizations $\mathbf{f}_t$ can be obtained by OLS giving

$$
\widehat{\mathbf{f}}_{t,OLS} = (\mathbf{B}'\mathbf{B})^{-1}\mathbf{B}'\mathbf{R}_t \tag{15.11}
$$

or

$$
\begin{pmatrix} \widehat{f}_{1t,OLS} \\ \vdots \\ \widehat{f}_{Kt,OLS} \end{pmatrix} = \begin{pmatrix} \frac{1}{N_1} \sum_{i=1}^{N_1} R_{it}^1 \\ \vdots \\ \frac{1}{N_K} \sum_{i=1}^{N_K} R_{it}^K \end{pmatrix}
$$

using (15.10) where R_{it}^k denotes the return on asset i if it is in industry k. Here, the estimated factor realizations $\widehat{f}_{kt}$ have nice interpretations. They represent an equally weighted average return in time period t on the industry k assets. Of course, this is expected given the nature of the binary industry factor beta values.

To get the time series of factor realizations, the cross-section regression (15.9) needs to be estimated for each $t = 1, \ldots, T$ giving the estimated factor realizations $(\widehat{\mathbf{f}}_{1,OLS}, \ldots, \widehat{\mathbf{f}}_{T,OLS})$.

---

[4]Notice that there is no intercept in the industry factor model. With K mutually exclusive industries, the intercept will be collinear with the factor betas and not identifiable.

Estimation of Factor Realization Covariance Matrix

Given the time series of factor realizations, the covariance matrix of the industry factors may be computed as the time series sample covariance

$$\widehat{\mathbf{\Omega}}_{OLS}^F \;=\; \frac{1}{T-1}\sum_{t=1}^{T}(\widehat{\mathbf{f}}_{t,OLS}-\overline{\mathbf{f}}_{OLS})(\widehat{\mathbf{f}}_{t,OLS}-\overline{\mathbf{f}}_{OLS})', \quad (15.12)$$

$$\overline{\mathbf{f}}_{OLS} \;=\; \frac{1}{T}\sum_{t=1}^{T}\widehat{\mathbf{f}}_{t,OLS}$$

Estimation of Residual Variances

The residual variances, $var(\varepsilon_{it}) = \sigma_i^2$, can be estimated from the time series of residuals from the T cross-section regressions given in (15.9) as follows. Let $\widehat{\boldsymbol{\varepsilon}}_{t,OLS}$, $t = 1,\ldots,T$, denote the $(N \times 1)$ vector of OLS residuals from (15.9), and let $\widehat{\varepsilon}_{it,OLS}$ denote the ith row of $\widehat{\boldsymbol{\varepsilon}}_{t,OLS}$. Then σ_i^2 may be estimated using

$$\widehat{\sigma}_{i,OLS}^2 \;=\; \frac{1}{T-1}\sum_{t=1}^{T}(\widehat{\varepsilon}_{it,OLS}-\overline{\varepsilon}_{i,OLS})^2, \; i=1,\ldots,N \quad (15.13)$$

$$\overline{\varepsilon}_{i,OLS} \;=\; \frac{1}{T}\sum_{t=1}^{T}\widehat{\varepsilon}_{it,OLS}$$

Estimation of Industry Factor Model Asset Return Covariance Matrix

The covariance matrix of the N assets is then estimated by

$$\widehat{\mathbf{\Omega}}_{OLS} = \mathbf{B}\widehat{\mathbf{\Omega}}_{OLS}^F\mathbf{B}' + \widehat{\mathbf{D}}_{OLS}$$

where $\widehat{\mathbf{D}}_{OLS}$ is a diagonal matrix with $\widehat{\sigma}_{i,OLS}^2$ along the diagonal.

Remarks

1. Multivariate regression may be used to compute all of the factor returns in one step. The multivariate regression model is

$$\mathbf{R} = \mathbf{BF} + \mathbf{E},$$

where $\mathbf{R}$ is a $(N \times T)$ matrix of cross-sectionally demeaned asset returns, $\mathbf{F}$ is a $(K \times T)$ matrix of parameters to be estimated (factor returns) and $\mathbf{E}$ is a $(N \times T)$ matrix of errors such that $E[\mathbf{EE}'] = \mathbf{D}$.

2. Robust regression techniques can be used to estimate $\mathbf{f}_t$, and a robust covariance matrix estimate of $\mathbf{\Omega}_f$ can be computed.

3. The industry factor model may be extended to cover cases where an asset may be classified into several industry categories.

4. Given the estimated factor realizations, a time series regression may be run to assess the constructed model. The estimated factor loading may be compared to the imposed values and the proportion of asset variance attributable to all of the factors may be computed.

Weighted Least Squares Estimation

The OLS estimation of the factor realizations $\mathbf{f}_t$ is inefficient due to the cross-sectional heteroskedasticity in the asset returns. The estimates of the residual variances from (15.13) may be used as weights for weighted least squares (feasible GLS) estimation:

$$\widehat{\mathbf{f}}_{t,GLS} = (\mathbf{B}'\widehat{\mathbf{D}}_{OLS}^{-1}\mathbf{B})^{-1}\mathbf{B}'\widehat{\mathbf{D}}_{OLS}^{-1}(\mathbf{R}_t - \overline{R}_t\mathbf{1}), \; t = 1, \ldots, T \qquad (15.14)$$

Given the time series of factor realizations, $(\widehat{\mathbf{f}}_{1,GLS}, \ldots, \widehat{\mathbf{f}}_{T,GLS})$, the co-variance matrix of the industry factors may be computed as the time series sample covariance

$$\widehat{\mathbf{\Omega}}_{GLS}^{F} = \frac{1}{T-1}\sum_{t=1}^{T}(\widehat{\mathbf{f}}_{t,GLS} - \overline{\mathbf{f}}_{GLS})(\widehat{\mathbf{f}}_{t,GLS} - \overline{\mathbf{f}}_{GLS})', \qquad (15.15)$$

$$\overline{\mathbf{f}}_{GLS} = \frac{1}{T}\sum_{t=1}^{T}\widehat{\mathbf{f}}_{t,GLS}$$

The residual variances, $var(\varepsilon_{it}) = \sigma_i^2$, can be re-estimated from the time series of residuals from the T cross-section GLS regressions as follows. Let $\widehat{\varepsilon}_{t,GLS}$, $t = 1, \ldots, T$, denote the $(N \times 1)$ vector of GLS residuals from the industry factor model (15.9) and let $\widehat{\varepsilon}_{it,GLS}$ denote the ith row of $\widehat{\varepsilon}_{t,GLS}$. Then σ_i^2 may be estimated using

$$\widehat{\sigma}_{i,GLS}^{2} = \frac{1}{T-1}\sum_{t=1}^{T}(\widehat{\varepsilon}_{it,GLS} - \overline{\varepsilon}_{i,GLS})^2, \; i = 1, \ldots, N \quad (15.16)$$

$$\overline{\varepsilon}_{i,GLS} = \frac{1}{T}\sum_{t=1}^{T}\widehat{\varepsilon}_{it,GLS}$$

The covariance matrix of the N assets is then estimated by

$$\widehat{\mathbf{\Omega}}_{GLS} = \mathbf{B}\widehat{\mathbf{\Omega}}_{GLS}^{F}\mathbf{B}' + \widehat{\mathbf{D}}_{GLS}$$

where $\widehat{\mathbf{D}}_{GLS}$ is a diagonal matrix with $\widehat{\sigma}_{i,GLS}^2$ along the diagonal.

Remarks

1. Since $\mathbf{B}$ and $\widehat{\mathbf{D}}_{OLS}$ are time invariant, $(\mathbf{B}'\widehat{\mathbf{D}}_{OLS}^{-1}\mathbf{B})^{-1}\mathbf{B}'\widehat{\mathbf{D}}_{OLS}^{-1}$ only needs to be computed once, and this greatly speeds up the computation of $\widehat{\mathbf{f}}_{t,GLS}$ $(t = 1, \ldots, T)$.

2. In principle, the GLS estimator may be iterated. Iteration does not improve the asymptotic efficiency of the estimator, and it may perform better or worse than the non-iterated estimator.

3. Weighted robust regression techniques can be used to estimate $\mathbf{f}_t$, and a robust covariance matrix estimate of $\boldsymbol{\Omega}_f$ can be computed.

Factor Mimicking Portfolios

The GLS estimates of the factor realizations (15.14) are just linear combinations of the observed returns in each industry. Further, these linear combinations sum to unity so that they can be interpreted as *factor mimicking portfolios*. Notice that they are simply weighted averages of the returns in each industry where the weights on each asset are based on the size of the residual variance. The $(N \times 1)$ vector of weights for the ith factor mimicking portfolio is given by

$$\mathbf{w}_i = \mathbf{H}_i = \left((\mathbf{B}'\widehat{\mathbf{D}}_{OLS}^{-1}\mathbf{B})^{-1}\mathbf{B}'\widehat{\mathbf{D}}_{OLS,}^{-1} \right)_i, \ i = 1, \ldots, K$$

where $\mathbf{H}_i$ denotes the ith row of $\mathbf{H}$.

Seemingly Unrelated Regression Formulation of Industry Factor Model

The industry factor model may be expressed as a *seemingly unrelated regression* (SUR) model. The cross section regression models (15.9) can be stacked to form the giant regression

$$\begin{pmatrix} \mathbf{R}_1 \\ \vdots \\ \mathbf{R}_T \end{pmatrix} = \begin{pmatrix} \mathbf{B} & 0 & 0 \\ 0 & \ddots & 0 \\ 0 & 0 & \mathbf{B} \end{pmatrix} \begin{pmatrix} \mathbf{f}_1 \\ \vdots \\ \mathbf{f}_T \end{pmatrix} + \begin{pmatrix} \varepsilon_1 \\ \vdots \\ \varepsilon_T \end{pmatrix}.$$

The giant regression may be compactly expressed using Kronecker products as

$$vec(\mathbf{R}) = (\mathbf{I}_T \otimes \mathbf{B})\mathbf{f} + \varepsilon$$
$$E[\varepsilon\varepsilon'] = \mathbf{I}_T \otimes \mathbf{D}$$

where $vec(\mathbf{R})$ is a $(NT \times 1)$ vector of returns, $\mathbf{f}$ is a $(TK \times 1)$ vector of factor realizations, and ε is a $(NT \times 1)$ vector of errors. The GLS estimator of $\mathbf{f}$ is

$$\widehat{\mathbf{f}}_{GLS} = \left[(\mathbf{I}_T \otimes \mathbf{B})'(\mathbf{I}_T \otimes \mathbf{D})^{-1}(\mathbf{I}_T \otimes \mathbf{B}) \right]^{-1} (\mathbf{I}_T \otimes \mathbf{B})'(\mathbf{I}_T \otimes \mathbf{D})^{-1}\mathbf{R}$$
$$= \left[\mathbf{I}_T \otimes (\mathbf{B}'\mathbf{D}^{-1}\mathbf{B})^{-1}\mathbf{B}'\mathbf{D}^{-1} \right] \mathbf{R}$$

or

$$\begin{pmatrix} \widehat{\mathbf{f}}_{1,GLS} \\ \vdots \\ \widehat{\mathbf{f}}_{T,GLS} \end{pmatrix} = \begin{pmatrix} (\mathbf{B}'\mathbf{D}^{-1}\mathbf{B})^{-1}\mathbf{B}'\mathbf{D}^{-1}\mathbf{R}_1 \\ \vdots \\ (\mathbf{B}'\mathbf{D}^{-1}\mathbf{B})^{-1}\mathbf{B}'\mathbf{D}^{-1}\mathbf{R}_T \end{pmatrix}$$

which is just weighted least squares on each of the cross section regressions (15.9). Hence, equation by equation GLS estimation of (15.9) is efficient.

Of course, the above GLS estimator is not feasible because it requires knowledge of the firm specific variances in **D**. However, using the techniques described above to estimate σ_i^2, feasible GLS estimation is possible.

Example 103 *Estimating an industry factor model using S–PLUS*

Consider creating a three industry factor model for the fifteen assets taken from the S+FinMetrics "timeSeries" berndt.dat. The three industries are defined to be "technology", "oil" and "other". The 15×3 matrix **B** of industry factor loadings are created using

```
> n.stocks = numCols(returns)
> tech.dum = oil.dum = other.dum = matrix(0,n.stocks,1)
> tech.dum[c(4,5,9,13),] = 1
> oil.dum[c(3,6,10,11,14),] = 1
> other.dum = 1 - tech.dum - oil.dum
> B = cbind(tech.dum,oil.dum,other.dum)
> dimnames(B) = list(colIds(returns),c("TECH","OIL","OTHER"))
> B
integer matrix: 15 rows, 3 columns.
```

	TECH	OIL	OTHER
CITCRP	0	0	1
CONED	0	0	1
CONTIL	0	1	0
DATGEN	1	0	0
DEC	1	0	0
DELTA	0	1	0
GENMIL	0	0	1
GERBER	0	0	1
IBM	1	0	0
MOBIL	0	1	0
PANAM	0	1	0
PSNH	0	0	1
TANDY	1	0	0
TEXACO	0	1	0
WEYER	0	0	1

The multivariate least squares estimates of the factor realizations are

```
> returns = t(returns)
> F.hat = solve(crossprod(B))%*%t(B)%*%returns
```

The multivariate GLS estimates are computed using

```
> E.hat = returns - B%*%F.hat
> diagD.hat = rowVars(E.hat)
```

```
> Dinv.hat = diag(diagD.hat^(-1))
> H = solve(t(B)%*%Dinv.hat%*%B)%*%t(B)%*%Dinv.hat
> F.hat = H%*%returns
> F.hat = t(F.hat)
```

The rows of the matrix H contain the weights for the factor mimicking portfolios:

```
> t(H)
numeric matrix: 15 rows, 3 columns.
          TECH     OIL    OTHER
 [1,]  0.0000 0.00000 0.19918
 [2,]  0.0000 0.00000 0.22024
 [3,]  0.0000 0.09611 0.00000
 [4,]  0.2197 0.00000 0.00000
 [5,]  0.3188 0.00000 0.00000
 [6,]  0.0000 0.22326 0.00000
 [7,]  0.0000 0.00000 0.22967
 [8,]  0.0000 0.00000 0.12697
 [9,]  0.2810 0.00000 0.00000
[10,]  0.0000 0.28645 0.00000
[11,]  0.0000 0.11857 0.00000
[12,]  0.0000 0.00000 0.06683
[13,]  0.1806 0.00000 0.00000
[14,]  0.0000 0.27561 0.00000
[15,]  0.0000 0.00000 0.15711
```

Notice that the weights sum to unity

```
> rowSums(H)
 TECH OIL OTHER
    1   1     1
```

The factor realizations are illustrated in Figure 15.3.

The industry factor model covariance and correlation matrices are computed using

```
> cov.ind = B%*%var(F.hat)%*%t(B) + diag(diagD.hat)
> sd = sqrt(diag(cov.ind))
> cor.ind = cov.ind/outer(sd,sd)
> print(cor.ind,digits=1,width=2)
        CITCRP CONED CONTIL DATGEN DEC DELTA GENMIL GERBER
CITCRP     1.0   0.4   0.10    0.2 0.2   0.1    0.3    0.2
 CONED     0.4   1.0   0.14    0.2 0.3   0.2    0.4    0.3
CONTIL     0.1   0.1   1.00    0.1 0.1   0.2    0.1    0.1
DATGEN     0.2   0.2   0.12    1.0 0.3   0.2    0.2    0.1
   DEC     0.2   0.3   0.14    0.3 1.0   0.2    0.2    0.2
 DELTA     0.1   0.2   0.20    0.2 0.2   1.0    0.2    0.1
```

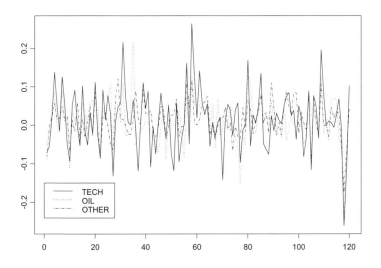

FIGURE 15.3. Estimated industry factor realizations from Berndt data.

GENMIL	0.3	0.4	0.12	0.2	0.2	0.2	1.0	0.3
GERBER	0.2	0.3	0.10	0.1	0.2	0.1	0.3	1.0
IBM	0.2	0.3	0.18	0.4	0.5	0.3	0.3	0.2
MOBIL	0.2	0.2	0.22	0.2	0.2	0.3	0.2	0.2
PANAM	0.1	0.2	0.15	0.1	0.2	0.2	0.1	0.1
PSNH	0.2	0.3	0.08	0.1	0.1	0.1	0.2	0.2
TANDY	0.2	0.2	0.12	0.3	0.3	0.2	0.2	0.1
TEXACO	0.2	0.2	0.22	0.2	0.2	0.3	0.2	0.2
WEYER	0.3	0.3	0.10	0.2	0.2	0.1	0.3	0.2

The industry factor model global minimum variance portfolio is

```
> w.gmin.ind = solve(cov.ind)%*%rep(1,nrow(cov.ind))
> w.gmin.ind = w.gmin.ind/sum(w.gmin.ind)
> t(w.gmin.ind)
numeric matrix: 1 rows, 15 columns.
     CITCRP  CONED  CONTIL   DATGEN     DEC  DELTA GENMIL
[1,] 0.0905 0.2409 0.02232 0.006256 0.01039 0.05656 0.1416

      GERBER    IBM   MOBIL  PANAM    PSNH   TANDY
[1,] 0.07775 0.02931 0.07861 0.02972 0.04878 0.006455

     TEXACO  WEYER
[1,] 0.0794 0.08149
```

15.5   Statistical Factor Models for Returns

In statistical factor models, the factor realizations $\mathbf{f}_t$ in (15.1) are not directly observable and must be extracted from the observable returns $\mathbf{R}_t$ using statistical methods. The primary methods are *factor analysis* and *principal components analysis*. Traditional factor analysis and principal component analysis are usually applied to extract the factor realizations if the number of time series observations, T, is greater than the number of assets, N. If $N > T$, then the sample covariance matrix of returns becomes singular which complicates traditional factor and principal components analysis. In this case, the method of *asymptotic principal component analysis* due to Connor and Korajczyk (1988) is more appropriate.

Traditional factor and principal component analysis is based on the $(N \times N)$ sample covariance matrix[5]

$$\widehat{\boldsymbol{\Omega}}_N = \frac{1}{T}\mathbf{R}\mathbf{R}'$$

where $\mathbf{R}$ is the $(N \times T)$ matrix of observed returns. Asymptotic principal component analysis is based on the $(T \times T)$ covariance matrix

$$\widehat{\boldsymbol{\Omega}}_T = \frac{1}{N}\mathbf{R}'\mathbf{R}.$$

15.5.1   Factor Analysis

Traditional factor analysis assumes a time invariant *orthogonal factor structure*[6]

$$
\begin{aligned}
\underset{(N\times 1)}{\mathbf{R}_t} &= \underset{(N\times 1)}{\boldsymbol{\mu}} + \underset{(N\times K)}{\mathbf{B}}\underset{(K\times 1)}{\mathbf{f}_t} + \underset{(N\times 1)}{\boldsymbol{\varepsilon}_t} &&(15.17)\\
cov(\mathbf{f}_t, \boldsymbol{\varepsilon}_s) &= 0, \text{ for all } t, s\\
E[\mathbf{f}_t] &= E[\boldsymbol{\varepsilon}_t] = 0\\
var(\mathbf{f}_t) &= \mathbf{I}_K\\
var(\boldsymbol{\varepsilon}_t) &= \mathbf{D}
\end{aligned}
$$

where $\mathbf{D}$ is a diagonal matrix with σ_i^2 along the diagonal. Then, the return covariance matrix, $\boldsymbol{\Omega}$, may be decomposed as

$$\boldsymbol{\Omega} = \mathbf{B}\mathbf{B}' + \mathbf{D}$$

---

[5] The matrix of returns is assumed to be in deviations about the mean form. In some applications, a mean correction is not used because the means are small.

[6] An excellent overview of factor analysis is given in Johnson and Wichern (1998). Factor analysis using S-PLUS is described in the *S-PLUS 6 Guide to Statistics Vol. 2*, chapter 21.

Hence, the K common factors $\mathbf{f}_t$ account for all of the cross covariances of asset returns.

For a given asset i, the return variance variance may be expressed as

$$var(R_{it}) = \sum_{j=1}^{K} \beta_{ij}^2 + \sigma_i^2$$

The variance portion due to the common factors, $\sum_{j=1}^{K} \beta_{ij}^2$, is called the *communality*, and the variance portion due to specific factors, σ_i^2, is called the *uniqueness*.

The orthogonal factor model (15.17) does not uniquely identify the common factors $\mathbf{f}_t$ and factor loadings $\mathbf{B}$ since for any orthogonal matrix $\mathbf{H}$ such that $\mathbf{H}' = \mathbf{H}^{-1}$

$$\begin{aligned}
\mathbf{R}_t &= \boldsymbol{\mu} + \mathbf{B}\mathbf{H}\mathbf{H}'\mathbf{f}_t + \boldsymbol{\varepsilon}_t \\
&= \boldsymbol{\mu} + \mathbf{B}^* \mathbf{f}_t^* + \boldsymbol{\varepsilon}_t
\end{aligned}$$

where $\mathbf{B}^* = \mathbf{B}\mathbf{H}$, $\mathbf{f}_t^* = \mathbf{H}'\mathbf{f}_t$ and $var(\mathbf{f}_t^*) = \mathbf{I}_K$. Because the factors and factor loadings are only identified up to an orthogonal transformation (rotation of coordinates), the interpretation of the factors may not be apparent until suitable rotation is chosen.

Estimation

Estimation using factor analysis consists of three steps:

- Estimation of the factor loading matrix $\mathbf{B}$ and the residual covariance matrix $\mathbf{D}$.

- Construction of the factor realizations $\mathbf{f}_t$.

- Rotation of coordinate system to enhance interpretation

Traditional factor analysis provides maximum likelihood estimates of $\mathbf{B}$ and $\mathbf{D}$ under the assumption that returns are jointly normally distributed and temporally *iid*. Given estimates $\widehat{\mathbf{B}}$ and $\widehat{\mathbf{D}}$, an empirical version of the factor model (15.2) may be constructed as

$$\mathbf{R}_t - \widehat{\boldsymbol{\mu}} = \widehat{\mathbf{B}}\mathbf{f}_t + \widehat{\boldsymbol{\varepsilon}}_t \tag{15.18}$$

where $\widehat{\boldsymbol{\mu}}$ is the sample mean vector of $\mathbf{R}_t$. The error terms in (15.18) are heteroskedastic so that OLS estimation is inefficient. Using (15.18), the factor realizations in a given time period t, $\mathbf{f}_t$, can be estimated using the cross-sectional generalized least squares (GLS) regression

$$\widehat{\mathbf{f}}_t = (\widehat{\mathbf{B}}'\widehat{\mathbf{D}}^{-1}\widehat{\mathbf{B}})^{-1}\widehat{\mathbf{B}}'\widehat{\mathbf{D}}^{-1}(\mathbf{R}_t - \widehat{\boldsymbol{\mu}}) \tag{15.19}$$

Performing this regression for $t = 1, \ldots, T$ times gives the time series of factor realizations $(\widehat{\mathbf{f}}_1, \ldots, \widehat{\mathbf{f}}_T)$.

The factor model estimated covariance matrix is given by

$$\widehat{\boldsymbol{\Omega}}^F = \widehat{\mathbf{B}}\widehat{\mathbf{B}}' + \widehat{\mathbf{D}}$$

Remarks:

- Traditional factor analysis starts with a $\sqrt{T}$- consistent and asymptotically normal estimator of $\boldsymbol{\Omega}$, usually the sample covariance matrix $\widehat{\boldsymbol{\Omega}}$, and makes inference on K based on $\widehat{\boldsymbol{\Omega}}$. A likelihood ratio test is often used to select K under the assumption that ε_{it} is normally distributed (see below). However, when $N \to \infty$ consistent estimation of $\boldsymbol{\Omega}$, an $N \times N$ matrix, is not a well defined problem. Hence, if N is large relative to T, then traditional factor analysis may run into problems. Additionally, typical algorithms for factor analysis are not efficient for very large problems.

- Traditional factor analysis is only appropriate if ε_{it} is cross-sectionally uncorrelated, serially uncorrelated, and serially homoskedastic.

Factor Mimicking Portfolios

From (15.19), we see that the estimated factor realizations $\widehat{\mathbf{f}}_t$ are simply linear combinations of the observed returns $\mathbf{R}_t$. As such, it is possible to normalize the linear combination so that the weights sum to unity. The resulting re-scaled factors are the factor mimicking portfolios and are perfectly correlated with the factor realizations.

Tests for the Number of Factors

Using the maximum likelihood estimates of $\mathbf{B}$ and $\mathbf{D}$ based on a $K-$factor model and the sample covariance matrix $\widehat{\boldsymbol{\Omega}}$, a likelihood ratio test (modified for improved small sample performance) of the adequacy of K factors is of the form

$$LR(K) = -(T - 1 - \frac{1}{6}(2N + 5) - \frac{2}{3}K) \cdot \left(\ln |\widehat{\boldsymbol{\Omega}}| - \ln |\widehat{\mathbf{B}}\widehat{\mathbf{B}}' + \widehat{\mathbf{D}}| \right).$$

$LR(K)$ is asymptotically chi-square with $\frac{1}{2}\left((N - K)^2 - N - K \right)$ degrees of freedom.

Example 104 *Estimating a statistical factor model by factor analysis using S-PLUS*

Factor analysis in S-PLUS is performed using the function `factanal`, which performs estimation of $\mathbf{B}$ and $\mathbf{D}$ using either the *principal factor method* or the *maximum likelihood method*, and it takes as input either raw

data or an estimated covariance or correlation matrix. A robust version
of factor analysis can be computed if the inputted covariance matrix is a
robust covariance matrix (MCD, MVE or M-estimate). If the maximum
likelihood method is used, then the LR test for the adequacy of the K
factor model is computed.

A factor model with $k = 2$ factors for the fifteen returns from `berndt.dat`
computed using maximum likelihood method is

```
> factor.fit = factanal(returns,factors=2,method="mle")
> class(factor.fit)
[1] "factanal"
> factor.fit
Sums of squares of loadings:
 Factor1 Factor2
   3.319   2.471

The number of variables is 15 and the number of observations
is 120

Test of the hypothesis that 2 factors are sufficient
versus the alternative that more are required:
The chi square statistic is 118.25 on 76 degrees of freedom.
The p-value is 0.00138

Component names:

 "loadings" "uniquenesses" "correlation" "criteria"


 "factors" "dof" "method" "center" "scale" "n.obs" "scores"


 "call"
Call:
factanal(x = returns, factors = 2, method = "mle")
```

The likelihood ratio test for determining the number of factors indicates
that two factors is not enough to adequately explain the sample return
covariance. A factor model with $k = 3$ factor appears to be adequate

```
> factor.fit = factanal(returns,factors=3,method="mle")
> factor.fit
Sums of squares of loadings:
 Factor1 Factor2 Factor3
   3.137   1.765   1.719
```

The number of variables is 15 and the number of observations
is 120

Test of the hypothesis that 3 factors are sufficient
versus the alternative that more are required:
The chi square statistic is 71.6 on 63 degrees of freedom.
The p-value is 0.214
...

A summary of the three factor model is

```
> summary(factor.fit)
Importance of factors:
                Factor1 Factor2 Factor3
   SS loadings  3.1370  1.7651  1.7185
Proportion Var  0.2091  0.1177  0.1146
Cumulative Var  0.2091  0.3268  0.4414
```

The degrees of freedom for the model is 63.

```
Uniquenesses:
 CITCRP  CONED CONTIL DATGEN     DEC  DELTA GENMIL GERBER
 0.3125 0.8506 0.7052 0.4863 0.3794 0.6257  0.592 0.5175

    IBM  MOBIL  PANAM   PSNH  TANDY TEXACO  WEYER
 0.6463 0.2161 0.7643 0.9628 0.5442 0.3584 0.4182
```

```
Loadings:
       Factor1 Factor2 Factor3
CITCRP  0.518   0.217   0.610
 CONED  0.116           0.356
CONTIL  0.173   0.195   0.476
DATGEN  0.668   0.206   0.160
   DEC  0.749   0.236
 DELTA  0.563           0.239
GENMIL  0.306           0.556
GERBER          0.346   0.600
   IBM  0.515   0.224   0.197
 MOBIL  0.257   0.847
 PANAM  0.427           0.219
  PSNH  0.115           0.133
 TANDY  0.614           0.264
TEXACO  0.140   0.787
 WEYER  0.694   0.200   0.247
```

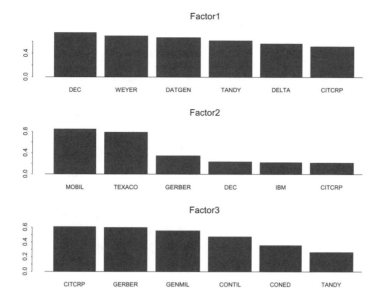

FIGURE 15.4. Estimated loadings from three factor model fit to Berndt data by factor analysis.

The three factors explain about forty four percent of the total variance of returns. The reported uniqueness for each asset is standardized such that the sum of the uniqueness and the communality is unity. Therefore, assets with uniqueness values close to zero are well explained by the factor model.

The factor loadings may be extracted using the generic `loadings` function. The extracted loadings have class "`loadings`" and may be visualized with `plot`

```
> plot(loadings(factor.fit))
```

Figure 15.4 gives the resulting plot. The first factor appears to be market-wide factor, and the second factor is concentrated on oil stocks. Since the factors are only defined up to an orthogonal rotation, the factor may be rotated to aid interpretation. The generic function `rotate` performs such rotation. For example, to rotate the factor using the `quartimax` rotation and view the rotated loadings use

```
> factor.fit2 = rotate(factor.fit,rotation="quartimax")
> loadings(factor.fit2)
       Factor1 Factor2 Factor3
CITCRP  0.722   0.108   0.393
 CONED  0.233  -0.153   0.268
CONTIL  0.351   0.113   0.398
```

```
DATGEN   0.693    0.168
   DEC   0.734    0.212   -0.193
 DELTA   0.610
GENMIL   0.485   -0.164    0.382
GERBER   0.299    0.243    0.578
   IBM   0.566    0.181
 MOBIL   0.307    0.829
 PANAM   0.472   -0.112
  PSNH   0.150   -0.101
 TANDY   0.673
TEXACO   0.205    0.767    0.103
 WEYER   0.748    0.148
```

See the online help for **rotate** for a description of the supported rotation methods.

The factor realizations (15.19) may be computed using the generic **predict** function:

```
> factor.ret = predict(factor.fit,type="weighted.ls")
```

The estimated factor model correlation matrix may be extracted using

```
> fitted(factor.fit)
numeric matrix: 15 rows, 15 columns.
          CITCRP    CONED  CONTIL  DATGEN     DEC   DELTA
CITCRP 1.0000  0.25701 0.42245 0.48833 0.47656 0.43723
 CONED 0.2570  1.00000 0.17131 0.11533 0.08655 0.15095
CONTIL 0.4224  0.17131 1.00000 0.23205 0.20474 0.21099
DATGEN 0.4883  0.11533 0.23205 1.00000 0.55841 0.41386
   DEC 0.4766  0.08655 0.20474 0.55841 1.00000 0.43597
 DELTA 0.4372  0.15095 0.21099 0.41386 0.43597 1.00000
GENMIL 0.4825  0.24043 0.30402 0.27919 0.24681 0.30570
GERBER 0.4693  0.18728 0.36267 0.20404 0.15936 0.17371
   IBM 0.4354  0.10893 0.22663 0.42116 0.45030 0.33649
 MOBIL 0.3278 -0.04399 0.21832 0.34861 0.39336 0.14722
 PANAM 0.3396  0.13446 0.16438 0.30585 0.31682 0.29320
  PSNH 0.1237  0.06825 0.06786 0.08206 0.07588 0.09689
 TANDY 0.5000  0.15650 0.25080 0.47188 0.49859 0.40868
TEXACO 0.2712 -0.04208 0.19960 0.26285 0.29353 0.08824
 WEYER 0.5531  0.14958 0.27646 0.54368 0.58181 0.44913
...
```

To obtain the estimated factor model covariance matrix, the estimated loadings and uniqueness values must be re-scaled. One way to do this is

```
> S.hat = diag(factor.fit$scale)
> D.hat = S.hat%*%diag(factor.fit$uniqueness)%*%S.hat
> D.hat.inv = diag(1/diag(D.hat))
```

```
> B.hat = S.hat%*%loadings(factor.fit)
> cov.factor = B.hat%*%t(B.hat)+D.hat
> dimnames(cov.fa) = list(colIds(returns),colIds(returns))
```

The factor analysis global minimum variance portfolio is then

```
> w.gmin.fa = solve(cov.fa)%*%rep(1,nrow(cov.fa))
> w.gmin.fa = w.gmin.fa/sum(w.gmin.fa)
> t(w.gmin.fa)
numeric matrix: 1 rows, 15 columns.
        CITCRP   CONED   CONTIL    DATGEN          DEC   DELTA
[1,]   -0.0791  0.3985  -0.02537  -0.04279  -0.002584  0.04107


        GENMIL   GERBER     IBM   MOBIL    PANAM     PSNH     TANDY
[1,]   0.1889  0.01321  0.2171  0.1027  0.01757  0.07533  -0.03255


        TEXACO    WEYER
[1,]   0.1188  0.009147
```

15.5.2 Principal Components

Principal component analysis (PCA) is a dimension reduction technique used to explain the majority of the information in the sample covariance matrix of returns. With N assets there are N principal components, and these principal components are just linear combinations of the returns. The principal components are constructed and ordered so that the first principal component explains the largest portion of the sample covariance matrix of returns, the second principal component explains the next largest portion, and so on. The principal components are constructed to be orthogonal to each other and to be normalized to have unit length. In terms of a multifactor model, the K most important principal components are the factor realizations. The factor loadings on these observed factors can then be estimated using regression techniques.

Let $\widehat{\Omega}$ denote the sample covariance matrix of returns. The first sample principal component is $\mathbf{x}_1^{*\prime}\mathbf{R}_t$ where the $(N \times 1)$ vector $\mathbf{x}_1^*$ solves

$$\max_{x_1} \mathbf{x}_1' \widehat{\Omega} \mathbf{x}_1 \text{ s.t. } \mathbf{x}_1' \mathbf{x}_1 = 1.$$

The solution $\mathbf{x}_1^*$ is the eigenvector associated with the largest eigenvalue of $\widehat{\Omega}$. The second principal component is $\mathbf{x}_2^{*\prime}\mathbf{R}_t$ where the $(N \times 1)$ vector $\mathbf{x}_2^*$ solves

$$\max_{x_2} \mathbf{x}_2' \widehat{\Omega} \mathbf{x}_2 \text{ s.t. } \mathbf{x}_2' \mathbf{x}_2 = 1 \text{ and } \mathbf{x}_1^{*\prime} \mathbf{x}_2 = 0$$

The solution $\mathbf{x}_2^*$ is the eigenvector associated with the second largest eigenvalue of $\widehat{\Omega}$. This process is repeated until K principal components are computed.

The estimated factor realizations are simply the first K principal components

$$\widehat{f}_{kt} = \mathbf{x}_k^{*\prime} \mathbf{R}_t, \ k = 1, \ldots, K. \tag{15.20}$$

The factor loadings for each asset, $\boldsymbol{\beta}_i$, and the residual variances, $var(\varepsilon_{it}) = \sigma_i^2$ can be estimated via OLS[7] from the time series regression

$$R_{it} = \alpha_i + \boldsymbol{\beta}_i' \widehat{\mathbf{f}}_t + \varepsilon_{it}, \ t = 1, \ldots, T \tag{15.21}$$

giving $\widehat{\boldsymbol{\beta}}_i$ and $\widehat{\sigma}_i^2$ for $i = 1, \ldots, N$. The factor model covariance matrix of returns is then

$$\widehat{\boldsymbol{\Omega}} = \widehat{\mathbf{B}} \widehat{\boldsymbol{\Omega}}^F \widehat{\mathbf{B}}' + \widehat{\mathbf{D}} \tag{15.22}$$

where

$$\widehat{\mathbf{B}} = \begin{pmatrix} \widehat{\boldsymbol{\beta}}_1' \\ \vdots \\ \widehat{\boldsymbol{\beta}}_N' \end{pmatrix}, \ \widehat{\mathbf{D}} = \begin{pmatrix} \widehat{\sigma}_1^2 & 0 & 0 \\ 0 & \ddots & 0 \\ 0 & \cdots & \widehat{\sigma}_N^2 \end{pmatrix},$$

and

$$\begin{aligned} \widehat{\boldsymbol{\Omega}}^F &= \frac{1}{T-1} \sum_{t=1}^{T} (\widehat{\mathbf{f}}_t - \overline{\mathbf{f}})(\widehat{\mathbf{f}}_t - \overline{\mathbf{f}})', \\ \overline{\mathbf{f}} &= \frac{1}{T} \sum_{t=1}^{T} \widehat{\mathbf{f}}_t. \end{aligned}$$

Usually $\widehat{\boldsymbol{\Omega}}^F = \mathbf{I}_K$ because the principal components are orthonormal.

Factor Mimicking Portfolios

Since the principal components (factors) $\mathbf{x}_i^*$ are just linear combinations of the returns, it is possible to construct portfolios that are perfectly correlated with the principal components by re-normalizing the weights in the $\mathbf{x}_i^*$ vectors so that they sum to unity. Hence, the weights in the factor mimicking portfolios have the form

$$\mathbf{w}_i = \left(\frac{1}{\mathbf{1}'\mathbf{x}_i^*} \right) \cdot \mathbf{x}_i^*, \ i = 1, \ldots, K \tag{15.23}$$

where $\mathbf{1}$ is a $(N \times 1)$ vector of ones.

---

[7] OLS estimation is efficient even though assets are contemporaneously correlated because the time series regression for each asset has the same regressors.

Variance Decomposition

It can be shown that

$$\sum_{i=1}^{k} var(R_{it}) = \sum_{i=1}^{k} var(f_{it}) = \sum_{i=1}^{k} \lambda_i$$

where λ_i are the ordered eigenvalues of $var(\mathbf{R}_i) = \mathbf{\Omega}$. Therefore, the ratio

$$\frac{\lambda_i}{\sum_{i=1}^{N} \lambda_i}$$

gives the proportion of the total variance $\sum_{i=1}^{N} var(R_{it})$ attributed to the ith principal component factor return, and the ratio

$$\frac{\sum_{i=1}^{K} \lambda_i}{\sum_{i=1}^{N} \lambda_i}$$

gives the cumulative variance explained. Examination of these ratios help in determining the number of factors to use to explain the covariance structure of returns.

Example 105 *Estimating a statistical factor model by principal components using S-PLUS*

Principal component analysis in S-PLUS is performed using the function princomp. The S+FinMetrics function mfactor simplifies the process of estimating a statistical factor model for asset returns using principal components. To illustrate, consider estimating a statistical factor model for the assets in the S+FinMetrics "timeSeries" berndt.dat excluding market portfolio and the thirty-day T-bill

```
> returns.ts = berndt.dat[,c(-10,-17)]
```

To estimate a statistical factor model with the default of one factor use

```
> pc.mfactor = mfactor(returns.ts)
> class(pc.mfactor)
[1] "mfactor"
```

The result of the function mfactor is an object of class "mfactor", for which there are print and plot methods and extractor functions factors, loadings, residuals and vcov. The components of an "mfactor" object are

```
> names(pc.mfactor)
[1] "factors"      "loadings"      "k"
[4] "alpha"        "Omega"         "r2"
[7] "eigen"        "call"          "sum.loadings"
```

where `factors` contains the estimated factor returns (15.20), `loadings` contains the asset specific factor loadings $\hat{\beta}_i$ estimated from (15.21), `alpha` contains the estimated intercepts α_i from (15.21), `r2` contains the regression R^2 values from (15.21), `k` is the number of factors and `eigen` contains the eigenvalues from the sample covariance matrix.

The `print` method gives a brief summary of the PCA fit

```
> pc.mfactor

Call:
mfactor(x = returns.ts)

Factor Model:
 Factors Variables Periods
       1        15     120

Factor Loadings:
       Min. 1st Qu. Median  Mean 3rd Qu.   Max.
F.1 0.0444   0.139   0.25 0.231   0.308 0.417

Regression R-squared:
  Min. 1st Qu. Median  Mean 3rd Qu.   Max.
 0.032 0.223   0.329 0.344 0.516   0.604
```

Notice that all of the estimated loadings on the first factor are positive, and the median R^2 is around thirty percent. These results are very similar to those found for the single index model. The factor loadings and factor regression R^2 values may be extracted using the functions `loadings` and `mfactor.r2`

```
> loadings(pc.mfactor)
numeric matrix: 1 rows, 15 columns.
     CITCRP   CONED CONTIL DATGEN    DEC  DELTA GENMIL
F.1 0.2727 0.04441 0.3769 0.4172 0.3049 0.2502 0.1326

     GERBER    IBM  MOBIL  PANAM    PSNH  TANDY TEXACO
F.1 0.1672 0.1464 0.1552 0.3107 0.08407 0.4119 0.1323

     WEYER
F.1 0.2649
> mfactor.r2(pc.mfactor)
 CITCRP  CONED CONTIL DATGEN    DEC  DELTA GENMIL GERBER
 0.6041 0.1563 0.3285 0.5633 0.516 0.3665 0.2662 0.2181

    IBM  MOBIL  PANAM    PSNH  TANDY TEXACO  WEYER
 0.3408 0.2277 0.2922 0.03241 0.5643 0.1635 0.5153
```

The factor returns (15.20) and the residuals from the regression (15.21) may be extracted using the functions `factors` and `residuals`, respectively.

The function `vcov` extracts the PCA covariance matrix (15.22). The corresponding correlation matrix may computed using

```
> cov.pca = vcov(pc.mfactor)
> sd = sqrt(diag(cov.pca))
> cor.pca = cov.pca/outer(sd,sd)
> print(cor.pca,digits=1,width=2)
        CITCRP CONED CONTIL DATGEN DEC DELTA GENMIL GERBER
 CITCRP    1.0  0.16    0.4    0.6 0.5   0.5   0.36   0.34
  CONED    0.2  1.00    0.1    0.2 0.1   0.1   0.09   0.09
 CONTIL    0.4  0.12    1.0    0.4 0.4   0.3   0.27   0.25
 DATGEN    0.6  0.15    0.4    1.0 0.5   0.4   0.35   0.33
    DEC    0.5  0.14    0.4    0.5 1.0   0.4   0.33   0.31
  DELTA    0.5  0.12    0.3    0.4 0.4   1.0   0.28   0.26
 GENMIL    0.4  0.09    0.3    0.3 0.3   0.3   1.00   0.20
 GERBER    0.3  0.09    0.2    0.3 0.3   0.3   0.20   1.00
    IBM    0.4  0.11    0.3    0.4 0.4   0.3   0.26   0.25
  MOBIL    0.3  0.09    0.3    0.3 0.3   0.3   0.21   0.19
  PANAM    0.4  0.11    0.3    0.4 0.4   0.3   0.25   0.23
   PSNH    0.1  0.04    0.1    0.1 0.1   0.1   0.08   0.08
  TANDY    0.6  0.15    0.4    0.6 0.5   0.4   0.34   0.32
 TEXACO    0.3  0.08    0.2    0.3 0.3   0.2   0.18   0.16
  WEYER    0.5  0.14    0.4    0.5 0.5   0.4   0.33   0.31
```

The PCA global minimum variance portfolio is

```
> w.gmin.pca = solve(cov.pca)%*%rep(1,nrow(cov.pca))
> w.gmin.pca = w.gmin.pca/sum(w.gmin.pca)
> t(w.gmin.pca)
numeric matrix: 1 rows, 15 columns.
        CITCRP  CONED CONTIL   DATGEN      DEC DELTA GENMIL
[1,]  0.02236 0.3675 -0.021 -0.06549 -0.01173 0.0239 0.1722


        GERBER    IBM   MOBIL     PANAM    PSNH    TANDY
[1,]  0.07121 0.2202 0.09399 -0.006415 0.06427 -0.06079


        TEXACO   WEYER
[1,]    0.105 0.02472
```

The `plot` method allows a graphical investigation of the PCA fit

```
> plot(pc.mfactor)
```

Make a plot selection (or 0 to exit):

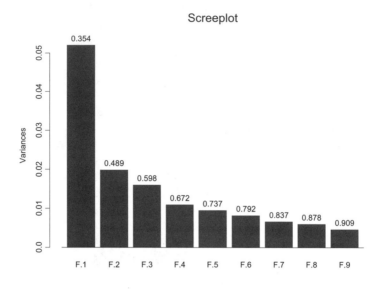

FIGURE 15.5. Screeplot of eigenvalues from PCA of Berndt returns.

```
1: plot: All
2: plot: Screeplot of Eigenvalues
3: plot: Factor Returns
Selection:
```

The Screeplot of Eigenvalues is illustrated in Figure 15.5. The first principal component explains about thirty five percent of the total variance, and the first two components explain about half of the total variance. It appears that two or three factors may be sufficient to explain most of the variability of the assets. The screeplot may also be computed directly using the S+FinMetrics function screeplot.mfactor.

The PCA factor model is re-estimated using two factors with

```
> pc2.mfactor = mfactor(returns.ts,k=2)
> pc2.mfactor

Call:
mfactor(x = returns.ts, k = 2)

Factor Model:
 Factors Variables Periods
       2        15     120

Factor Loadings:
```

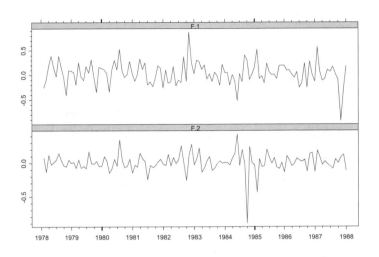

Factor Returns

FIGURE 15.6. Estimated factors from PCA of Berndt data.

```
     Min. 1st Qu. Median    Mean 3rd Qu.   Max.
F.1  0.0444  0.1395 0.2502  0.23143   0.308 0.417
F.2 -0.8236 -0.0671 0.0124 -0.00245   0.142 0.365
```

```
Regression R-squared:
  Min. 1st Qu. Median  Mean 3rd Qu.   Max.
 0.033 0.253   0.435  0.419 0.577   0.925
```

The first factor is the same as before and has all positive loadings. The second factor has both positive and negative loadings. The median regression R^2 has increased to about forty four percent. The factor returns are illustrated in Figure 15.6, created by selecting option 3 from the plot menu.

The factor return plot may also be computed directly by first extracting the factors and then using the S+FinMetrics function fplot:

```
> fplot(factors(pc2.mfactor))
```

The factor loadings are shown in Figure 15.7, created by

```
> pc2.betas = loadings(pc2.mfactor)
> par(mfrow=c(1,2))
> barplot(pc2.betas[1,],names=colIds(pc2.betas),horiz=T,
+ main="Beta values for first PCA factor")
> barplot(pc2.betas[2,],names=colIds(pc2.betas),horiz=T,
+ main="Beta values for second PCA factor")
```

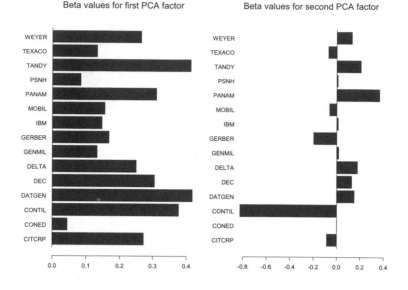

FIGURE 15.7. Estimated loadings on PCA factors for Berndt data.

The factor mimicking portfolios (15.23) may be computed using the S+FinMetrics function `mimic`

```
> pc2.mimic = mimic(pc2.mfactor)
> class(pc2.mimic)
[1] "mimic"
> pc2.mimic
            F.1        F.2
CITCRP  0.07856     2.3217
 CONED  0.01279    -0.0324
...
 WEYER  0.07630    -3.5637
attr(, "class"):
[1] "mimic"
```

These weights in these portfolios may be summarized using

```
> pc2.mimic.sum = summary(pc2.mimic,n.top=3)
> pc2.mimic.sum
```

```
Factor   1
  Top.Long.Name Top.Long.Weight Top.Short.Name Top.Short.Weight
1        DATGEN             12%          CONED             1.3%
2         TANDY             12%           PSNH             2.4%
```

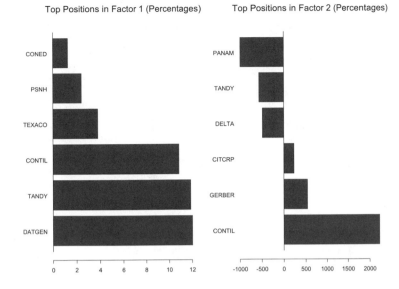

FIGURE 15.8. Weights in factor mimicking portfolios from PCA fit to Berndt data.

3	CONTIL	11%	TEXACO	3.8%

Factor   2

	Top.Long.Name	Top.Long.Weight	Top.Short.Name	Top.Short.Weight
1	CONTIL	2200%	PANAM	-990%
2	GERBER	540%	TANDY	-560%
3	CITCRP	230%	DELTA	-490%

The optional argument `n.top=3` specifies that the three assets with the largest and smallest weights in each factor mimicking portfolio are displayed. For the first factor, the assets `DATGEN`, `TANDY` and `CONTIL` have the highest weights and the assets `CONED`, `PSNH` and `TEXACO` have the lowest weights. Examination of the weights helps to interpret the factor mimicking portfolio. For the first portfolio, the weights are all positive (long positions in all assets) and are roughly equal suggesting the interpretation of a market-wide factor. The second factor has both positive and negative weights (long and short positions in the assets), and it is not clear how to interpret the weights. The weights may also be examined graphically using

```
> par(mfrow=c(1,2))
> plot(pc2.mimic.sum)
```

which produces the plot in Figure 15.8.

15.5.3 *Asymptotic Principal Components*

Asymptotic principal component analysis (APCA), proposed and developed in Conner and Korajczyk (1986) and based on the analysis in Chamberlain and Rothschild (1983), is similar to traditional PCA except that it relies on asymptotic results as the number of cross-sections N (assets) grows large. APCA is based on eigenvector analysis of the $T \times T$ matrix $\widehat{\mathbf{\Omega}}_T$. Conner and Korajczyk prove that as N grows large, eigenvector analysis of $\widehat{\mathbf{\Omega}}_T$ is asymptotically equivalent to traditional factor analysis. That is, the APCA estimates of the factors $\mathbf{f}_t$ are the first K eigenvectors of $\widehat{\mathbf{\Omega}}_T$. Specifically, let $\widehat{\mathbf{F}}$ denote the orthornormal $K \times T$ matrix consisting of the first K eigenvectors of $\widehat{\mathbf{\Omega}}_T$. Then $\widehat{\mathbf{f}}_t$ is the tth column of $\widehat{\mathbf{F}}$.

The main advantages of the APCA approach are:

- It works in situations where the number of assets, N, is much greater than the number of time periods, T. Eigenvectors of the smaller $T \times T$ matrix $\widehat{\mathbf{\Omega}}_T$ only need to be computed, whereas with traditional principal component analysis eigenvalues of the larger $N \times N$ matrix $\widehat{\mathbf{\Omega}}_N$ need to be computed.

- The method allows for an approximate factor structure of returns. In an approximate factor structure, the asset specific error terms ε_{it} are allowed to be contemporaneously correlated, but this correlation is not allowed to be too large across the cross section of returns. Allowing an approximate factor structure guards against picking up local factors, e.g. industry factors, as global common factors.

Refinement

Connor and Korajczyk (1988) offer a refinement of the APCA procedure that may improve the efficiency of the procedure.

1. Estimate the factors $\mathbf{f}_t$ $(t = 1, \ldots, T)$ by computing the first K eigenvalues of $\widehat{\mathbf{\Omega}}_T$.

2. For each asset, estimate the time series regression (factor model) by OLS

$$R_{it} = \alpha_i + \boldsymbol{\beta}_i' \widehat{\mathbf{f}}_t + \varepsilon_{it}, \ t = 1, \ldots, T$$

and compute the residual variances $\widehat{\sigma}_i^2$. Use these variance estimates to compute the residual covariance matrix

$$\widehat{\mathbf{D}} = \begin{pmatrix} \widehat{\sigma}_1^2 & 0 & 0 \\ 0 & \ddots & 0 \\ 0 & \cdots & \widehat{\sigma}_N^2 \end{pmatrix}$$

3. Form the $N \times T$ matrix of re-scaled returns

$$\mathbf{R}^* = \widehat{\mathbf{D}}^{-1/2}\mathbf{R}$$

and recompute the $T \times T$ covariance matrix

$$\widehat{\mathbf{\Omega}}_T^* = \frac{1}{N}\mathbf{R}^{*\prime}\mathbf{R}^*$$

4. Re-estimate the factors $\mathbf{f}_t$ by computing the first K eigenvalues of $\widehat{\mathbf{\Omega}}_T^*$.

Example 106 *Estimation of a statistical factor model by asymptotic principal component analysis using S-PLUS*

The S+FinMetrics function mfactor estimates a statistical factor model by asymptotic principal components whenever the number of assets, N, is greater than the number of time periods, T. To illustrate, consider fitting a statistical factor model using the S+FinMetrics "timeSeries" folio.dat, which contains weekly data on 1618 stocks over the period January 8, 1997 to June 28, 2000. For this data, $N = 1618$ and $T = 182$. To compute the APCA fit with $k = 15$ factors use

```
> folio.mf = mfactor(folio.dat,k=15)
> folio.mf

Call:
mfactor(x = folio.dat, k = 15)

Factor Model:
 Factors Variables Periods
      15      1618     182

Factor Loadings:
         Min. 1st Qu.    Median     Mean 3rd Qu.   Max.
 F.1  -0.977 -0.4261 -0.314658 -0.33377 -0.2168 0.160
 F.2  -0.420 -0.1041 -0.014446  0.06519  0.1628 1.110
 F.3  -0.463 -0.0784 -0.011839 -0.00311  0.0392 0.998
 F.4  -0.556 -0.0588  0.004821  0.00866  0.0771 0.495
 F.5  -1.621 -0.0622  0.015520  0.01373  0.0858 0.467
 F.6  -0.835 -0.0635 -0.001544  0.00307  0.0665 0.468
 F.7  -0.758 -0.0633 -0.006376 -0.01183  0.0509 2.090
 F.8  -0.831 -0.0685 -0.012736 -0.01413  0.0479 0.517
 F.9  -0.464 -0.0466  0.006447  0.01200  0.0640 1.095
 F.10 -0.640 -0.0659 -0.008760 -0.01050  0.0482 0.687
 F.11 -1.515 -0.0540 -0.001114 -0.00457  0.0539 0.371
 F.12 -1.682 -0.0637 -0.005902 -0.01068  0.0451 0.515
```

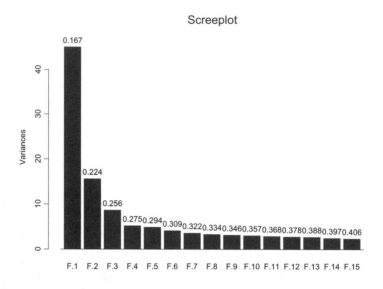

FIGURE 15.9. Screeplot of eigenvalues from APCA fit to 1618 assets.

```
F.13 -0.462 -0.0480  0.001901  0.00164  0.0516 0.685
F.14 -0.912 -0.0523 -0.001072 -0.00443  0.0472 0.436
F.15 -0.681 -0.0505 -0.000977 -0.00366  0.0473 0.548

Regression R-squared:
  Min. 1st Qu. Median  Mean 3rd Qu.  Max.
 0.066 0.265   0.354  0.372 0.459   0.944
```

By default, the APCA fit uses the Connor-Korajczyk refinement. To compute the APCA fit without the refinement, set the optional argument refine=F in the call to mfactor. The factor loadings appear to be reasonably scaled and skewed toward negative values. The loadings for the first factor appear to be almost all negative. Multiplying the first factor by negative one would make it more interpretable. The median regression R^2 is about thirty five percent, which is a bit higher than what one would expect from the single index model.

Figures 15.9 and 15.10 show the screeplot of eigenvalues and factor returns for the APCA fit, computed using

```
> screeplot.mfactor(folio.mf)
> fplot(factors(folio.mf)
```

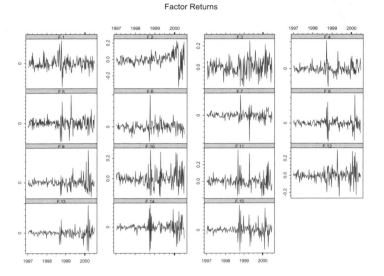

FIGURE 15.10. Estimated factors returns from APCA fit to 1618 assets.

The first two factors clearly have the largest explanatory power, and the fifteen factors together explain roughly forty one percent of the total variance.

The factor mimicking portfolios are computed using

```
> folio.m = mimic(folio.mf)
```

which is an object of class "mimic" of dimension 1618×15. It is difficult to concisely summarize the factor mimicking portfolios when the number of assets is large. This is why the **summary** method for "mimic" objects has an option for displaying only the largest and smallest **n.top** weights for each factor mimicking portfolio. To view the top five largest and smallest weights for the fifteen factors use

```
> folio.ms = summary(folio.m,n.top=5)
> folio.ms
```

Factor   1

	Top.Long.Name	Top.Long.Weight	Top.Short.Name	Top.Short.Weight
1	OWC	0.23%	BBY	−0.15%
2	FNV	0.22%	SCON	−0.14%
3	MT	0.22%	PUMA	−0.12%
4	BAC	0.21%	THDO	−0.11%
5	CACC	0.21%	AVTC	−0.11%

...

```
Factor   15
   Top.Long.Name Top.Long.Weight Top.Short.Name Top.Short.Weight
1            ALXN            79%           SCTC            -85%
2            AVID            59%           MCLL            -82%
3            LTXX            53%           WLNK            -65%
4             IDX            52%           LRCX            -63%
5            SEAC            51%           TSCC            -63%
```

The summary information may be visualized using the generic `plot` function

```
> plot(folio.ms)
```

which generates a fifteen page graph sheet, with one page for each factor.

The correlations of the assets giving the largest and smallest weights for a given factor may be visualized using an image plot. To do this, first compute the correlation matrix for all of the assets

```
> folio.cov = vcov(folio.mf)
> sd = sqrt(diag(folio.cov))
> folio.cor = folio.cov/outer(sd,sd)
```

Extract the names of the assets in the summary for the first factor

```
> top.names = c(as.character(folio.m[[1]][,1]),
+ rev(as.character(folio.ms[[1]][,3])))
```

and call the S+FinMetrics function `image.plot`

```
> image.plot(folio.cor[top.names, top.names],
+ sub="Risk factor 1", main="Correlations of top positions")
```

The resulting plot is shown in Figure 15.11.

15.5.4   Determining the Number of Factors

The statistical methods described above are based on knowing the number of common factors. In practice, the number of factors is unknown and must be determined from the data. If traditional factor analysis is used, then there is a likelihood ratio test for the number of factors. However, this test will not work if $N > T$. Connor and Korajczyk (1993) describe a procedure for determining the number of factors in an approximate factor model that is valid for $N > T$ and Connor (1995) applies this method to a variety of factor models. Recently Bai and Ng (2002) have proposed an alternative method.

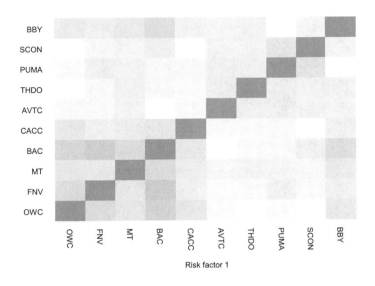

FIGURE 15.11. Image plot correlations between assets with top five largest and smallest weights in first factor mimicking portfolio.

Connor and Korajczyk Method

The intuition behind this method is that if K is the correct number of common factors then there should be no significant decrease in the cross-sectional variance of the asset specific error, ε_{it}, in moving from K to $K+1$ factors. The procedure is implemented as follows:

1. Given observed returns on asset i and a time series of $K+1$ factors, estimate the time series regression models

$$
\begin{aligned}
R_{it} &= \alpha_i + \boldsymbol{\beta}_i'\widehat{\mathbf{f}}_t + \varepsilon_{it} \\
R_{it} &= \alpha_i + \boldsymbol{\beta}_i'\widehat{\mathbf{f}}_t + \beta_{K+1,i}f_{K+1,t} + \varepsilon_{it}^*
\end{aligned}
$$

giving residuals $\widehat{\varepsilon}_{it}$ and $\widehat{\varepsilon}_{it}^*$.

2. Calculate degrees-of-freedom adjusted squared residuals

$$
\widehat{\sigma}_{it} = \frac{\widehat{\varepsilon}_{it}^2}{1-(K+1)/T-K/N}
$$

$$
\widehat{\sigma}_{it}^* = \frac{\widehat{\varepsilon}_{it}^{*2}}{1-(K+3)/T-(K+1)/N}
$$

3. Calculate the cross-sectional difference in squared errors based on odd and even time periods

$$\widehat{\Delta}_s = \widehat{\mu}_{2s-1} - \widehat{\mu}_{2s}^*, \ s = 1, \dots, T/2$$

$$\widehat{\mu}_t = \frac{1}{N} \sum_{i=1}^{N} \widehat{\sigma}_{it}$$

$$\widehat{\mu}_t^* = \frac{1}{N} \sum_{i=1}^{N} \widehat{\sigma}_{it}^*$$

and compute the $T/2 \times 1$ vector of differences

$$\widehat{\boldsymbol{\Delta}} = \left(\widehat{\Delta}_1, \widehat{\Delta}_2, \dots, \widehat{\Delta}_{T/2} \right)'$$

4. Compute the time series sample mean and variance of the differences

$$\overline{\Delta} = \frac{T}{2} \sum_{s=1}^{T/2} \widehat{\Delta}_s$$

$$\widehat{\sigma}_\Delta^2 = \frac{2}{T-2} \sum_{s=1}^{T/2} \left(\widehat{\Delta}_s - \overline{\Delta} \right)^2$$

5. Compute the t-statistic

$$t = \frac{\overline{\Delta}}{\widehat{\sigma}_\Delta}$$

and use it to test for a positive mean value.

Bai and Ng Method

Bai and Ng (2002) propose some panel C_p (Mallows-type) information criteria for choosing the number of factors. Their criteria are based on the observation that eigenvector analysis on $\widehat{\boldsymbol{\Omega}}$ or $\widehat{\boldsymbol{\Omega}}_N$ solves the least squares problem

$$\min_{\beta_i, \mathbf{f}_t} \ (NT)^{-1} \sum_{i=1}^{N} \sum_{t=1}^{T} (R_{it} - \alpha_i - \boldsymbol{\beta}_i' \mathbf{f}_t)^2$$

Bai and Ng's model selection or information criteria are of the form

$$IC(K) = \widehat{\sigma}^2(K) + K \cdot g(N, T)$$

where

$$\widehat{\sigma}^2(K) = \frac{1}{N} \sum_{i=1}^{N} \widehat{\sigma}_i^2$$

is the cross-sectional average of the estimated residual variances for each asset based on a model with K factors and $g(N, T)$ is a penalty function depending only on N and T. The preferred model is the one which minimizes the information criteria $IC(K)$ over all values of $K < K_{\max}$. Bai and Ng consider several penalty functions and the preferred criteria are

$$
\begin{aligned}
PC_{p1}(K) &= \widehat{\sigma}^2(K) + K \cdot \widehat{\sigma}^2(K_{\max}) \left(\frac{N+T}{NT} \right) \cdot \ln \left(\frac{NT}{N+T} \right), \\
PC_{p2}(K) &= \widehat{\sigma}^2(K) + K \cdot \widehat{\sigma}^2(K_{\max}) \left(\frac{N+T}{NT} \right) \cdot \ln \left(C_{NT}^2 \right),
\end{aligned}
$$

where $C_{NT} = \min(\sqrt{N}, \sqrt{T})$.

The implementation of the Bai and Ng strategy for determining the number of factors is a follows. First, select a number $K_{\max}$ indicating the maximum number of factors to be considered. Then for each value of $K < K_{\max}$, do the following:

1. Extract realized factors $\widehat{\mathbf{f}}_t$ using the method of APCA.

2. For each asset i, estimate the factor model

$$
R_{it} = \alpha_i + \boldsymbol{\beta}_i' \widehat{\mathbf{f}}_t^K + \varepsilon_{it},
$$

   where the superscript K indicates that the regression has K factors, using time series regression and compute the residual variances

$$
\widehat{\sigma}_i^2(K) = \frac{1}{T - K - 1} \sum_{t=1}^{T} \widehat{\varepsilon}_{it}^2.
$$

3. Compute the cross-sectional average of the estimated residual variances for each asset based on a model with K factors

$$
\widehat{\sigma}^2(K) = \frac{1}{N} \sum_{i=1}^{N} \widehat{\sigma}_i^2(K)
$$

4. Compute the cross-sectional average of the estimated residual variances for each asset based on a model with $K_{\max}$ factors, $\widehat{\sigma}^2(K_{\max})$.

5. Compute the information criteria $PC_{p1}(K)$ and $PC_{p2}(K)$.

6. Select the value of K that minimized either $PC_{p1}(K)$ or $PC_{p2}(K)$.

Bai and Ng perform an extensive simulation study and find that the selection criteria PC_{p1} and PC_{p2} yield high precision when $\min(N, T) > 40$.

Example 107 *Determining the number of factors for a statistical factor model estimated by asymptotic principal components*

To determine the number of factors in the "timeSeries" folio.dat using the Connor-Korajczyk method with a maximum number of factors equal to ten and a significance level equal to five percent use[8]

```
> folio.mf.ck = mfactor(folio.dat,k="ck",max.k=10,sig=0.05)
> folio.mf.ck

Call:
mfactor(x = folio.dat, k = "ck", max.k = 10, sig = 0.05)

Factor Model:
 Factors Variables Periods
       2      1618     182

Factor Loadings:
       Min. 1st Qu.    Median   Mean 3rd Qu. Max.
F.1 -0.177  0.2181   0.31721 0.3317   0.419 0.95
F.2 -0.411 -0.0958  -0.00531 0.0777   0.181 1.12

Regression R-squared:
  Min. 1st Qu. Median  Mean 3rd Qu.   Max.
 0.000 0.124    0.188 0.206 0.268    0.837
```

Two factors are selected by the Connor-Korajczyk method. Notice that most of the loadings on the first factor are positive.

Similarly, to determine the number of factors using the Bai-Ng method use

```
> folio.mf.bn = mfactor(folio.dat,k="bn",max.k=10,sig=0.05)
> folio.mf.bn$k
[1] 2
```

Again, two factors are determined.

15.6   References

[1] ALEXANDER, C. (2001). *Market Models: A Guide to Financial Data Analysis*, John Wiley and Sons.

[2] BAI, J. AND NG, S., (2002), "Determining the Number of Factors in Approximate Factor Models." *Econometrica*, 70, 191-221.

---

[8]For a data set with a large number of assets, the Connor-Korajczyk and Bai-Ng methods may take a while.

[3] CHAMBERLAIN, G. AND ROTHSCHILD, M. (1983), "Arbitrage, Factor Structure and Mean-Variance Analysis in Large Asset Markets, *Econometrica*, 51, 1305-1324.

[4] CHAN, L.K., KARCESKI, J. AND LAKONISHOK, J. (1998), "The Risk and Return from Factors," *Journal of Financial and Quantitative Analysis*, 33(2), 159-188.

[5] CHAN, L.K., KARCESKI, J. AND LAKONISHOK, J. (1999), "On Portfolio Optimization: Forecasting Covariances and Choosing the Risk Model," *Review of Financial Studies*, 5, 937-974.

[6] CHEN, N.F., ROLL, R., AND ROSS, S.A. (1986), "Economic Forces and the Stock Market," *The Journal of Business*, 59(3), 383-404.

[7] CAMPBELL, J.Y., LO, A.W., AND MACKINLAY, A.C. (1997). *The Econometrics of Financial Markets*. Princeton University Press.

[8] CONNOR, G. (1995). "The Three Types of Factor Models: A Comparison of Their Explanatory Power," *Financial Analysts Journal*, 42-46.

[9] CONNOR, G., AND KORAJCZYK, R.A. (1986), "Performance Measurement with the Arbitrage Pricing Theory: A New Framework for Analysis," *Journal of Financial Economics*, 15, 373-394.

[10] CONNOR, G., AND KORAJCZYK, R.A. (1988), "Risk and Return in an Equilibrium APT: Application of a New Test Methodology," *Journal of Financial Economics*, 21, 255-289.

[11] CONNOR, G. AND KORAJCZYK, R.A. (1993). "A Test for the Number of Factors in an Approximate Factor Model," *The Journal of Finance*, vol. 48(4), 1263-92.

[12] ELTON, E. AND M.J. GRUBER (1997). *Modern Portfolio Theory and Investment Analysis, 5th Edition*. John Wiley & Sons.

[13] FAMA, E. AND K.R. FRENCH (1992). "The Cross-Section of Expected Stock Returns", *Journal of Finance*, 47, 427-465.

[14] GRINOLD, R.C. AND KAHN, R.N. (2000), *Active Portfolio Management: A Quantitative Approach for Producing Superior Returns and Controlling Risk, Second Edition*. McGraw-Hill, New York.

[15] JOHNSON AND WICHERN (1998). *Multivariate Statistical Analysis*. Prentice-Hall, Englewood Cliffs, New Jersey.

[16] SHARPE, W.F. (1970). *Portfolio Theory and Capital Markets*. McGraw-Hill, New York.

[17] SHEIKH, A. (1995), "BARRA's Risk Models," mimeo, BARRA.

16
Term Structure of Interest Rates

16.1 Introduction

In financial markets, the term structure of interest rates is crucial to pricing of fixed income securities and derivatives. The last thirty years have seen great advances in the financial economics of term structure of interest rates. This chapter will focus on interpolating the term structure of interest rates from discrete bond yields. Refer to Campbell, Lo and MacKinlay (1997) for basic concepts in fixed income calculations and Hull (1997) for an introduction to theoretical term structure modeling.

Section 16.2 first defines different rates, such as spot or zero coupon interest rate, forward rate, and discount rate, and documents how one rate can be converted to another. Section 16.3 shows how to interpolate term structure data using quadratic or cubic spline. Section 16.4 illustrates how to use smoothing splines to fit term structure data. Section 16.5 introduces the parametric Nelson-Siegel function and its extension and shows how it can be used to interpolate term structure data. Bliss (1997) and Ferguson and Raymar (1998) compared the performance of these different methods. Section 16.6 concludes this chapter.

16.2 Discount, Spot and Forward Rates

16.2.1 Definitions and Rate Conversion

Although many theoretical models in financial economics hinge on an abstract interest rate, in reality there are many different interest rates. For example, the rates of a three month U.S. Treasury bill are different from those of a six month U.S. Treasury bill. The relationship between these different rates of different maturity is known as the term structure of interest rates. The term structure of interest rates can be described in terms of spot rate, discount rate or forward rate.

The *discount function*, $d(m)$, gives the present value of $1.00 which is repaid in m years. The corresponding *yield to maturity* of the investment, $y(m)$, or *spot interest rate*, or *zero coupon rate*, must satisfy the following equation under continuous compounding:

$$d(m)e^{y(m)\cdot m} = 1$$

or

$$d(m) = e^{-y(m)\cdot m} \tag{16.1}$$

Obviously, the discount function is an exponentially decaying function of the maturity, and must satisfy the constraint $d(0) = 1$.

The above equation easily shows that under continuous compounding

$$y(m) = -\frac{\log d(m)}{m}.$$

If discrete compounding is used instead, one can similarly show that

$$y(m) = p[d(m)^{-\frac{1}{p\cdot m}} - 1]$$

where p is the number of compounding periods in a year.

The spot interest rate is the single rate of return applied over the maturity of m years starting from today. It is also useful to think of it as the average of a series of future spot interest rates, or *forward rates*, with different maturities starting from a point in the future, and thus:

$$e^{y(m)\cdot m} = e^{\int_0^m f(x)dx}$$

from which one can easily obtain:

$$y(m) = \frac{1}{m}\int_0^m f(x)dx \tag{16.2}$$

with $f(m)$ denoting the forward rate curve as a function of the maturity m.

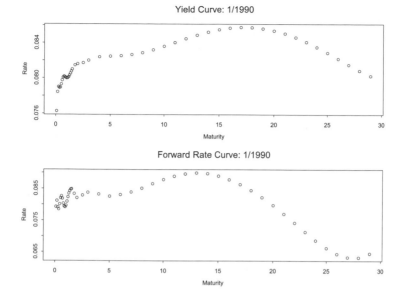

FIGURE 16.1. Yield curve and forward rate curve for January 1990.

From (16.1) and (16.2), the relationship between the discount function and forward rate can be derived:

$$d(m) = \exp\{-\int_0^m f(x)dx\}$$

or

$$f(m) = -\frac{d'(m)}{d(m)}.$$

Hence the forward rate gives the rate of decay of the discount function as a function of the maturity m. The relationship between these different rates under discrete compounding can be similarly obtained.

16.2.2 Rate Conversion in S+FinMetrics

To facilitate the interpolation of term structure from any of discount rate, spot rate, or forward rate, S+FinMetrics provides a group of functions for converting one rate into another rate. These functions will be illustrated using the mk.zero2 and mk.fwd2 data sets in S+FinMetrics, which contains the U.S. zero coupon rates and forward rates, respectively, as computed by McCulloch and Kwon (1993).

Both mk.zero2 and mk.fwd2 are "timeSeries" objects with 55 columns, with each column representing the rate with the corresponding maturity in the 55×1 vector mk.maturity. For example, the first element of the vector mk.maturity is 0.083, so the first columns of mk.zero2 and mk.fwd2 correspond to the rates with maturity of one month. Use the following code to plot the yield curve and forward rate curve for January 1990, and the graph is shown in Figure 16.1:

```
> par(mfrow=c(2,1))
> plot(mk.maturity, mk.zero2[54,], xlab="Maturity", ylab="Rate")
> title(paste("Yield Curve:", positions(mk.zero2[54,])))
> plot(mk.maturity, mk.fwd2[54,], xlab="Maturity", ylab="Rate")
> title(paste("Forward Rate Curve:", positions(mk.fwd2[54,])))
> par(mfrow=c(1,1))
```

To convert the spot interest rate or forward rate into the discount rate, use the S+FinMetrics function bond.discount. For example, to convert the first 48 spot rates in Figure 16.1 to discount rates, use the following command:

```
> disc.rate = bond.discount(mk.zero2[54, 1:48],
+ mk.maturity[1:48], input="spot", compounding=2)
```

The bond.discount function takes two required arguments: the first is a vector of rates, and the second is a vector of the corresponding maturity. Note that the optional argument input is used to specify the type of the input rates, and compounding to specify the number of compounding periods in each year. So compounding=2 corresponds to semi-annual compounding.[1] If the input rates are forward rates, simply set input="forward".

The functions bond.spot and bond.forward can be called in a similar fashion to compute the spot interest rate and forward rate, respectively, from different input rates. For all those three functions, the rates should be expressed as decimal numbers, and the maturity should be expressed in units of years. For example, to convert disc.rate back into the spot rates, use the following command:

```
> spot.rate = bond.spot(disc.rate, mk.maturity[1:48],
+ input="discount", compounding=2)
```

It can be easily checked that spot.rate is the same as mk.zero2[54, 1:48].

16.3 Quadratic and Cubic Spline Interpolation

The interest rates are observed with discrete maturities. In fixed income analysis, the rate for a maturity which is not observed can sometimes be

---

[1] To use continuous compounding, specify compounding=0.

used. Those unobserved rates can usually be obtained by interpolating the observed term structure.

Since the discount rate should be a monotonically decreasing function of maturity and the price of bonds can be expressed as a linear combination of discount rates, McCulloch (1971, 1975) suggested that a spline method could be used to interpolate the discount function, or the bond prices directly. In particular, use k continuously differentiable functions $s_j(m)$ to approximate the discount rates:

$$d(m) = a_0 + \sum_{j=1}^{k} a_j s_j(m) \tag{16.3}$$

where $s_j(m)$ are known functions of maturity m, and a_j are the unknown coefficients to be determined from the data. Since the discount rate must satisfy the constraint $d(0) = 1$, set $a_0 = 1$ and $s_j(0) = 0$ for $j = 1, \cdots, k$. Note that once the functional form of $s_j(m)$ is determined, the coefficients a_j can be easily estimated by linear regression. Thus the discount rate, or forward rate, or spot rate, associated with an unobserved maturity can be easily interpolated using the above functional form, as long as the maturity is smaller than the largest maturity used in the estimation.

Figure 16.1 shows that there are usually more points in the short end of the term structure, and less points in the long end of the term structure. To obtain a reliable interpolation using the spline method, the functional form of $s_j(m)$ should be chosen so that it adapts to the density of maturity m. McCulloch (1971) gives a functional form of $s_j(m)$ using quadratic spline, which is based on piecewise quadratic polynomials, while McCulloch (1975) gives a functional form of $s_j(m)$ using cubic spline, which is based on piecewise cubic polynomials.

Term structure interpolation using quadratic or cubic spline methods can be performed by calling the **term.struct** function in S+FinMetrics. The arguments taken by **term.struct** are:

```
> args(term.struct)
function(rate, maturity, method = "cubic", input.type = "spot",
        na.rm = F, plot = T, compounding.frequency = 0,
        k = NULL, cv = F, penalty = 2, spar = 0, ...)
NULL
```

Similar to **bond.spot**, **bond.discount** and **bond.forward** functions, the first argument **rate** should be a vector of interest rates, while the second argument **maturity** specifies the corresponding maturity in units of years. The type of the input interest rate should be specified through the optional argument **input.type**. Note that the quadratic or cubic spline methods operate on discount rates. If the input interest rates are not discount rates, the optional argument **compounding.frequency** should also be set for proper conversion, which is set to zero for continuous compounding

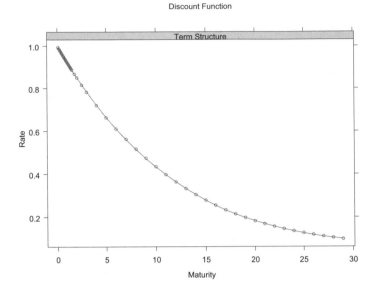

FIGURE 16.2. U.S. discount function for January 1990: quadratic spline.

by default. The optional argument k determines the number of functions in (16.3), also known as *knot points*. By default, follow McCulloch (1971, 1975) and set $k = [\sqrt{n}]$ where n is the length of the input rates. Other optional arguments will be discussed in later sections.

To illustrate the usage of the spline methods, in order to interpolate the term structure corresponding to January 1990, using mk.zero2, use the following command:

```
> disc.rate = term.struct(mk.zero2[54,], mk.maturity,
+ method="quadratic", input="spot", na.rm=T)
```

Note that na.rm=T is set to remove the missing values at the long end of the term structure. By default, the interpolated discount rate is plotted automatically, which is shown in Figure 16.2. The points in the figure represent the original discount rates, while the line represents the spline interpolation.

The returned object disc.rate is of class "term.struct". As usual, typing the name of the object at the command line invokes its print method:

```
> class(disc.rate)
[1] "term.struct"
> disc.rate
```

Call:

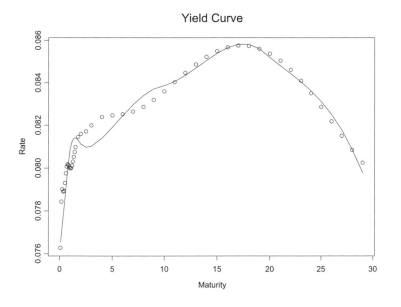

FIGURE 16.3. U.S. yield curve for January 1990: quadratic spline.

```
term.struct(rate = mk.zero2[54,  ], maturity = mk.maturity,
      method = "quadratic", input.type = "spot", na.rm = T)
```

```
Coefficients:
     a1       a2       a3       a4       a5       a6
 -0.0761  -0.0791  -0.0688  -0.0373  -0.0146  -0.0045
```

```
Degrees of freedom: 48 total; 42 residual
Residual standard error: 0.001067688
```

Since the unknown coefficients a_j of the spline are estimated by linear regression, the output looks very much similar to linear regression output. Since there are 48 spot rates available for January 1990, the number of knot points is chosen to be 6 by default.

The plot generated in Figure 16.2 shows the interpolated discount function because the quadratic or cubic spline methods are designed to operate on discount function. This plot can be later regenerated by calling the generic **plot** function on a "**term.struct**" object. However the yield curve or forward rate curve is usually of more interest. These can also be easily plotted using the components of a "**term.struct**" object. For example, use the S-PLUS **names** function to find out the components of **disc.rate**:

```
> names(disc.rate)
 [1] "coefficients" "residuals"   "fitted.values" "effects"
```

```
[5]  "R"              "rank"        "assign"       "df.residual"
[9]  "contrasts"      "terms"       "call"         "fitted"
[13] "knots"          "method"      "maturity"     "rate"
```

The first 10 components are inherited from an "lm" object, because the S-PLUS lm function is used for the linear regression. The fitted (instead of the fitted.values) component represents the estimated discount rates associated with the maturity component. To plot the interpolated yield curve or forward rate curve, simply convert the estimated discount rates into the rates you want. For example, use the following code to plot the interpolated yield curve:

```
> spot.rate = bond.spot(disc.rate$fitted, disc.rate$maturity,
+ input="discount", compounding=0)
> plot(mk.maturity[1:48], mk.zero2[54,1:48],
+ xlab="Maturity", ylab="Rate", main="Yield Curve")
> lines(disc.rate$maturity, spot.rate)
```

and the plot is shown in Figure 16.3. Note that in the plot the points represent the original zero coupon rates, while the line represents the quadratic spline interpolation.

16.4   Smoothing Spline Interpolation

The previous section demonstrated that the polynomial spline methods proposed by McCulloch (1971, 1975) can fit the discount rate and yield curve very well. However, since the methods operate on (linear combinations of) discount functions, the implied forward rate curve usually has some undesirable features. For example, use the following code to generate the implied forward rate curve from the object disc.rate fitted in the previous section:

```
> fwd.rate = bond.forward(disc.rate$fitted, disc.rate$maturity,
+ input="discount", compounding=0)
> plot(disc.rate$maturity, fwd.rate, type="l",
+ xlab="Maturity", ylab="Rate", main="Forward Rate")
> points(mk.maturity[1:48], mk.fwd2[54, 1:48])
```

The plot is shown in Figure 16.4. The implied forward rate is way off at the long end of the term structure.

In addition to the undesirable behavior of implied forward rate, the choice of knot points for polynomial splines is rather *ad hoc*. For a large number of securities, the rule can imply a large number of knot points, or coefficients a_j. To avoid these problems with polynomial spline methods, Fisher, Nychka and Zervos (1995) proposed to use *smoothing splines* for interpolating the term structure of interest rates.

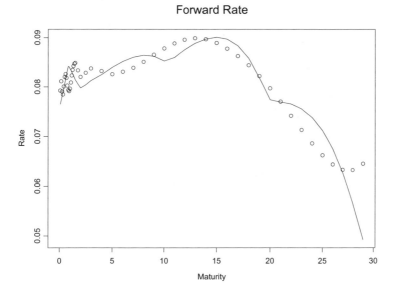

FIGURE 16.4. U.S. forward rate for January 1990: quadratic spline.

In general, for an explanatory variable x_i and a response variable y_i, the smoothing spline tries to find a smooth function $f(\cdot)$ to minimize the penalized residual sum of squares (PRSS):

$$\text{PRSS} = \sum_{i=1}^{n}[y_i - f(x_i)]^2 + \lambda \int [f''(t)]^2 dt \qquad (16.4)$$

where the first term is the residual sum of squares (RSS), and the second term is the penalty term, and the parameter λ controls the trade-off between goodness-of-fit and parsimony. By using the penalty term, the spline function can be over-parameterized, while using λ to reduce the effective number of parameters.

Let S denote the $n \times n$ implicit smoother matrix such that $f(x_i) = \sum_{j=1}^{n} S(x_i, x_j)y_j$. Fisher, Nychka and Zervos (1995) suggested using generalized cross validation (GCV) to choose λ. That is, λ is chosen to minimize

$$\text{GCV} = \frac{\text{RSS}}{n - \theta \cdot \text{tr}(S)}$$

where θ is called the *cost*, and $\text{tr}(S)$ denotes the trace of the implicit smoother matrix and is usually used as the measure of effective number of parameters.

Interpolation of term structure using smoothing spline can also be performed using the **term.struct** function by setting the optional argument

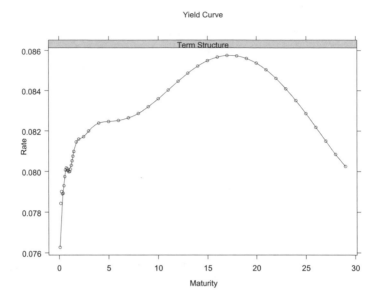

FIGURE 16.5. U.S. yield curve for January 1990: smoothing spline.

`method="smooth"`. The procedure uses the S-PLUS `smooth.spline` function as the workhorse.[2] In particular, for all the arguments taken by the function `term.struct`, `cv`, `penalty` and `spar` are specifically used for smoothing spline methods and passed to the `smooth.spline` function. By default, use GCV by setting `cv=F` and thus `spar`, which specifies the value of λ, is ignored.[3] The optional argument `penalty` is used to specify the value for θ. Following Fisher, Nychka and Zervos (1995), set $\theta = 2$ by default.

For example, use the following command to interpolate the yield curve for January 1990, with the smoothing spline method:

```
> fnz.fit = term.struct(mk.zero2[54,], mk.maturity,
+ method="smooth", input="spot", na.rm=T)
```

Again, the interpolated yield curve is plotted automatically, as shown in Figure 16.5. Although the returned object `fnz.fit` is of class "`term.struct`", its components are different from the `disc.rate` object fitted in the previous section, because now the `smooth.spline` function is used as the workhorse:

---

[2] Refer to Hastie (1993) and *S-PLUS Guide to Statistics* for the description of `smooth.spline` function.

[3] For further details regarding these arguments, see the on-line help file for `smooth.spline` function.

```
> class(fnz.fit)
[1] "term.struct"
> names(fnz.fit)
 [1] "x"         "y"         "w"         "yin"       "lev"       "cv.crit"
 [7] "pen.crit"  "df"        "spar"      "fit"       "call"      "method"
[13] "maturity"  "rate"
```

The first 10 components are inherited from a "smooth.spline" object, while the last four components are generated by the term.struct function. For the same reason, the print function now shows different information:

```
> fnz.fit
Call:
term.struct(rate = mk.zero2[54,  ], maturity = mk.maturity,
        method = "smooth", input.type = "spot", na.rm = T)

Smoothing Parameter (Spar): 4.767984e-11
Equivalent Degrees of Freedom (Df): 47.57122
Penalized Criterion: 4.129338e-10
GCV: 3.605842e-14
```

which shows the optimal smoothing parameter λ, and its associated GCV, penalized criterion, and equivalent degrees of freedom.

For "term.struct" objects, S+FinMetrics also implements a predict method, which can be used to obtain the interpolated rate associated with an arbitrary vector of maturity. For example, to recover the fitted spot rates from fnz.fit, use the predict method as follows:

```
> fnz.spot = predict(fnz.fit, fnz.fit$maturity)
```

From the fitted spot rates, one can compute the implied forward rates for the smoothing spline:

```
> fnz.forward = bond.forward(fnz.spot, fnz.fit$maturity,
+ input="spot", compounding=0)
> plot(mk.maturity[1:48], mk.fwd2[54,1:48],
+ xlab="Maturity", ylab="Rate", main="Forward Rate")
> lines(fnz.fit$maturity, fnz.forward)
```

The "real" forward rates and the smoothing spline interpolations are shown together in Figure 16.6. The interpolations agree very well with the "real" forward rates. The slight difference is partly caused by the fact that mk.zero2[54,] and the spot rates implied by mk.fwd2[54,] are slightly different.

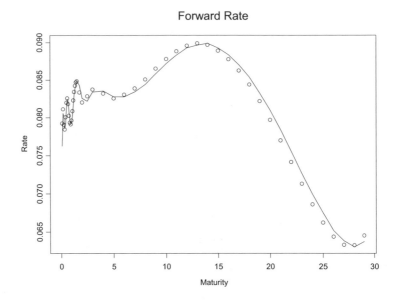

FIGURE 16.6. U.S. forward rate for January 1990: smoothing spline.

16.5   Nelson-Siegel Function

The previous sections have shown that both the polynomial and smoothing spline methods can fit the term structure very well, except that the implied forward rates from polynomial spline methods have some undesirable features at the long end of the term structure. However, the non-parametric spline based methods usually do not generate good out-of-sample forecasts. There is substantial evidence showing that a parametric function suggested by Nelson and Siegel (1987) has better out-of-sample forecasting performance.

Using a heuristic argument based on the expectation theory of the term structure of interest rates, Nelson and Siegel (1987) proposed the following parsimonious model for the forward rate:

$$f(m) = \beta_0 + \beta_1 \cdot e^{-m/\tau} + \beta_2 \cdot m/\tau \cdot e^{-m/\tau}.$$

They suggested that the model may also be viewed as a constant plus a Laguerre function, and thus can be generalized to higher-order models. Based on the above equation, the corresponding yield curve can be derived as follows:

$$y(m) = \beta_0 + \beta_1 \frac{1 - e^{-m/\tau}}{m/\tau} + \beta_2 \left[\frac{1 - e^{-m/\tau}}{m/\tau} - e^{-m/\tau} \right]. \qquad (16.5)$$

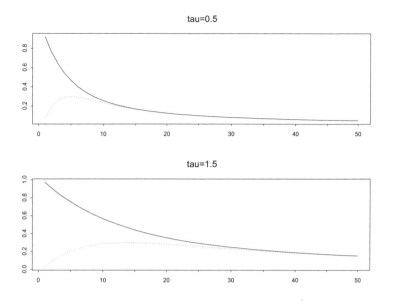

FIGURE 16.7. Short term and medium term components of Nelson-Siegel function.

For a given constant τ, both the forward rate curve and the yield curve are linear functions of the coefficients β_0, β_1 and β_2. Nelson and Siegel (1987) showed that, depending on the values of β_1 and β_2, the yield curve can assume the common shapes of observed yield curves, such as upward sloping, downward sloping, humped, or inverted humped. In addition, consistent with stylized facts of the yield curve, the three components in (16.5) can be interpreted as the long term, short term and medium term component, or the level, slope, and curvature component of the yield curve.[4]

Example 108 *Interpretation of Nelson-Siegel function*

The function `term.struct.nsx` in `S+FinMetrics` can be used to generate the regressors in (16.5) given a vector of maturity and a value for τ. Use the following code to visualize these components for different values of τ:

```
> ns.maturity = seq(1/12, 10, length=50)
> ns05 = term.struct.nsx(ns.maturity, 0.5)
> ns15 = term.struct.nsx(ns.maturity, 1.5)
> par(mfrow=c(2,1))
> tsplot(ns05[,2:3], main="tau=0.5")
> tsplot(ns15[,2:3], main="tau=1.5")
```

---

[4]Refer to Diebold and Li (2002) for a detailed explanation.

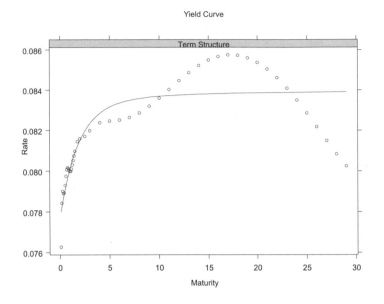

FIGURE 16.8. U.S. yield curve for January 1990: Nelson-Siegel function.

```
> par(mfrow=c(1,1))
```

A vector of maturity was created from one month to ten years. The regressor matrix has three columns, and only the last two columns were plotted because the first column is always one, and the plot is shown in Figure 16.7. The parameter τ controls the rate of decay of those components. When τ is smaller, the short and medium term components decay to zero at a faster rate. Asymptotically, both the short and medium term components approach zero, and thus β_0 can be interpreted as the long term component, or the level of the yield curve.

To interpolate yield curves using the Nelson-Siegel function, choose the value of τ which gives the best fit for equation (16.5). The `term.struct` function employs this procedure if the optional argument `method` is set to `"ns"`. For example, use the following command to interpolate the yield curve for January 1990:

```
> ns.fit = term.struct(mk.zero2[54,], mk.maturity,
+ method="ns", input="spot", na.rm=T)
> ns.fit

Call:
term.struct(rate = mk.zero2[54,  ], maturity = mk.maturity,
       method = "ns", input.type = "spot", na.rm = T)
```

```
Coefficients:
      b0       b1       b2
  0.0840  -0.0063   0.0044
```

```
Degrees of freedom: 48 total; 45 residual
Residual standard error: 0.001203026
Tau estimate: 1.7603
```

Again, the fit is plotted by default as shown in Figure 16.8. The graph shows that although the Nelson-Siegel generally captures the shape of the yield curve, the in-sample fit is usually not as good as the non-parametric spline methods because it only uses three coefficients. The output shows the estimates of those coefficients, along with the estimate of τ.

Since the Nelson-Siegel function does not fit the data very well when the yield curve has a rich structure as in the above example, Svensson (1994) proposed to extend the Nelson-Siegel forward function as follows:

$$f(m) = \beta_0 + \beta_1 e^{-m/\tau_1} + \beta_2 \cdot m/\tau_1 \cdot e^{-m/\tau_1} + \beta_3 \cdot m/\tau_2 \cdot e^{-m/\tau_2}$$

which adds another term to the Nelson-Siegel function to allow for a second hump. The corresponding yield function can be shown to be:

$$y(m) = \beta_0 + \beta_1 \frac{1 - e^{-m/\tau_1}}{m/\tau_1} + \beta_2 \left[\frac{1 - e^{-m/\tau_1}}{m/\tau_1} - e^{-m/\tau_1} \right]$$
$$+ \beta_3 \left[\frac{1 - e^{-m/\tau_2}}{m/\tau_2} - e^{-m/\tau_2} \right]. \quad (16.6)$$

To use the above function for interpolating yield curve, simply call the function term.struct with method="nss":

```
> nss.fit = term.struct(mk.zero2[54,], mk.maturity,
+ method="nss", input="spot", na.rm=T)
> nss.fit
```

```
Call:
term.struct(rate = mk.zero2[54, ], maturity = mk.maturity,
      method = "nss", input.type = "spot", na.rm = T)
```

```
Coefficients:
      b0      b1      b2      b3
  0.0000  0.0761  0.1351  0.0104
```

```
Degrees of freedom: 48 total; 44 residual
Residual standard error: 0.0005997949
Tau estimate: 21.8128 0.5315
```

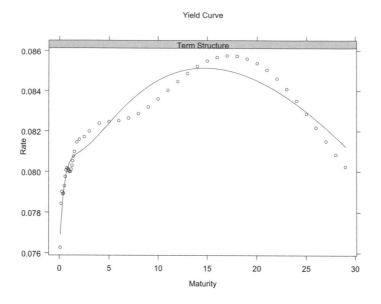

FIGURE 16.9. U.S. yield curve for January 1990: Svensson function.

The output now shows two estimates for τ and one more coefficient for the additional term. The plot of the interpolated yield curve is shown in Figure 16.9.

16.6   Conclusion

For all the term structure interpolation methods discussed in this chapter, they all work with the yield curve for a given time, and thus do not consider the time series aspect of the yield curve. Recently Diebold and Li (2002) considered estimating the three components β_0, β_1 and β_2 of the Nelson-Siegel function for each available time, and building a time series model (in particular, an AR(1)-GARCH(1,1) model) for the estimated β_0, β_1 and β_2. By employing the times series forecasts of β_0, β_1 and β_2, they are able to generate reliable forecasts of yield curve. However, in this approach, the coefficients β_0, β_1 and β_2 are still estimated ignoring the time series aspect.

In recent years, many researchers have proposed to use state space models and Kalman filter to estimate the term structure of interest rates using a panel data, for example, see Duan and Simonato (1999), Geyer and Pichler (1999), Babbs and Nowman (1999), de Jong and Santa-Clara (1999) and de Jong (2000). Most of these models are special cases of the affine term structure model proposed by Duffie and Kan (1996), which can be readily expressed in a state space model by discretizing the continuous-time models. These models can be easily implemented using the state space modeling functions in S+FinMetrics.

16.7 References

[1] BABBS, S. H., AND NOWMAN, K. B. (1999). "Kalman Filtering of Generalized Vasicek Term Structure Models", *Journal of Financial and Quantitative Analysis*, 34 (1), 115-129.

[2] BLISS, R. R. (1997). "Testing Term Structure Estimation Methods", in P. Boyle, G. Pennacchi, and P. Ritchken (eds.), *Advances in Futures and Options Research*, Volume 9, 197-231.

[3] CAMPBELL, J. Y., LO, A. W., AND MACKINLAY, A. C. (1997). *The Econometrics of Financial Markets*, Princeton University Press.

[4] DE JONG, F. (2000). "Time Series and Cross Section Information in Affine Term-Structure Models", *Journal of Business and Economic Statistics*, 18 (3), 300-314.

[5] DE JONG, F., AND SANTA-CLARA, P. (1999). "The Dynamics of the Forward Interest Rate Curve: a Formulation with State Variables", *Journal of Financial and Quantitative Analysis*, 34 (1), 131-157.

[6] DIEBOLD, F. X., AND LI, C. (2002). "Forecasting the Term Structure of Government Bond Yields", mimeo.

[7] DUAN, J.-C., AND SIMONATO, J. (1999). "Estimating and Testing Exponential-Affine Term Structure Models by Kalman Filter", *Review of Quantitative Finance and Accounting*, 13, 111-135.

[8] DUFFIE, D., AND KAN, R. (1996). "A Yield-Factor Model of Interest Rates", *Mathematical Finance*, 6 (4), 379-406.

[9] FERGUSON, R., AND RAYMAR, S. (1998). "A Comparative Analysis of Several Popular Term Structure Estimation Models", *Journal of Fixed Income*, March 1998, 17-33.

[10] FISHER, M., NYCHKA, D., AND ZERVOS, D. (1995). "Fitting the Term Structure of Interest Rates with Smoothing Splines", Finance and Economics Discussion Series #1995-1, Board of Governors of the Federal Reserve System.

[11] GEYER, A. L. J., AND PICHLER, S. (1999). "A State-Space Approach to Estimate and Test Multifactor Cox-Ingersoll-Ross Models of the Term Structure", *Journal of Financial Research*, 22 (1), 107-130.

[12] HASTIE, T. J. (1993). "Generalized Additive Models", in J. M. Chambers and T. J. Hastie (eds.), *Statistical Models in S*, Chapman & Hall.

[13] HULL, J. C. (1997). *Options, Futures, and Other Derivatives*, Prentice Hall.

[14] MCCULLOCH, J. H. (1971). "Measuring the Term Structure of Interest Rates", *Journal of Business*, 44, 19-31.

[15] MCCULLOCH, J. H. (1975). "The Tax-Adjusted Yield Curve", *Journal of Finance*, 30 (3), 811-830.

[16] MCCULLOCH, J. H., AND KWON, H.-C. (1993). "U.S. Term Structure Data: 1947-1991", Department of Economics, Working Paper #93-6, Ohio State University.

[17] NELSON, C. R., AND SIEGEL, A. F. (1987). "Parsimonious Modeling of Yield Curves", *Journal of Business*, 60 (4), 473-489.

[18] SVENSSON, L. E. O. (1994). "Estimating and Interpreting Forward Interest Rates: Sweden 1992-1994", NBER Working Paper No. 4871.

17
Robust Change Detection

17.1   Introduction

In time series analysis, autoregressive integrated moving average (ARIMA) models have found extensive use since the publication of Box and Jenkins (1976). For an introduction to the standard ARIMA modeling in S-PLUS, see *S-PLUS Guide to Statistics*. Regression models are also frequently used in finance and econometrics research and applications. For example, as "factor" models for empirical asset pricing research and for parsimonious covariance matrix estimation in portfolio risk models. Often ARIMA models and regression models are combined by using an ARIMA model to account for serially correlated residuals in a regression model, resulting in REGARIMA models.

In reality, most time series data are rarely completely well behaved and often contain outliers and level shifts, which is especially true for economic and financial time series. The classical maximum likelihood estimators of both ordinary regression model parameters and ARIMA model parameters are not robust in that they can be highly influenced by the presence of even a small fraction of outliers and/or level shifts in a time series. It is therefore not suprising that classical maximum likelihood estimators of REGARIMA models also lack robustness toward outliers and/or level shifts.

S+FinMetrics provides functions that compute robust alternatives to the classical non-robust MLE's for robust fitting and diagnostics of RE-GARIMA models. In particular, the robust procedure `arima.rob` allows reliable model fitting when the data contain outliers and/or level shifts. In addition, it also detects the types and locations of the outliers in the time series and thus can be used to perform robust change detection.

This chapter is organized as follows: Section 17.2 gives a brief introduction to REGARIMA models, and Section 17.3 shows how to fit a robust REGARIMA model using functions in S+FinMetrics. Section 17.4 shows how to predict from a robustly fitted REGARIMA model, while Section 17.5 illustrates more options which can be used to control the robust fitting of REGARIMA models. Finally in Section 17.6, some technical details are given about how REGARIMA model parameters are estimated robustly in the procedure arima.rob.

17.2 REGARIMA Models

The REGARIMA model considered in this chapter takes the following form:

$$y_t = \mathbf{x}_t' \boldsymbol{\beta} + \epsilon_t, \text{ for } t = 1, 2, \cdots, T \tag{17.1}$$

where $\mathbf{x}_t$ is a $k \times 1$ vector of predictor variables, and $\boldsymbol{\beta}$ is a $k \times 1$ vector of regression coefficients. The error term ϵ_t follows a seasonal ARIMA process:

$$\Phi(L)(1-L)^d(1-L^s)^D \epsilon_t = (1 - \theta^* L^s)\Theta(L)u_t \tag{17.2}$$

where L is the lag (or backshift) operator, d the number of regular differences, D the number of seasonal differences, s the seasonality frequency, $\Phi(L) = 1 - \phi_1 L - \cdots - \phi_p L^p$ a stationary autoregressive operator of order p, $\Theta(L) = 1 - \theta_1 L - \cdots - \theta_q L^q$ a moving average operator of order q and θ^* a seasonal moving average parameter. Note that currently only one seasonal moving average term is allowed in the discussions in this chapter. The innovations u_t are assumed to be i.i.d. random variables with distribution F.

In practice, observed time series data are rarely well behaved as assumed in the REGARIMA model (17.1) and (17.2). An observed time series y_t^* is usually some kind of variant of y_t in equation (17.1). When the observed time series y_t^* might be influenced by some outliers, the classical maximum likelihood estimates as implemented in the S-PLUS function arima.mle are not robust. In contrast, the S+FinMetrics function arima.rob allows the robust estimation of the model parameters $(\boldsymbol{\beta}, \boldsymbol{\lambda})$, where $\boldsymbol{\lambda} = (\boldsymbol{\phi}, \boldsymbol{\theta}, \theta^*)$, $\boldsymbol{\phi}$ is a vector of the autoregressive parameters and $\boldsymbol{\theta}$ is a vector of the moving average parameters. Furthermore, it will detect three kinds of outliers in the original data y_t^*:

Additive outliers (AO): An additive outlier occurs at time t_0 if $y_{t_0}^* = y_{t_0} + c$, where c is a constant. The effect of this type of outlier is restricted to the time period t_0.

Innovation outliers (IO): An innovation outlier occurs at time t_0 if $u_{t_0} = v_{t_0} + c$, where v_{t_0} is generated by the distribution F. Usually it is assumed that F is the normal distribution $N(0, \sigma^2)$. Note that the effect of an innovation outlier is not restricted to time t_0 because of the structure of an ARIMA model. It also has influence on the subsequent observations.

Level shifts (LS): If one level shift occurs at time t_0, the observed series is $y_t^* = y_t + c$ for all $t \geq t_0$, with c being a constant. Note that if the series y_t^* has a level shift at t_0, the differenced series $y_t^* - y_{t-1}^*$ has an additive outlier at t_0.

In all those three cases c is the size of the outlier or level shift. Without any potential confusion, the general term "outlier" may refer to any of the three types of behavior.

17.3 Robust Fitting of REGARIMA Models

The S+FinMetrics function `arima.rob` computes the so-called "filtered τ-estimates" of the parameters (β, λ, σ) of REGARIMA model (17.1)-(17.2) when a time series is influenced by outliers. The technical details of this type of estimation can be found in Section 17.6.

S+FinMetrics comes with a "timeSeries" data `frip.dat`, which represents monthly industrial production of France from January 1960 to December 1989. This data set will be used to illustrate the usage of `arima.rob` function. First, a plot of the data will show the general properties of the time series:

```
> plot(frip.dat)
```

A few characteristics of the time series can be seen from Figure 17.1: (i) there are three big outliers around 1963 and 1968; (ii) it appears that a level shift happened around 1975; (iii) there is an obvious trend in the time series, and the trend looks like a exponential one, especially in the last five years. For diagnostic purpose, a robust ARIMA(2,1,0) model can be tried on the logarithm of `frip.dat`, due to the exponential-looking trend:

```
> frip.rr = arima.rob(log(frip.dat)~1, p=2, d=1)
```

Note that the `arima.rob` function has only one required argument: a formula specifying the regression model. The optional argument p specifies the autoregressive order, and d specifies the order of difference. In this case, the only predictor variable is the intercept term.

> **Caveat:** The interpretation of the intercept term in `arima.rob` is different from that for other formulas in S-PLUS. When both d

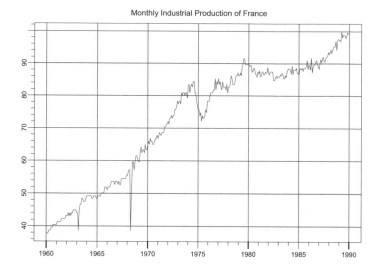

FIGURE 17.1. Monthly industrial production of France.

and **sd** (seasonal difference) are zero (which is the default), the intercept is the constant term as usual. However, when either **d** or **sd** is positive, the intercept is the coefficient of the lowest order time trend that can be identified. For instance, in the above example, the intercept corresponds to the coefficient of the trend term t. One can easily verify this using the following command:

```
> frip.t = 1:length(frip.dat)
> tmp = arima.rob(log(frip.dat)~frip.t-1, p=2, d=1)
```

which should give the same fit as **frip.rr**. The reason for this modification is obvious: some coefficients are not identifiable when differencing is involved.

The object returned by the function **arima.rob** is of class "arima.rob", which has **print** and **summary** methods, just like most modeling objects. For "arima.rob" objects, there is one additional advantage of using the **summary** method instead of the **print** method: if the data object is of class "timeSeries", the outliers will be lined up in a table with the time stamps of the observations, the types of the outliers, the impacts of the outliers, and the t-statistics. For example,

```
> summary(frip.rr)
```

```
Call:
arima.rob(formula = log(frip.dat) ~ 1, p = 2, d = 1)

Regression model:
 log(frip.dat) ~ 1

ARIMA model:
Ordinary differences: 1 ; AR order: 2 ; MA order: 0

Regression Coefficients:
            Value Std. Error t value Pr(>|t|)
(Intercept) 0.0024 0.0005     4.6558  0.0000

AR Coefficients:
        Value Std. Error t value Pr(>|t|)
AR(1) -0.3099  0.0537     -5.7742  0.0000
AR(2) -0.0929  0.0537     -1.7310  0.0843

Degrees of freedom: 360 total; 356 residual

Innovations standard deviation: 0.01311

 Number of outliers detected:  9

Outliers detected:

          |Time     |Type    |Impact   |t-value|
   -------+---------+--------+---------+-------+
1         |Mar 1963|AO      |-0.1457 |13.76  |
   -------+---------+--------+---------+-------+
2         |May 1968|AO      |-0.3978 |38.1   |
   -------+---------+--------+---------+-------+
3         |Jun 1968|AO      |-0.1541 |14.55  |
   -------+---------+--------+---------+-------+
4         |Sep 1968|AO      |-0.04516| 4.41  |
   -------+---------+--------+---------+-------+
5         |Apr 1969|LS      | 0.04511| 3.814 |
   -------+---------+--------+---------+-------+
6         |Sep 1974|LS      |-0.04351| 3.767 |
   -------+---------+--------+---------+-------+
7         |Nov 1974|LS      |-0.04844| 4.092 |
   -------+---------+--------+---------+-------+
8         |Sep 1976|AO      | 0.0382 | 3.829 |
   -------+---------+--------+---------+-------+
```

```
9        |Apr 1986|AO      | 0.03935| 3.932 |
-------+--------+-------+--------+-------+
```

```
Innovation scale estimate before correcting outliers:
  0.01311
```

```
Innovation scale estimate after correcting outliers:
  0.01215
```

The output generated by the **summary** method actually has two sections. The first section contains the parameter estimates in the REGARIMA model. In this section, one can see that the intercept (which, again, is actually the slope of the first order time trend) and the first autoregressive coefficient are very significant (that is, they have very small P-values), while the second autoregressive coefficient is not very significant.

The second section contains a summary of the outliers automatically detected by the **arima.rob** function. In this case, nine outliers are found: the first four and the last two are additive outliers, while the middle three are level shifts. The three additive outliers shown in Figure 17.1 are all detected with very large t-statistics.

A picture is always better than a thousand words. A visual diagnostic of the model fit **frip.rr** can be obtained by using the generic **plot** function:

```
> plot(frip.rr)

Make a plot selection (or 0 to exit):

1: plot: all
2: plot: Robust ACF of Innov.
3: plot: Robust PACF of Innov.
4: plot: Normal QQ-Plot of Innov.
5: plot: Original and Cleaned Series
6: plot: Detected Outliers
Selection:
```

Selections 2 and 3 will plot the robustly estimated autocorrelations and partial autocorrelations of the innovations u_t, respectively. Selection 4 produces the normal QQ-plot of the innovations, as shown in Figure 17.2, from which one can see that the three additive outliers are far away from the bulk of the data. Selection 5 plots the original response time series together with the series obtained by cleaning the original series of additive outliers using a robust filter, which is shown in Figure 17.3. Finally, Selection 6 plots the detected outliers, as shown in Figure 17.4.

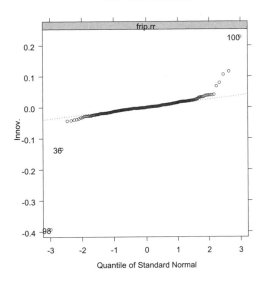

FIGURE 17.2. Normal QQ-plot of robust innovations.

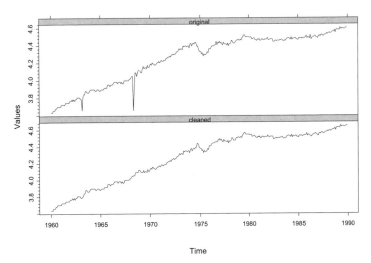

FIGURE 17.3. Original and cleaned series of `frip.dat`.

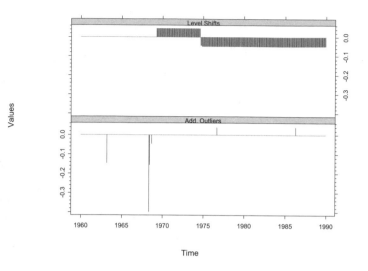

FIGURE 17.4. Detected outliers in `frip.dat`.

17.4   Prediction Using REGARIMA Models

One of the main applications of a REGARIMA model is to predict future values of response variable y_t based on past values of y_t and the corresponding future values of x_t. If future predictions are intended, then the call to the `arima.rob` function should specify the optional argument `n.predict`. This argument should be set to a number equal or greater than the number of predictions, the default of which is set to 20.

Prediction from REGARIMA models will be illustrated using the data set `import.dat` in S+FinMetrics, which contains two monthly time series from January 1983 to December 1990. The first series `taxes` corresponds to Argentinian import taxes and the second `import` to Argentinian imports. Another data frame `newtaxes.dat` contains the values of the variable `taxes` from January 1992 to October 1992. First fit a REGARIMA model with ARIMA(2,1,0) errors:

```
> import.rr = arima.rob(import~taxes-1, data=import.dat,
+ p=2, d=1)
```

Now with the new data of the predictor variable `taxes` in `newtaxes.dat`, one can predict `import` from January 1992 to October 1992 as follows:

```
> import.hat = predict(import.rr, 10, newdata=newtaxes.dat, se=T)
> class(import.hat)
```

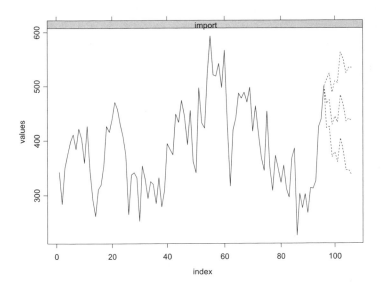

FIGURE 17.5. Fitted values ± 2· standard deviation.

```
[1] "forecast"
> names(import.hat)
[1] "values"   "std.err"
```

The optional argument se=T to the predict method tells the procedure to return the standard errors of the forecasts. The returned object import.hat is a "forecast" object with two components: values are the predicted values of import, and std.err are the standard errors of the prediction. Since import.hat is a "forecast" object, as we have seen from earlier chapters, the predictions can be easily plotted together with the original data:

```
> plot(import.hat, import.dat[, "import"])
```

The plot is shown in Figure 17.5.

17.5   Controlling Robust Fitting of REGARIMA Models

17.5.1   Adding Seasonal Effects

The arima.rob function allows for two kinds of seasonal effects options: the order of seasonal difference and the inclusion of a seasonal moving average term, controlled by the optional arguments sd and sma, respectively. For example, frip.dat is a monthly series, and you might expect that there are some seasonal effects in the series. Toward this end, you can add a seasonal moving average term by specifying the optional argument sma:

```
> frip.srr = arima.rob(log(frip.dat)~1, p=2, d=1, sfreq=12,
+ sma=T)
> summary(frip.srr)

Call:
arima.rob(formula = log(frip.dat) ~ 1, p = 2, d = 1,
    sfreq = 12, sma = T)

Regression model:
 log(frip.dat) ~ 1

ARIMA model:
Ordinary differences: 1 ; AR order: 2 ; MA order: 0
Seasonal differences: 0 ; Seasonal period: 12 ; Seasonal MA: 1

Regression Coefficients:
            Value Std. Error t value Pr(>|t|)
(Intercept) 0.0024 0.0004      5.3946  0.0000

AR Coefficients:
        Value Std. Error t value Pr(>|t|)
AR(1) -0.3135  0.0518     -6.0494  0.0000
AR(2) -0.1124  0.0518     -2.1697  0.0307

Seasonal MA Coefficient:
      Value Std. Error t value Pr(>|t|)
[1,] 0.0945 0.0519       1.8208  0.0695

Degrees of freedom: 360 total; 355 residual

Innovations standard deviation: 0.01304

 Number of outliers detected:   10

Outliers detected:

          |Time     |Type   |Impact  |t-value|
-------+--------+-------+--------+-------+
1        |Mar 1963|AO      |-0.1438 |13.58  |
-------+--------+-------+--------+-------+
```

```
2         |May 1963|LS     |  0.03988|  3.545  |
--------+---------+--------+---------+--------+
3         |May 1968|AO      |-0.3952  |38.67    |
--------+---------+--------+---------+--------+
4         |Jun 1968|AO      |-0.1519  |14.27    |
--------+---------+--------+---------+--------+
5         |Sep 1968|AO      |-0.04653|  4.615  |
--------+---------+--------+---------+--------+
6         |Apr 1969|LS     |  0.04602|  4.005  |
--------+---------+--------+---------+--------+
7         |Sep 1974|LS      |-0.04247|  3.739  |
--------+---------+--------+---------+--------+
8         |Nov 1974|LS      |-0.04914|  4.24   |
--------+---------+--------+---------+--------+
9         |Sep 1976|AO     |  0.038  |  3.891  |
--------+---------+--------+---------+--------+
10        |Apr 1986|AO     |  0.03792|  3.946  |
--------+---------+--------+---------+--------+
```

Innovation scale estimate before correcting outliers:
    0.01304

Innovation scale estimate after correcting outliers:
    0.01199

From the first section of the summary, one can see that the seasonal moving average term is relatively significant, and the estimates of other parameters are not altered very much. However, in the second section of the summary, one more level shift is detected, which corresponds to May 1963.

17.5.2   Controlling Outlier Detection

The outlier detection procedure used in `arima.rob` is similar to those proposed by Chang, Tiao and Chen (1988) and Tsay (1988) for ARIMA models, and the one used in the X12-REGARIMA program of U.S. Census Bureau. The main difference with those procedures is that `arima.rob` uses innovation residuals based on the filtered τ-estimates of β and λ, instead of the classical maximum likelihood estimates.

To detect the presence of an outlier at a given time t_0, the outlier detection procedure in `arima.rob` computes:

$$\mathcal{T} = \max_{t_0}\ \max\{T_{t_0,\mathrm{AO}},\ T_{t_0,\mathrm{LS}},\ T_{t_0,\mathrm{IO}}\},$$

where $T_{t_0,\text{AO}}$, $T_{t_0,\text{LS}}$ and $T_{t_0,\text{IO}}$ are the statistics corresponding to an AO, LS and IO at time t_0 respectively. The test statistic is defined as follows:

$$T = \frac{|\hat{\omega}|}{\hat{V}(\hat{\omega})^{1/2}},$$

where $\hat{\omega}$ is an estimate of ω, the size of the outlier, based on the residuals of the filtered τ-estimates and $\hat{V}(\hat{\omega})$ an estimate of its variance. If $T > \xi$, where ξ is a conveniently chosen critical value, one declares that there is an outlier. The time t_0 where the outlier occurs and the type of the outlier are those where the double maximum is attained.

The critical value ξ is similar to the constant used by Chang, Tiao and Chen (1988). They recommend using $\xi = 3$ for high sensitivity in outlier detection, $\xi = 3.5$ for medium sensitivity and $\xi = 4$ for low sensitivity, when the length of the series is less than 200. For arima.rob the critical value ξ is specified by the optional argument critv. The default value of critv is set as follows:

$$\xi = \begin{cases} 3 & \text{if} \quad T \leq 200, \\ 3.5 & \text{if} \quad 200 < T \leq 500, \\ 4 & \text{if} \quad T > 500. \end{cases}$$

More details of this procedure can be found in Bianco, Garcia Ben, Martinez and Yohai (1996, 2001).

So far none of the outliers detected is an innovation outlier. This is not a coincidence. By default, the outlier detection procedure in arima.rob does not consider innovation outliers. To allow for innovation outliers, use the optional argument innov.outlier:

```
> frip.nrr = arima.rob(log(frip.dat)~1, p=2, d=1, sma=T,
+ sfreq=12, innov.outlier=T)
```

S+FinMetrics also provides a function outliers to extract the information of the detected outliers from an "arima.rob" object. The object returned by outliers is of class "outliers". The methods print and summary are available for an "outliers" object. For example,

```
> summary(outliers(frip.nrr))
```

Number of outliers detected: 10

Outliers detected:

	Time	Type	Impact	t-value
1	Mar 1963	AO	-0.1438	13.58
2	May 1963	LS	0.03988	3.545

```
-------+--------+-------+--------+-------+
3        |May  1968|AO     |-0.3952 |38.67  |
-------+--------+-------+--------+-------+
4        |Jun  1968|AO     |-0.1519 |14.27  |
-------+--------+-------+--------+-------+
5        |Sep  1968|AO     |-0.04653|  4.615 |
-------+--------+-------+--------+-------+
6        |Apr  1969|LS     | 0.04602|  4.005 |
-------+--------+-------+--------+-------+
7        |Sep  1974|LS     |-0.04247|  3.739 |
-------+--------+-------+--------+-------+
8        |Nov  1974|LS     |-0.04914|  4.24  |
-------+--------+-------+--------+-------+
9        |Sep  1976|AO     | 0.038  |  3.891 |
-------+--------+-------+--------+-------+
10       |Apr  1986|AO     | 0.03792|  3.946 |
-------+--------+-------+--------+-------+
```

```
Innovation scale estimate before correcting outliers:
  0.01304
```

```
Innovation scale estimate after correcting outliers:
  0.01199
```

In this case, still no innovation outlier is detected even though we allowed for innovation outliers.

17.5.3 Iterating the Procedure

After the outlier detection, one can clean the original series of additive outliers and level shifts. If all the outliers in the data have been detected, and **arima.rob** is called on the cleaned data again, one should not find any new outliers. By this line of argument, the process of robust estimation and outlier detection can be iterated to obtain a more thorough detection of outliers. Before illustrating how this can be done using **arima.rob** function, we want to warn that this procedure is *ad hoc*, and sometimes the results may not be easily interpretable.

To carry out the iteration process, simply set the optional argument **iter=T** when calling **arima.rob** function. For example,

```
> frip.irr = arima.rob(log(frip.dat)~1, p=2, d=1, iter=T)
> summary(frip.irr)
```

```
Call:
arima.rob(formula = log(frip.dat) ~ 1, p = 2, d = 1, iter = T)
```

Regression model:
 log(frip.dat) ~ 1

ARIMA model:
Ordinary differences: 1 ; AR order: 2 ; MA order: 0

Regression Coefficients:
              Value Std. Error t value Pr(>|t|)
(Intercept) 0.0023 0.0005   4.6027 0.0000

AR Coefficients:
         Value Std. Error t value Pr(>|t|)
AR(1) -0.2861   0.0577   -4.9542 0.0000
AR(2) -0.0728   0.0577   -1.2608 0.2082

Degrees of freedom: 360 total; 356 residual

Innovations standard deviation: 0.01178

 Number of outliers detected: 10

Outliers detected:

	Time	Type	Impact	t-value
1	Mar 1963	AO	-0.1457	13.76
2	May 1968	AO	-0.3978	38.1
3	Jun 1968	AO	-0.1541	14.55
4	Sep 1968	AO	-0.04516	4.41
5	Apr 1969	LS	0.04511	3.814
6	Sep 1974	LS	-0.04351	3.767
7	Sep 1974	LS	0.04162	3.598
8	Nov 1974	LS	-0.04844	4.092
9	Dec 1975	LS	0.04037	3.534
10	Dec 1975	LS	0.0414	3.619

```
11       |Sep 1976|AO     | 0.0382 | 3.829 |
-------+--------+-------+--------+-------+
12       |Apr 1986|AO     | 0.03935| 3.932 |
-------+--------+-------+--------+-------+
```

Innovation scale estimate before correcting outliers:
    0.01311

Innovation scale estimate after correcting outliers:
    0.01176

In the first section of the output, the parameter estimates are from the last iterated model. In the second section of the output, it is stated that 10 outliers have been detected altogether, though there are 12 outliers listed in the table. The difference comes from the fact that some outliers are detected repeatedly during the iteration process. For example, two level shifts have been detected corresponding to September 1974.

To obtain a summary of the outliers detected for each iteration, one can use the `outliers` function with an `iter` argument. For example,

```
> summary(outliers(frip.irr, iter=2))
```

    Number of outliers detected: 2

Outliers detected:

```
         |Time      |Type    |Impact |t-value|
-------+--------+-------+-------+-------+
1        |Sep 1974|LS      |0.04162|3.598  |
-------+--------+-------+-------+-------+
2        |Dec 1975|LS      |0.04037|3.534  |
-------+--------+-------+-------+-------+
```

Innovation scale estimate before correcting outliers:
    0.01202

Innovation scale estimate after correcting outliers:
    0.01176

which summarizes the outliers detected in the second iteration.

17.6 Algorithms of Filtered τ-Estimation

This section briefly introduces filtered τ-estimates for REGARIMA models. The technical details can be found in the references cited in this chapter.

17.6.1 Classical Maximum Likelihood Estimates

For the REGARIMA model in equations (17.1) and (17.2), the model parameters are usually estimated by maximum likelihood estimation (MLE). The MLE can be computed using prediction error decomposition, for example, see Chapter 14.

First, let $d_0 = d + sD$. Note that we will lose the first d_0 observations because of the ARIMA differencing and/or seasonal differencing. For the moment, consider only equation (17.2). Let

$$\hat{\epsilon}_{t|t-1}(\boldsymbol{\lambda}) = E_{\lambda}[\epsilon_t|\epsilon_1, \ldots, \epsilon_{t-1}], \text{ for } t \geq d_0$$

be the one-step-ahead predictor of ϵ_t given the knowledge of historic values of ϵ_t. Then

$$\hat{u}_t(\boldsymbol{\lambda}) = \epsilon_t - \hat{\epsilon}_{t|t-1}(\boldsymbol{\lambda}) \quad (17.3)$$

will be the one-step-ahead prediction error, and the variance of $\hat{u}_t(\lambda)$ is of the form

$$\sigma_t^2(\lambda) = E_{\lambda}[\epsilon_t - \hat{\epsilon}_{t|t-1}(\lambda)]^2 = a_t^2(\lambda)\sigma_u^2,$$

where $\lim_{t \to \infty} a_t(\lambda) = 1$.

Second, for the REGARIMA model considered, the prediction error $\hat{u}_t(\boldsymbol{\beta}, \boldsymbol{\lambda})$ can be obtained similarly as in equation (17.3), replacing ϵ_t with $\epsilon_t(\boldsymbol{\beta}) = y_t - \mathbf{x}_t'\boldsymbol{\beta}$.

Now, let $L(\boldsymbol{\beta}, \boldsymbol{\lambda}, \sigma^2)$ be the conditional likelihood function of the sample observations, and let

$$Q(\boldsymbol{\beta}, \boldsymbol{\lambda}) = -2 \operatorname*{argmax}_{\sigma^2} \log L(\boldsymbol{\beta}, \boldsymbol{\lambda}),$$

which is -2 times the log-likelihood concentrated with respect to σ^2. Using prediction error decomposition, it can be easily shown that

$$Q(\boldsymbol{\beta}, \boldsymbol{\lambda}) = \sum_{t=d_0+1}^{T} \log a_t^2(\boldsymbol{\lambda}) + (T - d_0)s^2\left(\frac{\hat{u}_{d_0+1}(\boldsymbol{\beta}, \boldsymbol{\lambda})}{a_{d_0+1}(\boldsymbol{\lambda})}, \ldots, \frac{\hat{u}_T(\boldsymbol{\beta}, \boldsymbol{\lambda})}{a_T(\boldsymbol{\lambda})}\right),$$

$$(17.4)$$

up to a constant, where

$$s^2(u_1, \ldots, u_T) = \frac{1}{n}\sum_{t=1}^{n} u_t^2 \quad (17.5)$$

is the square of the scale estimate.

The classical maximum likelihood estimates of $\boldsymbol{\beta}$ and $\boldsymbol{\lambda}$ are obtained by minimizing $Q(\boldsymbol{\beta}, \boldsymbol{\lambda})$, that is,

$$(\hat{\boldsymbol{\beta}}, \hat{\boldsymbol{\lambda}}) = \operatorname*{argmin}_{\beta, \lambda} Q(\boldsymbol{\beta}, \boldsymbol{\lambda}),$$

and the maximum likelihood estimate of σ^2 is given by

$$\hat{\sigma}^2 = s^2(\hat{\boldsymbol{\beta}}, \hat{\boldsymbol{\lambda}}).$$

17.6.2   Filtered τ-Estimates

It is well known that the classical maximum likelihood estimates in the previous section are not robust and can produce poor estimates when the data contain outliers. Bianco, Garcia Ben, Martinez and Yohai (1996) proposed a class of robust estimates for REGARIMA model called *filtered τ-estimates*. See also Martin and Yohai (1996). These estimates are based on a robustification of the log-likelihood function. The robustification is accomplished through two steps: (1) use the filtered prediction error instead of the usual prediction error; (2) use a robust τ-estimate of the scale in equation (17.4).

The filtered τ-estimation uses a robust filter proposed by Masreliesz (1975) which eliminates the influence of previous outliers or bad observations. That is, the robust prediction error $\tilde{\epsilon}_{t|t-1}$ is computed based on cleaned series $\tilde{\epsilon}_{t|t}$ instead of the contaminated series ϵ_t. For an AR(1) model, the two series $\tilde{\epsilon}_{t|t-1}$ and $\tilde{\epsilon}_{t|t}$ are obtained simultaneously by a recursion procedure as follow:

$$\tilde{\epsilon}_{t|t} = w_t \epsilon_t + (1 - w_t)\tilde{\epsilon}_{t|t-1},$$

where

$$w_t = w\left(\frac{|\epsilon_t - \tilde{\epsilon}_{t|t-1}|}{m\hat{\sigma}_t}\right)$$

and $w(\cdot)$ is an even and non-increasing weight function, m is a tuning constant, and $\hat{\sigma}_t^2$ is an estimate of the prediction variance σ_t^2. For the general case the robust filtering procedure is based on the state space representation of the ARIMA model. The details can be found in Martin, Samarov and Vandaele (1983).

The filtered τ-estimation replaces the statistic s^2 in equation (17.5) with a robust τ-estimate of scale. For details of how τ-estimates of scale can be computed, see Yohai and Zamar (1983).

In summary, the filtered τ-estimates are defined by

$$(\hat{\boldsymbol{\beta}}, \hat{\boldsymbol{\lambda}}) = \operatorname*{argmin}_{\boldsymbol{\beta}, \boldsymbol{\lambda}} Q^*(\boldsymbol{\beta}, \boldsymbol{\lambda}),$$

where

$$Q^*(\boldsymbol{\beta}, \boldsymbol{\lambda}) = \sum_{t=d_0+1}^{T} \log a_t^2(\boldsymbol{\lambda}) + (T - d_0)\tau^2\left(\frac{\tilde{u}_{d_0+1}(\boldsymbol{\beta}, \boldsymbol{\lambda})}{a_{d_0+1}(\boldsymbol{\lambda})}, \ldots, \frac{\tilde{u}_T(\boldsymbol{\beta}, \boldsymbol{\lambda})}{a_T(\boldsymbol{\lambda})}\right),$$

with $\tilde{u}_t = \epsilon_t - \tilde{\epsilon}_{t|t-1}$, and $\tau^2(\cdot)$ is the square of the τ-estimate of scale.

17.7   References

[1] BIANCO, A., GARCIA BEN, M., MARTINEZ, E., AND YOHAI, V. (1996). "Robust Procedure for Regression Models with ARIMA Er-

rors", in A. Prat (ed.) *COMPSTAT 96 Proceedings Computational Statistics*, Physica-Verlag, Heidelberg.

[2] BIANCO, A., GARCIA BEN, M., MARTINEZ, E., AND YOHAI, V. (2001). "Outlier Detection in Regression Rodels with ARIMA Errors Using Robust Estimates," Journal of Forecasting, 20, 565-579 .

[3] BOX, G., AND JENKINS, G. (1976). *Time Series Analysis: Forecasting and Control*, San Francisco, Holden-Day.

[4] CHANG, I., TIAO, G. C., AND CHEN. C (1988). "Estimation of Time Series Parameters in the Presence of Outliers", *Technometrics*, 30, 193-204.

[5] MARTIN, R. D., SAMAROV, A., AND VANDAELE, W. (1983). "Robust Methods for ARIMA Models", in E. Zellner (ed.) *Applied Time Series Analysis of Economic Data*, U.S. Census Bureau, Government Printing Office.

[6] MARTIN, R.D., AND V. J. YOHAI (1996). "Highly Robust Estimation of Autoregressive Integrated Time Series Models," Publicaciones Previas No. 89, Facultad de Ciencias Exactas y Naturales, Universidad de Buenos Aires.

[7] MASRELIESZ, C. J. (1975). "Approximate non-Gaussian Filtering with Linear State and Observation Relations", *IEEE Transactions on Automatic Control*, AC-20, 107-110.

[8] TSAY, R. S. (1988). "Outliers, Level Shifts and Variance Changes in Time Series", *Journal of Forecasting*, 7, 1-20.

[9] YOHAI, V. J., AND ZAMAR, R. H. (1988). "High Breakdown-Point Estimates of Regression by Means of the Minimization of an Efficient Scale", *Journal of the American Statistical Association*, 83, 406-413.

Index